A History
of the
Canadian
Peoples
FOURTH EDITION

J.M. BUMSTED

OXFORD
UNIVERSITY PRESS

OXFORD
UNIVERSITY PRESS

8 Sampson Mews, Suite 204, Don Mills, Ontario M3C 0H5
www.oupcanada.com

Oxford University Press is a department of the University of Oxford.
It furthers the University's objective of excellence in research, scholarship,
and education by publishing worldwide in

Oxford   New York
Auckland   Cape Town   Dar es Salaam   Hong Kong   Karachi
Kuala Lumpur   Madrid   Melbourne   Mexico City   Nairobi
New Delhi   Shanghai   Taipei   Toronto

\With offices in
Argentina   Austria   Brazil   Chile   Czech Republic   France   Greece
Guatemala   Hungary   Italy   Japan   Poland   Portugal   Singapore
South Korea   Switzerland   Thailand   Turkey   Ukraine   Vietnam

Oxford is a trade mark of Oxford University Press in the UK and in certain other countries

Published in Canada by Oxford University Press

Library and Archives Canada Cataloguing in Publication

Bumsted, J. M., 1938–
A history of the Canadian peoples / J.M. Bumsted. — 4th ed.

Includes bibliographical references and index.

ISBN 978–0–19–543931–1

1. Canada—History—Textbooks.   2. Canada—Biography.

I. Title.

FC165.B862 2011   971   C2010-907712-1

Cover credit: City of Toronto Archives, Fonds 1244, Item 21B

This book is printed on permanent (acid-free) paper ∞
which contains a minimum of 10% post-consumer waste.

Printed and bound in the United States of America

1 2 3 4 — 14 13 12 11

Contents

Maps

Preface

From the Publisher

Oxford University Press is delighted to present the fourth edition of Jack Bumsted's *A History of the Canadian Peoples*. For over ten years, the textbook has offered students of Canadian history a rich and nuanced picture of Canada from pre-contact times to the present, through a balanced selection of historical perspectives and primary-source documents brought together into an articulate overarching narrative. The new edition has been thoroughly revised and updated with the addition of many new full-colour images, expanded coverage of Aboriginal peoples and immigration, and up-to-date treatment of the twenty-first-century events that have shaped the cultural and political landscape of this country.

Outstanding Features of the Fourth Edition

• **Wide-ranging, accessible coverage.** The stories of Canada's social, political, cultural, economic, and military past are carefully integrated into a well-structured, compelling narrative, prefaced by a unique essay on the importance of studying history today.

Harold Cardinal

Alberta Indian Association President Harold Cardinal watches as Queen Elizabeth emerges from a teepee at an Indian Village in Calgary, 5 July 1973. CP Picture Archive/ Chuck Mitchell.

Harold Cardinal (1945–2005) was a member of the Sucker Creek Reserve band who became president of the Indian Association of Alberta at the young age of 23. He had read widely in the American rhetorical literature of the 1960s regarding Aboriginal peoples, and he responded to the federal government's 1969 White Paper on Indian policy—which called for the advancement

The 'Book of Negroes'

In 1783 a regular weekly meeting occurred at a New York tavern between the American and British governments. At issue were the fates of more than 3,000 blacks, most of whom had escaped from slavery by crossing into British lines. The Americans wanted them returned, but General Guy Carleton refused to consent. Instead, he agreed to keep a record of all blacks being removed and to allow the Americans to dispute any name. Only 14 cases were in the end disputed as Carleton's 'Book of Negroes' was being prepared. Those who were included thought that they were now proper Loyalists, which would prove not quite the case. Copies of the 'Book of Negroes' survive in the Public Archives of Nova Scotia, the New York Public Library, and the Public Archives of Canada. Here is a transcription of one of the pages.

Ship *Spring* bound for St. John's [Saint John]

George Black, 35, (Lt. Col. Isaac). Freed by Lawrence Hartshorne as certified

Ann Black, 25, ([Lt. Col. Isaac Allen]). [Freed by Lawrence Hartshorne as certified.]

Billy Williams, 35, healthy stout man, (Richard Browne). Formerly lived with Mr. Moore of Reedy Island, Caroline, from whence he came with the 71st Regiment about 3 years ago.

Rose Richard, 20, healthy young woman, (Thomas Richard). Property of Thomas Richard, a refugee from Philadelphia.

Daniel Barber, 70, worn out, (James Moore). Says he was made free by Mr. Austin Moore of little York nigh 20 years ago.

Sarah Farmer, 23, healthy young woman, (Mrs. Sharp).

Free Negress indented to Mrs. Sharp for one year.

Barbarry Allen, 22, healthy stout wench, (Humphry Winters). Property of Humphrey Winters of New York from Virginia.

Elizabeth Black, 24, mulatto from Madagascar, (Mr. Buskirk). Free, indented when nine years of age to Mrs. Courtland.

Bob Stafford, 20, stout healthy Negro, (Mr. Sharp). Taken from Mr. Wilkinson in Virginia by a party from the Royal Navy about four years ago.

Reuben, 7, ([Lt. Col. Isaac Allen]. [Freed by Lawrence Hartshorne as certified.]

Sukey, 5, ([Lt. Col. Isaac Allen]). [Freed by Lawrence Hartshorne as certified.]

Ship *Aurora* bound for St. John's [Saint John]

Harry Covenhoven, 24, [stout healthy Negro], (Mr. Buskirk). Came in two years ago from Mr. Covenhoven in Jersey.

John Vans, 39, healthy, blind of his right eye, (Mr. Buskirk, Jr.). Taken in Pennsylvania a party of the British Army about 67 years ago; lived there with Sam Barber who he says had eight months before given him his freedom.

Anthony Haln, 27, stout Negro, (Nicholas Beckle). His own property willed

Joyce, 12, healthy Negress, (James Moore). Lived with James Moore for 6 years; her father died in the King's service.

Simson McGuire, 23, stout healthy Negro man, (John Buskirk). Came in to General Arnold in Virginia from Benjamin Hill.

Bristol Cobbwine, 14, stout healthy Negro boy, (Richard Browne). Came from Woodbury, Charlestown, South Carolina, with Major Grant of the King's American regiment about 4 years ago.

Paul, 19, [stout] mulatto, ([Richard Browne]). Came from Woodbury, Charlestown, South Carolina, with Major Grant of the King's American regiment.

- **Biographical portraits.** A wealth of boxes profile the women and men, both famous and lesser known, who played a role in the story of Canada's past.
- **Primary-source material.** A new selection of excerpted historical documents—from maps and journal entries to white papers and Royal Commission reports—gives students the chance to work with the raw materials of Canadian history.

Timeline

1886 W.S. Fielding introduces legislation in Nova Scotia calling for secession from the union. The first CPR transcontinental arrives in Manitoba.

1887 Honoré Mercier leads nationalite Liberals to victory in Quebec. St Catharines opens first electric streetcar system in Canada.

1890 Manitoba government abolishes public funding for Catholic schools. CPR builds rail line through Maine to connect Moncton with Montreal.

1891 Sir John A. Macdonald dies.

1892 A great fire destroys St John's, Newfoundland.

1896 Wilfrid Laurier leads the Liberal Party to a national electoral victory. Gold is discovered in the Klondike. The Manitoba Schools Question becomes a national issue.

1898 A national referendum is held on prohibition of alcoholic beverages. Newfoundland completes a railway across the island.

1899 Canadian Northern Railway is incorporated. Alaska Boundary Dispute is referred to an international tribunal. Canada agrees to send volunteer troops to South Africa.

1900 Art Museum of Toronto is founded. Prohibition legislation is passed on Prince Edward Island.

1901 The first wireless message transmitted across the Atlantic is received on Signal Hill near St John's, Newfoundland.

1902 Ernest Thompson Seton founds Woodcraft Indians.

of Africville, a black community on the outskirts of Halifax, and insists it was improper and unnecessary.

Desbiens, Jean-Paul. *The Impertinences of Brother Anonymous.* Toronto, 1962. The famous critique of Quebec politics and culture that caused a furor when first published.

Forsyth, Dennis, ed. *Let the Niggers Burn: The Sir George Williams University Affair and Its Caribbean Aftermath.* Montreal, 1971. An account of the most famous Canadian incident of student protest.

Handler, Richard. *Nationalism and the Politics of Culture in Quebec.* Madison, Wis., 1981. A detailed analysis of the manifold ways in which Quebec nationalism has influenced Quebec culture and cultural policy.

Kinsman, Gary. *The Regulation of Desire: Sexuality in Canada.* Montreal, 1987. A pioneering study of sexuality and its treatment by the state.

Levitt, Kari. *Silent Surrender: The Multinational Corporation in Canada.* Toronto, 1970. The most notorious statement of the nationalist critique of foreign investment and the multicultural corporation in Canada.

Morton, W.L. *The Canadian Identity.* Toronto, 1961. An effort to discover the essence of Canada by one of its leading historians.

Royal Commission on Bilingualism and Biculturalism. 1969. *Report*, 6 vols. Ottawa: Queen's Printer. The key document in the struggle for bilingualism and biculturalism.

Saywell, John. *Quebec 70: A Documentary Narrative.* Toronto, 1971. A useful account of the FLQ crisis of 1970.

Simeon, Richard. *Federal–Provincial Diplomacy: The Making of Recent Policy in Canada.* Toronto, 1972. A fascinating study of the international implications of Canadian federalism.

Vallières, Pierre. *White Niggers of America.* Toronto, 1971. A brilliant polemical memoir about living as a French Canadian.

Weaver, Sally M. *Making Canada's Indian Policy: The Hidden Agenda 1968–1970.* Toronto, 1981. A sober account of Canadian Aboriginal policy in a crucial period of re-evaluation.

Study Questions

1. Identify at least one way in which Canadian manners were emancipated during the 1960s in each of the following areas: religion, the media, literature, sexuality, and the law.
2. Explain why the 'counterculture' was mainly a youthful phenomenon.
3. Canada was never directly involved in the Vietnam War. Why did this war have such a strong impact on Canadian society?
4. Identify four militant collectivities that arose in the 1960s. For each, summarize briefly their goals.
5. What do Tables 10.1 and 10.2 tell us about unemployment in the 1960s?
6. In what ways did the 'Quiet Revolution' change Quebec society?
7. Of the factors listed in the text as changing Canada's immigration policy, which in your view was most important?
8. What three policies did the Pearson government develop to deal with Quebec's aspirations? Comment on the effectiveness of these policies.

www.oupcanada.com/Bumsted4e

Visit the companion website for *A History of the Canadian Peoples*, fourth edition for further resources.

Panning for gold. During the gold rushes in the Canadian Northwest of the last half of the nineteenth century, culminating with the Klondike discovery in 1896 in Yukon, prospectors and camp followers flocked to the region, hoping to strike it rich. Mining communities sprang up frequently and disappeared when the gold ran out. Corbis, MH001907.

- **Chapter-opening timelines.** Each chapter begins with a timeline of the events and themes that marked the historical period covered, providing a framework for the discussion and an excellent revision tool for students.
- **End-of-chapter learning tools.** A discussion of changing historical perspectives, a short annotated bibliography, and a set of study questions, presented together at the end of every chapter, challenge students to consider the evolving interpretation of historical moments and engage critically with the subject matter.

Canada in 1882.

Quebec: 'View of the Bishop's house with the ruins as they appear in going down the Hill from the Upper to the Lower Town', by Richard Short from a drawing made at the siege in 1759. LAC, C-000352

By 1767, when a detailed census of Nova Scotia was taken, the colony was well-populated, with 11,072 people in Nova Scotia proper, another 707 in Cape Breton, 1,196 in the northern section (now New Brunswick), and 519 on the Island of Saint John. The census also demonstrated that a heterogeneous population was already in place, consisting of 11,228 Protestants and 2,246 Catholics, and several ethnic groups (see Table 3.1). In addition,

the returns showed 95 'Negroes' and a scattering of 'Indians' (apparently no serious attempt was made to count them). Within a few years, substantial numbers of Scots would come to the region from the Lowlands but especially the Highlands, adding Gaelic to the English, German, French, and Mi'kmaq already freely spoken throughout the region.

Land speculation also dominated the development of the Island of Saint John. The entire land

Place	English	Irish	Scottish	Americans	Germans	Acadians
Nova Scotia	686	1,831	143	5,799	1,862	650
Cape Breton	70	169	6	170	21	271
North (NB)	25	53	17	874	60	147
Saint John	130	112	7	70	3	197
Totals	912	2,165	173	6,913	1,936	1,265

Table 3.1   Population of Nova Scotia in 1767 by Ethnicity

- **Abundant use of illustrations.** A dynamic array of maps, photos, paintings, and figures—many of them new, and set within a stunning new full-colour design—help bring history alive for readers.

Canada and the Refugees from Nazi Germany, 1933–1939

From Adolph Hitler's assumption of office as German chancellor, it was clear that the Jews would be a target for persecution. Those Jews who could escape Germany did so, although they were unable to flee swiftly enough to escape the German annexations of the Rhineland, Austria, and Czechoslovakia. Most countries sheltering refugees made clear that they were providing only temporary shelter, and Canada felt it could not open its doors to a flood of people from Europe. Canadian policy was put in the hands of Frederick Charles Blair, a lifetime bureaucrat and well-known anti-Semite, who saw Jewish people as unassimilable. Blair kept the Jews out with the full approval of the Canadian cabinet. In 1938 he decided that the few Jews admitted to Canada as farmers were not really agriculturalists. That same year Canada reluctantly attended a conference at Evian, France, sponsored partly by the United States, to discuss the refugee problems of Europe. Canada was a nation with large amounts of vacant land, and many of its politicians and population feared—quite accurately—that the world community would be quite satisfied to resolve its problems with displaced persons by sending them to Canada. From Canada's perspective, there was no reason to become involved in a European mess not of its own making. Unfortunately, isolationism did not suit the times.

A handful of Jewish members of Parliament (there were only three after 1935), with the support of J.S. Woodsworth of the Co-operative Commonwealth Federation, proposed to the Canadian cabinet that Canada offer at this conference to admit 5,000 Jewish refugees over four years, with all costs to

be assumed by the Jewish community [...] including guarantees that the newcomers [...] become charity cases. The cabinet reject[...] chiefly on the grounds that such action [...] as the thin edge of the wedge. By 1938 [...] there were at least a million refugees to be [...] Canadian Undersecretary of State for Ext[...] O.D. Skelton told the Americans that 'g[...] with unwanted minorities must . . . no[...] aged to think that harsh treatment at h[...] key that will open the doors to immigra[...] (quoted in Abella and Troper, 1991: 27[...] conference accomplished nothing exce[...] onstrate to the Nazis the lack of intern[...] port available to the Jews, thereby proba[...] further persecution, including the 'K[...] pogrom of late November 1938. On 23 [...] 1938 a delegation of Jews met with Pri[...] William Lyon Mackenzie King and T.A. [...] minister of immigration, to plead for th[...] of 10,000 refugees totally financed by [...] community. They were rebuffed, and [...] immigration regulations, which admitted [...] ers with capital. Highly skilled profe[...] intellectuals (including doctors, scientist[...] cians) were thus rejected as 'inadmissible[...]

In May of 1939, nearly 1,000 Germ[...] Hamburg on a luxury liner, the St Louis, [...] entrance visas for Cuba. The Cubans re[...] of the passengers, and while Canada sat [...] lines, the ship was forced to return to E[...] most that could be said for the Canadia[...]

and Mormons, had higher rates than the overall Catholic one. Finally, Aboriginal birth rates were at least twice the national average.

Another important new factor was divorce. The year 1918 saw 114 divorces in all of Canada, a rate

of 1.4 per 100,000 people. By 1929 [...] rate had reached 8.2 per 100,000, ris[...] per 100,000 in 1939 and to 65.3 per [...] 1947. Higher rates occurred partly be[...] Canadians gained access to divorce cou[...]

political) consciousness that development had to take into account the needs of Native peoples in a more thoroughgoing manner than had previously been the case. His report even became a best-seller (Berger, 1977). This was, arguably, the watershed event that brought Aboriginal issues into broad public awareness. It certainly made it impossible for the politicians to ignore Aboriginal peoples just a few years later when it came to crafting the Charter.

Immigration

While the Canadian population continued to drift off the farms, westward, and into the cities and surrounding suburbs, because of declining birth rates it also became increasingly dependent for its growth on immigration. That inflow increased its shift from the highly industrialized and earlier preferred nations of Western Europe and North America that had once represented Canada's sources of newcomers. Canada was no longer a special land of opportunity for citizens of the European Community, who lived in economies as prosperous. The new immigrants were largely from Third World countries in Africa, the Caribbean, Latin America, and Asia. The shift was facilitated by the changes in Canadian immigration policy and procedures. In 1973, Hong Kong, the Philippines, Jamaica, Trinidad, and India appeared among the top 10 countries of origin for Canadian immigrants.

In 1975 Immigration Minister Robert Andras tabled another government discussion document in the House of Commons, the so-called 'Green Paper'. A special joint committee of the House of Commons and Senate held almost 50 public hearings across Canada on the Green Paper. The hearings seemed to confirm that Canadians wanted to continue accepting relatively large numbers of new immigrants but not to open the nation's doors to unrestricted admissions. The result of the national discussion was another major Immigration Act, that of 1976, which stated Canadian goals regarding immigration and insisted on the need to plan for the future. The Act recognized three classes of immigrants: the family class (relatives of Canadian residents), the humanitarian class (refugees and displaced persons), and an independent class.

Immigration regulations were revised in 1978 to alter the points system by placing greater importance on practical experience and to change the refugee situation by creating a new program of refugee sponsorship. Most of the Vietnamese boat people, about 50,000, entered Canada under this plan between 1979 and 1984. Quebec was the only province to take full advantage of federal opportunities built into the legislation of 1976 and 1978 to assume new provincial powers in immigration matters. As a result, Quebec could now in practice select its own immigrants. Ontario and Nova Scotia also signed more limited immigration agreements with Ottawa. Whether or not Quebec could attract and hold its share of the immigration total was another matter entirely. Many immigrants were not enthusiastic about education in French for their children. Tough

By the mid-1980s, the majority of immigrants arriving in Canada came from countries in Asia. In this photo, a young Vietnamese boy waits with his family to be processed at an immigration centre in Montreal. © Owen Franken/Corbis.

- **Expanded coverage of immigration, multiculturalism, and racism.** New material adds depth to the detailed account of key topics while highlighting the change in historical perspectives.

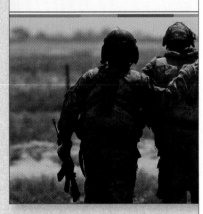

- **Broader coverage of women in Canada.** New insights into women's roles and contributions to Canadian history provide a rich, balanced account of Canada's past.

- **Updated coverage of twenty-first-century events.** Enlightening discussions of Canada's role in Afghanistan, the G20 and G8 summits held in Ontario, the Vancouver 2010 Olympics, and current cultural trends help students understand Canada's present-day political, economic, and socio-cultural identities.

Supplements

Instructors and students alike will benefit from the rich suite of ancillary materials available on the textbook's companion website: www.oupcanada.com/Bumsted4e.

FOR THE INSTRUCTOR

- An **Instructor's Manual** features chapter summaries, suggestions for lectures and further readings, and annotated lists of key figures, places, terms, research topics, and recommended resources.
- A **Test Generator** provides a comprehensive selection of multiple-choice, true–false, short-answer, and essay questions.
- **PowerPoint® slides**, fully updated to reflect the content of this edition, summarize key points from the text and provide a framework for course lectures.

FOR THE STUDENT

- A **Student Study Guide** offers a variety of useful learning tools, including chapter summaries, learning objectives, self-grading quizzes, recommended print and online resources, study and research tips, sample exams, and interviews with historians.
- An **Online Primary-Source Library** features 60 canonical and lesser-known primary sources from both pre- and post-Confederation history. Each source is accompanied by an introduction offering students a contextual and social perspective that will enrich their study of Canadian history.
- **Visual History Online** is a dynamic new resource comprising images with captions grouped in units that correspond to each chapter of the textbook. Images are accompanied by provocative questions designed to encourage students to consider the importance of visual history.

COMPANION WEBSITE

J.M. Bumsted

A History of the Canadian Peoples, 4e
ISBN 13: 9780195439311

Inspection copy request

Ordering information

Contact & Comments

About the Book

Now in a new fourth edition, this concise volume covers the whole of Canadian history from pre-contact times to the present, integrating social, cultural, political, and economic history into a coherent and compelling narrative. New to the fourth edition is additional coverage of multiculturalism, immigration, and racism, as well as women and work in the twenty-first century. Many new historical images have been added throughout to support the already robust photo and image program, engaging the readers and drawing them into each time period discussed. Engrossing, thorough, and timely, J.M. Bumsted's narrative provides a comprehensive look at this country's fascinating history.

Instructor Resources

You need a password to access these resources. Please contact your local Sales and Editorial Representative for more information.

Student Resources

Introduction
Understanding History

Every experienced historian has at some point encountered someone from a totally different background who assumes that 'anyone can do history'. In the sense that anyone can research, write, and even publish historical work without specialized training, that assumption is correct. History is one of those fields—creative writing is another—where the standards of achievement can be flexible and intuitive, and where much of the methodology is based on plain common sense. History's accessibility to almost all of us, not simply as readers but as actual researchers, is one of its great charms and greater merits. And many people do engage in historical research without calling it by that name. Everyone who tries to trace her ancestry through the labyrinth of historical records (often called 'genealogy') is involved in a form of historical research. Everyone who tries to research the background to a business project as part of a report on its present status, or to explain how a sports team achieved a championship season, is in a sense 'doing history'. Every criminal trial (and almost every civil one) is at some level a historical reconstruction. The historical mode is one of the most common ways through which we attempt to understand the world we live in.

To say that nearly all of us engage in some form of historical reconstruction, often unconsciously, is not to say that there are no fundamental rules to such activity. Most of us know instinctively that witnesses can be biased or mistaken, that human motivation is complex, and that in the chronological sequence of events—the establishment of which many non-professional historians regard as the centre of the enterprise—the cause must precede the effect. But history is not a laboratory science. Even the simplest rules of evidence and argument can be difficult to apply in specific situations, particularly if the researcher is operating intuitively. Understanding what causes these difficulties is important, and becoming sensitive to the problems of history is one of the chief benefits of formal historical study.

A good many Canadians (probably nearly as many as commonly read fiction or poetry) read history, for recreation and for information. Unfortunately, general readers often approach historical writing in much the same way they approach fiction, judging a work's value by its success in telling 'a good story'. But of course storytelling is only one of numerous ways in which history can be written. Although, as with fiction, there is great pleasure to be had from reading history simply at the level of entertainment, to remain at that level would be to miss much of the best modern historical writing. It is possible without training or formal critical tools to recognize that a Harlequin romance offers a far less complex view of the world than a Margaret Atwood novel; it is somewhat more difficult to appreciate a parallel difference in history. Readers who expect writers of fiction to have distinctive voices and world views still often assume that all historians participate equally in the effort to recover the truth of the past through application of some unspecified 'scientific' method: if history is about truth, then all historical writing must be more or less equally true, at least if the historian has 'the facts' right. The ordinary reader is frequently unable to distinguish between 'facts' and 'truth', failing to appreciate on one level that factual accuracy is in itself a complex issue and on another level that it has limited value as a critical test.

In addition, many readers fail to distinguish between history as everything that has happened before the present moment (also commonly known as 'the past') and history as the record (usually written) of the unfolding of some event(s) in that past. Yet that past can never be recovered, for reasons I shall discuss. All we can do is attempt to recreate and analyze discrete parts of that past, refracted through the historian's prism. Only this history can be studied and investigated. As a further confusion, history can mean not only the historian's account of the past, but the systematic study of the past as a discipline or a craft. The study of either the work of individual historians or the discipline itself is often known as historiography. Just as filmmakers make a surprising number of movies about the process of making movies, so historians devote more of their energy to examining the making of history than they do to any other single project.

The processes of both reading and researching history can obviously be greatly enhanced by some understanding of the problems that engage historians as they pursue their craft. Before we turn to some of those problems, however, it might be well to consider the question of the value of history.

The Value of History

Once upon a time, especially in the nineteenth and earlier twentieth centuries, most people did not question the value of historical study or wonder how it was relevant to their lives. They did not doubt the value of the liberal arts or the humanities, much less debate the benefits of studying languages like Greek or Latin. There are really two separate but related issues inherent in the 'value of history' question. One is whether or not historical study has a sufficient grip on truth and meaning in our modern world to have any value at all, intrinsic or extrinsic. Ultimately, this question involves us in high philosophy and theory, but it also has a particular Canadian edge. The other question is whether or not historical work has a sufficiently attractive vocational payoff to justify its study at the university. Perhaps we should turn to the latter question first, since it is easier to answer and may be of more interest to the beginning historian.

For many centuries, the opportunity to attend a university was available only to those of outstanding intellectual abilities or privileged socio-economic standing. In a world that did not question the importance of religion, the original purpose of universities was to educate clerics. The university gradually

became the centre of humanistic scholarship and enterprise generally, but so long as society valued education for its own sake—chiefly because it was something available only to the privileged few—its specific vocational role was quite insignificant. Universities turned out educated and 'cultured' men (not women until well into the nineteenth century) into a world that took it for granted that such people were important to the society. Specific occupational training was not part of the university's function, and preparation even for such elevated professions as law and medicine was done outside its doors. Yet gradually the notion of vocational training did enter the cloistered world of the university, particularly in North America, and by 1940 it was possible to prepare for nearly any occupation through specialized studies at a university, although such opportunities were still limited to members of the elites. Despite the new vocational bent of the university, occupational studies were largely confined to the post-graduate level; most undergraduate students at universities (as opposed to acknowledged vocational centres such as teachers' training colleges) still expected An Education rather than A Vocation.

The great change in the nature of the university really came after 1945, when the idea took hold that all Canadians were entitled to attend university and the number of university places was greatly expanded. A dynamic relationship has existed between the democratization of the university and the introduction of the idea that there should be some demonstrable economic value to a university degree. Thus specific occupational training now starts at the undergraduate rather than the graduate level. Today at many universities it is likely that the majority of students are enrolled in such programs, and even those who are not in such programs themselves commonly expect a university education to provide some kind of occupational entrée or advantage. In the new occupational sweepstakes, a field like history is of less obvious relevance than one like management or accounting or pharmacy or computing. Some historians would prefer to ignore the question of occupational relevance altogether, but the days of a simple liberal arts education for most university students are probably gone forever. History may not ever compete with accounting or pharmacy or medical school as preparation for employment, but it is still superb preparation for many professional programs (assuming that they do not insist on specialization from day one). And one can do more in the workforce with a history specialization than most students might at first think.

There are numerous history-related occupations besides teaching. They include work in archives, libraries, and museums, as well as in government service. 'Heritage' in itself is a major industry in Canada. Other occupations, such as law, journalism, and some branches of the civil service (the diplomatic corps, for example), have traditionally recruited heavily among history graduates, but any job requiring the ability to gather and analyze evidence and then communicate the findings is ideally suited to someone with a background in history. One individual with a graduate degree in history, Mike Smith, has become the general manager of several National Hockey League teams. What students have to do is learn to translate their historical training into the jargon of the contemporary job market. 'Researching term essays in history', for example, can be translated into 'using documentary resources to abstract and analyze complex information'. (At one recent 'interview' for a summer job with a government department, the student applicant was simply asked to summarize a complex document quickly and accurately.) To the extent that history is a discipline that teaches students both to think and to communicate, it should improve their qualifications for almost any job.

Beyond developing essential skills in research, analysis, and communication, what are the uses of history? Certainly few historians today believe—if they ever did—in the use of historical 'laws' of human conduct for predictive purposes. Most historians who have employed historical laws, such as Arnold Toynbee in *A Study in History*, Oswald Spengler in *The Decline of the West*, or Karl Marx in *Capital*, have done so on such an abstract level that it is difficult to translate those laws into specific terms. Toynbee's notion that civilizations pass through recognizable stages paralleling the human life cycle is attractive, but it does not tell us when our civilization will die. Employing the insights of Karl Marx,

no reader could have concluded that the 'dictatorship of the proletariat' would come first in Russia, or that it would eventually lead not to a classless society but to the collapse of the Soviet Union. No discipline has worked harder than economics to achieve scientific status, but the whole world has come to appreciate that economists constantly disagree on even the most general level of prediction and analysis.

Yet if history cannot predict, it can help us to understand the difficulty of prediction. In the same way it can help us to recognize the recurrent and ongoing nature of many of society's problems. By and large, historians were far more sanguine about the outcome of the 1992 referendum on the Charlottetown constitutional accord than were the scaremongers on either side of the debate or many of the journalists covering the 'crisis'. Indeed, those with an understanding of Canadian history, constitutional and otherwise, were bound to find the very concept of a 'crisis' suspect, just as they would any other popular journalistic concept, such as 'conspiracy'. The historical record tells us that there have been crises and conspiracies, but equally that these terms have so often been used without justification that they have lost any real meaning.

History provides us not only with a social context but with a personal one as well. The genealogical search for 'roots' has become important for many Canadians seeking to trace their family backgrounds and to understand the circumstances that drove their ancestors across the ocean, or the ways their ancestors' lives changed as a result of the newcomers' arrival. Nor is the question of personal identity merely an individual matter. It is no accident that as minority groups in Canada work to develop themselves as collectivities, they need to establish and assert their historical experience. Over the past 30 years some Canadians have lost interest in the historical mode, adopting what we might call the 'irrelevance of history' position. But this has not been the case with collective 'minorities' such as women, Native peoples, blacks, and ethnic minorities. For these groups, establishing their rightful place in Canadian history has been an absolutely primary function. That these groups' interpretations of their histories have often run counter to the traditional versions of Canadian history does not render them any less consequential—or less historical.

The Elusive Fact

More than 50 years ago a television series called *Dragnet* became famous for a catchphrase used by one of its characters, a police detective named Sergeant Joe Friday. When questioning witnesses, Friday always repeated the same request, delivered in an emotionless monotone: 'All I want is the facts, just give me the facts.' The monotone was intended to indicate Friday's objectivity and to extract from his witness a response devoid of personal bias and colouration. Of course he seldom got 'just the facts'—which from our perspective is exactly the point. Somehow, just as the popular mind in the 1950s associated Joe Friday with facts, so it has more recently come to think of historians as dealing in the same coin. The equation of facts and history has doubtless been assisted by the traditional way of teaching history in the schools, by marching out one name, date, event after another for students to commit to memory and regurgitate at the appropriate time in the course of an examination. Of course, historians do rely on facts as their basic building blocks; but they do not think of them the way Sergeant Friday did, nor do they use them the way common opinion believes they do.

The *Canadian Oxford Dictionary* offers several meanings for 'fact'. The most familiar is probably number 1: 'a thing that is known to have occurred, to exist, or to be true', although number 4—'truth, reality'—is also very common. Facts, as *Dragnet* suggested, are true things, unsullied by any process of interpretation or conclusion. Such things may exist, but they are much harder to come by than one might expect, for several reasons. One problem is the language in which 'facts' must be stated. Another is the context in which they become significant.

Over the last century we have become increasingly aware that language is not a neutral instrument, but one that carries with it a heavy freight of cultural experience and usage. 'John Cabot discovered Newfoundland in 1497' may seem a straightforward statement of fact, but at least half of the words in

it conjure up a whole host of meanings. One of those words is 'discovered'. The implication is that what Cabot found was previously unknown—but of course an Aboriginal population had been living in the area for millennia. Even qualifying 'discovered' by saying that Cabot 'was the first European to discover Newfoundland' doesn't help much, since we now know that the Vikings had settled at L'Anse aux Meadows in the eleventh century, and even they may not have been the first Europeans to cross the Atlantic. 'Discovery' is a complex concept. The term 'Newfoundland' is equally problematic, since in modern geographic terms Cabot was not at all precise about his movements, and the land he sighted may not have been part of the island that we know as Newfoundland today. Indeed, Cabot called the land he saw 'the New-Founde Land', and it was only later that the label was applied to the island. Moreover, Cabot's sightings were not confirmed by anything other than vague self-declarations. To top matters off, there are questions about the identity of John Cabot himself, who started in Italy as Giovanni (or Zuan) Caboto and became John Cabot Montecalunya, a resident of Valencia, in the early 1490s, before he called himself John Cabot of Bristol. Almost all but the most simplistic statements are subject to the same difficulties. Philosophers have spent thousands of years trying to formulate 'true' statements, with very little success, and historians are unlikely to do much better. Almost any 'factual' statement worth making has to be expressed in a language heavily weighted with values and contexts. Language is only one of the challenges in the quest for the fact.

Even if facts could be expressed in a neutral language, such as numbers, we would still need to decide which facts are important. At any given moment there exists a virtual infinity of pieces of information that could be isolated and stated. Most 'historical facts' are simply labels of events and dates, names and movements, which by themselves do not tell us very much. They are not statements in which anything is asserted, and therefore they have no standing as facts. Only when their significance is implicitly or explicitly understood do they acquire any utility or susceptibility to truth. 'The Battle of Vimy Ridge' is not a fact since it does not assert anything capable of being either true or false. 'The Battle of Vimy Ridge in 1917 was won by the Canadian army' is an assertion the validity of which can be assessed. Whether it is false or true (and hence 'a fact') is another matter entirely. The validity of the statement requires a detailed account of the battle in the context of the war.

One of the chief benefits of modern historical study is that it promotes a healthy skepticism about the neutrality and ultimate truth of the notorious fact. Taken by itself, in isolation, the fact has little meaning. It is only when facts are arranged into some larger picture—some sort of interpretive account—that they acquire significance. Those interpretive pictures themselves are subject to change over time. Anyone today who reads a Canadian history textbook written 30 years ago will be struck by the almost complete absence of any reference to women as important historical figures. Yet 30 years ago the majority of readers—even female readers—took that absence for granted. The absence of women does not mean that women were not present. It simply means that historians of that generation did not regard their activities as worthy of attention. The historian can uncover whole constellations of new facts simply by asking a new question of the historical record, as happened when some scholars asked: 'What about the women?' History is not the study of something eternally fixed, of something that can be 'discovered', but rather the continual dynamic re-investigation and re-evaluation of the past.

If historians can recover new facts, however, they are still limited to those facts that have been recorded in some way. The records need not be in written form; sometimes they take the form of oral history, sometimes of artifacts. Whatever form the evidence takes, it has to have been preserved. Preservation may be deliberate or serendipitous, but in either case certain biases may be observed. If we think about our own personal history, we realize that not every part of it has been recorded, let alone recorded with equal care; and much of the individual record that does exist has been preserved not through personal choice but to serve bureaucratic purposes. Not every society keeps public records, however, and even in the record-keeping societies, not everyone produces an equal quantity of evidence. Only a relative

handful of historical actors, for example, have left behind their own written accounts. Personal evidence tends to be limited to those involved in self-consciously important activity, as defined by any particular society. Such recorders usually represent that society's elite, and what they record represents what the elites think needs recording. We know far more about taxation in the Middle Ages than we do about sexual behaviour, for example. Whatever their limitations, it is with the records that historians must start. They are the primary sources for historical investigation, as distinguished from secondary sources (usually other historians' research gleanings and interpretations). In working with primary sources, historians face two problems: the first one of authenticity, the second one of credibility.

For understandable reasons, historians have to be certain that the records they study are genuine. Historians thus prefer to work with original documents, the so-called 'manuscript' sources (although not all manuscripts are necessarily handwritten). The republication of such material often raises questions of accuracy, which become even more problematic when the documents have been translated from one language to another. Even the most scrupulous of editors may subtly alter the meaning of a document through changes in punctuation or spelling, and until our own time the editors of historical documents often intervened in other ways as well. A famous editor of Shakespeare named Thomas Bowdler expurgated material that he considered to be in bad taste (his name is now commemorated in the verb 'to bowdlerize'). Other editors silently rewrote texts to what they regarded as the advantage of their authors. Even the appearance of authenticity is no guarantee; many skilful forgeries have been designed to pass close inspection. The famous Shroud of Turin (supposedly showing the imprint of the body of Christ) is not necessarily a deliberate forgery, but recent scientific investigation has found that it could not be authentically associated with the crucifixion. As for the supposedly fifteenth-century 'Vinland Map', discovered in the 1960s, it still has not been satisfactorily authenticated, and many scholars think it is a fake.

Even if we are dealing with an 'authentic' document, there are still many potential problems to face before we can use it as evidence. Many documents cannot be precisely dated or attributed to a specific author. But these questions must be addressed before the historian—acting all the parts in a court of law except that of witness—can determine the document's credibility. Was the author in a position to be authoritative? Are there reasons, obvious or subtle, for suspecting bias of some kind? Bias may appear in many forms. Authors may seek to justify themselves; they may place their interpretation of events in a context resulting from their place in society or from their ideological assumptions; they may report hearsay; they may adjust their accounts for literary reasons or simply to tell 'a good story'. Evidence is best if it can be corroborated by more than one source; but supporting evidence is not always available, particularly for specific details. Like the 'facts' derived from them, the documents themselves are seldom unassailable as sources. Historians work with probabilities rather than certainties, and the more evidence is available, the more likely it is that there will be complications. In any event, students of history need to be both skeptical and critical of what they read, whether documentary evidence itself or interpretations of such material.

The Conventions of History

Historians have developed a series of conventions for dealing with their raw data. Historical information presented in its unexplicated form—as a series of unrelated facts—is not history as historians understand it, and insufficient attention to interpretation and context is one of the most common faults of beginning historians. Traditionally, the chief mode for historians has been narrative, the recounting of past events in the sequence in which they occurred. Like all aspects of historical work, narrative requires selection—cutting into the seamless web of the past to isolate a particular sequence of events involving a limited number of characters. Narrative deals with the passage of time, and—since it is axiomatic that cause and effect must be in the right sequence—chronology is critical to historical understanding. Many great historians of the past concentrated almost exclusively on narrative, appropriately embellished with description and context; an example is Francis Parkman, who wrote extensively on the early conflict of the French and British in North America. But most modern historians would agree with Arthur Marwick (1970: 144) that 'the historian must achieve a balance between narrative and analysis, between a chronological approach and an approach by topic, and, it should be added, a balance between both of these, and, as necessary, passages of pure *description* "setting the scene", providing routine but essential information, conveying the texture of life in any particular age and environment.' Some historians have even dropped narrative entirely, although the sequence of events remains implicitly crucial to their work.

Despite the common use of the term 'causation' in historical writing, particularly among beginners, philosophers of history have long emphasized that historians really do not deal much in the sort of cause-and-effect relationships usually associated with scientific work. The past is too complex to isolate factors in this way. Instead, historians talk about 'explanation', which is not quite the same as scientific causation. Explanation requires the inclusion of enough context and relevant factors to make it clear that the events in question were neither totally predetermined nor utterly capricious. As E.H. Carr (1964: 103–4) has observed:

. . . no sane historian pretends to do anything so fantastic as to embrace 'the whole of experience'; he cannot embrace more than a minute fraction of the facts even of his chosen sector or aspect of history. The world of the historian, like the world of the scientist, is not a photographic copy of the real world, but rather a working model which enables him more or less effectively to understand it and to master it. The historian distils from the experience of the past, or from so much of the experience of the past as is accessible to him, that part which he recognizes as amenable to rational explanation and interpretation, and from it draws conclusions.

In their efforts at narrative and/or explanation, historians also use many other conventions. Among them, let us focus on periodization. The division of the past into historical 'periods' serves purposes beyond the organization of a teaching curriculum. By focusing attention on units of time, periodization serves to narrow and limit the range of material to be considered and helps to provide a structure for what would otherwise be a meaningless jumble of events and dates. The choice of beginning and end dates for larger historical sequences is hardly arbitrary, but it is still a matter of interpretation. Take, for example, the standard decision to divide Canadian history at 1867, the year of Confederation. This fundamental periodization reflects the assumption not only that political and constitutional development shaped everything else, but also that the creation of a national state called the Dominion of Canada was the critical point in that development. However, it makes little sense for many other themes in Canadian history. Historians of Canada continually debate the question of relevant periods. The authors of the first survey of the history of women in Canada, for example, were forced to find a new way of periodizing their account, since the standard political and constitutional periodization reflected a chronology that was mainly masculine in emphasis.

New Interpretations

Like all academic disciplines, history is constantly reinterpreting its subject matter. Some of the pressure for reinterpretation is a simple matter of growth: within the past quarter-century, the number of academic positions for historians in Canada has more than quadrupled, with the result that more individuals are now researching and writing within the field. At the same time, technological advances (in computers and photocopiers, for example) and the advent of the relatively inexpensive airline ticket have made it possible for historians to examine and process documentary materials in ways and quantities that would have been unthinkable at the beginning of the 1960s. Other pressures for revision, of course, come from changes in the social context, which is continually raising new questions for historians to explore and causing shifts in the climate of opinion.

In history, revisionist movements usually arise out of new developments in three (often related) areas: subject matter, conceptual frameworks, and methodologies. A new development in any one of these areas may be enough on its own to provoke significant revision. When two or three come together (as is often the case), they can completely alter our understanding of the past.

Addressing new subject matter involves asking new questions about hitherto neglected aspects of the past. In Canadian history, with its traditional focus on the political and constitutional ways in which a national state was created, the opportunities for new questions have been quite substantial. Out of a variety of new subjects, we can perhaps offer three examples: women, Aboriginal peoples, and ethnic groups. While each of these subjects would today be regarded as central to any contemporary understanding of Canadian history, they were virtually neglected until recent years. As we have seen, lack of attention to women in the past did not reflect lack of information but lack of interest on the part of historians. With the simple act of focusing attention on women, a new field of study was opened. In the case of Aboriginal peoples, the subject had not been entirely neglected, but it had virtually always been approached from the perspective of the developing national state. Thus many of the new questions raised today are aimed at understanding the First Nations' perspectives. As for ethnic groups, research has tended to involve scholars from a variety of disciplines, such as sociology and geography, and has been encouraged by the availability of grant money from governmental agencies at both the federal and provincial levels. Ethnic studies have proved to be politically popular within Canada.

New areas of study often suggest—if not require—new conceptual contexts. In general, all three of the new areas noted above fall under the rubric of 'social history'. As early as 1924, an article on 'The Teaching of Canadian History' advocated the study of the 'actual life of the Canadian people' in 'their efforts to secure a livelihood and then to provide for the higher demands of mind and spirit' (McArthur, 1924: 207). Until recent years, however, much of the research in the social history area concentrated on the upper echelons of society in Canada, the so-called 'elites'. Broadening the social base to include individuals outside the ranks of those whose lives were normally documented (women, Aboriginal people, racial and ethnic minorities, ordinary working folk) involved a substantial reconceptualization of the nature of Canada's past.

Studying those 'inarticulate' groups often required new methodologies as well. Perhaps the most important methodological innovation was quantification: generating new data sets by processing existing information not previously practicable for historical purposes out of data such as name-by-name census returns. At its worst, quantification could be little more than mindless number-crunching, but at its best it enabled historians to open up whole categories of hitherto unusable documentation. The information collected by the Dominion Bureau of the Census or the various provincial departments of Vital Statistics has provided much new insight into the way ordinary Canadians have lived (and loved) in the past. Computers have made it easier for historians to process large amounts of aggregate information—although the axiom 'Garbage In, Garbage Out' continues to apply. The complex processes of collecting and analyzing new categories of data have been contentious, and beginning historians should understand that the apparently simple act of producing a new set of information involves many steps and many disagreements. 'Hard' numbers and percentages are no more sacrosanct than information that appears 'softer'. Moreover, quantified data still require interpretation and are subject to all the standard rules that apply to historical explanation.

Although explicit controversies do arise within the field of Canadian history, they are probably less common than controversies among historians of other nations, notably the United States and Great Britain. To some extent the profession has avoided confrontations by allowing each practitioner his or her own area of specialization (or 'turf'). This has made good sense because the number of questions not yet adequately explored in the history of Canada is considerable. Whatever the reasons for the muting

of controversy, disagreements in Canadian historiography have had less to do with specific points and interpretations within a single tradition than with first principles and underlying assumptions. Thus Canadian historians tend to disagree only at the mega-level, as in the current debate over Canadian 'national history', which is really a debate among scholars with different sets of assumptions about the role of narrative in the past. Those on the moving frontier of scholarship are in some ways far less embattled than those still working in older traditions, since they can simply add their 'new' interpretations on to the old ones.

But at the same time, the interpretation and practice of history, in Canada as elsewhere, is constantly changing, presenting new issues and questions. As noted above, research over the past half-century has been greatly altered by a variety of technological developments, including the photocopier, the computer, and most recently, the Internet. This last tool, which few fully understand in all its complexity, can alter research processes and provides access to vast amounts of mostly unsorted information, and while it raises new possibilities for acquiring documentation and exchanging information it also opens a Pandora's box of new questions. Its users must develop new ways of authenticating what is credible in essentially unsupervised and uncontrolled material. We must figure out how to protect intellectual property in a world where a mere click of a mouse can copy and transfer thousands of pages of material from one file to another, and the resulting risks of plagiarism are enormous. New techniques for documenting the past will have to be developed so that we can be assured that what we are reading online is not simply another 'urban myth'. Contemporary teachers and students of history are thus faced with many new challenges.

The search for a credible past has been recently influenced not simply by the emergence of a totally unsupervised database, but, on the other hand, by new efforts on the part of public bodies to shape what we accept as 'truth'. Over the years, most historical arguments and interpretations have always been judged in the free marketplace of opinion by one's historical peers, and there has seldom been a 'final judgement'. The philosophical problems involved when complex historical questions are actually adjudicated by the judicial process are many. In court cases, increasingly employed in Canada in Aboriginal land claims disputes, the judge listens to a variety of expert testimony and pronounces a verdict that appears to rely on and thus to validate one or more particular historical interpretations or methodological approaches. Does this court approval mean that the judge's verdict takes on the character of the truth? Is it susceptible to revision? Has anything actually been validated? Apart from court pronouncements are others of an official nature. The Canadian government has recently (November 2009) issued a revised guide for new citizens that undertakes to summarize Canadian history in 10 pages. That history is now formally allowed to include the abuse of Aboriginal peoples and the mistreatment of several ethnic communities, although few details are given. Whether it has managed to be sufficiently vague so as not to introduce a new level of misconceptions is another matter entirely.

Simply because history is a cumulative subject, students should not think that the latest books and journal articles are necessarily better by virtue of their dates of publication. Many older works of historical scholarship can still be regarded as the best treatments of their topics. This is particularly true in traditional areas of study that have not attracted much attention from modern scholars, such as the military history of the War of 1812. Earlier generations were fond of publishing editions of documents, which, if well-transcribed, translated, and edited, are just as valuable today as they were a century ago. The complete (and most commonly used) edition of the *Jesuit Relations* in English was published between 1896 and 1901 (and, as times do change, that entire 73-volume collection is now available online in facsimile from Creighton University, a Jesuit institution in Omaha, Nebraska). On some topics our only sources are earlier documents; for example, Richard Hakluyt's sixteenth-century accounts are still essential for any study of English overseas voyages.

By now it should be clear that both the writing and the reading of history are extremely complicated enterprises. Whole books with titles like *Understanding History* or *The Nature of History* have been devoted to introducing students to the complexities of the craft, and in the space of a few pages it is impossible to explore all the potential dimensions. In any case, readers of this book should understand that every work of history involves a series of decisions to hold various contradictions in dynamic tension. Among the most important issues held in tension in this book are the following.

1. *Interpretive complexity versus authority.* Virtually every sentence in this work (or any other work of history) could be hedged in with conflicting evidence and interpretation. The result would almost certainly be incomprehensible. I have chosen to favour readability over total academic accuracy. This is not to say that I do not recognize the issues of interpretive complexity. Rather, I have consciously addressed them in two ways: by introducing questions of interpretation into the text on a regular basis, and by including essays on historiography—'How History Has Changed'—at the end of each chapter.

2. *Individual biography versus groups and forces.* One problem that all historians face (or ought to face) is how to make the material interesting to readers. As any newspaper editor will tell you, readers like their stories to have people in them. This work uses the experiences of individual people to represent and suggest the complex groups and forces that lie behind them. I do not subscribe to the Great Person theory of history, but I do believe in personalizing history as much as possible.

3. *Overarching master narrative versus the complex voices of social and cultural history.* Whether or not Canadian history has a single narrative is a hotly debated issue today, sometimes posed in the form of the question 'Is there a national history?' The single narrative is also related to the problem of authority, although the two are not the same. A coherent and connected single narrative could be based on the concept of the development of the nation, or on viewing events from the perspective of that nation, or on something quite different. The point is that any such narrative line represents an abstraction. Critics of the abstract,

single narrative approach associate it with the imposition of a hegemonic 'master principle' that in turn is often taken to represent the sequence of events preferred by the 'men in suits' or the 'ruling class' or the 'politicians in Ottawa'. Many groups are commonly left outside such a master narrative: workers, racial and cultural minorities, women, inhabitants of marginalized regions, inhabitants of alienated regions (e.g., Quebec for much of the twentieth century). Over the past 30 years, Canadian historians have concentrated on recovering the voices of these groups. But if those voices were all we heard, telling their own stories in their own tongues, the resulting cacophony would be unintelligible; and to establish chronology and meaningful periodization, we need a structure that will provide some common reference points. Hence a master narrative of some kind is still essential.

The master narrative around which this book is structured, into which all the other stories are woven, is a highly abstract one that may be labelled 'a history of Canada'. I hope this discussion will help readers to understand the chapters that follow.

J.M. Bumsted
Winnipeg, 2010

A History

of the

Canadian
Peoples

1 The Beginnings

Timeline

Major Events in the Early History of the First Nations

12,000 BCE (Before Common Era)

Mammal retaining stone weapon killed in New Mexico.

11,000 BCE

Glacial retreat escalates with warming trend.

10,000 BCE

Continued warming alters physical environment as ice retreats.

9000 BCE

Fluted Point people spread across North America.

7000 BCE

Maritime Archaic culture develops the harpoon.

5500 BCE

Maritime Archaic culture develops burial mounds. Notched projectile points appear in British Columbia.

3000 BCE

Forest reaches its northernmost extension.

2000 BCE

Paleo-Eskimos and other Archaics begin displacing Maritime Archaics on eastern seaboard and in Arctic regions.

1000 BCE

Ceramic pottery appears in Great Lakes area and spreads east.

500 BCE

Dorset people appear in Arctic Canada. Climate deteriorates.

500 CE (Common Era)

Maize cultivation begins in southern Ontario. Climate improves.

600 Beothuk culture replaces the Dorset Eskimos in Newfoundland.

1000 Norse settle briefly in eastern North America.

1150 Dorset culture is replaced by Thule culture among Inuit.

1350 Squash and bean cultivation appears in southern Ontario.

1497 First recorded European arrival in North America since Norse.

1634 Beginning of the destruction of Huronia.

These petroglyphs, located near Bella Coola, British Columbia, are thought to have been made between 5,000 and 10,000 years ago by the Nuxalk people. Although most petroglyphs are carved on vertical surfaces, many of the Bella Coola petroglyphs were carved on flat rock outcrops. Wolfgang Zintl © iStockphoto.com.

Timeline

Major Events in the Early European History in Northern North America

982–5 CE

Eric the Red explores Greenland.

c. 1000

L'Anse aux Meadows is established by the Norse.

1497   John Cabot reaches Newfoundland.

1500   Gaspar Corté-Real lands at Tierra Verde (Newfoundland).

1501   Gaspar Corté-Real brings the first Aboriginals to Europe.

1534   Jacques Cartier erects cross at Gaspé Harbour.

1576   First voyage of Martin Frobisher to Baffin Island.

1585   John Davis enters Davis Strait.

1605   Port-Royal established.

1608   Champlain builds habitation at Quebec.

1610   First English settlers arrive in Newfoundland.

1615   Étienne Brûlé investigates New York and Pennsylvania.

1616   Robert Bylot sails through Davis Strait.

1618   Champlain proposes major French colony on St Lawrence.

1628   Scottish settlement expedition arrives in Maritime region.

At one time, a history of Canada typically would begin with the arrival of the European 'discoverers' at the end of the fifteenth century. These events, at best, mark only the moment at which the inhabited land and its people enter the European historical record, not the beginning of their history. Thousands of years of human development preceded the appearance of the Europeans. The First Nations of North America also have their history. The work of countless modern specialists, chiefly linguistic scholars and archaeologists, has only begun to uncover the barest outlines of the pre-European period. The record of human settlement in Canada clearly does not begin with the Europeans.

The First Immigrants

Unlike other continents on planet Earth, North America did not produce indigenous archaic human forms going back thousands of generations. No evidence suggests that any of the many ancestors of *Homo sapiens* developed on this continent. There were no Old Stone Age people as in Africa, Asia, or Europe. Instead, the first humanlike inhabitant of North America was *Homo sapiens* himself, probably arriving as an immigrant in the New World during the last Great Ice Age—which ended 10,000 years ago—perhaps across a land bridge stretching between what is now Siberia and Alaska.

Until very recently, the 30,000 years or more of the human occupation of the North American continent before the arrival of the Europeans usually were labelled 'prehistoric'. That term has fallen out of common usage, however, because it produces so many misconceptions. No written record of North American development may have existed before the Europeans, but to assume that 'history' begins only with writing is misleading. Plenty of earlier records of human activity exist, including oral traditions of the First Nations. From them a fascinating picture of the early history of what is now Canada can be reconstructed. That picture is hardly a static one. Instead, it displays constant movement, adaptation, and change. These early people did not attempt to modify their environment so much as adapt to it. That environment was continually shifting, perhaps not over a single season but over several generations.

One of the chief factors influencing the early inhabitants of North America was climate. Until very recently—as the history of the planet goes—most of what is now Canada was covered with glacial ice, which began retreating about 10,000 years ago. Several ice-free corridors ran from Alaska south, through which the first immigrants from Asia probably travelled into the warmer regions of the continent. While some inhabitants adapted to ice and snow, most people began moving northward only as the ice began to melt. By the time of Christ, around 2,000 years ago, most of Canada had acquired the natural environment recognizable to us today. The land had also acquired permanent inhabitants. What we know about these people comes to us in the form of physical artifacts.

Because of the limited nature of the evidence, the early history of humankind in Canada is often described in terms of surviving tools and weapons, especially projectile points. Archaeologists can infer much from tool-making technology and its geographical spread across the continent. Using various dating techniques, including laboratory testing of organic substances to determine what remains of a radioactive isotope called carbon-14, it has been possible to provide some overall sense of chronological development. The first incontestable evidence of human habitation in northern North America comes in the form of fluted projectile points chipped from various rocks by taking long flakes (or flutes) from the base to the tip. Evidence from other parts of the Americas suggests that habitation occurred long before 9500–8000 BCE, when people using these points spread from Alaska through the central plains and eastern woodlands. They were hunters and gatherers who lived in small units, although not in total isolation from neighbours. Evidence survives of trade and the exchange of goods.

As the ice melted and the glaciers moved northward, the hunters who made the fluted points spread more widely across the continent. These people have come to be known by archaeologists as the Plano People because of their distinctive projectile-point technology. They flourished from 8000 to 6000 BCE. By 4000 BCE a number of regional offshoots of the Plano People had developed. Over the next 3,000 years these cultures stabilized to some extent, although there was still substantial physical movement. On the western plains, a culture organized around communal bison-hunting emerged, perhaps as early as 3000 BCE. The High Arctic was occupied by Paleo-Eskimos, who gradually moved to the south into the Barren Lands west of Hudson Bay. The northeastern seaboard was occupied between 2000 and 1000 BCE. On the west coast, a semi-sedentary lifestyle based on the salmon had developed by 2000 BCE.

From 1000 BCE to 500 CE, substantial cultural changes occurred across North America. Once we stop trying to compare these developments with what was going on in Europe and see them instead in their own terms, we can appreciate how substantial the technological innovations of this period were. The bow and arrow spread rapidly, for example, profoundly altering hunting techniques. In the same years, pottery-making moved from the Yukon to eastern districts. The introduction of the pot changed food preparation substantially, but pottery also provides evidence of rapidly changing aesthetic sensibilities, as ornamentation was added to design.

Archaeologists have shifted their classification systems from the projectile point to the pot to characterize peoples of this era. Another new development was the rapid expansion from the south of new funeral practices, chiefly burial in large mounds. This change, of course, helped provide a new self-consciously created richness of physical evidence.

The First Nations Population around 1500

Although on the eve of European intrusion all Aboriginal peoples lived in a reciprocal relationship with nature, not all experienced the same relationship. Much depended on the resources of the region in which they lived and the precise combination of survival skills they possessed. Most of the

Kennewick Man

Tri-City Heral/André Ranieri

In 1996 two young men found a human skull in the Columbia River near Kennewick, Washington. Over the next month, other parts of the skeleton were found by archaeologist James C. Chatters. Within the skeleton's right hipbone was embedded a projectile point, possibly of great antiquity. Forensic examination disclosed that the nearly complete skeleton, which included a full set of teeth, was of a male between 40 and 55 years, of tall but slender build. He had suffered numerous injuries over his lifetime. Radiocarbon dating of a bone fragment indicated that this man had lived about 7,500 years before the birth of Christ. The skull lacked mongoloid characteristics and displayed many signs associated with modern caucasoids, as a forensic reconstruction illustrates. The skeleton was caught up for some years in a legal dispute between modern American Indian tribes and scientists, which tended to obscure the purely scientific significance of the find. How did this example of early man—so unlike our picture of those humans migrating south from Asia and diffusing across America—come to be in Washington state? What did this find mean for conventional interpretations of how the Americas were peopled? We do not yet have the answers.

many groups were hunters and gatherers, organized into mobile bands that followed the seasons and the cycles of game. On the coasts, fishing was the principal means of collecting a food supply. In the North, as in many other areas, whether one fished or hunted depended on the season. On the Pacific Slope, the rich resource base of salmon and cedar made possible considerable accumulations of wealth and social gradation. These Pacific peoples demonstrated that it was not essential to farm in order to prosper. Only those people living in the area of the Great Lakes pursued horticulture. The planting of corn, tobacco, beans, squash, and sunflowers led to the establishment of semi-permanent villages.

Despite the differences in their lifestyles, all First Nations were remarkably adept and ingenious at adapting to their environment. None were more successful than the Inuit, who inhabited an ice-bound territory in the North. At sea they used the speedy kayak and on land the dogsled. They lived in domed snow-huts (igloos) in winter and in skin tents in summer. Caribou hides served as the basic clothing material and provided much protection from the inclement weather. The Inuit were extremely skilful at making tools and weapons. Their use of bone and ivory for such equipment was extensive, and their aesthetic sense highly developed.

With the possible exceptions of the horticulturalists of south-central Canada and the fisherfolk of the Pacific Slope, the economies of the First Nations were quite simple ones. They were organized around the food supply, offering semi-nomadic

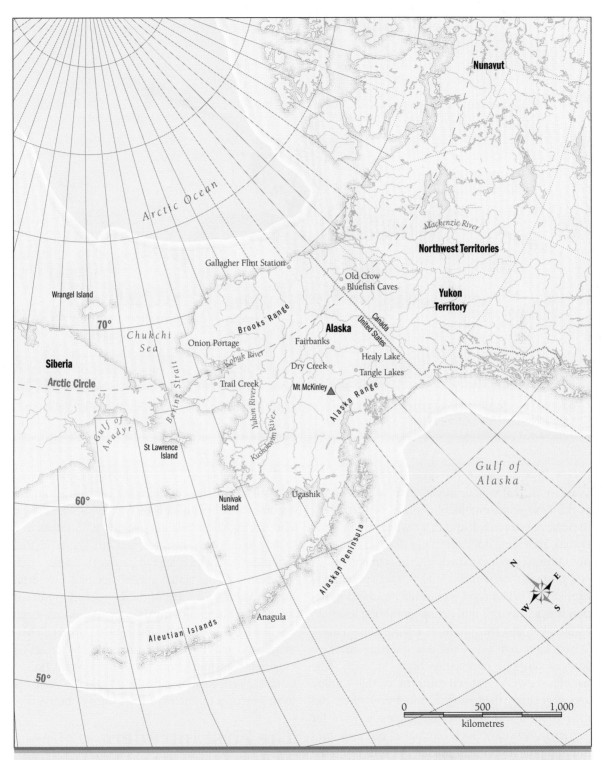

Beringia: the 'land bridge' at its greatest extent. Shaded area was above sea level approximately 20,000 years ago. Adapted from Brian M. Fagan, *The Great Journey: The Peopling of Ancient North America* (London: Thames and Hudson, 1987), 100

Sadlermiut man paddling an inflated walrus-skin boat, watercolour, c. 1830, artist unknown. LAC (Peter Winkworth Collection of Canadiana), W304.

people little scope for the acquisition of material possessions that would only have to be abandoned at the next—and imminent—move. Nevertheless, these were economies, and those within them functioned according to their inner logic. Food was not cultivated but pursued. The movement of fish and game had certain rhythms, but was potentially capricious. When food was available, the population was galvanized into action, gathering as much as possible and consuming it almost immediately. When food ran out, energetic questing for new sources did not necessarily begin at once. The people knew the general patterns of the wildlife and vegetation they sought, and hurry often did little good. It was, for example, useless to hunt for berries in February. Such economies put little premium on the disciplined pursuit of goals, or on the deferral of expectations. Nor did they encourage the sort of unremitting hard labour familiar to the European newcomers.

The number of First Nations peoples living in Canada on the eve of European intrusion has become the subject of debate. One point seems clear. The Aboriginal population, lacking immunities to a variety of European diseases, was quickly decimated by epidemics, which spread across the land, often in advance of the actual appearance of a European human carrier. The size of the population observed by the first European arrivals may have already been modified by disease brought by the earliest fishermen, who may well have preceded the recorded explorers. The indigenous pre-contact population of Canada was probably substantially larger than the most generous estimates of first-contact observers.

The First Intruders

As every Canadian schoolchild knows, Norsemen made the first documented European visitations to North America. Contemporary evidence of these visits is contained in the great Icelandic epic sagas, confirmed in our own time by archaeological excavations near L'Anse aux Meadows on the northern tip of Newfoundland. The sagas describe the landings to the west of Greenland made by Leif Ericsson and his brother Thorvald. They also relate Thorfinn Karlsefni's colonization attempt at a place Leif had called Vinland, an attempt that was thwarted by hostile residents labelled in the sagas as 'Skraelings'. It is tempting to equate Vinland with the archaeological discoveries, although there is no real evidence for doing so.

Later Greenlanders may have timbered on Baffin Island. They may also have intermarried with the Inuit. Attempts have been made to attribute the Thule culture of the Inuit to such relationships. But Greenland gradually lost contact with Europe, and the Icelandic settlement there died away in the fifteenth century. The Norse activities became part of the murky geographical knowledge of the late Middle Ages.

In our own time the uncovering of a world map executed in the mid-fifteenth century, showing a realistic Greenland and westward islands including inscriptions referring to Vinland, created much speculation about Europe's geographical knowledge before Columbus. This Vinland map has never been definitively authenticated, and many experts have regarded it with skepticism. The current scholarly view, however, has turned back to a positive evaluation of the map.

Like the Vinland map, none of the various candidates for North American landfalls before Columbus—except for the Norse in Newfoundland—can be indisputably documented. In the fifteenth century, Portuguese and possibly English fishermen may have discovered the rich fishing grounds off the Grand Banks. An occasional vessel may even have made a landfall. The fishermen did not publicize their knowledge, although many scholars insist that awareness of lands in the western Atlantic was

Sketch of an ocean-going Viking vessel of the eleventh century. In the 1950s archaeologists began excavating a collection of five Viking ships sunk between 1070 and 1090 to create a blockade across a narrow channel at Skuldelev, Denmark. One of these ships was a double-decked cargo carrier with higher sides (called a 'knarr') of the sort the Norse would have sailed in the open Atlantic. It had extra trusses and a sheltered cargo space below deck for people and animals. Source: The Viking Ship Museum, Denmark. Illustration: Morten Gøthche.

probably in common circulation in maritime circles by the end of the fifteenth century.

Europe around 1500

The arrival of Europeans in the Americas at the end of the fifteenth century was a collaborative effort by mariners and contemporary scholars of many nations, behind which were profound changes in economies and polities. The ambition to visit new lands was fuelled by the surge of intellectual confidence and the explosion of knowledge associated with the Renaissance. By the end of the fifteenth century, geographers—led by Paolo dal Pozzo Toscanelli, an Italian cosmographer in Portuguese service—were convinced that Europe and Asia were closer than the ancients had conjectured. The schemes of Christopher Columbus were influenced both by Toscanelli and by Portuguese notions of oceanic islands. Geographical speculation and ship

Karlsefni and the Skraelings

The Norse sagas began as manuscripts of the history of the Icelandic Norsemen collected in the thirteenth century. The following selection is from a manuscript called in English 'Eirik the Red's Saga', which is a reworking of original material in agreement with well-established rules of the saga tradition. Despite its title, 'Eirik the Red's Saga' is much more interested in the Icelanders Gudrid and Karlsefni than in the family of Eirik the Red.

Karlsefni sailed south along the land with Snorri and Bjarni and the rest of their company. They journeyed a long time till they reached a river which flowed down from the land into a lake and so on to the sea. There were such extensive bars off the mouth of the estuary that they were unable to get into the river except at full flood. Karlsefni and his men sailed into the estuary, and called the place Hop, Landlock Bay. There they found self-sown fields of wheat where the ground was low-lying, and vines wherever it was hilly. Every brook there was full of fish. They dug trenches at the meeting point of land and high water, and when the tide went out there were halibut in the trenches. There were vast numbers of animals of every kind in the forest. They were there for a fortnight enjoying themselves and saw nothing and nobody. They had their cattle with them.

Then early one morning when they looked about them they saw nine skin-boats, on board which staves were being swung which sounded just like flails threshing—and their motion was sunwise.

'What can this mean?' asked Karlsefni.

'Perhaps it is a token of peace,' replied Snorri. 'So let us take a white shield and hold it out towards them.'

They did so, and those others rowed towards them, showing their astonishment, then came ashore. They were small, ill-favoured men, and had ugly hair on their heads. They had big eyes and were broad in the cheeks. For a while they remained there, astonished, and afterwards rowed off south past the headlands.

Karlsefni and his men built themselves dwellings up above the lake; some of their houses stood near the mainland, and some near the lake. They now spent the winter there. No snow fell, and their entire stock found its food grazing in the open. But once spring came in they chanced early one morning to see how a multitude of skin-boats came rowing from the south round the headland, so many that the bay appeared sown with coals, and even so staves were being swung on every boat. Karlsefni and his men raised their shields, and they began trading together. Above all these people wanted to buy red cloth in return for which they had furs to offer and grey pelts. They also wanted to buy swords and spears, but this Karlsefni and Snorri would not allow. They had dark unblemished skins to exchange for the cloth, and were taking a span's length of cloth for a skin, and this they tied round their heads. So it continued for a while, then when the cloth began to run short they cut it up so that it was no broader than a fingerbreadth, but the Skraelings gave just as much for it, or more.

The next thing was that the bull belonging to Karlsefni and his mates ran out of the forest bellowing loudly. The Skraelings were terrified by this, raced to their boats and rowed south past the headland, and for three weeks running there was neither sight nor sound of them. But at the end of that period they saw a great multitude of Skraeling boats coming up from the south like a streaming torrent. This time all the staves were being swung anti-sunwise, and the Skraelings were all yelling aloud, so they took red shields and held them out against them. They clashed together and fought. There was a heavy shower of missiles, for the Skraelings had war-slings too. Karlsefni and Snorri could see the Skraelings hoisting up on poles a huge ball-shaped object, more or less the size of a sheep's paunch, and blue-black in colour, which they sent flying inland over Karlsefni's troop, and it made a hideous noise when it came down. Great fear now struck into Karlsefni and all his following, so that there was no other thought in their heads than to run away up along the river to some steep rocks, and there put up a strong resistance.

Source: Gwyn Jones, *The Norse Atlantic Saga: Being the Norse Voyages of Discovery and Settlement to Iceland, Greenland, America* (London: Oxford University Press, 1964), 181–3. Reprinted by permission of the publisher.

design pointed towards transatlantic voyages. Some time in the twelfth century, the Germans developed the cog, a single-masted ship decked over and fitted with rudder and tiller. In the early fifteenth century the cog's hull was lengthened and the vessel was given two additional masts, becoming the carvel (or caravel). Early explorers found smaller ships more manoeuvrable than larger ones and came to prefer them on their voyages. Rigging also improved, particularly with the addition of the square sail to the earlier lateen (triangular) variety.

The art of navigation showed development parallel to ship design, a gradual result of trial and error by countless mariners. The greatest advance was in written sailing directions based on taking latitudes in relation to Polaris (the North Star) and the sun. Longitudes still were based largely on guesswork, mainly on a mariner's estimates of his vessel's speed. In addition to the compass, seamen used quadrants and astrolabes to determine latitude, and were familiar with the need to transfer their data on latitude and longitude onto charts ruled for these variables. *Routiers*—coastal pilot charts of European waters—were readily available, but none of the early explorers who reached North America had the faintest idea of the hazards he was risking. The most remarkable feature of the first known voyages was the infrequency with which mariners ran into serious problems with rocks, shoals, and tides. Such master mariners had an instinctive 'feel' for the sea. They were able to read and deduce much from its colour and surface patterns.

Though the early explorers had their blind spots, they were without exception skilled sailors, suitably cautious in uncharted waters, which may explain many glaring failures to uncover rivers and bays obvious on any modern map. Once ashore, however, the first Europeans to reach North America threw caution to the winds, particularly in collecting rumours of rich mineral deposits or routes to Asia. Neither they nor their sponsors were at all interested in the scientific accumulation of knowledge. What they sought was wealth, equivalent to the riches the Spaniards were already taking out of their territories to the south. While other motives—such as national advantage and missionary fervour directed against the resident inhabitants—also entered the picture, the easy and rapid exploitation of the resources of the New World long remained the principal attraction.

The assumption of sovereignty by European states in the early period of exploration consisted chiefly of the performance of various symbolic acts or ceremonies of possession. Such ceremonies were intimately bound up with the culture and language of a particular nation, so that no two nations meant quite the same thing by their actions. The Portuguese, for example, thought that mere discovery was sufficient to establish legitimate dominion, and the word 'discovery' in Portuguese carried that nuanced meaning, while other nations had quite different concepts of what produced a legitimate right to rule. For the English, settlement in the form of 'first building and habitation' was one important test, as was 'replenishing and subduing' a land that had previously existed in common and was seemingly undeveloped (Seed, 1995: 9, 31). Every European nation had its own understanding of the meaning of 'possession'.

An astrolabe. By turning the sighting rod to point at the sun or a bright star, a mariner could estimate its altitude above the horizon and use that information as an aid to navigation. © Canadian Museum of Civilization, 989.56.1, image no. 594-37602.

Among those European powers who explored in North America, the French were the most likely to take into account the feelings of the indigenous peoples they encountered. Indeed, the French—whose monarchical political customs at home relied heavily on the use of ritual and ceremony—often incorporated the consent of the Aboriginal people into their ceremonies as a central component. The early French explorers assumed that physical gestures and body language could be universally understood, and made sure that the Aboriginal people either gave appropriate signs of agreement, or better still, actually participated in the ceremonies of possession. Thus, the French explorers did not simply

L'Anse aux Meadows

In 1961 the Norwegian explorer Helge Ingstad announced that he had found Norse buildings in northern Newfoundland. Many were skeptical, but in excavations executed between 1961 and 1968 by Ingstad and his wife Anne (and continued by Parks Canada in the 1970s), eight ruined buildings were uncovered in a grassy cove overlooking the Strait of Belle Isle. Seven of the buildings are grouped into three complexes located on a north–south axis. Each complex includes a hall of several rooms and a smaller one-room hut. Each of the huts may represent housing for a different vessel. Radiocarbon dating indicates an occupation between 980 and 1020. The buildings are substantial, with sod walls and permanent roofs. They were obviously constructed to be lived in year-round by up to 100 people. Each hall had a workshop: the southernmost one a smithy, the middle one a carpentry shop, and the northern one a boat-building lean-to. This was not a typical Norse arrangement, for there were no signs of livestock or domestic animals. The settlement was apparently not intended for farming, but probably as a base for further exploration of the region. The short duration of the season of navigation in these northern waters demanded that the Norse winter over in Vinland in order to scout out the region. The settlement was abandoned fairly swiftly in an orderly manner, leaving behind little equipment and no burial site. Archaeologists speculate that the site was the headquarters of Leif Ericsson himself, for the population here represented as much as 10 per cent of the Greenland Norse colony, mainly comprising workmen. Apparently this location (and the region surrounding it) was not sufficiently attractive to produce a permanent colony, both because of the

Source: William Fitzhugh and Elisabeth I. Ward, eds., *Vikings: The North Atlantic Saga* (Washington and London: Smithsonian Institution Press, 2000). Reprinted by permission of Smithsonian Books.

climate and because of the unfriendly local inhabitants. But it co-ordinates well with what is known of the Norse experience in Vinland as reported in the Vinland sagas.

John Cabot Reaches Land across the Atlantic, 1497

Over the winter of 1497–8, the English merchant John Day wrote a letter to 'El Gran Almirante' (probably Christopher Columbus), giving him an account of a recent voyage by John Cabot. This account provides some of our best evidence for Cabot's landfall.

From the said copy [of 'the land which has been found', which is no longer extant] your Lordship will learn what you wish to know, for in it are named the capes of the mainland and the islands, and thus you will see where land was first sighted, since most of them was discovered after turning back. Thus your Lordship will know that the cape nearest to Ireland is 1800 miles west of Dursey Head which is in Ireland, and the southernmost part of the Island of the Seven Cities is west of Bordeaux River, and your Lordship will know that he [Cabot] landed at only one spot of the mainland, near the place where land was first sighted, and they disembarked there with a crucifix and raised banners with the arms of the Holy Father and those of the King of England, my master; and they found tall trees of the kind masts are made, and other smaller trees, and the country is very rich in grass. In that particular spot, as I told your Lordship, they found a trail that went inland, they saw a site where a fire had been made, they saw manure of animals which they thought to be farm animals, and they saw a stick half a yard long pierced at both ends, carved and painted with brazil, and by such things they believe the land to be inhabited. Since he was with just a few people, he did not dare advance inland beyond the shooting distance of a cross-bow, and after taking in fresh water he returned to his ship. All along the coast they found many fish like those which in Iceland are dried in the open and sold in England and other countries, and these fish are called in English 'stockfish'; and thus following the shore they saw two forms running on land one after the other, but they could not tell if they were human beings or animals; and it seemed to them that there were fields where they thought might also be villages, and they saw a forest whose foliage looked beautiful. They left England toward the end of May, and must have been on the way 35 days before sighting land; the wind was east-north-east and the sea calm going and coming back, except for one day when he ran into a storm two or three days before finding land; and going so far out, his compass needle failed to point north and marked two rhumbs below. They spent about one month discovering the coast and from the above mentioned cape of the mainland which is nearest to Ireland, they returned to the coast of Europe in fifteen days. They had the wind behind them, and he reached Brittany because the sailors confused him, saying that he was heading too far north. From there he came to Bristol, and he went to see the King to report to him all the above mentioned; and the King granted him an annual pension of twenty pounds sterling to sustain himself until the time comes when more will be known of this business, since with God's help it is hoped to push through plans for exploring the said land more thoroughly next year with ten or twelve vessels—because in his voyage he had only one ship of fifty 'tonnes' and twenty men and food for seven or eight months—and they want to carry out this new project. It is considered certain that the cape of the said land was found and discovered in the past by the men from Bristol who found 'Brasil' as your Lordship well knows. It was called the Island of Brasil, and it is assumed and believed to be the mainland that the men from Bristol found. Since your Lordship wants information relating to the first voyage, here is what happened: he went with one ship, his crew confused him, he was short of supplies and ran into bad weather, and he decided to turn back.

Source: J.A. Williamson, ed., *The Cabot Voyages and British Discoveries under Henry VII* (Cambridge: Hakluyt Society of the University Press, 1962), 211–14. (The Hakluyt Society was established in 1846 for the purpose of printing rare or unpublished Voyages and Travels. For further information please see their website at www.Hakluyt.com.)

raise objects of possession like crosses and pillars, but sought to communicate something of their meaning to the Native witnesses and interpreted Native responses as evidence of acceptance or even enthusiasm of the French ceremonialism.

French accounts of ceremonies usually include detailed descriptions of the bodily movements and sounds of the indigenous observers, which were taken to mean formal consent. For the English, on the other hand, cultural symbols of land possession usually involved signs of successful occupation, such as housing, fencing, and cultivation of the land. Such actions had their own justification. Since the local inhabitants in most places obviously did not exhibit such signs of permanent occupation, they were not regarded as having proper jurisdiction over the country in which they resided (Seed, 1995: 41–68).

The European Entry into North America

John Cabot went briefly ashore at the 'newfoundland'. Cabot, originally an Italian, had convinced Henry VII of England to finance one small ship of 50 tons and a crew of 18 to sail west and find a short route to Asia. Cabot was lost at sea on a second voyage, and his mantle fell to a number of Portuguese mariners, some in English service, who produced a more clearly defined understanding of Newfoundland. Most of the sixteenth-century place names in Newfoundland were Portuguese rather than English. Portugal actually attempted to settle a colony on the Newfoundland coast under the leadership of Juan Fagundes, who had earlier sailed as far as the Gulf of St Lawrence. Fagundes ended up on Cape Breton Island, where his little settlement was apparently destroyed by the local residents, who 'killed all those who came there'. Nevertheless, by 1536 Newfoundland was sufficiently familiar, if exotic, to Europeans that a tourist voyage to the island was organized. London merchant Richard Hore (fl. 1507–40) signed 120 passengers, 'whereof thirty were gentlemen'. When provisions ran short on the Newfoundland coast, some participants allegedly resorted to eating their compatriots. Those surviving were understandably relieved to get back to England.

In 1523 the French entered the picture through the activities of Italian master mariner Giovanni da Verrazzano (c. 1485–c. 1528). Of high birth, Verrazzano persuaded Francis I to sponsor a voyage of exploration. He made three voyages in all, opening a French trade with Brazil and convincing himself that what he was investigating was not Asia but a totally new continent. Verrazzano was succeeded by Jacques Cartier (1491–1557), who had allegedly been to Brazil and Newfoundland. In 1534 Francis I ordered him to uncover new lands, 'where it is said that a great quantity of gold, and other precious things, are to be found.' Little concern was given to the conversion of Aboriginal peoples in Cartier's efforts. He, too, made three voyages: the first to make a great 'discovery', a second to locate some mineral resource there that would attract investors and the royal court, and a final large-scale effort that failed to produce any profit.

On his first voyage in 1534 Cartier explored the Gulf of St Lawrence. His second voyage in 1535 took him upriver as far as Mont Royal. He visited several First Nations villages and wintered at one of them, Stadacona. Here he heard about the fabulous kingdom of the Saguenay, somewhere farther west. A third voyage was actually headed by a great nobleman, the Sieur de Roberval (c. 1500–60). It was a disaster, finding little wealth to exploit and accomplishing nothing. The gold and diamonds Cartier brought back turned out to be iron pyrites and quartz. 'False as Canadian diamonds' became a common French expression of the time. Despite the lack of accomplishment, a French claim to the St Lawrence region had been established, and the French ultimately would return there.

The next major adventurer to what is now Canada was the Englishman Martin Frobisher (1539?–94), who spent several years searching for the Northwest Passage and great wealth in the Arctic region. Frobisher was a leading English 'sea dog'— part pirate and part merchant. In 1576 he raised the funds for an expedition to sail west to Asia through northern waters. He did not find the passageway, but did bring back mineral samples from Baffin Island. These were pronounced to be gold-bearing, leading to a second expedition in 1577, which brought back 200 tons of ore. About the first of October in 1578, a third fleet returned to England from the land called

'Meta Incognita'. Its principal cargo consisted of 1,350 tons of rocks, collected with great effort and at considerable expense on Baffin Island. Accounts of the return appeared in print before the experts had a chance to examine the cargo. Everyone was demanding to be paid. The owner of one vessel

Jacques Cartier Meets with Aboriginal People, 1534

In the summer of 1534, the French mariner Jacques Cartier cruised along the northern coast and St Lawrence region of North America. His original journal or log of this expedition does not survive, but a printed version appeared in Italian in 1565. Various versions of the journal were collated and translated by Henry Percival Biggar and published in 1924.

On Thursday the eighth of the said month [of July] as the wind was favourable for getting under way with our ships, we fitted up our long-boats to go and explore this [Chaleur] bay; and we ran up it that day about twenty-five leagues. The next day, at daybreak, we had fine weather and sailed on until about ten o'clock in the morning, at which hour we caught sight of the head of the bay, whereat we were grieved and displeased. At the head of this bay, beyond the low shore, were several high mountains. And seeing there was no passage, we proceeded to turn back. While making our way along the shore, we caught sight of the Indians on the side of a lagoon and low beach, who were making many fires that smoked. We rowed over to the spot, and finding there was an entrance from the sea into the lagoon, we placed our long-boats on one side of the entrance. The savages came over in one of their canoes and brought us some strips of cooked seal, which they placed on bits of wood and then withdrew, making signs to us that they were making us a present of them. We sent two men on shore with hatchets, knives, beads, and other wares, at which the Indians showed great pleasure. And at once they came over in a crowd in their canoes to the side where we were, bringing furs and whatever else they possessed, in order to obtain some of our wares. They numbered, both men, women, and children, more than 300 persons. Some of their women, who did not come over, danced and sang, standing in the water up to their knees. The other women, who had come over to the side where we were, advanced freely towards us and rubbed our arms with their hands. Then they joined their hands together and raised them to heaven, exhibiting many signs of joy. And so much at ease did the savages feel in our presence, that at length we bartered with them, hand to hand, for everything they possessed, so that nothing was left to them but their naked bodies; for they offered us everything they owned, which was, all told, of little value. We perceived that they are people who would be easy to convert, who go from place to place maintaining themselves and catching fish in the fishing-season for food. Their country is more temperate than Spain and the finest it is possible to see, and as level as the surface of a pond. There is not the smallest lot of ground bare of wood, and even on sandy soil, but is full of wild wheat, that has an ear like barley and the grain like oats, as well as of pease, as thick as if they had been sown and hoed; of white and red currant-bushes, of strawberries, of raspberries, of white and red roses and of other plants of a strong, pleasant odour. Likewise there are many fine meadows with useful herbs, and a pond where there are many salmon. I am more than ever of opinion that these people would be easy to convert to our holy faith.

Source: H.P. Biggar, ed., *The Voyages of Jacques Cartier: Published from the originals with translations, notes and appendices* (Ottawa: F. Acland, 1924), 54–7.

wrote desperately to the government for money to pay his crew, noting, 'Chrystmas beynge so nere, every man cryythe out for mony' (Stefansson, 1938). No money was forthcoming and for five years the sponsors of the expedition tried without success to find evidence of value in the cargo. The rock proved to be nothing more than sandstone flecked with mica. The business degenerated into an unseemly exchange of recriminations and accusations among the investors, and the rock was used eventually in Elizabethan road construction.

Frobisher's quest for the Northwest Passage in Arctic waters inspired a series of explorers, mainly Englishmen backed by English capital, over the next 50 years. The best-known of these adventurers was Henry Hudson (d. 1611), who sailed under both English and Dutch auspices. On his last voyage in 1610 he entered Hudson Bay and navigated its eastern coastal waters southward to James Bay before his crew mutinied against him and cast him adrift on a small boat, never to be seen again. Most of the great voyages of discovery had been completed by the end of the sixteenth century, even though much of the North American continent remained to be mapped and charted. They occurred against a complex European backdrop of dynastic manoeuvring, the rise of the modern nation-state, the religious disputes of the Protestant Reformation and Catholic Counter-Reformation, and the growth of capitalistic enterprise fuelled by the infusion of new wealth in the form of gold and silver bullion from the Indies. In the sixteenth century Henry VII and Elizabeth I of England joined Francis I of France as important patrons of master mariners who set sail for the West hoping to obtain wealth and national advantage from the voyages they sponsored. The dissolution of an earlier alliance between Spain and England in the wake of the latter nation's becoming Protestant, as well as the complex relationships between the ruling houses of the two countries, encouraged Elizabeth to turn her 'sea dogs' (like Frobisher) loose upon the Spanish empire. English exploration was inextricably bound up with 'singeing the Spanish beard' and with political hostility to Spain heightened by religious grievances. English adventurers often combined the roles of explorer, pirate, and even colonizer. The French had entered the American sweepstakes in the hopes of competing with the Spaniards and Portuguese. After Cartier's pioneering (and unsuccessful) voyages of 1534, 1535–6, and 1541–2, France was preoccupied with its internal dynastic struggles more than with overseas adventuring. The French government did not show much interest in North America until the end of the century, by which time France's Henry IV had stabilized the monarchy.

The frontispiece to *The Voyages of Jacques Cartier*, edited by H.P. Biggar. This portrait of Cartier—if such it is—is imaginary, since we do not have a likeness. Thomas Fisher Rare Book Library, University of Toronto.

Top: Cartier's first voyage, 1534.
Bottom: Cartier's second voyage, 1535–6.

Three Baffin Island Inuit—a man, a woman, and her child—who were taken prisoner by Frobisher on his expedition to the Arctic in 1577. All three died a month or so after arriving in England. Copyright © The Trustees of the British Museum 205220 and 234062.

In both France and England, overseas investment by an emerging mercantile class took over gradually from the earlier efforts of intrepid mariners backed by the Crown. Cartier's third voyage marked for France the transition from public to private enterprise, and the 1576 voyage of Martin Frobisher in search of the Northwest Passage to the East demonstrated the new importance of mercantile investment to the English.

By the end of the sixteenth century Europe had established that there were no wealthy Aboriginal civilizations to be conquered on the eastern seaboard, nor any readily apparent sources of rich mineral wealth to be exploited. When it was clear that what the continent had in abundance were fish and furs, a more complex pattern of exploitation had to be developed that required the year-round presence of settlers. Both France and England shifted their energies from maritime thrusts to colonization.

Map of the North Pole, 1595, by Gerardus Mercator. LAC, NMC-016097.

Henry Hudson

Like many another early European explorer, Hudson has left no paper trail beyond the events of the years at the high point of his reputation. We do not know where he was born or when, except that he was apparently an Englishman. In 1607 he was employed by the Muscovy Company (an English company trading with Russia) to seek a Northeast Passage to China across the North Pole, and he followed this voyage up with another in 1608, which sailed to the Russian Arctic but found nothing. This employment has been taken to mean that, whatever his background, he was regarded as highly competent. The Dutch East India Company hired him in 1609 to continue searching for the Northeast Passage in his ship *Half Moon*. His crew mutinied near Norway, and he changed his course as a result, crossing the Atlantic to search instead for the Northwest Passage and sailing up the Hudson River, which still bears his name.

Hudson subsequently was hired by a consortium of English merchants to search for a route to Asia through North America. His ship *Discovery* was manned by a number of experienced seamen, including Robert Bylot, who had earlier sailed with William Baffin. The crew was quite quarrelsome, and the voyage was replete with open conflict and at least one mutiny in which the mutineers backed down only at the last minute. As was the case with the notorious Captain Bligh less than two centuries later, Hudson was a better mariner than a manager of men. He took reprisals against the mutineers. For reasons unknown, he exhibited blatant and continual favouritism to one young man, who eventually turned against him in consort with several others. Hudson refused to pause to replenish provisions at Digges Island, apparently expecting to be in China very shortly. On 23 June 1611, shortly after beginning the voyage back from a winter on Hudson Bay and desperately short of food, the conspirators, led by the former favourite, cast Hudson, his son, and seven other men into a small shallop and cut it adrift. They persuaded Robert Bylot (if his story is to be believed) to pilot the ship back to England. Nothing more is known of the passengers on the shallop, but Bylot brought the *Discovery* back to England after a desperate battle with the Inuit at Digges Island in which several mutineers were killed. Most of what we know about the post-mutiny adventures of the *Discovery* comes to us via a narrative by one of the participants, the curiously named Abacuk Pricket. Bylot was pardoned by a court and went on to a distinguished Arctic career; the other mutineers were eventually tried on a charge of murder and acquitted. Hudson's widow, Katherine, impoverished by her husband's disappearance, had to fight hard to receive compensation from the East India Company, which called her 'that troublesome and impatient woman'. Finally, it allowed her to trade in India on her own account. She returned in 1622 with considerable wealth. Considering the discontent aboard the *Discovery*, Hudson's accomplishment in navigating through Hudson Strait and hundreds of miles into Hudson Bay was outstanding, although his leadership skills left much to be desired.

The Impact of Disease on the Aboriginal Peoples

However rapidly European artifacts and animals (such as the horse) may have spread ahead of the newcomers, what dispersed across the continent with even greater rapidity was disease. North America in the sixteenth century was relatively isolated in a geographical sense. A host of communicable diseases common to the 'known world' of international trade and commerce either did not exist or were not so virulent on the North American continent, and the population had less immunity to them.

Measles, smallpox, typhus, typhoid, mumps, and venereal disease—the last perhaps first contracted by Europeans in the Caribbean region—were as much European introductions as the gun and the horse. Although these diseases spread unusually quickly among an Aboriginal population that had little immunity to them, we must not think that communicable disease was totally unknown in early North America or that the pre-contact population lived in an Edenic state of robust health. In any case,

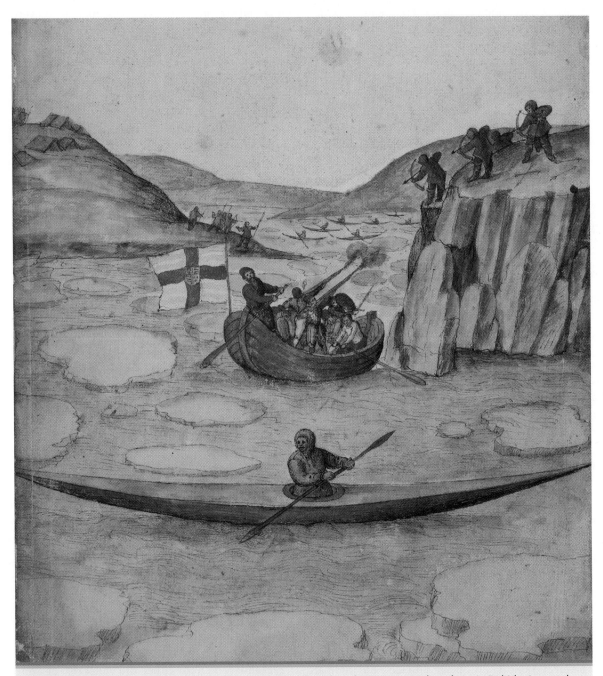

A confrontation between Inuit and English sailors, 1577. The artist, John White, was a member of Martin Frobisher's second expedition in search of a Northwest Passage.

trade and war, including the Aboriginal custom of replenishing population losses by adopting captive women and children, spread new and virulent diseases far beyond points of actual European contact. In fairness to the newcomers, they simply did not understand that their sexual promiscuity with First Nations women, or their taking Aboriginals back to Europe as prize specimens or informants, would be devastating to the Native populations. Europeans themselves had become callous about epidemic disease; it was part of life, and they did not understand the concepts of contagion and immunity. They had no reason to view the Aboriginal propensity for dying in captivity as something resulting from European intervention. For their part, the Aboriginals did not understand that crowding around a sick person to offer affection only spread disease, or that sitting in a sweat lodge and then plunging into cold water was not an effective remedy for a disease like smallpox.

As James Axtell points out, the Aboriginal peoples used three techniques to respond to the demographic disaster. The first, the employment of warfare to replenish the population through captivity and adoption, was of mixed success, particularly when extended to the Europeans. While the process worked well in some ways, it also helped to spread disease, and it certainly increased the hostility of European settlers to the First Nations. The second strategy was intermarriage, which ignored colour bars and many of the social assumptions of

Henri Membertou

Membertou claimed to have been a grown man when he met Jacques Cartier, which would mean that he had been born in the early years of the sixteenth century. Regardless of his exact birth date, Membertou was a venerable age when the French appeared at Port-Royal in 1605. He was the leader of a small band of Mi'kmaq whose hunting and fishing territory included Port-Royal. The opportunities afforded his band by the arrival of the Europeans were the envy of other Aboriginal leaders, and Membertou was a firm friend of the newcomers. He certainly looked like a leader. Father Biard described him as being taller and larger-limbed than his colleagues, and he apparently sported a beard. Much of what has been written about Membertou by the early chroniclers falls properly into the category of legend, but it was true that he was the first Aboriginal to be baptized in New France, as opposed to being carried to France and baptized there. The ceremony was performed by the newly arrived priest Jessé Fléché on 24 June 1610. All of Membertou's immediate family were baptized as well, without any proper preparation because the missionary could not speak the Algonquian language and the Aboriginals could not speak enough French. Membertou was given the European name of the king, Henri. After his baptism Membertou appeared eager to become a proper Christian. He wanted the missionaries to learn Algonquian so that he could be properly educated. However, by 1611 he had contracted dysentery, one of the many infectious diseases brought by the Europeans, and by September of that year he was clearly very ill. He insisted on being buried among his ancestors, which annoyed the missionaries, but they gave him extreme unction anyway, and at the end he apparently requested burial among the French. He died on 18 September 1611. The closing year of his life illustrates a pattern often repeated among the indigenous people who were 'Christianized' by the first European missionaries. Unable to understand properly the precepts of Christianity, they could hardly have been said to be converted, and they often died shortly after baptism, succumbing to contagious diseases probably introduced by the missionaries themselves.

European society. The third strategy was to move after depopulation, often joining with other tribes and peoples. The attraction of the Catholic reserves around Montreal and Quebec after the 1640s was in large part a result of the population devastations of the preceding period throughout the Northeast region of the continent.

The introduction of new diseases renders all attempts to estimate the size of the indigenous population at the time of first contact on the eastern seaboard highly problematic. Estimates for the population of North America north of the Rio Grande River at the beginning of the sixteenth century range as high as 18 million and beyond (Dickason, 2002: 9). We have already noted that the indigenous pre-contact population of Canada was substantially larger than the most generous estimates of all the first-contact observers, most of whom spoke of great numbers but were not very specific. The east coast population had probably been seriously reduced by epidemic disease during the sixteenth century, and demographic disaster preceded the Europeans right across the country. At the same time, this inadvertent introduction of the early pandemics should not be allowed to dominate the story of North America in the immediate pre-contact and early contact periods. In the first place, there was no 'Golden Age' in pre-European America in which contagious disease did not exist at all. In the second, infectious antigens were not the sole cause of the ultimate reduction (in size and power) of the Aboriginal population. Europeans took deliberate actions apart from epidemics that led to significant reductions in indigenous populations.

European Contact and the Development of Cultural Conflict

The intrusion of Europeans greatly altered the dynamics of First Nations development, while providing us with a somewhat misleading version of the nature of the population at the moment of contact and beyond. Recorded history was, after all, monopolized by those who had written languages and could make records. In the centuries following European arrival, virtually everything written about the indigenous population of Canada was produced from the European perspective. That perspective, moreover, tended to involve considerable misunderstanding of First Nations culture and behaviour.

Whatever technological glitter Europe had (the extent of its actual superiority is debatable), it would prove relatively useless in the wilderness of the New World. For several centuries, Europeans in Canada who were successful in surviving adopted First Nations technology. European inventions may have helped give the intruders a sense of superiority, as did their emerging capitalist economic order, their new political organization into nation-states, and especially their Christian system of values and beliefs. These pronounced differences between Europeans and indigenous Canadians prevented the visitors from fully comprehending the people they encountered. The Europeans quite unconsciously, often quite subtly, judged First Nations by their own standards.

At the same time, the process of early communication between Europeans and the Aboriginal peoples was a much more difficult business than we might think, or than the contemporary documents would suggest. Europeans and Aboriginals spoke different languages—a good many of them. In Europe, most countries lacked a single national language that was understood in every part of the country. Dialects had both regional and class origins. The great European sea captains, many of whom had connections at the royal court, were likely to have a different pronunciation and vocabulary than the common sailors, although technically both groups spoke the same language. The First Nations spoke several hundred different local languages in a myriad of dialects. Fifty different languages were spoken in what is now Canada, although most of these fell into a few language families. In what is now eastern Canada, the three principal language families were Algonquian, Iroquoian, and Siouan. But the differences in language between two tribes speaking an Algonquian tongue might be as great as the differences between Spanish and Portuguese. Moreover, local patois would vary from place to place. The Aboriginal

Father Biard on the Mi'kmaq, 1616

In 1616 the Jesuit missionary Pierre Biard (c. 1567–1622), who had been at Port-Royal since 1611, wrote a 'Relation', which was published in France, describing his experiences with the Aboriginals of the region. It was subsequently translated and republished by Reuben Gold Thwaites.

They are astonished and often complain that, since the French mingle with and carry on trade with them, they are dying fast and the population is thinning out. For they assert that, before this association and intercourse, all their countries were very populous and they tell how one by one the different coasts, according as they have begun to traffic with us, have been more reduced by disease; adding, that why the Armouchiquois do not diminish in population is because they are not at all careless. Thereupon they often puzzle their brains, and sometimes think that the French poison them, which is not true; at other times that they give poisons to the wicked and vicious of their nation to help them vent their spite upon some one. This last supposition is not without foundation; for we have seen them have some arsenic and sublimate which they say they bought from certain French Surgeons, in order to kill whomsoever they wished, and boasted that they had already experimented upon a captive, who (they said) died the day after taking it. Others complain that the merchandise is often counterfeited and adulterated, and that peas, beans, bread, and other things that are spoiled are sold them; and that it is that which corrupts the body and gives rise to the dysentery and other diseases which always attack them in Autumn. This theory is likewise not offered without citing instances, for which they have often been upon the point of breaking with us, and making war upon us. Indeed there would be need of providing against these detestable murders by some suitable remedy if one could be found.

Nevertheless the principal cause of all these deaths and diseases is not what they say it is, but it is something to their shame; in the Summer time, when our ships come, they never stop gorging themselves excessively during weeks with various kinds of food not suitable to the inactivity of their lives; they get drunk, not only on wine but on brandy; so it is no wonder that they are obliged to endure some gripes of the stomach in the following Autumn. . . . These are their storehouses. Who is to take care of them when they go away? For, if they stay, their stores would soon be consumed; so they go somewhere else until the time of famine. Such are the only guards they leave. For in truth this is not a nation of thieves. Would to God that the Christians who go among them would not set them a bad example in this respect. But as it is now, if a certain Savage is suspected of having stolen anything he will immediately throw this fine defense in your teeth, We are not thieves, like you.

Source: Reuben Gold Thwaites, ed., *The Jesuit Relations and Allied Documents: Travels and Explanations 1610–1791*, 73 vols (Cleveland, 1896–1901), III, 105–9.

tongues were often difficult for Europeans to pronounce, and there were at the outset no dictionaries.

The niceties of grammar and the nuances of language frustrated both Natives and newcomers for centuries. Some Aboriginals who were educated in missionary schools learned to speak and understand European languages very well, and a few Europeans who grew up among the Aboriginals (sometimes willingly, often as captives) became equally adept at the Native tongues. But most people came to communicate in new 'pidgin' languages composed by reducing speech to its simplest elements and amalgamating parts of both European and Aboriginal languages. Pidgin languages were capable of sophistication as time went on, and they eliminated the potentially inflammatory business of preferring one

Distribution of Aboriginal peoples and language areas in the sixteenth century.

people's language over another. One very venerable pidgin language was spoken on the coasts of the Gulf of St Lawrence, where Basque fishermen had traded with local Natives from the early sixteenth century. 'Since their languages were completely different,' wrote one observer in 1710, 'they created a form of lingua franca composed of Basque and two different languages of the Indians, by means of which they could understand each other very well' (Bakker, 1989: 259). Marc Lescarbot in the early seventeenth century recorded that the Mi'kmaq spoke to the French in a simplified version of their language mixed with 'much Basque'. In the later fur trade in the interior of the continent, pidgin tongues were a complex amalgam of French, Gaelic, English, Cree, and Assiniboine.

Not surprisingly, as relations between Europeans and Aboriginal peoples became more formalized, the need for skilled official interpreters acquired a new urgency. An interpreter who was trusted by both sides in complex negotiations to translate accurately the meaning and nuances of language was a rare commodity and highly prized. As late as 1873, when Treaty No. 6 was being negotiated between the Canadian government and the Saskatchewan Cree, the question of interpreters remained a critical issue. The government had brought two interpreters of its own, and argued it was unnecessary to add another brought by the Cree. The Cree chief answered, 'Very good. You keep your interpreters and we will keep ours. We will pay our own man and I already see that it will be well for us to do so' (Christensen, 2000: 229).

The First Nations economies did not produce political institutions on a European scale. Semi-sedentary people had no need for political organizations larger than the band, which was based on the consolidation of a few family units. Even where horticulture was developed, with its large semi-permanent villages, political structure was not complex by European standards. 'Chiefs' were not kings. They may not even have been 'head men' in any European sense. Such a concept of rulership was in most places introduced and imposed on the indigenous population by the newcomers. As is now well known, the Aboriginal notion of property, especially involving land, was beyond the comprehension of the European. While some First Nations groups could conceive of territory as 'belonging' to them, the concept was one of usage rather than of ownership. The indigenous people erroneously identified as kings were quite happy to 'sell' to the European newcomers land that neither they nor their people owned, at least as Europeans understood ownership.

Lacking much inclination to create hierarchical political organizations, the First Nations practised war according to different rules than those employed in Europe, where institutions of church and state went to war for 'reasons of state'. Aboriginal wars were mainly raids by a few warriors, conducted partly because success in battle was an important

'Homme acadien': a Mi'kmaq hunter, hand-coloured etching, c. 1788–96, from original by Jacques Grasset de Saint-Sauveur, published in *Tableaux des principaux peuples de l'Europe, de l'Asie, de l'Afrique, de l'Amérique et les découvertes des Capitaines Cook, La Pérouse, etc.* (Paris et Bordeaux, 1796–8). LAC, C-21112.

test of manhood. They were often used to capture women and children to replace those lost within the band. Individual prowess in battle was valued, while long-term military strategy and objectives were not. First Nations had their own military agendas, and were notoriously fickle allies from the European perspective. Only the Iroquois—who in the seventeenth century may have developed a militarily viable form of political organization partly based on European models—were able to compete with the newcomers and withstand their military power.

Nowhere was the gulf between First Nations and newcomers more apparent than in the spiritual realm. Aboriginal religious beliefs were complex, although not readily apparent to the outside observer. They were part of an intricate religio-magical world that the First Nations inhabited and shared with the flora and fauna. Given the hunting orientation of most groups, it is hardly surprising that animals were endowed with spiritual significance. The very act of food consumption often acquired deep religious meaning, becoming a form of worship of the spirit

Where the First People Came From: A Cree Legend from the West Coast of James Bay

So then, I shall tell another legend. I'll tell a story, the legend about ourselves, the people, as we are called. Also I shall tell the legend about where we came from and why we came . . . , why we who are living now came to inhabit this land.

Now then, first I shall begin.

The other land was above, it is said. It was like this land which we dwell in, except that the life seems different; also it is different on account of its being cold and mild [here]. So then, this land where we are invariably tends to be cold.

So that is the land above which is talked about from which there came two people, one woman and one man, . . . they dwelt in that land which was above. But it was certainly known that this world where we live was there.

Now then at one time someone spoke to them, while they were in that land of theirs where they were brought up. He said to them, 'Do you want to go see yonder land which is below?'

The very one about which they were spoken to is this one where we dwell.

'Yes,' they said, 'we will go there.'

'The land,' they were told, 'is different, appears different from this one where we dwell in, which you dwell in now during your lifetime. But you will find it different there, should you go to see that land. It is cold yonder. And sometimes it is hot.

'It fluctuates considerably. If you wish to go there, however, you must go see the spider at the end of this land where you are. That is where he lives.'

The spider, as he is called, that is the one who is the net-maker, who never exhausts his twine,—so they went to see him, who is called the spider.

Then he asked them, 'Where do you want to go? Do you want to go and see yonder land, the other one which is below?'

'Yes,' they said.

'Very well,' said the spider. 'I shall make a line so that I may lower you.'

So then, he made a line up to,—working it around up to, up to the top.

'Not yet, not yet even half done,' he said.

Then he spoke to them, telling them, better for him to let them down even before he finished it the length it should be.

world through everyday activity. Many peoples had legends about the origins of the world, and some may have believed in a single Creator. The mixture of authentic Aboriginal lore with European thought and missionary teaching has coloured First Nations legends and tales over the last 350 years. It has made it difficult—perhaps impossible—to separate one from the other. Formal religious ceremonies were not readily apparent to the visitors, except for the activities of the shamans, who claimed supernatural powers and engaged in several kinds of folk medicine ranging from herbal treatment to exorcism. Shamans were no more priests than other leaders were kings, but Europeans tended to consider their activities to be at the core of First Nations religion. The newcomers found it impossible to grasp that inanimate objects in nature could be considered to be alive and have their own powers, or that rituals connected with the ordinary round of daily life could have deep spiritual significance. That First Nations religion had no buildings, no clerical hierarchy, and no institutional presence thoroughly disoriented the Europeans.

Then he told them, 'That land which you want to go and see is cold and sometimes mild. But there will certainly be someone there who will teach you, where you will find a living once you have reached it. He, he will tell you every thing so you will get along well.'

So he made a place for them to sit as he lowered them, the man and the woman.

They got in together, into that thing which looked like a bag.

Then he instructed them what to do during their trip. 'Only one must look,' he said to them. 'But one must not look until you have made contact with the earth. You may both look then.'

So, meanwhile they went along, one looked. At last he caught sight of the land.

The one told the other, 'Now the land is in sight.'

The one told the other, 'Now the rivers are in sight.'

They had been told however, that 'if one, . . . if they both look together, before they come to the land, they will go into the great eagle-nest and they will never be able to get out and climb down from there.'

That's where they will be. That's what they were told.

Then the one told the other, 'Now the lakes are in sight. Now the grass.'

Then they both looked before they arrived, as they were right at the top of the trees. Then they went sideways for a short while, then they went into the great eagle-nest. That's where they went in, having violated their instructions. . . .

Then the bear arrived.

So he said to them, . . . and they said to him, 'Come and help us.'

The bear didn't listen for long; but then he started to get up on his hind legs to go and see them. Also another one, the wolverine as he is called. They made one trip each as they brought them down.

But the bear was followed by those people.

That was the very thing which had been said to them, 'You will have someone there who will teach you to survive.'

This bear, he taught them everything about how to keep alive there.

It was there that these people began to multiply from one couple, the persons who had come from another land. They lived giving birth to their children generation after generation. That is us right up until today. That is why we are in this country.

And by-and-by the White People began to arrive as they began to reach us people, who live in this country.

That is as much as I shall tell.

Source: C. Douglas Ellis, ed. and trans., *Cree Legends and Narratives from the West Coast of James Bay* (Winnipeg: University of Manitoba Press, 1995), 3–7.

Tolerance for alternative spiritual values and belief systems was hardly one of Europe's strong suits in the Age of Discovery. The period of European arrival in North America coincided with the Protestant Reformation and the Catholic Counter-Reformation. Christianity was undergoing profound alteration, with traditional Catholicism subjected to reform from both within and without. Protestants and Catholics alike were quite capable of fierce persecution of any deviation from official belief and practice. Both could agree that what was being encountered in Canada was pagan supernaturalism that needed to be uprooted as quickly as possible and replaced with a 'true faith'. That Europeans could not agree on the truth among themselves perplexed some First Nations people, such as the Iroquois, who were exposed to competing French, English, and Dutch missionaries.

The European intruders could not grasp the notion that Christianity was embedded in an intricately developed European value system, or that indigenous religious beliefs and practices were integral to First Nations existence. Views of the world and of one's place in it were as integral to life for Aboriginals as they were for Europeans, and the way in which First Nations related spiritually to their environment was a critical part of their culture. Europe could not convert First Nations to Christianity without undermining the very basis of their existence. Naturally, the First Nations resisted.

While commenting on the freedom that children were allowed, European observers of every First Nations group in northern North America from coast to coast also wrote that women were badly exploited. European society at the time could hardly be called liberal in its treatment of women. What the newcomers saw as exploitation reflected their inability to comprehend the divisions of labour within a warrior society. Men hunted and fought, while women were responsible for just about everything else. Interestingly enough, when European women were captured by raiding parties and integrated into Aboriginal life, many chose to remain with their captors instead of accepting repatriation back into colonial society. Those captives who were brought home and who wrote about their experiences emphasized that the Aboriginals had a strong sense of love and community and offered—as one set of repatriates acknowledged—'The most perfect freedom, the ease of living, [and] the absence of those cares and corroding solicitudes which so often prevail with us' (Axtell, 2001: 213).

Almost from the outset, European newcomers to Canada had two contradictory responses to the peoples they were contacting and describing. On the one hand, much of what they saw in First Nations life, particularly beyond mere superficial observation, struck them as admirable. The First Nations exhibited none of the negative features of capitalistic society. On the other hand, there was the equally powerful image of the First Nations as brutal savages and barbarians, particularly in the context of war. This dichotomy of response was particularly keen among the missionaries, who kept trying to 'civilize' the First Nations by converting them to Christianity and forcibly educating them in European ways. Mère Marie de l'Incarnation, the head of the Ursuline School for girls at Quebec, wrote of her charges in 1668 that there was 'docility and intelligence in these girls, but when we are least expecting it, they clamber over our wall and go off to run with their kinsmen in the woods, finding more to please them there than in all the amenities of our French houses' (Marshall, 1967: 341).

In the eighteenth century, an idealized and romanticized view of Aboriginal society was used by many European philosophers as a literary convention and fictional device for criticizing contemporary European society. As Peter Moogk has pointed out, conditions of press censorship, particularly in France, made it advisable to use fictitious foreigners, including Amerindians, to express negative opinions about church and state (Moogk, 2000: 48–9). The first such character probably was Baron de Lahontan's 'Huron' named Adario, who in 1703 observed that the Ten Commandments were routinely ignored in France, while the Aboriginals practised innocence, love, and tranquility of mind. Lahontan's books went through numerous editions and led to the Enlightenment notion of the *bon sauvage* advanced by Voltaire and Rousseau. The First Nations possessed none of the worst traits of European capitalistic society, such as covetousness and rapaciousness; and they revered freedom, while eschewing private property. What relationship the 'noble savage' bore to the realities of existence in North America is another matter entirely.

Europeans would blunder on for centuries in their attempts to come to terms with the indigenous peoples of North America. The First Nations would prove tenacious in maintaining their own identity and culture in the face of much effort to Europeanize them, but they lacked the physical power to prevent either constant encroachment on their territory, or the continual undermining of the basic physical and spiritual substance of their way of life. The cultural contact between Native and newcomer truly was a tragedy. Reconciliation of the two cultures proved quite impossible, and the failure of reconciliation resounds still today.

The First European Communities

When generations of painful experience taught Europeans that there was no quick road to wealth by exploiting the indigenous peoples or the resource base of North America, hopes turned to transplanting Europeans who could take advantage of fish and furs. The shift occurred at the beginning of the seventeenth century. A variety of motives jostled in the minds of the early promoters of settlement, few of whom ever planned to set foot on North American soil. National advantage, religion, humanitarianism, greed, personal ambition, and sheer fantasy were present in various combinations. European monarchs and their supporters were flattered by the 'enlarging of Dominions'. Missions to the First Nations and the possibilities of refuge from religious persecution at home excited the pious. Many a promoter saw colonization as a way to rid Europe of unwanted paupers and petty criminals. Investors were tempted with talk of titles and large land grants. In the pursuit of great profits, common sense was lost easily. Although large-scale colonization activities were begun by the English in Virginia in 1607, the ventures undertaken in the northern latitudes typically were more modest. They consisted mainly of trading posts and fishing settlements.

English familiarity with Newfoundland led London merchants to attempt colonization there beginning in 1610. The London and Bristol Company for the Colonization of Newfoundland (usually known as the Newfoundland Company) was organized by 48 subscribers who invested £25 each. The plan was that permanent settlers employed by the company would quickly dominate the fishery over those who came in the spring and went home in the autumn. Europe was desperately short of a protein food for the poor, and dried cod found a ready market, especially in Catholic countries. The first settlement of the company was established by John Guy (d. 1629), who led 40 colonists from Bristol to Cupid's Cove on Conception Bay in July 1610, only months after the company was granted the entire island. The venture was funded by sale of stock. The company did not appreciate how difficult local agriculture would be, given the soil and the climate, or how unlikely it was in the vast expanses of the New World that settlers could be kept permanently as landless employees labouring solely for the profit of their masters.

The Newfoundland Company's fishing settlements prospered no more than did those of courtiers like George Calvert, First Baron Baltimore (1579/80–1632), who began a plantation at Avalon in 1623. Calvert discovered to his surprise, as he wrote his monarch in 1629, that 'from the middest of October, to the middest of May there is a sadd face of wynter upon all this land, both sea and land so frozen for the great part of the tyme that they are not penetrable, no plant or vegetable thing appearing out of the earth untill it be about the beginning of May nor fish in the sea besides the ayre so intolerable cold, as it is hardly to be endured' (Cell, 1982: 295–6). Not long after penning this complaint, he left for Virginia. In 1632 Calvert was granted the land north of the Potomac River that would become Maryland.

The French were marginally more successful than the English at establishing colonies in the northern regions, both in Acadia (the region vaguely bounded by the St Lawrence to the north, the Atlantic Ocean to the east and south, and the St Croix River to the west) and in Canada (the St Lawrence Valley). An

Champlain's drawing of the habitation at Port-Royal, built in 1605 on the north shore of the Annapolis Basin. The parts of the complex are identified in an accompanying key. For example, building 'A' was the artisans' quarters, and 'B' was a platform for cannon. Champlain's own quarters were in building D. LAC, C–7033.

early effort by the Marquis de La Roche de Mesgouez (c. 1540–1606) on Sable Island failed dismally, with rebellious settlers murdering their local leaders over the winter of 1602–3. The island was subsequently evacuated. A similar result occurred at a settlement at the mouth of the Saguenay River. In May 1604 Pierre Du Gua de Monts (1558?–1628) arrived on the Nova Scotia coast with a young draftsman named Samuel de Champlain (c. 1570–1635). The two men were searching for a suitable site to establish a settlement, a condition of de Monts's grant of a trading monopoly in the region. They tried first on an island in the St Croix River. In 1605 the settlement was moved to Port-Royal in the Annapolis Basin, where de Monts built a habitation, a supposed replica of which still exists today as a historic site. In 1606 the

Paris lawyer Marc Lescarbot (c. 1570–1642) joined the colony and wrote a narrative of its development, published in 1609 as *Histoire de la Nouvelle France*. In this work Lescarbot noted the foundation of L'Ordre de Bon Temps in 1607, a sort of dining club with extemporaneous entertainment. He also described the masque he wrote for it (the first stage play composed and performed in North America). The colonists were obliged to leave in 1607 when de Monts was forced to relinquish his monopoly, but a French presence would continue in Acadia from the first establishment of Port-Royal, usually in the form of a handful of individuals trading with the First Nations.

As for Samuel de Champlain, he headed up the St Lawrence in 1608 to found a new trading post for de Monts at Stadacona. Another habitation was erected, this one including three buildings of two storeys—connected by a gallery around the outside, 'which proved very convenient', wrote Champlain—surrounded by a moat and palisades. Champlain provided a careful drawing of this habitation in his *Voyages*. He was forced to put down a conspiracy and face a devastating attack of scurvy in the first year. The post survived, however, and Champlain gradually allied himself with the local First Nations, who supplied him with furs and drew the French into war against the Iroquois. Champlain had little alternative to an alliance against the Iroquois, and they became mortal enemies of the French.

Only about 50 Frenchmen resided on the St Lawrence by 1615. Among the early settlers, only Louis Hébert (1595?–1627), who came to Quebec in 1617 after lengthy service as a surgeon at Port-Royal, showed an interest in cultivating the land. But Hébert was most useful for his medical and apothecary skills; the trading company actually attempted to discourage him from agriculture. Not until 1618—when Champlain outlined a grand scheme for the colonization of New France in reports to the king and the French Chamber of Commerce—did anything approaching the plans of the Newfoundland Company enter the French vision. Earlier French activities, including those of Champlain himself, had been underfinanced by a succession of individual entrepreneurs and small syndicates. Trading posts, rather than settlement colonies, were the goal.

Until 1618, Champlain had served as an agent for others rather than as a colonial promoter in his own right. In that year, however, he combined arguments for major investment with a scheme designed to appeal to the imperial pretensions of the Crown. New France and the St Lawrence not only held the possibility of a short route to Asia but could produce 'a great and permanent trade' in such items as fish, timber, whale oil, and furs. The annual income was

The Order of Good Cheer

It would be tedious to attempt to particularise all that was done among us during the winter [of 1606–7] . . . . But I shall relate how, in order to keep our table joyous and well-provided, an Order was established at the board of the said M. de Poutrincourt, which was called the Order of Good Cheer, originally proposed by Champlain. To this Order each man of the said table was appointed Chief Steward in his turn, which came round once a fortnight. Now this person had the duty of taking care that we were all well and honourably provided for. This was so well carried out that, though the epicures of Paris often tell us that we had no Rue aux Ours [meat-market district] over there, as a rule we made as good cheer as we could have in this same Rue aux Ours and at less cost. For there was no one who, two days before his turn came, failed to go hunting or fishing, and to bring back some delicacy in addition to our ordinary fare. So well was this carried out that never at breakfast did we lack some savoury meat of flesh or fish, and still less at our midday or evening meals; for that was our chief banquet, at which the ruler of the feast or chief butler, whom the savages called Atoctegic, having had everything prepared by the cook, marched in, napkin on shoulder, wand of office in hand, and around his neck the collar of the Order, carrying each a dish. The same was repeated at dessert, though not always with so much pomp. And at night, before giving thanks to God, he handed over to his successor in the charge the collar of the order, with a cup of wine, and they drank to each other.

Source: Marc Lescarbot, *The History of New France*, trans. W.L. Grant, intro. H.P. Biggar (Toronto: Champlain Society, 1911), II, 342–3.

projected at 5,400,000 livres, virtually none of it coming from agriculture and less than 10 per cent coming from furs. Champlain requested that priests, 300 families of four people each, and 300 soldiers be sent to his base on the St Lawrence. Amazingly enough, the French response was enthusiastic, and Louis XIII instructed the syndicate employing Champlain to expedite his plans. The partners and Champlain, however, were unable to agree upon terms or to make any progress in establishing the colony. Not until 1627, when Cardinal Richelieu assumed supervision of New France and established the Company of One Hundred Associates, did Champlain's grandiose schemes receive substantial backing.

The Beginnings of Overland Exploration

The geographical shakedown of European colonization activity in the late sixteenth and early seventeenth centuries determined that it would be the French who would take the lead in exploring the northern interior of the continent, and their activities would extend far beyond the boundaries of what is now Canada. While the English, Scots, Dutch, and Swedes established settlements along the eastern seaboard, the French founded their settlements on the St Lawrence River, in the interior of the continent. Providing access to the Great Lakes and to most of the major river systems of North America, this river would confer enormous power and influence on the nation that controlled it. The St Lawrence focused the French need for new sources of furs to supply the major export commodity of New France. The river's access to the interior ensured that most of the great feats of inland exploration would be executed by the French. The ability of young Frenchmen to adapt themselves to the ways of the First Nations was also critical.

Champlain himself was active in moving inland to investigate territory previously unknown to Europe, but he was not a typical figure. The first major French overland explorer, in many ways quintessential, was Étienne Brûlé (c. 1592–1633), who lived with the Huron near Georgian Bay, Lake Huron, in 1612, and may have been the first European to sight Lakes Superior and Erie. A shadowy, elusive figure, Brûlé, like many early explorers, left no written accounts of his life or adventures. It is likely that he had volunteered in 1610 to live with the First Nations and learn their language. He was probably the young man to whom Champlain referred in 1611 as 'my French boy who came dressed like an Indian' (DCB, 1966: I, 131). In 1615 Brûlé accompanied a party of Huron braves into the territory of the Susquehanna to the south of the Iroquois, in what is now southwestern New York state. He took advantage of the opportunity to investigate the neighbouring regions, perhaps reaching Chesapeake Bay and certainly tramping around modern Pennsylvania. Brûlé subsequently journeyed to the north shore of Georgian Bay, and then in the early 1620s along the St Mary's River to Lake Superior. Like many Europeans who 'went native', Brûlé was respected by his compatriots as an interpreter, although they were intensely suspicious of his new persona. In Brûlé's case, his moral character and behaviour were criticized by Champlain even before his final 'treachery' in 1629 when he entered the employment of the Kirke brothers after they successfully captured the tiny French colony at Quebec. By pursuing his own agenda rather than observing the abstract national loyalties dear to European hearts and values, he established what would become a familiar pattern among Europeans coming to terms with North America. By 1633 Brûlé was dead, reportedly killed and eaten by the Huron.

Over the course of the seventeenth century, the interpreters, as represented by Brûlé, would be transformed into the coureurs de bois—the 'runners of the woods' or 'bushlopers'—as the English often called them. These men would be responsible for most of the constantly broadening geographical knowledge of the North American continent. Their desire was less to improve cartography than to exploit new sources of wealth, particularly furs, and above all to enjoy an adventurous life in the woods. Whether or not these wilderness bravoes became completely assimilated into First Nations life and culture (some did), they all learned skills from the Aboriginals that made them crucial figures in the economy of

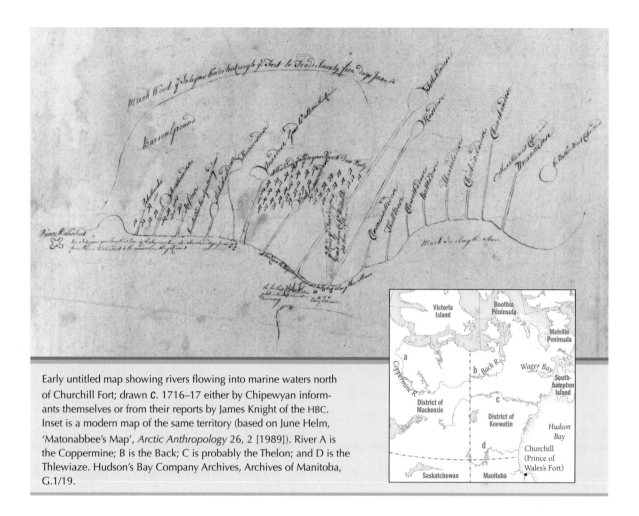

Early untitled map showing rivers flowing into marine waters north of Churchill Fort; drawn c. 1716–17 either by Chipewyan inform-ants themselves or from their reports by James Knight of the HBC. Inset is a modern map of the same territory (based on June Helm, 'Matonabbee's Map', *Arctic Anthropology* 26, 2 [1989]). River A is the Coppermine; B is the Back; C is probably the Thelon; and D is the Thlewiaze. Hudson's Bay Company Archives, Archives of Manitoba, G.1/19.

New France. Marine skills like sighting latitude or reading the surface of the water were replaced by the ability to live off the land, to paddle a canoe for long distances with few breaks, to hunt animals for food, and of course to communicate successfully with a local First Nations population, not merely at the level of language but at one of genuine empathy. These inland explorers travelled in exposed parties and had no defensive structure such as a ship to pro-tect them from attack. They lived by their wits and had to be constantly adaptable. They made splendid guerrilla warriors when Europe moved into warfare for control of the continent.

As Canadian schoolchildren are only too painfully aware, there were a good many overland explorers in the seventeenth and eighteenth centuries, some of whom have had automobiles and hotel chains named after them. While most Canadians could, if pressed, name one or two of these explorers, it is very doubtful whether they could offer the name of a single comparable First Nations explorer. Does this mean that the First Nations did not do any travel-ling in North America? Of course not. The Native geographical knowledge of the continent—much of which predated the arrival of the Europeans, who relied very heavily on it—has been ignored by most writers on exploration. The First Nations became part of the fuzzy background rather than the sharply focused foreground. Historians of exploration have long known of the great assistance provided by the First Nations in the 'discoveries' of the Europeans. The Aboriginals provided much geographical infor-mation—even maps—and typically served as guides, interpreters, and canoe paddlers.

Historic Sites

EASTERN CANADA

0   500   1,000
kilometres

1. Frobisher National Historic Site: On Kodlunarn Island in Frobisher Bay (close to Iqaluit). This tiny island has the remains of Martin Frobisher's habitation and the smelting plant he operated between 1576 and 1578.
2. L'Anse aux Meadows National Historic Park: At the northern tip of Newfoundland; contains the remains of seven buildings, cook pits, and a smithy.
3. Gaspé, Quebec: The site of a 30-foot granite cross commemorating the cross erected by Jacques Cartier in 1534.
4. Cartier-Brébeuf National Historic Park: Facing the St Charles River, where Cartier wintered his three ships in 1535–6.
5. McGill University (Montreal): A plaque marks the site of the village of Hochelaga.
6. Port au Choix (Newfoundland) National Historic Park: Burial sites of the 'red paint people' who inhabited the region about 5,000 years ago.
7. Port-Royal National Historic Site: Reconstruction of the 'habitation' and other buildings of the first French colony established on the banks of the Annapolis River by Champlain in 1605.

Conclusion

By the mid-1620s the first period of European intrusion into what is now Canada had been completed. Exploration of the new continent's eastern seaboard was done, and Europe could construct a fairly decent map of its coastline. What lay beyond was beginning to be investigated. Europe was on the verge of deciding that major transplantations of people were going to be necessary if this new northern land were to be exploited. As for the indigenous population, they had been buffeted by epidemic disease, the causes of which were beyond their comprehension, but they had not yet been marginalized. The First Nations could still meet the newcomers on something approximating equal terms. In retrospect, we can see how ephemeral this equality really was.

How History Has Changed

Early Disease in North America

As late as 1964, a book entitled *The Americas on the Eve of Discovery* could be published with no index entries for 'disease' or 'epidemics' and containing only brief references to those topics in discussions of other matters. Today, no subjects seem so important in the story of European intrusion into the New World.

The change has come from two directions. One was the modern attempt to ascertain the pre-European population of the Americas. The key breakthrough here came in 1966, when demographer Henry F. Dobyns published in *Current Anthropology* an article entitled 'Estimating Aboriginal American Population: An Appraisal of Techniques with a New Hemispheric Estimate'. Dobyns was highly critical of the methods used by earlier scholars to determine population numbers, insisting that they all shared the common result of greatly understating the size of the Aboriginal American population. Instead, he read backward from the various factors that reduced the population after conquest, including war and epidemic, and ended up with a hemispheric figure of 'approximately 90,000,000 persons immediately prior to discovery'. The preliminary assertions of a major population disaster at the time of intrusion were fleshed out for eastern North America in Dobyns's subsequent book, *Their Numbers Become Thinned: Native American Population Dynamics in Eastern North America* (1983), and in a number of other studies by younger anthropologists.

Many of the revisionists took some of their arguments from another strand of scholarship that had developed parallel to the detailed demographic studies. This work tended to be 'metahistorical' in emphasis, looking at large expanses of the world's area over long periods of time. The key item here was William McNeill's *Plagues and Peoples*, published in 1976, a sweeping study of the importance of epidemics in world history. Its arguments were expanded and extended for the whole period of European expansion by Alfred W. Crosby in 1986 in his *Ecological Imperialism: The Biological Expansion of Europe 900–1900*. McNeill had appreciated that epidemic disease was an inevitable result of the spread of 'civilization', for communicable disease was greatly enhanced by large agricultural populations, urban conditions, and the interchange of peoples across continents and oceans. Crosby added that not only disease but other biological intrusions into a virgin world were bound to be disastrous. By the twenty-first century, books like Charles Mann's *1491* went so far as to insist that the western hemisphere before European arrival had been a better place to live than the Old World. As often happens in history, a few new insights can spark a veritable deluge of fresh interpretations.

Short Bibliography

Axtell, James. *Natives and Newcomers: The Cultural Origins of North America*. New York, 2001. A series of penetrating essays by North America's leading historian of cultural contact.

Bailey, A.G. *The Conflict of European and Eastern Algonkin Cultures, 1534–1700: A Study in Civilization*, 2nd edn. Toronto, 1969. First produced as a doctoral dissertation in 1934, this pioneering study is one of the classics of the field, still as relevant as ever.

Cell, Gillian. *English Enterprise in Newfoundland, 1577–1660*. Toronto, 1969. Still the standard account of early settlement in Newfoundland and its mercantile connections.

Dickason, Olive Patricia. *Canada's First Nations: A History of Founding Peoples from Earliest Times*, 3rd edn. Toronto, 2002. Easily the best general survey of the history of the First Nations, current and full of detail. A revised and updated abridged edition—*A Concise History of Canada's First Nations*—was published in 2006 and a second edition appeared in 2010. A fourth edition of Dickason's original work, with David T. McNab, came out in 2009 with updates to that year and a new concluding chapter.

Fagan, Brian. *The Great Journey: The Peopling of Ancient America*. New York, 1987. A bit dated, but still the best account of the prevailing scholarly interpretations of the subject.

Fitzhugh, William, and Elizabeth Ward. *Vikings: The North American Saga*. Washington and London, 2000. A splendidly illustrated and authoritative account of the Norse in America.

Harris, R. Cole, ed. *Historical Atlas of Canada*, vol. 1. Toronto, 1987. This is one of the great collaborative works of scholarship in Canada, presenting a visual and cartographic record of the period to 1800.

Hunter, Douglas, *Half-Moon: Henry Hudson and the Voyage that Redrew the Map of the New World*. New York, Berlin, London, 2009. A new look at one of the most elusive figures of early European exploration.

Jaenen, Cornelius. *Friend and Foe: Aspects of French-Amerindian Culture Contact in the Sixteenth and Seventeenth Centuries*. Toronto, 1976. An early classic, still the best single work on the early contact between the French and the First Nations.

Nuffield, Edward. *The Discovery of Canada*. Vancouver, 1996. A recent survey.

Paul, Daniel. *We Were Not the Savages: A Micmac Perspective on the Collision of European and Aboriginal Civilization*. Halifax, 1993. Probably the first analysis of early cultural contact in Canada written by a First Nations scholar from a First Nations perspective.

Reid, John. *Acadia, Maine, and New Scotland: Marginal Colonies in the Seventeenth Century*. Toronto, 1981. A stimulating comparative approach to the early settlement of the Maritimes.

Seed, Patricia, *Ceremonies of Possession in Europe's Conquest of the New World, 1492–1640*. Cambridge, 1995. More important than its title suggests, this book distinguishes the various national approaches to conquest taken by the major European nations.

Trigger, Bruce. *Natives and Newcomers: Canada's 'Heroic Age' Reconsidered*. Montreal and Kingston, 1986. A revisionist account of early Canadian culture contact by Canada's leading expert.

Trudel, Marcel. *The Beginnings of New France 1524–1663*. Toronto, 1975. Still the authoritative account of the early years of New France, written by a scholar who spent his lifetime working on the period.

Wright, J.V. *A History of the Native People of Canada*, 3 vols. Ottawa, 1995–2000. An encyclopedic survey of Canada's ancient history.

Study Questions

1. Give three examples of ways in which the First Nations lived in a 'reciprocal relationship with nature'.
2. Explain the basic cultural, religious, and political factors behind the European misinterpretation of the First Nations.
3. Comment on the account from Cartier's *Voyages*, 'Jacques Cartier Meets with Aboriginal Peoples, 1534'. Did Cartier make any assumptions about the Aboriginal peoples that would lead to cultural conflicts later? Explain.
4. What can we learn about cultural conflict from Karlsefni's encounter with the Skraelings? What was the principal cause of the conflict between the Norse and the Skraelings?
5. On what grounds could you defend the European intrusion into North America? Identify three grounds and explain each of them.

 www.oupcanada.com/Bumsted4e

Visit the companion website for *A History of the Canadian Peoples*, fourth edition for further resources.

2

Struggling for a Continent, 1627–1758

Timeline

1627 Cardinal Richelieu establishes the Company of One Hundred Associates.

1628 The Kirke brothers capture Quebec.

1632 Treaty of St-Germain-en-Laye restores Canada and Acadia to France.

1633 Champlain returns to the St Lawrence.

1634 The Jesuits set up permanent missions in Huronia.

1635 Champlain dies.

1639 The Jesuits establish Ste-Marie-aux-Hurons.

1640 The Iroquois begin attacking the Huron.

1642 Montreal is established.

1645 Company of One Hundred Associates surrenders its monopoly to local interests. Madame La Tour surrenders Fort La Tour.

1647 Canada adopts government by central council.

1649 Iroquois destroy St-Louis and St-Ignace. Martyrdom of Jean de Brébeuf and Gabriel Lalemant.

1654 English capture Acadia.

1659 Bishop Laval arrives in Canada.

1662 French establish first Newfoundland colony at Placentia Bay.

1663 Earthquake strikes Canada. French royal government takes over New France and institutes the Coutume de Paris.

1664 Carignan-Salières regiment arrives in New France. Jean Talon arrives as first intendant.

1667 English return Acadia to France.

1670 Hudson's Bay Company is granted a charter by Charles II.

1689 War of the League of Augsburg begins.

1690 Port-Royal captured by the English; Quebec is unsuccessfully invaded.

1697 Treaty of Ryswick ends War of the League of Augsburg.

1702 War of Spanish Succession begins.

1713 By the Treaty of Utrecht, which ends the War of the Spanish Succession, France surrenders Nova Scotia, Newfoundland, and Hudson Bay claims to Great Britain.

1720 Establishment of Louisbourg.

1737 First iron forge at St Maurice is established.

1744 War of the Austrian Succession begins.

1745 Louisbourg is captured by joint Anglo-American military force.

1748 Treaty of Aix-la-Chapelle ends the War of the Austrian Succession.

1749 Halifax established.

1755 General Braddock is defeated on the Monongahela River; Acadians are expelled from Nova Scotia.

1756 Seven Years War officially begins.

1758 Louisbourg taken by force under General James Wolfe; Acadians are rounded up and again expelled from the Maritime region; Nova Scotia's first elected assembly meets. Nova Scotia's government advertises for settlers in New England.

◀ The fortress (centre background) at Louisbourg exchanged hands multiple times before finally being captured in 1758 by the British, led by General James Wolfe. Painting by Pierre Canot (1762). LAC, 2895021.

In 1627 Cardinal Richelieu, Louis XIII's 'grey eminence', assumed supervision of New France and established the Company of One Hundred Associates. However, Richelieu's company, unlike the English Newfoundland Company, was organized from the top of the government rather than from grassroots interest in the profits of colonization. It was to be capitalized at 300,000 livres, each participant contributing 3,000, and profits were not to be distributed initially. Of the 107 members listed in May 1629, only 26 were merchants and businessmen, mainly from Paris. The remainder were courtiers and state officials. The company's initial venture—at a cost of 164,270 livres—was to send to Quebec in 1628 four ships containing 400 people and carrying 'all necessary commodities & quantities of workmen & families coming to inhabit & clear the land and to build & prepare the necessary lodging' (quoted in Trudel, 1973: 118). Unfortunately, England and France had gone to war in 1627, and in July 1628 the company's ships were captured off Gaspé by an Anglo-Scottish armed expedition led by the brothers Kirke. Thus began a military struggle between France and Britain for control of North America lasting more than a century.

The nineteenth-century American historian Francis Parkman wrote of a 'Half Century of Conflict', but in truth the imperial struggle was much more protracted. The struggle would transcend a straightforward European rivalry, increasingly involving as it did both the population of the colonies and the First Nations of the continent—each fighting with individual agendas—as well as other parts of the world. The French colonies of North America felt the effects of this contest far more than did their British counterparts to the south. The much smaller population in New France was more often in the front lines of the fighting, which frequently occurred on French territory. Between 1627 and the final military defeat of New France more than 130 years later, the French experienced only one extended period (from 1713 to the early 1740s) when they were not constantly at war or under severe military pressure, either from Aboriginal peoples or from the British. The pervasiveness of the international rivalry came equally to affect British colonists and British policy in the northern region. At its greatest extent, 'New France' consisted of a number of colonies and regions, including a fishing base in Newfoundland (Placentia), Acadia, Canada, the 'pays d'en haut' or frontier country in the West, and Louisiana. Canada was the most important part of New France, but not of the French Empire in the New World, for sugar islands were preferred to 'arpents of snow'. Table 2.1, which shows the amount of correspondence from France's Bureau

Table 2.1 Volume of Correspondence of the Bureau of Colonies, 1713				
Destination	No. of Folios	Per cent	No. of Letters	Per cent
Îles français de l'Amérique*	225	37.1	440	57.9
New France (Canada)	118	19.5	126	16.6
Louisiana	10	1.7	15	2.0
St Domingue	114	18.8	73	9.6
Martinique and the Îles du Vent	122	20.1	81	10.7
Cayenne	10	1.7	21	2.8
Indes Orientales	7	1.2	4	0.5
Totals	606	100	760	100

*Correspondence pertaining to the Marine's shipping to colonial ports.

Source: Kenneth J. Banks, *Chasing Empire across the Sea: Communications and the State in the French Atlantic, 1713–1736* (Montreal and Kingston: McGill-Queen's University Press, 2002), 51, Table 2.1 In addition, a single letter was written to the 'Indes d'Espagne' (presumably the Spanish Main), but not included in the microfilmed set analyzed at the National Archives of Canada in Ottawa.

of Colonies for 1713, indicates the extent to which New France was only one of several pieces in the French overseas portfolio.

New France Fights for Survival

In July 1629 David Kirke sent his brothers Lewis and Thomas at the head of an Anglo-Scottish armed expedition that forced Champlain's little outpost on the St Lawrence to surrender. Later that same year, an attempt by the Company of One Hundred Associates to reoccupy Quebec failed dismally. The colony was restored to France in 1632 under the Treaty of St-Germain-en-Laye. One of the first French arrivals that year was Father Paul Le Jeune (1591–1664), recently appointed superior-general of the Jesuit missions in Canada. The Jesuits were to be the principal missionary order in the colony. Le Jeune soon began sending the first of the annual reports, the famous *Jesuit Relations*, which were forwarded to the provincial father of the Society of Jesus in Paris to explain and promote in the mother country the missionaries' efforts. They combine a wealth of detail about life in New France, the First Nations, Iroquois warfare, the Huron missions, exploration and travel, as well as accounts of various miracles. Champlain returned to Quebec in May 1633 after a four-year exile, tired but optimistic. He would die on Christmas Day 1635, his vision of a prosperous colony still beyond his grasp. At the time there were but 150 settlers along the St Lawrence.

Over the next few decades, the forces along the St Lawrence that met in bitter rivalry were less French and British and more Catholic evangelical energy on the one hand and resistance from the indigenous population on the other. The prize was control of the fur trade. Conflict along the Atlantic seaboard had more traditional European overtones, while in Canada the long rivalry between the Iroquois and the Algonquian trading allies of the French created

Champlain's New France

In 1603 Pierre Du Gua de Monts (1558?–1628) was granted a trading monopoly in northeastern North America in return for an obligation to settle 60 colonists each year and to establish missions among the Aboriginals. Among the first settlers he recruited was a young draftsman, Samuel de Champlain (*c.* 1570–1635), who had been to Tadoussac in 1603 and would serve as geographer and cartographer for de Monts's expedition. Champlain continued a commitment to explore and colonize the New World that would end only with his death (on Christmas Day, 1635). Unlike his English contemporaries, William Bradford at Plymouth Plantation and John Winthrop at Boston, Champlain had not been able to lead a prospering colony through the problems of internal growth and the establishment of permanent institutions. Instead, much of his career was spent dealing with the preliminaries of settlement, in the interests of which he sailed to France nine times to further his plans for colonization or to resist attempts to negate them.

As a successful geographer and intrepid explorer who was equal to the most arduous demands of wilderness life, and who was capable in complex dealings with Native peoples, Champlain also left a literary legacy. The three volumes of his *Voyages* (published in Paris in 1613, 1619, and 1632) provide much of what we know about New France during this period. Champlain's map of New France (facing page) appeared in the last volume of his *Voyages*. It includes the territories he explored, which are rendered quite accurately, along with inevitably inaccurate renderings of regions for which he had only second-hand information.

much fear and havoc, with disastrous consequences for the Huron people caught in the middle.

The Huron had access to a seemingly inexhaustible supply of furs from the northwest, and the French were determined to keep the flow moving to Montreal and Quebec. The Huron had outnumbered the Iroquois, but in the 1630s their numbers were greatly reduced by diseases contracted from the French missionaries who lived among them. In 1634, the year the Jesuits set up permanent missions in Huronia, the Huron suffered an epidemic of measles. In 1639 the Jesuits oversaw the building of an elaborate fortified headquarters, Ste-Marie-aux-Hurons, on the Wye River. It eventually comprised 20 buildings, including a residence for priests, a church, a hospital, outbuildings for farming, and residences for lay workers and Huron converts, as well as a canal with three locks.

The Iroquois—supplied by the Dutch with firearms, which the French were reluctant to give to their First Nations allies—were equally determined to control the flow of furs. They ambushed the Huron fur-fleets on the Ottawa River, and between 1640 and 1645 they blockaded the river, while also from 1643 onward attacking the settlements on the St Lawrence. Under the force of the assault, the Company of One Hundred Associates virtually withdrew from New France in 1645, giving its fur-trading monopoly to the Communauté des Habitants, an organization of Canadian merchants, which agreed to continue to pay for the administration of the colony. While the devolution of the fur trade to local interests was probably a positive move for the colony, the new company felt the effects of Iroquois hostility, which limited the fur trade for an entire decade.

The Iroquois soon turned their full attention to Huronia. In July 1648 Senecas destroyed the mission of St-Joseph and killed 700 Huron. In March 1649 a party of 1,200 Iroquois destroyed St-Louis and St-Ignace, where the priests Jean de Brébeuf (1593–1649) and Gabriel Lalemant (1610–49) were tortured to death. The weakened Huron surrendered, fled, or were killed. Before the Iroquois could reach Ste-Marie, the Jesuits there 'applied the

Champlain's map of New France, 1632. LAC, NMC–15661.

torch to the work of our own hands' and fled with some 300 families to Christian Island in Georgian Bay. Most died of starvation or malnutrition. The next year the missionaries returned to Quebec with a few hundred Huron, the pathetic remnant of a once-powerful nation.

The Huron were early victims of European ethnocentrism. As for the missionaries themselves, only the Jesuits' profound faith and misguided intentions—to educate the First Nations in French ways and induct them into a completely alien form of religion—kept them on their indomitable rounds of travel and life under extremely harsh and tense conditions. Many of the Huron turned against the missionaries, blaming their problems with disease and with the Iroquois on the Christian interlopers. Indeed, in exposing the Huron to disease and weakening their culture by introducing alien spiritual

Father le Jeune on the Conversion of the 'Savages', 1634

This selection by Father Paul le Jeune (1591–1664), the founding editor of the *Jesuit Relations*, offers some insight into the thinking of the fathers regarding their mission in the early 1630s.

The great show of power made at first by the Portuguese in the East and West Indies inspired profound admiration in the minds of the Indians, so that these people embraced, without any contradiction, the belief of those whom they admired. Now the following is, it seems to me, the way in which to acquire an ascendency over our Savages.

First, to check the progress of those who overthrow Religion, and to make ourselves feared by the Iroquois, who have killed some of our men, as every one knows, and who recently massacred two hundred Hurons, and took more than one hundred prisoners. This is, in my opinion, the only door through which we can escape the contempt into which the negligence of those who have hitherto held the trade of this country has thrown us, through their avarice.

The second means of commending ourselves to the Savages would be to send a number of capable men to clear and cultivate the land, who, joining themselves with others who know the language, would work for the Savages, on condition that they would settle down, and put their hands to the work, living in houses that would be built for their use. . . . I may be mistaken but if I can draw any conclusion from the things I see, it seems to me that not much ought to be hoped from the Savages as long as they are wanderers; you will instruct them today, tomorrow hunger snatches your hearers away, forcing them to go and seek their food in the rivers and woods. Last year I stammered out the Catechism to a goodly number of children; as soon as the ships departed, my birds flew away. . . .To try and follow them, as many Religious would be needed as there are cabins, and still we would not attain our object; for they are so occupied in seeking their livelihood in these woods, that they have not the time, so to speak, to save themselves. . . .

The third means of making ourselves welcome to these people, would be to erect here a seminary for little boys, and in time one for girls, under the direction of some brave mistress, whom zeal for the glory of God and a desire for the salvation of these people, will bring over here, with a few Companions animated by the same courage. May it please his divine Majesty to inspire some to so noble an enterprise, and to divest them of any fear that the weakness of their sex might induce in them at the thought of crossing so many seas and of living among Barbarians.

Source: Reuben Gold Thwaites, ed., *The Jesuit Relations and Allied Documents: Travels and Explorations of the Jesuit Missionaries in New France 1610–1791* (New York, 1959), vol. VI, 145–53.

elements, the missionaries may have inadvertently contributed to the destruction of Huronia.

If the missionaries had only limited success with the First Nations, their influence on the early European population of Canada was far more positive. The missionary enterprise in Canada had two basic wings, often only loosely connected: that of the Jesuits and that of the lay missionaries.

The Society of Jesus was founded by Ignatius Loyola in 1540 as a militant (and militarily organized) order devoted largely to missionary activity around the world. The Jesuits travelled around the globe, especially in the period 1550–1650, preaching and teaching among indigenous people ranging from the Aztecs to the Japanese. They developed a reputation for being able to adapt Christianity to the customs of the local people, and they were probably less rigid than most missionaries in their views

of what had to happen for true conversion to take place. Members of the order actually looked forward to martyrdom, although they were not supposed to go out of their way to seek it. As soldiers of Christ, they believed that conversion of pagans occurred only through bloodshed. The Jesuits were obviously highly disciplined and committed; to the usual vows of poverty, chastity, and obedience, they added one of loyalty to the Pope. Despite the suspicions of the Crown, they were given a monopoly of religious service in Canada in 1632. The Jesuits tended to be more involved with missionary outreach than with the European population.

The lay missions were organized as part of the French Counter-Reformation, in which lay people discovered they had enormous depths of piety that they were anxious to share with others, including the First Nations in North America. When the widow

'Mort héroique de quelques pères de la Compagnie de Jésus dans la Nouvelle France', lithograph by Et. David, 1844. LAC, C-4462. This rendering tells us much about how the French interpreted these events.

Marie de l'Incarnation

Marie de l'Incarnation, oil portrait attributed to Abbé Hugues Pommier (1637–86). Archives des Ursulines de Québec.

Born in Tours, the daughter of a master baker, Marie Guyart (1599–1672) was a devout child who married at the age of 17. Her husband died two years later, leaving her with a son. Soon after, she had a mystical experience of conversion. Taking vows of chastity, poverty, and obedience, she lived for some years with her sister and brother-in-law and worked with them in their business. At the age of 27, she had another experience of the 'inner paradise' and joined the Ursuline Order of nuns. After taking her vows in 1633, Marie had a dream in which God told her to go to Canada. She sailed there in 1639, founded her school, and spent the remainder of her life running it successfully. Mère Marie had an extraordinary ability to combine her fervent spiritual life with her skills as a competent administrator and perceptive observer of the secular life around her. She wrote extensively, in addition to educating young girls, catechizing the local Native people, learning their languages, and preparing dictionaries in French-Algonquin and French-Iroquois as well as an Iroquois catechism. Her writings include spiritual autobiographies, lectures on faith, notes on prayer, and over 13,000 letters (most of them to her son), of which relatively few survive. In her correspondence, Mère Marie dealt not only in spiritual matters but with the business of the entire colony. Her letters are one of the two best sources, along with the *Jesuit Relations*, for the history of New France in the mid-seventeenth century.

Marie-Madeleine de Chauvigny de la Peltrie (1603–71) recovered from a serious illness in 1635, she made a vow to establish a school for Native girls in New France. She persuaded Marie de l'Incarnation to join her, put much of her fortune in trust for the foundation, and even financed a vessel and some immigrants to accompany her. Once in New France, she founded the Ursuline convent in Quebec. Another noblewoman sponsored three nursing sisters of the order of Augustinian Hospitalières on the same ship as the Ursulines. They founded a hospital at Sillery to care for dozens of Aboriginals, most of whom were Montagnais, Algonquin, and Abenaki, with only a few Huron. The Société Notre-Dame de Montréal organized a missionary effort in 1639 that led to the establishment of Montreal in 1642. This work was financed by donations from wealthy lay people. Thirty-four of the 46 members were lay people, and 12 were women. For much of the mid-seventeenth century, Canada would be largely dominated by the energy of its leading women missionaries: Marie de l'Incarnation, Jeanne Mance (founder of the Hôtel-Dieu hospital), and Marguerite Bourgeoys (founder of the Congrégation de Notre-Dame).

François de Laval

Portrait of François de Laval, first bishop of New France, from 1674 to 1688. Bishop of Canada (oil on canvas), French School, (17th century) / Societe des Missions Etrangeres, Paris, France / Giraudon / The Bridgeman Art Library.

Born at Montigny-sur Abre, his father a member of a younger branch of the distinguished Montmorency family and his mother descended from Rouen legal nobility, François de Laval (1623–1708) was marked from childhood for the Church. He studied for some years at the Jesuit College at La Fléche, then at Paris. His studies were briefly interrupted by a family crisis, but he was ordained as a subdeacon in 1646 and as priest in 1647. As archdeacon of Évreux from 1648, he proved indefatigable in his work, and he seemed destined for missionary work in Indochina.

Before the politics of such an appointment could be negotiated, however, Laval found himself the Jesuit candidate for the post of bishop of New France, an appointment in the giving of the archbishop of Rouen. Again caught up in ecclesiastical politics, Laval found himself ultimately appointed a vicar apostolic rather than a bishop, and thus subject to the papacy rather than to the archbishop of Rouen. He sailed for his new post in April 1659. His first task was to get his authority recognized. This proved easier than expected, thanks to a letter from Louis XIV to the governor, which ordered Laval's authority recognized everywhere. His next job was to organize the church, which before his arrival had been a decentralized missionary operation. In 1662 he returned to consult with Louis XIV, returning to Canada with increased powers, an ordinance founding the seminary of Quebec, and an edict creating a Conseil Souverain.

Gradually the Church in Louis XIV's royal province of Canada took shape under his direction, and he was named the first bishop of Quebec in 1674. Laval organized a parochial system, which increased from five parishes in 1659 to 35 in 1688, with 102 clergy. He encouraged missionary activity, especially by the Jesuits, and he took the lead in opposing the liquor trade with the Aboriginals, a battle that he and the missionaries lost eventually. Laval became notorious for his constant disagreements with the governors of the colony over a variety of matters, both moral and political.

In 1684 he sailed for France to resign his bishopric, but after having his resignation accepted, he attempted to remain on the job for fear his successor would undo much of his work. Abbé Saint-Vallier was consecrated bishop early in 1688, and Laval returned to Canada as 'Monseigneur l'Ancien', beloved of his people but mainly retired from the fray at his seminary. He permitted his successor to reform the seminary without raising any opposition, and in later years he occasionally performed episcopal functions in the absence of Saint-Vallier, who was away from Canada from 1700 to 1713. Laval died in 1708 from a chilblain on his heel that became infected.

In 1647 Canada adopted government by a central council, with elected representatives of the districts of Quebec, Trois-Rivières, and Montreal employed for consultative purposes. Such a government was both responsive to the wishes of the inhabitants and autonomous of the mother country, but the arrangement was more a result of emergency conditions than a genuine reform. With the Huron destroyed, the Iroquois turned the full brunt of their fury on the French at Montreal. François Dollier de Casson (1928: 155) observed that 'not a month of this summer [1651] passed without our roll of slain being marked in red at the hands of the Iroquois.' The attacks subsided over the course of the decade, but the menace never entirely disappeared.

The period of the Iroquois wars was a difficult one for the French fur traders, and many headed north-westward to avoid the enemy. Among these adventurers were Pierre Radisson (*c.* 1640–1710) and his brother-in-law Médard Chouart Des Groseilliers *c.* 1618–96?). Radisson was born in France, but had been captured by Mohawks in 1651. Adopted by a prominent family, he was forced to learn Aboriginal ways in order to survive. In 1659 the brothers-in-law took a journey to Lake Superior that excited their interest in exploring the fur-producing region that they knew extended as far north as Hudson Bay. They returned to Montreal in 1660 with a vast haul of beaver skins, which was seen as the colony's salvation. The two fur traders were not well received, however; their furs were confiscated and both men were prosecuted for trading without official permission. Not surprisingly, they wound up in Boston in 1664, where the English were quite enthusiastic about the Hudson Bay fur trade. Eventually the pair would head for London, where their enthusiastic reports about conditions at the Bay led in 1670 to the establishment by the English of the Hudson's Bay Company, which would contend with the French for control of the region until the French conceded it to the English in 1713.

By the early 1660s the tensions within the colony on the St Lawrence seemed to be manifesting in strange forms. A general state of panic was produced by an incident of alleged witchcraft, and in the midst of carnival season in February 1663 the colony was struck by a serious earthquake. Mère Marie de

Marguerite Bourgeoys, 'Le Vrai Portrait', painted the day after her death in January 1700 by Pierre Le Ber. This work was not discovered until the mid-twentieth century, when x-rays of a work believed to be an authentic likeness revealed the 'true portrait' under several layers of paint. Musée Marguerite-Bourgeoys, Montreal.

l'Incarnation noted, 'we were all so frightened we believed it was the eve of Judgement, since all the portents were to be seen' (Marshall, 1967: 288–9). About this time the French Crown formally withdrew trading privileges and landownership from the Company of One Hundred Associates and made New France a Crown colony. Given the anxieties and problems of the colony, most of its 3,035 inhabitants were happy to trade autonomy for French financial and military assistance.

In June 1665 four companies of the Carignan-Salières regiment arrived to quell the Iroquois. In September of that year an intendant (or chief administrative officer)—Jean Talon (1626–94)—arrived to revitalize the colony. One of the royal government's first aims was to increase the population, and the *filles du roi* (orphan girls raised at the king's expense) were sent over for that purpose. Mère Marie reported that 100 girls had arrived in 1665, and more would come later. How long the French Crown would continue such support was uncertain, but it certainly rejuvenated the colony. The government had begun making a concerted effort to deal with the Iroquois menace and to reform both the administrative and economic structure of New France. It would shortly attempt to establish a foothold in Newfoundland and later regain control over Acadia. Although success would hold within it the seeds of destruction, the French in 1665 were on the eve of almost a century of expansion and dominance in North America.

The Maritime Region to 1667

In the Atlantic region, overtones of European imperial rivalries could be detected in the complex conflicts of the seventeenth century, although local factors were equally important. Much of the confusing history of Acadia after 1624 is wrapped up in the activities of the La Tour family, which illustrate the fluid and violent nature of the period. In 1629, when Quebec was captured by the Kirkes, a tiny trading post on Cape Sable (at the southwestern tip of present-day Nova Scotia) was all that was left of the French presence in North America. It was headed by Charles de Saint-Étienne de La Tour (1598–1666). His father, Claude de La Tour (c. 1570–after 1636), had already returned to France to plead for assistance, but on the return voyage was captured and taken to England, where he quickly made himself at home. Accepted at court, he married one of the Queen's ladies-in-waiting. (The English Queen Henrietta was a French princess and surrounded by women from France.) Claude also accepted Nova Scotia baronetcies for himself and his son from Sir William Alexander, a Scottish courtier, who had been granted Nova Scotia in 1621 by James VI of Scotland (who also was James I of England).

Returning with his bride to Acadia in May 1630 as part of a Scots-English expedition, Claude stopped at Cape Sable to persuade his son to join him. Charles replied that 'he would rather have died than consent to such baseness as to betray his King' (MacBeath,

1966: 593). Declaring his son an enemy, Claude led an unsuccessful attack on the fort at Cape Sable and retreated to Port-Royal, only to discover that the English planned to abandon it. He was forced to throw himself on his son's mercy and confess to his wife that he could not return to Europe. Acadia, like Canada, was returned to France by the English with the Treaty of St-Germain-en-Laye in 1632. The English monarch Charles I needed French financial subsidies as he attempted to govern without meeting Parliament, a policy that led to the English Civil War.

In Acadia, Charles de La Tour continued to lead an embattled life, coming into conflict with others who claimed royal authority in the region. In 1645 he was defeated by his chief rival, Charles de Menou d'Aulnay (c. 1604–50) and sought refuge in Canada. D'Aulnay controlled Acadia until his death in 1650.

Charles de La Tour returned to France after d'Aulnay's death to demand an inquiry into his case. He was completely vindicated and again received into royal favour. Returning to Port-Royal with a few new settlers in 1653, he successfully courted d'Aulnay's widow. Pursued by creditors, he was forced in 1654 to surrender his garrison of 70 at Fort La Tour to an invading English expedition of 500 men. La Tour was taken to England, where Oliver Cromwell (by now head of the English state) refused to restore his Acadian property but did agree to recognize the long-dormant baronetcy of Nova Scotia (negotiated earlier by Claude) if Charles would accept English allegiance and pay his English debts. Twenty-five years after denying his father and asserting his loyalty to the French Crown, Charles de La Tour accepted Cromwell's terms. He eventually sold his rights in Acadia to English partners and retired to Cape Sable with his wife and family.

For more than 40 years La Tour and his family had kept French interests alive in Acadia, but he was at best a trader and not a colonizer. The few settlers he brought to the New World were only incidental to his economic and military activities. Unlike Champlain in Canada, La Tour had no vision of a settled agricultural presence in Acadia, perhaps because he had to contend with the spillover from complex European rivalries. After his surrender to the English in 1654, the scattered few hundred Acadian residents

Françoise-Marie Jacquelin La Tour

According to her husband's chief enemy, Françoise-Marie Jacquelin La Tour (1602–45) was the daughter of a barber who became a Paris actress, but little is known of her background and it is at least as likely that she was a member of a family of lesser nobility in France. In 1640 she received a proposal of marriage in absentia from Charles de La Tour, who claimed the governorship of Acadia in competition with Charles de Menou d'Aulnay, and sailed to Port-Royal to join him. Whether the two had met earlier in France is not clear. After a marriage ceremony was performed at Port-Royal, the couple repaired to La Tour's trading post near Saint John. There Françoise-Marie gave birth to a son. In August 1642 d'Aulnay returned to Acadia with an official order that La Tour appear before the king to answer charges of treason. La Tour decided to send his wife, Françoise-Marie, to represent him at the royal court, suggesting that she had some connections there. She successfully argued her husband's case in 1642, then returned to Acadia in a French warship, carrying supplies for La Tour.

In 1644 she went again to France, but this time was unable to protect her husband's interests against d'Aulnay's charges. Escaping to England with borrowed money, Madame La Tour chartered an English ship to carry her and supplies back to her husband. Off Cape Sable the ship was detained and searched by d'Aulnay, but Madame La Tour hid in the hold. Arriving in Boston, she successfully sued the ship's captain for unwarranted delay, using the money to hire ships to reinforce La Tour at Fort La Tour.

Early in 1645, with her husband again off in Boston seeking fresh assistance, Madame La Tour commanded the defence of Fort La Tour against an attack by d'Aulnay. Her 45 defenders held out for four days against an invading force of 200, but she eventually surrendered on the understanding that d'Aulnay would 'give quarter to all'. The victor, however, went back on his word. All the captives except one man, who served as the executioner, were hanged. Madame La Tour, who was forced to witness the executions with a rope around her own neck, died scant weeks later.

She was probably the first European woman to have made her home in what is now New Brunswick, but as her experiences demonstrated, early life in the region was dangerous and complicated for both men and women.

were left to their own defences until formal French occupation was restored in 1667. While the period of English control from 1654 to 1667 left little internal mark on the region, it did isolate Acadia from the French court's rethinking of its American empire in the early 1660s. Acadia was not initially part of the Crown's decision in 1663 to take a more active interest in its American colonies. As a result, its subsequent status was never properly clarified, leading to an administrative weakness that encouraged its population to have an autonomous outlook and encouraged France (in 1713) under pressure to surrender large parts of the region to the English.

Newfoundland

Neither John Guy's settlement of Newfoundland in 1610 nor a series of successors sponsored by the Newfoundland Company and private promoters were spectacularly successful. But by the 1660s several communities of permanent settlers totalling 1,500 had taken hold along the rocky coast of the 'English Shore'. The society of these settlements was considerably more elaborate than historians once assumed, consisting of servants, planter employers, and a planter gentry of literate merchants. Incomes from fishing were reasonably good, and the local

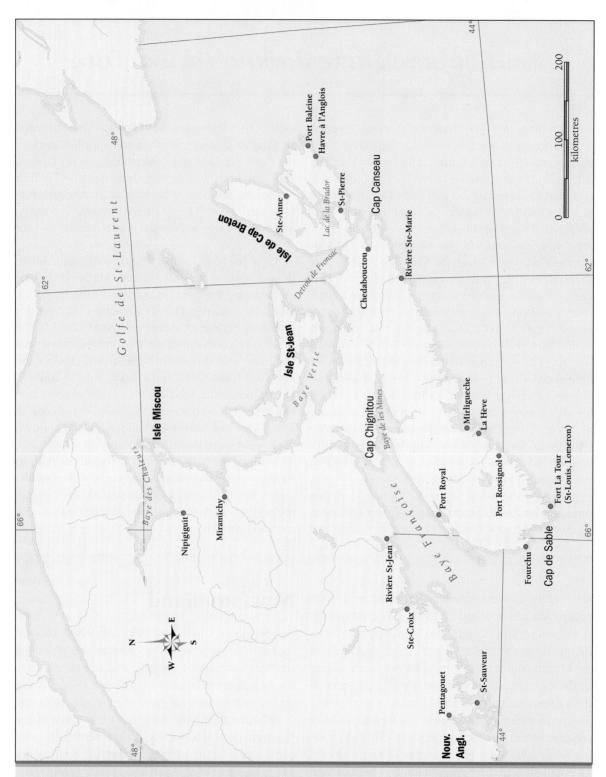

Acadia and environs to 1670. Adapted from A.H. Clark, *Acadia: The Geography of Early Nova Scotia to 1760* (Madison: University of Wisconsin Press, 1968), 76.

communities were no less stable than comparable ones in New England. The elite was dominated by the Kirke family, which was active in the Canadian trade (and buccaneering in the 1620s) and in the Newfoundland sack trade of the 1630s and 1640s, later becoming original investors in the Hudson's Bay Company. In 1675 the widow of Sir David Kirke and her son operated 10 fishing boats, and the Kirke family had 17 boats, employing 81 crew members. Indeed, on the English Shore of Newfoundland, as in many other early communities of North America, widows found opportunities for autonomy in business enterprises that they would not have enjoyed at home. Although Newfoundland had been one of the earliest sites in the New World for English colonization, the focus had quickly shifted south to New England, where the English by 1650 had developed a number of successful colonies with a total population in excess of 100,000. The 'new-found' land continued to provide enormous wealth to the British Empire in the form of fish, however, while remaining an unorganized jurisdiction and a marginal area of English settlement.

In the seventeenth century, almost all the year-round residents were of English origin, chiefly from the West Country counties of Cornwall, Devon, and Dorset. As late as 1732, 90 per cent of the permanent population remained English, but most of the eighteenth-century additions came from southern Ireland through the increasing links between Newfoundland and the Irish ports of Waterford and Cork. One census of wintering inhabitants in 1753 showed 2,668 Irish and 1,916 English. The Irish were being pushed out of Ireland by famine and unemployment, and were attracted to Newfoundland by the cheap fare for the voyage combined with work prospects. By 1750 Newfoundland had become a conduit by which Irish Catholics made their way to North America, and it remained so until 1815. Not all who jumped ship on the island remained in residence there.

Parallel to the increase of permanent population in Newfoundland came a shift in fishing practice. After 1714 the English summer visitors abandoned the inshore fishery and turned instead to fishing directly from the offshore banks. By 1750 the inshore fishery was controlled by local residents, but by this time there were already signs of depletion of the inshore fish stocks. The result was not conservation but diversification, with many Newfoundlanders moving into the seal fishery.

Canada, 1663–1760

That part of New France along the St Lawrence known as 'Canada' mixed French origins and North American environment in a way that defied easy characterization. The French background provided institutions, a terminology with which to express them, and a set of assumptions about how society ought to be organized and operated. The French assumed an ordered and hierarchical society in which the various social orders stayed in their places and duly subordinated themselves to the good of the whole, as defined by the Crown. As a complication, the French Crown was not satisfied simply to replicate the familiar institutions of the Old World in North America, but sought to reform them by stripping them of centuries of European tradition that had decentralized power and limited royal authority. At the same time, the environment provided a set of daily realities that worked against European institutions and assumptions, modifying and altering—while never totally negating—efforts to imitate the mother country. The result was a society that refracted the metropolis in France through the dual prisms of royal reform and North American experience. The external observer was struck at first by the presence of familiar European patterns and terminology, while beneath the surface different social designs constantly were evolving.

The royal takeover of 1663 put French administrative policy for the colonies and its execution in the hands of two men, the governor, Jean-Baptiste Colbert, and the intendant, Jean Talon. Colbert was Louis XIV's chief bureaucrat, a highly experienced civil servant. His major tasks both at home and abroad were to strengthen royal government and expand the French economy. As minister of marine, he served as the seventeenth-century equivalent of colonial secretary, in addition to a myriad of other responsibilities. To implement policy in America, Colbert decided to establish the position of intendant, a royal official

Sir David Kirke

Sir David Kirke, c. 1597–1654. Courtesy of the Centre for Newfoundland Studies Archives (MF231–411), St John's, Newfoundland. Image modified by Wendy Churchill, 1999.

Sir David Kirke (c. 1597–1654) was one of the notorious Kirke brothers who captured Quebec in 1629. This incident is probably the only one for which most Canadians remember him—if they remember at all. But there was more to his complex North American career than one buccaneering expedition. Kirke was the son of an English merchant who worked out of the French port of Dieppe, and David was apparently born in the French town. In 1627 Kirke's father was one of a consortium of English merchants who financed an expedition, led by David, to drive the French from Canada. David commanded a fleet of three vessels and was accompanied by several of his brothers; hence the common reference to the 'Kirke brothers' seizing Quebec. He apparently sailed with a fleet carrying Scottish settlers to Nova Scotia. In 1627 Champlain refused to surrender and Kirke did not press the issue. In the Gulf of St Lawrence, however, his ships met and defeated a French fleet, and Kirke returned to Europe with considerable booty.

The French in Paris protested because they regarded the Kirkes as French citizens. Kirke was rewarded by the British with the exclusive right to trade and settle in Canada, to which Sir William Alexander objected, however. Kirke and Alexander nevertheless negotiated a compromise to establish an Anglo-Scots colony at Tadoussac. The fleet sent out for this purpose (six ships, three pinnaces) also carried Claude de La Tour back to Nova Scotia. Kirke learned from a French deserter of the parlous state of the French garrison in Quebec, and this time Champlain surrendered. The Kirkes not only evacuated the colony but seized all the furs stored in Quebec. They subsequently attempted to work the fur trade with the assistance of a number of bushlopers, including Étienne Brûlé. Quebec was returned to the French by the Treaty of Saint-Germain-en-Laye in 1632, but Kirke was knighted a year later for his services to the Crown.

His North American activities had made Kirke aware of Newfoundland, and in 1637 he was part of a consortium (the Company of Adventurers to Newfoundland) that was made proprietor of that island. In 1639 he became first governor of Newfoundland and moved into Lord Baltimore's house at Ferryland. The four Kirke brothers were made English citizens at about the same time. Sir David began to recolonize Newfoundland, particularly Ferryland, and he attempted to control summer visiting along the island's coasts. He became one of the principal leaders of the Planters on the island, although his political actions always were controversial. In 1651 he was called home and charged with withholding taxes. Throughout the early 1650s he was under a cloud until his death in 1654, although his family continued to live in Newfoundland as merchants. Kirke's heirs, led by Lady Kirke, fought a number of legal battles for compensation (partly for the return of Quebec) after his death. Kirke was a good example of the extremely fluid legal situation among explorers and adventurers in northern North America in the first half of the seventeenth century.

who, in France, had been designated to cut through the accretion of centuries of devolution of royal power and to act decisively on behalf of the state. Beginning with Talon's first appointment as intendant in 1665, the colony's administration was greatly reorganized and centralized. The governor, though the titular head, was responsible for military affairs, external relations, and the colony's connections with the Church (including education). Subsequently, the governor invariably would be a member of the French aristocracy and an experienced military man, while routine administration devolved to the intendant, a career civil servant whose social origins were in the middle class. Classic confrontations between intendants and governors would ensue, particularly during the regime of Louis Buade de Frontenac (1620–98, governor 1672–82 and 1689–98). But the royal regime consistently backed the intendant.

Colbert and Talon not only managed to put the colony on its feet, but established its administrative and institutional structure for the entire century of French royal control. Their task was no easy one. Political institutions had to be established that were simultaneously responsive to the royal will and satisfactory to the populace. External threats had to be confronted. Population growth had to be stimulated. Some kind of economic viability had to be developed that would not endanger the mother country. Out this complex of factors would emerge a society and culture of enormous tenacity, possessing many resources for regeneration and change.

Canada was ruled by the Sovereign Council, made up mainly of the colony's elite and presided over by the intendant. No regularly elected political body represented the inhabitants. Instead, the colony used informal means to test public opinion, including the public protest (or 'riot'), which was a typical feature of life in both Europe and America at the time. Most Canadian riots were over food shortages, to which the government usually responded favourably. The Church was a major component of the government. Its main political task was to help establish, within the ranks of its communicants, due subordination to spiritual and secular authority. During the French regime the Church often found this job beyond its capabilities, partly because it was chronically understaffed. In 1759, for example, there were only 73 parish priests among 200 clergymen, hardly enough to provide religious services for everyone in the colony, especially outside the towns. In the symbiotic relationship between Church and state, moreover, the state dominated. It appointed bishops, granted seigneuries, and provided most of the revenue for religion. At the same time, the subordinate role of the Church did not mean that Canada was irreligious or secular, or that Catholicism did not permeate the lives of most of its inhabitants. Canada had been born in deep Catholic piety, and Catholic orthodoxy remained the norm.

Because Canada was continually in a state of siege, the role of the military was crucial. France was prepared to spend money on the military that it would not have allowed for civilian matters. The soldiers' pay was an important source of money for the Canadian economy, and the army was the best local customer for Canadian merchants. Regular soldiers served as a source of labour and as potential additions to the civilian population, which they were

Jean Talon, intendant of New France. This portrait is a nineteenth-century copy, attributed to Théophile Hamel, of a seventeenth-century painting by Frère Luc. LAC, C-7100.

encouraged to join at the expiration of their enlistments. Regular troops were not regarded as a sufficient military force, however, and from 1669 the entire adult male population of the colony between the ages of 16 and 60 was required to serve in the militia, locally commanded by *capitaines de milice* chosen democratically from the ranks of the inhabitants. After 1684 the militia was employed in every war. Much of this militia service was in collaboration with the First Nations in the form of raiding parties, designed to keep the English colonies off balance and to prevent them from using their superior numbers to invade the St Lawrence. Foreign observers were impressed with the martial spirit of the Canadians. For many Canadian elite families, as in France, military service in an officer class was preferable to entrance into commerce and industry. By the eighteenth century, the Canadian elite provided most of the officers for the Troupes de la Marine and even expected commissions to be reserved for the sons of serving officers.

One of Canada's major disadvantages in its constant wars against the English was the small size of its population. After 1660 French Canada matched the English colonies by doubling in population every 25 years, but it could never keep pace numerically. In 1715 the population of New France was 20,000, while that of the English colonies was 434,000. By 1754 the gap had widened, with 70,000 in New France and 1,485,000 in the American colonies to the south. After 1672 few French immigrants arrived in the colony, either publicly sponsored or privately motivated. The reasons for the lack of immigration have been much debated among scholars. One constellation of reasons revolves around the unfavourable publicity that Canada—despite or perhaps because of the *Jesuit Relations*—continually received in France. The colony had a reputation for a harsh climate and an absence of amenities, which did not dispose the French to emigrate. Another set of reasons involved conditions in France itself. Both the absence of agrarian dislocation and the insatiable demands of the French military for manpower prevented the development of a discontented and displaced population available for colonial migration on a massive scale. At the same time, the traditional juxtaposition

of the French and British colonial experiences is in many ways misleading. In relation to the colonies of most European nations in America—those of the Dutch Republic, Sweden, Scotland—New France was successful. The British colonies were unusual in their numbers and dynamism. Unfortunately for the French, the British did not have a mere handful of colonies in America, but a large number on the mainland and more in the Caribbean, which were both economically vibrant and located on the exposed flanks of New France and Louisiana. In the imperial rivalries that inevitably ensued, the French were at a substantial disadvantage.

At the time of the royal takeover in 1663, both Colbert and Talon had attempted to diversify the economy. They were especially concerned about the colony's heavy dependence on the fur trade. Colbert even saw the fur trade as a menace. 'It is to be feared', he wrote, 'that by means of this trade, the habitants will remain idle a good part of the year, whereas if they were not allowed to engage in it they would be obliged to apply themselves to cultivating their land' (quoted in Eccles, 1983: 104). What the French authorities wanted was an agricultural surplus and the exploitation of timber resources, which would enable the colony to supply the French West Indies with goods currently being obtained from the English. But the economy was slow to diversify. Part of the problem was that the fur trade kept expanding, contributing to a circular effect. The successful French quest for furs not only deflected attention from other enterprises but brought Canada into conflict with the English to the south. The ensuing struggle made it virtually impossible to limit the fur traders, since they were the ideal shock troops for engaging the enemy.

The numbers involved in the fur trade (the voyageurs and *engagés*) grew in number from 200 at the end of the seventeenth century to nearly 1,000 by the mid-eighteenth century. The work was both physically and emotionally demanding. Perhaps as many as one-quarter of able-bodied Canadian males were involved in the fur trade at some point in their lives, usually in their younger years before they settled down with a wife and family in more sedentary occupations along the St Lawrence. Many left First

Nations wives and mixed-blood families behind in the forest when they retired to their first families. A few rose to be specialists in the trade, some remaining in the West throughout their lives. A few became *marchands équipeurs* (outfitters), organizing the parties and providing the credit for the voyageurs. Unlike the colony's transatlantic merchants, the fur trade merchants were almost exclusively Canadian-born.

The constant quest for furs also drove Canada inexorably westward into the *pays d'en haut*, where some sort of satisfactory relationship had to be worked out with the First Nations. The upper country was the territory upriver from Montreal, beginning beyond Huronia and stretching through the Great Lakes and then south to Louisiana. This territory was claimed by the French by right of exploration and usage. It was originally an important fur-trading region, inhabited almost exclusively by Aboriginals who were mainly Algonquian speakers. Many of the traditional Native groups of the region had been joined by those fleeing westward from the Iroquois in the seventeenth century. These refugees re-established themselves in the country between the Ohio River and the Great Lakes to the west of Lake Michigan. This was an area that had been reduced in population by the Iroquois. The expansion of the fur trade could continue only as far as the western country of the Sioux, another military people. Gradually, some of the fur traders, especially those who had married Native women and started families, began to establish themselves in settlements along the river systems. A series of forts and towns, the former deliberately constructed by French policy, the latter

'Montreal from the West'. Although agriculture was still the primary form of economic activity in the seventeenth century, a commercial and artisan life emerged in urban centres, such as Montreal, seen in the distance in this painting by Philip John Bainbrigge. Library and Archives Canada, Acc. No. 1983-47-87.

mostly accidental creations, grew up in the region. The most prominent were Detroit, Michilimackinac, Green Bay, Cahokia, and Kaskakia. French fur traders travelled as far west as the Rocky Mountains in the first half of the eighteenth century.

A complex commercial and small-scale artisanal life did develop in New France. A small merchant class supported itself, particularly at the transatlantic level. Overseas trade was complicated and dangerous, and most merchants operated through family and clan connections. Marriage alliances established new branches of family firms in distant ports, and after the deaths of their husbands, women frequently took over the local enterprise. The trading economy over which the merchants presided required peace and stability to perform at its best. It also suffered

from a chronic shortage of a medium of exchange, which led the colony to produce its own paper money by using decks of playing cards inscribed in various denominations and signed by the intendant. Officially the cards were promissory notes, but they and the military *ordonnances* that circulated as legal tender after 1735 were inflationary. A constant demand existed for the local productions of skilled artisans, particularly those master craftsmen who worked for the Church, providing the furniture, ornaments, and decorations for the many church buildings in the colony. Artisans also made many things that would have been too bulky and expensive to import. Two major attempts to industrialize New France were made, both in the 1730s. One was an ironworks near Trois-Rivières (the 'forges du

Intendant Raudot on the Card Money, 1706

Beginning in 1685, New France dealt with its shortage of metallic coins by issuing decks of cards signed by the intendant and inscribed in various denominations. In 1706 Jacques Raudot, who was intendant of New France from 1705 to 1711, wrote a memorandum justifying the practice. It offers a little lesson in mercantilist monetary policy.

Memorandum on the Cards of Canada, Quebec, September 30, 1706

The cards which are issued in Canada serve as money just as coin does in France.

The Kingdom of France derives a certain utility from these cards, since, by this means, the King is not obliged to send funds in coined money for the expenditures which he has the goodness to incur. If it were necessary to send this, it would withdraw from the Kingdom annually 100,000 écus. Consequently this currency leaving the country would render money scarcer. It is true one would not appreciate this disadvantage during the abundance of money, nevertheless it is certain that it would effect a diminution. Moreover, France, by this device, not sending coined money, runs no risk as to it either from the sea or from enemies.

If coined money were sent to Canada, it would afterwards leave the country by two avenues, one part would return to France, the other would go to New England to purchase certain merchandise, which may be had cheaper there than from France. The part of this money returning to France would run the risks of the sea and enemies. The vessels may be taken or lost, and consequently the money they carry is lost to France, and there can be no greater injury to the Kingdom than the loss of its money.

The other part of this money being carried to New England for the purchase of merchandize, results in a considerable injury to France in the loss of its coinage and the advantage which it would produce among her enemies. . . .

St-Maurice'), the other a shipyard at Quebec. Both required large amounts of state subsidy to survive, but both demonstrated that Canadian workmen could be mobilized for industrial activity and could manufacture serviceable goods on a large scale.

Despite the growth of trade and industry, agriculture was always the dominant form of economic activity along the St Lawrence, functioning around the seigneurial system brought to the valley in 1627 and governed after 1663 by the Coutume de Paris. Seigneurialism in New France probably worked less to order society than to provide a means of settlement. The state made property concessions to landlords, who were supposed to find settlers to serve as tenants. Although the *censitaire* (tenant) owed various rents and feudal dues to his seigneur, these amounted to very little so long as there was more land than settlers. After the Edict of Marly in 1711, the seigneur could no longer withhold land from settlement in anticipation of price increases if there were settlers demanding it. Since they did not own the means of production, the *censitaires* seldom treated agriculture as a long-term business enterprise. The seigneurial system did not tie settlers to the soil and did not encourage large-scale, staple-crop farming so much as family farms on small holdings. The system was not really feudal, since military obligation in the colony was not tied to land occupation or tenure. Not until the end of the French regime was there sufficient pressure on the land to benefit the seigneur economically. He did acquire social status, however, and by the mid-eighteenth century the

Furthermore, there is no fear that money may be carried to New England, which would be very difficult to prevent if there were any in the colony, there being as in France persons who to gain something would risk much.

It is even a matter of policy for kings to attach the prosperity of their subjects to their own persons, in order to render the former more submissive and to take care that all the means which the colonies may have in money are always in the kingdom on which they are dependent. Canada, having nothing but cards, which are secured only on the word of the King, and seeing no other resource except in the good faith of the sovereign, will be still more submissive to him and still more attached to France for the reason that all the supply it can have in money depends on it. Hence, it appears to me that one cannot do better than to permit the continuation of the card money in Canada.

There may arise great abuses regarding these cards; they may be counterfeited in the country; this, however, can be prevented by a close attention, the easier bestowed as the resources of every person are known. Counterfeits may also be sent from France and so exactly imitated that one cannot distinguish the true from the false. That is almost impossible to do here, there not being clever people enough of that type. But even if there were some counterfeits they could not remain long without being recognised. To prevent this abuse one has only to change the dies, and shape of the cards every year after the departure of the vessels for France.

It is true that the colony of Canada will suffer somewhat by these cards, it being quite certain that it will buy French merchandise cheaper if it pays for them in coined money and not in cards, for which the merchants receive only bills of exchange which for the most part are not met at maturity. But it is proper that the colony of Canada suffer for the sake of the kingdom from which it receives its benefits, and it is only fair that this kingdom should run no risk of losing its money by the possible loss of its vessels bound for it. . . .

RAUDOT

Source: Adam Shortt, ed., *Documents Relating to Canadian Currency, Exchange and Finance during the French Period* (Ottawa: F.A. Acland, 1925), vol. 1, 157–9.

typical seigneur was an absentee landlord who lived in town and was involved in a variety of economic and political activities. A seigneury became part of a diversified portfolio of investment for those of the elite, within whose ranks little specialization of function had yet occurred.

By the mid-eighteenth century, Swedish visitor Peter Kalm could describe the heartland of French Canada along the St Lawrence as 'a village beginning at Montreal and ending at Quebec, which is a distance of more than one hundred and eight miles, for the farmhouses are never above five arpents [293 metres] and sometimes but three apart, a few places excepted' (Benson, 1937, II: 416–17). Each farmhouse, usually of three or four rooms built of stone and timber, stood alone. A few tiny villages formed, usually around churches. Three towns punctuated this continuous settlement: Quebec towards the eastern end, Trois-Rivières in the middle, and Montreal towards the west. Quebec and Montreal contained impressive and concentrated public and private buildings, often built of stone, but by our standards both towns were quite small in population and area. On their peripheries, the dominant landscape pattern of the separate but contiguous farmstead resumed. Narrow lots ran back for long distances from the river, and while there were new rows (*rangs*) of lots available behind the riverfront

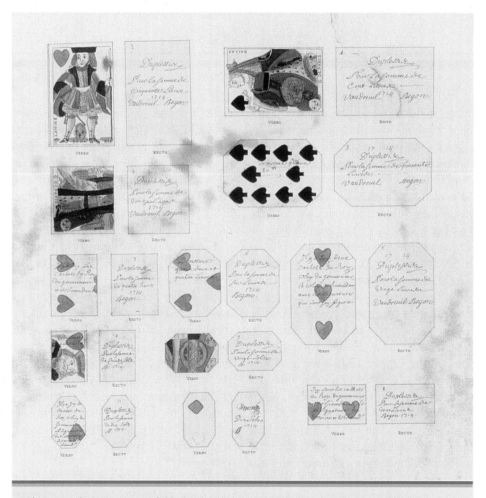

'Playing Card Money', pen with black ink with watercolour by Henri Beau (1863–1949), an employee of the Public Archives of Canada who was employed in the Paris office specifically to copy views, portraits, etc., and to carry out iconographic research. LAC, C-17059.

The iron forges on the St-Maurice, by Joseph Bouchette from his book *The British Dominion in North America* (London, 1832). LAC, C-4356

ones, population was slow to move inland. Thus French Canada replicated neither the French medieval village, whence many of its rural settlers had come, nor the English colonial tendency towards isolated farmsteads in the middle of large holdings separated from one another by considerable distances. Instead, in Canada its limited population sought to cover as much territory as possible.

Although Montreal and Quebec were not large, they did give Canada an urban life and a proportionately larger urban population than that of most North American colonies. These towns were the centres of government, of the direction of economic activity, and of the Church and its social services, such as health care and education. They inevitably included a heavy concentration of the upper classes of French Canada, and had an impressive polite society. While there were, doubtless, gradations of wealth and status, French North America was fundamentally divided into two orders: those with and those without access to government largesse and patronage. The law was available to all, but only some could expect public and military appointments, government contracts, and seigneurial grants. Upward mobility was a possibility, but most observers agreed that the typical Canadian worked no harder than was necessary, spent a disproportionate amount of time pursuing his own pleasures and interests (which included racing horses and disappearing into the bush), was far more prosperous than his European counterpart, and enjoyed a good deal more liberty.

Slavery was never prohibited in Canada, but it never flourished because there were no large plantations to employ a slave workforce. What slaves existed were mainly domestic servants. Not all were blacks, although 540 blacks have been identified in Canada during the French regime. Aboriginal prisoners (*panis*) sold to the French were also kept in bondage. The colonial New Englander John Gyles was technically a slave when he was transferred from his Aboriginal captor to a French merchant on the Saint John River at the beginning of the eighteenth century. The image of plantation slavery in the American South or in the Caribbean bears no relationship to the slave situation in French America, where many levels of bondage were possible.

New France in 1688. The cartographer, Jean-Baptiste-Louis Franquelin, worked at Quebec from 1671 to 1692 as both geographer and hydrographer to the king. LAC, Cartographic and Architectural Archives Division PH/1000/1688.

As for the roles and status of women, they did not undergo any remarkable transformation in the New World, although some modification of dependence may have occurred for some women, especially widows. The organization of society continued to be fundamentally patriarchal, with the woman in the traditional role of helpmate and child-bearer. Both the shortage of marriageable women and the frequent absence of men to the frontier or in the military somewhat moderated the oppression. There was some limited protection for the property rights of married women, and the autonomous rights of widows were safeguarded by law and custom. In truth, however, historians do not know very much about the ordinary lives of ordinary women in early Canada, chiefly because of the male orientation of the available documentation. While Canada always had a substantial number of women in holy orders, most women in the colony married (at the average age of 22) and raised a family. If marriage and remarriage rates were high, so, too, were birth rates and the number of children. Throughout the eighteenth century, birth rates ran over 50 per 1,000 inhabitants per annum, and women on average bore seven children. These demographic characteristics were typical of all colonial and frontier societies, however. Childbirth was certainly difficult and dangerous. Canada's men were constantly exposed to the dangers of wartime battle, but their wives faced equal or greater danger every time they gave birth.

In many ways the most difficult feature of New France to comprehend is its culture. In Canada, the language came to be the French of the Paris region of that period, spoken extremely well, although with a modified accent and incorporating vocabulary adopted from the indigenous people. The French spoken by Acadians was far more archaic and regionalized, coming mainly from the west of France. The French spoken in the Canadian interior was heavily laced with words taken over from Aboriginal languages. Recognizing the importance of spoken language rather than the written word is linked to the circumstance that New France never had a printing press or a newspaper. The transmission of French

The village of Château-Richer (on the north shore of the St Lawrence northeast of Quebec City), 1787, watercolour by Thomas Davies. Included in this pastoral scene are whitewashed stone farmhouses, wooden barns, and eel traps in the river. © National Gallery of Canada, 6275.

The Île d'Orléans and north and south shores of the St Lawrence, showing the boundaries of the land grants with the names of the seigneurial families in 1709; detail from a larger map of the Quebec region by Gédéon Catalogne and Jean-Baptiste de Couagne. LAC, NMC-0048248.

Plaisance (Placentia)

One of the least well-known North American colonies of Europe was Placentia or Plaisance, established on the gulf side of the Avalon Peninsula of Newfoundland in the early 1660s by the French. The middle years of the seventeenth century were a particularly confusing period on the northern Atlantic coast. The English Commonwealth under Oliver Cromwell had expanded its naval resources in the region, and had taken over most of Acadia. As a result, French access to the Atlantic region was being challenged, especially on the beaches of Newfoundland, where the English fishing fleet required increasingly large expanses of beach to dry its catch. The fishery remained an important imperial factor for all European nations, since mercantilism cherished it both as a training ground for a merchant marine and as a source of protein for hungry citizens. The French decided that a fortified post on the Newfoundland coast would be the best way to demonstrate their claims to the Newfoundland fishery and to protect their subjects in it. A very young Thalour Du Perron was sent ashore at the site about 100 kilometres south of St. John's in October 1662 with a few soldiers and a supply of food. He was murdered over the following winter by a drunken party of his men; the culprits were eventually brought to justice in Quebec. France spent over 10,000 livres a year before 1670 maintaining the tiny colony, but was unsuccessful in establishing much of an agricultural base; a summering population of 256 was fed by only 30 domestic animals and almost no cultivated ground. Basque merchant vessels visiting the colony charged what the traffic would bear, since they were virtually the only source of supplies and labour until the inhabitants managed to develop a trade with other French traders and eventually with vessels from Boston. A deep chasm between the settlers and the visitors soon emerged which lingered throughout the colony's existence. The soldiers of the garrison were quartered on the inhabitants and disarmed lest they become unruly, which rendered them virtually useless in times of crisis. The settlement was constantly beset with instability, and easily succumbed in 1690 to a small English party. Restored to France, it survived another two decades, serving as the base for French naval raiders in Newfoundland, until it was turned over to the English in 1713.

The control of Placentia, seen in this 1786 drawing, shuffled between the English and French for over 50 years until the English gained permanent control of the colony in 1713. Sketch by James S. Meres, 'The Log Book of His Majesty's Ship Pegasus'. Library and Archives Canada C-002525.

colonial culture, as that among peasants in France of the same period, was oral and visual rather than via print and literacy.

The locus of much of the formal artistic and aesthetic life in Canada was the Church, which required decorative and ritual ornaments. A great emphasis was placed on music, by the Church and among the people, who brought with them a rich heritage of song, dance, and music for dance. Culture was expressed through folktales and fairy stories, but these, too, were oral rather than written. Most expressions of culture among ordinary Canadians were part of the business of everyday life and experience in habitant households in rural parishes. Sometimes the North American environment changed the imported French culture, but in many cases—such as the use of oaths and pejorative slang—French usage still prevailed. Both the decoration of churches and the few examples of early wooden house furnishings that survive reveal a strong aesthetic sense. The churches preferred the baroque style of the French seventeenth and eighteenth centuries, while the everyday furniture featured simple, elegant, and functional designs.

The First Three Anglo–French Wars

Although sporadic warfare had occurred in North America since the earliest settlements, a protracted struggle for the continent between the European imperial powers—in which the First Nations were important players—began only in 1689. North American hostilities had their own dynamic, although they were always associated with the larger international rivalries of the mother countries. There were four wars. The first three were the War of the League of Augsburg (1689–97), settled by the Treaty of Ryswick; the War of the Spanish Succession (1702–13), settled by the Treaty of Utrecht; and the War of the Austrian Succession (1744–8), settled by the Treaty of Aix-la-Chapelle. The North American aspects of these first three wars shared a good deal in common. The North American fighting in these first conflicts was conducted mainly by the colonists

themselves employing their own military methods. Occasionally, the mother country would undertake a brief initiative, usually disastrous. Much of the fighting occurred in the backcountry and along the frontier. Such conflict involved the First Nations, who joined the battles for reasons of their own.

The strategy of the French was to send out raiding parties on land and sea to keep the British colonies disunited and off balance. The French hoped that the British would not be able to utilize their superior manpower, resources, and command of the sea (the British controlled the Atlantic for all but brief periods throughout these wars) to invade and capture French territory. The British unsuccessfully—and disastrously—attempted to invade the St Lawrence in the first two wars. In the third, New England troops and British naval forces captured Louisbourg in 1745, leading to the dispatch of a major French fleet to North America in 1746. The fleet met bad weather and experienced epidemic disease, limping back to France without ever engaging the enemy. France hoped to make sufficient military gains around the world so that any territory lost in North America would be returned in the peace treaty. This strategy was not always successful. In 1713 it was forced to give up Acadia and its claims to Newfoundland, although in 1697 and 1748 it surrendered nothing of substance in North America. Neither mother country considered the North American theatre anything but a sideshow until the 1750s, when the British, after settling Nova Scotia at government expense, decided to take the New World seriously.

Acadia and Nova Scotia

Acadia, that ill-defined geographical region that included more than peninsular Nova Scotia, had been contested ground between the British and the French since the early days of European settlement. Returned to France in 1670, Acadia and especially the village of Port-Royal often were attacked by New Englanders. Port-Royal was captured in 1690 but returned to France by the Treaty of Ryswick in 1697. New England failed to take Port-Royal in 1707, but succeeded in 1710. Port-Royal was not typical of

European possessions in North America after the peace of Utrecht (1713).

The Capture of Louisbourg, 1745

The capture of Louisbourg by New England militiamen in 1745 was one of the great military success stories of the colonial wars. The Americans celebrated in thanksgiving sermons and in broadside poetry (probably intended to be sung) sold in single printed sheets on the streets of Boston. Here is one of those broadsides.

New England Bravery

Come all New England's gallant Lads,
And lend to me an Ear,
And of your Brethren's Acts
I will in short declare.
Brave Pep'rell with Three Thousand Men,
(perhaps some hundreds more)
Did land the very first of May,
upon Cape Breton Shore:
And tho' opposed by Morepang
with full two hundred Men,
A handful of our gallant Lads
did drive them back again.
Some few were taken Prisoners,
And many kill'd out-right
Which taught the French at Louisbourg
New England Men can fight.
The Monsieurs all astonished
to see our Armament,
Were griev'd to see that they must be
within Stone Walls all pent.
In haste they call in to their Aid
the Men upon the Isle
Forgetting their own Poverty,
(such things would make one smile)
But what is vastly more absurd
Than anything like this,
They quitted the Grand Battery,
The Glory of the Place.
Of which our English Lads did take
Possession quietly,
And with the Guns did ever since
the Enemy annoy.

They also did with mighty Toil
their Batteries erect,
Against the Town and Citadel
which play'd with good Effect.
They sent such Showers of Bombs and Balls
as made the Frenchmen quake,
And sputter out such words as these,
Those Dogs the Place will take.
Our men did also batter down
The West Gate and the Wall,
And made therein so large a Breach
That to the French they'd call,
Come out, Jack Frenchmen, come to us,
And drink a Bowl of Punch.
Jack Frenchman cries, you English Dogs,
come, here's a pretty Wench,
But by and by they change their Tones,
and after Terms of Peace,
Which if consented to they would
surrender up the Place.
(For they were so severely maul'd
by Cannon Shot and Shells,
That they no Place of Safety found
on Platforms or in Cells. . . .)
Our Gen'ral upon this Success
did send Monsieurs Words,
If they would not give up the Place,
He'd put them to the Sword.
And now not daring to withstand
The Force of all our Bands,
They gave up all their Fortresses
into our English Hands.

Louisbourg

After 1713 the French had turned their attention to Île Royale, and particularly to building a large fortress at Louisbourg on the southeastern coast.

In 1716 Louisbourg contained about 600 people, mainly fishermen brought there from Placentia in Newfoundland, which had been evacuated. After

Louisbourg in 1734.
Source: A.J.B. Johnston, *Control and Order in French Colonial Louisbourg, 1713–1758* (East Lansing: Michigan State University Press, 2001), xlii. Direction des Archives de France/Centre des Archives d'Outre-Mer.

Acadia, however. Between 1660 and 1713 Acadians expanded in numbers and increased the amount of territory cultivated. A population of about 500 in 1660 had grown to more than 1,500 in 1710, mostly through natural increase, and had planted settlements along the Minas Basin, Cobequid, and Chignecto Bay. Most of Acadia's people came from a relatively small area of southwestern France. Younger members of families moved to new communities, which featured dykes that controlled the inundation of lowland areas by the high tides of the Bay of Fundy. Marsh was drained for farming. Farms were small but richly prosperous. Livestock, especially cattle, was the chief produce, traded illegally by the Acadians with New Englanders. A few outlying fishing communities existed on the southwest coast. Acadia had few roads and little overland transportation. Movement was by canoe and small boat.

Government sat fairly lightly upon this population. The French never really asserted tight administrative control over the region, and the Church operated solely through missionaries who provided some contact with Canada. Culturally and politically, the Acadians remained isolated from French Canada. The family (*clan*) and the local community were the important units for a closely knit peasant society. Acadia had developed an inherent sense of autonomy when—in the chess game of eighteenth-century

1720 it grew rapidly as the French government fortified the town, garrisoned it, and employed it as the military and economic nerve centre of the Atlantic region. By 1734 the townsite—four east–west streets on about 100 acres—was surrounded by walls on three sides, with impressive gates. The fortifications—poorly located and poorly built—were never completed. Inside the walls were the huge and stately King's Bastion and barracks (the largest building in New France), and numerous stone dwellings and other structures. In the 1740s the Louisbourg population was made up of 600 soldiers (increased to 3,500 in the 1750s) and some 2,000 administrators, clerks, innkeepers, artisans, fishermen, and families.

We know a substantial amount about Louisbourg, much more than about Acadia, partly because as a fortress it generated a considerable volume of records and partly because its reconstruction as a National Historic Site has produced a minor industry of subsidized historical research. Its complex urban society—consisting of people who came from various parts of France as well as from New France (see Table 2.2)—was heavily subsidized by the Crown and included a wide variety of tradesmen and a substantial servant-keeping class, headed by

20 marchands. Always a major fishing port, serving as the centre of the French fishery after the surrender of Placentia in 1713, Louisbourg in its prime was also an important naval station harbouring French warships as well as fishing vessels. Since its hinterland was completely undeveloped, supplies had to be imported from afar: from Canada, France, Acadia, and New England. The Yankees even supplied much of the building material for its fortifications, which cost 5 million livres incompleted.

By the time open warfare was resumed between Great Britain and France on 27 April 1744, Louisbourg had become a major military and commercial entrepôt in northern North America. The fortress was attacked in 1745 by a joint Anglo-American force under the command of Sir William Pepperell and Sir Peter Warren. Weakened by bad garrison morale that led to mutiny earlier in the winter of 1744–5, the fortress surrendered after only token resistance, leaving the victors to squabble over credit for the success. The fortress was returned to France in 1748 at the Treaty of Aix-la-Chapelle in exchange for Madras in India, but despite considerable reinforcement of fortifications and garrison in the 1750s, it fell quickly to the British again in 1758.

Table 2.2	Origins of the Habitants of Louisbourg					
	1724		**1726**		**1734**	
	No.	%	No.	%	No.	%
New France	18	16.8	25	16.3	31	21.2
Normandy/Brittany	16	15.0	31	20.3	28	19.2
Southwest France	12	11.2	18	11.8	16	11.0
West France	29	27.1	36	23.5	24	16.4
Île de France	10	9.4	14	9.2	11	7.5
France (elsewhere)	21	19.6	25	16.3	27	18.5
Foreign	1	0.9	4	2.6	9	6.2
Total	107	100	153	100	146	100

Source: Adapted from A.J.B. Johnston, *Control and Order in French Colonial Louisbourg, 1713–1758* (East Lansing: Michigan State University Press, 2001), xlii.

imperial warfare—France was obliged to surrender territory in North America with the Treaty of Utrecht (1713). Acadia was one of the pawns given up to the British that year. The *anciennes limites* of Acadia mentioned in the treaty were not defined, and the French subsequently insisted that they had surrendered only peninsular Nova Scotia, informally retaining northern Maine and New Brunswick, and formally retaining Île Royale (Cape Breton) and Île St-Jean (Prince Edward Island). As for the population of the ceded territory, which the British called Nova Scotia to emphasize Britain's historic claims there, the inhabitants were given one year to remove to French territory or to remain as subjects of their new masters.

Nobody except the French wanted the Acadians removed, so they were tacitly allowed to remain in Nova Scotia on sufferance. Questions such as their land, language, and religious rights, as well as their political and military obligations to the new rulers, were unresolved. The government of Nova Scotia dealt with the Acadians on an ad hoc basis, accepting their insistence on political neutrality and failing to exercise much authority within the Acadian community. The Acadians were not the first nor would they be the last group to translate unofficial tolerance born of irresolution, into enshrined 'rights'. The dealings of the Nova Scotian authorities with the Acadians on the question of loyalty before 1740 were never authorized in London, but they led the Acadians to believe that they had an understanding.

Unfortunately for the French population of Nova Scotia, their loyalties were tested constantly by the French, who had begun after 1720 to construct a fortress at Louisbourg on the southeastern coast of Île Royale.

The British capture of Louisbourg in 1745 and its return in 1748 had several important effects in Nova Scotia. One was to encourage the British to counter Louisbourg with some military settling of their own. Another was to turn the attention of the local authorities to the Acadians. The Nova Scotia Council in 1745 declared of the Acadians that 'if they are not absolutely to be regarded as utter Enemies to His Majesty's Government they cannot be accounted less than unprofitable Inhabitants for

their conditional Oath of Allegiance will not entitle them to the Confidence and Privileges of Natural British Subjects' (Library and Archives Canada, 1745: A27). British settlement and Acadian removal were commonly coupled in the minds of British officials on both sides of the Atlantic. With the founding of Halifax, a sequence of events was set in motion that would result in the forcible expulsion of 6,000 Acadian residents from the colony.

The decision of the British government to use the public purse to populate a British colony—the first time Britain had done so in America and at a cost of more than £600,000 between 1749 and 1764—marked a new British interest in the Atlantic region. In 1749 Britain recruited some 2,500 people, including soldiers and sailors recently disbanded and some London artisans, and shipped them to Nova Scotia. They arrived to find huts, tents, and primitive conditions. The new governor, Lord Edward Cornwallis (1713–76), complained that most of the new arrivals were 'poor idle worthless vagabonds' (quoted in Bell, 1990: 344n). The British government soon sought a new source of more reliable settlers, turning to 'foreign Protestants' from Switzerland, France, and Germany. It employed as recruiting agent the young Scotsman John Dick (d. 1804), who was empowered by the Board of Trade over the winter of 1749–50 to recruit up to 1,500 'foreign Protestants', who would receive land, a year's subsistence, arms, and tools, but not free transportation. Dick protested that free passage would be the main inducement, but he managed to fill the order. There were again complaints about the recruits, who were labelled 'in general old miserable wretches' (Bell, 1990: 344n). In the end Dick sent over 2,700 Germans and Swiss, many of the latter actually French Huguenots from Lorraine. These immigrants were mainly farmers and skilled labourers. Uncertainty over land titles confined them to shantytown Halifax until the Nova Scotia government determined to remove them to a site 50 miles (80 km) west of Halifax, renamed Lunenburg. There they resettled, an unhappy crowd that was 'inconceivably turbulent, I might have said mutinous', according to the officer in charge of the relocation, Major Charles Lawrence (*c.* 1709–60) (Bell, 1990: 435).

The Porte Dauphine, the entrance to the reconstructed Louisbourg, with the clock tower of the King's Bastion and barracks in the distance. Parks Canada, Fortress of Louisbourg National Historic Site of Canada, 01 A 339.

The settlement of Halifax was only one of a series of new pressures brought upon the province's Acadians. The French were reinforcing Louisbourg and constructing new forts (Fort Beauséjour and Fort Gaspéreau) on the disputed Chignecto Peninsula. The French also began encouraging the Acadians in Nova Scotia to remove to French territory, especially the previously neglected Île St-Jean, which grew to more than 2,000 residents by 1752. The bulk of Nova Scotia's Acadians remained where they were, but after the renewal of undeclared war in North America in 1754, the government of the colony decided to settle the question. In July 1755 the Executive Council of Nova Scotia summoned

Acadian deputies into a meeting room in Halifax and informed them that conditional fealty was impossible. The Acadians must immediately take the oath of allegiance in its common form. The Acadian representatives temporized overnight. When they were told that if they refused to take an unconditional oath, 'effectual Measures' would be taken 'to remove all such Recusants out of the Province', some offered to concede (Akins, 1869: 259–60). The council then refused to administer the oath, however, saying 'that as there was no reason to hope their proposed Compliance proceeded from an honest Mind, and could be esteemed only the Effect of Compulsion and Force, they could not now be indulged with such Permission' (Akins, 1869: 259–60). A classic confrontation between the civic inflexibility of the state and a collective minority demanding special treatment was in the closing stages of resolution. The council decided not only to expel the Acadians but to distribute them to several British colonies in the south.

More than 6,000 Acadians were summarily rounded up in the late summer and early autumn of 1755 by the British military and transported by ship to the south. There was little resistance, although many escaped to the woods and headed for French territory or to the inhabited north. The Acadians were not received with great enthusiasm in the British colonies, which had not been warned to expect them, and many eventually returned to the province. The British government never commented on the action of the Nova Scotia government, which it had never authorized, except to note that the colony had regarded it as 'indispensably necessary for the Security and protection of the Province' (quoted in Brebner, 1927: 230). As for those who did escape to the French, after the British forced the surrender of Louisbourg in July 1758 another expulsion began. A further 6,000 Acadians, including 3,500 on Île St-Jean, were summarily rounded up by the British military and sent back to France. A storm at sea destroyed many of the vessels carrying the Acadians, and perhaps as many as half of them drowned. The British never succeeded in eliminating the French presence from the region, however. Many Acadians escaped into the bush, others returned from their exile. What the expulsion did accomplish was to remove the Acadians from their traditional lands and force them to the unsettled margins of the Maritime colonies.

The founding of Halifax also had a substantial impact on the First Nations of Nova Scotia, especially the 1,000 Mi'kmaq remaining in the colony. The Mi'kmaq had attempted to pursue their own best interests during the years of warfare between the French and the English. They understood that British concepts of landownership and settlement were disastrous to them. As a result they declared war against the British in 1749 and were met with a policy of extermination ordered by Lord Cornwallis.

A final peace treaty with the Mi'kmaq in 1761 did not deal with land rights. No longer a military threat, the First Peoples would soon cease to be regarded as important in the colony.

In the wake of the final conquest of Louisbourg, the Nova Scotia government in October 1758 sent out advertisements to New England, offering to those who would settle in the colony free land, free transportation to it, and initial assistance in the form of food and tools. A few days before these advertisements were published, a legislative assembly—the first widely elected governing body in what is now Canada—met in Halifax. Nova Scotia was now a full-fledged British colony, the fourteenth mainland colony in Britain's North American empire. This point had been reached with brutal measures that were characteristic of the age.

The Seven Years War

Officially, the Seven Years War began in 1756 in Europe, although the North American contestants had been engaged in open conflict for several years. In 1754, a desperate struggle between the British and the French for the allegiance of the Aboriginal peoples in the Ohio country and for sovereignty over the region came to a head. The French had tried to assert their claim in 1749 by sending a military expedition, led by Pierre-Joseph Céleron de Blainville (1693–1759), which planted lead tablets all along the Ohio and Allegheny rivers stating the French claims to the region. The French in 1752 and 1753 built military posts in the area. In the latter year the British sent George Washington with a small party to deliver a letter to the French commandant at one of the French posts, Fort Le Boeuf, claiming the Ohio Valley and requesting the French to leave. They refused. In turn, the British governor of Virginia was authorized to use force to expel the French. He sent Washington back a year later with a force of 159 men, backed by a party of Aboriginals, to establish a fort on the Ohio. On the way, the expedition confronted a small French party of 30 men commanded by Joseph Coulon de Villiers de Jumonville (1718–54), who were travelling east to see whether Washington had entered what the French regarded

A Contemporary Acadian Account

Many of the Acadian exiles ended up in the colony of Pennsylvania, which in 1758 collected a number of their narratives, including the following.

A Relation of the Misfortunes of the French Neutrals, as laid before the
Assembly of the Province of Pennsylvania, by John Baptist Galerm, one of the said People.

. . . Almost numberless are the Instances which might be given of the Abuses and Losses we have undergone from the French Indians, on Account of our steady Adhearance to our Oath of Fidelity: and yet notwithstanding our strict Observance thereof, we have not been able to prevent the grievous Calamity which is now come upon us, which we apprehend to be in a great Measure owing to the unhappy Situation and Conduct of some of our People settled at Chignecto, at the bottom of the Bay of Fundi, where the French, about four Years ago, erected a Fort; those of our People who were settled near it, after having had many of their Settlements burnt by the French; being too far from Halifax and Annapolis Royal to expect sufficient Assistance from the English, were obliged, as we believe, more through Compulsion and Fear than Inclination, to join with and assist the French. . . . As these People's Conduct had given just Umbrage to the Government and created Suspicions, to the Prejudice of our whole Community, we were summoned to appear before the Governor and Council at Halifax, where we were required to take the Oath of Allegiance without any Exception, which we could not comply with because, as that Government is at present situate, we apprehend that we should have been obliged to take up Arms; but we are still willing to take the Oath of Fidelity, and to give the strongest Assurance of continuing peaceable and faithful to his Britannic Majesty, with that Exception, But this, in the present Situation of Affairs, not being satisfactory, we were made Prisoners, and our Estates, both real and personal, forfeited for the King's Use; and Vessels being provided, we were some time after sent off, with most of our Families, and dispersed amongst the English Colonies. The Hurry and Confusion in which we were embarked was an aggravating Circumstance attending our Misfortunes; for thereby many, who had lived in Affluence, found themselves deprived of every Necessary, and many Families were separated, Parents from Children, and Children from Parents.

John Baptiste Galerm

Source: 'Relation of the French Neutrals, 1758. Pennsylvania Archives, 1758. First series, vol. 3', as reprinted in N.E.S. Griffiths, *The Acadian Deportation: Deliberate Perfidy or Cruel Necessity* (Toronto: Copp Clark, 1969), 151.

as their territory. If he had, he was to be ordered formally to withdraw. Jumonville's party was specifically ordered not to provoke trouble; he was on a diplomatic mission, not a military one.

On 28 May 1754, Washington and some of his men entered the French camp, which was not well guarded. In the course of the ensuing melee, Jumonville (who had been wounded) was dispatched in traditional Aboriginal fashion with a tomahawk by one of the warriors. 'You are not yet dead, my father', Tanacharison said to the wounded Frenchman in the ritual language of the time, and so he killed him (White, 1991: 241). Washington subsequently did his best to deny that Jumonville had been murdered, arguing that the French had hostile intentions—putting his reputation for

Letter from Charles Lawrence regarding the expulsion of the Acadians, 11 August 1755. LAC, MG53, No. 71 2–4.

never telling a lie in jeopardy. The incident led the French to send out a much larger force from Fort Duquesne, which in early July forced the Virginians to surrender. This surrender in turn led the British to dispatch two regiments under General Edward Braddock to America, and they were devastated at the Monongahela River in the early summer of 1755. News of this defeat—war still not having formally been declared—contributed to the British decision in Nova Scotia to expel the neutral Acadians from their province. Thus did the imperial struggle in the west impact the maritime region, demonstrating that however marginal these regions were, their domestic development was affected by larger events.

In the beginning, the French seemed to be doing well. They had destroyed General Braddock's army of British regulars in 1755. On this occasion, the French tactics of ambush and guerrilla warfare easily triumphed over professional soldiers. A year later, under General Montcalm, they took 1,700 prisoners at the surrender of the three forts associated with Fort Oswego (on the southern shore of Lake Ontario, known to the French as Fort Chouaguen). Hit-and-run raiders kept the American backcountry in a constant uproar along the Ohio frontier. General Montcalm and other French officers were not happy with the brutality of these military actions. Given their naval weaknesses, however, the French needed to keep the

'A Map of the South Part of Nova Scotia and its Fishing Banks', by Thomas Jefferys, 1750. Inset at the upper right is 'A Plan of the new town of Halifax Surveyed by M. Harris'; at the lower right, 'A View of Halifax drawn from ye top masthead'. LAC, NMC 1012.

British off balance to prevent a buildup of forces that would lead to an invasion.

In 1757 the French concentrated on New York as the major battlefield. Montcalm won several more notable victories, putting the French in control of the lake route into Canada. But the British continued to pour men and supplies into North America. A year later, the British managed to force the surrender of the garrison at Fort Frontenac on the north shore of Lake Ontario. A sideshow in the Ohio region saw the British capture Fort Duquesne on the Ohio River. The British further increased the number of troops at their disposal, employing their naval superiority to besiege successfully the exposed French fortress at Louisbourg in 1758. The French garrison held out just long enough to prevent the enemy from continuing on to an invasion of Quebec that same year, but the French were pulling back militarily. The situation in New France was becoming desperate. The government was unable to get reinforcements of men or fresh supplies, especially of arms and munitions, because the British controlled the sea. Moreover, the colony was in terrible shape financially, with runaway inflation. The civilian government and the military leadership were at constant loggerheads, and morale was very low.

A map by Thomas Jefferys showing the British claims to Acadia. Library of Congress, Prints and Photographs Division, 705008.

Conclusion

At the beginning of 1759, the situation was very grave for New France. After more than a century and a half of successful struggle against the environment, First Nations enemies, French neglect, and British hostility, the Canadians had their backs to the wall. The Acadians had been forcibly removed from Nova Scotia and Louisbourg had been captured. A series of powerful British armies, backed by a wealthy government determined to win, was gathering for the invasion of the St Lawrence. The locus of power was about to shift, to the detriment of the French in North America.

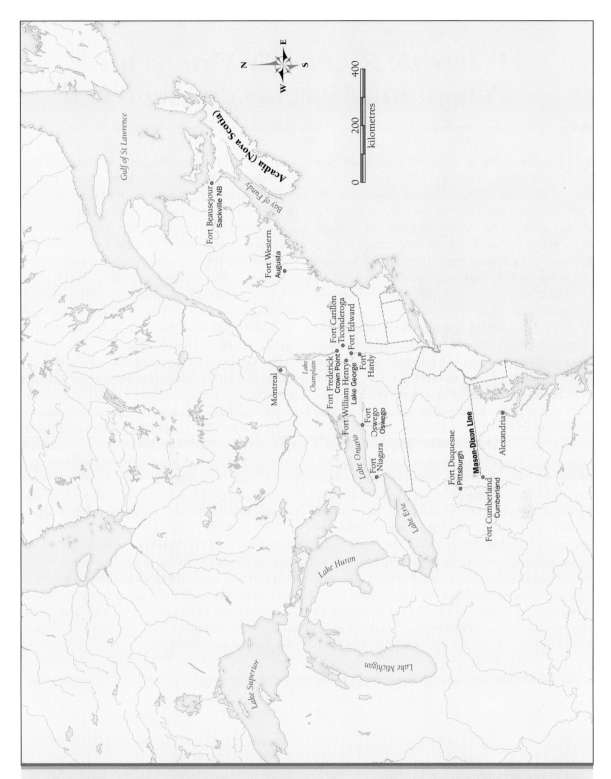

The war in 1755. Adapted from Seymour Schwartz, *The French and Indian War 1754–1763: The Imperial Struggle for North America* (New York: Simon & Schuster, 1994), 37.

Pierre de Rigaud de Vaudreuil de Cavagnial, Marquis de Vaudreuil

His father served as Governor General of New France from 1703 to 1725, and Pierre de Vaudreuil (1698–1778) advanced quickly in the French military service. After his father's death, his mother arranged for him the appointment as major of the troops in Canada. On a visit to France in 1728 he made a favourable impression on the Minister of Marine and received a promotion. In 1733 he became Governor of Trois-Rivières, the first rung on the ladder of political advancement in New France. After successful service in this appointment, in 1742 he was made Governor of Louisiana, where he was quick to take advantage of the independent authority the distance from Quebec gave him, and he boasted both of his reforms and of his diplomatic successes with the local Indian nations, especially the Choctaws.

In 1746, already in middle age, he married a woman considerably older than himself. The two had a very happy marriage. Vaudreuil's responsibilities included the Ohio Valley and the Illinois country, which became a hotbed of intrigue and imperial contention in the 1750s and brought him to the attention of Quebec. His major success in Louisiana was improving the economic situation, stressing the production of indigo and other goods and attracting a larger French expenditure on defence.

He was recalled to Paris in 1753, and in 1755 he was appointed Governor General of New France. While in Paris he missed the conflict in the Ohio Valley at Fort Duquesne, but he acquired the responsibility for defending New France against the British. His plan was to defend his territory tenaciously by gathering all authority in his hands and employing interior lines of communication to advantage, while simultaneously hoping that the British would remain as disunified as they had been in the past. This strategy worked for awhile, but it took a heavy toll on Vaudreuil, who was complaining about ill health by late 1756. In this war the British took over from the colonials and put much pressure on New France.

The Governor General became on increasingly bad terms with his military commander, the Marquis of Montcalm, over a variety of issues, including the French regulars' disrespect for the people and for the militia. In 1758 he convinced the King's ministers to replace Montcalm, but the King rejected the order and promoted Montcalm to a military rank higher than the Governor General, which made him Montcalm's subordinate. The two were still disputing while the British were at the colony's door.

The death of Montcalm on the battleground made it necessary for Vaudreuil to order the capitulation of Montreal in 1760 to prevent further bloodshed and also ensured that Vaudreuil and Intendant Bigot would be made the scapegoats for the loss of France's American empire. After a long trial the tribunal declared him innocent and restored his pension. He retired in Paris.

How History Has Changed

The Expulsion of Acadians in 1755 and the Evangeline Myth

Contemporaries at the time of the Acadian deportations were aware of their existence. Indeed, one Abbé Raynal, in his *Histoire philosophie et politique des établissements et du commerce des Européens dans les deux Indies*, published in Paris in 1766, gave a rather full account of the British treatment of the Acadians. For Raynal the story was one of 'jalousies nationales' and 'cupidité des gouvernments' destroying a simple, innocent, and devout people who lived in a virtual Garden of Eden. For their part, nineteenth-century Nova Scotians were not totally ignorant of what had happened. In his *An Historical and Statistical Account of Nova Scotia*, published in Halifax in 1829, Thomas Chandler Haliburton gave a lengthy historical account of their treatment—based both on Raynal and his own researches—which emphasized the lengthy period of conflict between Nova Scotia's authorities and the Acadians over allegiance, and concluded that the Acadians were 'an unfortunate and deluded people'.

In the winter of 1840–1, the American poet Henry Wadsworth Longfellow at a dinner party heard a story about the Acadian experiences. It concerned a girl who was separated from her lover in the deportation and who spent her life searching for him. The two were reconciled in old age in a hospital in which the lover was dying. Longfellow was so taken with the story that he wrote a poem about it, completed as *Evangeline: A Tale of Acadia* in February 1847. *Evangeline* became instantly a best-seller. Longfellow had hoped to write a poem about a virtuous female that emphasized the 'faithfulness and constancy of women', but what readers took from *Evangeline* instead was an idealized and romanticized image of a simple bucolic community that had been brutally mistreated by the English in Nova Scotia and met its fate with stoic acceptance.

Longfellow set his poem squarely in 1755, the year of the expulsion. The context in which he placed Evangeline was not the complex history of British–Acadian relations over more than 40 years, but the immediate suffering of Evangeline, her family, and the Acadian people. In 1848 the poet wrote to one correspondent, 'you will be astonished at the tragedy enacted in the little Acadian village, not one feature of which have I darkened or deepened.' He described the 'columns of shining smoke' and 'flashes of flame . . . Thrust through their folds, and withdrawn, like the quavering hands of a martyr.' Evangeline's family are treated as poor innocents caught up in a web of brutality not at all of their own making.

Nova Scotians understood perfectly well the political implications of Longfellow's setting of the Acadian experience, particularly in the context of the ultimate return to the province of many of those involved or their descendants. Any progressive history of the development of Nova Scotia had been challenged. The settlement of the New England Planters had been built on a terribly wrong policy. Nevertheless, a whole generation passed before the Longfellow approach was challenged in print. In the meantime, Thomas Beamish Akins had used the lack of context in the poem to press for preservation of the province's public records, including those necessary for such a context, and subsequently produced a volume of documents. Contextualization of the expulsion did not completely exonerate the British government of the day, however, and the historical controversy over the events of 1755 has continued unabated, today taking the form of disagreement over the use of modern language like 'ethnic cleansing' and 'genocide' to describe the expulsion.

Perhaps even more interesting than the attempt within anglophone Nova Scotia to set the record straight was the way in which the Longfellow story and version of the expulsion gained currency among the Acadian population of the Maritime region. After years of relative silence, the Acadians began in the 1860s to reassert their identity as a people. Acadian activists found Longfellow's 'soufflé mystique'—as one of them referred to it—a powerful weapon in the reconstruction of an Acadian identity. They were so successful in associating *Evangeline* with the Acadians that in the twentieth century most tourist publicity about the Acadian regions of the Maritimes spoke of 'the land of Evangeline'. This identification built to some extent on an awareness that *Evangeline* was a poem well-known to the American tourists the region wished to attract, largely because of its use in the schools of the United States. Thus, the American poet Henry Wadsworth Longfellow created one of Canada's most durable myths and provided the impetus for the reinvention of a Canadian ethnic identity.

Short Bibliography

Banks, Kenneth. *Chasing Empire across the Sea: Communications and the State in the French Atlantic, 1713–1763.* Montreal and Kingston, 2002. A fascinating study of the eighteenth-century French Empire in the New World.

Blackburn, Carole. *The Jesuit Missions and Colonialism in North America, 1632–1650.* Montreal and Kingston, 2000. A recent study of the missionary activities of the Jesuits with the Huron, placed in a contemporary perspective of colonialism.

Dechêne, Louise. *Habitants and Merchants in Seventeenth-Century Montreal.* Montreal and Kingston, 1992. An award-winning study of the development of early Montreal.

———. *Le people, l'État et la guerre au Canada sous le régime français.* Montreal, 2008. The product of a life's work of study by Quebec's leading social historian.

Delâge, Denys. *Bitter Feast: Amerindians and Europeans in Northeastern North America 1600–1664*, trans. Jane Brierly. Vancouver, 1993. An analysis of the early relationships between First Nations and European intruders.

Eccles, W.J. *France in America.* Markham, Ont., 1990. The best overview of the French Empire in North America.

Faragher, John Mack. *A Great and Noble Scheme: The Tragic Story of the Expulsion of the French Acadians from Their American Homeland.* New York, 2005. A recent synthesis by an American scholar.

Griffiths, Naomi. *The Contexts of Acadian History, 1587–1781.* Montreal, 1992. A series of fascinating essays by the leading specialist on early Acadia.

Handcock, Gordon. *'So Longe As There Comes Noe Women': Origins of English Settlement in Newfoundland.* St John's, 1989. The story of early English settlement in Newfoundland.

Harris, R.C. *The Seigneurial System in Early Canada: A Geographical Study.* Madison, Wis., 1966. The classic revisionist text on the subject, not yet superseded.

Head, C. Grant. *Eighteenth-Century Newfoundland: A Geographer's Perspective.* Toronto, 1976. An interesting example of what the historical geographer contributes to Canadian historical analysis.

Johnstone, A.J.B. *Control and Order in French Colonial Louisbourg.* East Lansing, Mich., 2001. A study of the administration of Louisbourg.

MacDonald, M.A. *Fortune and La Tour: The Civil War in Acadia.* Toronto, 1983. A well-written account of the La Tour family and its vicissitudes.

Moogk, Peter. *La Nouvelle France: The Making of New France—A Cultural History.* East Lansing, Mich., 2000. A fascinating new analysis made from the standpoint of culture and cultural studies.

Moore, Christopher. *Louisbourg Portrait: Life in an Eighteenth-Century Garrison Town.* Toronto, 1982. An award-winning book based on early court records, demonstrating how much fascinating material can be teased out of such sources.

Pritchard, J.S. *Anatomy of a Naval Disaster: The 1746 French Expedition to North America.* Montreal and Kingston, 1998. A wonderful account of the French navy in a time of crisis, demonstrating how difficult it was to coordinate military activities in the eighteenth century.

Simpson, Patricia. *Marguerite Bourgeoys and Montreal, 1640–1665.* Montreal and Kingston, 1997. A sympathetic account of one of the leading female figures of seventeenth-century Canada.

Steele, Ian. *Guerillas and Grenadiers: The Struggle for Canada, 1689–1760.* Toronto, 1969. A useful short history of the Canadian wars, emphasizing the roles of both the regular and irregular forces.

Trudel, Marcel. Introduction to New France. Toronto, 1968. A textbook summary of New France by its leading modern historian.

White, Richard. *The Middle Ground: Indians, Empire and Republics in the Great Lakes Region 1650–1815.* Cambridge, 1991. A revisionist work that takes the First Nations seriously in strategic and cultural terms.

Study Questions

1. Reread the excerpt from Father Le Jeune's *Relation.* Identify and explain the three techniques he recommends for converting the Aboriginal people. By what means did the missionaries hope to sell themselves to the Huron?
2. What were the advantages and disadvantages of card money?
3. Reread the poem 'New England Bravery'. How did the New England poet interpret the victory at Louisbourg?
4. Why was the Acadian Expulsion such a tragedy? Could it have been prevented?
5. Briefly explain why the Maritime region was a scene of such violence in the seventeenth century.
6. In the matter of its economic development, did Canada owe more to its European origins or to its North American location? Explain.
7. What were the three chief differences between the earlier colonial wars and the Seven Years War?
8. How does Intendant Raudot justify the use of card money?

 www.oupcanada.com/Bumsted4e

Visit the companion website for *A History of the Canadian Peoples,* fourth edition for further resources.

3 Becoming and Remaining British, 1759–1815

Timeline

1759 Battle of Quebec.

1760 Final French surrender.

1763 Treaty of Paris transfers New France and Acadia to Great Britain; King George III of England issues the Proclamation of 1763.

1773 The Island of Saint John calls its first assembly.

1774 Parliament passes the Quebec Act. It also passes Palliser's Act to regulate the Newfoundland fishery.

1775 The Americans invade Canada.

1776 An American party invades Nova Scotia.

1778 Peter Pond reaches the rich Athabasca country; James Cook arrives at Nootka Sound.

1781 The British surrender at Yorktown; a smallpox epidemic decimates the First Nations around Hudson Bay.

1782 The first Loyalist fleet departs for Nova Scotia.

1783 Treaty of Paris ends the War of the American Revolution by recognizing American independence.

1784 British North America is reorganized; New Brunswick is separated from Nova Scotia and given a separate government; Cape Breton gets a government but no assembly.

1786 Guy Carleton (now Lord Dorchester) is appointed Governor General of British North America.

1787 Charles Inglis, the first Anglican bishop in North America, arrives at Halifax.

1788 King's College is established by the Nova Scotia Assembly (it actually opens in 1790 in Windsor).

1789 The British and Spanish spar at Nootka Sound.

1791 Upper and Lower Canada are separated by the British Parliament's passage of the Constitutional Act of 1791.

1792 First legislature in Upper Canada is convened at Newark (Niagara-on-the-Lake). Captain George Vancouver begins his survey of the BC coast.

1793 Alexander Mackenzie of the North West Company reaches the Pacific Ocean via an overland route from Montreal.

1800 King's College (now the University of New Brunswick) is founded at Fredericton.

1806 *Le Canadien*, the first French-language newspaper, is published in Quebec.

1808 Simon Fraser reaches the Pacific via the Fraser River.

1809 First steam vessel (the *Accommodation*) begins service between Montreal and Quebec.

1811 Hudson's Bay Company makes a land grant of 116,000 square miles (300,429 km^2) to Lord Selkirk.

1812 Americans declare war on Great Britain and invade Canada; the first settlers arrive at Red River.

1813 York (Toronto) is sacked by the Americans.

1814 Treaty of Ghent inconclusively ends the War of 1812.

The Battle of Quebec, also known as the Battle of the Plains of Abraham, was a pivotal event in the Seven Years War. The battle ended in 1759, leaving towns destroyed and lives uprooted. A view of the Bishop's house with the ruins, as they appear in going up the hill from the Lower, to the Upper Town © McCord Museum.

The British established a foothold in Canada with their victory at the Battle of Quebec in 1759. They consolidated their position in 1760, and kept the conquest at the peace treaty in 1763. The theory was that eliminating the French would stabilize North America. It did not work out that way. Within a few years of the conquest, the American colonists had begun an armed rebellion and attempted unsuccessful invasions of Quebec and Nova Scotia. The British reorganized their North American empire after the Americans left it, taking advantage of the thousands of exiles and refugees, called Loyalists, the war had produced. Within a generation, in 1812, the Americans declared war on Great Britain and attempted another round of invasions of Canada, but they were beaten back by British regulars and colonial militia, albeit with considerable difficulty. The period from 1759 to 1815 was, thus, one of great turmoil and change. British North America would settle down only after 1815.

The Conquest and Its Aftermath

The series of abortive and aborted British attempts to seize Quebec, the administrative capital of New France (in 1690, 1711, and 1746), did not prevent another major expedition under General James Wolfe (1727–59) from trying again. The largest and best-equipped military force that North America had ever known assembled at Louisbourg over the winter of 1758–9, while the frozen ice of the St Lawrence isolated the French. The British force consisted of 8,600 troops, most of them regulars, and 13,500 sailors aboard 119 vessels, including 22 ships of the line and five frigates. This great armada required six days simply to clear Louisbourg harbour in early June 1759. On 27 June, Wolfe landed his army on the Île d'Orléans without serious French opposition. There followed over two months of skirmishing, as Wolfe attempted to land his army closer to the French forces, and the French commander-in-chief, the Marquis de Montcalm (1712–59), sought to prevent such a move. Meanwhile, Wolfe and the British admiral, Sir Charles Saunders (1713?–75), were

constantly at loggerheads, and Montcalm found evidence that his forces, mainly French-Canadian militiamen, would not stand up to offensive action.

Wolfe tried a number of plans, all without success. He was becoming desperate. As the end of summer approached, there was less time for the massive British fleet to remain in the St Lawrence, and its commanders were pressing for a final confrontation. Finally, after partially recovering from a fever, Wolfe made a final effort. His troops found a path up the cliffs to the plain above at the Anse au Foulon, and managed to pass the French sentries unmolested. The British drew their battle lines covering the plain above the cliffs. Inexplicably, Montcalm decided to attack the British army without waiting for reinforcements. The French ranks broke first, both Wolfe and Montcalm were mortally wounded, and the British possessed Quebec. The war was not ended, for the bulk of the French army escaped and would fight on valiantly for another year. The Battle of Quebec (or the Battle of the Plains of Abraham) was probably the first military engagement in North America that was fought almost entirely on European rather than on American terms. A fully professional army, disciplined and on the day well led, defeated a partly untrained one. Backed by a government at home with regular troops and naval support, the British finally breached the defensive position that the French had enjoyed for over a century.

British reinforcements and supplies arrived first on the St Lawrence in 1760, and a traditional three-pronged attack on Montreal—anchored by a large army led by General Jeffrey Amherst (1717–97) from New York—forced the surrender of that town, the final French stronghold, in early September. The 55 articles of capitulation would govern the British occupation of Canada until the governments in Europe finally settled matters by the Treaty of Paris in 1763. Until Europe made a final determination, Britain dealt with the colony with a fairly light hand. Canada was governed by military administrators who spoke French and accepted it as the 'language of the country'. A few of the French-Canadian elite departed for France, while a number of new suppliers (mainly American colonials tied to British and American trading patterns) made their inevitable appearance.

Peace negotiations in 1761 proved unsuccessful, not because the French had balked at sacrificing North American territory, but because war minister William Pitt had wanted more concessions around the world. When the French West Indies fell totally and the British began an assault on Spanish Havana—Spain had earlier foolishly entered the war on the side of France—the French and Spanish had their backs to the wall. The French offered to sacrifice more continental American territory. Louisiana east of the Mississippi was surrendered for Martinique and Guadeloupe. The French were granted fishing rights in Newfoundland and the tiny islands of St Pierre and Miquelon in exchange for the surrender of all other claims to territory in the northern part of the American continent. The Spanish proved no problem after the fall of Havana. In a complicated arrangement, Britain returned Havana and Puerto Rico and kept Spain's Florida, while France compensated Spain for its losses by ceding to it the western half of Louisiana and the port of New Orleans.

The final arrangement was 'sold' to the British public by emphasizing the great gains made in North America. Having stressed the security won for the American colonies as a result of the war—at monumental expense to the British people in manpower and money—the government needed an American policy. Its first effort at creating one was the notorious Proclamation of 1763. Like most British policy for its northern possessions produced over the next few years, the Proclamation of 1763 was not directly intended to effect fundamental changes for Britain's older seaboard colonies. Four new governments were created out of the American acquisitions, including Quebec, which was limited to its St Lawrence settlements. This truncated province was to be governed by British law and, as soon as possible, an elected assembly. The Island of Saint John and Cape Breton were attached to Nova Scotia. Land grants were to be readily available to retired officers and disbanded servicemen. In the West, beyond the river systems of the Atlantic coast, no land grants were to be made. This territory was to be reserved for the First Nations, and any trading in it was to be regulated by the imperial government.

The environs of Quebec, a 1760 map by Thomas Jefferys, who was then geographer to George III, illustrates the Quebec campaign in 1759. Wolfe set up camp on the Île d'Orléans (lower right); tried and failed to land at Montmorency, on the north shore (above the North Channel), in July; moved his fleet upriver past Quebec in September; and landed at l'Anse au Foulon (extreme left) to wage the brief battles on the Plains of Abraham (above). LAC, C-128079.

The Proclamation had ramifications beyond the territory ceded by the French. It was preceded by the beginning of a major Aboriginal uprising in the interior, known as Pontiac's Rebellion. Both the declaration of limits for American westward expansion and the need to finance Britain's new military responsibilities would enrage the American colonials. They began a series of provocative responses to Britain that would escalate into an organized colonial rebellion or 'revolution'. It became apparent that policy for the new territories could not be executed by Great Britain in isolation.

Although neither the Proclamation of 1763 nor any other British policy document ever elaborated a full settlement policy for what is now Canada, the outlines of that policy were perfectly plain. The British did not wish to populate their northernmost colonies with emigrants from the mother country. Great Britain was at the beginning of a major economic shift, usually called the Industrial Revolution. Instead of having excess population, it wanted to retain its people, both as a labour force and for military purposes. The British were prepared, however, to make land grants to disbanded soldiers, who were not regarded as very useful at home in peacetime. They also were willing to accept 'foreign Protestants' as settlers, although they hoped that colonial Americans, already acclimated to the New World, would become the principal newcomers. The creation of a First Nations reserve in the West would force land-hungry Americans south and north: south to Florida, north to Quebec and Nova Scotia. The British hoped that new immigration soon would outnumber and overwhelm the French in Quebec, but they were not prepared to subsidize the movement of settlers beyond making land available to them.

From the Proclamation to the Rebellion

In Nova Scotia, a third contingent of subsidized settlers was added to the first group at Halifax and to the 'foreign Protestants'. The New England 'Planters' came to the province between 1759 and 1762. Governor Charles Lawrence took advantage of a substantial annual parliamentary grant for Nova Scotia to recruit over 8,000 Yankees. He provided them with land, transportation, and subsidies until the financial tap was turned off in 1762. The New Englanders came mainly from land-hungry areas of Rhode Island, Connecticut, and southeastern Massachusetts. They saw migration to Nova Scotia as a particularly attractive alternative to moving to northern areas of New England because it was financed by the government. The migrants tended to move in kinship groups, often as entire communities. Most were farmers, although others were fishermen seeking improved access to superior fishing grounds. The farmers settled on Acadian land in the Minas Basin region at the top of the Annapolis Valley, while the fishermen moved to south-shore outports they named Yarmouth and Barrington after their New England counterparts.

Preparatory drawing for the engraved print 'The Death of Wolfe' by James Barry, watercolour, c. 1763. LAC (Peter Winkworth Collection of Canadiana), P3253.

The Planters had been promised not only cheap land but liberty of conscience and a government 'like those of neighbouring colonies', a guarantee they took to mean that they could replicate the participatory local democracy of their former homes (quoted in Bumsted, 1971: 8). They soon found that Nova Scotia had no intention of permitting strong local government. Political disillusionment was added to disappointment over the climate and the absence of markets. Perhaps half the newcomers left within a few years of the termination of subsidies, complaining of 'Nova Scarcity'. While Yankee farmers dealt in small parcels of land, the elite office-holding classes (both within and without the colony) acquired large grants of wilderness land—3 million acres (1,214,100 ha) in the last few days before the Stamp Act became effective in 1765. The Stamp Act put a tax—in the form of an embossed stamp—on all paper used in legal transactions; having to buy stamped paper would greatly increase the cost of obtaining the grants. Only a handful of these speculators became active in either settlement ventures or commercial development.

Brave Wolfe

The Americans celebrated the victory of Quebec in broadside poetry (often intended to be sung) that was sold in single printed sheets on the streets of Boston. Here is one of those broadsides. This song went through so many variations that it is probably America's first best-seller.

Then forth went this brave youth
And crossed the ocean,
To free America
Was his intention.
He landed at Quebec
With all his party,
The city to attack,
both brave and hearty.

Brave Wolfe drew up his men
In line so pretty,
On the Plains of Abraham
Before the city.
The French came marching down
Arrayed to meet them,
In double numbers 'round
Resolved to beat them.

Montcalm and this brave youth
Together walkéd;
Between two armies they
Like brothers talkéd,

Till each one took his post
And did retire.
'Twas then these numerous hosts
Commenced their fire.

The drums did loudly beat,
With colours flying,
The purple gore did stream,
And men lay dying.
Then shot from off his horse
Fell that brave hero.
We'll long lament his loss
That day in sorrow.

He raiséd up his head
Where the guns did rattle,
And to his aide he said,
'How goes the battle?'
'Quebec is all our own,
They can't prevent it.'
He said without a groan,
'I die contented.'

Source: Edith Fowke and Alan Mills, eds, *Canada's Story in Song* (Toronto: W.J. Gage, 1965), 49.

Quebec: 'View of the Bishop's house with the ruins as they appear in going down the Hill from the Upper to the Lower Town', by Richard Short from a drawing made at the siege in 1759. LAC, C-000352

By 1767, when a detailed census of Nova Scotia was taken, the colony was well-populated, with 11,072 people in Nova Scotia proper, another 707 in Cape Breton, 1,196 in the northern section (now New Brunswick), and 519 on the Island of Saint John. The census also demonstrated that a heterogeneous population was already in place, consisting of 11,228 Protestants and 2,246 Catholics, and several ethnic groups (see Table 3.1). In addition, the returns showed 95 'Negroes' and a scattering of 'Indians' (apparently no serious attempt was made to count them). Within a few years, substantial numbers of Scots would come to the region from the Lowlands but especially the Highlands, adding Gaelic to the English, German, French, and Mi'kmaq already freely spoken throughout the region.

Land speculation also dominated the development of the Island of Saint John. The entire land

Table 3.1   Population of Nova Scotia in 1767 by Ethnicity

Place	English	Irish	Scottish	Americans	Germans	Acadians
Nova Scotia	686	1,831	143	5,799	1,862	650
Cape Breton	70	169	6	170	21	271
North (NB)	25	53	17	874	60	147
Saint John	130	112	7	70	3	197
Totals	912	2,165	173	6,913	1,936	1,265

The Lords of Trade and Policy for the West

In the late spring of 1763, the British government turned its attention to what it should do with the new territories ceded to Britain by the Treaty of Paris. It was easily agreed that most of the territories could be included in old colonies or established in new ones, but one exception was 'that large Tract of Country bounded by the Mississippi and the Limits of the Hudson Bay Company on the one hand and on the other by the Limits of Canada, East and West Florida and His Majesty's ancient Colonies'. The Lords of Trade—the equivalent of a colonial office at the time—offered a different policy for this territory in a report of 5 August 1763. This report led directly to the Proclamation of 1763.

To the King's Most Excellent Majesty . . .

We have taken this important Subject into our most serious Consideration and do most humbly concur in Your Majesty's Opinion, of the propriety of putting this Country under a particular Government, by a Commission under Your Great Seal, with a most precise Description of its Boundaries, in Order to ascertain the actual possession of its Property, and with such Powers as may be necessary, as well to maintain and secure the free Exercise of the Indian Trade, which it is proposed all Your Majesty's Subjects shall enjoy within it, under proper Regulations, as to prevent its becoming a Refuge to Criminals and Fugitives.—But at the same time, we beg Leave to submit to your Majesty, the following Objections which have occurred to us, against the annexing this Country to any particular Government, especially to that of Canada.

1st We are apprehensive that, should this Country be annexed to the Government of Canada, a Colour might be taken on some future Occasion, for supposing that Your Majesty's Title to it, had taken its Rise, singly from the Cessions made by France, in the late Treaty, whereas Your Majesty's Title to the Lakes and circumjacent Territory as well as to the Sovereignty over the Indian Tribes, particularly of the six Nations, rests on a more solid and even a more equitable Foundation; and perhaps nothing is more necessary than that just Impressions on this Subject should be carefully preserved to the Minds of the Indians, whose Ideas might be blended and confounded if they should be brought to consider themselves as under the Government of Canada—

2d We are apprehensive as the whole of this Country would become subject to the Laws of a particular Government or Province, it would give that Province such superior Advantage in respect to the whole of the Indian Trade, which Your Majesty in Your Justice and Wisdom has determined to leave as open as possible to all Your Subjects, as might controul and obstruct it to the Prejudice of Your other Colonies—

3d If this great Country should be annexed to the Government of Canada, we are apprehensive, that the Powers of such Government could not be carried properly into execution, either in respect to the Indians or British Traders, unless by means of the Garrisons at the different Posts and Forts in that Country, which must contain the greatest Part of Your Majesty's American Forces and consequently the Governor of Canada would become virtually Commander in Chief or constant and inextricable Disputes would arise, between him, and the commanding Officers of Your Majesty's Troops—. . . .

We would further submit, whether the issuing such Commission and Instructions may not be delayed; till by the receipt of such Information, which your Majesty has been graciously pleased to direct, We are enabled to make a full and particular Report on that very important subject.—. . . In the mean time, We humbly propose that a Proclamation be immediately issued by Your Majesty as well on Account of the late Complaint of the Indians, and the actual Disturbances in Consequence, as of Your Majesty's fixed Determination to permit no grant of Lands nor any settlements to be made within certain fixed Bounds, under pretence of Purchase or any other Pretext whatever, leaving all that Territory within it free for the hunting Grounds of those Indian Nations Subjects of Your Majesty, and for the free trade of all your Subjects, to prohibit strictly all infringements or Settlements to be made on such Grounds, and at the same time to declare Your Majesty's Intentions to encourage all such Persons who shall be inclined to commence New Settlements from Your old Colonies, together with all foreign Protestants, coming by themselves or with such Undertakers, in Your new Colonies of East and West Florida or your old Colony of Nova Scotia . . . .

Source: Adam Shortt and Arthur G. Doughty, eds, *Documents Relating to the Constitutional History of Canada 1759–1791* (Ottawa: King's Printer, 1907), 110–12.

surface of the island was distributed to absentee owners (mainly British office-holders and military men) by lottery in 1767. These proprietors were supposed to settle the land in return for their grants, but most would merely hold it in the hopes that it would become more valuable. The British allowed the proprietors on the Island of Saint John, which was initially attached to Nova Scotia, to petition for a separate government in 1769, on the understanding that it would not cost the mother country a penny.

In Quebec, a number of military officers (and sometimes their men) took advantage of the British offer of land grants. The anticipated stampede of American settlers to Quebec did not occur, however. The Americans were put off partly by the presence of thousands of francophone Roman Catholics and the absence of familiar institutions such as representative government and universal freehold tenure. In a classic vicious circle, the laws, government, and culture of Quebec could not very well be reconstructed until large numbers of anglophones arrived, and this immigration was not likely to happen until change had occurred. Moreover, Americans did not move north into any of the British colonies after 1763. Most of the newcomers were British, mainly Scots, who began leaving their homes in the mid-1760s. The Scottish influx had only begun to gain momentum when it was closed down by the warfare of the American rebellion.

Everywhere in the northernmost colonies in these years, freehold land tenure and the concept of the yeoman farmer fought an uphill battle. The seigneurial system still controlled land in Quebec, the Island of Saint John had been distributed to proprietors who were expected to settle as tenant farmers did in Europe, and much of Nova Scotia was held by large landholders. In the absence of aggressive government settlement activity, those who acquired grants of land in North America in order to settle them were committed to replicating a European pattern of landholding, with aristocratic landlords and peasant tenants.

The administration of the new province of Quebec was greatly complicated not only by the small number of anglophones but by the emerging political turmoil to the south. The colonial authorities in Quebec began by introducing some British elements into the system, but ended by confirming many French ones. English criminal law was put into effect, but the French civil law was largely retained. The British in London agreed that British laws against Catholics did not extend to Quebec. Grand-Vicar Jean-Olivier Briand (1715–94) was chosen by his Canadian colleagues to head the Church in Quebec, and was consecrated bishop near Paris on 16 March 1766. Officially he would be only 'superintendant' of the Quebec Church, but in practice he was accepted as its bishop and the collecting of tithes was officially supported. There could be no elected assembly until there were more Protestants. The process of confirmation of the institutions of the Old Regime gained a real boost from Governor Guy Carleton (1724–1808). An Anglo-Irishman, Carleton was a firm believer in a landed aristocracy, the subordination of a tenant class, and a close connection between church and state. He came to see that, with adjustments to circumstance, his overall vision for society was quite compatible with that of

'Part of the Town and Harbour of Halifax in Nova Scotia, looking down Prince Street to the Opposite Shore', one of six prints of drawings of Halifax made by Richard Short in 1759. LAC, C-4294.

the Old Regime of New France. As the Americans to the south became increasingly restive and turbulent, Carleton became less eager for reform and more interested in pacification. Inevitably he turned to the handiest instruments at his disposal.

Instinctively grasping the need for collaborators to rule an 'alien' population, Carleton recognized the clergy and the seigneurs as natural leaders who could be won over if their rights and privileges were protected. In the process some of the damage to the economy resulting from the geographical dismemberment of Quebec in 1763 could be undone. The result was the Quebec Act of 1774. Most of the ancient boundaries of Quebec were restored to the colony. His Majesty's subjects in Quebec 'professing the Religion of the Church of Rome' were granted free exercise of their religion and exempted from the traditional oaths of supremacy (a new one was supplied). The Catholic clergy were allowed 'their

accustomed Dues and Rights, with respect to such Persons only as shall profess the said Religion'. Provision was made for the support of a Protestant clergy. All matters relating to property and civil rights were to be decided by the traditional laws of Canada. This clause, in effect, preserved the seigneurial system. English criminal law was continued, and the province was to be governed by a newly structured legislative council; there was no provision for an elected assembly.

Parliamentary critics of the administration that introduced this measure complained of its 'sowing the seeds of despotism in Canada' (Edmund Burke, quoted in Neatby, 1972: 38–9). The Americans assumed a direct connection between it and their own situation, including the Quebec Act as one of the 'Intolerable Acts' passed by the British Parliament at this time to punish the Americans for the Boston Tea Party. The legislation was certainly influenced by

Governor Guy Carleton, painted in 1923 by Mabel B. Messer 'from a copy that hung in Rideau Hall'; original artist unknown. LAC, C-002833.

the need to pacify Quebec, but it was not intended to aggravate the Americans. If the Act was supposed to secure the loyalty of the Canadians, however, the strategy was not entirely successful.

Implementing British policy in the old *pays d'en haut* was, if anything, even more difficult than coming to terms with the old and new subjects of Quebec. Part of the problem was that the British army, which was responsible for administering this region, did not really appreciate the extent to which the French and the Aboriginals had become connected with one another by trade and by marriage. One soldier commented of the French residents of the region— the British called them the 'Interior French'—that 'they have been in these upper Countrys for these twelve, twenty, or thirty years, [and] have adopted the very principles and ideas of Indians, and differ little from them only a little in colour.' The return

of British persons who had been taken prisoner by the Aboriginals would not be easy, since many had become thoroughly integrated into their adoptive tribes. The British did not trust these people, who often took Aboriginal names, and thus did not treat them with the same kindness that the people of Canada received. The British army had expected to be able to employ the sort of imperialistic policies that it thought proper to use with 'heathen savages'. The army did not understand the system by which the fur-trading country had long been governed. General Jeffrey Amherst, who was responsible for the West in the early 1760s, saw the region in the simple terms of British conquest and Native subjects. He sought to eliminate the whole mediation process that had governed the 'middle ground' under the French, including the gift-giving relationship. 'Purchasing the good behaviour, either of Indians or any others is what I do not understand', he wrote. 'When men of what race soever behave ill, they must be punished but not bribed' (Gage, 1772). As British fur trader George Croghan observed, 'The British and French Colonies since the first Settling America . . . have adopted the Indian Customs and manners by indulging them in Treaties and renewing friendships making them large Presents which I fear won't be so easey to break them of as the General may imagine' (quoted in White, 1991: 258).

Further complicating matters for the British conquerors was the emergence of an insurgency among the Aboriginal population of the Great Lakes region. This began in the prophetic teachings of Native leaders like Neolin, but soon became a general war against the British when they tried to fill the policy vacuum between the conquest of Canada and its actual cession in 1763. Amherst had no compunctions about suggesting in response that the Aboriginal people be given blankets infected with smallpox. But the uprising quickly burnt itself out. The ostensible leader, the Ottawa chief Pontiac, was unable to unite the many factions, and Amherst's successor, Thomas Gage, decided to try to mend some fences. Gage also determined to take advantage of Pontiac, and offered to treat him as if he really were an Aboriginal leader. In 1765 Pontiac accepted George III as his father and formally made peace. He would die in 1769 in the streets of the French village of Cahokia, clubbed from behind. Some Aboriginal leaders fought on, including Charlot Kaské, a Shawnee leader whose father was German and whose wife was a British captive adopted by the Shawnees since childhood. Kaské insisted that the British would strip his people of their land:

> The English come there and say that the land is theirs and that the French have sold it to them. You know well our fathers have always told us that the land was ours, that we were free there, that the French came to settle there only to protect us and defend us as a good father protects and defends his children. (White, 1991: 307)

Despite the Proclamation of 1763, the British army administrators on the spot were prepared to tolerate European settlement in the region, and the Algonquians knew it. The British administration also attempted to resurrect the old alliance of the region between the Europeans and Aboriginals, with the British in place of the French. This policy was limited by the failure of London to provide the money for presents. But its adoption meant that the British began to discourage their fur traders from moving into the lower Great Lakes. Instead, the British used forts to distribute trade goods to the Interior French, who continued to dominate the trade. British traders would have far more success in the Northwest, where trading networks had not yet been established.

The First American Civil War

In early April 1775 British troops, attempting to raid clandestine colonial arms depots in Massachusetts, were fired upon by the Americans. A long-festering imperial political crisis turned into a shooting war. From the vantage point of the American leadership, they were involved in a 'revolution' to secure their rights against the arbitrary authority of the British Crown. From the vantage point of the British government, the Americans were engaged in a 'rebellion' against duly constituted authority. Whatever its label, for many of the inhabitants in British North America the event meant involvement in an extended civil war in which brother fought brother, friend opposed friend, and many were eventually pushed into exile. Indeed, the proportion of exiles from the new United States (relative to population) exceeded that from France after 1789, from Russia after 1917, and from Cuba after 1955. Instead of seeing the people of the northernmost colonies as impotent victims of the American Revolution taking place to the south, it makes far more sense to view them as participants (although often at a distance) in a great civil war that affected the whole transatlantic region of Britain's vast empire.

The Americans moved quickly in 1775 to organize an alternative government and raise an army, under the command of George Washington of Virginia. While that force was still in embryo, the Second Continental Congress authorized an invasion of Quebec as a move to give 'the coup de grace to the hellish junto' governing Great Britain (quoted in Stanley, 1977: 27). Washington was somewhat more enthusiastic about this plan than he was about subsequent proposals to invade Nova Scotia. One army was ordered to proceed to Quebec by way of Lake Champlain and the Richelieu River. Another was authorized to travel across northern Maine and along the Chaudière River to the St Lawrence.

The sudden turn of events found the government of Quebec in a state of shock and confusion. Governor Carleton, only recently returned from London with the Quebec Act in his dispatch case, complained he had insufficient military force to withstand an invasion. A public *mandement* from Bishop Briand, ordering the population to ignore American propaganda under threat of denial of the sacraments, had little effect. The seigneurs appointed to raise a militia found it difficult to do so. Carleton's alliance with Quebec's traditional leaders proved useless, largely because he misunderstood the dynamics of the Old Regime. The Church never had much influence on habitant behaviour, and the seigneurs never had much to do with the militia. The British merchants of Quebec had never been cultivated by Carleton and proved singularly unco-operative. Not even the First Nations leapt into action on Britain's behalf; most of the Iroquois would remain neutral until they were forced to side with the British later in the war.

Fortunately for the British, the Americans were neither as well-organized nor as lucky as Wolfe's expedition had been in 1758–9, and the Québécois were not as enthusiastic about 'liberation from tyranny' as the invaders had hoped (Hatch, 1970: 60). General Richard Montgomery (1736–75), struggling to bring an invading army up the Lake Champlain route, wrote that 'the privates are all generals' and that those from different colonies did not get along together (quoted in Hatch, 1970: 60). Benedict Arnold (1741–1801), bringing his army across what is now Maine under horrendous late autumn conditions, lost nearly half his troops in the process. On 11 November, Montgomery and his troops arrived near Montreal and pressed on to Quebec, although his soldiers were constantly deserting. At the same time, the habitants were hardly rushing to enlist in the American army. In Quebec, Colonel Allan Maclean (1725–84), who had earlier organized two battalions of disbanded Highland soldiers, had stiffened resistance. Montgomery joined Arnold at Pointe-aux-Trembles on 3 December. He quickly determined that he lacked the force and the supplies to besiege Quebec. He decided, instead, to storm the town. The assault on 31 December was a desperate move by the Americans, who were suffering from smallpox as well as problems of logistics and morale.

The garrison held. The result, wrote one British officer, was 'A glorious day for us, as compleat a little victory as ever was gained' (quoted in Stanley, 1977: 27). General Montgomery's frozen body was found not far from the barricade against which he had led the charge. He subsequently was buried with military honours, with Guy Carleton, who had known him from earlier campaigns, as chief mourner. General Arnold took a ball through the left leg at the first battery, and over 300 Americans were taken prisoner. The American forces, now under Arnold's command, remained in military occupation of more than 50 parishes over the winter of 1775–6. Their desperate seizure of foodstuffs, sometimes paid for with worthless Continental currency, according to one American, cost the occupying army 'the affections of the people in general' (quoted in Dyer and Viljoen,

1990: 49). A commission from the Continental Congress, headed by Benjamin Franklin, pronounced from Montreal, 'Till the arrival of money, it seems improper to propose the Federal union of this Province with the others' (quoted in Dyer and Viljoen, 1990: 49). In May 1776 British reinforcements arrived at Quebec, and by mid-June the Americans had completely retreated, never to return. Quebec became an important centre for the British army, later serving as the staging point for a counter-invasion of the United States (equally unsuccessful) in 1778, led by General John Burgoyne.

The Americans had desperately wanted Quebec. George Washington wrote to Benedict Arnold early in 1776: 'To whomsoever it belongs, in their favour, probably will the balance turn. If it is ours, success, I think, will most certainly crown our virtuous struggles; if it is theirs, the contest, at least, will be doubtful, hazardous and bloody' (quoted in Dyer and Viljoen, 1990: 49). The Rebel leaders did not feel the same way about Nova Scotia, partly because of its protection by the British navy, partly because there was not enough visible evidence of enthusiastic residents ready to support an invading army. Some American sympathizers, including Jonathan Eddy (1726/7–1804) and John Allan (1747–1805), recruited a private army in Machias and Maugerville, consisting of 80 men, who marched overland from the Saint John River towards the British outpost at Fort Cumberland in late October and early November 1776. This 'invasion' was joined by a few residents from the area, but was quickly suppressed by British reinforcements, leaving those Nova Scotians who had supported the Americans either abjectly explaining away their actions or quickly departing for American lines, leaving behind their wives and families to be sworn at and 'often kicked when met in the street' (quoted in Clark, 1988: 49). Civil wars were truly nasty ones.

The affair at Fort Cumberland was more typical of this war than was the earlier invasion of Quebec. Away from the armies, the opposing parties—rebel and Loyalist—fought vicious little battles with one another for control of the uncommitted local population, often paying back old scores along the way. On the high seas, legalized pirates (called privateers)

'A Map of the Country which was the scene of operations of the Northern Army; including the Wilderness through which General Arnold marched to attack Quebec'. Metropolitan Toronto Reference Library.

captured unarmed ships and attacked unprotected settlements along the coasts. Between 1775 and 1781 the privateers literally brought commerce to a halt in the Atlantic region, causing a number of food shortages, particularly in Newfoundland and the Island of Saint John. Both these colonies went for long periods without the arrival of a single vessel from overseas. On the borders between Loyalist and Rebel territory, guerrilla raiders (often including Native allies) attacked farms and villages. Since most of the population of the northernmost provinces lived on the coast or near an American border, everyone lived in constant fear of attack.

Given the insecurity of the times, it is hardly surprising that the radical preacher Henry Alline (1748–84) had considerable success in the Maritime region in introducing a movement of Christian pietism and rejuvenation often called The Great Awakening. Alline rejected secular affairs in favour of the self-government of the godly, emphasizing that Christ had commanded his followers 'to salute no man by the way' (quoted in Bumsted, 1971: 93). He travelled the countryside, composing and singing hymns, regarding music as a way to attract and to hold an audience and as a useful vehicle on the road to salvation. At his death he left a legacy of evangelism

The Americans Attack Quebec, 1776

The following account of the assault on Quebec is from the diary of Captain Thomas Ainslie.

December 31st 1775:
It snow'd all night, it was dark, the wind was strong at N.E. About 4 o'clock in the Morning Capt: Malcom Fraser of the Royal Emigrants being on his rounds, saw many flashes of fire without hearing any reports; the sentries inform'd him that they had perceived them for some time on the heights of Abraham, the sentinels between Port Louis & Cape Diamond had seen fix'd lights like lamps in a street—these appearances being very uncommon & the night favouring the designs of the enemy, Capt: Fraser order'd the Guard and Pickets on the ramparts to stand to their arms. The drums beat, the bells rang the alarum, & in a few minutes the whole Garrison was under arms—even old men of seventy were forward to oppose the attackers.

Two Rockets sent by the enemy from the foot of Cape Diamond were immediately followed by a heavy & hot fire from a body of men posted behind a rising ground within eighty yards of the wall, at Cape Diamond, the flashes from their muskets made their heads visible—their bodies were cover'd: we briskly

return'd the fire directed by theirs. . . . Arnold's party was obliged to pass close under the pickets behind the Hotel Dieu & Montcalms house, where they were exposed to a dreadful fire of small arms which the Sailors pour'd down on them, as they passed. Arnold was here wounded in the leg & carried off:—his men proceeded, forced our guard, & got possession of our battery at Saut au Matelot.

Every power of Col: McLean was exerted on this occasion, he had his eye everywhere to prevent the progress of the attackers; his activity gave life to all who saw him—he follow'd the Gens: orders with military judgment. The Canadian militia shew'd no kind of backwardness,—a few of them stood to the last at a little breastwork near the battery at Saut au Matelot; when they were in the greatest danger of being surrounded, they retreated to the barrier.

The Flower of the rebel army fell into our hands. We have reason to think that many of Arnold's party were killed in advancing, & many killed & wounded in endeavouring to get back. Our fire from the Pickets gall'd them exceedingly.

Source: Sheldon S. Cohen, ed., *Canada Preserved: The Journal of Captain Thomas Ainslie* (Toronto: Copp Clark, 1968), 33–7.

and revivalism among his followers, who were called New Lights. In a period of confusion, Alline offered an alternative path to public involvement.

Not all residents of the northernmost colonies who did make a conscious choice selected the British side. One who did not was Moses Hazen (1733–1803), a native of Massachusetts, who had settled in the Richelieu Valley of Quebec after the Conquest. After a period of fence-sitting in 1775, Hazen committed himself to the United States and was appointed by the Continental Congress to command a regiment he was to raise in Canada. Hazen successfully recruited several hundred habitants, many of whom retreated with him from Canada in June 1776 and stayed together as a unit throughout most of the war. His men (and the Nova Scotia refugees) ultimately were compensated by the American Congress with land and financial assistance.

Molly (Mary) Brant

Molly Brant (Konwatsiʔtsiaié'nni, 1736?–96) was born to a Mohawk couple living in Canajoharie, New York, who were completely undistinguished in Mohawk society. We know very little of Molly Brant's early life. In 1753 her mother married a Mohawk sachem named Brant Canagaraduncka, a friend of Sir William Johnson, who brought her children Molly and Joseph into the upper reaches of Mohawk society.

Within a few years, Molly was Sir William's housekeeper and his chatelaine. He was by this time one of the richest men in New York, made a baronet by the King a few months before receiving the appointment as Colonel of the Six Nations and Superintendent of Indian Affairs for the colony in 1756. Johnson found it advantageous to have a Mohawk 'wife', who soon became a clan mother as well as a competent household manager and mother of Johnson's youngest children. In 1763 Sir William and his family moved into a grand new house at Johnson Hall. From the beginning he held councils with the Aboriginals at or in his house, including a large peace gathering in 1768 attended by thousands of Native peoples. The result was the peace treaty of Fort Stanwix, soon sundered by the American Revolution. Sir William died in 1774 shortly after another peace gathering at which he had exhausted himself.

Molly was no longer in charge of Johnson Hall, although she was left considerable property and was by now the head of the Iroquois clan matrons. She returned to Canajoharie and began a store. When rebellion began against the King, Molly remained loyal to the Crown. While most of the Johnson clan retreated from the Mohawk Valley in late 1775, Molly remained. Among the Mohawks she counselled loyalty, and she collected what information she could on Patriot plans, even warning her brother Joseph of a colonial army that was met and defeated at Oriskany.

From the beginning, she was suspected by the rebels, and she escaped Canajoharie only minutes ahead of arrest. After leaving her home she spoke publicly at a council meeting at Onondaga, opposing peace with the rebels and declaring the need for friendship with the King of England. She was soon pressed to come to Fort Niagara to help manage her people, and arrived there in late 1777. Gradually her interferences disturbed her hosts, and they encouraged her to move to Montreal. She subsequently went to a large Six Nations settlement at Carleton Island, NY, where she was credited with inducing 'uncommon good behaviour' on the part of her people.

She moved in 1783 to Kingston, Upper Canada, and remained there for the remainder of her life, worshipping at the local Anglican Church. In 1787 she contemptuously refused an American offer of compensation for her expropriated lands if she would return to the Mohawk Valley. Although her brother Joseph got most of the publicity, Molly Brant was equally and deeply a committed Loyalist.

Like many other North Americans, most Native people attempted to remain out of the conflict. For the Iroquois, neutrality proved impossible. One of the Mohawk leaders, Joseph Brant (Thayendanegea, 1742–1807), became persuaded that only continued active alliance with the British could protect the interests of Native people by preserving their land from the encroachment of European settlement. Brant and his sister Molly (head of the Iroquois clan matrons) were unable to convince the Iroquois councils, but he recruited a force of about 300 Aboriginal warriors and 100 Loyalist settlers, which was active in scouting and raiding operations, and in 1778 collaborated with Butler's Rangers (a Loyalist regiment) in guerrilla raids in the Mohawk Valley of New York. The Americans responded to such activity in 1779 with a major expedition into the land of the Iroquois, laying waste to the country. The Iroquois, including

An American Privateering Raid

Simeon Perkins (1734/5–1812) was born in Norwich, Connecticut, and migrated to Liverpool, Nova Scotia, in 1762. When the American Rebellion began, Perkins remained loyal to the Crown. As lieutenant-colonel of the Queen's County militia, he was responsible for the defence of Liverpool.

Thursday, April 9th, [1778]—Pleasant [sic] day. Wind N.W. Capt. Hopkins, and Capt. Gorham, Capt. Dean, B. Harrington, are about going to Halifax. Some of them get to the mouth of the Harbour and discover a privateer sloop at anchor back of the Island. . . . She continues at anchor till towards night she came into the Harbour, and the wind being small, rowed up into Herring Cove and sent a boat almost up to the Bar. I went on the Point to hail them but she tacked about and returned on board the sloop. Seeing a sloop full of men come into the Harbour it was truly alarming in our defenceless condition. . . . I had some men under arms, and kept a sentry on the Point, relieved every half hour. Soon after Mr Collins return I found that the sentry, Robert Bramham, was deserted. Had left his musket, and taken a skiff from shore, and no doubt remained but he was gone on board the privateer. This put us in some Consternation, as this Bramham . . . had heard all our Council. The sloop soon got under way, and stood athwart the Harbour, and finally went out of sight. I then ordered a guard of one sergeant and four privates[,] dismissed the remainder of the People, and went home. In less than two hours I was informed that the Privateer was coming in again. I immediately alarmed the People from one end of the street to the other, and mustered about 15 under arms. The sloop came in with Drum and fife going, and whuzzaing, etc. They anchored a little above the Bar, and sent a boat on board Mr Gorham's schooner, and Mr Hopkins schr. I gave orders not to speak to them or fire upon, except they offered to come on shore to rob the stores, etc. If they made any such attempt to engage them. They searched the two schrs. mentioned, and returned on board the Privateer, and hove up their anchor, and went out after daylight. They had boarded a sloop in Herring Cove, Benjamin Harrington, master, and demanded a hhd. of Rum, which was landed as she was coming in, but finally took up with 40 gallons, which Harrington produced. . . .

It is now Fryday morning, April 10th,—The Privateer is gone out. Wind S.E. All is quiet. A small schr., Prince Doan, Master, arrives from Barrington. The Privateer put a man on board her in the night, but released her this morning. I am mutch fatigued, and sleep a sound nap. In the afternoon I hear the Privateer is gone into Portmatoon.

Source: Harold A. Innis, ed., *The Diary of Simeon Perkins, 1766–1780*, vol. 1 (Toronto: Champlain Society, 1948), 139–41.

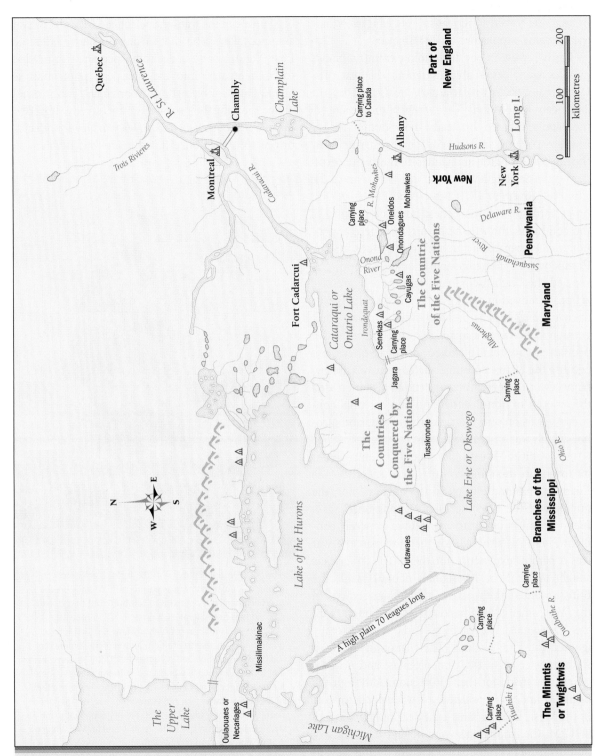

'The country of the Five Nations', based on the frontispiece to vol. 2 of *The History of the Five Indian Nations of Canada* (New York, 1902) by Cadwallader Colden (1688–1766), surveyor-general (1720) and lieutenant-governor (1761) of colonial New York.

Brant, were forced to retreat to Fort Niagara, where they became supplicants for British aid.

Farther west in the fur-trading country, Native peoples were better able to ignore the war. The western fur trade was relatively unaffected by the American Revolution. The western movement of the Montreal-based fur trade, now dominated by English-speaking traders, continued unabated. By the time of Lexington and Concord, they were pressing up the Saskatchewan River into the basin of the Churchill River. In 1778 Peter Pond (1740–1807?) broke through into the richest fur trade country of the continent: the Athabasca region. The competition, the 'Pedlars from Quebec', as one Hudson's Bay Company man contemptuously labelled them, galvanized the English company into more aggressive action. It moved inland from its posts on the Bay to open up ones on the Saskatchewan. Trading competition was always a mixed blessing to the Native peoples. It gave them a choice and lower prices, but because the Native consumer had a relatively inelastic need for trade goods, competition also increased the amount of non-material and non-essential consumer goods on offer, particularly tobacco and alcohol, which was a negative feature.

Any official British attempts to limit settler intrusions in the Ohio country were ended by the American assumption of independence. For the duration of the war, the First Nations once again found an opportunity to manoeuvre between conflicting powers, although for the most part the war was a painful experience for them. The Americans sought to keep the Aboriginals neutral, while the British wanted their active military assistance. In the West, small roving bands of settlers fought with the Aboriginals. The Treaty of Paris in 1783 totally ignored the First Nations. Their lands in the West were transferred to the United States, and no provision was made for their protection. Although the British would prove reluctant to evacuate their posts in the West, holding most of them until Jay's Treaty in 1794, the Aboriginals were now at the mercy of punitive American military expeditions and advancing settlement. Many of the more militant First Nations leaders (such as Tecumseh) would support the British in the War of 1812, finding little joy in the eventual military stalemate.

Outside of the trans-Appalachian West, the British assumed after 1763 that in most eastern places the First Nations were a declining people who needed to be integrated into the European population as quickly as possible. Those Aboriginals who insisted on maintaining their old ways were quickly shoved to the margins of society and, at least in Newfoundland, driven to extinction. The situation was different in

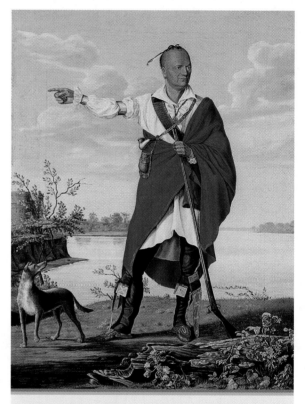

'Portrait of Joseph Brant', *c.* 1807, by William Berczy, oil on canvas. This portrait was painted after Brant's death in November 1807, perhaps as a tribute, but Berczy had painted him from life at least once. In 1799 he wrote of Brant: 'he is near 6 feet high in stance, of a stout and durable texture able to undergo all the inconvenience of the hardships connected with the difficulties to carry on war through immense woods and wildernesses—His intellectual qualities compared with the phisical construction of his bodily frame—he professes in an eminent degree a sound and profound judgement. He hears patiently and with great attention before he replies and answers in general in a precise and laconic stile. But as soon as it is the question of some topic of great moment, especially relative to the interest of his nation he speaks with a peculiar dignity—his speech is exalted energy and endowed with all the charm of complete Retorick.' Photo © National Gallery of Canada, 5777.

Upper Canada and in the vast northwestern regions of the continent. The core of British policy in this region since 1763 had consisted of maintaining an orderly frontier. In theory this involved a legal procedure for the orderly purchase of lands, the reservation to the Aboriginals of sufficient land on which to make a living, and, in Upper Canada, the full application of legal rights under the law wherever possible. This approach was taken partly to distinguish Canada symbolically from the United States. It involved the application of the common law to everybody, including the Aboriginals, both because the common law was a bulwark of Tory ideology and because it provided a framework for good government. The law-centred approach was meant to avoid unnecessary violence and warfare and to re-educate Aboriginal people into the new order. It worked better in theory than in practice. The law-centred approach assumed that the First Nations did not become a part of society until they were thoroughly integrated into Europe's hierarchies and authority structures.

The revolutionary period did see one curious development in Hudson Bay. A great French fleet had been beaten by the British off Jamaica in 1781, and three of the dispersed vessels ended up in the Bay, where they did significant damage to Hudson's Bay Company posts before returning to France. Far more serious than the French depredations, however, was the appearance in this region in 1781 and 1782 of a major epidemic of smallpox among the Native peoples, who lacked European immunities and suffered heavy mortalities.

On the Pacific coast, the American Revolution was even more remote than on Hudson Bay. From

Tecumseh

Tecumseh (the name means 'shooting star') was born around 1768 in present-day Ohio. He first distinguished himself at the Battle of Falling Timbers in 1794, and subsequently helped translate the prophetic teachings of his brother Tenskwatawa ('the Prophet') into a movement devoted to holding onto First Nations land. As he told one American 'Indian agent' in Ohio, 'The Great Spirit above has appointed this place for us, on which to light our fires, and here we will remain. As to boundaries, the Great Spirit above knows no boundaries, nor will his red people acknowledge any.'

Although the Americans blamed this resistance on the British, it is clear that the Natives had their own agenda. Tecumseh and his brother were active after 1808 in an effort to unite all the First Nations under one banner, but both 'the Prophet' and the movement lost credibility when they failed to halt the Americans and were badly beaten in battle by Governor William Henry Harrison at Vincennes late in 1811. When Tecumseh returned to his village from the Vincennes defeat, he found it devastated, and although he rebuilt, he was obviously determined to join the British in an effort of resistance against the Americans.

He led a war party into Upper Canada in June of 1812. At the head of 600 Native warriors, Tecumseh helped cut General William Hull's supply lines and eagerly supported Isaac Brock's aggressive scheme to attack Detroit. Brock would later comment that he never met 'a more sagacious or a more gallant Warrior' than Tecumseh. In 1813, Tecumseh was at the head of an even larger party of Aboriginal fighters that helped attack Fort Meigs. He stepped in to prevent his warriors from completing a slaughter of prisoners at this point and became known as a humane leader. Later, in 1813, at the Battle of Moraviantown, Tecumseh was killed. His body disappeared. The man himself quickly passed into myth and legend, one of the most popular figures of nineteenth-century Canadian verse and story, most of which attempted erroneously to make him out to be a Canadian patriot rather than a First Nations leader.

the European perspective, the major event was the appearance in March 1778 of Captain James Cook (1728–79) in Resolution Cove, Nootka Sound, off the western coast of Vancouver Island. Cook was on another quest for the Northwest Passage, spurred by new information that suggested one might exist. In Nootka Sound, he and his crews observed the Nuu-chah-nulth people. The visitors were much impressed with their trading acumen and especially their principal trading commodity: the sleek, thick fur pelt of the sea otter. Cook was killed on the return voyage through the Pacific to England. An impressive account of the voyage in 1784 included descriptions of the sea otter pelts. Soon there was a rush to cash in on their obvious value, for they offered something to trade in the otherwise difficult Chinese market.

While James Cook's crews were still on the high seas returning to England, the British lost the war of the American Revolution. Whether they could ever have won it remains an open question. Military suppression of movements of national liberation has never been a very successful strategy. The Americans managed to hold on, assisted by considerable British military stupidity and inefficiency, and they found allies in Europe. France joined the war in 1778. Unable to defeat the Americans with regular troops, the British turned increasingly to provincial Loyalist units to do the actual fighting, thus further enhancing the civil war aspect of the conflict. On the New York and Carolina frontiers, Loyalists and Rebels fought fierce battles in which no quarter was asked or given.

With the help of the French navy, the Americans finally succeeded in 1781 in trapping a large contingent of the British army under Lord Cornwallis in Virginia. The surrender of Cornwallis was really the end of the line for the British. The ministry could no longer pretend that victory was just around the corner. It surrendered, allowing its critics to negotiate the peace. The final agreement worked out with the Americans, signed on 30 November 1782, gave the Rebels most of what they wanted. It recognized the independence of the United States, allowed the new nation fishing rights in the Atlantic, and gave to it the entire Ohio Valley. Equally important, the British negotiators failed to insist on any real security for either their Aboriginal allies or the Loyalists.

'A Man of Nootka Sound', drawing by John Webber, c. 1778. The artist was a member of Captain Cook's expedition to the west coast of North America. LAC, C-013415.

Accommodating the Loyalists

From the beginning of the revolutionary conflict, some colonials had supported the British. As the war continued, many more were pressured by events into choosing sides and ended up with Great Britain. The struggle had been a bitter one, and officers of the provincial Loyalist regiments insisted that they be included in any Loyalist resettlement scheme, since 'The personal animosities that arose from civil dissension have been so heightened by the Blood that has been shed in the Contest, that the Parties can never be reconciled' (quoted in Wright, 1955: 41–2). The British authorities in New York, where most of the Loyalists had gathered, accepted this argument. They were allowed to join the contingents of Loyalists that departed by ship for Nova Scotia in 1782 and 1783. Other Loyalist regiments already in Quebec joined British regulars in settling there at the close of the hostilities. The British were prepared to make extensive grants of land to these new arrivals and to support them with supplies while they remade their lives. Perhaps 40,000 people received land grants and assistance as Loyalists, with about 30,000 settling in Nova Scotia (part of which would become the province of New Brunswick in 1784), 750 on the Island of Saint John, 1,000 on Cape Breton, and the remainder in Quebec—mainly in what would become Upper Canada.

The Loyalists were quite a disparate group of newcomers. Of the total of 40,000, well over 3,000 were blacks who settled in Nova Scotia, and almost 2,000 were Aboriginals who settled in Upper Canada. Over half of the 40,000 were civilian refugees and their families; those remaining were officers and men either from former Loyalist regiments or from British regiments disbanded in America. A large proportion of both groups were neither American nor English in origin. Quite apart from the blacks and the Aboriginals, a substantial number of the new settlers came from Scotland, Ireland, or various German principalities. Anglican clergyman Jacob Bailey (1731–1808) characterized his new neighbours in the Annapolis Valley of Nova Scotia as 'a collection of all nations, kindreds, complexions and tongues assembled from every quarter of the globe and till lately equally strangers to me and each other' (quoted in Bumsted, 1986: 34).

Some unknown number of the Loyalist settlers were women. Most of the records of the Loyalists list only the males, who got land grants, served in the military, and received stores. But of the 3,225 individuals who presented claims to the British government for compensation of losses during the war, 468 (or about 14 per cent) were women. Only a small percentage of these women had worked outside the home, and most of them obviously were most familiar with their immediate households. Many other women and their families accompanied their husbands into their new surroundings. The loss of homes and cherished contents was probably more traumatic for Loyalist women than were property losses for men. Certainly the gradual recreation of stability was much more difficult. Men could re-establish friendships and relationships in meeting places outside the home, but women usually could not. Women—who were often not consulted about the decision to support the King or to emigrate—had sacrificed a great deal for a principle. They had every reason to be bitter about their fate.

From the first days of the war, the British military authorities in America had attempted to enlist some of the half-million slaves to fight against their masters, chiefly by promising them their freedom. Thousands of blacks found their way to British lines by whatever means possible, drawn by promises only the British could possibly honour. Loyal blacks usually were evacuated when the British withdrew from an American district. Most of them ended up in New York with the other Loyalists and the British army. More than 3,000 were transported to Nova Scotia. Although they were free, they were not treated well. Only 1,155 of the black Loyalists in the province actually received land grants, which averaged less than 11 acres (4.5 ha) per grant. Blacks became part of the mobile population of the region, taking up whatever employment was available. They suffered many disabilities. In Nova Scotia they were not entitled to trial by jury. In New Brunswick they were not allowed to vote. Freed blacks were treated more harshly in the courts than European people convicted of the same or similar crimes. An unknown number of blacks, who were brought to British North America as slaves by Loyalist masters, continued in that status until the early years of the nineteenth century, when local courts ruled slavery out of existence in the colonies by extending English laws. Not surprisingly, in 1791 nearly half of the Nova Scotia black Loyalists would accept with alacrity a chance to immigrate to the African colony of Sierra Leone.

Throughout the war the British had played on the First Nations' fear that the Americans intended to settle in large numbers on their ancestral lands, which had never been recognized as belonging to them. Some Natives had joined the British, and all were punished for this choice by both sides. The Iroquois were driven from their lands in New York

The Diary of Sarah Frost

Sarah Frost and her husband William were natives of Stamford, Connecticut. William was involved in the guerrilla war between Long Island Loyalists and the Patriots of Connecticut. The two, with several of their children, embarked aboard a vessel of the 'Spring Fleet' in May of 1783. This diary is one of the few surviving kept by a Loyalist woman. Sarah gave birth to a daughter—Hannah—on 30 July 1783.

25 May 1783: I left Lloyd's Neck with my family and went on board the Two Sisters, commanded by Capt. Brown, for a voyage to Nova Scotia with the rest of the Loyalist sufferers. This evening the captain drank tea with us. He appears to be a very clever gentleman. We expect to sail as soon as the wind shall favor. We have very fair accommodation in the cabin, although it contains six families, besides our own. There are two hundred and fifty passengers on board. . . .

Wednesday, June 25: Still foggy; the wind is fair, but we are obliged to lie to for the rest of the fleet. The commodore fires once an hour. The frigate is near us, and judging by the bells, we are not far from some of the other ships, but we can't see ten rods for the fog. We have measles very bad on board our ship.

Thursday, June 26: This morning the sun appears very pleasant. The fog is gone to our great satisfaction. Ten of our ships are in sight. We are now nigh the banks of Cape Sable. At nine o'clock we begin to see land, at which we all rejoice. We have been nine days out of sight of land. . . . Our captain told me just now we should be in the Bay of Fund[y] before morning. He says it is about one day's sail after we get into the bay to Saint John's River. Oh, how I long to see that place, though a strange land. I am tired of being on

board ship, though we have as kind a captain as ever need to live. . . .

Saturday, June 28: Got up in the morning and found ourselves nigh to land on each side. It was up the river St. John's. . . . Our people went ashore and brought on board spruce and gooseberries, and grass and pie vines with the blossoms on them, all of which grow wild here. They say this is to be our city. Our land is five and twenty miles up the river. We are to have here only a building place of forty feet in the front and a hundred feet back. Mr. Frost has now gone on shore in his whale boat to see how the place looks, and he says he will soon come back and take me on shore. I long to set my feet once more on land. He soon came on board again and brought a fine salmon.

Sunday, June 29: This morning it looks very pleasant on the shore. I am just going ashore with my children to see how I like it. Later—It is now afternoon and I have been ashore. It is, I think, the roughest land I ever saw. It beats Short Rocks, indeed, I think that is nothing in comparison; but this is to be the city, they say! We are to settle here, but are to have our land sixty miles farther up the river. We are all ordered to land tomorrow, and not a shelter to go under.

Source: W.O. Raymond, ed., *Kingston and the Loyalists of the "Spring Fleet" of 1783 with Reminiscences of Early Days in Connecticut by Walter Bates to which is appended a diary written by Sarah Frost on her voyage to Saint John, New Brunswick, with the Loyalists of 1783* (Fredericton: Nonentity Press, 1980), 28–32.

state. The First Nations were abandoned by the British in the rush for extrication from an unpopular and expensive war. Britain transferred sovereignty over land south of the Great Lakes and as far west as

the Mississippi River to the Americans, totally ignoring the fact that most of that land was claimed by its Aboriginal allies, who would insist they had never surrendered it to the Americans. The Native refugees

'Encampment of the Loyalists at Johnston, a New Settlement on the banks of the St Lawrence River in Canada', watercolour by James Peachey, 6 June 1784. An officer in the 60th Regiment, Peachey was deputy surveyor-general at the time, surveying lots for disbanded troops and Loyalist refugees. 'Johnston' was the future Cornwall, Ontario. LAC, C-2001.

were given a grant of land along the Grand River in what would become Upper Canada. Here a 1785 census showed 1,843 Native residents, including more than 400 Mohawks.

Few of the Loyalists stayed where they were settled initially. The town of Port Roseway (or Shelburne), on the southwest coast of the Nova Scotia peninsula, became notorious as a place where almost all of the 10,000 people who had been transported there left within 10 years. The decade of the 1780s saw continual Loyalist relocation, sometimes within the colony of original settlement, sometimes in another colony of greater promise, and often eventually back to the United States after subsidies ran out and the initial American hostility had died down. Much of the land initially granted to the Loyalists had only limited agricultural potential, and everywhere homes had to be hewn out of a wilderness. The Loyalist settlement did reassert the principle of freehold tenure in all the colonies. The most stable newcomers were members of the office-holding elite, who tended to cluster in the provincial capitals.

If the Loyalists were a restless population physically, they were a discontented and highly vocal one politically. Only a small fraction would receive formal compensation for property lost in the United States. All felt that they had suffered for their allegiance to the Crown, and that this made them deserving of both land and government assistance. Since many of the Loyalists were former American colonials, they were accustomed to certain levels of political participation. They also shared many political assumptions with their former neighbours. Loyalists may have supported George III, but they expected to be admitted to full participation in the political process for which they had fought. Quebec Loyalists thus complained bitterly about the absence of a representative assembly in the province. Nova Scotia and Island of Saint John Loyalists were unhappy about the domination of government by earlier inhabitants. Furthermore, Loyalists were divided among themselves, with the chief divisions being between the old elite, who sought to re-establish themselves as the natural leaders of society, and the more articulate among the rank and file, who sought a more democratic and open future. The coming of the Loyalists finally provided the cadre of articulate anglophone settlers that the British had hoped for in 1763. The new settlers not only spoke English, but did so with an American accent. Patrick Campbell, on the Grand River in Upper Canada in 1792, was answered by a man 'in a twang peculiar to the New Englanders': 'I viow niew you may depen I's just a-comin.' When asked how far, the response was, 'I viow niew I guess I do'no,—I guess niew I do'no—I sear niew I guess it is three miles' (Campbell, 1837: 157). In

The 'Book of Negroes'

In 1783 a regular weekly meeting occurred at a New York tavern between the American and British governments. At issue were the fates of more than 3,000 blacks, most of whom had escaped from slavery by crossing into British lines. The Americans wanted them returned, but General Guy Carleton refused to consent. Instead, he agreed to keep a record of all blacks being removed and to allow the Americans to dispute any name. Only 14 cases were in the end disputed as Carleton's 'Book of Negroes' was being prepared. Those who were included thought that they were now proper Loyalists, which would prove not quite the case. Copies of the 'Book of Negroes' survive in the Public Archives of Nova Scotia, the New York Public Library, and the Public Archives of Canada. Here is a transcription of one of the pages.

Ship *Spring* bound for St. John's [Saint John]

George Black, 35, (Lt. Col. Isaac). Freed by Lawrence Hartshorne as certified

Ann Black, 25, ([Lt. Col. Isaac Allen)]. [Freed by Lawrence Hartshorne as certified.]

Reuben, 7, ([Lt. Col. Isaac Allen. [Freed by Lawrence Hartshorne as certified.]

Sukey, 5, ([Lt. Col. Isaac Allen]). [Freed by Lawrence Hartshorne as certified.]

Ship *Aurora* bound for St. John's [Saint John]

Billy Williams, 35, healthy stout man, (Richard Browne). Formerly lived with Mr. Moore of Reedy Island, Caroline, from whence he came with the 71st Regiment about 3 years ago.

Rose Richard, 20, healthy young woman, (Thomas Richard). Property of Thomas Richard, a refugee from Philadelphia.

Daniel Barber, 70, worn out, (James Moore). Says he was made free by Mr. Austin Moore of little York nigh 20 years ago.

Sarah Farmer, 23, healthy young woman, (Mrs. Sharp).

Free Negress indented to Mrs. Sharp for one year.

Barbarry Allen, 22, healthy stout wench, (Humphry Winters). Property of Humphrey Winters of New York from Virginia.

Elizabeth Black, 24, mulatto from Madagascar, (Mr. Buskirk). Free, indented when nine years of age to Mrs. Courtland.

Bob Stafford, 20, stout healthy Negro, (Mr. Sharp). Taken from Mr. Wilkinson in Virginia by a party from the Royal Navy about four years ago.

Harry Covenhoven, 24, [stout healthy Negro], (Mr. Buskirk). Came in two years ago from Mr. Covenhoven in Jersey.

John Vans, 39, healthy, blind of his right eye, (Mr. Buskirk, Jr.). Taken in Pennsylvania a party of the British Army about 6? years ago; lived there with Sam Barber who he says had eight months before given him his freedom.

Anthony Haln, 27, stout Negro, (Nicholas Beckle). His own property willed

Joyce, 12, healthy Negress, (James Moore). Lived with James Moore for 6 years; her father died in the King's service.

Simson McGuire, 23, stout healthy Negro man, (John Buskirk). Came in to General Arnold in Virginia from Benjamin Hill.

Bristol Cobbwine, 14, stout healthy Negro boy, (Richard Browne). Came from Woodbury, Charlestown, South Carolina, with Major Grant of the King's American regiment about 4 years ago.

Paul, 19, [stout] mulatto, ([Richard Browne]). Came from Woodbury, Charlestown, South Carolina, with Major Grant of the King's American regiment.

Table 3.2   Canada Census of 1784

Population, Sexes, Conjugal Condition

Districts	Population	Sexes		Married and Widowed			Children & Unmarried		
		Male	Female	Male	Female	Total	Male	Female	Total
Québec	44,760	22,064	20,570	7,911	7,280	15,291	14,153	13,190	27,347
Trois-Rivières	12,618	5,806	5,850	2,080	2,247	4,327	3,786	3,603	7,389
Montréal	55,634	26,134	24,339	10,140	9,272	19,867	15,994	14,612	30,606
Total	113,012	54,064	50,759	20,131	19,354	39,485	33,933	31,405	65,338

Apportionment by Ages &C.

Districts	Male	Female	Males		Females		Servants	Slaves	Infirm	Temporarily Absent	Total
			Under 15	Over 15	Under 14	Over 14					
Québec	7,911	7,380	10,041	4,112	8,984	4,206	1,795	88	150	93	44,760
Trois-Rivières	2,080	2,247	2,874	912	2,726	877	676	4	118	104	12,618
Montréal	10,140	9,727	11,637	4,357	10,803	3,809	4,020	212	625	304	55,634
Total	20,131	19,354	24,552	9,381	22,513	8,892	6,491	304	893	501	113,012

Buildings, Lands, Crops, and Cattle

Districts	Agriculture			Cattle					
	Houses	Arpents under Culture	Bushels Sown	Horses	Oxen	Young Cattle	Cows	Sheep	Swine
Québec	7,157	628,240	126,318	9,166	8,456	12,439	16,344	41,252	22,202
Trois-Rivières	1,973	214,875	39,349	3,155	1,602	3,147	5,368	10,206	6,458
Montréal	9,794	726,703	217,682	17,825	12,036	16,620	22,579	33,238	41,805
Total	18,924	1,569,818	383,349	30,146	22,094	32,206	44,291	84,696	70,465

most respects—except for loyalty to George III—the Loyalists were thoroughly Americanized.

Reinventing British North America

The loss of the American colonies, combined with pressure from the Loyalist leadership, gradually produced a political reorganization of British North America. It is at least arguable that since the Americans were the ones who had separated, what remained of British America carried on the imperial continuity in the New World. Stage one came in 1784, after the Treaty of Paris of 1783, when a governor-generalship was established to administer Britain's remaining North American colonies. Sir Guy Carleton, now

Lord Dorchester, was the first appointee to this post in 1786. Britain also created two new provinces in 1784. New Brunswick was hived off from Nova Scotia and given a set of political officials chosen from the 'needy' Loyalist elite. The capital, Fredericton, was laid out in 1785, the year the first governor, Thomas Carleton (brother of Guy), arrived. Cape Breton was given a separate government, administered by a lieutenant-governor and a council without an assembly—until it was reunited with Nova Scotia in 1820. No changes were made in the government of Newfoundland, which still was being administered by officials resident in St John's during only the summer months; there was yet no assembly. A court system was operating on the island, however. Nor were alterations made immediately in Quebec, although Dorchester arrived in 1786 with a new chief justice in the person of

Shelburne

At the conclusion of the military part of the War for American Independence in 1781 and 1782, a motley crew of Loyalists collected in New York City, the chief American jurisdiction still controlled by the Americans. They included Loyalist military units, British soldiers, civilian refugees, and loyal blacks who the British refused to return to their former masters. Unexpectedly, these people were totally abandoned by the British government in favour of peace with the Americans. Thanks to New York's military commandant, Sir Guy Carleton, they were shipped out of New York in the spring of 1783 and sent north, mostly to Nova Scotia. Virtually no advance preparation was made for their arrival, partly because it was so sudden and partly because the British government was not very good at responding to emergency conditions.

Some of the refugees had organized themselves into a private corporation that intended to settle at a place called Port Roseway in southwestern Nova Scotia, and they were joined by the passengers from a number of British evacuation vessels. Port Roseway, renamed Shelburne in an ironic tribute to the British politician who negotiated the humiliating peace treaty with the Americans, along with the mouth of the Saint John River, in what became New Brunswick, were the principal destinations of the New York ships. The first arrivals literally camped on the beach while a team of ill-trained surveyors attempted to allocate land for them to settle upon. Over the following 10 years Shelburne received more than 10,000 Loyalist refugees, sprang into life as a major eighteenth-century community upon which much British money was lavished, and was reduced to a veritable shell of itself as the British ended the subsidies and the settlers left.

Nearly everything that could go wrong had gone wrong, but several factors stand out in Shelburne's failure. One was the absence of any promise of successful economic activity; the land was poor for agriculture and the town isolated for commerce. The newcomers for the most part had no experience of pioneering and lived off government largesse until it ended. A second was the British government's failure to provide decent-sized landholdings for the blacks, who did have some agricultural background and many reasons for persistence. The final factor was the lack of a sense of community to provide the settlement with some sort of cohesion and stability. A number of different populations—representing different social classes and religious backgrounds—was set down in Shelburne, and they did not relate well to one another. The town never organized a proper government to provide political leadership, and the religious denominations, instead of providing a common experience, squabbled with one another.

Part of the Town of Shelburne in Nova Scotia, with the Barracks Opposite', pencil drawing by William Booth, 1789. LAC 1990-289-1.

William Smith (1728–93) of New York. Smith's political views were distinctly Anglo-American. He was known to have little sympathy for the Old Regime.

We will use the term 'British America' to distinguish the new version of the British colonies in America from the old 'British North America'.

In 1787 a former Loyalist pamphleteer, the Reverend Charles Inglis (1734–1816), arrived in Halifax as the first North American bishop of the Church of England. Although most Loyalists were not Anglicans, the British government wished to establish a close connection between church and state. Initially, the new bishop was responsible for Quebec. Inglis worked uphill for years to bring Anglicanism to a level worthy of state support. The Loyalists pressed hard for institutions of higher learning in the colonies. William Smith of Quebec advocated a secular university for his province, Inglis helped establish King's College in Windsor, Nova Scotia, and Benedict Arnold (who lived in Saint John as an unpopular Loyalist refugee from 1786–91) spearheaded a movement for a university in New Brunswick, which did not take root at that time.

In the western part of Quebec, demands for British institutions, particularly an assembly, produced the second stage of political reorganization: the Constitutional Act of 1791. This parliamentary legislation split Quebec into Upper and Lower Canada, giving the former a lieutenant-governor—the first one was John Graves Simcoe (1752–1806)—both an executive and a legislative council, and an assembly. In theory, Upper Canada's lieutenant-governor would be responsible to the governor of Quebec, and all the chief officials in the various colonies to the Governor General, but Britain's efforts to create an administrative hierarchy were not very effective. Each colony of British America continued to turn directly to the British government as the source of real authority.

Despite self-denying legislation by Parliament in 1777 that no direct taxes would be collected in British America without the consent of the governed in a legislative assembly, and however much eighteenth-century British statesmen remained committed to the principle of colonial assemblies, Great Britain was reluctant to universalize these institutions. French Canada obtained an assembly in 1791 less because Britain felt it was entitled to one than because the Loyalist settlers up-country insisted on having one, and symmetry between Upper and Lower Canada needed to be maintained. For the British, assemblies implied that colonies had come to full maturity, including the control of decent revenue. Cape Breton, because of its small size and remote location, would have to grow into an assembly, which it never did. As for Newfoundland, Britain still hesitated to grant it full colonial status, partly because of its large population of Roman Catholics. The Loyalist period, however, saw the achievement of full political privileges for Roman Catholics in most of British America, both through local legislative initiative and parliamentary fiat (for Quebec). Only on the Island of Saint John (which in 1786 passed laws permitting Catholics to own land but not to vote) and in New Brunswick until 1810 were Catholics still disenfranchised politically. In 1791 the British Parliament passed the Constitutional Act of 1791, which separated Quebec into Upper and Lower Canada and gave each a legislative assembly.

A less publicized development than the introduction of assemblies and the expansion of voting franchises was the elaboration of the legal system of the various colonies. This system was based chiefly on English law and English models except in Quebec, where English criminal law was joined to most aspects of French civil law. The establishment of colonial courts and assemblies meant that new English statute law extended to British America only where specifically authorized, but the colonial legal system took over earlier English statute law and the whole body of the common law, including its patriarchal treatment of women. The introduction of the law was necessary both to good government and especially to business, which would have been lost without the adjudication of the complex system of credit employed in commerce. While the law in British America would develop its own characteristics over time, it was always closely linked to its English origins. Here was the origin of what Lord Macaulay would later describe for England as a system where 'the authority of law and security of property were found to be compatible with a liberty of discussion and individual action'.

The Loyalist migration had ended by 1786, when compensatory land grants and provisioning ceased virtually everywhere in British America. In one decade the loyal provinces of British America had received a substantial contingent of American settlers, well-subsidized by the British government, that they had not previously been able to attract.

So-called 'late Loyalists' continued to come to Upper and Lower Canada, drawn by offers of land. The Atlantic region has not since then experienced a substantial American influx. For all colonies of British America, immigration and settlement would have crucial importance, but the post-Loyalist wave would have to be managed under quite different circumstances.

Immigration and Settlement, 1790–1815

Between 1790 and 1815 immigration to British America came from two major sources: the British Isles (mainly the Scottish Highlands and Ireland) and the United States (mainly upper New York state, Pennsylvania, and New England). The British newcomers settled everywhere, while the Americans were almost entirely confined to the Canadas. Most of the Scots were drawn to the Maritime region, where they had already established beachheads of settlement, but some went to Lower Canada and eastern Upper Canada to join Scottish communities there. The major movement from Britain occurred in a brief interlude of European peace between 1801 and 1803, chiefly to the northeast shore of Nova Scotia, to Cape Breton, and to Prince Edward Island (which the Island of Saint John became in 1799). Prosperity in Newfoundland and New Brunswick during the period 1812–15 drew many Irish to these colonies, more of whom were Protestant than Catholic because they came from northern Ireland.

Some of the American arrivals were pacifist Quakers and Mennonites encouraged by offers of exemption from military service in Upper Canada, but they soon were joined by a large influx of settlers who took up readily available land from government or private entrepreneurs. Lieutenant-Governor John Simcoe encouraged such grants. Some of these newcomers were fleeing American policies they disliked, including the new Constitution of 1789 and the severe repression of Pennsylvania whisky distillers in the 1790s, but most simply were part of the North American moving frontier. Until 1798 the Upper Canadian government treated these arrivals

as Loyalists. Between 1791 and 1812 the English-speaking population of Lower Canada (mainly American) tripled from 10,000 to 30,000 and represented 10 per cent of the province's population. The Americans were located mainly in the Ottawa Valley and the Eastern Townships. In Upper Canada, by the time of the War of 1812, Americans made up as much as 80 per cent of a population estimated by one contemporary at 136,000. As tensions grew between Britain and the United States after 1807, the British began to be worried by the predominance of Americans in Upper Canada. In both Canadas, Americans tended to recreate their own local culture and institutions rather than to insist on political and legal reform of provincial political systems they regarded as oligarchical and repressive.

Another distinctive population emerged from obscurity in the Maritime region in this period. Despite the best efforts of the British to eliminate the Acadians in the 1750s, the campaign had not been completely effective. We do not understand very well the process by which the Acadians regrouped in the region, since most of the movement occurred outside record-keeping and beyond the reach of central authority, which may well be the point. After the Treaty of Paris of 1763, British policy permitted Acadian resettlement, provided that oaths of allegiance were taken and that the population moved to designated places in small numbers. Acadians gradually returned to the Maritime region to farm and fish, usually in remote districts far from existing settlement and often on marginal land. The governments of the region made no attempt to assist or accept them, but they were tolerated and left to create their own institutions. Those institutions were dominated, as they always had been, by the nuclear family and kinship ties, and to a much lesser extent by the Church. The scattered Acadians had great difficulty in obtaining priests, especially French-speaking ones, from the Quebec Church, which claimed it had few priests to spare for missionary service. As a result, the Acadians became accustomed to a religion dominated by laymen and supplemented by the arrival of occasional missionaries. Many of the regulations of the Church, including those on marriage, were not enforced, and parochial organizations were

Elizabeth Posthuma Gwillim Simcoe

Elizabeth Simcoe (1762–1850) was born in Aldwincle, England, but her mother died giving her birth and her father had died earlier. As an orphan she was looked after by her mother's younger sister until her marriage to John Graves Simcoe in 1782. She had substantial inheritances from both sides of her family, sufficient to buy a 5,000-acre estate near Honiton, where she gave birth to a series of five daughters, after which a son was born in 1791.

Soon after this birth Simcoe was appointed lieutenant-governor of the new province of Upper Canada. Elizabeth and her two youngest children sailed with her husband for Canada. She spent the next few years travelling and living in rough conditions, keeping a diary (in three or more versions) of her experiences. Her years in Canada were Mrs Simcoe's Great Adventure, and she loved every minute of the experience, as her diary documented. She was the wife of the highest official in the province, and she knew it. But she was not dependent on her husband's protection, and she was quite willing to head off on her own. She enjoyed seeing new places and new things, she revelled in creating little social occasions (such as her whist parties) in the midst of the wilderness, and she had a keen eye for the unusual.

Like most English travellers of her day, Mrs Simcoe exploited what artistic talents she possessed to produce a number of sketches and watercolours of the sights that she was experiencing. 'I took no sketch of a place I never wish to recollect', she once recalled. The result was a diary of extraordinary richness, full of observations and views of the infant province. Mrs Simcoe was hardly a typical Canadian settler, but her descriptions were quite detailed, although she wrote much better about inanimate objects than people.

After the Great Adventure, Mrs Simcoe returned to her estate with her husband, who died in 1806 in England after contracting some disease in Portugal. She never remarried, and none of her seven daughters, who lived with her, ever married during her lifetime. She became one of the evangelical party of the Church of England, which gave her great satisfaction in later years. Mrs Simcoe was a perfect example of an educated Englishwoman who made herself at home in the vast Empire when given the opportunity.

Elizabeth Simcoe, *c.* 1790. Library and Archives Canada, Acc. No. 1972-118-2.

slow to develop. Despite the problems, by 1803 a religious census showed nearly 4,000 Acadians in Nova Scotia, nearly 4,000 in New Brunswick, and nearly 700 in Prince Edward Island.

It was certainly the case that government and politics everywhere in British America were, to say the least, cozy. The governments of the various provinces were dominated by a small cadre of well-paid

'Part of York the Capital of Upper Canada on the Bay of Toronto in Lake Ontario', 1804, by Elizabeth F. Hale. Looking east along Palace (now Front) Street, this view shows Cooper's Tavern (at left, facing what is now Jarvis Street) and the houses of Duncan Cameron (a merchant), William Warren Baldwin, and William Allan. In the distance are the government buildings and blockhouse (with flag). LAC, C-34334.

officials appointed chiefly in England, in collaboration with local elites represented on the councils. While serious political conflict between the elected assemblies and the provincial oligarchies that governed British America was almost inevitable, it was slow to develop. The oligarchy associated the aspirations of the assemblies with the worst aspects of levelling republicanism—after 1789 the French Revolution succeeded the American as the chief example. Criticism of government was immediately rejected and critics were silenced by any means necessary, including violence.

In most provinces, early political opposition was sporadic and usually conducted within the ranks of the elite according to well-defined rules. Many of the early opponents of government—men like James Glenie (1750–1817) in New Brunswick, William Cottnam Tonge (1764–1832) in Nova Scotia, Robert Thorpe (1764–1836) in Upper Canada, and William

Carson (1770–1843) in Newfoundland—were outspoken political gadflies who received very little consistent support from their colleagues. Only in Prince Edward Island and Lower Canada did anything resembling political parties develop before the War of 1812.

Lower Canada started its separate legislative existence with politics divided along class lines. The 'French Party' consisted chiefly of Canadian seigneurs, supported by the clergy and a few English officials. They wanted all of the French civil law restored and retained. The bulk of the French-Canadian population was not yet integrated into the political system. The opposition, mainly English merchants, wanted the introduction of English commercial law, radical constitutional changes, and the right of habeas corpus. Over the next few years, the ideas and controversies of the French Revolution gradually made their way to Canada, often assisted by deliberate propaganda and subversion from France via the United States. In 1796–7, the French government actually developed a plan for the invasion of Canada from Vermont, although it had little public support.

The English official elite in Lower Canada overreacted to the French threat, exaggerating the colony's importance to France and the disloyalty (or potential disloyalty) of the Canadian people. The elite acted as though the colony was constantly faced with insurrection, and then engaged in repressive tactics. In 1794, the assembly, opposed by only a few Canadian members, passed an Alien Act that suspended habeas corpus not only in cases of treason but also in cases of sedition. The legislation was used to conduct a witch hunt and jail many persons without recourse to bail.

As the French-Canadian population became more experienced at electoral politics—and their experience grew rapidly—they inevitably reacted to the suspicions and repressive tactics of the official elite. By 1796, the Canadians had won a majority of seats in the assembly. Official Lower Canada saw this election as a victory for treason and the revolt of

Pierre-Stanislas Bédard

Born into a prominent family in the Charlesbourg area near Quebec, Pierre-Stanislas Bédard (1762–1829) studied at the Petit Séminaire de Québec from 1777 to 1784 and became a lawyer in 1790. The daily practice of the law did not much interest him, although politics did. He was elected to the general assembly of Lower Canada from the rural riding of Northumberland in 1792 and became—as one of his contemporaries put it—'possessed by the demon of politics'. Bédard did not rise to prominence in the assembly until after 1804, when he began to define the political interests of the French-Canadian middle class while he built bridges to English-speaking politicians and between Montreal and Quebec.

From his first entrance into politics, Bédard was an admirer of the British constitution of balanced powers, and after 1806, when he began writing for *Le Canadien*, he argued that the administration of power in Lower Canada did not reflect this balance of interests. He also appreciated that the maladministration of the Château Clique under Governor Sir James Craig threatened the Governor's position in the balanced constitution, by laying 'the king's representative open to the danger of losing the people's confidence through his ministers' errors'. He also understood that in an ethnically divided province like Lower Canada, 'a governor cannot have the English party, the party of the government, on his side without adopting all its ideas, prejudices, and plans against the Canadians.' This became one of his central themes: that the English minority deliberately and malevolently misrepresented the French Canadians to the government of the mother country, which itself played little role in keeping down his people. Bédard was willing to accept the fur trade economy and those who dominated it as beneficial to the Empire, but he insisted that agriculture would be a better choice for building the economy.

Although not a very skilled political organizer, Bédard nevertheless defined the nascent political aspirations of his generation of French Canadians. He emphasized that patronage was employed to limit the Canadian role in government, and that the province was divided into the English party on one side and 'the mass of the people on the other'. In 1810 Sir James Craig had Bédard thrown into prison, where he languished for a year while new leaders came to the fore in the assembly. In 1812 he accepted a judgeship at Trois-Rivières and effectively took himself out of politics. Bédard's genius had been to use British political theory to make a political place for the French Canadians, a transitional position gradually succeeded by more radical views.

the Canadian lower orders. The new ethnic division was quickly made more permanent by the authorities' insistence on viewing the French Canadians as determined to turn the colony over to the French 'sans-culottes'. The ethnic division also ended any possibility of reform of the government created by the Constitutional Act of 1791. The Canadians continued to favour reform, while the former anglophone reformers now allied themselves with the English officials to form the 'English Party', which was devoted to preservation of the status quo. The French-Canadian reformers received little support from the Catholic Church, either. Virtually the only emigrants from France to Lower Canada during this period were clergymen, refugees from the anticlericalism of the Revolution who hardly were likely to preach revolution to their flocks.

By the end of the eighteenth century the ethnic division was probably irreparable, and it only became more entrenched in the years before the War of 1812. The English party in the assembly and the 'Château Clique', the anglophone oligarchy that ran the government, continued to fear an imminent French invasion, one that would be warmly supported by the Canadians. Such fears were encouraged by the deterioration of relations between the United States and Great Britain and by the increased pressure of the 'Parti Canadien' (as it came to be called) for a constitutional change that the English elite was certain represented the start of rebellion. Partisanship reached a new height during the 1810 elections, in which Governor Lieutenant-General Sir James Henry Craig seized newspaper printing presses and jailed both printers and leaders of the Parti Canadien, thus making himself a symbol of British tyranny. The French Canadians had quickly adopted the tactics of a popular party in a British-style legislature. But they had been forced to do more. They had also turned their popular party into one committed to the preservation of French-Canadian values and even the perpetuation of French-Canadian nationalism.

The period before 1815 also saw the beginnings of the settlement of the West. In 1811 the Earl of Selkirk (1772–1820) received from the Hudson's Bay Company a grant of 116,000 sq. mi. (300,417 km^2) covering parts of present-day Manitoba, North Dakota, and Minnesota. In return for this grant Selkirk was to supply the HBC with employees to aid in its bitter struggle with the North West Company for control of the western fur trade. Selkirk hoped to be able to keep the colony he intended to establish at the forks of the Red and Assiniboine rivers separate from the fur trade rivalry, but this would prove impossible. Miles Macdonell (c. 1767–1828) was named the first governor of Assiniboia, as the territory was called in June 1811. On 26 July he and the first contingent of colonists left for Hudson Bay, arriving two months later at York Factory. After wintering on the Nelson River until the breakup of ice (at the end of June), they did not arrive at the junction of the Red and Assiniboine rivers until 30 August 1812. The colony soon ran afoul of the North West Company, which used the Red River region as the source of pemmican for provisioning its traders on the vast inland canoe routes it had established.

Thomas Douglas, Earl of Selkirk. This painting was based supposedly on a portrait by the Scottish artist Henry Raeburn. The location of the original is unknown. LAC, C-1346.

The War of 1812

After some years of worsening relations, the Americans declared war on Great Britain on 18 June 1812. There were several factors behind the war. One was Britain's high-handedness in searching American ships on the high seas during the Napoleonic blockade, removing British subjects aboard them, and recruiting them into her navy. Another was the British failure to abandon the Ohio Valley, where military posts continued to monitor the fur trade. Most of all, the Americans coveted Canada and they proceeded again to invade in 1812 and in 1813. Invading armies successively were thrust back through the major entry points: the Detroit–Windsor corridor, the Niagara Peninsula, and Lake Champlain. A relatively small number of British regulars, assisted by colonial militia and Native peoples, held the province against American armies, which were neither well-trained nor well-led. A number of Canadian heroes emerged from the war, their reputations to be further mythologized after it was over: General Isaac Brock, Tecumseh, and Laura Secord.

The appearance of invading American armies posed a crisis of allegiance for many of the American

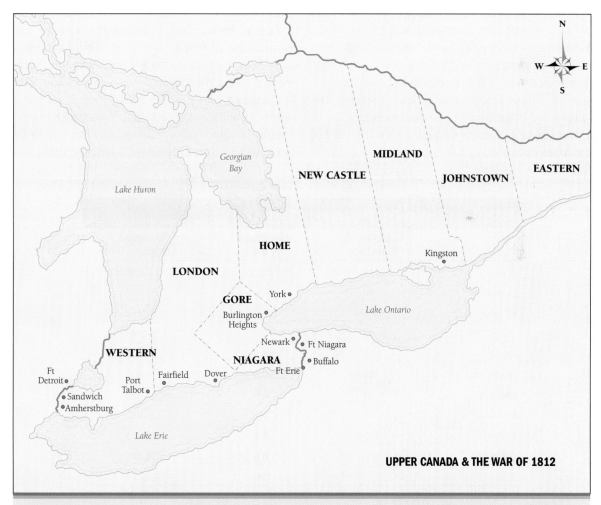

Upper Canada and the War of 1812. Drawing by Cy Morris. From George Sheppard Plunder, *Profit and Paroles: A Social History of the War of 1812 in Upper Canada* (Montreal and Kingston: McGill-Queen's University Press, 1994). Reprinted by permission of the publisher.

settlers in Upper Canada. Most remained silently on their farms, although some supported their countrymen and retreated across the border with them. A handful of Americans were arrested and tried for treason at Ancaster in 1814, but the Canadian authorities generally did a good job of avoiding unnecessary witch hunts. Civilian damage was heavy (Table 3.3).

The loyalty question would not emerge as an open political issue until after the war was over. Well-led British regulars were assisted by militiamen from both the Canadas and by a number of Aboriginal allies. The Upper Canadians came out of the war convinced that their militia had won the war single-handed, although most militia died of disease and fewer than 30 died in battle (*Niagara Spectator*, 11 Dec. 1817). When the ministry of Alexander Mackenzie decided in 1875 to grant pensions for War of 1812 veterans, it expected only a few hundred to come forward. Instead, almost 2,000 veterans claimed service. The 'militia myth' contributed to the emergence of an Upper Canadian identity through the middle years of the nineteenth century.

The naval war was fought on several fronts. The first and best-known one was on the Great Lakes, especially Lake Ontario, where both sides built substantial navies from scratch and fought to a standstill from 1812 to 1814. The Atlantic Ocean front consisted of a handful of legendary set battles between individual American and British naval vessels—which the Americans typically won—and a considerable quantity of prize-taking, both by the British navy and by privateers on both sides (Table 3.4). The British probably won the war of the prizes. Business-like privateers from Atlantic Canada made a substantial economic contribution to their communities and helped keep the economies of Nova Scotia and New Brunswick humming during the conflict (Kert, 1997).

Before the war had ended, York (Toronto) was burned, the American capital at Washington was sacked in retaliation, and Fort Michilimackinac (on western Lake Huron) was captured and held by Canadian voyageurs. The final struggle for naval control of the Great Lakes took place in 1814; the Americans appeared to be winning. The last battle of the war, at New Orleans on 8 January 1815, was

Table 3.3	Claims for Damages by District		
	Claims Submitted	Percentage of Total	Estimated Damages (£)
Western	415	20.2	65,196
London	296	14.4	50,797
Niagara	678	33.0	182,169
Gore	310	15.1	44,243
Home	80	3.9	12,379
Newcastle	13	0.6	2,633
Midland	21	1.0	6,938
Johnston	63	3.1	6,007
Eastern	167	8.1	12,065
Other*	12	0.6	18,301
Total	2,055	100	400,728

*There were 12 claims for damages outside the province.

Source: George Sheppard, *Plunder, Profit and Paroles: A Social History of the War of 1812 in Upper Canada* (Montreal and Kingston: McGill-Queen's University Press, 1994), 14, 123, from LAC, RG 19, E5 (a), Board of Claims. Reprinted by permission of the publisher.

Table 3.4	Privateering in the Atlantic Region			
Privateer Type	**Number**	**% of Total**	**Prizes**	**% of Prizes**
Schooner	26	55	182	81
Sloop	6	13	21	9
Brigantine/brig	6	13	18	8
Ship	2	4	0	0
Others*	4	11	5	2
Unknown	3	4	2	

*Includes jebacco boats, cutters, and a lugger.

Source: Faye Margaret Kert, *Prize and Prejudice: Privateering and Naval Prize in Atlantic Canada in the War of 1812* was originally published as Research in Maritime History No. 11 (St John's, NL, 1997), and excerpts are reprinted here with the kind permission of the International Maritime Economic History Association.

'The Battle of Queenston. October 18th, 1813 [*sic*]', by Major James B. Dennis, coloured lithograph, *c.* 1866, after the original print published in 1836 by J.W. Laird & Co. in London. The Battle of Queenston Heights actually took place on 13 October 1812. LAC, C-276.

A Common Soldier Fights in the War of 1812

Shadrach Byfield was born near Bradford, England, in 1789, and joined the British army in 1807. By 1812 he was serving in Canada as a private in the 41st Foot. In the following account, written years later, he describes a battle at Brown's Town in January 1813. The account was originally published in 1828.

Orders were given to cross the river St Lawrence. We landed at a place called Brown's Town, and then proceeded for the river Reasin, with about 500 of our troops and a few Indians. We had to contend with about 1400 of the enemy, under the command of General Winchester. When within about two miles of the enemy, we encamped for part of the night; early in the morning, we proceeded to meet them, and under cover of a wood, we approached near to them, unperceived; we formed the line, and had a view of them as they surrounded their fires. While we were forming, the Indians marched so as to get round their right flank. We had six field pieces, which led on in front of the line. We were then discovered by one of their sentries, who challenged and discharged his piece, which killed one of our grenadiers; we then gave three cheers, and the Indians followed with a war whoop; the fight then commenced very warmly. It was on the 22nd of January, 1813. . . . As the day approached, we discovered that what had been supposed to have been the enemy's line was a made fence behind which they were sheltered, with holes in it through which they fired at us. About this time my comrade on my left hand was killed. It being now light, I saw a man come from the fence when I said to my comrade, 'There is a man, I'll have a shot at him.' Just as I said these words and pulled my trigger, I received a ball under my left ear and fell immediately;

actually fought after a peace of stalemate had been signed at Ghent on 24 December 1814. Slow communications of the time kept the combatants from knowing that hostilities had ceased.

The Americans treated the War of 1812 as a second War of Independence, a necessary struggle to complete the process of separation from the mother country. National survival was taken as victory, perhaps not least because of Andrew Jackson's decisive victory over the attacking British fleet at New Orleans. From the British perspective, the war had been little more than a sideshow to the major struggle, which was against Napoleon in Europe. As for British America, in the lower provinces (as the Maritime region was coming to be called) the War of 1812 mainly represented an opportunity to serve as a conduit for illicit trade between Britain and the United States; the region was never actively involved in the military struggle. Only in the Canadas did the War of 1812 have any great impact. In Lower Canada, the support the French

Canadians gave the British demonstrated their loyalty. In Upper Canada, the war provided a demarcation point between the loyal and the disloyal, the latter composed almost entirely of Americans. During and after the fighting, the Canadian oligarchies (especially in Upper Canada) were able to appropriate Loyalism as their monopoly and use it against their American opponents. The great struggle between British and American allegiance was played out internally in Upper Canada between 1812 and 1815, and the British won. After 1815 the overt American influence on Upper Canada—and the prevalence of American culture—would gradually decline.

Despite the return to the status quo antebellum, the War of 1812 had considerable impact upon British America in several areas. One was in the domestic politics of Upper Canada. To earlier notions of loyalty to the British Crown inherited from the period of the American Revolution was added a new ideological stream. The Upper Canadian Tory elite became in falling I cut my comrade's leg with my bayonet. He exclaimed, 'Byfield is dead.' To which I replied, 'I believe I be,' and I thought to myself, is this death, or how do men die? As soon as I had recovered so as to raise my head from the ground, I crept away upon my hands and knees and saw a sergeant in the rear, who said, 'Byfield, shall I take you to the doctor?' I said, 'Never mind me, go and help the men.' I got to the place where the doctor was, who, when it came to my turn to be dressed, put a plaister to my neck and ordered me to go to a barn which was appointed for the reception of the wounded. As I was going, the blood flowed so freely as to force off the plaister. I now saw a man between the woods, and asked him what he did there. He told me he was wounded in the leg. I observed to him that if I had not been wounded worse than he was, I should be back, helping the men. I then asked him to give me a pocket handkerchief to tie round my neck, to stop the blood. He replied, 'I have not got one.' I said, 'If I do not get something, I shall bleed to death.' He immediately tore off the tail of his shirt, and wound it round my neck. I then got to the barn, and laid down with my fellow sufferers. I had not been there long before the doctor came and said, 'My dear fellows, you that can had better get away, for our men are terribly cut up, and I fear we shall be all taken.' He rode away, but soon returned saying, 'My dear fellows, we have taken all of them prisoners.' At which news I exclaimed (being quite overjoyed), 'I don't mind about my wound, since that is the case.' While in the barn, I was much affected by seeing and hearing a lad, about 11 or 12 years of age, who was wounded in one of his knees. The little fellow's cries from the pain of his wound; his crying after his dear mother; and saying he should die, were so affecting that it was not soon forgotten by me. He was a midshipman, belonging to one of the gunboats; I think his name was Dickenson.

Source: *Recollections of the War of 1812: Three Eyewitnesses' Accounts* (Toronto: Baxter Publishing, 1964), 15–18.

convinced that the province had been in great danger, as much from the internal menace of American residents as from the external one of American troops. That elite carried over into the post-war period their beliefs in the necessity of the simultaneous suppression of political opposition and the maintenance of social harmony, by force if necessary. These twin beliefs served as the basis for Upper Canadian Toryism for several generations (Mills, 1988).

Another important effect of the War of 1812 was upon the Aboriginal people, many of whom had supported the British. It was never quite clear how a British victory would contribute to the cause of Aboriginal unity or the dream of a First Nations state, but it was certainly plain that the maintenance of the status quo was—from the Aboriginal perspective—a victory for the American expansionists. The United States had used the war to solidify its control of the 'Middle Ground' in the Ohio Valley and to push the Aboriginals farther towards the margins.

One of the articles of the Treaty of Ghent stipulated that both the United States and Great Britain would endeavour not only to end hostilities with the Native peoples, but 'forthwith to restore to such tribes or nations respectively all possessions, right and privileges which they may have enjoyed or been entitled to in one thousand eight hundred and eleven, previous to such hostilities' (quoted in Allen, 1992: 169). This clause remained a dead letter. As it became clear that the British sought détente with the Americans in the wake of the war, many of the tribes near the border sullenly came to terms with the American government after the Treaty of Ghent, while others retreated farther west to continue a resistance they understood full well was doomed.

In the North-West, a little war between the Hudson's Bay Company and the North West Company ran its own course, occasionally touching on the larger Anglo–American conflict. In 1813, for example, Lord Selkirk very nearly succeeded in persuading the British government to finance the recruiting, equipping, and transporting to the Red River of a Highland regiment that he would command. The purpose of the unit was to protect the West from an American takeover. The scheme won ministerial approval, but was vetoed at the last moment by the commander-in-chief, the Duke of York, not because it would have crushed the North West Company but because it involved Highlanders. In 1816 Selkirk recruited as soldier/settlers a number of disbanded troops from several Swiss regiments that had fought for the British in North America, leading them to the Red River. As in the War of 1812, the western fur trade war was fought to an expensive draw. The two rival companies would settle matters by merging in 1821, shortly after Selkirk's death.

Conclusion

By a diplomatic convention in 1818, Great Britain and the United States would agree to declare the Great Lakes an unarmed zone and the forty-ninth parallel to be the Anglo–American border from the Lake of the Woods to the Rocky Mountains. British policy after the war would consistently be to seek entente rather than trouble with the Americans, so in a sense the Americans had won. The final defeat of Napoleon at Waterloo in 1815, rather than the Treaty of Ghent, marked the major watershed for Britain and her North American colonies, however. After 1815 the shift from an overheated war economy to a peacetime one in the British Isles produced substantial unemployment. Even after the post-war depression had ended, a new round of industrialization and agricultural rationalization left many without work in their traditional occupations and places of residence. The result was a new era of emigration and immigration. Between 1815 and 1860 more than a million Britons would leave their homes and come to British America. In the process they would help bring the colonies into maturity.

How History Has Changed

Loyalist Legends

The Loyalists are one of the few subjects that are as important in American as in Canadian history. For the Americans, the Loyalists are part of the opposition in the American Revolution, and American historians have always lost interest in them in the period after the States achieved independence in 1783. Canadian historians become interested in the Loyalists as they leave the United States. There are no clear definitions of what constitutes a Loyalist, but the traditional assumption has always been that Loyalists have to be American refugees. This poses several problems. One is how to categorize those resident in the northern colonies (Upper and Lower Canada, etc.) who remained loyal. Another is to determine when American refugees ceased to be Loyalists and became merely immigrants. Research and writing about Canadian Loyalists has passed through several stages over the centuries.

In the first stage, which began at the time of the American Revolution and continued until well into the twentieth century, the Loyalists were viewed as the founders of English Canada and given a special hagiographic cachet. The high point of Loyalist enthusiasm probably occurred in the 1870s and early 1880s, when the various centennials of the larger Loyalist migrations and settlements were celebrated. The key work was Egerton Ryerson's *The Loyalists of America and Their Times*, published in 1880. Loyalists naturally appeared in a favourable light in the dominant imperial and WASPish ideologies of the time.

In the second stage, which began about the middle of the twentieth century, Canadian historians reconsidered the questions of the composition of the Loyalists and of their importance in Canadian development. The aim was to recover a reasonably accurate picture of who the Loyalists actually were by freeing them from the legends and hagiography of the nineteenth century. The pioneer work, in 1955, was Esther Clark Wright's *The Loyalists of New Brunswick*, which relied on land settlement records to reconstruct the story of the Loyalists in the province. A series of works since have demonstrated that the Loyalists were an interesting if not completely representative cross-section of colonial American society. They included several racial minorities (blacks, Aboriginals), a number of ethnic groups, and a substantial minority of women. Many of the Loyalist settlers in British America were disbanded soldiers rather than civilian refugees. Not all Loyalists were political conservatives. The multi-racial and multi-ethnic composition of the Loyalists was well-suited for Canadians of the last decades of the twentieth century, who were busy establishing a multi-ethnic society in the nation. One unresolved question of Loyalist composition remained, and that was the extent to which the Loyalists were Americans, who brought American culture and American assumptions to Canada.

A third stage of Loyalist historiography began in the early 1970s. Instead of seeking to uncover the 'real Loyalists', it deliberately set out to explore and understand the Loyalist myths and legends that have developed in Canada, on the grounds that what people thought the Loyalists were was probably as important as their actual composition. The net result has been studies that examine the Loyalist celebrations in the 1870s, the merger of Loyalist legend into imperialist ideology, the Loyalist literary tradition, and the use of Loyalist sentiment by politicians, especially in the nineteenth century. This sort of analysis increasingly has taken on postmodernist overtones.

Short Bibliography

Boyd, Robert T. *The Coming of the Spirit of Pestilence: Introduced Infectious Diseases and Population Decline among Northwest Coast Indians, 1774–1874*. Vancouver and Seattle, 1999. A pioneering study.

Brown, Wallace, and Hereward Senior. *Victorious in Defeat: The Loyalists in Canada*. Toronto, 1984. Somewhat dated, but still the best survey of the Loyalists.

Bumsted, J.M. *The Peoples' Clearance: Highland Emigration to British North America 1770–1815*. Edinburgh and Winnipeg, 1982. A revisionist work that argues the early Scots came to British North America of their own volition.

Clarke, Ernest. *The Siege of Fort Cumberland: An Episode in the American Revolution*. Montreal and Kingston, 1996. A recent study that emphasizes that being loyal in revolutionary Nova Scotia was no easy matter.

Dowd, Gregory. *A Spirited Resistance: The North American Indian Struggle for Unity 1745–1815*. Baltimore and London, 1992. A book focusing on the conflicts in the Ohio country from the First Nations perspective.

Greenwood, F. Murray. *Legacies of Fear: Law and Politics in the Era of the French Revolution*. Toronto, 1993. A work making the point that British officialdom and its anglophone allies in Lower Canada helped create the province's ethnic division through their paranoid politics.

Greer, Allan. *Peasant, Lord and Merchant: Rural Society in Three Quebec Parishes 1740–1840*. Toronto, 1985. A detailed localized study of rural French Canada.

Kert, Faye Margaret. *Prize and Prejudice: Privateering and Naval Prize in Atlantic Canada in the War of 1812*. St John's, 1997. A thorough account of the importance of privateering in the War of 1812.

Kimber, Stephen. *Loyalists and Layabouts: The Rapid Rise and Faster Fall of Shelburne, Nova Scotia*. Toronto, 2008. A new look at the biggest failure in Loyalist resettlement.

Knowles, Norman. *Inventing the Loyalists: The Ontario Loyalist Experience and the Creation of Usable Pasts*. Toronto, 1997. A postmodern work more interested in Loyalist mythology than in Loyalist actuality.

Lawson, Philip. *The Imperial Challenge: Quebec and Britain in the Age of the American Revolution*. Montreal and Kingston, 1989. A well-researched study of Quebec in the British Empire.

Neatby, Hilda. *Quebec: The Revolutionary Age 1760–91*. Toronto, 1966. Old, but still the standard study.

Potter-MacKinnon, Janice. *While the Women Only Wept: Loyalist Refugee Women*. Montreal and Kingston, 1993. A pioneer work focusing on Loyalist women in Canada.

Sheppard, George. *Plunder, Profit and Paroles: A Social History of the War of 1812 in Upper Canada*. Montreal and Kingston, 1994. A revisionist study concentrating on the internal struggle in Upper Canada during the War of 1812.

Walker, James St G. *The Black Loyalists: The Search for a Promised Land in Nova Scotia and Sierra Leone, 1778–1870*. Halifax, 1976. The pioneering study of the black Loyalists and their fate.

Study Questions

1. How did the author of 'Brave Wolfe' present his subject to the audience?
2. How did the Proclamation of 1763 respond to the problems of the British in North America at the time? Why did it fail to avert the American Revolution?
3. What was the political effect of the American invasions of Canada in 1775–6?
4. Who were the Loyalists?
5. Were the Loyalists the 'founders' of English-speaking Canada? Explain your answer.
6. What does the 'Book of Negroes' (both its existence and contents) tell us about the black Loyalists?
7. What can you deduce about Canadian society in 1784 from the census data in Table 3.2? How does the colony compare with Nova Scotia in 1767 (Table 3.1)?
8. Identify three reasons to explain why the War of 1812 was so crucial to British North America.
9. Define the term 'oligarchy'. Explain how this concept operated in British North America, especially in Lower Canada, during this period.

 www.oupcanada.com/Bumsted4e

Visit the companion website for *A History of the Canadian Peoples*, fourth edition for further resources.

4 Relying on Resources, 1815–1840

Timeline

1816   Métis and Selkirk settlers clash at Seven Oaks.

1817   Bank of Montreal founded.

1818   Britain agrees to allow France to carry on a dry fishery on Newfoundland's west coast. Britain and the United States agree in principle to extend their boundary across the forty-ninth parallel from Lake of the Woods to the Rocky Mountains. Dalhousie University is founded in Halifax.

1820   Cape Breton is annexed to Nova Scotia.

1821   Hudson's Bay Company and the North West Company merge as the Hudson's Bay Company. Bank of Canada is chartered. Contract is let for the first Lachine Canal.

1824   Founding of Canada Company.

1825   Lachine Canal completed.

1826   Canada Company is chartered and purchases most of the Crown reserves and half of the clergy reserves of Upper Canada. Rideau Canal is begun.

1827   British Parliament rejects major government resettlement scheme for Canada brought forward by Robert John Wilmot-Horton. Hudson's Bay Company establishes Fort Langley on the Fraser River.

1829   First Welland Canal is opened. King's College is founded in Toronto.

1832   John Richardson publishes *Wacousta*. Newfoundland establishes its first assembly.

1833   Slavery is abolished by the British Parliament in the British Empire. First crossing of the Atlantic by a steamship (the *Royal William*). Cholera epidemic in Lower Canada.

1834   Village of York is incorporated as Toronto. The Rideau Canal is completed. Assembly of Lower Canada passes the Ninety-Two Resolutions.

1835   The Selkirk family's interests in Red River are sold to the Hudson's Bay Company and the General Quarterly Court of Assiniboia is established.

1836   T.C. Haliburton publishes *The Clockmaker* as a book. New Brunswick legislature gains control of Crown lands in the province. The first railway in Canada is completed, running 16 miles (26 km) from La Prairie to St John's, Quebec.

1837   Rebellions erupt in Upper and Lower Canada.

1838   Lord Durham is appointed Governor General to investigate colonial grievances. A second uprising in Lower Canada is brutally suppressed.

1839   Durham submits his report on British America. The Hudson's Bay Company establishes the office of Recorder of Rupert's Land.

Although tension existed between Aboriginal peoples and European settlers in Canada, trade between these groups was common in the early nineteenth century. Painting by John Richard Coke Smyth. Library and Archives Canada, C-001026.

After the end of the War of 1812 the various provinces of British America began to develop their economies. Not surprisingly, those economies were based almost exclusively on exploitation of the rich natural resource base of the country, with a rising merchant group providing commercial links to the outside world. In this period, the resource economy relied heavily on transatlantic (chiefly British) markets and took full advantage of imperial trade advantages whenever they could be found. Overseas trade to the Caribbean also expanded. While there was some trade with the United States, few in British America concentrated on the continental American market. The economies of the United States and British America were still too similar in their reliance on primary resources to develop much interdependence. The society that took shape within the resource economy depended heavily on immigration from the British Isles to fuel its growth. Like the economy itself, it had a fairly simple structure, dominated by a self-conscious elite that was challenged politically towards the end of the period. In cultural terms, French Canada continued to survive and even flourished. In several of the English-speaking provinces, there was a subtle but significant movement away from a highly derivative Americanized culture (chiefly attributable to the Loyalists) to a more hybrid culture that consciously looked to Great Britain for its priorities.

The Resource Economy

British America began the post-war period of peace after 1815 with an extremely limited economy, heavily dependent on British financial aid. By the 1840s it could boast a very active, even vibrant, commercial economy based on its rich inheritance of natural resources and a growing transatlantic carrying trade. The economic growth worked together with the appearance of new immigrants who flocked into its seaports and made their way onto its wilderness lands. Economic development was always complex, never straightforward. In most regions of European settlement it was anchored from the outset by natural resources. Fish, furs, timber, and grain—along with their ancillary industries—represented well over 90 per cent of all economic activity in British America during this period.

Natural resources required a market, and before the 1840s Britain's colonies found the market chiefly in the United Kingdom and within the British Empire, where trade policies tended to remain favourable to colonial raw materials. In the 1840s, when Britain shifted to a policy of international free trade, British America had significant adjustments to make to fit into the new economic and commercial patterns. But for infant colonies rapidly expanding in population, British preferential treatment for colonial raw materials constituted a major boost. The mother country provided not only the market but also much of the capital with which British Americans developed their resource base. British investment capital was never very adventuresome. It preferred known industries and may well have constricted colonial diversification. For a people desperately short of capital, however, no real alternative to British investment seemed possible. The Americans were using what capital they generated to develop their own internal economy. The British government also provided considerable cash in other forms. It continued to pay pensions to military officers, collectable by their widows until their deaths. It also paid the salaries of the officials of most of the colonies. The capital brought by immigrants totalled several million pounds over this period.

A colonial economy based on natural resources was inevitably one that depended on international and even transatlantic trade. Such an economy also had substantial implications for society and its structure. The extraction and production of the raw materials of trade was a seasonal business, for example. Rhythms depended on the commodities being produced. Fish and grain required summer labour, and while timbering flourished in the winter months shipbuilding was a warm-weather activity. Moreover, initial production was in the hands of small-scale commodity producers. These people exploited those working for them and were in turn exploited by the merchants who handled the commercial system of marketing. Most primary resource producers had little connection with the international market. They had no control over the prices they received for their products.

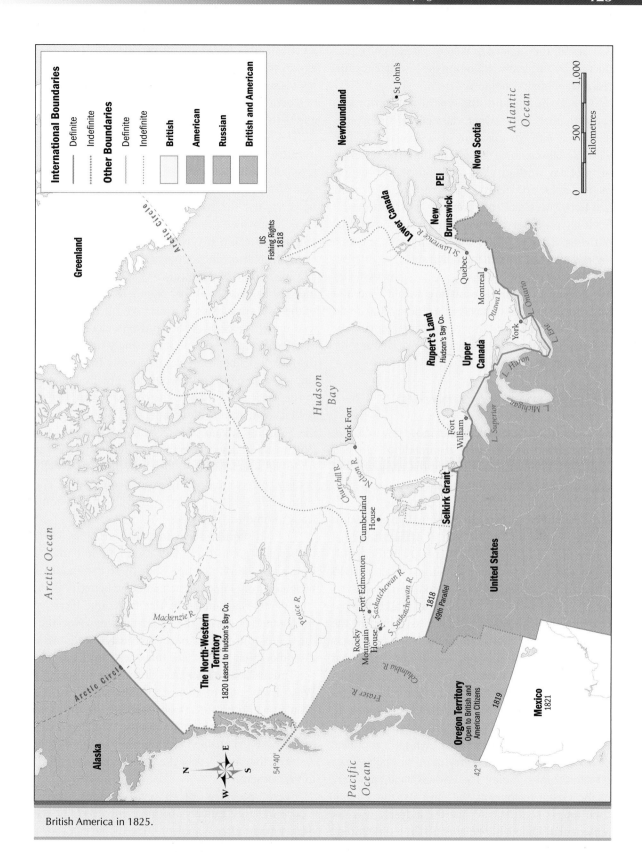

British America in 1825.

As a result, they tended to attempt to maximize production by ruthlessly exploiting the resource regardless of economic conditions.

As a small capitalist, the typical primary producer—whether boat owner, farmer, or timberer—identified with the commercial system rather than with his labour force, thus impeding the development of any working-class consciousness or the formation of an articulated class structure. Merchants had to be successful entrepreneurs, but found it difficult to move beyond their immediate commercial horizons. They were prepared to invest in processing raw materials within their own sphere of interest, but not outside it. The result was a highly exploitative and unadventurous economy, with a fluid and fuzzy social structure. It was an economy that could celebrate the values of an independent yeomanry at the same time that it took advantage of a labour force not composed of those yeomen.

The Staple Resources

The fishery was the oldest and most rewarding of British America's resource commodities. It had been successfully exploited since the early years of the sixteenth century. Traditionally associated with Newfoundland, it continued to dominate that colony's economic picture throughout the nineteenth century. By the end of the War of 1812, the actual production of fish was almost entirely in the hands of Newfoundland residents. Although after 1815 the market for Newfoundland cod remained stagnant for decades, the fishing economy experienced considerable change. Smaller buyers of fish in the outports were squeezed out by the larger merchants of Water Street in St John's. The fishery expanded into Labrador, and sealing became far more important, representing over one-third of the value of fishery exports by 1831. Newfoundland was unable to gain ground in the lucrative Caribbean trade. Nova Scotia merchants now had their own local suppliers of fish and were able to carry more diversified cargoes to the West Indies. The Lower Canadian fishery of the Gaspé region was the object of the agricultural interests' disdain. While the industry was not a particularly buoyant one after 1815, it did employ a considerable workforce. It produced a significant export trade, and it required a large number of sailing vessels both large and small. These characteristics contributed both to the shipbuilding industry and to the carrying-trade capacity of British America.

The fur trade was the other traditional resource industry. By the nineteenth century, the fur trade's economic value was very small in comparison with that of other resources. In a non-economic sense, however, the fur trade was of enormous importance. It provided the means by which Great Britain retained its claim to sovereignty over much of the northern half of the continent. It also supplied the administration of the British relationship with the indigenous peoples of that region. With the merger of the two great rivals in 1821, the fur trade stabilized under the aegis of the Hudson's Bay Company. The Pacific coast became increasingly important to the HBC. It deliberately over-trapped in the Far West since it assumed that it would eventually lose out to the Americans. Indeed, the company was able to hold its own against fur competitors, but not against the constant stream of American settlers into the Willamette Valley in the Oregon Territory. The fur trade had a remarkable influence in the West, chiefly because furs were its only export commodity. The entire region was organized politically and economically around the trade.

The old staples of fish and fur were replaced by timber and grain in primary economic importance in the nineteenth century. Both these commodities benefited from imperial preference, which gave them considerable advantage in the large and lucrative British market during their start-up years. Not until the 1840s did Britain begin seriously to eliminate the differential duty scales that the Corn Laws and the Timber Laws had created during the Napoleonic Wars. Every hint of change in imperial regulations brought a chorus of fears of economic disaster from the colonial mercantile community. While colonials may have been chained economically to the mother country, they revelled in the chains and were loath to break them.

Every province of British America except Newfoundland quickly became involved in the timber trade after Napoleon closed the Baltic (the

Sealing in Newfoundland

Joseph Jukes was an Englishman employed on a geological survey of Newfoundland in 1839. In a book about his experiences published in 1842, he recorded the following from his diary.

March 12th: Again foggy, with a southeast wind. As we stood on deck this morning before breakfast, we heard a cry down to leeward, like the cry of a gull, which some of the men said it was. It became, however, so loud and continued, that both Stuwitz and I doubted its being the cry of any bird, and one of the men took a gaff and went to look. We watched him for some distance with our glasses as he proceeded slowly through the fog till he suddenly began to run, and then struck at something, and presently returned dragging a young seal alive over the ice, and brought it on deck. It was of a dirty white colour, with short close fur, large expressive eyes, and it paddled and walloped about the deck fierce and bawling. A Newfoundland dog called Nestor, belonging to the captain, approached it, but it snapped at his nose and bit him, though its teeth were just beginning to appear. After taking it down below to show the captain and demand the usual quart of rum for the first man who caught a seal, one of the men knocked it on its head and skinned it. Stuwitz then cut off its 'flippers' or paws and its head, and after breakfast we took it into the 'after-hatch' or steerage where he drew and dissected it. In the middle of the day we heard from some of the men who had been out on the ice, that a vessel a few miles ahead of us had already 2500 seals on board, so we pushed on through the ice, and shortly came into a lake of water. On the borders of this many young seals were lying and two or three punts were hoisted out to despatch and collect them. I shot one through the head that was scuffling off a pan of ice, but the crew begged me to desist, as they said the balls might glance from the ice and injure some of the men who were about. Having picked up the few which were immediately about us, we hoisted in our punts again, as there were several vessels near us, and more coming up, and bore away farther north through an open pool of water. In passing through a thin skirt of ice, one of the men hooked up a young seal with his gaff. Its cries were precisely like those of a young child in the extremity of agony and distress, something between shrieks and convulsive sobbings. . . . We soon afterwards passed through some loose ice on which the young seals were scattered, and nearly all hands were overboard slaying, skinning and hauling. We then got into another lake of water and sent our five punts. The crews of these joined those already on the ice, and dragging either the whole seals or their 'pelts' to the edge of the water, collected them in the punts, and when one of these was full brought them on board.

Source: J.B. Jukes, *Excursions in and about Newfoundland*, 2 vols (London, 1842), as reprinted in Peter Neary and Patrick O'Flaherty, eds, *By Great Waters: A Newfoundland and Labrador Anthology* (Toronto: University of Toronto Press, 1974), 82–3.

traditional source of British supply) in 1807. Even tiny Prince Edward Island enjoyed a considerable boom from cutting down its trees, most of which were relatively accessible to open water. Primary-growth forest was cut as quickly as possible with no thought for either conservation or oversupplying the market, although the finest white pine forest in North America, in Norfolk County, Upper Canada, was ruthlessly chopped down for potash and firewood. In no province was the industry more important than in New Brunswick. Its dependence on timber as an export commodity had become almost complete by the mid-1820s. The needs of the industry controlled every aspect of the province's life.

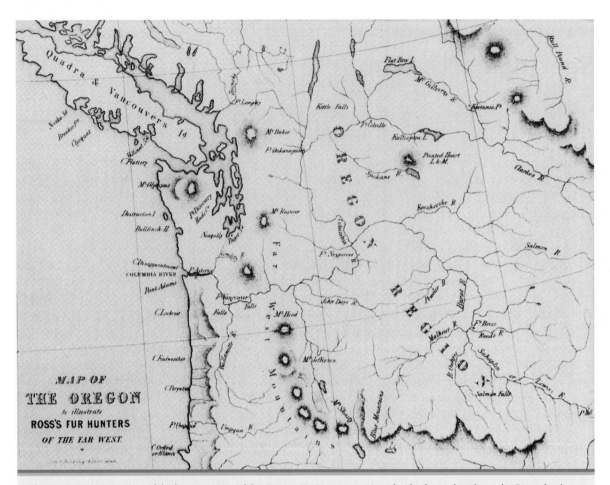

The Oregon Territory. One of the best accounts of the Oregon Territory was written by the fur trader Alexander Ross after he retired to Red River with his Okanagan wife and their children. *Fur-Hunters of the Far West* was first published in 1853. This map is from the 1855 edition. Metropolitan Toronto Reference Library.

Settlement was closely connected to the opening of new timber territory. It was no accident that the few timber princes who controlled the licences to cut on Crown land were also the leading politicians of the province. Under the large entrepreneurs worked a variety of local businessmen—storekeepers, brokers, and sawmill operators—who actually organized and dealt with the hundreds of small parties that wintered in the woods. Provisioning the timberers was a lucrative business. The industry preferred to do as much processing of the timber on the spot as possible, moving inexorably in that direction. As early as 1837 the sawmills of Samuel Cunard, on the Miramichi River in northeastern New Brunswick, were capable of cutting 42,471 feet (12,945 metres)

of boards per day, 'the produce of 320 logs and 50 workmen' (quoted in Wynn, 1980). Much timber also was processed into wooden sailing ships.

Before 1840 the export market for Upper Canadian timber was somewhat limited by transportation difficulties, but after that date the United States took all the timber Upper Canada could produce. The Ottawa Valley was a region of 8,000 square miles, most not arable but initially covered with primary-growth forest. It was timbered by professional crews who fostered a rough and violent society. The first serious ethnic conflicts in British America occurred in the 'Shiner's Wars' of the 1830s, as Irish timberers fought with French Canadians and others for dominance of the forests. Much of the forest in Upper

The forts of the recently merged Hudson's Bay and North West companies at the Forks at the junction of the Red and Assiniboine rivers, 1822, watercolour by Peter Rindisbacher. The NWC post, Fort Gibraltar, is on the left, the HBC post, Fort Douglas, on the right. LAC, C-001934.

Canada and elsewhere was timbered in advance of the arrival of settlement, with little except minimal license fees as the only charge for the cutting.

In the extensive agricultural lands of the St Lawrence Valley and Upper Canada, wheat quickly became the dominant crop. It met a growing demand abroad and it transported well as either grain or flour. Wheat quickly turned farmers into agricultural specialists, who exploited their soil much as did the timberers the forest. Lower Canada's wheat yields on rapidly exhausted soil often cropped for decades were frequently inadequate for home consumption. While Upper Canada was able to transform its wheat profits from great surpluses into non-agricultural investment, by the 1850s it, too, had exhausted its best soils and was looking westward. Most farmers also produced for their own consumption, of course, and some (such as those on Prince Edward Island) produced livestock and potatoes for export or supplied a local market with produce. Even Maritime farmers grew more wheat than was good for them, however.

The Mercantile System

The resource economy worked only because of its capacity to deal with the international market. The merchant capitalist looked after transportation and marketing in a world of totally unsophisticated credit and banking. Merchants operated at all levels of volume and capital investment. Some placed goods in a number of vessels and invested small amounts in other ships and voyages, as had been done in the colonies since the earliest days. The growing extent of the resource trade demanded entrepreneurs with more capital, however. Whether the merchant's business was large or small, international mercantile activity in the first half of the nineteenth century was extremely dangerous. Financial disaster lurked everywhere. Ships could be lost at sea, markets

These two photos from the New Brunswick lumber camps obviously postdate 1840 and the invention of the camera, but there is no reason to think that conditions in the timber trade changed much over the course of the nineteenth century. Top: a cookhouse; bottom: men with peaveys on a log-jam. From Adam Shortt and A.G. Doughty, eds, *Canada and Its Provinces* (Edinburgh, 1914), vol. 14. Courtesy of Toronto Public Library.

could be miscalculated, debtors could be unable to pay. Communications were incredibly slow. Because of the difficulties in finding trustworthy partners and agents abroad, the extensive family network was still the international basis of much mercantile activity. Few of the large merchant princes of this period avoided at least one bankruptcy, and fewer still left fortunes to their heirs. The sailing ship, filled with outgoing cargoes of resource commodities and incoming ones of manufactured goods and new immigrants, remained the backbone of British America's economic system in this period.

Some manufacturing activity did exist in British America. It involved relatively small establishments that engaged in two kinds of production. One was by artisans producing for local markets goods and services that either could not be imported profitably or could not be imported at all. Every town had its saddler, every village its blacksmith. The second type of production involved the processing of resource commodities. Grain was distilled into whisky, brewed into beer, and milled into flour. Wood from land being cleared by farmers was burned into potash, and timber was cut at sawmills into deals. Among many specialized manufacturing enterprises, shipyards that transformed timber into sailing vessels were the most extensive. The small shipyard was to be found wherever there was timber and open water; the commerce of the Great Lakes required as many sailing vessels as the transatlantic trade.

Shipbuilding was the ideal colonial processing industry. It relied primarily on a rich natural resource—timber—that British America had in abundance. It did not require excessive capital outlay for physical plant or materials, and its end product provided its own transportation to market. On

The Shipbuilding Industry

Shipyards could be found anywhere in British America where forests met open water. Scaffolding for ships dotted the Maritime region's landscape on beaches and rivers, and could also be found in Upper Canada along the Great Lakes. Occasionally, shipyards were owned by merchants, but in most cases they were controlled by master shipbuilders of limited capital resources. Building could be done any place with access to the water and did not require indoor facilities, which cut capital costs to the bare minimum. Only one ship under construction at a given site was quite common, although centres like Saint John built many ships simultaneously.

Merchants often placed orders for ships, and even supplied hardware and capital advances. Business arrangements sometimes were casual in the early years, and the merchants had little control over design or craftsmanship on the vessels they ordered, as their constant complaints to the builders testified. Vessels built before 1830 were often badly constructed of unseasoned wood, but gradually the quality of construction improved. As for the wood itself, white pine was valued for its lightness and freedom from knot, but both white and red pine initially were regarded in Britain as inferior to Baltic wood because of perceived structural weakness and susceptibility to dry rot. Most ships were built entirely of local wood by local carpenters (who frequently were paid in rum and other spirits) and then were finished with imported goods, such as iron fittings and sail cloth. The possibility of adding imported hardware at the completion of a ship reduced the opportunity for the creation of spinoff industries, such as the manufacture of finished iron goods.

Like timbering itself, shipbuilding was a seasonal activity, possible only during warmer weather, but ships were easily the most valuable export commodities of the provinces that built them in large numbers, particularly New Brunswick, Nova Scotia, and Prince Edward Island. By 1840 the merchant marine of the British American colonies was already one of the largest in the world.

the other hand, even during its heyday it was not an industry with either a future or a capacity to generate industrial development. As early as 1840 wood and sail were being overtaken by iron and steam. These technologies required an entirely different form of industrial organization than a handful of craftsmen employing hand tools, carefully assembling a wooden ship on the edge of open water. Neither the technology nor the industrial organization flowed logically out of the nature of colonial shipbuilding, which became instead the symbol of the mercantile resource economy's limitations.

Providing the infrastructure for trade and commerce was a gradual development. Banks were slow to expand because most colonials were suspicious of institutions that could, in effect, manufacture money. The Bank of Montreal was founded in 1817 and the Bank of Canada was chartered in 1821, opening at York in 1822. Early banks did not co-operate and their services were limited. An expanding internal economic system required roads, bridges, and canals to connect the population with their markets and

sources of supply. Most people wanted such facilities, but they did not want to pay for them out of taxes. Much road-building was done by labour levies on the local population. After the American success with the Erie Canal, canal-building became the craze in the Canadas. The early Canadian canals—the Lachine Canal, the Welland Canal, the Rideau Canal, and the Chambly Canal—either opened water access into Lake Ontario or improved the St Lawrence River system. Their thrust was to enable the economy to shift from a transatlantic focus to an internal one. This process really took hold with the introduction of the railroads in the 1850s.

Trade and commerce were the basis of urban growth, although the major cities of the British colonies in North America were centres of political activity as well as of commerce. It was easier to flourish, however, without being a capital (Montreal or Hamilton) than without trade (Fredericton). No city dominated more than its immediate region and none was very large. Nonetheless, most urban centres in British America were growing rapidly. York in 1795

Shipbuilding at Dorchester, New Brunswick, 1875. The technology of shipbuilding remained fairly constant throughout the nineteenth century. Over the years, Dorchester's river silted up, and the community is now landlocked. LAC, C-10103.

'View in King Street [Toronto], Looking East', hand-coloured lithograph, 1835, by Thomas Young. The buildings on the left (north) are the jail, the courthouse, and St James Church at Church Street. Library and Archives Canada, C-041602.

contained 12 cottages. By the time it was incorporated and renamed Toronto in 1834 it had over 1,000 houses, 100 shops, and a population of 9,252. The cities were small in area as well as in population, many being collections of tightly packed buildings radiating from a port facility. Such a city had little concept of zoning and not many amenities, although by the 1830s matters were improving. Toronto was fairly typical for 1830 in lacking sidewalks, drains, sewers, water supply, and street lighting, all developments of the 1830s and 1840s. Policing consisted at best of a few ward constables and a night watch. For most urban centres in British America, 1840 marked the break between remaining an eighteenth-century town and becoming a nineteenth-century city.

Immigration

After 1815 circumstances combined to alter patterns of immigration, especially from the British Isles. Resistance to emigration from both the British government and the British ruling classes was quickly broken down by unemployment and a new round of industrialization and agricultural rationalization. Pressures increased on Britain's relief system for the poor, and among those who governed the nation common wisdom again was that Britain was overpopulated. The burgeoning North American timber trade provided the shipping capacity for the transatlantic movement of immigrants at low cost. Immigrants came to British America chiefly to obtain access to land, something that was becoming increasingly difficult to obtain in the British Isles. Many Britons had an extremely idealized picture of the wilderness. The essayist Thomas Carlyle wrote in 1839 of the vastness of North America, 'nine-tenths of it yet vacant or tenanted by nomads, . . . still crying, Come and till me, come and reap me!' Despite the best efforts of a number of writers of immigration manuals, many newcomers failed to appreciate the need for capital or the difficulties involved in clearing much of this vacant land of trees and brush. In 1846, in her book *The Backwoods of Canada*, Catharine Parr Traill included 'some official information' 'to render this work of more practical value to persons desiring to emigrate'. Table 4.1 presents two examples: charts on the sale of Crown lands in Lower and Upper Canada, 'abstracted from Parliamentary documents'.

What we know about the numbers departing the British Isles suggests that Scottish emigration remained relatively steady throughout the period at 10–15 per cent of the total flow. A far higher proportion of Highlanders than Lowlanders departed in these years. Irish emigration was more variable, ranging annually from 30 to 70 per cent of the total numbers. Irish movement to North America before the 1840s was dominated by Protestants from Northern Ireland. Only in the mid-1840s did the Irish emigrants begin to include huge numbers of Catholic southerners. As a result, the whole nature of Irish emigration to British America was quite different from Irish emigration to the United States. British America received far more Irish emigrants in the early period than did the United States. The Irish flow to what is now Canada included far more Protestants and Orangists than did that to the United States, where the emigrants were almost exclusively Catholics from the south. Not all newcomers to British America came from the British Isles. A relative handful, for example, of Sephardic Jews arrived individually or in family groups from Europe after 1763 to form the first continuing synagogue in Montreal, founded in 1768.

The national and regional complexity of the population in the British Isles at this time produces several interesting questions and problems. It is tempting from a twenty-first-century perspective to assume, for example, that the British emigrants were a relatively homogeneous anglophone group of people. Nothing could be further from the truth. Each of the historic nations of Britain continued in the nineteenth century to preserve its own culture and history. There was homogeneity of neither language nor religion. Many of the Irish, especially in the south, spoke the Irish tongue. Almost all Scots from north of the Highland fault spoke Gaelic as a first language, while those in the Lowlands spoke a Scottish variant of English. Dialects and linguistic variants were

Table 4.1	The Quantity of Crown Lands Granted and the Conditions on which the Grants Were Given from 1823 to 1833				
Lower Canada					
Year	Number of acres granted to militia claimants	Number of acres granted to discharged soldiers and pensioners	Number of acres granted to officers	Number of acres granted, not coming within the previous descriptions	Total number of acres granted
1824	51,810	—	4,100	34,859	90,769
1825	32,620	—	1,000	16,274	49,894
1826	3,525	5,500	—	48,224	57,249
1827	7,640	6,300	800	38,375	53,118
1828	7,300	—	4,504	9,036	20,840
1829	3,200	—	—	5,282	8,482
1830	81,425	—	2,000	10,670	94,095
1831	9,400	8,273	3,408	9,900	30,981
1832	10,116	19,000	4,000	4,000	37,116
1833	5,200	22,500	1,200	—	28,900
Total	212,236	61,573	21,012	176,623	471,444

Settler's Conditions: That he do clear twenty feet of road on his lot within the space of ninety days.
Military and Militia Conditions: That he do, within the space of three years, clear and cultivate four acres of his lot, and build a dwelling-house thereon.

Table 4.1   *(continued)*

	Upper Canada					
Year	Number of acres granted to militia claimants	Number of acres granted to discharged soldiers and pensioners	Number of acres granted to officers	Number of acres granted, not coming within the previous descriptions	Number of acres granted to UE Loyalists*	Total number of acres granted
1824	11,800	5,800	5,500	134,500	30,200	187,800
1825	20,300	5,700	8,100	149,060	45,000	228,160
1826	16,600	3,100	4,700	19,390	24,800	68,590
1827	10,900	4,200	7,200	33,600	20,200	76,100
1828	10,800	900	3,000	4,304	30,800	49,804
1829	5,300	7,500	8,400	3,230	22,600	47,030
1830	6,400	12,500	12,600	9,336	27,400	68,236
1831	5,500	58,400	7,200	8,000	34,200	113,300
1832	19,300	97,800	7,600	6,100	62,600	193,400
1833	35,200	46,000	—	9,100	135,600	225,900
Total	142,100	241,900	64,300	376,620	433,400	1,258,320

Condition: Actual settlement.

*UE Loyalists means United Empire Loyalists—individuals who fled from the United States on the outbreak of the American war of independence. The grants in this column were mostly to the children of these individuals.

Source: C.P. Traill, *The Backwoods of Canada* (London: M.A. Nattali, 1846).

extensive in England and Wales, also. In the latter place, there was a north–south division whereby the northerners were more likely to speak Welsh than English. At the same time, the nineteenth century saw a considerable growth of a common 'Britishness' that to various extents overcame regional distinctions. On the other hand, acceptance of the concepts of Great Britain and Britishness was quite variable. Many of the southern Irish, for example, would not have agreed that they were British or that they were willing subjects of the British Crown.

Another difference between immigration to the United States and to British America occurred in the nature of the vessels employed in the transatlantic passage. This had certain ramifications for the sorts of emigrants who departed for each of the countries. Those going to the United States tended to travel in large vessels specifically designed to carry passengers, while those going to British America usually travelled in smaller vessels designed for the timber trade. These smaller ships carried passengers on the return voyage

in makeshift accommodations instead of sailing in ballast. The port of Quebec was the principal entry for immigrants into the Canadas because sailing vessels could collect a load of timber for the voyage to Britain. The result of the sort of passage provided was that the passage to British America cost significantly less than that to the United States. When this difference in cost is combined with the much shorter duration of the passage from the British Isles to the eastern seaports of British America (which meant that fewer provisions were required for the journey), it seems likely that far more immigrants to British America sailed on extremely limited budgets and without much capital in reserve than was typically the case for those who went to the United States. It is hard to generalize, because the rates for passengers varied substantially from time to time. One Belfast advertisement from 1820 put the charge for a family of husband, wife, and six children to the United States at 80 guineas, for example, and the cost for the same family to New Brunswick at 24 guineas. Either way, such rates meant

Philemon Wright

Philemon Wright (1760–1839) was born in Woburn, Massachusetts. He fought with the Americans in the Battle of Bunker Hill in 1775 and subsequently moved to the Vermont frontier. In 1796 Wright bought land in Lower Canada and a year later he petitioned the government there for the township of Hull on behalf of himself and a number of associates (who turned out to be fellow citizens of Woburn). Wright himself led a party of 63 settlers (presumably all Americans like himself) to Hull in March of 1800. Initially he had planned to establish himself as a squire in a new agricultural society, but he soon added timbering to the economic mix. From the beginning Wright took farming seriously, and in 1820 he became one of British America's first 'Wheat Kings', harvesting nearly 36,000 bushels of wheat on his farms. A few years later, his harvest reached over 71,000 bushels. As well as grain crops, Wright also raised large herds of cattle.

Whether Wright's lumbering activities were simply offshoots of his agricultural involvement—as were innkeeping, milling, and retailing—or whether timber was from the beginning the fulcrum of the entire enterprise is not entirely clear. In any event, by 1806 Wright was floating rafts of squared timber down the Ottawa River to Quebec. Initially, much of the wood came from settlers' land during clearance, but gradually Wright got the wood from land acquired specifically for the purpose. His businesses were a classic example of economic integration, both horizontal and vertical. He had a piece of virtually every economic enterprise remotely related to Hull Township, and he controlled the production of timber from woodlot to point of sale on the St Lawrence.

Wright showed little interest in provincial politics before 1830, but as a critical member of a regional elite he had a good deal of local power. He was an officer of militia and justice of the peace, and after 1817 commissioner for the summary trial of small causes. It was Philemon Wright who asked the Royal Institution for Advancement of Learning to begin a school at Hull, and although he began life as a Congregationalist he gradually moved towards the Anglican Church. Wright was master of the first Masonic lodge established in Hull in 1813. He was elected to the assembly in 1830, sat for four years, and went home without having become a member of the legislative council and the Château Clique. Wright was the perfect example of a 'Late Loyalist' who demonstrated how Yankee ambition and ingenuity could work in British America.

that only those with considerable capital—or who were willing to acquire considerable debt—could afford to sail at all. Many of those arriving in British American ports without capital may have intended to move on to the United States when they had acquired the means, but how many actually managed to do so is another matter entirely. Large numbers of those arriving with little or no capital were already in debt to friends or relatives at home. They had borrowed the price of steerage passage and were bound to repay the debt out of their first earnings.

Costs and geography also meant that British America rather than the United States throughout the period received the vast bulk of the emigrants from the Highlands of Scotland. Many of these Highlanders arrived virtually destitute in British America and could not afford to continue on to the United States. Sufficient numbers of Gaelic-speakers from Highland Scotland arrived in various parts of British America (notably parts of Upper Canada, the eastern townships of Lower Canada, Cape Breton Island, and Prince Edward Island) to make the language an important medium of communication in these areas. This simply did not happen in the United States, where newcomers were strongly encouraged to assimilate immediately to the dominant society.

Irish emigrants awaiting departure on the quay at Cork, as depicted in the *Illustrated London News*, 10 May 1851. LAC, C-3904.

Four patterns of organized emigration and settlement developed after 1815. The first pattern involved government assistance, which was often a combination of British official recruitment of emigrants and settlement, with public aid, on land made available by the several colonial governments. Such schemes, frequently involving either soldiers disbanded after the wars or excess Irish population, continued sporadically until 1830. What the various schemes best demonstrated was that the financial cost of establishing British emigrants in British America was high and the chances of successful transplantation were low. Even those who argued that the existing operations were unnecessarily profligate estimated £60 subsidy for a family of five. In the late 1820s the British government rejected a proposal for a major government resettlement scheme to be financed by local authorities as an alternative to poor relief. It was brought forward by the parliamentary undersecretary at the Colonial Office, Robert John Wilmot-Horton. Thereafter government policy abandoned public assistance for emigration.

The other three patterns were not mutually exclusive. Some emigrants could even combine all three. The second pattern emphasized settlement on the land. It involved private proprietors of land, usually large land companies. These occasionally offered financial assistance, but most frequently they made land on affordable terms available to emigrants who had managed to make their way to North America. This process was intended to appeal to emigrants with some financial resources. There were three large land companies: the Canada Company, the British American Land Company (in the Eastern Townships of Quebec), and the New Brunswick and Nova Scotia Land Company. In 1826 the Canada Company had purchased most of the Crown reserves and half of the clergy reserves of Upper Canada, thus providing revenue for the colony. It settled large numbers of emigrants on its lands.

A third pattern emphasized transport to North America but not settlement on the land. Private emigrant contractors would offer passage to North America in sailing vessels. The ships involved were usually in the timber trade, temporarily converted to provide accommodation on the outward passage. The contractor provided low rates of passage but as few services as possible. His passengers were

Advice for Immigrants

Numbers of books and pamphlets were published between 1800 and 1860 devoted exclusively to offering advice for immigrants. Most of the advice was useful, although few authors went into details on how difficult the passage and transition would be.

[Liverpool] is undoubtedly the best port to embark from, as vessels may there be met with at any time during the spring and summer months; and the expense of travelling to that town, even from places at a considerable distance, is not great . . . . In the winter and very early in the spring, there are also vessels constantly going to New York, from whence there are steam-boats to Albany, and a stage to Montreal, or to Sackett's harbour opposite Kingston, by Utica. This would be the best route for persons without families, or who had but little baggage, and who were desirous of leaving England in February or March. A considerable duty or per centage (as much, I believe, as thirty per cent) on the value of their baggage, is paid at New York by persons not intending to settle in the United States, but who were only passing through them in order to proceed to the British colonies. Persons with families, and a considerable quantity of baggage, had therefore better embark for Quebec; and the commencement of April would be soon enough to leave Liverpool, as vessels cannot proceed up the river St. Lawrence to Quebec before the middle of May, on account of the ice. . . .

Coarse warm clothing with flannel shirts, thick worsted or yarn stockings, and strong shoes or half-boots nailed, are most suitable for the climate of Canada in winter; and duck slops, duck trowsers, and calico or homespun linen shirts, for summer wear. Fur caps may also be brought out, as they are expensive here. Any old clothes will serve during the voyage out, and in travelling through the country. Beds may be taken out (without bedsteads). Curtains and curtainrings, cords, blankets, sheets, warm rugs or coverlets, and several spare bed-ticks. All these latter articles are extremely dear in Canada. Scarcely any thing else need be provided, as all articles of hardware, axes suitable for the country, plough-irons, harrow-teeth, Dutch and tin ovens, tea-kettles, kettles for cooking meat in, &c., &c., &c. may be purchased at Montreal at nearly the same prices as in England.

Every thing should be well packed in strong boxes, cases, or trunks, the more portable they are the better, each not exceeding three feet in length, eighteen inches in breadth, and one foot in depth, made water-tight if possible, or in barrels about the size of flour barrels, also water-tight; and all to be well lashed up or corded. Beds, bedding, curtains, &c. &c., may be sewed up in a wool-sack or very coarse harden, with a strong cord round them; this is the most convenient and best method of taking out beds. China or other earthenware may be packed in tow or the refuse of flax. . . .

All spare money must be brought out in guineas or Spanish dollars, which may be purchased for good bills at any bullion office in Liverpool. Dollars are bought for about 4s. 4d. or 4s. 6d. each.

Source: 'English Farmer Settled in Upper Canada', *A few plain directions for persons intending to proceed as settlers to His Majesty's province of Upper Canada, in North America* (London, 1820), as found in Harold Innis and A.R.M. Lower, eds, *Select Documents in Canadian Economic History 1783–1885* (Toronto, 1933), 96–8.

frequently deposited at seaports in British America and left to their own devices. The lucky ones managed to make their way to some destination where they could find employment.

The vast majority of emigrants, whatever their transport and settlement arrangements, fitted into the fourth pattern. They had arranged their own passage, frequently coming to British America without

'The Emigrant's Welcome to Canada', c. 1820. W.H. Coverdale Collection of Canadiana, LAC C-41067.

fixed plans or destination. Sometimes they intended to join relatives or friends who had preceded them. If they had capital, they found land. It was generally estimated that at least £100 (beyond the cost of passage) was required to establish a farm on wilderness land, and even more was required to purchase one already improved. Those who could not afford this expense joined the ranks of the labouring class or, in the case of unattached females, went into domestic service. Most immigrants apparently understood that their important baggage was cash money, good health, and family connections. The transatlantic passage in sailing ships lasted from six to eight weeks, and was long and arduous even for those who could afford cabin accommodation. For those in steerage (the vast majority), the discomfort and health hazards were high. After 1825 the British government abandoned attempts to regulate the traffic in any serious way.

Aside from the assisted settlement schemes, public policy was never really mobilized to settle British America. The major shift in policy after the mid-1820s, apart from the termination of assisted settlement, was the abandonment of the practice of giving colonial land away; now a 'sufficient price' was to be charged, to ensure a revenue for colonial improvement, and to guarantee that those acquiring land had some capital. In the end, settlement was achieved out of the trials and tribulations of the many who tried their luck, not always successfully. Apart from their physical energy, the immigrants were also a great source of wealth for the colonies they entered. If every immigrant brought on average only £10, between 1815 and 1845 that amount would have injected £10 million into the local economies.

The Resource Society

The resource society of the early nineteenth century was dominated by two overlapping elites. One governed; the other controlled international commerce.

'A First Settlement', by W.H. Bartlett, engraved by J.C. Bentley, from N.P. Willis, *Canadian Scenery* (London, 1842), vol. 2. LAC, C-2401

In most colonies their separate identities were easily confused when they battled politically, employing imported rhetoric that suggested deeper divisions than actually existed. By far the majority of the population was composed of the non-elite: small shopkeepers, artisans, minor civil servants; owners of small industries such as gristmills, tanneries, soap factories, and breweries; and resource workers and farmers. In the British sense of distinguishing between those who held land and those who did not, an important distinction in Europe, few 'landholders' in British America possessed anything but land that was in the process of becoming farms. Undeveloped land had little value. Most landowners were forced to hold multiple employments, often working side by side with the landless. Women in this society acquired the status of their husbands. Those without spouses had some autonomy, but were severely limited in any upward mobility. Finally, the indigenous peoples lived completely outside the social structure, although the missionaries constantly tried to bring them into it.

The governing elite included the leading appointed colonial officials of government, military officers, church leaders, and the merchants who lived in the capital city. The first three enjoyed the enormous advantage of a substantial guaranteed annual salary, usually paid in London in pounds sterling. This income, the access to credit, and the style of living it encouraged all enabled colonial officials to emulate the British values of the landed gentry. Their houses reflected their aspirations. The magnificent house of John Strachan (1778–1867) on Front Street in Toronto was popularly known as 'The Palace' even before he became bishop of Toronto in 1839. In 1819, the year after it was built, his brother visiting from Scotland is alleged to have commented, 'I hope it's a' come by honestly, John' (quoted in

Arthur, 1986: 44). Not surprisingly, colonial officials believed in the balance of interests and order, the maintenance of which John Beverley Robinson (1791–1863) once described as 'the foundation of good government in the social state' (quoted in Brode, 1984: 175). Such men were well-educated and very able. They governed British America with an extremely limited vision, usually without soiling themselves in sordid graft and corruption.

The most successful merchants (and a few professional men) shared the lifestyle of the major colonial office-holders, usually without their status. What really limited the social positions of the merchants was the impermanence of their incomes, which could be greatly affected by conditions in the market. The British associated status with land because an income from landed estates was rightly regarded as far more permanent and inheritable than income from trade or industry. British America was never able to generate a landed aristocracy. The colonial official's income was only for life, although a few offices were passed on from father to son. The typical seigneur in Lower Canada did not have enough income to cut much of a figure. The trouble with land in North America was its sheer availability. An Upper Canadian backwoods farm consisted of a larger acreage than many an English landed estate. Most land was held for speculation rather than status. Lacking an aristocracy based on land, British America instead began developing a social structure based on wealth and conspicuous consumption. Money might be temporary, but it could be made visible. British America also held in high regard education, professional training, and the life of the mind. The concentrations of leading professional men in the larger towns were admitted to the ranks of elite society, though in a subordinate position.

While the governing elite and their merchant partners lived mainly in the political capitals that were also the great commercial centres of British America, a sprinkling of others in the hinterlands also assumed the functions of leadership. Such regional leaders included local merchants and professional men, prominent farmers, and retired half-pay officers. These were the men who were elected to the provincial houses of assembly from the countryside,

where they inevitably came to contend with the governing elites for political control of the province. Regional prominence was recognized by election to the assembly and appointment to local civic office. Thus, these also were the men who served as local justices of the peace. They tended to be the militia officers as well. Before 1840 most would have described themselves as farmers, although they usually engaged in a variety of occupations, hoping to succeed and survive. One of the most striking features of the lives of most British Americans was their lack of occupational specialization. Over the course of a lifetime most colonials would hold many different jobs, both in succession and simultaneously.

Coming to terms with the remainder of society in British America is more complicated than dealing with the elite. Despite the vaunted availability of land, not everyone represented that British (and American) ideal: a land-holding yeoman farmer. In some places (Newfoundland, Prince Edward Island, and Lower Canada), freehold land was not easily available. Moreover, the land that was worth holding was not wilderness but an improved market farm. Cultivating land carved out of primary-growth forest was a tedious and laborious process. Such 'improvement' was hampered by the difficulties of finding a market for surplus agricultural products. Farmers inevitably embraced crops such as wheat, which could be transported into a regular market system. Improvement was further hampered by the availability of alternative employment in fishing, timbering, shipbuilding, and construction—which could sustain a farming family before it was plugged into the market—but would also slow down the land-clearing process essential to agrarian success.

At the bottom of colonial society were the poor. They fell into three categories: permanent, immigrant, and casual; and into two major groups: those who had relations or friends to look after them and those who did not. While British America was spoken of on both sides of the Atlantic as a 'land of opportunity' and a 'good poor man's country', it was absolutely essential to be healthy or to have kinfolk prepared to help with one's welfare. Those who through disability, incompetence, or misfortune (such as young orphans) could not look after themselves and had no one to do it for them became the objects of charity or lived permanently in squalor. Recent immigrants who arrived in port without capital resources joined the ranks of the poor wherever they disembarked. Unable to move onto the land, these newcomers merged into the third category, the casually employed. Because of the seasonal nature of most Canadian employment, winter saw the largest number of unemployed. Winter was also the worst time to be poor, for food costs increased and the need to keep warm in a Canadian winter was inescapable. Malnutrition and inadequate clothing, combined with inadequate heating, provided a recipe for the spread of illness and contagious disease. The poor were 'relieved' chiefly to prevent their turning 'by despair to commit depredations' (quoted in Fingard, 1988: 197). Contemporary society tended to identify poverty with the city and personal failure. It saw poverty as a moral rather than as an economic problem.

Between the poor and the prosperous fell a variety of occupational and social groups that defy ordering by almost any scheme. An examination of the Newfoundland fishing-boat owner suggests some of the difficulties. A property owner and an employer, the boat owner was probably landless except for a small house lot for which he held no deed. He was usually deeply in debt to the merchant who bought his fish and supplied him with essentials. Forced to contract debt, the fisher soon found himself in slavish servitude. The fishery's truck system also operated in the timber districts and the fur trade. In another guise it also worked in farming communities, where families accumulated large debts to local storekeepers who supplied goods that could not be made at home. Moreover, huge portions of British America consisted of uneconomic farms that were kept operating on a subsistence level, often by women and children, while the male landholder was off elsewhere working for wages. As with the elites, houses told the tale. Settlers hoped to progress from log hut (or shanty) to log house to permanent dwelling built of stone or brick or finished lumber in accordance with their prosperity. In 1831 Upper Canada had 36,000 dwellings, of which 75 per cent were constructed of logs and fewer than 1,000 built of brick and stone.

Colonial society also included a number of categories of people who were quite outside the social structure as it was then understood. One such group was women. The law in British America was quite different for men and for women. Women were citizens only in that they were inhabitants of British America whose civil rights had yet to be ultimately decided. They were for the most part 'non-legal entities'. A variety of disabilities operated against women. They could not be legislators, or lawyers, judges, magistrates, or members of juries that decided the fate of many women in both civil and criminal actions. Politically disenfranchised—several provinces even passed legislation in this period specifically depriving widows of the vote—women were especially disadvantaged by marriage. As the English jurist Sir William Blackstone put it, 'In law husband and wife are one person and the husband is that person.' All real property passed into the hands of the husband, who was entitled to control his spouse. Women were expected to produce many children in an age when maternal mortality ran very high. Despite the drawbacks, most women preferred marriage to the alternatives.

At least among the elite and the very prosperous, a process began of converting the home into the central social unit for cultural transmission and the pursuit of happiness. As British American society became more settled, and somewhat more urbanized, within the ranks of the middle and upper classes emerged a clear separation of work life and home life, and women withdrew into the privacy of the home. This growth of the concept of domesticity began in the ranks of the elite but gradually made its way into the middle class. It was connected with increasing prosperity and the construction of larger houses, which in turn encouraged new notions of social space. It became possible to conceive of reserving different rooms for different functions (and different people), to distinguish 'public' rooms from 'private' rooms, and to introduce ideas of privacy as well. Instead of spending his life almost entirely in public spaces, the husband and father now came 'home' from work to renew himself. Women were placed on a pedestal as keepers of culture and as civilizing influences.

For most women in British America, struggle with the pioneering conditions of carving farms out of the wilderness was the principal reality of life. An absence of labour-saving devices—except the domestic servant, for those who could afford one—meant that most work associated with the home involved heavy physical drudgery and long hours. Women were not only responsible for food preparation, but for much food production—gardening and berry-picking, churning butter and making cheese,

Clearing a Farm

The following appeared in Walter Johnstone, *A Series of Letters, Descriptive of Prince Edward Island, in the Gulph of St. Laurence, Addressed to the Rev. John Wightman, Minister of Kirkmahoe, Dumfries-shire* (Dumfries: J. Swan, 1822). Johnstone had travelled extensively on the Island as a missionary.

I may begin by observing, that the country is one entire forest of wood; all the exceptions to the truth of this literally are not much more, even including the present clearances, than the dark spots upon the moon's face, as they appear to the naked eye, compared with the brighter parts thereof. . . .

New settlers (who should always be here as early in the spring as possible) begin to cut down the wood where they intend to erect their first house. As the trees are cut the branches are to be lopped off, and the trunks cut into lengths of 12 or 14 feet. This operation they call junking them; if they are not junked before fire is applied, they are much worse to junk afterwards. Thus, when the space intended to be cleared is cut down, junked, and all lying in a promiscuous manner over the whole surface, fire is applied to it in as dry and windy a day as can be selected, and if the fire runs well, the greater part of the small branches will be consumed, but the trunks will only be scorched. These are next rolled together and made up in piles, lying flat upon the ground; then the remaining small branches are gathered up and thrown upon the heavier wood, to help it to kindle for burning a second time. The stronger part of the family then go on to make up more piles, while the weaker part set fire to those which are thus prepared. In this way they proceed till the whole of what was cut down is gone over; then when the piles go out they are kindled again, and those that continue to burn are thrust closer together, till all is consumed. I must say this is a piece of work of the most dirty and disagreeable nature, and when the wood is heavy, as tiresome as any I have seen in America.

I have often passed by the settlers when engaged in this employment, and what with smoke, sweat, and the dust of the burnt wood, their faces were little fairer than those of the negroes in the West Indies, while their clothes were much the same as if they had been dragged up a sooty chimney. After the wood is all burnt, the stumps are left standing about two feet high, scorched black with the first burning, like so many flocks, of a blacksmith's anvil. The people then begin planting their potatoes, which is done in the following manner;—with their hoes they scratch or rake a little of the [earth] to one side, about eight inches square, and after raking a little of the ashes lying upon the surface into this groove, they place four cuttings of seed potatoes in it in square form, and then cover them up with earth till it resembles a small mole-hill, and still repeating the same operation they go on putting all their seed into the ground by four at a time, and when the space cleared is all planted it looks as if it were all covered with small mole-hills. And this is the only labour bestowed upon the potatoes till they are ready for raising. But when the time for planting arrives, man, wife, children, and all that can handle a hoe, must work, as the season is short; and if the crop is not got in to a sufficient extent, want may stare them in the face, when a supply will be difficult to procure, and when there will be nothing in their pocket to pay for it.—This work of planting with the hoe is very laborious, for there are always a great number of small roots spread over the surface, which they have to cut to pieces with their hoes, otherwise they could not plant it at all. . . .

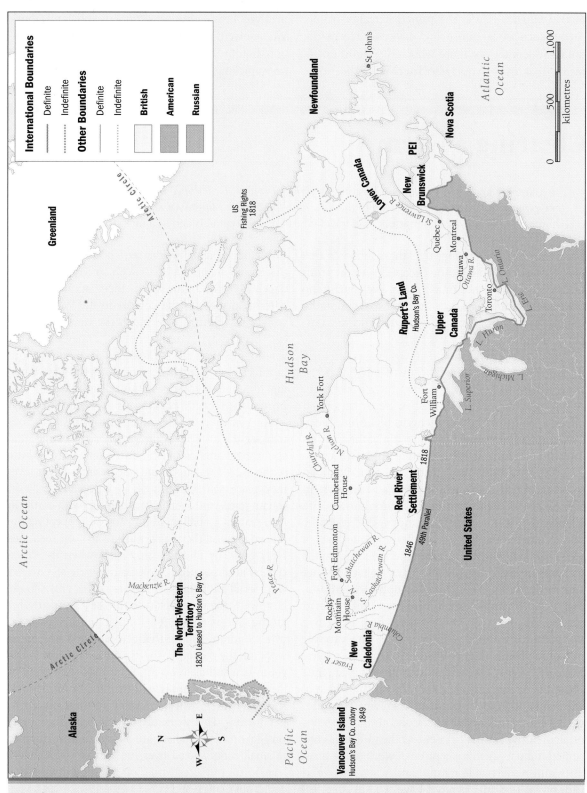

British America in 1849.

keeping chickens for eggs and meat—and for most of its preservation. In addition, women made soap and candles; they washed clothes; they tended the fires under the maple syrup vats. While conditions could become less primitive over time, there was never any appreciable reduction in the amount of a woman's labour required to keep the family going. She was also responsible for bearing and raising children. In a society in which infant mortality was high and labour outside the family hard to come by, a considerable incentive existed for the production of large families. Women were also expected to help their men in work in the male sphere when required. In the resource society of British America in the first half of the nineteenth century, men were away from home often and for long periods. In their absence,

Angélique Pilotte

Angélique Pilotte was born c. 1797 near Michilimackinac to Aboriginal parents. In 1815 she engaged as a servant and accompanied her mistress to France, returning in 1817 to Drummond Island (now Michigan), where she again became a 'waiting woman'. She went with her mistress to Chippewa, Upper Canada, where in early August the body of a dead baby was discovered in a shallow grave. Pilotte confessed that she was the mother and was subsequently put on trial for infanticide under a 1624 English statute, although there is little evidence that she had admitted to killing the child.

Pilotte had spent most of her life in Ojibwa society and does not appear to have understood much English or most of the legal niceties connected with the charge against her in the Niagara court. Several of the witnesses, including her mistress, thought that she was mentally challenged, although the problem may have been one of language, combined with racial prejudice, rather than mental acuity. In any event, she had admitted to concealing a pregnancy, to bearing a live child, and to burying it when it subsequently died—which were the key points in the law against infanticide. A jury quickly found her guilty but recommended mercy. Nonetheless, the judge—who over the years insisted that Aboriginals should be brought under English justice—sentenced her to be hanged, with the body subsequently given over for dissection.

Pilotte's lawyer, Bartholomew Beardsley, encouraged her to petition for mercy, partly on the grounds of substantial communications problems; Pilotte insisted that she had been misunderstood and misinterpreted. But Beardsley also emphasized that Pilotte was a victim of cultural misunderstanding. In Ojibwa society, the girl had acted perfectly appropriately in the way she had given birth. Pilotte knew only 'the customs and maxims of her own nation', which included 'the invariable custom of Indian women to retire and bring forth their children alone, and in secret'. The jury backed her plea for a pardon. One juror wrote to the local newspaper that the jury had recommended mercy because 'she was a savage and had no knowledge of the usages of the Christians.' A number of prominent citizens of Niagara, many of whom were involved in trade with Aboriginals, also supported her petition, as did Robert Gourlay (the Scots-born opponent of the Upper Canadian government at the time).

The appeal went to Upper Canada's chief executive, colonial administrator Samuel Smith, who sent it to London for a final decision. Pilotte waited in prison while the appeal crossed the Atlantic. The British authorities altered her sentence to one year's imprisonment. She had already served most of that time, and she was apparently released to return to her people. The Pilotte case could be read in a number of ways. It could be seen as an illustration of the harshness of the laws against women, as an example of the way in which minorities were treated (for the successful appeal was not common practice), or as an instance of the ultimate triumph of British justice.

their wives had to run households and farms, as well as to manage businesses. Although women's work was drudgery never done, they were never properly rewarded. Domestic duties were not regarded as a labour to be remunerated, and women's contributions to the success of the family estate were rarely taken into account in inheritance strategies. The typical pattern was for sons (usually eldest sons) to inherit the property, while the caring patriarch specified, at best, that the heir was responsible for the maintenance of his mother. Daughters counted for very little in this pattern of inheritance.

Other groups almost completely marginalized by colonial society included indigenous peoples and blacks. In much of the eastern region of British America, settlement had eliminated hunting grounds, and there was no place for the indigenous peoples to go. They were offered the choice of provisions of land in unsurveyed local reserves or general integration into the farming community. The year 1836 saw several major and contradictory developments in First Nations policy. In that year the first serious British attempt at co-ordinating policy came with a parliamentary inquiry that covered the entire empire. Canada featured prominently in this investigation, with a litany of abuses exposed from one colony to the next. The government of Nova Scotia refused to provide any information whatsoever. In its 1,000-page report, the committee concluded that First Nations policy should remain under British control. It also recommended against making treaties with local Aboriginals, on the grounds that the treaty process was so heavily weighted in favour of government that it could never produce a satisfactory result. This recommendation was never implemented, and treaty-making was instead transferred from imperial authorities to colonial governments in ensuing years.

Symptomatic of this transfer were developments in Upper Canada in 1836, when Lieutenant-Governor Sir Francis Bond Head decided that attempts at assimilation were a mistake. Instead, he argued that the 'greatest kindness we can perform towards these Intelligent, simpleminded people is to remove and fortify them as much as possible from all Communication with the Whites' (Dickason, 2002: 211). Head subsequently engineered the cession of 3 million acres of land by the Ojibwa in return for

a promise that Manitoulin Island and its adjacent islands would be protected as Aboriginal territory. The Ojibwa knew full well that the deal was a bad one, but reasoned that if they did not agree they might lose everything. For all the First Nations, the reverberations of extensive settlement could be felt at long distances from the actual European presence, and settlement was inexorably coming to the west as well as to the east.

Thousands of blacks flocked to Upper Canada between 1820 and 1860. Some were slaves seeking freedom, for it was well known in the United States that slavery was illegal in British America. By and large, the Upper Canadian authorities protected slaves who made their way into the province. After 1830, an increasing level of organization moved fugitive blacks from the United States. One key development was that of the 'Underground Railroad'. This was, of course, not a railroad at all, but a complex network of organizations, people—black and white, male and female—and safe houses through which black fugitives were smuggled northward and eventually across the border. Fugitive slaves were joined by thousands of freed northern blacks seeking a better life in British America. Many of the freed blacks were active in abolitionist activities and in the Underground Railroad. Harriet Tubman (1820–1913, known as 'Moses') made a number of trips into slave territory from her home in St Catharines, rescuing as many as 300 slaves over the course of her career. Unfortunately, all blacks faced prejudice and social disadvantage in their new land. They were granted civil liberty but were never really made to feel at home. The Reverend Thomas Kinnard, a Toronto-based abolitionist and former slave, wrote in 1863, 'If freedom is established in the United States, there will be one great black streak, reaching from here to the uttermost parts of the South' (quoted in Prince, 2009: 217). As he predicted, many blacks returned to the United States after the Emancipation Proclamation of 1863.

Religion and Education

The privileged elites were supported by the clergy of the established church, the Church of England, as well as by the Church of Scotland and the Roman Catholic Church. All these churches taught

Peter Jones

Peter Jones (Kahkewaquonaby). Peter Jones Collection, Victoria University Library (Toronto).

Peter Jones ('Kahkewaquonaby' or 'sacred feathers' in Ojibwa, 'Desagondensta' or 'he stands people on their feet' in Mohawk, 1802–56) was born near Burlington, Upper Canada, the son of a retired English surveyor and a Mississauga chief's daughter. He was brought up among the Mississaugas and then sent to school by his father, where he was called Peter Jones and acquired English. His father remarried a prominent Mohawk and Peter was adopted into a Mohawk family. Peter was converted to the Methodist Episcopal Church at a camp meeting in Ancaster in 1823, and he led a group of Mississauga Indians—including many of his own family—to a mission village on the Credit River in 1826. The village began farming successfully and had nearly 1,000 acres cleared by the 1830s.

Peter became a trial preacher in 1827 and in 1829 was elected one of the chiefs of this band. He went on circuit to raise money for mission activities, much of it for his own people. He and his brother John (who was for years his faithful assistant) refused at one point to join the Anglicans, despite a tempting offer to do so from Archdeacon John Strachan. Jones toured the United States in 1829 and in 1831 toured Britain, usually appearing in 'Indian' garb, where he had an audience with the King and met his future wife, Eliza Field, who came to Canada and assisted her husband in his missionary work. Jones was ordained in the Methodist Church in 1833. Jones and his people successfully refused to join other Ojibwa bands in removing to Manitoulin Island in the late 1830s, but some of the Credit people objected to the complete loss of Native identity that Jones preached. In the 1840s he lost much of his energy, and even confessed to his wife—on his third British missionary tour, in 1845—'I am getting heartily tired of begging.'

Jones also objected to posing as an Indian when at heart he felt himself to be totally Europeanized. Several years later he was able to lead 200 of his people to new land on the Grand River at New Credit. His health continued to deteriorate, but he spent his last years residing in a handsome brick Georgian villa constructed for him not far from Brantford. His funeral was quite spectacular, and after his death his wife edited his diaries and his historical papers for publication. He had published many sermons and speeches during his lifetime. Much of his most important work, however, was done in translating scripture and hymns into Ojibwa. Jones assisted his people to survive by adapting to European ways, but he appears to have paid a heavy psychological price for his own efforts to remain within both the Aboriginal and European worlds.

the doctrine of subordination to rightful authority. Those not associated with these churches found the pretensions of the ecclesiastical establishment,

particularly in maintaining such traditional monopolies as marriage rites and education, constant irritants that could be associated with the oligarchic constitutional system. Dissenters chafed under arrangements that granted 'liberty of conscience' to all Christians while denying them full powers to act in such matters as the solemnization of marriage. The Church of England fought an unsuccessful rearguard action to maintain its pretense to monopoly.

In Lower Canada, the Catholic Church solidified its position within the political structure, especially under Bishop Joseph-Octave Plessis (1763–1825, bishop and archbishop, 1806–25), who was appointed to the province's legislative council in 1817. Plessis presided over the devolution of the Church in British America. In 1819 Rome elevated him to an archbishopric at the same time that it created new dioceses in Upper Canada and Prince Edward Island, both headed by Highland Scots. Plessis was not himself an ultramontanist. He did not believe that the Church, although the guardian of moral law, must be heeded in all matters relating to politics. But he did attempt, with some success, to strengthen the structure of his Church by educating more clergy, by obtaining government recognition of its legal position (especially in Lower Canada), and by reforming its far-flung governance. His successors were more sympathetic to the pretensions of Rome than Plessis had been.

Dissenters in every colony not only chafed at the conservative social vision of the established churches and their support of hierarchy and privilege but also objected to the view of God they promulgated. The most numerous dissenters were Methodists and their itinerant preachers, although the Baptists also had a considerable following. Most dissenters were evangelicals who believed that God had to be experienced emotionally and spiritually rather than comprehended rationally. This awareness was 'awakened' at revivals and at the Methodist 'camp meetings that were so common in Upper Canada. The evangelicals were not only passionate but also populist in their attitude. For many in the establishment, passionate populism was viewed as tantamount to revolution. Education was another area of conflict between establishment privileges and the needs of an expanding population. The Church of England attempted to insist that it alone was entitled to the revenue from Crown lands set aside for the support of a Protestant clergy. It also tried to maintain close control over the institutions of higher education—universities, colleges, and academies—on the grounds that such education had to involve moral as well as technical knowledge. Only a relative handful of students had places at these institutions. For the authorities, education was seen as necessary for social order. For the common folk, it represented a means of mobility and liberation. Systems of education brought to the colonies after 1815 were based on teaching the older children, who in turn passed their lessons by rote to the younger. Only towards the end of the period was there much demand for broadly based public education. The curricula of such schools as existed were extremely eclectic. Despite the absence of regular schooling in most provinces, the population was surprisingly literate. Immigrants brought with them their educational experiences in England, Ireland, Scotland, or America. These experiences often were coloured by a substantial class bias as well as by ethnic and denominational ones.

Colonial Culture

Before 1840 the schools were not yet the bearers of the cultural aspirations of the resource society of British America. While a common stereotype identifies this period as one of extremely limited and primitive cultural and artistic production—particularly by European or American standards—such a view reflects a particular set of assumptions about culture. Locally based high culture was understandably rare. Foreign models were usually employed. There was, however, a substantial folk culture, which included a well-established oral tradition, in the form of tales and songs, handed down from generation to generation and from group to group. There was also a tradition of craftsmanship. The simple pine furniture of clean, uncluttered, functional lines produced by hundreds of anonymous craftsmen during the colonial period found little favour in succeeding generations, which regarded heavy ornamentation and the use of highly polished wood veneers as exemplary. But today we recognize that the aesthetic values of those anonymous furniture-makers were on a level with their high craftsmanship.

Most high culture was produced by people who made their living in some other way, and who often regarded their artistic activity as diversion or by-product rather than conscious art or professional activity. The majority of the producers of elite culture—like most of the elite of this period—were born abroad. Of the 538 people given entries in Volume VII of the *Dictionary of Canadian Biography*, covering those who died between 1835 and 1850, fewer than 200 were born in the colonies, and most of these were born in Lower Canada. Young people educated in British America were usually trained by those who were educated abroad, usually with emphasis on slavish reproduction of both form and content. Some respectable work was done within these constraints.

In literature, John Richardson (1796–1852) produced one unusual novel, *Wacousta, or, The Prophecy*, published anonymously in London and Edinburgh in 1832. Thomas McCulloch (1776–1843) had a literary success with short sketches, *The Letters of Mephibosheth Stepsure*, originally published in a newspaper and not collected in book form until 1960. Thomas Chandler Haliburton (1796–1865) wrote 21 sketches about Sam Slick in 1835–6, which became *The Clockmaker; or The Sayings and Doings of Samuel Slick of Slickville*. Haliburton went on to become an international best-selling writer. Both McCulloch and Haliburton produced their best work for a local colonial audience. When they wrote for international markets, they were less imaginative and inventive.

Another interesting development of this period was the emergence of middle-class female authors, often recent immigrants, who portrayed the colonial scene in their works. The first novel by a native

Foreign models of high culture were generally employed in the early nineteenth century, such as social dances, common in England and France. 'Dance in the Château St. Louis', by George Heriot, 1801. Library and Archives Canada, Acc. No. 1989-472-1.

British American—*St Ursula's Convent; or, The Nun in Canada*, published in Kingston in 1824—was written by Julia Catherine Hart (1796–1867), née Julia Beckwith, of Fredericton, New Brunswick. Nearly 150 subscribers paid 9s 4d for copies of the two-volume work. Hart published several other novels, all of which were characterized by unrealistic, often fantastic, plots and settings. In *St Ursula's Convent* she tapped a rich vein of Protestant suspicion of what Catholics 'got up to' in convents, although her tale was more of melodrama than of immorality.

The Strickland sisters—Catharine Parr Traill (1802–99) and Susanna Moodie (1803–85)—were more polished writers, and each sister wrote a work based on her experiences as an immigrant in Canada that is now a classic (Gray, 1999).

Traill's *The Backwoods of Canada* (London, 1836) is made of 18 letters home to family and friends in Suffolk. It is a sensitive early account of the pioneer experience. Never complaining, she left readers with an overall impression of cheerful adaptation to the rigours of life in a previously unsettled area of Upper Canada, where she willingly made do with whatever was at hand. Upper Canada itself, however, is portrayed as a land 'with no historical associations, no legendary tales of those that came before', and the impenetrable forest all around her is 'desolate', 'interminable', 'a maze'. It simultaneously isolates and liberates the author. Susanna Moodie's *Roughing It in the Bush: or, Forest Life in Canada* (1852) is the best-known of a number of works by Moodie that offer trenchant (and often discouraging) descriptions of the pioneering experience. Moodie was particularly good at the satirical description of the customs of the average immigrant, customs such as the 'bee' and the 'charivari'.

Another successful writer was Anna Brownell Jameson (1794–1860). More willing to flout the gender rules of her society than most females, Jameson was a frequently published author in 1825 when she married the lawyer Robert Jameson. She did not initially accompany her husband to Dominica or to Upper Canada when he received judicial appointments in the colonies, but joined him temporarily in 1836 as she attempted to negotiate a legal separation. While in Canada she travelled extensively, and the result of her journeys was the book *Winter Tales*

and Summer Rambles in Canada (1838). Jameson deliberately set out to relate her adventures from both a personal and a feminist point of view. As she records under the date of 13 March 1837, 'In these days when society is becoming every day more artificial and complex, and marriage, as the gentlemen assure us, more and more expensive, hazardous and inexpedient, women *must* find means to fill up the void of existence' (quoted in Gerry, 1990–1: 37). Most women from the elite classes did not attempt to publish their literary efforts, but instead composed lengthy and fascinating letters to friends and family or kept diaries that remained in family papers and have only in recent years been read and published.

In the non-literary arts, the official culture of British America was derivative and unadventurous. Painters inevitably emphasized European styles and techniques, which were sometimes acquired from working with established masters, and the market had little interest in anything else. Within this tradition a few fine painters emerged, such as William Berczy (1744–1813), Louis Dulongpré, and Joseph Légaré (1796–1855). In architecture, Late Georgian style predominated. It was not only what architects and craftsmen knew, it symbolized British authority and epitomized British standards.

Rather more interesting developments were occurring in the vernacular culture of the common people, which tended to be oral rather than written, traditional rather than imitative, and often connected either with artisan conventions or with religious energy. For all inhabitants of British America, singing religious hymns and secular songs was an important part of their lives. People sang as they worked in the fields, the voyageurs sang as they paddled their canoes, and fishermen sang as they pulled up their nets. Most of what was sung was inherited from Europe, although both music and lyrics were frequently altered by time and new circumstances. Many pioneers sprang from ethnic backgrounds in which the bard, a combination of poet and songster, represented important folk memory. Gaelic-speaking bards from the Highlands of Scotland not only carried on the tradition in British America but extended it. A rich heritage of crafting in wood produced not only furniture and useful ornamentation (such as the weather vane), but the sailing ship, a monument to

Thomas Chandler Haliburton's
The Clockmaker

In 1835–6 Thomas Chandler Haliburton wrote 21 sketches entitled 'Recollections of Nova Scotia' that appeared in Joseph Howe's *Novascotian*. They proved so popular that Howe brought them out as *The Clockmaker, or The sayings and doings of Samuel Slick of Slickville* (First ser., Halifax, 1836).

Now I find—here his lecture on 'soft sawder' was cut short by the entrance of Mrs. Flint. What, have you sold all your clocks? yes, and very low, too, for money is scarce, and I wished to close the concern; no, I am wrong in saying all, for I have just one left. Neighbor Steel's wife asked to have the refusal of it, but I guess I wont sell it; I had but two of them, this one and the feller of it, that I sold Governor Lincoln. General Green, the Secretary of State for Maine, said he'd give me 40 dollars for this one here—it has composition wheels and patent axles, it is a beautiful article—a real first chop—no mistake, genuine superfine, but I guess I'll take it back; and beside, Squire Hawk might think kinder harder; that I did not give him the offer. Dear me, said Mrs. Flint, I should like to see it, where is it? It is in a chest of mine over the way at Tom Tape's store, I guess he can ship it on to Eastport. That's a good man, said Mrs. Flint, jist let's look at it. Mr. Slick, willing to oblige, yielded to these entreaties, and soon produced the clock—a gawdy, highly varnished trumpery looking affair. He placed it on the chimney piece, where its beauties were pointed out and duly appreciated by Mrs. Flint, whose admiration was about ending in a proposal, when Mr. Flint returned from giving his directions about the care of the horses. The deacon praised the clock, he too thought it a handsome one; but the deacon was a prudent man, he had a watch, he was sorry, but he had no occasion for a clock. I guess you're in the wrong furrow this time, deacon, it ant for sale said Mr. Slick—and if it was, I reckon neighbor Steel's wife would have it, for she gives me no peace about it. Mrs. Flint said, that Mr. Steel had enough to do, poor man, to pay

his interest, without buying clocks for his wife. It's no concarn of mine, said Mr. Slick, as long as he pays me, what he has to do, but I guess I don't want to sell it, and beside it comes too high; that clock can't be made at Rhode Island under 40 dollars. Why it aint possible, said the Clock maker in apparent surprise, looking at his watch, why I'm alive it is 4 o'clock, and if I hav'nt been two hours here—how on airth shall I reach River Philip tonight? I'll tell you what, Mrs. Flint, I'll leave the clock in your care till I return on my way to the States—I'll set it a going, and put it to the right time. As soon as this operation was performed, he delivered the key to the deacon with a sort of serio-comic injunction to wind the clock up every Saturday night, which Mrs. Flint said she would take care should be done, and promised to remind her husband of it, in case he should chance to forget it.

That, said the clock maker as soon as we were mounted, that I call 'human natur!' Now that clock is sold for 40 dollars—it cost me just 6 dollars and 50 cents. Mrs. Flint will never let Mrs. Steel have the refusal—nor will the deacon learn until I call for the clock, that having once indulged in the use of a superfluity, how difficult it is to give it up. We can do without any article of luxury we have never had, but when once obtained, it is not 'in human natur' to surrender it voluntarily. Of fifteen thousand sold by myself and partners in the Province, twelve thousand were left in this manner, and only ten clocks were ever returned—when we called for them they invariably bought them. We trust to soft sawder to get them into the house, and to 'human natur' that they never come out of it.

Source: George L. Parker, ed., *The Clockmaker Series One, Two and Three* (Ottawa: Carleton University Press, 1995), 15–16.

the skills of carpenters and builders. Popular culture suggested some of the rich possibilities for creative adaptation. By 1840, for example, Scottish settlers familiar with the sport of curling had not only imported the game into a climate ideally suited for it but had made great strides forward in its popularization and regularization. So successful was the game that around 1840 the world's first indoor curling facility was constructed in Montreal.

The Politics of the Elite

Like the culture, the politics of the resource society were in flux. By 1820 the governments of the various provinces of British America were becoming well ensconced in power. The pattern was a fairly standard one, even for Newfoundland, which still did not have representative government and would not acquire it until 1832. Each colonial government was headed by a governor (or lieutenant-governor). Appointed in England, he was often a military man. No figureheads, governors of this period had considerable power and autonomy. The governor administered the province in association with the principal office-holders—also imperial appointments, although sometimes colonials were appointed—who, with the prominent merchants, comprised his council or councils. The resultant oligarchies were given various derisive labels. In Upper Canada there was the 'Family Compact', in Lower Canada the 'Château Clique', in Nova Scotia the 'System', and in Prince Edward Island 'the Cabal'. As administrations, these groups were not necessarily unenlightened Tories. They believed in the need to increase the prosperity of their colonies and usually attempted to mediate among the conflicting interests that emerged, provided they remained

'The Woolsey Family', William Berczy, 1809, oil on canvas. If the sitters in this portrait look oddly detached from one another, the reason is that the artist drew each one separately. Once all the figures had been transferred to the canvas, he painted in the background around them. National Gallery of Canada, Ottawa, 5875. © National Gallery of Canada, 5875.

orderly. Most of the oligarchies favoured government intervention in the economy, particularly through the creation of new infrastructure such as banks, roads, and canals. Not all members of the official factions in English-speaking colonies belonged to the Church of England, and not all members of the government in Lower Canada were Anglos. Under pressure from the Colonial Office, they surrendered the revenues in dispute between the assemblies and themselves, particularly those from the sale and lease of Crown lands. The popularly elected assembly, which comprised one part of the legislative system that also included the council (or in some provinces, a separate legislative council), had a very limited role in the process of government. In 1820 the assemblies did not yet have control of the revenue or finances of the provinces, much less any real involvement in their administration, although they gained control over more revenue in the 1830s.

Under this constitutional arrangement, political conflict could take a number of forms. One involved disagreement between the governor and the oligarchy that comprised the provincial administration. This could come about either because the governor was expected to implement unpopular instructions from the mother country, or because he sought to limit the self-perpetuating power of the oligarchs. More frequently after 1820, the conflict involved a fierce struggle between the administration and the leaders of an assembly eager to expand its prerogatives and authority. A new generation of political leaders emerged who were willing to invoke popular support on behalf of their attacks on the prevailing governments. Reform was no more monolithic than the oligarchies. It broke into several main camps with much overlap among them. One group of reformers represented the radicals, the other consisted of various factions with more moderate voices

'Curling on the lake near Halifax', c. 1867, from Lt Henry Buckton Laurence, *Sketches of Canadian Sports and Pastimes* (London, 1870). LAC (W.H. Coverdale Collection of Canadiana), C-041092.

who extolled the glories of the English Constitution and its supposed entrenchment of British rights and liberties. Moderate reformers did not wish to eliminate the imperial connection, but instead wanted to employ it to obtain a colonial constitution that more closely resembled what they thought was that of the mother country. Many of the members of the evangelical sects so critical of the Church of England were former Americans, and they would play a prominent role in the rebellions of 1837 and 1838. Four reformers stand out in this period: William Lyon Mackenzie (1795–1861) of Upper Canada, Louis-Joseph Papineau (1786–1871) of Lower Canada, Joseph Howe (1804–73) of Nova Scotia, and William Cooper (1786–1867) of Prince Edward Island. None of these men actually overturned the political system, but each did make some inroads against it, anticipating in a variety of ways a gradual democratization of politics in British America.

William Lyon Mackenzie, 1834, by an unknown artist; lithograph published in *Canadiana Military Events*, III, 337. LAC, C-24937.

All four reformers (and others) sounded radical in their rhetoric. All believed in the importance of the 'independent cultivator of the soil', displaying profound hostility to commerce, the merchant classes, and expensive economic development by the public sector (quoted in Halpenny, 1976: 156). Equality of conditions and opportunity was what mattered. William Cooper sought this equality through 'escheat', a process by which the large landholders of Prince Edward Island would be stripped of their ill-gotten holdings and the land redistributed to those who actually tilled the soil. In the 1830s both Papineau and Mackenzie turned to the American ideas of Jacksonian democracy when they found themselves unable either to persuade the British government of the inadequacy of existing constitutional arrangements or to alter the system by political activity. These reformers wanted to overturn the corrupt oligarchies that ran their respective provinces and replace them with administrations that would be responsible to the province as represented in the elected Houses of Assembly. They could also agree, as a result of their agrarian and anti-commercial assumptions, that public 'improvements' paid for by the public purse or sponsored by the government (such as canals and banks) represented an unnecessary financial burden on the taxpayer, being in effect 'class legislation'. As Mackenzie argued, the 'true source of a country's wealth' was 'labour usefully and prudently applied' (quoted in Fairley, 1960: 217). For Papineau in Lower Canada, an active economic state was being dominated not only by a mercantile class but by a British mercantile class, which promoted capitalism.

It is in the context of the struggle between commercial capitalism and agrarian idealism that we must understand both the Tory commitment to public involvement in economic activity and the reform opposition. These political reformers had no conception that economic development could be directed by government on behalf of the people, any more than they had a general conception of any positive role for the state in ensuring the social well-being of its citizenry. They were instead typical nineteenth-century liberal democrats who sought to reduce (rather than to increase) the influence of government on the lives of the population, as well as to limit the temptation of special privilege. As Mackenzie put it in a broadside entitled 'Independence' in late November 1837, 'We contend, that in all laws made, or to be made, every person shall be bound alike—neither should any tenure, estate, charter, degree, birth or place, confer any exemption from the ordinary course of legal proceedings and responsibilities whereunto others are subjected' (quoted in Fairley, 1960: 223).

Reform and Rebellion

Eventually, in 1837, the frustration of the reformers in the Canadas led to rebellion. Political violence was hardly new in 1837; it was endemic throughout this era. Though sometimes spontaneous, it could also be carefully calculated for partisan purposes. The mob was the political expression of the ordinary inhabitant, who was not usually at the centre of politics in this period. The difference in 1837 was the attempt to co-ordinate large-scale violence to overthrow the governments of the Canadas by force. The uprisings can be viewed in a variety of ways: as political events, as cultural manifestations, as examples of subterranean pressures resulting from agrarian discontent, or, in Lower Canada, as an expression of Anglo–French animosity. They were a combination of all these things. Had the rebellions not been

Joseph Howe

Joseph Howe (1804–73) was the son of a Halifax Loyalist printer, largely self-educated, who had entered the family firm and then began publishing his own newspaper, the *Novascotian*, in 1828. His paper increasingly pressed for political reform, and Howe was acquitted of criminal libel in 1835. This persecution encouraged him to enter politics in 1836 as a Reformer, and it was his government that in 1847 achieved responsible government. In 1855 he helped recruit in the United States for the Crimean War, making comments that cost him the Catholic vote in his province in 1857. He became premier again (1860–3), then imperial fishery commissioner (1863–6).

Although the young Howe had visions of a unified British America, the mature politician did not want Nova Scotia to become absorbed into Canadian expansion. Thus, Howe led the anti-confederate forces in Nova Scotia, focusing in 1866 particularly on the failure of the Tupper government to submit the question to an election. He led an anti-confederate party to success in the first dominion elections, but was unable to effect repeal in Ottawa and entered the federal cabinet in 1869. Howe was famed as one of the great orators of nineteenth-century Canada.

Joseph Howe in later life, 1871. LAC, C-22002.

Louis-Joseph Papineau

Louis-Joseph Papineau (1786–1871) was the son of a Montreal notary who purchased the seigneury of Petite-Nation from the Quebec seminary in 1802. He was educated at the Petit Séminaire and then trained as a lawyer.

In 1809 Papineau was first elected to the legislative assembly of Lower Canada, beginning an association of nearly 50 years with that body. He joined the Parti Canadien at the outset and was chosen speaker of the House in 1815. As leader of that party and its successor, the Parti Patriote, after 1826, he advocated political reform that would leave the traditional social system intact. Papineau was simultaneously a democrat and a social conservative suspicious of the economic and social transformations occurring in his province.

Over the years his commitment to British institutions decreased, and he became more attracted to the American model of Jacksonian democracy, which sought to eliminate political privilege without radical social change. Papineau's commitment to the survival of beleaguered French Canada also increased. He did not instigate the popular rebellion of 1837, but he did try (with limited success) to become its leader. His inability to lead the rebellion was intimately connected with his inability to understand the aspirations of the rebels. When threatened with arrest he fled to the United States, and he played little part in the renewal of insurrection in 1838. He spent some years in exile in France, returning to Canada in 1845 and to politics in 1848.

Louis-Joseph Papineau, lithograph by Antoine Maurin. LAC, C-5435.

so quickly and brutally suppressed, similar uprisings might well have broken out in the lower provinces, particularly in Prince Edward Island, where agrarian and political discontents were strong.

On one level the rebellions of 1837 were unsuccessful challenges to the stability of the urban elite political cultures of the Canadas. Their ostensible leaders, William Lyon Mackenzie and Louis-Joseph Papineau, had become totally frustrated in their attempts to wrest control of the government from the hands of the powerful cliques of Toronto and Quebec and put it in the hands of the popularly elected assemblies. Part of the frustration, particularly for Mackenzie, was that the assemblies themselves could be manipulated by the oligarchy. The so-called 'popular parties' in the assemblies of the colonies were in large part dominated by members of regional elites who were more representative of the grassroots countryside. The regional elites wanted a more open political culture. If home rule was one ambition of the reformers, the expansion of politics beyond the ranks of the governing elite (and their kin) was another. In this sense the rebellions marked the first of a series of movements in Canadian history to decentralize authority and political power. On another level, in both Canadas there was a popular resistance, mainly agrarian in origin, which was more interested in economic grievances, class issues, and land reform, particularly of the seigneurial system. The two resistances came more or less together in 1837, first in Lower Canada and then in Upper Canada. That they did not cooperate more closely was partly because politics in Lower Canada was by 1837 conducted mainly along ethnic lines. The Parti Patriote had lost most of its

Charles Duncombe to Robert David Burford

Charles Duncombe (1792–1867) was born in Connecticut, and came to Upper Canada after graduation from medical school in 1819. By 1830 he had a flourishing medical practice in Burford, Upper Canada, and was first elected to the legislative assembly in that year.

24 October 1837

Your favor of the 17th instant has this moment come to hand, in which you say that the time has come when reformers ought to be on the alert in forming political unions and in organizing for our common safety;

I heartily concur with you that it is high time for the reformers to be up and doing. When Sir Francis Head declares that the British Government never intended any such absurdity as giving us the British Constitution, (of course we are to continue to be governed by the Oligarchy of Toronto,) And when the doors of the Colonial Office are closed against reformers (or republicans as Sir Francis Head tauntingly styles us;) because we are guilty of the crime of appealing to His Majestys Government with our Complaints, and when we see [the] Province under the dynasty of a foreign Governor and an Orange Oligarchy, retrograding in one year as much as it had advanced in five, the only interest our oppressors have in the Province being the plunder they can amass and take away with them; I think any one not willfully blind, not interested in the continuation of the abuses, must see, that while this baneful domination continues we have not the slightest chance for prosperity and that if we will be well governed we must govern ourselves; Our oppressors have shown us more clearly than ever before, that their great object is to make the rich richer and the poor poorer, for if the people should become wealthy they would become intelligent and unwilling slaves; my maxim has always been educate the people, this can now be done only upon a few matters upon politics[;] we may do much by 'the assembling our selves together' and hearing political lectures, by the forming political unions, publishing periodicals and encouraging the circulation of reform news-papers—this can be best done by union and by our devoting the few pence we save from our grog bills to the purchase of correct information upon the subject of our own affairs—and the time formerly spent in drinking to reading and reflection; I shall be most happy to meet with you any time next week (as I have heard that there is to be a reform meeting in Oakland one day next week but have not heard what day)—and I must (God willing) be there; . . . I hope when you appoint the time you will let me know as the time has come when we are to decide whether we will be bondsmen or slaves— the reformers of Westminister have done nobly; your name I see among the immortal patriots who feel the oppressor's iron rod; thank God we are strong in the justice of our cause, and although we may suffer for a time, we shall assuredly in the end prevail; 'A nation never can rebel' those only are rebels who resist the will of the people; from them (the people) emenates all legitimate, constitutional government.

Source: Colin Read and Ronald Stagg, eds, *The Rebellion of 1837 in Upper Canada: A Collection of Documents* (Toronto: Champlain Society, 1985), 88–9. Reprinted by permission of the publisher.

British supporters, and one of its goals was a government—if not a state—with a *Canadien* majority.

In Lower Canada, the Parti Canadien and its successor, the Parti Patriote, more consistently dominated the lower house than had the reformers in Upper Canada. The reason was that the party conflict in Lower Canada had long since taken on racial overtones. The Parti Canadien was dominated by French-Canadian professionals who represented the regional elites and who had no hope of gaining admission to the ruling Château Clique. In February 1834, the Ninety-Two Resolutions, prepared by Papineau and three others, were adopted by the assembly of Lower Canada and submitted to London. They catalogued grievances and requests, among them the legislature's control of revenue, the executive's responsibility to the electorate, and the election of legislative councillors. These resolutions were in effect rejected by the British Parliament in March 1837, and the way was opened for rebellion.

The Battle of St Denis

The battle of St Denis was one of those accidental battles that have occurred in Canadian history—Seven Oaks in 1816 was another—when opposing forces meet by surprise and inflict damage upon one another. St Denis was a small village northeast of Montreal—it had less than 100 houses. But the village had a reputation as a centre of political agitation of assembly member Louis Bourdages, a loose cannon of reform since his support of Pierre-Stanislas Bédard in the early years of the century, and the 'hot Reformer' Wolfred Nelson.

Nelson was a member of a prominent Loyalist family who had married an aristocratic French Canadian and had converted totally to the Catholic and French-Canadian side, declaring himself (as his daughter said) a supporter of 'an oppressed race, which was not his own, but which he loved'. Nelson had organized a protest meeting in St Denis in the summer of 1837 and, subsequently, in September had led the Patriotes in a well-orchestrated demonstration against the government, hanging a number of public officials in effigy in the public square. Like many communities in Lower Canada, the families of St Denis, especially those with French–English marriage alliances, were divided in political terms. When one local widow (Madame Saint-Jacques) was critical of the September demonstration, Nelson produced a charivari against her which turned nasty when the inhabitants of the besieged house fired on the crowd and killed one of its members.

The authorities knew that conditions were inflammatory in the villages along the Richelieu, and a Patriote assembly at St Charles had heard extreme rhetoric from Papineau and Nelson. Fears of government action against the Patriote leaders led Papineau and his assistant, Dr E.B. O'Callaghan, to take refuge in St Denis with Wolfred Nelson. The Patriotes seized a strongbox from the parish church and stored it away, then the leaders met in Nelson's home, soon joined by men from all over the province. Conditions became tense as everyone waited for the authorities to act.

Sir John Colborne, the commander of the army, determined to bring one brigade from Sorel to St Denis and another to the village from Chambly, hoping to catch the rebel leaders in a pincer movement and to arrest them. The troop movements, led by Colonel Charles Gore on the night of 22 November, were carried out in the midst of a heavy storm. The rebels knew the troops were coming, and determined to fight. Papineau was advised to move out of the village so he could negotiate a settlement, but he said, 'since today the wine is poured, it is fitting that I drink it.' The orders to the rebel forces were not to fire first. The insurgents fortified a local hat factory. As one of the government columns of regular soldiers marched near the village, sharpshooters began firing. One of these sharpshooters later said, 'I fired without remorse. It was not so much from a sentiment of insults and injustices, but

Part of the reason for the ineffectuality of the rebellions was that there was little relationship between the reform leaders—who were operating within the elite system even while trying to change it—and popular opinion, which was responding to the economic collapse of the international wheat market in the mid-1830s. Both Mackenzie and Papineau persistently denied that they had planned an insurrection, although they were prepared to lead one when it emerged. Rural districts had been restive for several years in both provinces, and some protest meetings held in 1837 were attended by armed farmers. A rural uprising near Brantford, Upper Canada, led by Dr Charles Duncombe (1792–1867), dispersed on 13 December when he heard of the easy defeat of Mackenzie's motley crew of rebels at Montgomery's Tavern north of Toronto. Certainly the rural districts in Lower Canada provided their own rationale and impetus for rising in arms against the government. When political agitation turned to

the old instinct of traditional hatred of the races that awoke in us.' A British officer, who had earlier blundered into the village and had been captured, was killed in the midst of a melee. After hours of aimless shooting with a remarkably small number of casualties, eventually the British determined to withdraw, leaving their cannon behind.

After the battle, it transpired that 12 Patriotes had died, while the British counted six dead and six missing. The authorities blamed the loss on bad weather and bad leadership by Colonel Charles Gore, although it is clear that the Patriotes were successful fighters both at St Denis and elsewhere. Nonetheless, St Denis was the only Patriote victory in 1837.

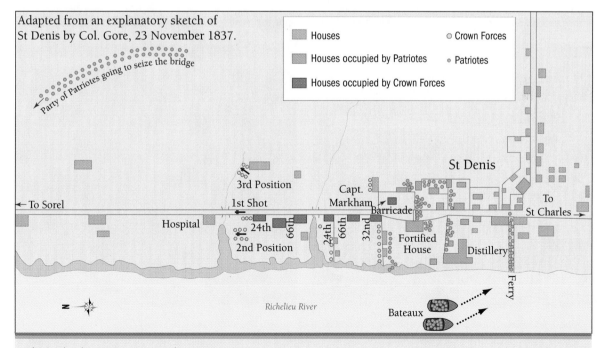

The Battle of St Denis, 23 November 1837.

Source: Based on an illustration by W. Constable. From the Battle of St Denis, by Elinor Kyte Senior, 1990, p. 25. © Canadian War Museum.

insurrection, many moderate members of the elite leadership of the reformers fell away, to be replaced by armed and angry farmers.

Unfortunately for the rebels in both the Canadas, their self-declared leaders had a fairly narrow agenda of political change and little notion of how to turn a spontaneous uprising into an organized rebellion. Mackenzie, Papineau, and Duncombe all became caught up in their own hysteria, panicked, and fled to leave others to face the music. Among these others was Samuel Lount (1791–1838), who first came to Upper Canada with his family in 1811 and later settled in Whitchurch Township in Simcoe County in 1815. Trained as a blacksmith, he was a typical Yankee 'jack of all trades'—besides shoeing horses and iron work, he was a woodsman, farmer, and businessman.

In 1834 he was elected to the legislative assembly and fell in with the reformers, but he attributed his defeat in 1836 to the corrupt practices of the Tories and Sir Francis Bond Head and was soon recruited to Mackenzie's cause of overturning the government. Lount helped prepare pikes for the revolt and led a party from the Lake Simcoe area to Toronto in December 1837, although he quickly became disillusioned with the violence—he personally stopped Mackenzie from burning down the house of Sheriff William Botsford—and fled. He was captured on the Canadian side of Lake Erie in an attempt to row a small boat across the lake to safety on the American side, and subsequently was charged with treason.

Large numbers of rebels were released under the Pardoning Act (I Vic. C. 10), which was intended to

(above left) Execution of Lount and Matthews [date and artist unknown]. LAC, C-001242.

(above right) 'The Insurgents at Beauharnois, Lower Canada', 1838, watercolour by Katherine Jane Ellice (1814–64). The artist was visiting her father-in-law's seigneury at Beauharnois when it was captured by Patriote rebels on the night of 4 November. She made this sketch during the week that she and other members of the household were held hostage before British troops arrived to free them and set fire to the village. The next day, Ellice recorded in her diary that the fire was 'still burning; women and children flying in all directions. Such are the melancholy consequences of civil war.' LAC, C-013392.

Southwestern Lower Canada in 1837, showing the region of Lower Canada in which the major fighting of the 1837 rebellion occurred. Villages are indicated by dots. The battles, mainly the result of local rural uprisings, are marked with crossed swords. Based on a map from A.D. Decelles's *The Patriotes of '37: A Chronicle of the Lower Canadian Rebellion* (1916).

meet the injunctions of the British government to be as lenient as possible with the rebels while also providing a form of summary justice that avoided contentious jury trials—in order to be eligible for a pardon the accused rebel had to confess his crimes. Still, the Tories wanted the leading culprits punished, and Lount was the biggest fish the government had managed to find who was still in the country. His confession under the Pardoning Act effectively signed his own death warrant, for an innocent plea was hardly credible thereafter. Despite the petition of thousands of Upper Canadians on

Historic Sites

1. Saint-Denis, Quebec: A cairn marks the site of Maison Saint Germain, where Patriotes fought the British regulars on 23 November 1937.
2. Saint-Eustache, Quebec: Saint-Eustache Church, at 123 St-Louis Street, was the site of a battle on 14 December 1837, where 250 Patriotes attempted unsuccessfully to hold off nearly 2,000 British soldiers. The church was virtually destroyed by cannon and fire in the battle, and has been extensively rebuilt.
3. Montebello, Quebec: Here is the Manoir Papineau National Historic Site, encompassing the seigneury on the Ottawa River of Louis-Joseph Papineau, including his stone house and chapel.
4. Prescott, Ontario: Fort Wellington National Historic Park contains the 66-foot stone tower built as a windmill and captured by 'Patriot Hunters' on 12 November 1838 at the Battle of the Windmill.
5. Toronto, Ontario: The Toronto Necropolis, at 200 Winchester Street, is the final resting place of William Lyon Mackenzie and Samuel Lount and contains a 20-foot granite monument to Samuel Lount and Peter Matthews. The monument has a broken peak, symbolizing life cut short.
6. Scotland, Ontario: At the corner of Talbot and Simcoe streets is a plaque marking the spot where Charles Duncombe rallied 'the Patriots' in 1837.

his behalf and admission by government members that he was hardly the worst offender or real ringleader, Lount and a fellow prisoner, Peter Matthews, were executed on 12 April 1838 in the courtyard of the Toronto jail. His property was then confiscated. British justice had been served.

More justice remained to be meted out, especially after a second uprising in Lower Canada in November 1838, which was brutally suppressed by the authorities. As in the earlier rebellion, the government allowed the leaders to escape and went instead after the rank and file. This time 753 men were captured and 108 brought to court martial, resulting in 99 death sentences. In the end, 12 were executed and 58 banished to Australia. In both Canadas the ruling elite was still very much in charge. The militia, which prided itself on having fought off the Americans in 1815, had another mark of its loyalty.

After reports of the first rebellions had reached Britain, the authorities dispatched a fact-finding commission headed by John George Lambton, Lord Durham (1792–1840). Although he did not remain long in Canada, his famous 'Report on the Affairs in British America', filed in January 1839, was a thorough and eloquent examination of the problems in Canada based on information from local reformers. Durham recommended two political solutions: the introduction of responsible government and the unification of the two Canadas. He also wanted changes in land policy, including a general system for the sale of Crown land at sufficient price and the elimination of the proprietorial system in Prince Edward Island.

Conclusion

While the rebellions accomplished little more in the short run than to focus Great Britain's attention on the need for change in her American colonies, Durham's recommendations for the union of the Canadas and for responsible government were adopted over the next few years. Nevertheless, other forces would profoundly help remake British America. Free trade, railroads, economic expansion, and industrialization were, in the end, more powerful engines of change than either political uprisings or constitutional reform.

How History Has Changed

Emigration and Immigration

In some ways, the history of immigration and settlement in early Canada has not changed very much over the years. The overall story told in older works is still recognizable in the twenty-first century, although, as in so many other areas, we could use a new synthesis. While the old works are still relevant, constant revision has occurred in important but scattered parts of the story. The older works are much more important for telling us about government policy than about immigrant decision-making, for example.

One of the most important questions for students of transatlantic movement has always been whether to concentrate on 'emigration'—the process of leaving the homeland—or 'immigration'—the process of coming to a new land and adapting to it. The traditional tendency had been for historians based in Europe to treat the process as emigration and those in North Americans to investigate it as immigration. Traditionally, one set of scholars took the migrants to the boats, another set picked them up at the boats on the other side, and the matter of the transatlantic passage was negotiable for both sets, with its own distinct literature. By and large, the view from Europe has always been less favourable to and less enthusiastic about the transatlantic movement of population than has been the view from North America. The current trend is to recognize both sides of the Atlantic as one integrated whole; as one recent study has put it, 'Emigrant Worlds and Transatlantic Communities'.

Developments in funding and technology have made it possible for Canadians to do detailed research in the British archives, including the local study necessary to investigate carefully the origins of immigrants and then to follow them to their Canadian destinations. Along the way, Canadian scholars have made a significant contribution to understanding why it was that people sought to leave—or were pushed from—their homeland. They have helped us understand how and why these people settled where they did on the other side of the ocean. The tendency for the research to become much more microscopic has made it possible to understand and highlight new aspects of the process. Modern treatments understand the importance of the communication of information within the population likely to emigrate, particularly letters from North America and word-of-mouth linkages among family and community groups. Modern discussions appreciate the 'chain' nature of most immigration. They also understand the importance of the economic situation of the immigrant, and especially the amount of cash money he or she was able to bring to the transplantation process.

There has also in recent years been much more concentration on the cultural baggage of the immigrants and the adaptation of this culture in the new homeland. Modern Canadian scholarship on transatlantic movement, with its increasing focus on origins of immigrants as well as on destinations, has had to come to terms with the regional complexities of the British Isles. There were at least three Irelands, at least two Scotlands, at least two distinctive peoples in Wales, and a number of distinctive regions within England. In the beginning, not all of these people spoke English as their first language, and religious preferences were complex. The question of the impact of this regionalism on Canadian development is being considered in the literature now in ways that go beyond the traditional ethnic approach of 'The Scot in Canada' or 'The Irish in Ontario'. The question of the cultural identities of the immigrants from the British Isles is a complex one, not least because on one level there was an overarching British identity and on other levels a series of regional and national ones.

More attention is now being paid to the literature of immigration—particularly to the substantial number of publications purporting to give advice to prospective immigrants—and to the letters home of immigrants, both those published at the time and those unpublished until recently. Lurking under all the analysis is the question of whether immigration to British America actually fulfilled the expectations of the immigrants. Scholars are only now turning to examine the return flow of disappointed immigrants to their areas of origin, and this subject is not yet well understood.

Short Bibliography

Brown, Jennifer. *Strangers in Blood: Fur Trade Company Families in Indian Country*. Vancouver, 1980. A fascinating study of family life in the fur trade in the first half of the nineteenth century.

Cadigan, Sean T. *Hope and Deception in Conception Bay: Merchant–Settler Relations in Newfoundland 1785–1855*. Toronto, 1995. A revisionist analysis of socio-economic relations in Newfoundland, based largely on underutilized court records.

Cameron, Wendy, and Maude McDougall. *Assisting Emigration to Upper Canada: The Petworth Project 1832–7*. Montreal and Kingston, 2000. A recent account of one of the largest assisted emigration schemes of the 1830s.

Creighton, Donald. *The Empire of the St Lawrence*. Toronto, 1958. The classic study of the old mercantile system of Canada.

Errington, Elizabeth Jane. *Emigrant Worlds and Transatlantic Communities: Migration to Upper Canada in the First Half of the Nineteen Century*. Montreal and Kingston, 2007. A recent synthesis of early migration to one important colony.

Greenwood, F. Murray, and Barry Wright, eds. *Canadian State Trials, vol. 2: Rebellion and Invasion in the Canadas*. Toronto, 2002. An important collection of essays focusing on the way the law was used in the rebellions.

Greer, Allan. *The Patriots and the People: Rebellion of 1837 in Rural Lower Canada*. Toronto, 1994. An account of the Lower Canadian rebellion of 1837, focusing on the rural community and popular agitation.

Houston, Cecil, and W.J. Smyth. *Irish Emigration and Canadian Settlement: Patterns, Links, and Letters*. Toronto, 1990. A useful study of the emigration of the Irish—from both north and south—to Canada.

Johnston, Hugh. *British Emigration Policy, 1815–1830: 'Shovelling Out Paupers'*. Oxford, 1972. The standard study of British policy in the era of pauper emigration.

Lower, A.R.M. *Great Britain's Woodyard: British North America and the Timber Trade 1763–1867*. Montreal, 1973. An important analysis of British America's timber trade.

McCalla, Douglas. *Planting the Province: The Economic History of Upper Canada 1784–1870*. Toronto, 1993. An excellent synthesis of the early economic history of a critical province.

McCallum, John. *Unequal Beginnings: Agriculture and Economic Development in Quebec and Ontario until 1870*. Toronto, 1970. A controversial and revisionist study that argues Ontario enjoyed advantages over Quebec because of its agricultural beginnings.

Macdonald, Norman. *Immigration and Settlement: The Administration of the Imperial Land Regulations, 1763–1840*. Toronto, 1939. An old but useful study of land policy and immigration.

Ouellet, Fernand. *Economic and Social History of Quebec, 1760–1850: Structures and Conjunctures*. Toronto,

1985. A provocative survey by the leading scholar of French Canada in the early nineteenth century, based on European historical conceptualizations.

Read, Colin. *The Rising in Western Upper Canada, 1837–8: The Duncombe Revolt and After*. Toronto, 1983. A good corrective to the notion that William Lyon Mackenzie led the only rebellion in Upper Canada in 1837.

Sager, Eric, and L. Fischer. *Shipping and Shipbuilding in Atlantic Canada, 1820–1914*. Ottawa, 1986. An innovative study, based on a massive collaborative project funded by the Social Sciences Research Council of Canada.

Stewart, Gordon. *The Origins of Canadian Politics: A Comparative Approach*. Vancouver, 1986. A provocative survey based on American and British political models.

Warkentin, Germaine, ed. *Canadian Exploration Literature: An Anthology*. Toronto, 1993. A rich collection of what was probably the most robust writing in British America before 1850.

Wilton, Carol. *Popular Politics and Political Culture in Upper Canada, 1800–1850*. Montreal and Kingston, 2000. A study focusing on popular politics in Upper Canada.

Wynn, Graeme. *Timber Colony: A Historical Geography of Early Nineteenth Century New Brunswick*. Toronto, 1981. A richly rewarding analysis of timbering in early New Brunswick.

Study Questions

1. Why was the relationship between land policy and immigration so critical?
2. How did the British attitude towards emigration change in the first half of the nineteenth century?
3. If you were contemplating immigration to British America in the first half of the nineteenth century, what would be the most important questions that you would want answered before you made a decision?
4. How might the data on Crown lands (Table 4.1) have assisted prospective immigrants? What could prospective immigrants have concluded from these figures?
5. Identify the four staple resources in British America at this time.
6. Identify and explain the most important characteristics of the resource economy of British America between 1815 and 1840.
7. How did elite society operate in British America in the first half of the nineteenth century?
8. What were the causes of the rebellions of 1837? Were they the same in both Upper and Lower Canada? Would you have supported the rebellions?

 www.oupcanada.com/Bumsted4e

Visit the companion website for *A History of the Canadian Peoples*, fourth edition for further resources.

5

Becoming a Nation, 1840–1867

Timeline

1841 Union of Upper Canada and Lower Canada proclaimed.

1842 Webster-Ashburton Treaty resolves the New Brunswick border. Great Britain experiments with partially elected, partially appointed legislature for Newfoundland.

1843 Fort Victoria established on Vancouver Island.

1846 Oregon Boundary Treaty settles western boundary. Corn Laws and Timber duties are repealed by British Parliament. St John's, Newfoundland, is destroyed by fire.

1848 Nova Scotia gets responsible government. Lord Elgin concedes responsible government to Canada. Newfoundland reverts to an elected assembly.

1849 Vancouver Island is leased by the British to the Hudson's Bay Company and becomes a Crown colony. Rebellion Losses Bill is enacted, leading to riots in Montreal. Annexation movement flourishes.

1851 James Douglas becomes governor of Vancouver Island. Cable is laid from New Brunswick to Prince Edward Island, which receives responsible government. Colonial government takes over post offices.

1852 Grand Trunk Railway is incorporated.

1854 Reciprocity Treaty with United States is signed, to last 10 years.

1855 Petroleum is discovered in southwestern Ontario. Newfoundland receives responsible government.

1856 The first legislature meets on Vancouver Island.

1857 British Parliament holds inquiry over the future of the Northwest. Palliser and Canadian Exploring Expeditions are sent West to investigate the region. Gold is discovered on the Thompson and Fraser rivers. Ottawa is chosen by Queen Victoria as the site for the capital of the Province of Canada. Canadian legislature passes an Act for the Gradual Civilization of the Indian Tribes in the Canadas.

1858 British Columbia becomes a colony.

1859 The first steamer is launched on the Red River. First newspaper is established in Red River.

1860 Cariboo Gold Rush begins in British Columbia. Prince Edward Island Land Commission convenes. Royal Tour of Prince Albert suggests that what would become Canada is already, in some senses, a political entity.

1861 American Civil War begins. Montreal and Toronto introduce horse-drawn cars for public transportation.

1862 Cariboo Road is begun in British Columbia.

1863 First non-Native salmon fishery on the Fraser River established.

1864 Reciprocity Treaty is terminated by a vote of the American Senate, to take effect in 1866. Charlottetown and Quebec Conferences are held to discuss union of British North America.

1866 Transatlantic cable laid from Newfoundland to Europe. Union of British Columbia and Vancouver Island implemented, with Victoria as capital.

1867 The British North America Act is passed by British Parliament to take effect 1 July 1867. Emily Howard Stowe obtains a medical degree in the United States, the first woman to do so.

Interior of a lumber ship in Quebec, 1872. While politicians and settlers in central Canada concerned themselves with territorial expansion during the mid-nineteenth century, those living in the Atlantic region were constrained to the older transatlantic way of life, of which shipping was integral.
© McCord Museum I-76318.

A seamless web of political and economic expansion, beginning around 1840, brought Canadian Confederation. Between 1840 and 1871, British America became 'British North America' and changed from a collection of loosely connected colonies in the northeastern sector of the continent, heavily dependent on the mother country both economically and politically, to a transcontinental nation—at least on paper—called 'Canada' with a rapidly diversifying internal economy in the early stages of industrialization. Because the Province of Canada took the lead in national unification, the beginning of the process can be identified as the Act of Union, which joined Upper and Lower Canada in July 1840.

British Americans had witnessed many changes over the centuries since first settlement. But in terms of technology, a settler of 1640 still would have been quite at home in the Canada of 1840. The era of political unification was the first period that experienced substantial technological advances, radically altering perceptions of distance and time in a vast domain separated from Europe by thousands of miles of ocean. With the railroad, travel not only sped up substantially, it acquired a predictable timetable. The invention of telegraphy and the laying of a transatlantic cable from Newfoundland in 1866 affected the perception of time as well as of distance. By 1870 the largest telegraph company in Canada had 20,000 miles (32,000 km) of wire extended across eastern Canada. Communication could take place in seconds instead of months. The ability to operate to a schedule and communicate instantly completely altered the world and the way people operated within it. These changes were not a necessary prerequisite for union, but they were clearly part of the facilitating background. In many respects, modern Canada began not in 1867 with political unification but in the 1840s, the first era of transforming technological change.

The Mobile Society

Throughout the 1840s and 1850s British immigration to North America continued at high levels, although its makeup was now quite different. The proportion of new arrivals from southern Ireland, mainly Roman Catholic, increased and the number of those landing in British America without capital was much higher; the most impoverished were usually forced into the cities since they could not afford to obtain land. Driving immigration were the potato famines in Ireland (and to a lesser extent in Scotland), which peaked in 1846. Between 1840 and 1860 well over 600,000 British immigrants arrived in British North America, many of them seeking land on which to build a new life.

In addition to the British immigrants came large numbers of immigrants from the continent of Europe, especially from what is now Germany. Most were on their way to the United States via the route from Quebec City along the St. Lawrence or from New York to Detroit via Lake Ontario. Using either route, the newcomers passed through Canada West where they were surprised to find German speakers, mainly Mennonite farmers who had arrived as Loyalists. After a major European famine began in 1847—the eastern extension of the potato famine—the German states of southwestern Germany dispatched excess population. By the later 1850s and 1860s, numbers of Germans and Poles were deliberately recruited by the Canadian government through agents in the German states. This German population contained small numbers of Jews, who settled in a number of cities and towns in Ontario and Quebec. By the first Canadian census in 1871, there were 202,991 persons of German ethnic origin in the Dominion of Canada. This German presence has gone largely unnoticed in the ethnic history of Canada because of the two world wars fought against Germany, which led many Canadians to suppress their German ethnic background.

Combined with the natural population increase within the colonies, the arrival of this horde of new settlers put enormous pressure on available agricultural land, particularly land suitable for staple crop farming for the market. Second-generation farmers accepted less desirable land or moved to the United States, where a more rapid industrialization than in British North America had created new employment and where the West was open to settlement. Thus, at the same time as thousands of land-hungry immigrants were moving in, thousands of disillusioned members of the younger generation within the colonies were moving out.

The first sign of serious out-migration came from the seigneurial districts of French Canada, the heartland of French-Canadian culture, language, and religion. Almost any opportunity was superior to a future on a farm of less than 100 acres (40 ha) of worn-out land. Over the course of the 1830s more than 40,000 left Lower Canada for the United States, and that figure jumped to 90,000 in the 1840s and to 190,000 in the 1850s. One clergyman called this population loss 'the cemetery of the race'. The visitor to New England can still see standing, usually empty and forlorn, the extensive brick buildings that housed the nineteenth-century factories employing these migrants. Thousands of French Canadians also moved into the Eastern Townships of Canada East, originally intended as anglophone enclaves. In the Upper St Francis district of the Eastern Townships, for example, the francophone population grew from 9.7 per cent of the district in 1844 to 64.1 per cent by 1871. Others continued to fill unpopulated regions in the Laurentians and around Lac St-Jean. State and church both promoted colonization of these regions as an alternative to migration to the United States. As well as moving out of the country or into new districts, thousands of French Canadians moved into the cities and expanding towns of the province where they often found employment as manufacturing workers. In Montreal, especially, many of the newcomers were female. Some found employment as domestic servants, but most worked in a few burgeoning industries, particularly clothing manufacture, textile production, and the making of tobacco products.

In Canada West, most of the movement into the United States before 1870 was into the rich agricultural districts of the American Midwest and beyond. A constant stream of Canadians crossed Ohio, Indiana, and Illinois onto the American prairies, contributing to the rapid settlement of Minnesota and the Dakotas. A key factor driving the migrants was the inability of the family farm to accommodate the needs of all family members. Successful farming required several children, but large families also

created pressures for the expansion of landholdings and eventually led to the departure of some of the younger generation. In this male-dominated society, only males, as a rule, had expectations of inheritance; hence the tendency in all British North American rural society was to send disproportionate numbers of females (usually between the ages of 15 and 21) into the cities and non-agricultural employment. Some farms in some districts were more divisible than others, but the pressures were always strong on the younger members of the next generation to seek their fortunes elsewhere. Elder sons (and the women they married) could look forward to becoming pillars of and local leaders in their communities. For most of the children of most farmers, however, coming of age meant moving on. Some new land within Canada West was available to the north. Settlement after mid-century moved rapidly up to Georgian Bay and into the Muskoka country, heedless of the prominent rock outcroppings of the Canadian Shield. For most who chose to remain in Canada West, however, cities and towns were the obvious destinations.

The years before 1860 saw considerable internal expansion in the Atlantic region. Settlers moved on to less desirable and more remote lands, while others moved into the major urban centres. Population growth rates continued to be extremely high despite decreasing immigration, although they had ominously begun to decline for Nova Scotia as early as the 1850s. By the end of that decade, very few of the older settled districts could support their natural increases in population, much less sustain incoming immigrants. In Newfoundland, for example, there was considerable movement into the largely unsettled western part of the island, and a vast increase in seasonal migration into the Labrador fisheries; in some outports over two-thirds of the working males became seasonal workers in Labrador. Neither expansion nor seasonal migration could, in the end, accommodate the growing population. Many began to migrate, often to the United States. By the 1860s over one-third of the counties in the Maritime provinces were losing people, mostly to the United States, particularly to New England. The correlation between rural counties (with economies largely dependent on fishing and farming) and depopulation

'Roxburgh Place, Residence of A. Marshall, Esq.', 1868. The unnamed artist who painted this farmstead—located in Oxford County, in southwestern Ontario   is thought to have been a local schoolteacher. Courtesy Michael S. Bird.

was very high. While out-migration was a general phenomenon, Scots and Irish were over-represented in the exodus and Acadians under-represented. Most of those departing were 15–25 years of age.

From Mercantilism to Free Trade

By 1840 the mercantile economy of British North America had reached its apex, and it began to undergo considerable change. That alteration resulted from a number of factors. The most important was clearly the British government's demolition of the imperial trading system, which had prevailed since the seventeenth century. Instead of mercantilism, Britain moved to free trade. In the process, the mother country wiped out protectionist advantages for her colonies. As a result, instead of a transatlantic economy based on the sailing ship, some of British North America began to think in terms of a continental economy. Fortunately, the railway came along at exactly this time, providing possibilities for internal development and internal markets. Equally fortunately, Britain resolved long-standing differences with the Americans, making possible the negotiation of a trade treaty, providing some access for British North America to the lucrative American market. An important factor in the reorganization of the commercial economy was the rise of industrialization. Internal markets within the continent required not raw materials but finished goods. Colonial business sought to oblige.

British economists, beginning with Adam Smith in *The Wealth of Nations* (1776), provided a thoroughly reasoned theoretical critique of the old mercantile system. They offered an alternative vision of international expansion based on free trade. In the years following Smith, a number of classical political economists in Britain—Malthus, Chambers, Ricardo, and Mill—expanded on earlier critiques of mercantilism, always insisting that freedom worked best, especially in the marketplace. Despite the intellectual demolition of protectionism in the first quarter of the nineteenth century, the British government found it hard to give up; it artificially assisted influential sectors of the economy, particularly agriculture. Eventually, the free traders won out, chiefly because of Britain's industrial successes after 1815. By the 1840s, the British industrial economy could no longer afford the luxury of protectionism, which limited its access to foreign raw materials and protected markets. The ministry, led by Sir Robert Peel, gritted its teeth and systematically removed protection for corn and other raw materials, including timber. The British still sought to emphasize importing cheap raw materials and exporting finished goods overseas. Instead of trading with colonies, however, they sought to trade with the entire world. Most colonial merchants appreciated the nature of the revolution that was occurring in Britain. The *Quebec Gazette* summarized several generations of argument in 1842 when it wrote of the timber trade, 'Our great ground of complaint is that British Acts of Parliament created the trade, caused capital to be invested in the trade, trusting to these acts, which by the uncertain character they now assume may ruin thousands. We never asked for protection; it was given on grounds of national policy' (quoted in Lower, 1973: 88). British free trade policies would have a tremendous psychological impact on colonial merchants.

In the short run, the British North American rush to export wheat and timber under the old system, before the repeal of the Corn Laws and Timber duties of 1846 took effect, resulted in a collapse of prices in 1847 that would last for the remainder of the decade. Further complicating matters for colonial governments was the arrival of thousands of impoverished Irish immigrants, refugees from the Great Famine of the 1840s. They brought sickness and expense to the colonies along with their anguish. The result of these blows was a conviction that the mother country had subverted the old empire. The crisis seemed much worse in the united Province of Canada because of its reliance on wheat exports. Canadian mercantile policy in the later 1840s was to attempt to come to terms with the Americans. The Canadians continued to improve their canal system. They argued for reciprocal free trade between British North America and the United States in the natural products of each.

Britain's industrial needs also contributed to the need for international peace and bilateral understandings. One of these understandings came with the United States. Since 1815 Britain had sought entente with the Americans, a process that gained momentum during the period of free trade. By 1846 most of the outstanding boundary questions between the two nations had been resolved. In 1842 the Webster-Ashburton Treaty had sorted out the complex eastern boundary issues along the Maine–New Brunswick border. The boundary question was even more complex west of the Rocky Mountains where the two nations had agreed in 1818 to share occupation until there was a need for a decision. Many Americans had settled in the Oregon Territory south of the Columbia River, and presidential candidate James K. Polk in 1844 had rattled American sabres with his campaign slogan of '54–40 or Fight'; 54' 40" is the latitude of what was the southernmost Russian boundary on the Pacific slope. Under the Oregon Boundary Treaty of 1846, the border across the West from Lake of the Woods continued at the forty-ninth parallel to the Pacific (excluding Vancouver Island). This 'compromise' allowed the Americans to possess the state of Washington, in which they had virtually no nationals and which had been occupied chiefly by the Hudson's Bay Company. The forty-ninth parallel artificially bisected the Pacific slope, where mountain ranges and river valleys ran north and south rather than east and west. While the geographical interests of British North America may have been sacrificed by the Oregon settlement, entente was good for business.

Along the way to reciprocity, for a short time some Canadians were seduced by the idea of annexation to the United States. Annexationism gained support after an intense political debate over compensation for Lower Canadians who had not rebelled but had lost property in 1837. It was a far less important movement than that of reciprocity. Both flourished in the economic and political uncertainties of the late 1840s. Many British North Americans saw annexation as the inevitable result of the failure to achieve reciprocity rather than as a desirable end in itself.

Canadians, especially those dependent on the wheat economy, viewed internal markets—which to them meant the United States—as the only alternative to those lost in Britain. The eastern provinces also saw advantages to gaining access to the American market. The Americans displayed no interest until 1852 when the British government decided to toughen its fishery policy. The resultant Reciprocity Treaty of 1854 was hardly a very broad free trade agreement. It removed tariff and other barriers on a variety of enumerated goods, chiefly raw materials common to both countries. It did not remove barriers on finished goods, although the Americans hoped that a more prosperous British North America would buy more American manufactures. The treaty was potentially much more beneficial to British North America than to the United States. This helps explain why the Americans were so eager to end it at the expiration of its initial 10-year term. It does not appear to have greatly increased trade in either direction while it was in effect. The Reciprocity Treaty of 1854, nevertheless, was of enormous psychological value to British North America.

The Rise of Industrialism

The Reciprocity Treaty encouraged merchants, entrepreneurs, and politicians (mainly in the Province of Canada) to continue reconceptualizing their economic orientation. They moved from an imperial context, in which the British market was critical, to a continental context, in which internal markets were dominant. Supplying the American market in preference to the British one was quite advantageous to the Canadas, especially Upper Canada/Canada West, since these provinces had little open access to the Atlantic Ocean. Once turned from its traditional transatlantic economy to a continental one, Canada began to industrialize. Indeed, one of the principal reasons why American trade in dutiable items did not expand during the 10 years of the reciprocity

agreement was that the manufacturing capacity of British North America—again, particularly in the Province of Canada—grew substantially in this period. The internal market permitted agriculture in Canada West to shift partially out of grain cultivation into mixed farming. The concern for modernization led to the elimination of the seigneurial system in the St Lawrence Valley by legislative fiat. A bill replaced traditional seigneurial obligations with a 'quit rent', which gave tenants the opportunity to purchase their lands.

The process of economic reorientation was not a uniform one. Canada and the Atlantic region moved in somewhat different directions. While the Canadians became immersed in internal development—even territorial expansion into the prairie West—the Atlantic provinces continued to find the older transatlantic economy quite comfortable. They based their prosperity on a shipping industry committed to the wooden sailing ship, which the region was still successfully producing. The period from 1840 to the early 1870s was the 'Golden Age of Sail' in the Atlantic region. With hindsight, it is possible to recognize the long-term technological weaknesses of the wooden sailing ship. So long as vessels that cost less than half as much to produce as iron steamers were more than half as profitable, however, they would flourish. The carrying trade provided employment for thousands. It also produced an outward-looking international orientation rather than one that focused on internal continental development. The Atlantic provinces sought to expand transportation links with Canada (mainly railways) in terms of transatlantic linkages.

The Province of Canada saw railways as a means to continental destinations rather than as transatlantic linkages. Canadian railway expansion would not occur in earnest until after 1850, after the complete demolition of the old imperial trade system. By 1850 only 60 miles (97 km) of track were in use in Canada. The obstacles were not technological; the technology had been available since the 1820s. Finance and psychology were the barriers. Railways were expensive capital investments, few routes in British North America promised to be immediately profitable, and investors shied away until the railway

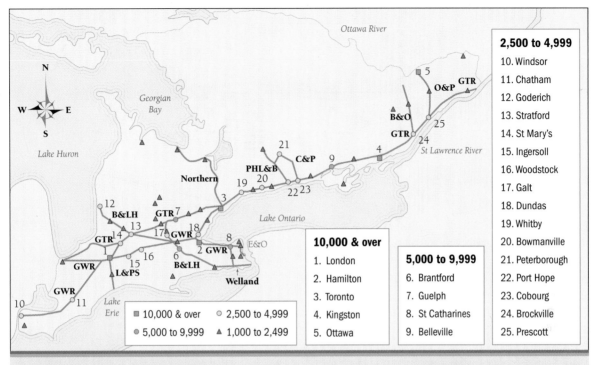

Canada West, railways and urban centres, 1861.

Source: Douglas McCalla, *Planting the Province: The Economic History of Upper Canada 1784–1870* (Toronto: University of Toronto Press, 1993).

boom of the 1850s. In that decade a mania for internal development totally captured the imaginations of Canadian politicians and investors, encouraged by exaggerated promises of profits resulting from railway expansion. Canadian railway tracks had to be built well on deep beds because of the climate variances that caused heaving. American railroads were less expensive to construct. By 1867 the total cost to Canada of 2,188.25 miles (3,520 km) of track was $145,794,853, or roughly $66,000 per mile. In order to pay for this construction, the railways borrowed on the British exchanges. Governments had to guarantee the loans and make contributions. The Canadian government, by 1867, had incurred a provincial debt on railway construction of over $33 million, and its municipalities added considerably more. The result, however, was the economic linking of cities and towns in a new way.

Vast expenditures brought out the worst in businessmen and politicians, who commonly served together on interlocking directorates and engaged in the various aspects of railway construction. Allan

MacNab (1798–1862), who was seven times chairman of the Canadian assembly's railway committee between 1848 and 1857 and served the province as co-premier in 1854–6, was at various times president of three railway companies, chairman of another, and director of two more. Small wonder he once commented, 'All my politics are railroads.' Bribes to politicians were common. Construction overruns were a way of life. Corruption ran rampant. The most serious problem, however, was that too much construction occurred in advance of a settled population that could sustain a profitable level of traffic. Perhaps the greatest disaster was the Bytown and Prescott Railway, financed by Boston interests in 1852 to carry timber from the Ottawa Valley into the United States but unable to find much other trade. This would always be the Canadian dilemma: trading off development against sustainability.

All railway promoters insisted that their lines would promote manufacturing by reducing transportation costs. Railways not only closed the distance between markets, they also served as a major

Old Montreal in 1860.

Source: Robert Lewis, *Manufacturing Montreal: The Making of an Industrial Landscape, 1850 to 1930* (Baltimore: Johns Hopkins University Press, 2000), 51. Reprinted with permission of the publisher.

market for industrial goods, often becoming industrial manufacturers themselves. The Grand Trunk Railway, incorporated in 1852 to build a railway from Toronto to Montreal, began by building its own rolling stock. By 1857 it had decided to produce its own rails as well, constructing an iron foundry and rolling mill in Hamilton. This was the heavy-industry section of the economy. Most railroads relied heavily on carrying Canadian timber, ultimately

into the American market. By 1853, no fewer than 51 ports in the Province of Canada were exporting at least a million feet of planks and boards into the United States. As manufacturing grew and required increasing amounts of capital investment, most of the large firms were relatively recent creations. Some of the old entrepreneurs successfully made the shift from the commercial economy. Many others did not. Canadian cities certainly changed in the process.

The growth of industrialization—the introduction of manufacturing and related commerce on a large scale—inevitably made labour relations an increasingly important issue in British North America. The resource economy had employed large numbers of men on a seasonal basis, offering little opportunity for organization. Industrialization rationalized and stabilized the labour market. Manufacturing tended to be more continuous, and much of it was conducted indoors. Overhead costs encouraged employers to seek a stable and experienced labour force. The rise of a capitalistic labour market stabilized and settled the workers but did little for their bargaining position. Those with highly developed skills were in the strongest position, and labour organization first developed in industries employing skilled workers, such as printing. Early trade unions emerged in certain skilled industries in various cities. Such unions almost never had any contact with one another. They could achieve only immediate and localized gains.

Like union organization, labour militancy was local and extremely limited. Most industrial action consisted of unsystematic rioting. Employers responded to industrial action of any kind by calling in the police or the military. Before the 1850s there was a tendency for unions to identify with their particular trades rather than with fellow workers in other trades in other places. The development of industry and the rise of factories employing mechanization brought considerable change to the incipient

Mechanics Institutes

A movement to supply adult educational opportunity for the working classes, who were virtually ignored in the school and university systems, began in Scotland at the end of the eighteenth century and spread to London, where George Birkbeck founded the London Mechanics Institute in 1823. The growth of the movement in Great Britain—over 100 local Institutes by 1826—was facilitated mainly by wealthy businessmen and industrialists, who sought to provide self-improving facilities for working men, thus enabling them to move up the social and economic ladder. The Mechanics Institutes movement was transferred to British America at the end of the 1820s, with the establishment of a Montreal Institute in 1828, one at Toronto in 1830, and one in Halifax in 1831. The movement spread across the colonies in the 1840s, with almost every prominent town and city establishing an Institute and constructing or taking over a building to house the activities of the organization.

Most of the Institutes served three functions: first, they housed libraries and reading rooms publicly accessible to the working classes, who were encouraged to borrow books; many of these facilities eventually provided the basis for public libraries in their respective cities. Second, they provided classroom and lecture space for adult education in the local community; and third, they provided space for local organizations and groups to meet informally. The Institutes offered venues for visiting lecturers and others to speak on important issues and movements of the day, and in the 1840s and 1850s much of public awareness of science in British America was spread by the Mechanics Institutes. Lectures featuring practical exhibitions of scientific principles were common activities at most Mechanics Institutes, and were very well attended. Few Mechanics Institutes remained solvent on the contributions of members of the working classes, relying instead increasingly on government grants and largesse from wealthy benefactors who saw the value of these institutions of adult education.

The Mechanics Institutes seldom served as active sponsors of workingmen's associations or unions, and were more likely to be involved in temperance activity than in labour agitation. Nevertheless, the Mechanics Institutes movement remained a powerful one in Canada throughout the nineteenth century, with more than 300 local Institutes established in Ontario alone before 1900, but the heyday of the Mechanics Institute was between 1840 and Confederation.

labour movement. A handful of international unions appeared, either British or American in origin. Unions with several local chapters also organized. Although mechanization encouraged unionization, the impersonality of the factory system created problems for labour, particularly when juveniles and women were drawn into the labour market. These workers were hard to organize.

Westward

By mid-century there were signs that the vast territory west of the Lakehead would not forever remain the monopoly of the fur trade. There were also signs of Canadian interest in the West, beginning with editorials in the Toronto *Globe* in 1850. One key development in western settlement was the establishment in 1848 of Vancouver Island as a British colony. Until then, Britain had been content to allow the Hudson's Bay Company to act as custodian of all British interests in the West. Earlier, the HBC had sent James Douglas (1803–77) from Fort Vancouver (now in the state of Washington) to establish Fort Victoria on Vancouver Island. This was a fallback position if the Oregon Territory were to be lost, as it was in 1846. In 1849 Vancouver Island was leased to the Company for an annual payment of seven shillings. The HBC would organize the colony there. James Douglas returned to Fort Victoria as chief factor of the Company, subsequently becoming its governor in 1851. Settlement on the west coast was slow. Most newcomers came from the British Isles. They sought to reproduce on the Pacific slope the life of the British gentry. This was not easy. The Colonial Office insisted on encumbering Vancouver Island with unworkable land policies. Land must be high-priced (a pound per acre) and settlement must be led by those who could afford to bring out labourers as settlers to work the lands.

The trouble with such notions was that the labourers constantly abandoned their masters, as they had done in the early seventeenth century in Newfoundland and in the eighteenth century on Prince Edward Island. Much of the early agricultural activity was conducted by the Puget's Sound Colonization Company, which had been transferred from the Cowlitz Valley and had its own colonization program. There were four farms, each managed

The Great Western Railway station, Hamilton, c. 1850–60. LAC, C-019415.

Sarah Lindley Crease

Sarah Lindley Crease (1826–1922) was born in the London, England, suburb of Acton Green, the daughter of an important English botanist who was a fellow of the Royal Society and later a professor at London University. She was raised in an educated household, was well-read, and was taught all the genteel arts appropriate to a woman of her time and station. Her father's continual use of botanical illustrators meant that she learned much about sketching and about pictorial reproduction through copper engraving and woodblock printing. The family was sufficiently well connected that Sarah accompanied her father to Westminster Abbey for Queen Victoria's coronation. She subsequently attended Mrs Gee's school at Hendon from 1838–42. After a lengthy engagement, she married a young lawyer, Henry Crease, in 1853. Crease was forced by a financial scandal (in which he was ultimately found innocent) to emigrate to British North America in 1856, and by 1858 he had managed to land on his feet as the first barrister in British Columbia. He rose rapidly to become the colony's Attorney General in 1861, and lived with his family in New Westminster from that date to 1868. The family then moved to Victoria and Henry subsequently became a Supreme Court justice in 1870.

The Creases had an extremely amicable marriage. They sketched together on their honeymoon, wrote love letters to one another while separated by the Atlantic from 1856 to 1860, and shared a common social life in Victoria. Both cradle Anglicans, the Creases taught Sunday school, organized charitable events, and continued their interest in sketching and painting. Their home in New Westminster—'Ince Cottage'—had a large garden and a white picket fence. Their house in Victoria—'Pentrelew'—was an Italianate three-storey brick house designed by a team of California architects and completed in 1875; it had a large garden. Typical representatives of the English upper-middle classes transported to British North America, the Creases used their houses to establish their credentials as leaders of society in New Westminster and Victoria, frequently entertaining and allowing their rooms to be used for meetings.

Despite their pretensions and their status, life was not necessarily easy for Sarah Crease, especially in the early years in British Columbia. The couple had seven children, all of whom had to be sent to England for schooling or long visits. Such family expenses, combined with their houses and the costs of servants to look after them, ensured that there would be continual financial worries. One of the characteristics of a middle-class marriage in the nineteenth century was domesticity, which of course meant that Henry was responsible for making the money through his outside employment and that Sarah was responsible for looking after the house and the children. Although there were servants, no woman in Sarah Crease's situation could sit back and rest, at least not while she had her health. Housekeeping on a daily basis was a major occupation, and seven pregnancies and childbirths between 1854 and 1872—plus the subsequent responsibility for the children—were constant drains on her energy. After 1880, Sarah was unable to continue with her sketching because of glaucoma, which resulted in several operations. She devoted much of her time in later years to maintaining a vast family correspondence.

by a 'gentleman bailiff' and worked by hired labour imported from Britain (mainly Scotland) for the purpose. A dour Scot, Kenneth McKenzie (1811–74), was put in charge of farming operations, and he found himself constantly struggling with the social pretensions of the bailiffs. 'Balls & parties every now & then for farmers in a new country will not do', he admonished one of his underlings, telling another, 'It is profits we want at as little outlay as possible' (Ormsby, 1958: 102–3). The HBC was astounded to

The Aurora gold mine, Williams Creek, BC, 15 August 1867, by Frederick Dally. Courtesy of Toronto Public Library, T14321.

discover that one of these bailiffs spent eight times his annual salary in 1854 on various expenses and purchases, including 1,606 pounds of sugar and 70 gallons of brandy, rum, whisky, and wine.

In 1838 the British government had extended the Hudson's Bay Company monopoly over the West for 21 years. A major parliamentary inquiry took place in 1857 before the government decided its ongoing policy in regard to the Company. The HBC officials had attempted to argue that the West was inhabitable only in river valleys limited in extent; most of the region was a vast desert too cold and too arid to be settled. The inquiry's report was not very favourable to the HBC. It acknowledged 'the desire of our Canadian fellow-subjects that the means of extension and regular settlement should be afforded to them over a portion of this territory' (quoted in Bumsted, 1969: 220). It recommended that the HBC cease to control Vancouver Island. It also encouraged the annexation to Canada of the districts on the

Red River and the Saskatchewan River. At the same time, the report maintained that for much of the West the continuation of the trading monopoly of the Company was desirable and appropriate. While the British Parliament was considering the future of the West, two scientific expeditions (one British and one Canadian) set out in 1857 to investigate the region first-hand. The leader of the British expedition was an Irishman, Captain John Palliser (1817–87). The Canadian Exploring Expedition was under the titular command of George Gladman (1800–63), assisted by Simon James Dawson (1820–1902) and Henry Youle Hind (1823–1908). The findings of these expeditions helped to end the public perception of this vast region as utterly unfit for human habitation. Both expeditions produced reports acknowledging the great agricultural potential of the West, once opened by a railway.

Meanwhile on the west coast, sheer serendipity brought the region to the attention of the world. In

1857 the discovery of gold on the mainland, along the Thompson and Fraser rivers, attracted fortune hunters from around the world. The amount of gold easily available was quite small by earlier California standards. The ensuing rush was a pale imitation of the American one. Nevertheless, hundreds of miners, mainly from California, made their way to the Fraser River in the interior of British Columbia in the spring of 1858. The quiet village of Victoria was transformed overnight into a major port. South of the forty-ninth parallel, talk of American annexation spread rapidly. The British government rushed through legislation putting New Caledonia under the direct jurisdiction of the Crown. The mainland colony of British Columbia came into formal existence on 2 August 1858, with James Douglas as Governor. The two colonies were at first administratively separate. The miners, however rough in appearance, were not really badly behaved and accepted British authority readily enough.

The extraction of most of the gold required proper machinery and capital expenditure. Many of the gold-seekers found employment in other ways, taking advantage of the developmental spinoff from

Gold Mining in British Columbia

The following account of the pre-industrial techniques of gold mining is taken from Matthew Macfie's *Vancouver Island and British Columbia*. Macfie had journeyed from Britain to British Columbia in 1859.

The metallic sand in which gold is found is primarily sought, and the peculiar quality of earth that contains the amalgam is technically called the 'colour'. While engaged in the pursuit of this indication of the presence of gold, the miner is 'prospecting'. The requisites for this task are a 'pan' and some quicksilver. When the miner comes to a spot on the bank of the river which he supposes to be auriferous, he proceeds to test the value of the 'dirt' in the following manner. Having filled the pan with earth, he gently dips it in the stream, and by the assistance of a rotatory motion which he gives to the contents, loosened by the introduction of water, the black sand with pebbles is precipitated to the bottom. The lighter earth is allowed to pass over the edge of the pan or basin. After all has been removed except the sand and any specks of gold that may be in combination with it, the pan is placed by a fire or in the sun to dry. The lighter particles of sand are blown away, and if the gold be very fine it is amalgamated with quicksilver. By thus ascertaining the value of the remaining particles of gold dust, skilful 'prospectors' conclude whether the ground would pay to work. In this rough method of searching for gold the superior specific gravity of that metal over every other, except platinum, is the basis of operations—auriferous particles, on this principle, settling at the bottom.

The readiest and most primitive contrivance for washing gold is the 'rocker', which is still used by Chinamen and a few white men, on the banks of the Fraser. The rocker is constructed like a child's cradle, with rockers underneath. The box is 3 1/2 to 4 feet long, about 2 feet wide and 1 1/2 feet deep. The upper part and one end are open, and the sides gradually slope toward the bottom. At the head is a section closely jointed with a sheet-iron bottom, perforated so as to admit of small stones passing through. Along the bottom of the rocker riffles [these are strips of wood or metal arranged after the manner of a Venetian blind] or cleets are arranged to arrest the gold. This apparatus placed on the margin of the river, the upper iron box is fed by one miner with earth, and by another is rocked and supplied with water. The gold and pebbles passing down to the bottom, the water carries away the latter, and the riffles detain the former. In case the gold is very fine, part of a blanket is often laid along the under box, covered with quicksilver to attract the gold dust. By this simple agency from 1 pound sterling to 10 pounds sterling per day and upwards to the hand has been realised. In an ordinary sluice 40 or 50 lbs. of quicksilver is employed daily, and in a rocker from 8 to 10 lbs. But after the gold has been retorted from it, the same quicksilver may be applied several times over.

The next method to be described, and the one most prevailing on the Pacific, is Sluicing. This is a process of mining that can be conducted on any scale and in connection with the labour of an indefinite number of men. It is almost invariably found in conjunction with a system of 'flumes' or wooden aqueducts of various extent, running parallel with the claims on a creek or river. It is necessary, in separating the earth from the gold which is mixed with it, that each sluice should be supplied with a fall of water, and if the stream contiguous to the mine run on too low a level to supply this want, miners . . . are often compelled to go considerable distances in quest of water sufficiently elevated to afford the object desired. Flumes are thus brought into requisition, and by openings made in that side of them opposite the mine, water is admitted to the sluice,

which is placed at such an angle that the water may have forced enough to carry off the earth, while leaving the gold behind.

Sluice-boxes are of various sizes, and are fitted closely together so as to form a strongly built and extended trough. The fall of the water in the sluice-box is adjusted to allow sufficient time for the riffles and quicksilver to arrest the gold as it passes, and the supply from the flume is regulated by a slide in the opening on the side of it. The bottom of each sluice is usually intersected with strips of wood, and in the interstices of this grating quicksilver is spread to intercept the fine gold in its descent, nuggets and grains of coarse gold being caught by the grating itself. The sluice is supported on trussels so as to raise or lower it to the level convenient for shoveling in the earth. Several miners introduced 'dirt' on either side, and others assist in loosening the heap and removing large stones, so that the gold may be easily precipitated. . . .

Source: Matthew Macfie, *Vancouver Island and British Columbia: Their History, Resources and Prospects* (London: Longman, Green, Longman, Roberts & Green, 1865), 267–70.

---

the rush. The discovery of gold irreversibly altered life for the indigenous peoples of the Pacific slope. Even remote regions could contain great mineral wealth. The settlers and the government ignored the land claims of indigenous peoples in the rush to exploit the land itself. Few settlers disagreed with the view that the 'indolent, contented savage, must give place to the busteling [*sic*] sons of civilization & Toil' (quoted in Fisher, 1977: 105). For the Aboriginal peoples the result was a very serious cultural disruption, recovery from which would be extraordinarily difficult, if not impossible.

The Fraser River gold rush presaged a new element in the resource economy of British North America: exploitation of the rich mineral wealth of the northern part of the continent. New technologies provided a constantly expanding market for British North America's mineral wealth. They also brought new means of extracting it from the ground. By the 1850s copper ore was being mined along Lake Superior, and petroleum was discovered in southwestern Ontario

in 1855. Production of crude oil in Canada by 1863 ran to 100,000 barrels a year. Unlike timbering, mineral production tended to be extremely capital-intensive, requiring specialized scientific knowledge. Until the twentieth century, production involved only a few minerals located conveniently for transportation in bulk. Coal seams on both coasts were obvious targets. The continent's burgeoning industrialization would demand ever larger quantities of minerals, and the future potential was indisputable.

Responsible Government and the Reorientation of Politics

The British government gradually resolved the constitutional problems of the commercial period in British North America over the decade following the unification of Upper and Lower Canada in July

1840. Legislative union did not by itself satisfy Lord Durham's other major recommendation for Canada, the right of the assembly to decide policy and its implementation through control of 'the persons by whom that policy was to be administered' (quoted in Craig, 1963: 141). Part of the problem was that nobody at the time understood the importance of political parties or how they could work in responsible government. Colonial governors served as party brokers rather than conceding responsible government. Finally, in 1848 the governor of Canada, Lord Elgin (1811–63), called on the leaders of the Reform parties, recently successful at the polls, to form a ministry. Louis LaFontaine (1807–64) and Robert Baldwin (1804–58) had allied their respective parties in 1842 on a Reform platform. In placing himself, as a representative of the Crown, above party politics and leaving government in the hands of leaders selected by their parties, Lord Elgin inaugurated responsible government in the Province of Canada.

The victory of responsible government in Canada did not begin the story or end it, however. Nova Scotia—where Joseph Howe had been agitating for responsible government as a Reformer since 1836—finally achieved it after an election on 5 August 1847, which focused on that single issue. The Reformers were victorious, and when a Reform administration took office in late January 1848, the province became the first colony to achieve responsible government. Prince Edward Island acquired responsible government in 1851 and New Brunswick in 1854. A British attempt at alternative constitutional arrangements complicated the situation in Newfoundland. In 1842 Britain gave the colony a legislature composed partly of elected and partly of appointed members, thus amalgamating the old council and assembly into one body. The experiment was not popular and never had a proper chance to work. The older Constitution returned in 1848. Newfoundlanders immediately began agitating for 'a form of Government . . . with a departmental Government and Executive Responsibility similar in character to that form lately yielded to . . . Nova Scotia' (quoted in Gunn, 1966: 315). The British reluctantly gave in to this demand in 1855.

The lower provinces, even including Newfoundland, were sufficiently homogeneous to be able to live with a two-party system. Canada was not so fortunate. It could and did create four parties, two for each section. The Reform alliance of Baldwin and La Fontaine was largely illusory. It quickly transpired that Canada East (the unofficial designation for the former Lower Canada) had slipped back into old voting patterns removed from Reform. The principle of governing by a coalition from each of the two sections of the united province was inherently unstable. By the mid-1840s the French had become enamoured of the principle of the 'double majority', in which the province would be governed by an assembly majority in each of its two main sections. Such an arrangement naturally appealed to French Canada's growing sense of nationality. It also required the parallel growth of political parties in the two sections. Two factors emerged to complicate matters for the Province of Canada.

One was the rise of a new political movement in Canada West at the end of the 1840s. A radical Reform group known as the Clear Grits, with whom the moderate Reformers gradually merged, appeared under the leadership of George Brown (1818–80). Centred in the western districts, the Grits were the heirs of William Lyon Mackenzie rather than of Robert Baldwin. They were democrats, populists, geographical expansionists, and opponents of close connections between church and state in a Protestant rather than a true secularist sense. Furthermore— and ominously—they were hostile to French Canada in traditional anglophone ways. In 1840, when the population of Canada East had been greater than that of Canada West, each section of united Canada got 40 seats in Parliament. When the census of 1851 showed that the population of the anglophone section was growing more rapidly, George Brown adopted 'representation by population'—'rep by pop'—as a campaign slogan when he stood as an independent Reformer in the general election of that year. He won easily. 'Rep by pop' came to epitomize the brassy reformism of the Clear Grits.

The growing pressures of the Grits contributed to, but did not by themselves produce, the second development of the 1850s. This was the gradual withdrawal of French Canada into its own agenda, centred on the development of nationalist aspirations and the preservation of French-Canadian

George Brown

Born in Alloa, Scotland, George Brown (1818–80) was educated in Edinburgh and joined his father's business. In 1836 Peter Brown was involved in the maladministration of public funds and a year later he left for North America with his son. The two opened a moderately successful store, but Peter turned to journalism, publishing the *British Chronicle* in New York beginning in 1842. The newspaper took a strong stance on the issues of the 'Great Disruption' in the Church of Scotland, supporting the reformers, and in 1843 George published the first issue of a new family paper in Toronto called the *Banner*. He soon established a reputation as a Reformer, and founded a new newspaper, the Toronto *Globe*, in 1844.

Brown quickly made his new paper a force to be reckoned with, combining new technology (a Hoe rotary press) with detailed news coverage and a branch office in London. By 1853 the *Globe* was a daily, and George Brown was an important Toronto businessman as well as a noted spokesman for the Reform party in Canada West; the *Globe*, after 1849, was the official organ for the government. Editorially, Brown supported the abolition of

George Brown. LAC, PA-6165.

culture and society. The leaders of the Catholic Church took upon themselves the mantle of nationalism. They used the Grits to separate nationalism from reform. In the context of Canada West, the Grit espousal of 'voluntaryism'—the separation of church and state—was directed chiefly against the Anglican Church. Such ultra-Protestantism had even more implications for the Catholic Church. Voluntaryism was not quite the same as secularism. The voluntaryists sought to free the state from 'religious privilege', but could contemplate with equanimity the passage of legislation controlling the availability of alcoholic beverages during the Sabbath (which they held sacrosanct). While God might not be eligible to hold land or be exempt from taxation, He could be used to justify state intrusion in matters of morality. Such ideas were very much at odds with the

principles of French-Canadian religious nationalists. The result was an alliance between the latter and the Upper Canadian opponents of the Grits.

The rise of denominational divisions as major factors in politics was not confined to the Canadas, although the sectional situation—Roman Catholicism in Canada East and evangelical Protestantism in Canada West—gave such matters a special edge in that province. To a considerable extent, denominational politics reflected the growing democratization of the political process. As the interest, involvement, and size of the electorate grew, politicians turned to issues that appealed to the voter. Denominations also reflected ethnic background and regional strengths. Infighting among religious denominations constantly tussling for advantage transferred easily into the political arena. In Nova Scotia such struggles had the clergy reserves and 'voluntaryism' in religion and public education, and he was elected to the Canadian legislature in 1851 as an independent Reformer, becoming the chief spokesman for the English-speaking community of Canada West against the francophone Roman Catholics of Canada East. Brown took the lead in arguing for representation by population, which would have given English Canada more parliamentary seats, but he was isolated by fresh coalitions of English-speaking politicians and left as the leader of the anglophone radicals, unable to form a proper alliance with the French-Canadian radicals (Rouges) because of confessional issues. He soon found a new cause by calling for the annexation to Canada of the vast western territories of the Hudson's Bay Company, and by 1857 found himself the unofficial leader of Reform in western Canada, invited to form a new government early in 1858 in alliance with the Rouges. The result was parliamentary defeat and years of political instability.

In 1864 Brown acted to break a long-standing political impasse by moving towards a new British American federal union and calling for a coalition government in Canada committed to this achievement. He took an active part in the negotiations for union, and was the one who explained to the delegates at Charlottetown how a new constitution might work. He defended the resulting scheme at Quebec as well, subsequently unveiling the actual plan for confederation worked out at Quebec to the Canadian people in a speech in Toronto.

Although a strong advocate of union, he resigned from the cabinet in 1866 over other issues and gradually came to oppose Sir John A. Macdonald's dream for the continuation of non-partisan coalition politics in the new nation. His newspaper encouraged the creation of a Liberal opposition under the leadership of his protégé, Alexander Mackenzie. Brown had labour problems with his newspaper in 1872, but he agreed in 1874 to go to the United States to negotiate a new reciprocity agreement on behalf of the Mackenzie government. His negotiations were successful but the Americans did not implement the agreement. In 1875 he became a senator, and in 1880 he was shot in the thigh in an altercation with an employee. The wound turned septic and he eventually died.

occurred for years over the creation of institutions of higher learning. No denomination could allow another an educational edge, and the result was the creation of a series of colleges and universities, one for each major denomination (and one for each ethnic branch of Catholicism in the province). By the 1850s the venue for denominational disagreements had shifted to public education. In Prince Edward Island the question began over Bible-reading in the schools, a practice pressed by the evangelical Protestants and opposed by the Roman Catholics. The 'Bible Question' helped realign island politics as Catholics and liberal Protestants, backed by the old Tories, joined against evangelical Protestants. By 1858 the principal issue in that year's election was between Protestantism and Romanism, and the result was a Protestant party and a Catholic party. In

Newfoundland as well, the contending political parties wore denominational as well as ethnic faces, the Liberals backed by the Irish Roman Catholics and the Tories supported by the English Protestants.

In Canada, John A. Macdonald (1815–91), the Scots-born lawyer from Kingston, came gradually to dominate the anglophone Conservatives. Macdonald was not a man to allow abstract principle, such as the double majority, to stand in the way of power. In 1856 he was able to forge a new coalition among the moderate (some said very pragmatic) Tories he led and the Bleus of French Canada, led after 1859 by George-Étienne Cartier (1814–73).

This alliance enabled the Tories to remain in power despite Grit victories in Canada West. It also led George Brown's *Globe* to comment in August of 1856 that 'If Upper and Lower Canada cannot

George-Étienne Cartier

Born at Saint-Antoine-sur-Richelieu, Lower Canada, George-Étienne Cartier (1814–73) attended the College of Montreal beginning in 1824 and started legal training in 1831. Becoming a lawyer in 1835, he had already gravitated towards the radicals, and he was clearly a Patriote in 1837, present at the battle of St-Denis. He then fled to the United States until October 1838, when he returned to Montreal and apparently was rehabilitated.

After a number of years of feverish legal activity, he entered the legislature in 1849 and subsequently worked increasingly for the Grand Trunk Railway, with which his name was always associated. He did not enter the debate on the Rebellion Losses Bill. Cartier became associated with the moderate reformers and entered the MacNab-Taché government as provincial secretary for Canada East in 1855. He won an election caused when his acceptance of office required him to seek a fresh mandate from the voters after vociferous opposition from the radical Rouges, and in the Taché-Macdonald cabinet of 1856 he became Attorney General for Canada East. When Taché withdrew from politics in 1857, he joined with John A. Macdonald to form a government. The two remained close political associates until his death. He was part of the 'double shuffle' of 1858, in which a defeated government returned to office by briefly accepting different portfolios and then resuming their former ones. In the years before 1862, when he and Macdonald were defeated on a militia bill, he was the guiding force behind a number of legislative measures that reshaped united Canada, including municipal reform, educational reform, and legal reform.

He returned to power in 1864 and became part of the Grand Coalition committed to the unification of British America. He was the chief spokesman for French Canada in the various discussions that produced the Quebec Resolutions, maintaining that only Confederation would do as an alternative to American annexation and insisting on the importance of a separate province for French Canada in which religious and linguistic rights would be preserved. He was also, of course, a strong advocate of a transcontinental railroad. When he entered the first cabinet of the Dominion he refused an honour inferior to Sir John A. Macdonald's knight of the Order of the Bath, and subsequently accepted a baronetcy. He served initially in both the federal and the provincial houses of Parliament, but was clearly Macdonald's

Sir George-Étienne Cartier. Notman & Son, LAC C-02162.

chief lieutenant in Quebec and co-leader of the government.

Cartier played a central role in the negotiations that brought the Red River Settlement into Canada, and was unquestionably more sympathetic to Louis Riel and his 'rebellion' than were most of the Macdonald cabinet members in 1870. He probably made promises to the delegates from Red River that he could not honour, but he was unable to gain approval for an amnesty for Riel and his government, despite Riel's relinquishment of a nomination to Parliament in 1872 in his favour. Cartier was a genial man who at the same time brooked no opposition to his will, especially in terms of political and religious innovation.

be made to agree, a federal union of all the provinces will probably be the result.' By 1863 most of Canada's leading politicians had come to concur on the need for some other form of union.

The New Imperial Relationship

The imperial government conceded responsible government in British North America because it had little choice, given its unwillingness in the era of free trade to devote unnecessary amounts of money to colonial administration. There was a feeling in both the Colonial Office and in the Parliament that the separation of colonies, particularly colonies populated with large numbers of British emigrants, was inevitable when those colonies had reached a point of sufficient 'maturity'. An equally strong feeling was that the costs of imperial administration were an unnecessary drain on the public purse. A student giving a cursory glance at the literature on the British Empire and British America between 1840 and the early 1860s could easily be forgiven for concluding that once responsible government had been conceded, nothing much happened on the imperial front until the British started pressing seriously for union of the colonies at the end of the 1850s. Such a conclusion would not be correct for a number of reasons.

Even when colonies were given internal self-government, the business of colonial administration continued, albeit in a somewhat different context. Moreover, not every colony in British North America had acquired self-government. The Colonial Office still had enormous power and responsibility in the West and ultimate authority over Aboriginal policy. It was the imperial administration that created the colony of Vancouver Island in 1849, for example, and the colony of British Columbia in 1857. As well, the British government still appointed colonial governors, and both it and they still had considerable moral authority in the colonies. Some historic issues, such as the clergy reserves in Upper Canada, were fought out in the context of responsible government and were resolved with its achievement. Others, such as the land question on Prince Edward Island, were not settled and continued to fester. Finally, Britain

was still in charge of the international situation of the colonies. This included diplomatic relations with the United States, which encompassed such business as the survey of the boundary line beginning in 1857. Britain was also responsible for the direction and financing of the land and sea defences of British North America. Under free trade and responsible government, Britain reduced its military establishment in British North America and attempted with mixed success to convince the colonials to take up the burden. When the American Civil War endangered the stability of the continent, the imperial authorities would respond by attempting to strengthen colonial defence through political and constitutional revisions.

Victorian Society

The relationship between political unification and social change was a complicated one. There were some obvious connections, however. A number of major themes dominated the society of these years.

John A. Macdonald, *c.* 1883–4, oil portrait by Thomas Horsburgh, from a photograph by William James. LAC, C-097288.

First, there was an unmistakable sense of geographical movement, as we have already discussed, mainly out of the older and more settled rural districts. Second, the class structure of society began to take shape and to solidify. The chief changes were the appearance of a new business class, the emergence of a working class associated with urbanization and industrialization, and the rapid professionalization of certain educated and skilled segments of the middle class. Along with the development of social classes went a strengthening of certain caste lines associated with class but not identical with it; many of these lines emphasized ethnicity. Finally, an enormous expansion of voluntary organizations of all sorts occurred, at least partly to maintain personal identities and a sense of belonging in a time of great mobility and social change.

Most British North Americans uprooted themselves at least once, and many were constantly on the move. Wilson Benson, an immigrant of the 1830s, tells the story in his autobiography. Beginning in Ireland at age 15, Benson changed his district of residence 11 times (six times in Ireland and Scotland between 1836 and 1838 and five times in Canada West between 1838 and 1851) before finally settling on a farm in Grey County in 1851 at age 30. He bought the farm not with his savings but with an inheritance from Ireland. Benson had changed jobs

The Orange Order

The Orange Order was founded as the Loyal Orange Association in the 1790s in County Armagh in response to the increasing disorder in Ireland. Protestants in Ulster created local societies devoted to the memory of William of Orange, who had intervened in Ireland militarily in 1688 to replace James II and to guarantee the Protestant succession in England, thus guaranteeing the position of the Protestant minority in Ireland. William's great victory at the Battle of the Boyne in 1690 was celebrated every 12 July with a parade and commemoration, including the festooning of everything imaginable in the colour orange.

In Ulster the Order existed as a hierarchy of local lodges devoted to the maintenance of the Protestant faith and loyalty to the Crown of England, and included a good deal of secrecy and costumed ritual similar to the Masons. In British America the Order downplayed its secrecy and emphasized various fraternal aspects, including life insurance and support for families of members. The first lodge in Canada was founded in Brockville, Upper Canada, in 1830 by Ogle Gowan, and thereafter it spread rapidly. By the later 1830s the Order had over 100 lodges, most of them in Upper Canada. Probably the most important ingredients in its Canadian spread were its transcendence of Irish ethnicity in favour of a non-denominational Protestantism encompassing immigrants from all over the British Isles, its identification with deep-seated fears of Roman Catholicism in many parts of British America, and its various fraternal aspects.

At its height the Orange Order probably had no more than 50,000 actual members, but its degree of popular support in Newfoundland and New Brunswick, as well as in Protestant Upper Canada/Ontario, made it seem much more ubiquitous. The Order had begun by opposing Irish Roman Catholicism through demonstrations and violence. Its leaders insisted that its enthusiasm was mainly a display of support for the Crown, but the Crown during the 1860 visit of the Prince of Wales to British America made clear that waving an orange flag did not find any favour with the monarchy. The Order gradually transferred its hostility from Irish to French-Canadian Catholics and, in Manitoba especially, to the Métis led by Louis Riel. After Confederation the Orange Order became much more constrained in its public demonstrations, but it always maintained a stance of hostility to Roman Catholicism and support for British values (especially the monarchy) in Canada.

29 times in those years and apprenticed to at least six different trades in the 1830s and 1840s before finally settling down to farming. In his later years, he also kept a store in his community. On the whole, transients like Wilson Benson were not economically successful. In both urban Hamilton and rural Peel County, Upper Canada, there was a remarkable correlation between transience and poverty. Whether such people failed because they were continually on the move, or constantly moved in search of a better life they never found, is debatable. So, too, is the question of whether their failure was so deep-rooted as to be transmittable to their children. In any case, the success stories in terms of the accumulation of wealth usually involved those who remained more or less permanently in one place.

The need for a sense of belonging in an era of change and mobility helps explain the enormous expansion in the number of private associations devoted to non-occupational and non-economic goals. Despite the growth of the state, even in Canada it did not weigh heavily on the lives of British Americans. Political allegiances were not as important to the average person as family, religion, and fraternal commitments. Churches continued to be important. They were increasingly dominated—especially on the Protestant side—by women, who made up the bulk of the attending congregations. Women also supported their own religious organizations with their own money, kept separate from the larger funds of the church, and these organizations offered many women their first glimpse of independent administration. British Americans also found a place in the temperance societies, which had begun in the 1820s but really expanded in the 1840s under the Sons of Temperance, a fraternal organization that served 'no liquor stronger than tea'. The temperance movement crusaded against drunkenness, but it was also a way of reacting against new immigration—mainly Irish— and asserting a sense of Protestant hegemony.

By 1870 few British Americans—whether urban or rural—could be found who did not belong to a good number of voluntary societies beyond their churches. In earlier eras, private fraternal organizations had supplemented or provided public services such as water, light, fire protection, and library facilities. By 1870, many organizations had virtually relinquished charitable and public goals in favour of entertainment and companionship for their members. Some of the new societies were created to provide a framework for sporting activities such as curling, lacrosse, or baseball.

Rural overpopulation produced some migrants who would settle and tame undeveloped regions and others who would provide a labour force for industrialization. While the farming pioneers remained small-scale commodity producers indeterminately related to the class structure, the urbanized workforce swiftly turned into a landless working class. At the other end of the scale, merchants turned into bankers, financiers, and industrialists, and became far wealthier. Over the middle decades of the nineteenth century, the older social structure of elites and non-elites disappeared, to be replaced by one far more clearly stratified.

Successful businessmen were highly esteemed in the era of economic transformation, achieving their high status partly by self-ascription and partly by their acknowledged economic and political power. Nowhere was the power more evident than at the municipal level, where businessmen formed a mutually supportive coterie that took the lead in all aspects of life in the city, including its development and land market. Most business leaders in this period were self-made men, not in the sense that they had risen from rags to riches, but in that they had achieved their position in the community by their own efforts. Scots were over-represented in business ranks, where Protestantism predominated. The new wealth was in finance and manufacturing. The wealthier business leaders of Montreal and Toronto began to adopt extravagant lifestyles that were in many respects comparable to those of their American counterparts.

As Canadian cities began the shift from commercial entrepôts to industrial and financial centres, they already contained significant inequalities in terms of wealth and income. In Hamilton, for example, the most affluent 10 per cent of the city held 88 per cent of its propertied wealth, drew nearly half its income, and controlled about 60 per cent of its wealth. On the other hand, the poorest 40 per cent earned only about 1 per cent of the city's total income and controlled about 6 per cent of its total wealth. A close relationship existed between wealth and emerging class status, and between class status and ethnicity. The last was an important determinant of status both because ethnic groups like the Southern Irish carried over their Old World poverty into the New World and because the poorer immigrants tended to arrive later when opportunity was less fluid. The Irish were by far the largest element of the working-class poor in Hamilton and were the most substantial non-Francophone part of the poor in Montreal.

Nevertheless, before 1860 rich and poor in both Hamilton and Montreal lived in close proximity to each other. Only as cities grew larger and developed an expanding middle class that could afford to move out of the urban centre and a working class desperate for housing would the industrial city emerge with its clear divisions between rich and poor and between one economic function and another. In the pre-industrial city the role of women and children in the labour force was fairly limited. Industry could and did employ both women and children for some of the simple repetitive tasks that supplemented the machines, however. Factory owners found that children worked for low wages. Families often insisted that employers take on the entire family, so they would earn enough to live, and the income of all members of the family—including older children—was crucial for survival. In the last analysis, the major characteristic of families on the unskilled side of industrialization was their vulnerability to poverty. Not all the working-class poor worked in factories. Opportunities for women were strong at the lower end of the labour force in domestic service, and increasingly as well as in business and clerical occupations. The mid-Victorian Age saw changes in the retail trade as well as in manufacturing. In 1840 retail establishments were relatively small. By 1870 general merchandising had begun to spawn the department store: the T. Eaton Company was founded in Toronto in 1869.

The relatively small physical size of cities before 1865 made residential segregation relatively difficult, and as various British ethnic communities turned into British North Americans, they came to share loyalty to their new homeland and to a common Empire and monarchy. At the same time, an increase of certain forms of ethnic conflict was imported from the British Isles. Ireland was a major arena for such conflict, as Protestants and Catholics in that land became constantly more aware of their antipathies for one another. The success of the Orange Order was a sign of the problem. As Irish immigration turned into a flood—especially after the potato famine drove thousands of impoverished and embittered Irish Catholics across the Atlantic—the Irish groups were increasingly forced into contact with one another. Irish ethnic differences were not simply confessional or geographical. They also were class-driven. In most places the Catholic Irish were both the latest and the poorest arrivals, forced to take the worst lands (often as tenants) in the countryside or the worst jobs in the cities. The Irish were looked down upon, and often responded with anger to their treatment. The Irish had a long-standing tradition of parades and public events to celebrate their major ethnic holidays, a tradition they brought to North America. Such occasions, particularly in New Brunswick, the Ottawa Valley, and the city of Toronto, which had especially large Irish Catholic populations, produced continual ethnic tensions.

Between rich and poor, the middle class—although it ranged from small urban merchants to small-town industrialists to well-to-do rural farmers—came increasingly to be anchored by members of the educated professional occupations. Professionals' relative dependability of income tended to set them apart. Guaranteeing that dependability through professionalization was the chief development within the middle classes in this period. The numbers of qualified practitioners were increased through formal education, and at the same time stringent licensing requirements were imposed, often set by the occupation itself. The doctors took the lead. An attempt to legislate the creation of a College of Physicians and Surgeons of Upper Canada failed in 1840, although another similar attempt in Canada East in 1847 was more successful. Perhaps significantly, doctors were one of the first groups to organize nationally: the Canadian Medical Association formed in the very year of Confederation. Lawyers engaged in a similar policy, with most provincial law societies formed between 1846 and 1877.

McCarthy's Song

This song is credited to Irish schoolmaster Michael McCarthy of Taylor's Bay Harbour, Nova Scotia. The story is a familiar one.

Long shall I remember one day last December,
My fob lined with silver, my heart full of glee,
Being out on a frolic, determined to travel,
Intending great Halifax city to see.

I crossed Taylor's Bay Harbour in very good order,
From back to Pope's Harbour both up hill and
   down;
I took into my noddle to get a full bottle,
Oh, at the Brian's tavern, that hole of renown.

At the hotel I arrived; I was kindly invited,
Led into the barroom as you may suppose,
With Brian's ale and water, and wine in the corner
They bid me sweet kindly with a how-do-you-do.

I called for a flagon, all hands then I treated,
All hands then I treated and paid the cash down.
Says this Brian, 'my dear fellow, come let us be
   mellow,
You have plenty of money, I pray you sit down.'

Being easily persuaded myself then I seated,
All hands again treated with full bumpers round.
Being fond of the cratur [creature?] my head got
   elated,
On the floor they soon made me a bed of
   shakedown.

It's there I lay groaning and horrors bemoaning,
Not one to control, not a heed to my call;
They battered and bruised me and sorely abused me,
I'm sure that they broke both my liver and all.

My room then I ordered in very poor quarters,
A chamber more fierce than the frozen north pole.
No friend to come near me, and no one to cheer me
But a bucket of cold water to nourish my soul.

Oh, early next morning the landlord gave warning
To pay for my quarters and what I did call.
I paid to each farthing each treat that was called on,
He swore black and blue I paid nothing at all.

Then my guardian angel cries, 'Flee from the danger,'
He told my heart it was time to be gone.
Like Lot leaving Sodom and wicked Gomorrah
For home then I started quite feeble alone.

Each step as I walked I staggered and halted,
My heart's blood been gushing through his mouth
   and nose,
When Hilshy and Glawson like big kind Samaritans
Conducted me safely to old Mrs Haws.

Next day I was greeted and most kindly treated,
On my wounds that was bleeding she poured oil
   and wine;
With mother's feeling she nursed and relieved me,
Her words full of sweetness, they seemed divine.

My health being regained I offered her payment,
She freely forgave me her labour and time.
May the great God reward her both here and
   hereafter
Then in glory eternal I hope she may shine.

Now my frolic is over, no more I'll be rover,
Good-bye to Pope's Harbour and Halifax town.
Here I'll die easy with Henry and Sarah,
A bonnie Scotch laddie that cares not a frown;

And Brian's ale and water I'll ne'er taste hereafter,
But home keep a bottle my sorrows to drown.
My Irish blood would scorn at the name of the
   informer,
Excise men I'll call on to pull this house down

Source: Helen Creighton, *Songs and Ballads from Nova Scotia* (New York: Dover Publications, 1966), 288–90.

Outside the class structure entirely were women, Aboriginal peoples, people from Asia, and blacks (or Negroes, as they were then called). In Victorian Canada the woman, as the bearer and nurturer of children, was regarded as belonging in the home as wife, helpmate, and mother. Women had few legal rights. A woman could not expect automatically to inherit a deceased husband's property. In most provinces, a husband could sue a wife for divorce on grounds of adultery, but a wife could sue a husband only if he were adulterous and had committed some other heinous offence. The courts expected women to reform violent husbands rather than to prosecute them. Mothers had a better chance to rights of guardianship over children even if they were unwed. Despite the domestic ideal, many women worked. The most invisible women workers were the domestic servants. The typical domestic servant in the census of 1871 was a single woman in her twenties who lived in the house and could both read and write. The most prestigious occupation to which most women could aspire was that of schoolteacher. Actively recruited into the teaching ranks, they then remained at the lower end of the ranges of both salary and responsibility. There was little opportunity for entry into the professions. Emily Howard Stowe (1831–1903) obtained a medical degree from the New York Medical College for Women in 1867, but she could not achieve proper accreditation until 1880. The first woman lawyer would not appear until the next century.

Blacks and Chinese joined the Aboriginal peoples in suffering from widespread racial prejudice and

Orange Order parade along King Street, Toronto. Courtesy of Toronto Public Library, T13222.

discrimination in British North America. Chinese migration before 1870 was relatively small, and confined to British Columbia. But thousands of blacks fled the United States for freedom north of border, often encouraged by blacks like Harriet Tubman. After 1840 governments pressured the indigenous peoples of the settled provinces to become freehold farmers. While governments recognized some Native rights, that alone did not lead to much protection. In 1850 the Canadian Parliament passed legislation that operationally defined who was and who was not an 'Indian' within the meaning of the Acts involved. The process of legislating for Aboriginals rapidly escalated after 1850. In 1857 the legislature of Canada passed the Act for the Gradual Civilization of the Indian Tribes in the Canadas. It contained many provisions that ran against the expressed wishes of the Aboriginals. Canadian policy became devoted to removing Natives from the paths of settlement, by coercion and compulsion if necessary. Most of these policies—which defined 'Indians', made them citizens when properly educated, and provided for land grants—passed on to the Dominion of Canada from the Province of Canada in 1867.

Few British North Americans believed that the state would come to their assistance in times of trouble. For some, politics and government were a source of employment or patronage, but for the average person the government (whether local, provincial, or federal) existed mainly to act as an impartial and somewhat distant umpire. Government mostly affected events outside the citizen's personal experience. Nevertheless, the exodus from older settled districts with traditional agrarian and resource-oriented economies into towns and cities demonstrated two points. First, it showed the extent to which the older mercantile economy was failing to support the rate of population growth. Second, it showed the extent to which new economic development was essential. By the 1860s politicians were extremely conscious of out-migration, particularly to the United States. Territorial expansion westward was one solution. A more sophisticated economy was another. In the view of many political leaders across British North America both seemed to require new political arrangements.

The first Eaton catalogue, 1884. According to a prefatory note, it was published in response to 'the immense increase in our Mail Order Department'. Courtesy of Toronto Public Library.

The Creation of Cultural Infrastructure

The conscious cultivation of mind, creativity, and aesthetic taste—which is what most people have in mind when they think of 'culture'—is obviously something that does not come easily to a pioneer society living on the edge of a vast wilderness and spending most of its energy on survival. Such culture requires a complex infrastructure in order to flourish. While small parts of that infrastructure had been in place almost from the beginning of settlement in North America, the elaboration of substantial institutional support for culture was slow to develop. The years

Mrs E.J. Jarvis to Mrs William Jarvis, 1837

Anna Maria Boyd was born in New Brunswick, and married Edward Jarvis in 1817; the couple had eight children. In 1837 Jarvis was Supreme Court justice of Prince Edward Island and the owner of an impressive new house. Anna Maria describes the preparations for the housewarming in the following letter.

Charlotte Town, Prince Edward Island
February 13, 1837

My Dear Caroline,

. . . I fear you have thought me negligent about writing to you. I believe my last to St. John & Halifax were dated in November. I had a great deal to attend to in December. The miss Grays came to us on New Years day & remained nearly four weeks & during that time I cut out my two drawing room Curtains & partly made them, assisted in putting them up, in addition to the window curtains of four other rooms each with two windows. The blinds (chintz) were also made & fixed & we had a House warming on the first day of February (Cornelia's birthday), which hurried the Ball & myself as I wished to celebrate it. She has my affectionate good wishes for many happy returns of it. There were eighty-one persons at the Ball including our children. We invited one hundred & ten. The dancing was kept up with great animation until nearly four o'clock in the morning & every one expressed themselves delighted with their entertainment. Sir John & Lady Harvey, Capt. & Miss Harvey and the two young men honoured us. Lady Harvey expressed herself much gratified by our inviting the two Boys. Sir John left us soon after Supper, but her Ladyship remained for the sake of her children. She is a most devoted Mother. The Curtains were much admired & I am told the effect of the two rooms was exceedingly good. I received the Company in the dining room & when Sir John and Lady Harvey were ushered into the Ball rooms by the Chief Justice & myself the music struck up God Save the King, & after walking round the rooms Miss Harvey opened the Ball with Major Lane. The whole thing went off with style & astonished many present. I borrowed a dining table the length of our own & had the two set up for supper in the room that Mary occupies as a bed room. I wish Mary could write a good description of the whole to you, as to myself I was too much fatigued in mind and body to attempt it & even the repetition is painful to me for I was more disposed to cry than to be cheerful & yet I was obliged to force my spirits. After supper my anxiety eased & I danced several quadriles & felt rested towards morning. You will be astonished that I am alive when I tell you that in one week six rooms were furnished with window curtains, three of them & the Hall window with chintz blinds. Pictures were hung round the dining room, Carpets taken up, four room floors cleaned & two put down again, bell ropes put up in the bedrooms & the Clock in the Hall, added to which I stood by while seven hogs were cut up. (Hams & shoulders cut by myself.) I assisted in the salting & packing down, I hired a woman to assist me to prepare the supper & she with the rest of their servants did their duty most faithfully to the last and every individual including the musicians left the house gratified by the attention shown to them by the Host & Hostess. One of the Musicians came as a particular favour to us. . . .

I unfortunately broke my spectacles just before Christmas & I cannot read with the pair I am writing with only by putting the reading glass before them. In this stupid place there are none for sale & I am puzzled to know how I am to get such articles to suit my eyes by sending to foreign parts for them. It is only occasionally that I write a decent letter, but for the above mentioned circumstances I am unable to do so & I shall make Mary use her pen oftener than she has done. . . .

Yours very affectionately, A.M. JARVIS

Source: Jarvis Papers, Saint John Museum, Saint John, New Brunswick.

between 1840 and 1870 were important in terms of that elaboration, if only because they witnessed such a striking growth in urban populations. Only a few illustrative examples can be discussed here.

Until the 1830s most newspapers had been published weekly, but biweekly editions for papers in the larger cities began in the late 1830s. The Saint John *News* introduced a penny edition in 1839, and dailies started in the 1850s. Most early papers were four page-sheets and had relatively small circulations, printing no more than 1,000 copies, although readership could be far greater. Susanna Moodie described the typical newspaper of her day as 'a strange mélange of politics, religion, abuse, and general information', adding that it 'contains, in a condensed form, all the news of the Old and New World, and informs its readers of what is passing on the great globe, from the North Pole to the Gold Mines of Australia and California' (quoted in Rutherford, 1982: 38). One modern content analysis of four papers from this era corroborates this description (Rutherford, 1982: 39). George Brown published the first daily in 1853, printing it on a steam-powered cylinder press, and he reached a hitherto unheard of circulation of 28,000 by 1861. In British North America Brown was a pioneer in the regular serialization of popular fiction, including the works of Charles Dickens. He also aggressively covered the arts, especially in the local community. All newspapers, especially the dailies, benefited from the introduction of telegraphy to British America in the late 1840s.

In history everything connects. Critical to the emergence of the daily newspaper and the development of a larger and more sophisticated arts community was the introduction of mass education. This began in the 1840s, especially in anglophone British North America. Mass education was a product of the introduction of publicly supported schooling combined with the principle of universality. The result was that increasing numbers of people learned to

Chinese CPR construction workers in camp at Kamloops, BC. LAC, C-2880C.

Harriet Tubman

Born Araminta Ross to slave parents on a Maryland plantation, Harriet Tubman (c. 1820–1913) worked in the fields as a child and was subject to many abuses. On one occasion she was struck in the head by an object thrown by an overseer, and thereafter was subject to seizures. She took her mother's Christian name (Harriet) at an early age, and around 1844 married a freed black named John Tubman. In 1849 she escaped from the plantation and removed without her husband to Philadelphia, where she worked as a cook and began her activities of slave liberation with the Underground Railroad. She started with members of her own family. Although she was both illiterate and physically handicapped, Tubman never let these obstacles interfere with her activities, and, indeed, they probably served as a persuasive disguise for her many clandestine exploits. Who could be suspicious of such a person?

In 1851, after the passage of the Fugitive Slave Act, Harriet went to St Catharines, Canada, thereafter making a number of journeys back into the United States to lead fugitive slaves to freedom. During these years a reward was offered by slaveholders of $40,000 for her capture, dead or alive. In 1857 she returned to Maryland to lead her parents to Canada, subsequently removing them to a house in Auburn, New York, which she bought with the financial assistance of sympathizers, notably William Seward, later the American Secretary of State. Tubman opened a boarding house in St Catharines in 1858, and the notorious abolitionist zealot John Brown stayed there in the early part of that year. Brown described Tubman in a letter to his wife as 'the most of man, naturally, that I ever met with'. She soon began to use the Auburn home of her parents as a permanent residence, however, although she continued to retain contacts in Canada and received financial assistance from there for many years.

During the American Civil War she acted for the Union Army in a number of capacities, including that of spy, returning to Auburn after the cessation of hostilities. The American Congress refused to give her a pension in 1868. That same year she married Benjamin Davis, and after his death began receiving his pension. Tubman became a mythical figure in the black community from a relatively early period, especially after the publication of a biography in 1869 by Sarah Elizabeth Hopkins Bradford—*Harriet Tubman: The Moses of Her People*—described her exploits (which are essentially undocumentable) in considerable detail.

read and write, and this increased the audience and market for the arts and culture. Census data from 1861 suggest that more than 90 per cent of the population of Canada West could read, a tribute to the early introduction of free schooling. The figures were lower in Canada East, where over one-third of the population could not read in 1861, and in the Maritimes, where 22.6 per cent could not read and 32.7 per cent could not write. The 1871 census indicated that only just over 12 per cent of Ontarians could not write; the figure for Quebec was 45.8 per cent and for the Maritimes 23.3 per cent. The data suggest that French Canada remained a much more oral society than English Canada. Naturally, the younger members of society were more literate than their elders, and males in most places were more literate than females. Raw literacy data do not tell us much about how individual people employed their skills, but combined with increases in the number of libraries and the availability of books and newspapers, the figures suggest a marked increase in the audience for cultural productions.

Higher education is just as important as mass education for the development of elite culture, since

Petition of a Number of Colored Inhabitants of the City of Montreal

One way of showing loyalty to Canada in the nineteenth century was by offering to organize a militia company, as did a number of blacks in Montreal in 1860. We do not know whether the petition was successful.

To His Excellency Sir Edmund Walker Head, Governor General of British North America and Captain General and Governor in Chief of the Provinces of Canada, New Brunswick, Nova Scotia, and the Island of Prince Edward, &c. &c.

The humble Petition of a number of the Colored Inhabitants of the City of Montreal, Canada East,—

Montreal, 19th February 1860.

Respectfully Sheweth,

That the undersigned Petitioners, loyal and dutiful subjects of Her Gracious Majesty Queen Victoria, and residing in the City of Montreal, Canada East, are desirous of proving their attachment to the British Crown under which they hold their rights and privileges as Free Citizens, in common with their brethren of European origin, humbly and respectfully solicit the Authority of Your Excellency as the Representative of Her Majesty in this part of Her Dominions, to allow your Petitioners to raise and organize from themselves a Volunteer Militia Company of Foot, in class B, to be dominated, if it should please Your Excellency, the Colored Company of Montreal Volunteer Rifles; to be drilled & exercised in conformity with the regulations of the Service in all respects.

That Your Petitioners pledge themselves should Your Excellency feel disposed to favor their views, to cloth themselves at their own expense, in a neat and appropriate uniform (subject to the approval of Your Excellency), and to conform in every way to the Militia Rules & Regulations,

That Your Petitioners venture most respectfully to bring to Your Excellency's notice, that in the West India Island belonging to Her Majesty, there exist many Companies of Militia composed entirely of the Colored population, who have at all times been found ready to do their duty when called on; and that the Regular Colored Colonial Regiments in the West Indies volunteered their Services to a man on the outbreak of the Indian Mutiny; thus proving that the Colored race, under a free and enlightened Government like that of Great Britain, are second to none in loyalty, fidelity and truthfulness to their Country and their Queen.

Your petitioners, in conclusion, would most respectfully entreat Your Excellency to grant them a favorable reply to this their earnest Petition, to be allowed to participate as Citizens, in the duties of the Militia Force of this valuable Colony; and should your Excellency under all the circumstances of Your Petitioners case, view the same in a favorable light, they, as in duty bound will ever pray—

Proposed Strength of Company

1 Captain	3 N.C. Officers
1 Lieutenant	1 Bugler
1 Ensign	59 Rank & File

[signed with 38 names]

Source: Gary Collison, *Shadrach Minkins: From Fugitive Slave to Citizen* (Cambridge, Mass.: Harvard University Press, 1997), 227–8.

The Testimony of Maria Thomas, 1863

In 1863 a well-known Anglican clergyman in Red River was put on trial for attempting an abortion on his 15-year-old mixed-blood serving girl, who accused him of rape. The transcript of the trial was carried in full in the local newspaper and represents the most detailed account that we have of any such trial in British North America. The clergyman was found guilty of procuring an abortion, but was freed by his followers and returned to England.

Maria Thomas sworn.—I know prisoner have been in his service. Engaged April 1, 1861. Was engaged for one year—was engaged one month more. Wages for year 8 pounds wages for extra month 13s; I engaged then for a second month, at, I think, the same rate of wages. I stayed after the second month as Mr Corbett told me two weeks. I left because Mrs Corbett could not agree with me. Mr Corbett and I were always together at the byres feeding the cattle. Mr Corbett daed [sic] always have something to do with me at the byre. He had dealings with me there. He lay with me—he had connections with me, up on the loft of the stable over where his mare was kept. The loft was made of round sticks with hay on them. There was a hole in the wall, which Mr Corbett made after he first had connection with me. He took a broad chisel and hammer and made it. It was mudded up by old Tom Swain. The hole was made for Mr Corbett to watch through. He said he made this hole to watch his wife—that he might see her when she came towards the byre. After it was closed it was re-opened by Mr Corbett with the same chisel. He told me he had re-opened it. Mr Corbett first had connection with me one day last winter, in my bed in the kitchen of his own house, I was washing that day. When I finished, Mr Corbett made up a little wine, put medicine in it, and told me to drink it before anybody would see me.

I drank it and when I was kneeling at prayers I fell asleep. Little Polly (a girl employed about the house) pushed me when they were done, and I got up and went into the kitchen. While I was putting away the things I felt as if I would fall asleep; as soon as I had finished I went and laid down and fell fast asleep. When I awoke in the morning it was late and I felt as if I could not move. Little Polly who slept with me that night, pulled me up when I told her. When I got out of bed I felt as if my inside would all fall out. I saw blood lying in the bed and I said what can be the matter with me? I went out to the porch, met Mr. Corbett and told him my troubles were coming on. He smiled and said he had been with me that night, and said it would be all right. I told him I would tell the Bishop. He shed tears, and told me, like a good girl not to do it; he said he would give me money and get me things whenever he went down to the Fort. He gave me a French Merino dress and a black one. I cannot tell how long after he first had connection with me. Afterwards on the stable-loft, more than once, he lay with me, I cannot say how often: but it was nearly every time we went to feed the cattle. He would tell me to go up to the stable-loft to throw down hay, and as soon as I would go up, he would go after me. He also examined me with his fingers in the byre. He did so twice.

Source: 'The Trial of G.O. Corbett', *The Nor'-Wester*, Feb. 1863.

it helps create an interest in the life of the mind. By 1867 there were 17 degree-granting institutions in the colonies, as well as a number of colleges that provided some higher education but did not actually confer degrees. Virtually every province (and even Red River) had at least a college or two, and several provinces (such as Nova Scotia) had a plethora of them. Colonial institutions of higher learning had their limitations. With few exceptions they were small, with enrolments of fewer than 100 students.

Except for Dalhousie (1818), McGill (1821), New Brunswick (1828, secularized 1859), and the University of Toronto (1827, secularized 1850), all the remaining institutions of higher learning were church-related and church-governed. One of the reasons for a large number of small colleges and universities was that every major denomination insisted on founding a school where its own students could be educated, free from the doctrinal influence of the competition, and also for the ministry. Only a few of these colleges taught science seriously, partly because of the expense of proper laboratories, partly because of the origins of higher learning in the traditional arts curriculum. Most teachers did not have higher degrees and had no pretensions to interest in research or in independent scholarship. They taught

Jean-Baptiste Meilleur

Jean-Baptiste Meilleur (1796–1878) was born on Montreal Island and was educated at the College of Montreal. He subsequently studied medicine in Vermont, receiving his doctorate in 1825 from Middlebury College. He also studied at Dartmouth, apparently supporting himself by giving French lessons and writing 'A Treatise on the Pronunciation of the French Language' (1825). He returned to medical practice at L'Assomption in 1826, acquiring the usual accoutrements of a successful doctor at the time, including a militia rank of lieutenant and election to the Lower Canadian assembly in 1838. He sympathized with political reform in 1837, but not with violence. He wrote extensively on educational and scientific topics, and began in 1828 a series of letters on education in *La Minerve*, which led to the establishment of a college at L'Assomption in 1834.

Meilleur responded to Lord Durham's challenge for educational improvement in Lower Canada in an exchange of letters with Arthur Buller in Montreal's *Le Populaire* in 1838 and with a famous series of letters published in Quebec's *Le Canadien* that same year. These letters outlined a system of public schooling for the province, in which at least the primary grades would be free. He recommended supplementing Jesuit funding, the source for most schooling in the province, with various duties and licences to finance education. He was heavily critical of the existing state of education and recommended a series of levels ranging from primary school through classical teaching (at the high school level) to academic teaching of practical subjects (also at the high school level) to training at normal schools. When Canada passed an Education Act in 1841, Meilleur applied to be superintendent, and was so appointed—without pay—for Lower Canada. Meilleur served in this onerous post for 13 years, administering the original Education Act and six subsequent revisions. In 1845 he became Superintendent of Education for Lower Canada under an Act that made the parish the basis of the school system. An 1846 Act provided for parish school commissions, which were to match educational grants from the province. This Act was much opposed by various local districts as an introduction of taxation for education and led to sporadic rioting over education taxes.

Meilleur was a hard man to work with, for he was an intellectual loner rather than a political animal, and he was not happy in his job. In 1853, the report of a committee chaired by Louis-Victor Sicotte called for further reforms in education to provide some energy for the system, and eventually in 1855 Meilleur took the hint and resigned. He subsequently served as director and then inspector of the Montreal post office, then provincial deputy registrar. After he retired Meilleur found more time for intellectual activity, and in 1860 he published *Mémorial de l'éducation du Bas-Canada*, which summarized the educational record of the province. In 1870 he became president of the Natural History Society of Quebec. Meilleur was something of a polymath, and—whatever his flaws—the founder of the educational system in Quebec.

The Victorian era was fond of graphic illustrations of progress. Here four schoolhouses illustrate the improvements made from the early days of settlement to the 1860s. Top: two 'First Settlers' School-houses'; bottom left: 'Country District School-house'; bottom right: 'Village School-house'. From H.Y. Hind, *The Dominion of Canada: Containing a Historical Sketch of the Preliminaries and Organization of Confederation* (1869).

many hours a week, usually by lecture and with an insistence on rote memorization. Nevertheless, a sense of connection to the wider world of humanistic culture permeated the system and helped to create an audience for advanced study.

The Road to Confederation

The political problems of the Canadas were the immediate stimulus for Canadian politicians to begin to explore the possibility of a larger union with the eastern provinces, beginning at the famous Charlottetown Conference of September 1864. Such

a solution did not come out of thin air, however. Politicians had discussed the political unification of the provinces of British North America on and off since the days of the Loyalists. Few of the early proposals were very elaborate. Most gave no consideration to whether the proposed union would result in an independent national state. Most came from Tories concerned with enhancing the power of the Crown or providing a basis for economic development. By the 1850s, however, particularly in the Canadas, some sense was emerging of 'a true Canadian feeling—a feeling of what might be termed Canadian nationality, in contradistinction to a feeling of mere

Table 5.1   Schedule of the Course of Study, University of Toronto, 1868

Matriculation

Xenophon's Anabasis, book i.
Sallust's Catilina
Virgil's Aeneid, book ii.
Latin Prose Cosmopolitan

Arithmetic, to end of square root
Algebra, first four rules
Euclid, book i.
English Grammar
Outlines of English History

Not including the honour course, which includes options, etc.

Outlines of Roman History, to death of Nero
Grecian History, to death of Alexander
Ancient and Modern Geography

First year

Homer's Illiad, book vi
Lucian's Vita and Charon
Virgil's Aeneid, book vi.
Cicero, de Amicitia
Latin Prose Composition
Arithmetic
Algebra
Euclid, books i–vi
Plane Trigonometry
English Composition
English Language and Literature
French Grammar
Montesquieu's Grandeur et Décadence des
        Romains
Ancient History
British History
Elements of Chemistry
Elements of Physiology
Elements of Botany
Paley's Natural Theology
Paley's Evidences

Second year

Homer's Odyssey, book xi
Demosthene's Olynthiacs
Horace, Odes
Cicero, two orations
Latin Prose Composition
Statics, Dynamics
English Composition
English Literature
French Composition
La Bruyère Caractères
French Literature
German Grammar
Adler's German Reader
German Literature
German Composition
Schiller's William Tell, etc.
German Literature
Medieval History
British History
Chemistry and Chemical Physics

Mineralogy and Geology
Murray's Logic
Wayland's Moral Philosophy
Locke, books ii, iii, and iv.

Third year

Sophocles, Oedipus Rex
Herodotus, book ii
Horace, Satires and Epistles
Livy, book v
Latin Prose Composition
Hydrostatics, Optics
French Composition
Racine's Phèdre and Athalie
Bossuet's Oraisons Funèbres
French Literature
German Grammar, etc.
German Composition
Lessing's Minna von Barnhelm
German Literature
Modern History
British History
Chemistry
Comparative Physiology
Vegetable Physiology, etc.
Ried's Intellectual Powers
Stewart's Moral and Active Powers
Whately's Political Economy

Final examination

Euripides, Medea
Thucydides, book vii
Juvenal, sat. iii, vii, viii, and x
Tacitus, Germania and Agricola
Latin Prose Competition
Acoustics, Astronomy
English Composition
English Language and Literature
French Composition
Corneille's Le Cid
De Staël's De l'Allemagne
French Literature
Chemistry, Mineralogy, Geology, Physical Geography,
        and Meteorology
Smith's Wealth of Nations

colonial or annexation vassalage', as the Montreal *Pilot* put it on 6 April 1850. Sometimes these sentiments were couched in high-flown rhetoric. Often economic or cultural protectionism dominated the phraseology, but a new Canadian nationalism was growing in power after mid-century. It flourished partly on changing communications technology that made it possible to transmit fast-breaking news across the provinces in moments. The royal tour of Prince Albert in 1860 suggested that British North America was already in some senses a political entity.

Neither the bind of the double majority nor the beginning of national sentiment was sufficient, however, to propel British North Americans to national unification. As so often had been the case, events in the United States provided the catalyst. The American federal union broke apart with surprising suddenness in 1861. The southern states seceded into their own Confederacy. The American Civil War began. Many Canadians quietly rooted for the Confederacy despite its maintenance of slavery. Britain adopted an official policy of neutrality. The British watched warily while public opinion in the northern states, whipped up by American newspapers, talked openly of finding compensation for the lost Confederacy by annexing British North America.

Britain could hardly leave her North American colonies unprotected. Defending them at great expense was not something the British faced with relish, however. By the 1860s the British ruling classes believed that colonies like British North America would inevitably separate from the mother country. Why not hasten the process and save money? An independent British North America could organize its own defences. In 1864 the military situation in the United States turned more dangerous for British North America, as the Union forces gained clear victories over the Confederacy. In several respects the efforts of the Canadians to create a larger union fitted very well with British desires for reduced colonial responsibility and expense. The full weight of the still considerable influence of the British colonial system came down on the side of unification.

In Canada the difficulty of agreeing to military mobilization was one of the many factors that led George Brown to propose a political coalition with his enemies. The understanding rested on a commitment to a British–American federal union. This Great Coalition—a ministry formed by a union of the Conservatives under Macdonald and the Bleus under Cartier, with the Grits led by Brown, announced in the Canadian Parliament on 22 June 1864—broke the political deadlock. The new government moved on a variety of fronts over the summer of 1864. Most important was to prepare the outlines of federal union for a conference of Maritime delegates called at Charlottetown in September to discuss Maritime union. The Maritime region contained a good deal of abstract support for unification with Canada, tempered by two realities: any Maritime participation in a larger union must not work to the disadvantage of the provinces, and many felt strongly that the Maritimes were doing pretty well within the existing imperial structure. Historians sympathetic to central Canada have tended to view the Maritime defence of local interests as parochial. Such an interpretation misses the point. One problem with the Canadian initiative was that Canada was so much bigger and more powerful than the other provinces that almost any union would seem more like annexation than confederation. The Maritimes, moreover, were already part of a larger political and economic system known as the British Empire. Many Maritimers had travelled on sailing ships to the far corners of the world, and in many ways Maritime voters were far more cosmopolitan than the Canadians. At the time, the case against Confederation was quite reasonable. Unification seemed an impracticable visionary scheme, proposed by politicians in the Province of Canada to meet their needs. It was not necessarily in the best interests of the other colonies.

Considerable ingenuity was required in 1864 to explain to delegates from smaller constituencies how the Canadian proposal really worked to their benefit. The union as finally developed was somewhat different from the one initially proposed. The biggest difference was in the place of the provinces. The Canadians originally intended to create a strong central government by consolidating all the provincial legislatures (and their powers) into one grand Parliament. This procedure of legislative union was how Great Britain had earlier incorporated Scotland

Another Canadian principle was legislative sovereignty. 'We the People' would not create this union, as in the United States. Instead, an Act of the British Parliament would create Canada. Conveniently enough, this denial of popular sovereignty meant that Confederation did not go before the public in the form of an election, a ratification convention, or a referendum/plebiscite. But at the same time, the union had been worked out totally in a parliamentary context. The public debate on the Quebec resolutions did not always take into account the niceties of political theory. Critics understood the basic thrust of the proposals well enough, however, and the debate did affect their interpretation and ultimate implementation. While the Canadians had initially intended to reduce the provincial governments to municipal proportions, both French Canada and the Maritimes made clear that the provinces would have to survive relatively intact. The proponents of union in Canada East emphasized that Confederation meant giving French Canadians their own province, with—as the *Courrier de St-Hyacinthe* put it in September 1864—the two levels of government both 'sovereign, each within its jurisdiction as clearly defined by the constitution'. An informal adjustment addressed this matter. On the other hand, the

George Brown on the Charlottetown Conference of 1864

. . . Having dressed ourselves in correct style, our two boats were lowered man-of-war fashion—and being each duly manned with four oarsmen and a boatswain, dressed in blue uniform, hats, belts, etc. in regular style, we pulled away for shore and landed like Mr. Christopher Columbus who had the precedence of us in taking possession of portions of the American Continent. Our brother delegates were there before us. Five from Nova Scotia, five from New Brunswick and five from Prince Edward Island. Newfoundland goes heartily with the movement, but was not notified in time to take part in the proceedings.

At two o'clock the Conference was organized by the appointment of Col. Gray, Prime Minister of Prince Edward Island, as President of the Convention. You are aware that the Conference was originally summoned merely to consider the question of a union of the Maritime Provinces and that Canada was no party to that Arrangement and had no interest in it. We came their [sic], not as recognized members of the Conference, but unofficially to discuss with them the propriety of extending their scheme and seeing whether the whole of British America could not be included in one government. The Conference was accordingly organized without us, but that being done we were formally invited to be present and were presented in great style to the Conference. Having gone through the shake elbow and the how dyedo and the fine weather— the Conference adjourned to the next morning at 10 when to meet for the serious despatch of business. In the evening the Governor, Mr. Dundas, gave a large Dinner party to as many of the party as he could conveniently receive—I being one. . . .

On Friday we met in Conference and Canada opened her batteries—John A. and Cartier exposing the general arguments in favour of Confederation— and this occupied the time until the hour of adjournment at three. At four o'clock Mr. Pope gave us a grand déjeuner à la fourchette. . . .

On Saturday the Conference resumed its deliberations and Mr. Galt occupied the sitting in opening up the financial aspects of the Federation and the manner in which the financial disparities and requirements of the several Provinces ought to be arranged. When the Conference adjourned, we all proceeded on board our steamer and the members were entertained at luncheon in princely style. Cartier and I made eloquent speeches—of course—and whether as the result of our eloquence or of the goodness of our champagne, the ice became completely broken, the tongues of the delegates wagged merrily, and the banns of matrimony between all the Provinces of BNA having been formally proclaimed and all manner of persons duly warned their [sic] and then to speak or forever after to hold their tongues—no man appeared to forbid the banns and the union was thereupon formally completed and proclaimed! In the evening Col. Gray gave a grand dinner party at his beautiful mansion. . . .

On Monday the Conference resumed its sittings, when I addressed the members on the Constitutional aspects of the question—the manner in which the several governments general and local should be constructed—the Judiciary should be constituted— what duties should be ascribed to the general and local legislatures respectively—and so forth. My speech occupied the whole sitting. . . . On Tuesday

the Conference resumed its deliberations—earnestly discussing the several details of the scheme. The Canadians this day closed their case, and left the Conference to decide what course it would take on their propositions. At four o'clock Mr. Palmer, Attorney-General, gave the delegates a grand luncheon at his residence. . . .

On Wednesday, the Conference gave the Canadian Delegates their answer—that they were unanimous in regarding Federation of all the Provinces to be highly desirable, if the terms of union could be made satisfactory—and that they were prepared to waive their own more limited questions until the details of our scheme could be more fully considered and matured. It was agreed that the Conference should stand adjourned until Monday the 12th Sept. then to meet at Halifax. . . .

Source: LAC, Brown Papers, George Brown to Anne Brown, 13 Sept. 1864.

opposition fulminated unsuccessfully to the end over the refusal of the proponents of Confederation to take the scheme to the people.

Newspapers, pamphlets, and debates held in the legislatures of each of the provinces discussed the Quebec resolutions. What these demonstrated most of all was the success of the proponents of union in capturing most of the positive ground. Critics could reduce the proposals to rubble, but had little to put in their place. For Canada, the absence of alternatives was particularly striking. The debates also demonstrated that the Quebec resolutions were, on the whole, far more acceptable to Tories than they were to Reformers. Although the debates in the Canadian Parliament were lengthy and long-winded, the ultimate result was approval. The eastern provinces could stand pat, however, and some did. Newfoundland— convinced it would be little more than 'the contemptible fag-end of such a compact' with Canada after an election fought on the question in 1869—remained outside Confederation until 1949. Prince Edward

Island felt insufficiently compensated for 'the surrender of a separate Government, with the independent powers it now enjoys'. It would not join until 1873.

The situation in New Brunswick and Nova Scotia was more complex. In the former province, a coalition of opponents to union headed by A.J. Smith (1822–83) blew away the pro-Confederation government of Samuel Leonard Tilley (1818–96) in an 1865 election. A year later another election was held against the background of threatened invasion by thousands of Irish nationalists (the Fenians), many of them veterans of the American Union army who had kept their arms when disbanded. The threat was sufficient to return Tilley to office. The new administration moved an address favouring Confederation, not, it must be noted, as embodied in the Quebec resolutions but 'upon such terms as will secure the just rights and interests of New Brunswick, accompanied with provision for the immediate construction of the Intercolonial Railway'. When this motion carried, opposition disappeared.

In Nova Scotia, which owned one ton of sailing ship for each of its 350,000 inhabitants, there was much concerted opposition to union. Joseph Howe led the opponents of Confederation. He attacked the union's Canadian origins from the vantage point of someone perfectly content with the British Empire. Confederation smacked too much of Canadian self-interest. It gave Upper Canada rep by pop and Lower Canada provincial autonomy, but offered nothing to Nova Scotia. The Nova Scotia legislature never did approve the Quebec resolutions. The government, led by Charles Tupper (1821–1915), introduced a motion calling for a 'scheme of union' in which 'the rights and interests of Nova Scotia' would be ensured (quoted in Pryke, 1979: 27). It passed by a vote of 31 to 19. Unlike their counterparts in New Brunswick, the opponents of Confederation in Nova Scotia did not melt away. They eventually went on to elect full slates of candidates provincially and federally that promised to take Nova Scotia out of the union in which it had become involved.

Although neither Nova Scotia nor New Brunswick ever actually approved the Quebec resolutions—which all but the most ardent unionists recognized would consign the smaller provinces to national impotence—the fundamentals laid down at Quebec became the basis of the new Constitution. Small wonder that the region later complained about the deal they had made. In November 1866 delegates from Canada, Nova Scotia, and New Brunswick met in London to work out the final details, essentially the Quebec resolutions with more money for the Maritimes and the Intercolonial Railway. All agreed that the name of the new country should be that of its principal progenitor, thus openly declaring the primacy of Canada in the arrangement and causing confusion ever afterwards for students of Canadian history. The resulting legislation, the British North America Act, passed quickly through the British Parliament in 1867. The MPs barely looked up from the order paper as they voted. The Queen signed the bill into law on 29 March 1867, with the date of proclamation 1 July. Governor General Lord Monck (1819–94) called upon John A. Macdonald, the man everyone most closely associated with the union, to be the first Prime Minister.

On the morning of 1 July—a day of celebration and military parades in all four provinces—the new country was proclaimed in the recently completed Parliament buildings in Ottawa. Macdonald received a knighthood. The ceremonial launching of the new nation did not, however, guarantee its success. Much work still would be needed to make Canada an integrated nation.

Conclusion

The road to Confederation was a complex one, with many paths coming together. The British cut British North America free from their mercantile system. The British North Americans naturally were drawn to the continental economy, and began to build railroads and industrialize. The Province of Canada cast covetous glances westward, where the hold of the Hudson's Bay Company was weakened by the beginnings of settlement. A unified Canada was not only more powerful but also a leader in achieving responsible government and in producing a new imperial relationship. Immigration to British North America continued, producing much mobility, which in turn led to a need for roots. Population growth brought a new cultural infrastructure. By the 1860s, the Canadians were ready to take the lead in creating an expanded nation, which they did against the judgement of many in the Atlantic region.

How History Has Changed

Achieving Responsible Government

By and large, Canadian historians are no longer much fascinated with politics and constitutional development in either the domestic or the imperial sense. Nevertheless, the shifting interpretations of British North America's political development between 1840 and 1860 tell us a good deal about changing fashions in Canadian historical writing. The traditional view, which prevailed well into the twentieth century, saw the colonies (especially Upper and Lower Canada) dominated by a liberal reformist ideology and rebelling against Britain's failure to allow them colonial self-government. As a solution to the discontent, which involved rebellions in the Canadas in 1837 and 1838, Lord Durham recommended responsible government—colonial legislative autonomy. This answer was eventually adopted after considerable pressure from colonial reformers in the early 1840s. Little serious attention was paid by historians either to Toryism or to radicalism in the onward march to autonomy. We can perhaps call this the Whig interpretation. There was always some disagreement over whether responsible government came in 1841 or 1848, chiefly because there were different interpretations of what was required before responsible government actually was in place. Was it legislative autonomy from the Colonial Office or the triumph of party government freed from the governors? Gradually this question of different interpretations became essential for a new interpretation that developed over the period from 1920 to 1950. This interpretation argued that the British had resisted party government throughout the 1840s, and responsible government as party government was won by politicians in British North America only after a hard struggle over the course of that decade. We can label this the neo-Whig interpretation.

After 1950, much more work was done on imperial policy and imperial politics, with the result that the old views of a backward and oppressive British imperial government—against which the colonials had to rebel—became much harder to sustain. On the colonial side, additional research had emphasized that the political situation in the colonies was much more complex than anyone had previously imagined. The colonial reformers were not necessarily 'the good guys', and the British were not necessarily 'the bad guys'. The move to free trade took on new importance, and British imperial policy (rather than Lord Durham) became the crucial element in the achievement of responsible government. This, of course, produced its own problems (by downgrading the pressures exerted on the imperial system by colonial politicians) and led ultimately to an interpretation that attempted to balance imperial and domestic influence.

Since the 1980s, less and less interest has been shown by Canadian historians in either domestic or imperial political matters. This probably reflects in part the severing of most of Canada's imperial ties, in part a general cynicism about modern politics, and in part the fact that politics, imperial or domestic, in the pre-Confederation era were almost exclusively focused in the legislature. Instead, there has been a growing focus on other developments that resonate more in the modern world. Radicalism has become more acceptable as an expression of popular politics opposed to the increasing power of the executive. Perhaps the most important of the alternative nineteenth-century developments is the growth of the administrative state, a subject that has increasingly fascinated historians of Europe and North America as they have come to realize that in many ways the key figures in government were not the politicians after all but the bureaucrats who administered the day-to-day routine of government. This recognition is perhaps not as fully developed in Canada for the pre-Confederation period as it is in British, German, or American historiography, but it does clearly represent the direction of new interpretation.

Short Bibliography

Bradbury, Bettina. *Working Families: Age, Gender, and Daily Survival in Industrializing Montreal*. Toronto, 1993. An exciting work on early industrialization in Montreal from the twin perspectives of women and the working classes.

Buckner, P.A. *The Transition to Responsible Government: British Policy in British North America 1815–59*. Westport, Conn., 1985. Now the standard study, based on detailed research and elegantly argued.

Courville, Serge, and Normand Séguin. *Rural Life in Nineteenth-century Quebec*. Ottawa, 1989. A middle-level synthesis of an important topic.

Curtis, Bruce. *Building the Educational State: Canada West, 1836–1871*. Sussex and London, 1988. A revisionist work that argues the importance of educational policy for state formation in this period.

Gagan, David. *Hopeful Travellers: Families, Land, and Social Change in Mid-Victorian Peel Country, Canada West*. Toronto, 1981. The product of a huge quantification project, this book attempts to explain the relationship between land and mobility in rural English Canada.

Galbraith, John S. *The Hudson's Bay Company as an Imperial Factor*. Toronto, 1957. The classic statement of the imperial role of the Hudson's Bay Company in the nineteenth century.

Greer, Allan, and Ian Radforth, eds. *Colonial Leviathan: State Formation in Mid-Nineteenth Century Canada*. Toronto, 1992. A collection of essays informed by international thinking about the nineteenth-century state.

Hodgetts, J.E. *Pioneer Public Service: An Administrative History of the United Canadas, 1841–1867*. Toronto, 1955. A pioneer work decades ahead of its time.

Katz, Michael. *The People of Hamilton, Canada West: Family and Class in a Mid-Nineteenth-Century City*. Cambridge, Mass., 1975. The first attempt to apply American quantitative methodology on a large scale to a Canadian subject.

Lewis, Robert, *Manufacturing Montreal: The Making of an Industrial Landscape, 1850 to 1930* Baltimore, 2000. A study from a geographer's perspective of the growth of industrial Montreal.

Lucas, Sir Charles, ed. *Lord Durham's Report on the Affairs of British North America*, 3 vols. Oxford, 1912; reprinted New York, 1970. The scholarly edition of the complete Durham Report.

Masters, D.C. *The Reciprocity Treaty of 1854*. Ottawa, 1963. Still the standard account of this important treaty.

Metcalfe, Alan. *Canada Learns to Play: The Emergence of Organized Sport 1807–1911*. Toronto, 1987. An important work that documents the development in Canada of organized sport in the nineteenth century.

Monet, Jacques. *The Last Cannon Shot: A Study of French-Canadian Nationalism*. Toronto, 1969. The classic study of the emergence of nationalism, under the watchful eye of the Church, in Lower Canada/Canada East.

Saddlemyer, Ann, ed. *Early Stages: Theatre in Ontario 1800–1914*. Toronto, 1990. A collection of pioneering essays that demonstrate how much is to be learned about Canadian culture in the nineteenth century if one chooses to look.

Shippee, L.B. *Canadian–American Relations 1849–1874*. New Haven, 1939. Still the best overall study of the topic.

Tucker, Gilbert. *The Canadian Commercial Revolution 1845–1851*. Ottawa, 1970. The most useful survey of this question.

Waite, Peter B. *The Life and Times of Confederation, 1864–1867: Politics, Newspapers, and the Union of British North America*. Toronto, 1962. Still the best account of the central period of unification.

Winks, Robin. *Canada and the United States: The Civil War Years*. Montreal, 1971. Old, but still the standard work; a thorough account of Canadian–American relations during the war years.

Zeller, Suzanne. *Inventing Canada: Early Victorian Science and the Idea of a Transcontinental Nation*. Toronto, 1987. A work with a controversial argument—that science helped unite British North America—and a good deal of material on colonial science.

Study Questions

1. Explain how Britain's espousal of the free trade doctrine affected markets for Canadian wheat in the late 1840s.

2. Explain why the free trade doctrine led to the Reciprocity Treaty between British North America and the United States. How did this lead to more railway-building and the rise of industrialism in British North America?

3. Identify three reasons why people in Canada West were so anxious to move into the Canadian West.

4. Outline the political consequences of the move to responsible government in Canada East.

5. Why did volunteer and fraternal organizations become so popular in British North America?

6. Explain how the infrastructure of an educational system and a publishing industry contributed to Canadian cultural production during this period.

7. What is important about George Brown's observation that the Maritime delegates agreed that union was desirable 'if the terms of union could be made satisfactory'?

8. Give two reasons to explain why people in the Maritimes might think of Confederation as a 'Canadian plot'.

 www.oupcanada.com/Bumsted4e

Visit the companion website for *A History of the Canadian Peoples*, fourth edition for further resources.

6

Expanding the Nation, 1867–1885

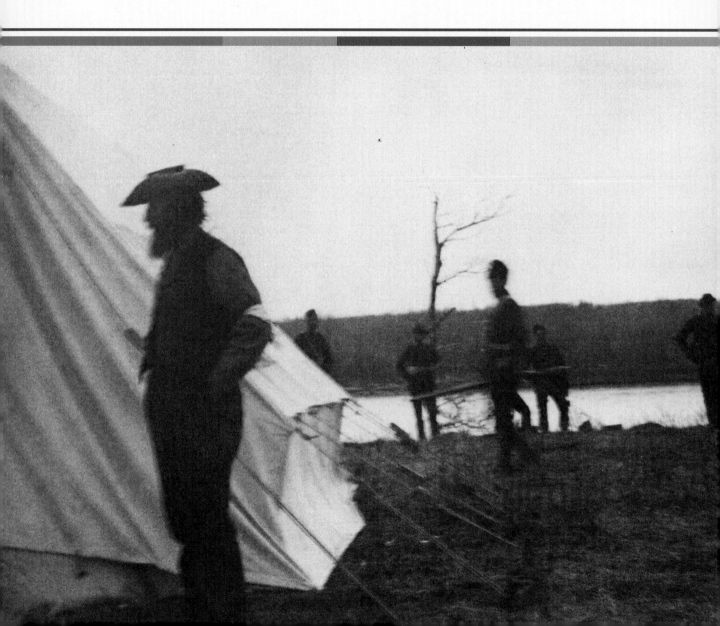

Timeline

1867 British Columbia's legislative council resolves to request that the province be allowed eventual admission into Canada, which officially comes into existence on 1 July 1867 under an all-party government headed by Sir John A. Macdonald. Resolutions for territorial expansion are passed by the Canadian Parliament in December. The Americans purchase Alaska from Russia.

1868 Canada First is founded in Ottawa. Five hundred and seven Zouaves are recruited in Quebec for the papal army.

1869 Resistance to Canada, led by Louis Riel, begins in Red River. Newfoundland election produces an anti-confederate assembly.

1870 Louis Riel allows execution of Thomas Scott. The Manitoba Act is passed by the Canadian Parliament. The Wolseley Expedition is sent to Red River. Negotiations are begun with British Columbia for admission to Canada. Dominion Notes Act of 1870 is passed.

1871 British Columbia enters Confederation on 20 July 1871. The Washington Treaty is signed with the United States. The Bank Act of 1871 is passed.

1872 In a federal election, Conservatives win 103 seats to 97 for the Liberals. Ontario Society of Artists is formed.

1873 Prince Edward Island enters Confederation. The Macdonald government resigns over the Pacific Scandal. Liberals under Alexander Mackenzie take over federal government.

1874 Liberals win a clear majority in Parliament (133 to 73) over Conservatives. Woman's Christian Temperance Union is founded in December in Picton, Ontario.

1876 Intercolonial Railway is completed, linking Saint John, Halifax, and Montreal. Alexander Graham Bell invents a workable telephone. The first wheat crop is exported from Manitoba.

1877 Saint John fire leaves 13,000 homeless.

1878 Conservatives returned to power, electing 137 members to 69 for the Liberals. Sir John A. Macdonald returns to power.

1880 Royal Academy of Arts is formed. Canadian government signs contract with the Canadian Pacific Railway.

1881 CPR reaches Winnipeg. The boundaries of Manitoba are expanded. 15,000 Chinese workers are allowed into Canada.

1882 Royal Society of Canada is formed. Conservatives are re-elected, winning 139 seats to 71 for the Liberals, now led by Edward Blake. Macdonald remains Prime Minister.

1883 CPR construction crews discover nickel near Sudbury, Ontario. Canadian Labour Congress is founded.

1884 Louis Riel returns to Canada.

1885 The second resistance led by Louis Riel (the North West Rebellion) is crushed. Riel is executed. The last spike is driven in the CPR.

Louis Riel at the camp of Major General Frederick Dobson Middleton after surrendering to Middleton, c. 16 May 1885. Riel was later tried for treason and executed, but he remains one of the most influential figures in Canadian history. Glenbow Archives NA-363-53.

Although 1 July 1867 would be celebrated a century later as the date for Canada's 100th birthday, it was in the larger sense only an interim point. The new union consisted of four provinces—Ontario, Quebec, Nova Scotia, and New Brunswick—carved from the three that had created it. Sir John A. Macdonald's government was conscious that a lot of British territory on the continent had been excluded. The new government was also quite obviously the old Canadian coalition, with a few Maritime faces added. Its organization was the former Canadian departments. It used buildings erected in Ottawa for the old Province of Canada. If the new administration seemed familiar, so did many of its policies. It bought off the malcontents in Nova Scotia with better terms that were entirely financial. It started building the Intercolonial Railway along the eastern coast of New Brunswick. With the prodding of the British, the Hudson's Bay Company would sell Rupert's Land and the Northwest Territory to the new nation. Canada devoted much of its energy to rounding up the strays and expanding from coast to coast.

In many respects, the two decades from 1867 to 1885 would focus on tying up the myriad loose ends created by unification. There was the need to create new policies for the new Canada. In the end, too many policies continued from the older Canada, occasionally writ larger to accommodate the other provinces. The creation of new identities was even more difficult. The easiest identities to accept were the old provincial ones. Collectively, these provincial identities grew to provide one alternative to the national identity envisioned by the founding fathers.

Adding New Territory

One of the earliest legislative actions of the new Canadian government in December 1867 was the passage of resolutions calling for transcontinental expansion. Most of the legislators regarded such expansion as the nation's inevitable right, a sort of Canadian version of manifest destiny. As a result, in 1868 a ministerial delegation went to London to arrange the Hudson's Bay Company's transfer of the Northwest to Canada. While complex negotiations continued, the Canadian government began building a road from Fort Garry to Lake of the Woods. This was part of a proposed road and water system linking Red River with Canada. The road builders established informal connections with Dr John Christian Schultz (1840–96), the influential leader of the local faction that had been agitating for Canadian annexation for years. Nobody paid any attention to the Métis who constituted the bulk of the local population of the settlement. The Canadian delegation in London finally worked out a deal for the transfer. The British government received the territory from the Hudson's Bay Company (the Canadians put up £300,000 and agreed to substantial land grants for the Company) and subsequently transferred it intact to Canada.

Since the arrangements for the West were made without bothering to inform the Red River people of their import, it was hardly surprising that the locals were suspicious and easily roused to protest. The Métis were concerned on several counts. The road-building party had been involved in a number of racist incidents. There was transparent haste on the part of the Canadian government to build a road and to send in men to survey land. This rush suggested that Canadian settlement would inundate the existing population without regard for their 'rights'. Canada made clear that it intended to treat the new territory as a colony. Furthermore, some of the road builders bought land cheaply from the Aboriginal peoples—land that the Métis thought was theirs. The Métis quickly perceived the Canadians as a threat to their way of life, perhaps even to their existence. The Canadian government received a number of warnings in 1869 that trouble was brewing. The warnings came from the Anglican archbishop of Rupert's Land, Robert Machray (1831–1904); from the governor of the Hudson's Bay Company, William Mactavish (1815–70); and from Bishop Alexandre Taché (1823–94), the Catholic bishop of St Boniface. Ottawa received all such reports with little or no interest. Subsequent events were largely a consequence of avoidable Canadian blunders and insensitivities. In colonial thralldom itself until only a few years previously, Canada had little experience in managing imperial expansion. It handled the project very clumsily, and the entire nation would pay dearly for its mistakes.

In October 1869 a leader of the Métis emerged in the person of Louis Riel (1844–85), a member of a leading family in the community. His father, for whom he was named, had successfully led a Métis protest in 1849 against the Hudson's Bay Company, which had won the right to trade freely in furs. The young Riel spoke out publicly against the surveys. He then led a party that stood on the surveyors' chains and ordered them to stop. In the meantime, William McDougall (1822–1905) was on his way from Canada to assume office as lieutenant-governor of the North-West. A newly formed National Committee of the Métis resolved that McDougall should not be allowed to enter the country. The Métis made it clear that they would oppose him by force if necessary. Canada responded to the unrest by refusing to take over the territory until it was pacified. Riel escalated the conflict. In early November he and a large band of armed Métis took possession of Upper Fort Garry, the Hudson's Bay Company central headquarters. The Métis then invited the anglophone inhabitants of the settlement, most of whom were mixed bloods themselves, to send delegates to meet and co-ordinate policy. Riel managed to get tacit consent for the establishment of a provisional government and approval of a 'list of rights'. On 7 December he and his men surrounded Dr Schultz's store, taking Schultz and 48 Canadians to Fort Garry as prisoners. The next day Riel issued a 'Declaration of the People', announcing a provisional government. He declared that the people of Red River wanted to be allowed to negotiate their own entry

A Red River Letter

This letter, dated 6 October 1869, represents the earliest written statement of the Métis case for opposition to Canada. The letter was probably drafted by Louis Riel. It claims no authority except 'the people themselves', meeting in an assembly composed of two representatives of each parish. The letter claims 'indisputable rights' that are unspecified.

St Boniface, 6 Oct., 1869

Dear Mr Editor,

. . . Several newspapers of Upper and Lower Canada have freely published their views on what inconveniences might arise in the organization . . . [of a territorial government by Canada for Red River]. And now that the Canadian people have heard these different discussions, would they not be glad to know what the people of Red River themselves think of all that? Here it is:

They do not appear to be at all ready to receive a Canadian governor. A Council chosen and constituted outside the country cannot hope, we think, to see its decrees highly respected. One perhaps can judge by the demonstrations which the Métis population of Red River has just made. Each parish has elected two representatives in order that they might pronounce in its name on the proceedings of the Canadian government with respect to the people of Red River, and the following are the resolutions that these representatives have passed in their first assembly:

1. These representatives declare in the name of the Métis population of Red River that they are loyal subjects of Her Majesty the Queen of England.

2. These representatives acknowledge themselves, in the name of the Métis population of Red River, beholden to the Honourable Hudson's Bay Company for the protection which they have received under the government of that Company whatever the nature of that government may have been.

3. The people of Red River having till now upheld and supported the government of the Honourable Hudson's Bay Company, which has been established in the country by the Crown of England, the said representatives declare, in the name of the Métis population of Red River, that Snow and Dennis have disregarded the law of nations in coming to carry out

public work here in the name of an alien authority without paying any attention to the authority to-day existing in the country.

4. The Honourable Hudson's Bay Company being about to lay down the government of Red River, the said representatives declare, in the name of the Métis population of Red River, that they are ready to submit to that change. But at the same time, being settled, working and living on the lands which they have assisted the Company [to open up, the people] of Red River, having acquired in the above manner [indisputable rights in that country,] the representatives of the Métis population of Red River loudly proclaim those rights.

5. The colony of Red River having always been subject to the Crown of England, and having developed in isolation, through all the hazards of its situation, the said representatives declare in the name of the Métis population of Red River, that they will do everything necessary to have the privileges accorded so liberally by the Crown of England to every English colony respected on their behalf.

There, Mr Editor, is what we would like to communicate to you. And those who take the liberty to send these things to you will not be the last to ensure that the rights of the people of Red River may be respected.

TWO MÉTIS SETTLERS OF RED RIVER

Source: Louis Riel, a carte-de-visite portrait taken in Ottawa following his election as member of Parliament for Provencher, Manitoba, in 1873. LAC, 002048.

Source: *Courrier de Saint-Hyacinthe*, 28 Oct. 1869, as translated in W.L. Morton, ed., *Alexander Begg's Red River Journal* (Toronto: Champlain Society, 1956), 411–13. Reprinted by permission of the publisher.

into Confederation on the basis of the 'rights' already agreed to by the residents. William McDougall made a fool of himself with an illegal proclamation of his government—Canada having refused to take possession of the territory—and then returned home.

Louis Riel marshalled his forces brilliantly. A convention of 40 representatives, equally divided between the two language groups, debated and approved another 'list of rights'. The convention endorsed Riel's provisional government. It appointed three delegates to go to Ottawa to negotiate with the Macdonald government. So far, so good. But in early March, Thomas Scott, a prisoner who was an Orangeman, got into trouble with Riel and his guards. A Métis court martial condemned Scott to death without offering him a chance to be heard. Riel accepted the sentence, commenting, 'We must make Canada respect us.' The 'murder' of Scott would have enormous repercussions in Orange Ontario, which was looking desperately for an excuse to condemn the Red River uprising. The three-man delegation from Red River, headed by Abbé Noël Ritchot (1825–1905), gained substantial concessions from the Canadian government. If honoured, they would

This photograph shows Louis Riel at the centre of his provisional government sometime in early 1870. In the top row, left to right, are Bonnet Tromage, Pierre de Lorme, Thomas Bunn, Xavier Page, Baptiste Beauchemin, Baptiste Tournond, and Thomas Spence. In the middle row are Pierre Poitras, John Bruce, Louis Riel, John O'Donoghue, and François Dauphenais. In the front row are Robert O'Lone and Paul Proulx. Although Canada had not annexed Red River in December 1869 as planned, it never admitted that the provisional government was legal. LAC, C-12854.

guarantee some protection for the original inhabitants of Red River against the expected later influx of settlers and land speculators. In what the Canadians always regarded as an act of extortion at the point of a gun, the Métis obtained the Manitoba Act of 1870. This legislation granted provincial status to a Manitoba roughly equivalent to the old Red River settlement, with 1.4 million acres (566,580 ha) set aside for the Métis and bilingual services guaranteed. The remainder of the North-West became a territory of Canada. One of its government's principal tasks was to extinguish Aboriginal title through the negotiation of treaties with the indigenous peoples. These agreements would open the way for settlement by people of European origin.

In May 1870 the Canadian government sent a so-called peaceful military expedition to Red River. The troops occupied the province for Canada in late August, forcing Riel and his associates to flee for their lives. The Scott execution provided the Canadian government with the excuse to deny Riel and his lieutenants an official amnesty for all acts committed during the 'uprising'. Those who negotiated with Canada always insisted that such an amnesty had been unofficially promised. The result was that Louis Riel went into long-term exile instead of becoming premier of the province he had created. (An amnesty was granted Riel in 1875, on the condition that he be banished from the country for five years.) Whether the government would keep better faith over its land guarantees to the Métis was another matter.

After the postage-stamp province called Manitoba was taken out, the remainder of the territory transferred to Canada by the Hudson's Bay Company—the North-West Territories—was initially administered under the original legislation passed by the Canadian

Ambroise Lépine

Ambroise Lépine (1840–1923) was born in St Boniface, his father a well-to-do French-Canadian farmer and his mother a Saskatchewan métisse. Ambroise was educated at St Boniface College, and so was hardly the illiterate 'savage' he was often made out to be by later Canadians in Manitoba. He married Cécile Marion in 1859; the couple would have 14 children. The Lépines farmed a riverside lot (number 272) not far from the Riel family, but Ambroise also participated in the buffalo hunt. He was described as 'of magnificent physique, standing fully six foot three and built of splendid proportion, straight as an arrow, with hair of raven blackness, large aquiline nose and eyes of piercing brilliance'. In 1869, Lépine became an important figure in the uprising against the Canadian annexation of Red River, not surprising in view of his family position and his reputation for hunting prowess, as well as his imposing size. He returned to the settlement around the end of October, just in time to be ordered to the border to make sure the Canadian governor, William McDougall, did not cross it to assert Canadian control over the territory. Nobody knew who was in charge of this party, he later remembered, 'and I was made leader.' Lépine very nearly did not get his assignment right. He initially allowed McDougall to cross the border, and then returned the next day to escort him back into the United States.

Lépine continued to be associated with Louis Riel, and was the commander of the Métis who surrounded the house of John Christian Schultz in early December. He later helped Riel and W.B. O'Donoghue raise the flag of the provisional government over Upper Fort Garry on 10 December. On 8 January, Lépine was named adjutant general of the provisional government, given the responsibility for the administration of justice. He was the equivalent of the chief of police in the settlement. He later represented St Boniface in the Convention of Forty, which met to formulate the demands to be made of the Canadian government, and chaired the Military Council of the convention. It was Lépine who led the Métis forces out of Upper Fort Garry to confront the men from Portage la Prairie returning from a military gathering at Kildonan. The Métis were on horseback and the Portage boys on foot. The latter surrendered. Their captain, Charles Arkoll Boulton, was initially condemned to death by Riel, but was reprieved. Later, Lépine presided at the hearing that sentenced Thomas Scott to death, casting the deciding vote in favour of execution over the objections of his brother, Baptiste. The next day, he refused to listen to pleas for Scott's life and stood by stoically as the Canadian was shot by a firing squad.

Lépine later had trouble with his men at Upper Fort Garry, and at one point both he and they went home. According to Alexander Begg, he was brought back on the understanding that he would not be so overbearing in his manner. When the Canadians took over Manitoba in late August of 1870, Lépine went on the run with Louis Riel. No amnesty for the leaders of the provisional government had been publicly declared, and the Canadians regarded the death of Scott as a murder, not a political crime. Lépine helped Riel in 1871 to raise a Métis militia force against a possible Fenian invasion, and later that year was paid by the Canadian government to leave Manitoba with Riel. He soon returned from St Paul, Minnesota, and in 1873 was arrested at his home for the death of Scott. His trial, which was really intended to test the government's case against Riel, ended in a conviction for murder by a half English-, half French-speaking jury. Lépine did not testify at the trial, but issued a statement that denied the competence of the court to try him, while insisting that he had acted as a member of a de facto government; both assertions were dismissed by the court. He was sentenced to be hanged, but was spared by the Canadian Governor General, who commuted the sentence to two years in prison and permanent loss of civil rights. Lépine declined an amnesty conditional on leaving Manitoba for five years and decided to serve his sentence. He was released in 1876, spending the remainder of a long life in poverty and obscurity. He was conspicuous by his absence from the rebellion of 1885. In 1909 he helped A.-H. Trémaudan in the writing of a history of the Métis nation.

Canada First

In April of 1868, a young man named Charles Mair headed to Ottawa to see his first book through the press. He soon fell in with an old friend, Henry J. Morgan, a clerk in the office of the secretary of state and author of the 1862 book *Sketches of Celebrated Canadians*. Morgan introduced Mair to three other visitors to Ottawa: George Taylor Denison III, William Alexander Foster, and Robert Grant Haliburton. All five men were writers, all were bachelors, and only Haliburton was over 30. They quickly discovered their common interests and fell into the habit of spending the early evening listening to the parliamentary debates in the House of Commons before returning to Morgan's rooms at the Revere Hotel to discuss public affairs over smokes and drinks. During the period between 15 April and 20 May 1868, the five young bachelors formed a secret society later called 'Canada First'. Inspired by the assassination of D'Arcy McGee, they agreed on the evil of provincialism and the need to inculcate a new 'national spirit'. They also agreed on the necessity of securing for the new Dominion the vast territory west of Ontario. Except for Haliburton, who was from Nova Scotia, the remaining four were Upper Canadians who were sensitive about being colonials and who wanted increased Canadian autonomy under an imperial umbrella.

Like many Canadians of their day, the five young men also believed in the innate superiority of white Anglo-Saxon Protestants. Haliburton was one of the earliest exponents of the notion that Canadians were the heirs of the Aryan northmen of the Old World. He told the Montreal Literary Club in March 1869 that the new Canadian nationality comprised 'the Celtic, the Teutonic, and the Scandinavian elements', and embraced 'the Celt, the Norman French, the Saxon and the Swede'. Canada Firsters looked down their noses at Aboriginal peoples and the Métis. They saw the French as the great 'bar to progress, and to the extension of a great Anglo-Saxon Dominion across the Continent', as the Toronto *Globe* put it on 4 March 1870. They were utterly contemptuous of 'half-breeds'.

Canada First remained only a debating society until the spring of 1870, when it determined to orchestrate public sentiment to the execution of Thomas Scott by the provisional government of Red River headed by Louis Riel. The reaction in Ontario to Riel before Scott's death had been fairly quiet, but by denouncing the execution of Scott, a member of the Orange Lodge, in editorials planted in leading newspapers—it was 'like putting a match to tinder', George Denison later wrote—the Canada Firsters managed to inflame Protestant Ontario against Louis Riel and his Métis followers.

In a huge public meeting in Toronto in April, Canada First introduced three resolutions that were passed easily. The first endorsed resistance of the usurpation of power by 'the murderer Riel'. The second advocated decisive measures to suppress the uprising, and the third declared that it would be gross injustice to negotiate with emissaries of a government who 'have robbed, imprisoned and murdered loyal Canadians, whose only fault was zeal for British institutions, whose only crime was devotion to the old flag.' As a result of the Canada First intervention, negotiations between Ottawa and Red River had to be conducted unofficially, the military expedition to Red River was allowed to go forward, and the leaders of the Red River resistance received no amnesty for their deeds in 1869–70.

Parliament in 1869 to deal with the West. It clearly envisioned a region held in colonial tutelage, with both government and natural resources under the strict control of Canada. The lieutenant-governor of Manitoba also served as lieutenant-governor of the Territories. The temporary legislation of 1869 was renewed without change in 1871. Not until 1872 were the Territories actually given even an appointed council. It consisted of 11 members, only two of which resided in the region. The other nine lived

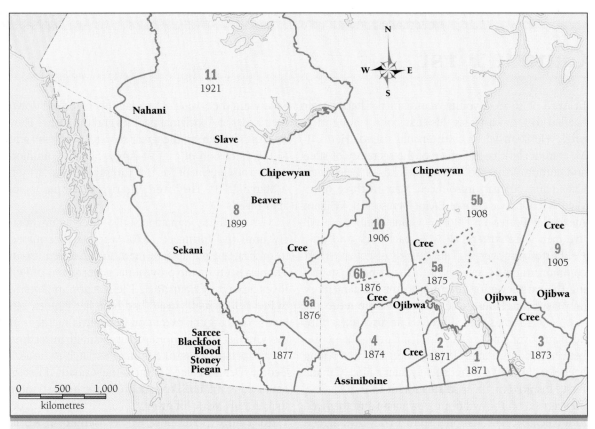

The numbered treaties, 1871–1921. Adapted from J.R. Miller, *Skyscrapers Hide the Heavens: A History of Indian–White Relations in Canada*, rev. edn (Toronto: University of Toronto Press, 1991), 166.

in or near Winnipeg, and initial meetings of the council were held there. Only in 1905—long after a second rebellion, in 1885—was provincial status finally granted to the Territories, which became Saskatchewan and Alberta.

While the question of Rupert's Land dragged slowly to its conclusion, the Canadian government was presented with an unexpected (although not totally unsolicited) gift. It consisted of a request from British Columbia—to which Vancouver Island had been joined in 1866—for admission into the new union. The initiative from the Pacific colony had originated with the Nova Scotia-born journalist Amor De Cosmos (William Alexander Smith, 1825–97), a member of the colony's legislative council. As early as March 1867 he had introduced a motion that the British North America Act, then about to be passed by the British Parliament, allow for the eventual admission of British Columbia. Entry into Confederation would introduce responsible government and resolve the colony's serious financial difficulties, which resulted partly from the interest on debts incurred for road building during the gold rushes. Union with Canada received an additional impetus when—coterminous with the passage of the British North America Act but quite independent of it—the American government purchased Alaska from the Russians. The purchase touched off demands in the American press for the annexation of British Columbia as well. Officially the British notified the colony in November 1867 that no action would be taken on its relationship with Canada until Rupert's Land had been duly incorporated into the new nation.

Union with Canada was debated by the British Columbia Legislative Council in March 1870. This

'Red River Settlement' to *Montreal Herald*, 4 December 1869

This is part of one of a series of letters sent from Red River to the *Montreal Herald* by J.J. Hargrave, writing as 'Red River Settlement' in 1869.

Fort Garry
Red River Settlement
4th Dec., 1869

In my last letter I explained that the delegates representing the English and French sections of the Settlement had separated on the afternoon of the 23rd November, appointing the 1st December as the day of their next meeting, in order to give the former an opportunity of meeting their constituents and receiving their sanction to act in the formation of a temporary or 'Provisional Government'.

Meetings of a public nature had, in accordance with this design, been held in the various parishes inhabited by the Protestant population of the Colony. I mentioned that one had also been held in the village of Winnipeg, and I would now begin to trouble you with a few matters of detail regarding it. It was held in the Fire Engine House in the village, on the evening of Friday, 26th ult [last, i.e., 26 November].

The room was well filled with a crowd of American citizens, local residents, and Canadian new arrivals and others late of the Government. The Post Master, Mr. Bannatyne, was chairman. Louis Riel, the most active spirit among the French half-breeds, was present, with his body guard. He did not, I believe, intend to take part in the debate; but Mr. Michael Powers, a Chelsea Out-Pensioner of the rank of Sergeant from a regiment of Dragoon Guards, requested him to state to the people the source whence he drew the authority under which he is at present acting.

After some apparent reluctance, overcome by the encouraging demonstrations of those present, Riel stepped forward, and in the course of a somewhat protracted speech in English, stated substantially that he drew his authority, as did all other constitutional rulers, from the people. He said the French did not wish to impose their Provisional Government on any or all of the English, and that any one who did not wish to own allegiance to it was at liberty to remain beyond its pale. He and his friends wanted no money, and were ambitious only to serve their countrymen. He stated that his widowed mother was suffering the consequences of the action he was taking, as they were very poor; and his was by no means a solitary case, for all his assistants and followers were poor men and their families were suffering while their time was occupied with public service and duties. Above all, the government was not one of religion, as he said had been rumoured. . . .

As an instance of the state in which society exists here at present, I beg to mention the following facts: Talking over the events of the meeting with three friends, with whom I spent the subsequent part of the evening, I rather ridiculed the idea expressed in my hearing, that almost every one present at the meeting had been armed, and that there had been certain critical moments when a general discharge of pistols had been imminent. I must confess, however, to a modification of opinion when my three friends pulled, each man from a belt concealed under his coat, a revolver pistol. In one of these three instances, certainly, only one chamber was loaded, and as the hammer was laid down on the corresponding nipple, the instrument, on being cocked, would, of course, have turned, so as to let it fall on any empty chamber, and the person covered by that instrument would probably have run no very serious risk; but the other two were fully charged and capped, and had only to be cocked, after which, to use the expression of one of the parties, 'one trigger, sir, would do the business.' After such a demonstration I affect not to doubt the truth of the assertion that more than fifty revolvers were in readiness for use at the meeting; but the position of a non combatant spectator, in the centre of such a shower of leaden hail as might have burst forth in a crowded chamber from all these instruments, would have been far from pleasant.

Source: From *Montreal Herald and Daily Commercial Gazette*, 25 Dec. 1869.

debate was different from earlier ones in the eastern legislatures, for the British North America Act was already in place and in operation. British Columbia could not hope to influence the shape of Confederation, only to decide whether it would enter the union and upon what terms. The debate was a bit curious. The opponents of Confederation wanted the issues of popular elections (in an elected assembly) and responsible government cleared up in advance of union, while the pro-confederates—the government party—were quite satisfied with the local status quo.

Negotiations between British Columbia and Canada took place in the late spring of 1870. The Canadians were generous to a fault. Of course, British Columbia could have responsible government. Of course, the debt would be wiped out. Of course, there would be subsidies and grants, as well as federal support for the naval station at Esquimalt. And, of course, British Columbia could have a rail link with Canada, to be begun within two years and completed within 15 years. The promise was audacious, although Canada obviously needed a transcontinental railroad to match the lines rapidly being constructed across the United States. The terms were far better than expected, and on 20 July 1871 British Columbia entered Confederation as the sixth province. While in most respects the new province remained isolated until the completion of the rail link in 1885, Confederation encouraged the development of a new land policy for the province.

Confederation Complete

To-day, British Columbia passed peacefully and, let us add, gracefully into the confederated empire of British North America. Perhaps it would be more proper to put it thus: To-day the confederated empire of British North America stretches to the shores of the Pacific, 'whose limpid waters' to quote the poetic language of Mr. J. Spencer Thompson, 'leave in baptismal welcome to brow of the new-born Province which forms the last link in the transcontinental chain—the last star in the constellation which is destined hereafter to shine so brightly in the northern hemisphere.' To-day the great scheme of Confederation in British North America may be regarded as practically complete. It is true that two islands of the Atlantic (Prince Edward and Newfoundland) still stand aloof. But Confederation can get on without them much better than they can get on without it. . . . To-day British Columbia and Canada join hands and hearts across the Rocky Mountains, and John Bull the younger stands with one foot on the Atlantic and the other on the Pacific—with his back to the North Pole and his face looking southward—how far we will not now venture to predict. Let the larger political union which we celebrate to-day be symbolic of a union of parties, of purpose and of action. Let the people of this Pacific Province accustom themselves to think of the Dominion as a second edition of Great Britain, and let all learn to regard each other as a band of brothers upon whom has devolved the honor and the responsibility of laying the foundations of empire. There is a feeling in the minds of some that the day which celebrates the nuptials of British Columbia

The provincial government opened its Crown lands to massive pre-emption and free land grants; the largesse of British Columbia would far exceed that of the federal government.

Prince Edward Island's acceptance of terms in 1873 was almost anticlimactic. The tiny province had tried to survive without much support from the British, who made clear their lack of enthusiasm for a Crown colony. The imperial refusal to pay the salary of the lieutenant-governor was seen as a 'confederate screw unfairly put upon us'. Both the Americans and the Canadians actively wooed the island. In the end, it entered Confederation in the wake of a profligate policy of railway construction, which many saw as a scheme to force it into union. As well as offering to take over the debt and the railway, Canada agreed to guarantee continuous communication with the mainland and to help buy out the last of the old landed proprietors. Only one island MLA, the crusty farmer Cornelius Howatt, refused to vote for the Canadian offer.

Unlike Prince Edward Island, Newfoundland was not persuaded to join the union at all. In 1869 Newfoundland held an election fought on the issue of Confederation with Canada. The economy improved in the period before the election, while the opponents of Confederation employed every argument in their rhetorical arsenal. These included rumours that Canada would use Newfoundland children as wadding for their cannons. The 1869 election went decisively against the pro-confederates. The island's Catholics opposed union. In one Catholic area, a pro-confederate candidate was greeted by priest and populace carrying pots of pitch and bags of feathers. The Protestant vote split equally. In the end the election returned nine confederates and 21 antis. The confederates blamed their defeat on the nasty campaign tactics of the opposition, but Newfoundland's union with Canada was not a matter of high priority for anyone. Both the British and Canadian governments acquiesced in Newfoundland's continued autonomy—despite sporadic union discussions as in 1887 and 1895—until 1949.

As well as dealing with the strays, the Canadian government had also to pacify Nova Scotia and New Brunswick. This was especially true of Nova Scotia, where pledged anti-confederates took both federal and provincial seats in the election that accompanied union. The British government refused to allow reconsideration of the initial decision to join

and Canada at the same time celebrates the divorce of the former from the parent empire, and this feeling may tend to damp the enthusiasm of such as are the subjects of it: and we readily confess that, did not ground for the idea exist, we would sympathise with the feeling it is calculated to beget. Not only is there no ground for the idea, but the reverse is actually true. Instead of the union we celebrate weakening those bonds which connect us with the parent empire, it will impart additional strength and vitality to them. It will release us from the red tape and sealing wax of Downing street, it is true—but then, it will draw us nearer to the throne. It will do more. It will draw together all the peoples of British North America into one common brotherhood and beget a national sentiment, a sentiment more truly British than would be compatible with isolation and discontent. Let the union we celebrate be suggestive of a drawing together, a harmonizing and a nationalizing of all those sometime discordant elements which have culminated in local faction; and while joining hands with Canada in the grand and patriotic work of building up a second British Empire on this continent, let us join hands among ourselves in a friendly but firm resolve to begin our new political life a united and harmonious band for the purpose of making British Columbia—what Nature designed her to be—the Queen Province of the Dominion. With one common nationality, one common interest, one object should now actuate every heart and obliterate all those lines created by the factions of the past.

Source: From *The British Colonist* (Victoria), 20 July 1871.

Canada in 1873.

Canada, chiefly on the grounds that such important political actions should not be taken at the whim of local electorates. The leading anti, Joseph Howe, eventually accepted that there was no alternative to accepting confederation. In February 1869 Howe ran as a pro-confederate in a federal election in Hants County, which was hotly contested. He won with a comfortable majority and headed off to Ottawa, joining the federal cabinet within weeks. In some ways this grudging acquiescence in a situation with which he did not agree may have been the most important political act of his career.

The Development of National Policies

As well as completing the creation of a transcontinental nation, the Macdonald government gradually improvised some national policies with which to govern the new Dominion. Confederation was encouraging to foreign investment. From its inception, Canada was able to import large amounts of capital to help create its infrastructure. Between 1865 and 1869 Canada raised $16.5 million in Great Britain, a figure that rose to $96.4 million in 1870–4, $74.7 million in 1875–9, and $69.8 million in 1880–4.

The government obtained some recognition of Canadian diplomatic autonomy by its acquiescence to the Treaty of Washington in 1871. Outstanding issues with the Americans included the *Alabama* claims. The *Alabama* was a Confederate raider built in Britain for the southern states. The Americans, half-seriously, demanded the cession of British-American territory in compensation for the losses it inflicted on northern shipping. In 1871 the British government made Macdonald a member of an international joint commission set up in 1870 to deal

Dominion Day in Charlottetown

On Tuesday, whether for weal or woe, Prince Edward Island became a province of the Dominion of Canada. At 12 o'clock noon, the Dominion flag was run up on the flag staffs at Government House and the Colonial Building, and a salute of 21 guns was fired from St. George's battery and from H.M.S. Spartan now in port. The Church and City bells also rang out a lively peal, and the Volunteers under review at the City Park, fired a feu de joie. So far as powder and metal could do it there was for a short time a terrible din. But among the people who thronged the streets there was no enthusiasm. A few moments before 12, Mr. Sheriff Watson stepped forward on the balcony of the Colonial Building and read the Union Proclamation. He was accompanied by two ladies and about half a dozen gentlemen. The audience below within hearing consisted of three persons, and even they did not appear to be very attentive. After the reading of the Proclamation was concluded, the gentlemen on the balcony gave a cheer, but the three persons below—who like the Tooley street tailors who claimed to be 'the people of England,' at that moment represented the people of Prince Edward Island,—responded never a word. Most of the shops in the city were shut, and a good deal of bunting was displayed. HMS Spartan, and some of the merchant shipping in the harbor, were gaily decked with flags. At night the Colonial and new Post Office Buildings were illuminated, and presented a fine appearance. A few sky rockets were also fired off from the top of the latter building about 10 o'clock, with good effect. But the most beautiful sight of the day was the illumination of the Spartan, between 9 1/2 and 10 o'clock. With her ports all lit up, and various kinds of lights in the rigging, she was really an object worth looking at. . . .

We have already remarked that there did not appear to be any enthusiasm among the people. Probably no effort the Government could have put forth would have made the celebration of Dominion Day a grand success, but we beg leave to express the opinion the arrangements were very lame indeed. The public were not notified that the Sheriff was to read the union Proclamation in front of the Building at 12 o'clock, consequently no person was there except two or three people who happened to be passing by at the time. Had one of the 'able men' been called upon to prepare an oration for the occasion, and due notice thereof given there might have been a crowd on Queen Square to listen to both it and the proclamation. . . .

The great majority of the people of the Island, it is pretty evident, have accepted Confederation as a necessity. They did not take up the question con amore and when the day arrived that the union was a fait accompli, they had not a cheer to give. Many of our citizens look upon last night's illumination as but the complement of the one which took place when the Railway Bill was passed. We have a shrewd suspicion that their view of the case is tolerably correct; but now since Confederation is a fact—since the Island is now part and parcel of the Dominion, the duty of our people is to make the best of their position. We are now with the Sister Provinces in regard to political institutions; let us perform our part so that we may do more than merely keep pace with them in the march of intelligence and reform.

Source: From *The Patriot* (Charlottetown), 3 July 1873.

with the fisheries question. The British made clear they were willing to surrender Canadian interests in the fisheries to settle outstanding Anglo–American differences. Macdonald signed the resulting treaty.

On the domestic front, the banking system of the new nation grew rapidly from 123 chartered bank branches in 1869 to 279 in 1879 and 426 by 1890. Two major pieces of national legislation were the

The Reminiscences of Dr John Sebastian Helmcken

In 1892, Dr John Sebastian Helmcken (1824–1920) of British Columbia wrote in manuscript a lengthy collection of his memories. The manuscript ended up in the Provincial Archives of British Columbia in Victoria, and was edited for publication by Dorothy Blakey Smith, appearing in print in 1975. Here Helmcken discusses the election of 1868, fought over the issue of Confederation. His use of what we would regard as racist language was quite common in the nineteenth century.

. . . [A] general election was ordered; Confederation being the burning question, everyone rampant on one side or the other; of course the American element being against the Union. At this time no distinct terms had been proposed, but if I recollect rightly De Cosmos and the colored man Gibbs and [John Norris] had been to the 'Yale Convention'; a Convention for the purpose of an organization for Confederation purposes. The Convention was ridiculed and lambasted by opponents—the colored man [Gibbs] having a good share. By the bye I had been a means of getting the coloured man elected to the House of Assembly and really he was in some measure a superior man and very gentlemanly withal. I think he claimed being a West Indian.

I came out against Confederation distinctly, chiefly because I thought it premature—partly from prejudice—and because no suitable terms could be proposed. The tariff was a sticking point: although we had at this time a tariff but could change it to suit ourselves. Our income too would be diminished and there at this time appeared no means of replenishing it by the [British] North America Act. Our population was too small numerically. Moreover it would only be a confederacy on paper for no means of communication with the Eastern Provinces existed, without which no advantage could possibly ensue. Canada was looked down upon as a poor mean slow people, who had been very commonly designated North American chinamen. This character they had

Dominion Notes Act of 1870 and the Bank Act of 1871. The former allowed the government to issue circulating notes of small denominations, only partly backed by specie. The latter exerted control over the banking system. The Bank Act specified capital requirements for banks, prohibited new foreign-owned banks, and supplied general regulation. Canada accepted the international gold standard, but the government would share the issuance of currency (and the control of the creation of money) with the banks until well into the twentieth century.

One of the major new developments of the Macdonald government was a new federal system of justice for the new nation commensurate with Confederation's division of the administration of justice between federal and provincial governments.

It began in 1868 with the establishment of a Department of Justice, creating the post of minister of justice to administer it as well as an attorney general; the minister of justice was given the task of reviewing provincial legislation and the attorney general the supervision of the criminal law. Other renovations to the administration of justice followed. The creation of a national penitentiary system also began in 1868, with the enactment of a statute that envisioned a prison system where punishment and deterrence were meted out through discipline and rewards (Swainger, 2000). The Canadian government established the North West Mounted Police in 1873 to act as its quasi-military agent in the West. It modelled the NWMP on the Irish constabulary. Its officers, drawn from the elites of eastern Canada, achieved from their necessarily thrifty condition for long years, and indeed they compared unfavourably with the Americans and with our American element, for at this time and previously very many liberal-handed and better class of Americans resided here, many in business—some on account of the Civil War necessitating their remaining even after the frightful internecine killing had ceased. Our trade was either with the U.S. or England—with Canada we had nothing to do. Of course my being an Anti-confederationist, led to my being dubbed an Annexationist, but really I had no idea of annexation, but merely wished the Colony to be let alone under HM Govt and to fight her way unhampered. I had nothing whatever to do with annexation petitions, and do not know who signed them—tho I have heard that some who now hold or have held official positions have done so. This petition doubtless went to the President of the U.S. but no one has ever been able to see a copy of it since, altho it is said to exist in Victoria somewhere. There is no doubt the Americans had a contempt for Canada and this feeling extended to the colonists.

I suppose the election was one of the fiercest ever fought in Victoria, everyone seemed crazy, I among the number—these were the days of great excitements. I had the British and American elements and Jewish element on my side and after a time the election came on. Numberless ladies wore my colours, red, white and blue, in shape according to their taste, the men likewise. Ladies were at the windows waving their handkerchiefs, every hack in the place was frightfully busy. The polling went actively on, but there were no rows, or if there were, they were insignificant. Various committees had districts under control; they had to get the voters up and were responsible therefore. The cry went round that both sides had a number of voters locked up and were feeding them with whisky, to get them into proper trim; altho this accusation was not strictly true, still voters came to the polling place, where the Courts of Justice now stand, in files. Notwithstanding all this there were no rows outside the polling places, the matter was too serious for this. At length 4 o'clock struck—the polls closed; everyone tired—thirsty, hoarse and expectant. The Anti-confederates had won handsomely. . . .

Source: Reprinted with permission of the Publisher from *The Reminiscences of Doctor Sebastian Helmcken* by Dorothy Blakey Smith © University of British Columbia Press 1975. All rights reserved by the Publisher.

believed in a notion of public stability that associated crime and violence with the 'lower orders' and the Aboriginal peoples. The Mounties kept ahead of settlement and have always been seen as the chief instruments of a more peaceful process of western expansion than occurred in the neighbouring United States. Certainly in Canada there was less overt violence, but this was often owing to the early exertion of state power and control.

Much capital would be invested in railways. The opportunity for railway expansion was one of the principal arguments for Confederation. Railways were a prime target of foreign investors. The Macdonald government was slow to move on a transcontinental line, chiefly because of the enormous expense involved in building so far ahead

of population needs. To some extent, the offer to British Columbia cast the die. There followed an unseemly scuffling over a charter, awarded in 1873 by Parliament to the Canada Pacific Railway Company of Sir Hugh Allan (1810–82). Then the Pacific Scandal broke. Allan had provided the government with money for its 1872 election campaign. Macdonald was unable to steer totally clear of the corrupt dealings. In November 1873 the government resigned. Replacing it was a Liberal government headed by a Scottish-born former stonemason, Alexander Mackenzie (1822–92). He sought to build a transcontinental line more gradually, using public funds. He also encouraged private interests to hook up with American western lines. Trains began running from Minnesota to Winnipeg late in 1878.

Alexander Mackenzie

Alexander Mackenzie, c. 1878. The Canadian Press.

Born and raised in Perthshire, Scotland, Alexander Mackenzie (1822–92) grew up speaking English and Gaelic. Like most Scots, he received the rudiments of an education in a village school but was largely self-taught. He came to adulthood in a Scotland plagued by financial depression and political discontent, and in 1842, as a stonecutter and stonemason, he joined thousands of other Scots (including members of his own family) in immigrating to Canada. From his arrival, Mackenzie behaved as an archetypal Scot, committed to family, a joyless nonconformist religion, teetotalism, and a utilitarianism that manifested itself in a strong work ethic and sense of duty.

In 1847 he moved to Sarnia, where he became a highly successful building contractor and an active supporter of the Clear Grit movement led by fellow Scot George Brown, who became his political mentor. In 1861 he was elected to represent Lambton and Kent (the riding that included Sarnia) in the Canadian assembly. Here he supported Confederation but strongly opposed both the 'Great Coalition' that brought it about and the attempt of John A. Macdonald to continue non-partisan government after 1 July 1867. Mackenzie's insistence on the importance of party and its management—he led the Reform party in Parliament after Confederation—was one of his major contributions to the new nation; it was particularly crucial since the Canadian Constitution made no mention of political parties, leaving early practice to establish the conventions. Mackenzie became federal leader of the Liberal opposition in Parliament in May 1873, and before the year was out became Prime Minister when Macdonald suddenly resigned on 5 November.

Mackenzie was almost the mirror opposite of his predecessor, austere and humourless, obsessed with detail rather than the big picture. He worked very hard at demonstrating that the Canadian nation could be governed by alternate visions and different national policies. His government granted amnesty to the Red River rebels and a provisional pardon to Louis Riel. It created the Supreme Court of Canada (in 1875) and the Auditor General's office (1878), and built more than 2,500 miles of railway track. Mackenzie's legislative successes included the secret ballot, an improved post office, and standardized weights and measures. He supported provincial rights, greater national powers within the British Empire, and free trade. Not long after his party was defeated in the election of 1878, at least partly because of one of Macdonald's grand visions—the 'National Policy'—Mackenzie resigned as party leader and resumed life as a backbench member of Parliament. On numerous occasions he refused knighthood and died as an ordinary citizen.

Mackenzie's government was also largely responsible for the initial funding of western railway construction. It gave the railway companies large land grants along the right of way. Although Canada developed a seemingly generous homestead policy by which pioneers could receive free land grants in return for developing the land, the generosity was deceptive. Almost no homestead land was available within easy access to the rail lines. Most early settlers ended up purchasing their land, either from the railways or from the Hudson's Bay Company.

Mackenzie's government had a number of positive achievements to its credit. It resolved the Louis Riel question in 1875 by granting the Métis leader an amnesty, conditional on his residence in exile for five years. It established the Supreme Court of Canada that same year, and subsequently created the office of the Auditor General. But the real importance of the Mackenzie government was its demonstration that the nation could be governed without serious upheaval by another political party with different policies from the one led by Sir John A. Macdonald. Mackenzie was a man without charisma, however, and many critics thought he spent too much energy micromanaging the budget.

The probity of his government did not save Alexander Mackenzie in 1878. Sir John A. Macdonald returned to power. Recognizing the temper of the times, Macdonald worked hard to restore in the public mind a sense of identification between his party and the process of nation-building. Decisiveness and flamboyance were part of the image. Even before the election was called, Macdonald had his platform. He introduced into the House of Commons a resolution

Sir John A. Macdonald on the National Policy, 1882

Canadian political parties did not adopt official platforms until late in the nineteenth century. In earlier elections, voters could glean some notion of the parties' policies from the speeches of their leaders, which were widely reported in the press. The following excerpts are taken from various campaign speeches made by Sir John A. Macdonald and reported in the Toronto *Mail* in May and June 1882.

WHY THE GOVERNMENT GOES TO THE COUNTRY

Because we thought it was of the greatest consequence to Canada, and to the future prosperity of the manufacturers of Canada, that the people should have an opportunity of expressing their opinion whether our policy is wise or not. A good many manufactures have been commenced, but they would have been quadrupled, four times as many manufactures would have been started in Canada, if it were not for the dread that the policy of 1878 would be destroyed and upset by a free trade Parliament in 1883.

THE ISSUE

We desire that the people may at once declare whether they wish to have fair trade, plenty of work, and prosperity, or free trade, want of labour, and poverty.

We place that fairly before the people and say:—If you want to reverse that policy, do; if you want a continuance of prosperity, declare so at the polls, and you will have five years ahead during which that policy cannot be reversed. We have had three years now and at the end of five years more the manufacturing interest will be so strong that, as in the United States, it will be able to fight its own battles, and there is no fear of that policy being reversed to ruin the manufacturer who has put his money, his means, his credit, and his capital into such enterprises.

Why, sir, the true National Policy is this—to find, at all events, a home market for as much as we can, and if in consequence of our industry and of good seasons we raise more in the country than we can consume ourselves, to send the surplus abroad.

'That this House is of the opinion that the welfare of Canada requires the adoption of a National Policy, which, by a judicious readjustment of the Tariff, will benefit and foster the agricultural, the mining, the manufacturing, and other interests of this Dominion' (quoted in Easterbrook and Watkins, 1962: 238). The Tory leader invented neither the policy nor the term used to describe it. Both went well back into the history of the Province of Canada, which had begun using a tariff as an instrument of both protection and revenue in the late 1840s. Nor did John A. Macdonald ever articulate the version of the National Policy as it was later lovingly described by economic historians and textbook writers. But he certainly recognized some relationship involving tariffs, manufacturing, employment, and national prosperity. He also wanted a transcontinental railway and the accompanying western settlement necessary to make it a reality. All these features had been and remained a traditional part of Canadian economic expansionism.

What Macdonald achieved was masterful in its own way. He succeeded in persuading a large number of Canadians in all provinces that policies strongly driven by the economic self-interest of some of the people in some of its constituent parts were in the best interest of the nation as a whole. He then persuaded the electorate that his party was the one that had successfully built the nation and would continue to do so. The fact that the opposition party took the lead in developing a different and less overt version of nation-building helped in this identification.

The responsibility for immigration policy had been divided between the Dominion and the provinces by the British North America Act. Both the Macdonald governments and the Mackenzie government sought to develop federal supremacy over immigration policy, in large measure to make possible the rapid settlement of the West. The Dominion also began to set rules indicating which immigrants would be acceptable. The federal Parliament passed its first immigration legislation in 1869 and, in 1872, prohibited the entry of criminals and other 'vicious classes'. That same year Parliament passed the Dominion Lands Act, which created homesteading privileges on western lands. The Dominion then began extensive advertising in Europe for new settlers. While the Canadian government discouraged the Métis from settling in concentrated blocks of land, in the mid-1870s it negotiated with several European groups, including the Mennonites and the Icelanders, for group settlement in Manitoba.

The first successful arrangements for block settlement were conducted by the Canadian government with Russian Mennonites beginning in 1872 and 1873. These Mennonites were European Quakers committed to pacifism who had originated in Prussia and Poland in the sixteenth century. They were driven out of their homes by threats of military conscription in Frederick the Great's Prussia, finding an asylum in Russia, where Catherine II offered them generous conditions of resettlement, including land, freedom of religion, their own schools, and permanent exemption from military service. By 1870s the Mennonites were again threatened, this time by a rising Russian nationalism that resented a people set apart. The Canadian government offered inducements similar to the earlier Russian ones: exemption from military service, religious liberty, control of education, free homesteads of 160 acres, and the right to purchase additional land at one dollar per acre. Canada set aside two blocks of townships for the Mennonites in southern Manitoba. One block of eight townships was on the east side of the Red River southwest of Winnipeg, and another block of twelve townships ('The West Reserve') was located along the international boundary west of the Red River. The blocks of reserves signalled to the Mennonites that they could live in their own communities (and hold land in common) apart from their neighbours; about 8,000 Mennonites settled in 1874 in southern Manitoba.

In 1879, a federal Order-in-Council prohibited the entrance of paupers and destitute immigrants. Not long afterwards, the government began to admit large numbers of Chinese immigrants (over 15,000), approximately half of them as labourers on the transcontinental railroad. In 1882, a public response to Russian pogroms led to the admission of a contingent of 247 Jews leaving London for Manitoba and the North-West to establish a 'New Jerusalem' in what would become Saskatchewan. They did not receive land until 1884, by which time their numbers had been greatly reduced, and the settlement soon failed. By the early 1880s demands for

The Republic of New Iceland

People from Iceland had been coming to Canada from the early 1870s, prompted by both volcanic eruptions and grassland shortages in their homeland and a general population excess pressing on available resources. The first arrivals had come to Ontario and Quebec, but were attracted west by promises from the Canadian government of an autonomous settlement in the west. The land they chose was on the west side of Lake Winnipeg, about 15 miles wide and 40 miles long stretching from present-day Selkirk to Hecla Island and including the modern community of Gimli. This territory was beyond the then northern boundary of the province of Manitoba, and the newcomers were allowed autonomous settlement, 'the Republic of New Iceland', with its own laws and judicial system. The Canadian government accepted a provisional council ('Thing') set up by the Icelanders, and allowed them to produce a fully articulated system of self-government. This entity became part of Manitoba when the boundaries of the province were expanded in 1881, but self-government remained until 1887. Although the territory the Icelanders chose was good for fishing on Lake Winnipeg, it contained some of the poorest agricultural land in the region. The Icelanders were struck by epidemic disease and spring flooding, and in the later 1870s a religious dispute emerged as well. Many moved to the United States or to Winnipeg. Most who remained made a living by fishing. Icelanders were generally well-educated and committed to preservation of their language. Schools and newspapers were established in New Iceland within months of settlement, and the community over the next half-century would produce a number of poets, journalists, and writers who employed the Icelandic language before the area was absorbed gradually into Manitoba.

Many Icelanders who settled in Manitoba hoped to make a living through agriculture, but due to flooding and disease, as well as settlement on marginal land for farming, most were unsuccessful. Archives of Manitoba, New Iceland 312 (N11314).

further restrictions on the number of immigrants surfaced in Canada, particularly of those outside previous Canadian experience regarded as 'unassimilable'. Sir John A. Macdonald told the House of Commons in 1883 that 'It will be all very well to exclude Chinese labour, when we can replace it with white labour, but until that is done, it is better to have Chinese labour than no labour at all' (quoted in Magocsi, 1999: 359). As soon as the railroad was completed, Macdonald gave in to pressures from British Columbia and elsewhere to deal with the Chinese, who were blamed for a variety of social and economic evils. A Royal Commission on Chinese immigration in 1885 recommended restrictions on the number of Chinese workers, and Macdonald instituted a head tax of $50 on every Chinese person entering the country. His legislation also restricted the number of Chinese people who could be carried on individual vessels entering Canadian ports. (On 22 June 2006, Prime Minister Stephen Harper formally apologized to the Chinese community for this policy, which continued until 1923.) The federal legislation was added to numerous provincial statutes (especially in British Columbia) to limit the rights of the Chinese in Canada.

The Quest for Regional and National Identity

The British North America Act had no guarantees that political unification would necessarily create a nation. After 1867 Canadians made various attempts to locate themselves in their world. Some of these attempts were political and constitutional. Others were cultural, with intellectuals and artists playing their part by providing rhetorical flourishes as well as creating national institutions in which the arts could operate.

The development of nationhood in the years after 1867 did not mean that all Canadians shared in the same vision (or version) of the meaning of the nation. One of the major questions was whether Canada was an indissoluble new creation or the product of a compact among the provinces that they could modify or even leave. Since the time of the debate over Confederation in the 1860s, people had disagreed over the nature of the union. While most Canadians in 1867 saw the British North America Act as creating a strong central government, provincial legislatures still existed. They would quickly assert more than the merely local power accorded them by the Quebec resolutions. One of the arch-critics of Confederation, Christopher Dunkin (1812–81), had prophesied in 1865 that 'In the times to come, when men shall begin to feel strongly on those questions that appeal to national preferences, prejudices and passions, all talk of your new nationality will sound but strangely. Some older nationality will then be found to hold the first place in most

people's hearts' (quoted in Waite, 1963: 511). Even Sir John A. Macdonald had admitted in Parliament in 1868 that 'a conflict may, ere long, arise between the Dominion and the States Rights people' (quoted in Cook, 1969a: 10).

Ontario initially spearheaded the provincial-rights interpretation of the new union. The seeds of this interpretation were inherent in the constitutional arrangements, and the movement could have begun anywhere. As early as 1869 Ontario became distressed at 'the assumption by the Parliament of Canada of the power to disturb the financial relations established by the British North America Act (1867), as between Canada and the several provinces' (quoted in Cook, 1969a: 11). Not surprisingly, the old Reform Party of Canada West, in the persons of George Brown, Edward Blake (1833–1912), and Oliver Mowat (1820–1903), took the lead. They demanded—in Blake's phrase of 1871—'that each government [Dominion and provincial] shall be absolutely independent of the other in its management of its own affairs' (quoted in Cook, 1969a: 13). The Rouges of Quebec soon joined in the same call, adding the identification of French-Canadian 'national' rights to Ontario's 'provincial' ones. Before long, Liberals in most provinces—many of whom had either opposed Confederation or been luke-warm about it—had embraced provincial rights.

Provincial rights often seemed interchangeable with Ottawa-bashing for local political advantage, lacking in any other principle than the desire to pressure Ottawa into fiscal concessions. In its early years, Quebec did not dominate the movement. There was little insistence that Confederation was a cultural deal between two distinct societies. In 1884, for example, the Honourable Honoré Mercier (1840–94) tabled resolutions in the Quebec legislature stating merely that 'the frequent encroachments of the Federal Parliament upon the prerogatives of the Provinces are a permanent menace to the latter' (quoted in Cook, 1969a: 31). The ensuing debate involved no more cultural nationalism than one backbencher's assertion that 'le Québec n'est pas une province comme les autres' (quoted in Cook, 1969a: 33). Although the Riel affair of 1885 (discussed later in this chapter) pushed Quebec towards the brink of arguments of cultural distinctiveness, when Mercier (by this time Premier of Quebec) invited the provinces to the Interprovincial Conference in 1887 to re-examine the federal compact, broad agreement could be reached on demands for better terms and constitutional change by the five provinces attending without the need for such concepts.

Provincial rights involved on one level a political-constitutional struggle over revenue and power. On another level they were a reflection of the continued identification of the people of Canada with their province of residence as much as, if not more than, with their nation. The educational structure of Canada certainly encouraged this identification. In all provinces education passed from private to public financial support at the same time that schooling became increasingly universal. However, section 92 of the British North America Act left education completely in the hands of the provinces. It is almost impossible to talk about any integrated national movements. Indeed, education would become one of the most divisive issues in the new nation. A major question was whether provinces would have a single public school system for all students or would support separate religious (and linguistic) education as well. Educational diversity was still the norm after Confederation. There were, at best, provincial educational systems and norms, not national ones.

Although a sense of nationalism was beginning to develop, it did not pose a serious challenge to provincial loyalties. The movement calling itself Canada First, for example, did not have a program that was particularly attractive outside Protestant circles in Ontario. Canada First was an exclusive secret society rather than a broad-based organization. It did not help that its vision of Canada was really that of Canada West writ larger. While Canada First's notions were compatible, to some extent, with the westward thrust of Canada West, they were, fortunately, not totally typical of the conscious development of Canadian nationalism. The French-Canadian poet Octave Crémazie (1827–79), for example, lamented ironically that Canada's major literary languages were entirely of European origin. He continued: 'if we spoke Huron or Iroquois, the works of our writers would attract the attention of the old

world. . . . One would be overwhelmed by a novel or a poem translated from the Iroquois, while one does not take the trouble to read a book written in French by a native of Quebec or Montreal' (quoted in Rasporich, 1969: 225). The search for an essential 'Canadian-ness' went on in many corners of the new Dominion. It was nowhere so successful as in the somewhat remote New Brunswick town of Fredericton, home of the University of New Brunswick. There the rectory of St Anne's Parish (Anglican) produced Charles G.D. Roberts (1860–1943), while not far down the road lived his cousin Bliss Carman (1861–1929). Along with Ottawa's Archibald Lampman (1861–99) and Duncan Campbell Scott (1862–1947), these men comprised the first school of Canadian poets, designated 'Confederation Poets' by modern literary critics. Roberts, Lampman, Carman, and Scott brought Canadian themes into their writing, notably the local or regional landscape, with some degree of skill and sensitivity. As Crémazie had suggested, however, the European origins of their literary influences limited their efforts.

While many intellectuals and artists sought ways to articulate Canadian-ness in their work, others took a more prosaic route towards the realization of a Canadian national identity. Curiously enough, it was the painters, not normally known for their political acuity, who took the lead in organizing national groups to maintain professional standards and publicize Canadian achievement. The Ontario Society of Artists, formed in 1872 and incorporated in 1877, was at the forefront of this effort. The OSA was instrumental in the formation of the Royal Canadian Academy of Arts in 1880—in collaboration with the Governor General, Lord Lorne (1845–1914)—and in the establishment that same year of the National Gallery of Canada. One of the founders of this organization wrote, 'We are bound to try to civilize the Dominion a little' (quoted in Williamson, 1970: 64). The year 1880 was doubly important in art circles, for in that year the Canadian Society of Graphic Art was also founded.

The first president of the Royal Canadian Academy, the painter Lucius O'Brien (1832–99), was art director of an elaborate literary and artistic celebration of the young nation. *Picturesque Canada*

(1882) was based on the highly successful books *Picturesque America* and *Picturesque Europe*. It was the idea of two Americans, the Belden brothers, who had established themselves in Toronto. The editor of the project—George Monro Grant (1835–1902), principal of Queen's University—stated in the preface: 'I believed that a work that would represent its characteristic scenery and history and life of its people would not only make us better known to ourselves and to strangers, but would also stimulate national sentiment and contribute to the rightful development of the nation.' The two large volumes of *Picturesque Canada*—which can sometimes be found in second-hand bookshops—contain 540 illustrations. They included wood engravings based on paintings and, for the West, photo engravings of photographs that offered serene vistas fulfilling the promise of the title. The descriptive texts by Grant, Charles G.D. Roberts, and others presented an idealized, complacent view of the cities, towns, and regions of Canada, praising the present and pointing to a glorious future.

The Royal Society of Canada was founded in 1882 to promote research and learning in the arts and sciences. Lord Lorne again provided much of the impetus, replicating a British institution to establish the importance of cultural accomplishments in creating a sense of national pride and self-confidence. The first president, J.W. Dawson (1820–99), principal of McGill University (another Nova Scotian transported to central Canada), emphasized in his presidential address a sense of national purpose. Dawson stressed especially 'the establishment of a bond of union between the scattered workers now widely separated in different parts of the Dominion' (quoted in Royal Society of Canada, 1932: 91–2). Thomas Sterry Hunt (1826–92), a charter member and later president, observed that 'The occasion which brings us together is one which should mark a new departure in the intellectual history of Canada' (Royal Society of Canada, 1932: 91–2). He added that 'the brightest glories and the most enduring honours of a country are those which come from its thinkers and its scholars' (Royal Society of Canada, 1932: 91–2). However romantic that praise might sound, what mattered was Hunt's emphasis on the country as a whole. Like the Royal Canadian Academy, the Royal Society had its headquarters in Ottawa.

Other Identities

We can easily make too much of the political arena. The elaboration of a number of competing and occasionally incompatible identities by and for its citizens characterized the Victorian Age. As well as their national and provincial loyalties, most Canadians had firm allegiances to their ethnic origins, whether these were French Canadian, Acadian, or British. French Canada further elaborated its cultural identity in this period, and the Acadians began self-consciously to develop one. As for those people whose origins were in the British Isles, they simultaneously thought of themselves as British as well as Welsh, Scotch, Irish, or English. Indeed, British Canadians may well have thought of themselves as more British (as opposed to Welsh or Scottish) than did their compatriots at home.

The state did not weigh heavily on the daily lives of most Canadians in this era, although the administrative state had begun its development before Confederation. Taxation had not yet become ubiquitous and occurred mainly as tariffs and duties. Moreover, the state—as represented by province, nation, or city—did not normally provide social benefits or solace when people got sick, lost jobs, retired, or died. For some, politics and government were a source of employment or patronage. For most Canadians, however, government had very little to do with their lives. For many people, political allegiance to the state was therefore not as important as loyalty to the caring institutions: family, ethnic group, religion, and fraternal organization. Churches and religion were most important. Canada was a Christian country and few of its citizens openly defied Christian norms and values. By the 1880s the mobility of many Canadians contributed to the tendency to belong to a good many other voluntary organizations beyond the church. In an earlier period, voluntary organizations supplemented or provided municipal services such as water, light, fire, and libraries as well as charity. By the 1880s some organizations had begun providing entertainment and companionship for their members.

Charles G.D. Roberts's 'Canada', 1886

In 1886 Charles G.D. Roberts published a small volume of verses in Boston, entitled *Divers Tones*. The following is one of the first poems in the book.

Canada

O Child of Nations, giant-limbed,
Who stand'st among the nations now
Unheeded, unadorned, unhymned,
With unanointed brow,—

How long the ignoble sloth, how long
The trust in greatness not thine own?
Surely the lion's brood is strong
To front the world alone!

How long the indolence, ere thou dare
Achieve thy destiny, seize thy fame –
Ere our proud eyes behold thee bear
A nation's franchise, nation's name?

The Saxon force, the Celtic fire,
These are thy manhood's heritage!
Why rest with babes and slaves? Seek higher
The place of race and age.

I see to every wind unfurled
The flag that bears the Maple-Wreath;
Thy swift keels furrow round the world
Its blood-red folds beneath;

Thy swift keels cleave the furthest seas;
Thy white sails swell with alien gales;
To stream on each remotest breeze
The black smoke of thy pipes exhales.

O Falterer, let thy past convince
Thy future,—all the growth, the gain,
The fame since Cartier knew thee, since
Thy shores beheld Champlain!

Montcalm and Wolfe! Wolfe and Montcalm!
Quebec, thy storied citadel
Attest in burning song and psalm
How here thy heroes fell!

O Thou that bor'st the battle's brunt
At Queenston, and at Lundy's Lane,—
On whose scant ranks but iron front
The battle broke in vain! –

Whose was the danger, whose the day,
From whose triumphant throats the cheers,
At Chrysler's Farm, at Chateauguay,
Storming like clarion-bursts our ears?

On soft Pacific slopes,—beside
Strange floods that northward rave and fall,—
Where chafes Acadia's chainless tide –
Thy sons await thy call.

They wait; but some in exile, some
With strangers housed, in stranger lands;—
And some Canadian lips are dumb
Beneath Egyptian sands.

O mystic Nile! Thy secret yields
Before us; thy most ancient dreams
Are mixed with fresh Canadian fields
And murmur of Canadian streams.

But thou, my Country, dream not thou!
Wake, and behold how night is done,—
How on thy breast, and o'er thy brow,
Bursts the rising sun!

Source: Charles G.D. Roberts, *Divers Tones* (Boston: Lothrop, 1886), 2–5.

Lock no. 1, new Welland Canal', from volume I of *Picturesque Canada* (Toronto, 1882), 385. LAC, C-083047.

The mid-Victorian period was a crucial era for Roman Catholicism in Canada. Within French Canada the period witnessed the emergence of the Church as the leading voice of French Canada's national aspirations and the assumption of local leadership by the curé. It also saw the Church take on the ultramontane character that would remain with it for many years. In Quebec, the man who symbolized the ultramontane Church in the mid-Victorian period was Bishop Ignace Bourget (1799–1885). Bourget was consecrated coadjutor to the Bishop of Montreal in early 1837, on the very eve of rebellion, and succeeded to the see in 1840. He died in June 1885, on the eve of the second Riel uprising, although he had retired a few years earlier. Bourget was always an active defender of both the papacy and the position of the Church in Canada. He introduced the Roman liturgy and fervently opposed the principles of the European revolutions of 1848. Gradually, he became the leading opponent of liberal thinking in the province, particularly as it was represented by the Institut Canadien in Montreal. Bourget carried on a lengthy battle against the Institut and especially its library, which contained many prohibited books. Equally important was his expansion of the ecclesiastical administration of his diocese, so that nearly every parish had a priest and nearly half the priests had an assistant. The clergy were now able to mobilize public opinion, as they did in 1868 when they helped raise 507 Zouaves in Quebec (and over $100,000 to support them) to serve in the papal army. Quebec bishops strongly supported the doctrine of papal infallibility at the First Vatican Council in 1870.

English-speaking Catholicism had succeeded by 1840 in separating itself from francophone control. At about the same time, the hierarchy had also

Robert Harris

Born in Tyn-y-groes, Wales, Robert Harris (1849–1919) accompanied his family to Prince Edward Island in 1856. Robert's father was a 'gentleman' without any occupational qualifications who became a partner in a canning factory. Robert took advantage of local education and culture, and left for Liverpool at the age of 21 to sample the art scene there, since he had decided to become an artist. He soon returned to Charlottetown, but left again in 1873 for Boston, where he spent two years drawing from life at the Lowell Institute and the Boston Atheneum.

Harris supported himself on various commissions from the Island and Nova Scotia, including one to paint portraits of members of the Island's legislative assembly from photographs. Between 1871 and 1875 he painted 61 portraits and had begun to make a reputation for himself. In 1876 he once again headed for Europe, first to England and then to Paris, where he attached himself to the Atelier Bonnat and taught himself. Because of bad eyesight, he spent most of his life husbanding his sight for his work. He returned to Canada in 1879, heading for Toronto and the Ontario Society of Artists. A friendship struck up with the OSA's vice-president, Lucius O'Brien, led to a nomination as a founding member of the Canadian Academy of Art, and he began to add other genres to his portraiture.

Back in Paris in 1881 he first learned of a government commission for a painting of the Fathers of Confederation, and he pursued it for several years, signing a contract in 1883. The setting was to be the Charlottetown Conference, although it was later changed to the Quebec Conference. In the end the contract was a source of much bitterness for Harris, since he accepted a low fee on the grounds that he would make money from reproductions, but then he never got the rights. Harris did not work from life in this painting, but mainly from photographs and research on such matters as hair and eye colour. It was a jigsaw puzzle of smaller work assembled by the artist. The painting was finished in 1884 and quickly became an icon of Confederation. It was destroyed by the fire in the east block of the Parliament buildings in 1916.

Harris married in 1885 and continued to paint incessantly, mainly portraits but occasionally other observational studies. His fees for portraits were quite high but were paid willingly, since he was regarded as Canada's finest painter of likenesses. In 1893 he became president of the Canadian academy and remained in office for 13 years. He lobbied the Canadian government to assist financially with the participation of Canadian artists in foreign exhibitions. In 1916 he refused to repaint the Confederation work, fearing such an effort would injure his health.

re-established its control over the laity, which had previously assumed considerable autonomy in the absence of local bishops and clergy. Anglophone bishops from the Maritime region were among those who attempted unsuccessfully to prevent the issue of papal infallibility from being decided at the Vatican Council. Contemporaries often overlooked the importance of anglophone Catholicism in the nineteenth century. Only in Canada West/Ontario were Protestants in such a clear numerical ascendency and position

of power that the regional culture assumed obvious Protestant dimensions. This Ontario culture, especially as it expanded westward onto the prairies, began to be confused with Canadian culture in some circles.

By 1840 Protestantism everywhere in British North America had largely cut itself free from its foreign origins in either Great Britain or the United States. The major development of the mid-Victorian period, notably in an Ontario where Protestantism emerged as a distinct and all-embracing culture, was the construction of a broad alliance among the major denominations: Anglican, Presbyterian, and Methodist. The gradual elimination of the major points of public friction between the established churches and the dissenters made this possible. The result was a Victorian Protestant culture in Ontario that emphasized the relationship between social stability and Protestant morality. A firm belief in God and his millennium formed the basis for the latter. Gradual social change was progressive, offering a way of understanding the events and changes that swirled around the individual in the Victorian era. The moral code was strict, but chiefly voluntary and individualistic.

The churches, especially the Protestant ones, were also a key to the growth of a vast network of clubs, societies, and charities. By the mid-nineteenth century women members were implicitly challenging the male governance of the churches. Evangelically oriented churches frequently employed their ladies' aid or women's auxiliary groups to sponsor missionary activity. By 1885 there were over 120 Baptist Women's Missionary Aid Societies scattered across the Maritimes. Women generally used their own money to support their religious organizations, which kept separate accounts and offered many women their first opportunity at independent administration.

Technically independent of the churches, but closely connected in overlapping membership and social goals, were reform organizations like the Woman's Christian Temperance Union. Letitia Youmans (1827–96), a public school teacher and Sunday school teacher in the Methodist Church, founded the first Canadian local of the WCTU in December 1874 in Picton, Ontario. The WCTU spread rapidly across Canada in the 1880s, preaching that alcohol abuse was responsible for many of the social problems of contemporary Canada and campaigning for public prohibition of the sale of alcoholic beverages. Most of its members came from the middle class, and much of its literature was directed at demonstrating that poverty and family problems among the lower orders could be reduced, if not eliminated, by cutting off the availability of alcohol to the male breadwinner.

Canadians of the time tended to associate Orangism with political matters—organizing parades on 12 July, opposing Roman Catholics, objecting to the 1870 execution of Thomas Scott—and with the Irish. Nevertheless, the order's real importance and influence continued to rest on the twin facts that its membership united British Protestants of all origins and that it served as a focal point on the local level for social intercourse and conviviality. As a 'secret' society, it had elaborate initiation rites and a ritual that appealed to men who spent most of their lives in drudgery or dull routine. Lodges provided a variety of services for members, including an elaborate funeral. But if local fraternity was the key to Orangism's success, its public influence was enormous. In 1885 John A. Macdonald's government would prefer to risk alienating Quebec by executing Louis Riel than alienating Orange Ontario by sparing him.

The Orange Order was not the only fraternal organization that grew and flourished in Canada. Because most of these societies were semi-secret, with rites based on Freemasonry, they appealed mainly to Protestants. The Masons themselves expanded enormously during the mid-nineteenth century. They were joined by a number of other orders, such as the Independent Order of Oddfellows (founded in England in 1813 and brought to Canada by 1845), the Independent Order of Foresters (founded in the United States in 1874 and brought to Canada in 1881), and the Order of Knights of Pythias (founded in Washington, DC, in the early 1860s and brought to Canada in 1870). The Knights of Labor was an all-embracing labour organization that owed much to the lodges. Fellowship and mutual support were the keys to the success of all of these societies. Their success led to the formation in 1882 of the Knights of Columbus as a similar fraternal benefit society for Roman Catholic men, although the first chapters in Canada were probably not founded until the early 1890s. While few of these societies admitted women directly, most had adjunct or parallel organizations for women. By the 1880s many Canadians belonged to one or more of these societies. Membership offered a means of social introduction into a new community, provided status and entertainment to members, and increasingly supplied assurance of assistance in times of economic or emotional crisis.

Cultural Life

The creation of the nation did not directly affect all aspects of cultural life. Indeed, most culture in Canada existed quite apart from political considerations. Despite their new self-consciousness about the need for cultural achievements to match their political accomplishments, most Canadians probably did not appreciate how much progress was being made in many cultural spheres. Only a brief sampling of cultural activity in Victorian Canada—focusing on painting, theatre, music, and organized sports—can be included here.

Painting was the most vibrant and productive of the arts in the era immediately after Confederation, with many artists producing large numbers of canvases, some of them key works in the history of Canadian painting. The beginning of the period coincided roughly with the end of a tradition of landscape painting that had become dominant partly in response to the developing quest for national identity and the topographical beauties of the new country that were just being discovered. Lucius O'Brien (1832–99) and John A. Fraser (1838–98) were two of numerous painters who travelled west in 1880 at the invitation of the Canadian Pacific Railway to paint the Rockies. O'Brien's most famous painting, however, is *Sunrise on the Saguenay* (1880). It is a remarkable depiction of the sublime in nature, while in its poetic, moody treatment of the romantic scene it is also an outstanding Canadian example of a style, popular in the United States, that came to be called

'Sunrise on the Saguenay', oil on canvas, 1880, by Lucius O'Brien. National Gallery of Canada, Ottawa. Photo © National Gallery of Canada, 113.

'luminism'. This painting was hung in the inaugural exhibition of the Royal Academy, of which O'Brien was the first president, and deposited in the new National Gallery of Canada.

Homer Watson (1855–1936) and his friend Horatio Walker (1858–1936) both came to concentrate on Canadian landscapes that romanticized rural scenes. Oscar Wilde, after seeing Watson's work in Toronto, called him 'the Canadian Constable'. In fairness to Watson, he was no imitator, since at the time he had never heard of Constable. Walker, who was born in Listowel, Canada West, wintered in New York and summered on the Île d'Orléans just north of Quebec in the St Lawrence. He specialized, with great commercial success, in striking, sentimentalized interpretations of Quebec farm life in the style of the French painter Jean-François Millet. Walker himself described his preoccupations:

The pastoral life of the people of our countryside, the noble work of the Habitant, the magnificent panoramas which surround him, the different aspects of our seasons, the calm of our mornings and the serenity of our evenings, the movement of ebb and flow of our tides which I have observed on the shores of my island which is truly the sacred temple of the muses and a gift of the gods to men: such are the preferred subjects of my paintings. I have passed the greatest part of my life in trying to paint the poetry, the easy joys, the hard daily work of rural life, the sylvan beauty in which is spent the peaceable life of the habitant, the gesture of the wood cutter and the ploughman, the bright colours of sunrise and sunset, the song of the cock, the daily tasks of the farmyard, all the activity which goes on from morning to evening, in the neighbourhood of the barn. (Quoted in Harper, 1966: 204)

By 1880 young Canadian painters sought to study in the academies of Paris, the centre of the art world of the time. There they learned to paint large, richly detailed, subtly coloured, naturalistic canvases featuring the human figure and sentimental subtexts. Robert Harris's studies of everyday life were exemplars of this approach. They included: The

Chorister (1880), showing a young man singing in a church choir; Harmony (1886), a portrait of a young woman (his wife) playing the harmonium, a popular musical instrument in rural Canada; and A Meeting of the School Trustees (1885) in which a young woman teacher, doubtless with 'newfangled ideas', faces the suspicious gazes of a small group of men.

Perhaps the most important development in Canadian theatre in this period was the extension of railroad construction, which would make possible extensive touring across the nation by theatrical and vaudeville companies. By the 1880s, most Canadian cities could look forward to visits by professional performers, which undoubtedly raised the standard of presentation and provided models worthy of emulation. At the same time, the arrival of professionals and the raising of standards could be damaging to local amateurs, who had previously dominated the theatrical scene and occasionally even produced homegrown plays and musicals.

Although only a few trained musicians existed in British North America, the mid-Victorian era saw the development of a widespread musical life. Garrison bands and choral groups were the chief components. In British Columbia the band of the Royal Engineers brought new standards of musical performance when it arrived in the colony in 1859. From that year until 1863 (when it was reposted to Britain) it entertained as militia band, fire-brigade band, brass band, and even a dance band. In British Columbia, as elsewhere, brass bands were the most common and popular instrumental ensembles throughout the nineteenth century. Few band musicians were professional or professionally trained. A number of brass bands were organized in the province in Aboriginal communities and residential schools. At least 33 sprang to life between 1864 (when the Oblates founded the St Mary's Mission Band near Mission City) and the end of the century. In Red River, a brass band from St Boniface played as the Métis provisional government raised its new flag in December 1869.

By the time of Confederation, larger cities were producing substantial numbers of musical societies, chiefly choral in their orientation. In 1864, for example, the Mendelssohn Choir and the Société

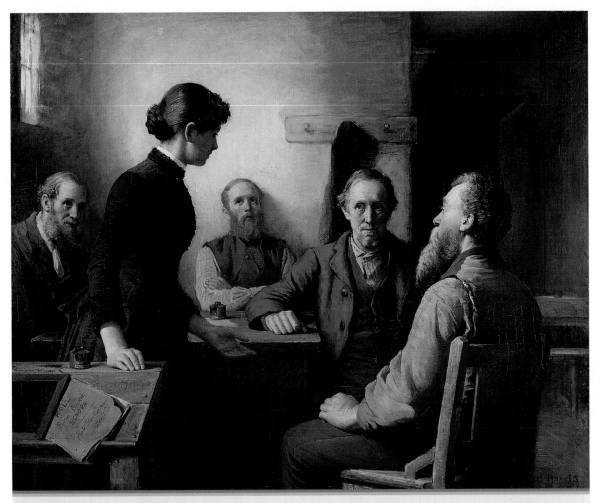

'A Meeting of the School Trustees', oil on canvas, 1885, by Robert Harris. National Gallery of Canada, Ottawa. Purchased 1886, #6. Photo © National Gallery of Canada, 6 R.

Musicale des Montagnards Canadiens, as well as Les Orphéonistes de Montréal, joined the Montreal Oratorio Society. Montreal also helped produce the first well-known Canadian composer, Calixa Lavallée (1842–91), best known today for the music to 'O Canada'. He made his debut at the piano in Montreal at age 13, spending much time in the United States until he went to Paris in 1873. Returning to settle in Quebec, Lavallée wrote a grand cantata for the reception of Governor General Lord Lorne and his wife. It concluded with a stirring contrapuntal arrangement of 'God Save the Queen' and 'Comin' thro' the Rye'. Unable to make a living in Canada, the composer spent the last years of his life in exile in the United States. Although Canada was not often generous to its professional musicians, it embraced amateur musical performance with gusto. Most music-making occurred in the home, with people gathering around the piano to sing hymns and popular songs of the day.

The mid-Victorian period in Canada saw a continued development of organized sports and games. Most were imported, although some (like lacrosse) had local origins. Lacrosse had begun as an Aboriginal game called *baggataway* or *tewaarathon*, and was played by many tribes under various rules. In 1833 the First Nations near Montreal played lacrosse, and in 1856 the Montreal Lacrosse Club was organized, to be joined by two others before 1860. A Montreal dentist, William George Beers (1843–1900), codified the game in Montreal and promoted it across the country. Lacrosse flourished between 1868 and 1885, achieving great success as a spectator sport until it was overtaken by baseball and hockey. Snowshoeing, which became very popular as an organized winter activity in the 1860s (often among the summer lacrosse crowd), was another obviously Aboriginal development. The Montreal Snow Shoe Club was organized in 1843, and in Winnipeg a snowshoe club, begun in 1878, was the major winter diversion for members of the city's elite by the early 1880s.

The formulation of rules for these and other sports occurred in most cases between 1840 and 1880, which was the great era of codification of sports. Precise dates are very contentious, with many communities advancing their own claims for 'firsts'. Certainly by 1880 most sports and games familiar to us today had reached a stage of rule development that would have made them comprehensible to a modern Canadian. What is important about the development of sports is not simply the introduction of standardized rules, techniques, and equipment, but the sheer scope and ubiquity of sporting activity on the part of both participants and spectators. While many Canadians participated, many more gathered to watch sporting activity. The development of any of the major games followed roughly the same path of regularization, which made it possible for teams from one place to play teams from another.

By 1885 two aspects of sports in Canada had evolved: participation and spectacle. Sports still had not achieved an overt political meaning. There was not yet the creation of either national leagues or national teams to play in international competitions. Expansion, sophistication, and growing organization matched the development of the nation. The mobility of the population moved various sports and games around the country and made the standardization of rules both possible and necessary. Both the development of official rules and growing hierarchies of teams and players pointed to the future.

Caughnawaga (Kahnawake) Mohawks, lacrosse champions of Canada, 1869, James Inglis. LAC, C-001959.

The Struggle for the West

Sincere efforts were made in the new Dominion to encourage a sense of nationhood transcending the linguistic barriers between French and English and the geographical barriers of the provinces and the regions. Nevertheless, the new Canadian nationality remained fragile, more than a bit artificial, and very racist. In addition, at least outside French Canada, it tended to express the prejudices and values of British Ontario. The crucible for the new Canada, many believed, was in the vast expanse of territory west of the Great Lakes. Here its limitations were most clearly evident.

The interests of the Canadian government in the North-West Territories, especially under Sir John A. Macdonald, were focused on agricultural settlement. This would provide both an outlet for excess eastern population and the means of encouraging the development of a truly transcontinental nation. The process of settlement and government policy pushed the Aboriginal inhabitants of the region out of the way as quickly as possible. The federal government continued the pre-confederation policy of the Canadas by establishing an Indian Department and insisting on the rule of law in its westward expansion and in its dealings with the Native peoples. Foremost in the rule-of-law approach were the creation of the North West Mounted Police and the working out of treaties with the First Nations that extinguished Aboriginal claims to the land as first inhabitants in exchange for reserves on the most marginal and least attractive land. Eleven 'numbered' treaties were negotiated between 1871 and 1930, the first five of which were land cession agreements covering most of the Canadian West, except for British Columbia. As well as reserves, the Aboriginals received cash money, allowances for blankets and tools, seed and livestock, and the right to hunt on land not otherwise utilized by Canadians. The government's hope was to convert the First Peoples into settled farmers, and its rhetoric featured an insistence on its humanitarianism and paternalism, under which a good deal of racism and prejudice flourished. As one Indian Commissioner wrote in 1887, the government was engaged in 'the slow and tedious work of uplifting a savage race and eradicating the nomadic and other inherent tendencies which centuries of a wild and barbarous life have firmly planted' (quoted in Titley, 2009: 207). While the Aboriginal people might eventually aspire (with Canadian government assistance) to full citizenship by assuming all the characteristics of the European colonizers, in the meantime they would be denied full citizenship and given a special inferior status experienced by no other Canadians.

Administration of the treaties and of Dominion 'Indian policy' in the West left a good deal to be desired. The Aboriginal peoples were obviously caught in an inexorable process that was going to change forever their traditional way of life. The buffalo were rapidly disappearing, the victims of overhunting and of the arrival of settlement and new technology. Most Aboriginal leaders saw the handwriting on the wall clearly enough. They did not get anywhere near enough help from the Department of Indian Affairs, however. The government expected the Aboriginals to be able to become self-sufficient virtually overnight. It did not supply the reserves with enough food to prevent starvation and disease, and it complained when the Natives slaughtered their livestock for something to eat. The reserve land tended to be marginal, the assistance supplied was inadequate—often for financial reasons—and the attitude of many of the government's Indian agents was unsympathetic. By the early 1880s, the North-West was a virtual powder keg of Aboriginal discontent. Cree leaders in what is now Alberta sent a letter to John A. Macdonald (who was Minister of the Interior and head of Indian Affairs as well as Prime Minister) complaining of destitution and noting that the motto of their people was: 'If we must die by violence let us do it quickly.' The winter of 1883–4 was particularly harsh and severe, and many were starving. Some Indian agents wrote to Ottawa, but nothing was done. In June 1884, Big Bear and his followers, with many others, travelled to Poundmaker's reserve to hold a big meeting. They discussed the serious state of affairs, after which some 2,000 Aboriginals held a Thirst Dance, a religious ritual.

Like the First Nations, settlement drove the Métis to the margins. By 1885 Ontario-born settlers outnumbered the Métis five to one in Manitoba, and only 7 per cent of the population of the province was of mixed-blood origin. Many Métis drifted farther west, to the Saskatchewan Valley, where they formed small mission settlements including Qu'Appelle, Batoche, and Duck Lake. The buffalo were becoming scarce everywhere. Government surveyors caused uncertainty and fear, as they had in Red River a decade earlier. Over the harsh winter of 1883–4, many Métis and Aboriginals starved. The Métis turned in despair to Louis Riel. He had apparently put his life back together after years of exile in the United States and hospitalization for mental disturbance in 1876–8 at Longue Pointe, Quebec. He became an American citizen and was teaching in St Peter's, Montana (where he had married), when a delegation from the Saskatchewan country visited him on 4 June 1884. They told him of the grievances that were burdening the peoples of the region, explained that agitation was developing against the Canadian government, and pleaded with him to return to Canada to lead them. Why Riel agreed to do so is one of the many mysteries surrounding his life. However,

Poundmaker

Poundmaker (Pitikwahanapiwiyin, *c.* 1842–86) was born to a Plains Cree father and a mother of French extraction. In 1873 Crowfoot, a Blackfoot chief, lost a son in battle with the Cree. His wife saw Poundmaker at the peacemaking and was struck by his resemblance to the dead man. Crowfoot adopted Poundmaker and gave him a Blackfoot name. Returning to the Cree, Poundmaker's position was enhanced by his Blackfoot connections and especially by the horses it provided him.

When the Aboriginals of central Saskatchewan negotiated a peace treaty with Canada at Fort Carlton, Poundmaker was a minor chief. He actually objected to the terms of the treaty (No. 6), saying he had no knowledge of farming and was not clear how he would be able to survive. He did sign, however. He continued to hunt the buffalo for several years, but settled on a reserve in 1879.

Two years later, he guided the Marquess of Lorne, Canada's Governor General, on a tour in the central region. The two were mutually impressed. The Governor General came to appreciate Poundmaker's knowledge of his own culture, and Poundmaker understood that the Europeans could not be chased away. 'Our only resource is our work, our industry, our farms', he told his people.

Beginning in 1883, rations to the Aboriginals were reduced as an economic measure, despite a heavy winter in 1883–4. Poundmaker was unable to keep his young warriors under control. More than 1,000 dissidents met on Poundmaker's reserve to engage in a Thirst Dance. Poundmaker was forced to offer himself as a hostage to prevent the NWMP from arresting in the midst of the ritual a young warrior accused of assaulting a farm instructor on a neighbouring reserve.

Poundmaker was not among those who invited Louis Riel to the region, but his reputation attracted many young warriors in the spring of 1885. At Battleford he could not prevent his hot-bloods from attacking the village, and thereafter he lost control over the warriors. When Lieutenant-Colonel William Dillon Otter decided to punish Poundmaker for the Battleford incident, he led over 300 men to attack Poundmaker's camp. Otter's men were badly defeated by the Aboriginals, and Poundmaker, who had not been involved in the earlier fighting, managed to prevent his warriors from following the retreat. Poundmaker offered to negotiate a peace after Batoche, but was ordered to surrender by Major General Frederick Dobson Middleton. On 26 May he did, and he was put on trial for treason at Regina. After a trial that was in many ways a travesty of British justice, he was sentenced to prison. Released after a year's incarceration, he died soon after.

Canada in 1882.

Legend:
- Provinces
- North-West Territories: Districts
- North-West Territories: Unorganized
- Newfoundland
- Disputed Area

Greenland

Arctic Ocean

Arctic Circle

Alaska (USA)

Pacific Ocean

North-West Territories

District of Keewatin 1876

Hudson Bay

District of Athabasca 1882

District of Alberta 1882

District of Saskatchewan 1882

District of Assiniboia 1882

British Columbia

Victoria   Vancouver

United States of America

Manitoba

Area Claimed by Ontario and Manitoba

Ontario

Toronto

Ottawa

Montreal

Quebec

St. Lawrence R.

Newfoundland

Quebec

New Brunswick

PEI

Nova Scotia

Atlantic Ocean

N E S W

0   500   1,000
kilometres

within a month he and his family were in Batoche. By December 1884, Riel and W.H. Jackson (secretary of the Settlers' Union) had finished drafting a long petition (with 25 sections), which they sent to Ottawa. It concluded by requesting that the petitioners 'be allowed as in [1870] to send Delegates to Ottawa with their Bill of rights; whereby an understanding may be arrived at as to their entry into confederation, with the constitution of a free province'. Ottawa acknowledged the petition, but gave no other response.

In March 1885 events took a menacing turn. Riel's military leader, Gabriel Dumont (1836–1906), intercepted a small NWMP detachment near Duck Lake. The engagement turned into a full-fledged battle in which fatalities occurred on both sides. Riel called upon the First Nations to assist him, and there were incidents of Aboriginal violence connected less to Riel's resistance than to younger warriors' discontent with conditions. Poundmaker's people broke into buildings in Battleford, terrifying settlers. The Cree warrior, Wandering Spirit (Kapapamahchakwew,

'All That I Used To Live On Has Gone'

At a meeting with the visiting Governor General of Canada, the Marquess of Lorne, at Fort Carlton in 1881, Chief Ahtahkakoop of the Plains Cree addressed Lord Lorne.

I have reason to be thankful to see His Excellency and since this [treaty] medal was put on my neck from the Great Mother I am thankful—& all my tribe—to see the Great Mother's representative here that I will speak for her as I speak for my children. I am a poor man and now will express my views on this subject, but as I look round I do not see anything I could live by. I see nothing, all that I used to live on has gone. Where I used to get my [living] was the animal the buffalo, and also I had horses, now the buffalo and the horses have left me. I say with that I am a poor man.

You may have seen the poverty of the land as regards the animal—that was my hunting ground. I used to find them all I wanted. Now it is a solitary wilderness. I find nothing there, when I look at all this I see but one thing left, that is to work the ground. I am too old to work but I think of my children & grandchildren they may learn.

The first thing [we want] is some strength, i.e., farm implements & cattle—these are necessary. If we don't progress faster than in the past years, we shall move very shortly and my Grandchildren will

not see it for we walk very slowly now. Why I say this is that the crops we have raised the half was spoilt as sickness came on us and my people could not work. I remember right on the treaty it was said that if any famine or trouble came the Government would see to us and help. My trouble arose from partly starvation and sickness. The remedy I ask for now. We want nets, we want guns. I ask for these only for living. There is another thing we lack. When I take a flail to thrash I lose part of my wheat. I want a thrashing machine. A thrasher and a reaper and the power to work them. There is no end to my losses. I loose [lose] in the thrashing. I have miles sometimes to go through the snow to have my grain ground, and I am only about to bring back a handful. I make no doubt that his Excellency will sympathize with us, that he will open his heart towards the trouble of his Indian Children. What we want is speedy help on my farms. I have no more to say. I wish to be remembered to the Great Mother & to the Princess and please remember me in the cold winter days & give me covering for my women and children.

Source: 'Report of the Marquis of Lorne's Trip', quoted in Deanna Christensen, *Ahtahkakoop: The Epic Account of a Plains Cree Head Chief, His People, and Their Struggle for Survival 1816–1896* (Shell Lake, Sask.: Ahtahkakoop Publishing, 2000), 422–3.

Marguerite Monet de Bellhumeur (or Bellehumeur) Riel

Marguerite Monet de Bellhumeur. Library and Archives Canada/C-15468.

Louis Riel met Marguerite Monet de Bellhumeur (1861–86) somewhere near Carroll, Montana, in 1881. Her father, Jean Monet de Bellehumeur, was a native of Lower Canada who had married Marie Malaterre, probably in Red River. Marguerite had been born in St François Xavier on 15 January 1861. She was a very pretty dark-skinned young woman. Her only photograph shows off her oval face and her black hair, with fashionable ringlets in the front and what looks like a ponytail behind. Although apparently illiterate, she spoke Cree, French, and English. Riel fell in love with the quiet young métisse and married her (with her father's permission) around 28 April 1881 'according to the fashion of the country'; their marriage was solemnized by Father Joseph Damiani on 6 March 1882. Marguerite's dowry was scrip for 240 acres of Métis land allotment southeast of Portage la Prairie, which Riel tried to sell in 1883 and probably did sell in 1884.

Marriage seemed to stabilize Riel, and he began to write to his family in Manitoba again after the birth of his son. Marriage and family also increased his financial worries, however. Whether the marriage was a passionate one is impossible to measure. Riel described Marguerite in a poem: 'Her faith so deep and her righteousness / Are a beauty to behold / Ah! . . . she is a tender creature / Always attentive to her duty. / I have the privilege of knowing / that her love is unfailing. / When she loves, she loves through and through / Her gaze beckons me on.' In another poem Riel indicated that the Métis teased him about Marguerite in some way. He wrote of their opposing his wishes in wanting a woman and in gossiping behind his back. He also wrote angrily about another Métis who tried to seduce Marguerite. Marguerite bore two children with Riel—Jean (b. 4 May 1882) at Carroll; Marie Angelique (b. 17 Sept. 1883)—and lost one child at birth while Riel was in prison in 1885.

She had journeyed to Saskatchewan from St Peter's Mission in 1884 with her two small children, travelling for three weeks before being able to spend a night indoors and then living with Charles Nolin 15 miles north of Batoche until early November. She and the children cowered in a cave after Batoche. The ordeal contributed to her illness (tuberculosis) and to the death of the couple's third child, born on 21 October, who lived only a couple of hours.

Riel wrote poetry in English about Marguerite as he waited to die, often upon religious themes: 'Marguerite be fair and good / Consider now the sacred wood / On which the perfect Jesus / Died to save us. . . . Margaret! we be the prey / Of bad spirits? no let us pray . . . / Be sweet to my words and listen / When I write you with a golden Pen.'

According to Riel's prison guard in 1885, writing in the *Empire* in 1896, she 'was a very dark Cree woman. She possessed all the characteristics of the ideal Indian. She was extremely proud, gentle, and self-sacrificing.' She spoke to Riel for two hours in prison in Cree before his death. Presumably they spoke in Cree to be able to converse without being understood by the guards; there is no evidence that Cree was their normal language of discourse, although it might well have been. Riel's brother Joseph took Marguerite and the children back to St Vital before Louis's execution. Riel told a guard on his last day that his only regret was that he was leaving his wife and children unprovided for. Riel's last letter to his wife is a powerful one of suppressed emotions. Riel told his wife to 'take good care of your little children', included a 'word of kindness according to God' for his son, and 'a word of kindness and tenderness also' to his little daughter. She died in Manitoba at 1886. Marie-Angélique died of diphtheria in 1897, and Jean, who was given a trust fund raised in Quebec, died in a buggy accident in 1908.

The Battle of Batoche

With rumours of armed trouble rife across western Canada, a contingent of militia from Winnipeg was mustered and ordered west before the encounter at Duck Lake near Prince Albert, where a column of Mounties and special constables were badly beaten by a force of Métis commanded by Gabriel Dumont. After Duck Lake, Major General Frederick Middleton, arriving in Winnipeg via American rail lines, left the city with the 90th Rifles, 260 strong and badly equipped. The railroad got the troops only as far as Qu'Appelle, whence they marched north to Fort Qu'Appelle to practise firing rifles before heading further north to Batoche, a village on the east bank of the South Saskatchewan River, where Middleton had decided to confront the Métis.

The troops made about 25 miles a day under adverse conditions. It was over 200 miles from the end of the railway line to the Métis strongholds, and so the CPR played very little active role in the campaign. By 24 April they had made Fish Creek and found signs of smouldering Métis campfires in a ravine between bluffs. The troops suffered heavy casualties from a crossfire from Métis sharpshooters, who disappeared into the bush of a ravine and withdrew as their ammunition ran out. Middleton camped on the site of this first battle for 12 days, waiting for reinforcements from eastern Canada and a detachment manning a Gatling gun.

The village of Batoche was a scattered settlement of houses and outbuildings on both sides of the river, connected by a ferry operated on a cable. On 5 May the paddlewheel steamer the *Northcote* arrived on the river and was ambushed by the sharpshooters, then damaged severely when its smokestacks hit the ferry cable. Middleton had 800 men, most of them infantry but including about 100 horsemen. He also had four field guns and the Gatling gun. Gabriel Dumont later estimated he had 200 effectives (Métis), and perhaps 200 Aboriginal warriors to fight with him. Louis Riel and Dumont disagreed over tactics. Riel prayed for divine assistance, while Dumont dug into rifle pits across a two-mile front.

The initial encounters impressed General Middleton, but he was afraid to fall back because he doubted his inexperienced troops could sustain their discipline in retreat. The Canadians held their ground, constructing a little fort of wagons in the midst of the prairie. Middleton wanted a decisive victory and was prepared, if necessary, to starve out Batoche. He ordered his troops to fire away, but did not yet order an assault. Finally Middleton ordered a battle plan for 12 May. He would attack the village from two sides, using mounted troops from the north and the infantry from the south. The men on horseback were to be the feint, the infantry assault the major attack. The feint went well, but the infantry attack did not occur, apparently because the order to advance had not reached Colonel van Straubenzie, the officer in charge.

In the meantime Middleton had met emissaries from Riel, asking him to stop shelling the houses harbouring women and children. Middleton responded by telling them to gather the women and children in a house marked with a white flag, which would not be shelled. But he would not negotiate and would only accept unconditional surrender. It was never clear who gave the infantry the order to advance, but once the order was given the troops quickly overran the rifle pits and headed for the village. The battle was over within half an hour. Batoche was taken and the resistance melted away.

On this last day the army lost five dead and 25 wounded, while the Métis casualties were never counted. Mounted riders quickly brought the news of the victory back to the telegraph lines and then east to a victory-starved Canada. The army soon rounded up the Aboriginals who were independently fighting the settlers, the NWMP, and the Canadian military. The Last Stand of the Aboriginal West had ended.

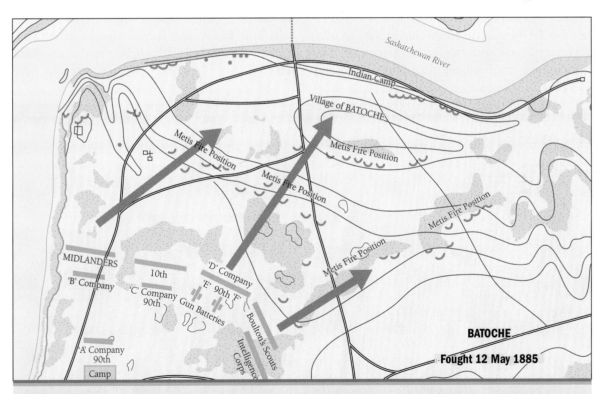

Battle of Batoche.

Source: Bruce Tascona and Eric Wells, *Little Black Devils: A History of the Royal Winnipeg Rifles* (Winnipeg: n.p., 1983), p. 50). Courtesy of The Royal Winnipeg Rifles.

c. 1845–85), one of Big Bear's war chiefs, led a band that attacked Frog Lake, killing nine. Prime Minister Macdonald determined to crush this rebellion quickly, sending an armed force under Major General Frederick Dobson Middleton (1825–98) by way of the new Canadian Pacific Railway. The Canadian force of 800 men arrived at Batoche on 9 May. They quickly defeated Riel and about 200 Métis. The uprising was over by 12 May. Dumont and others fled to the United States. The government arrested Riel. In order to achieve this result, the Canadian government had mustered '5,546 soldiers in three columns, 586 horses, 2 Gatling Guns, 6,000 Snider Enfield, 50 calibre rifles, 2 field hospitals, 70,000 Gatling Gun rounds, 1,500,000 rifle cartridges and 2,000 cannon shells', at a cost of $4,451,584.38 (Barnholden, 2009: 13).

A formal charge of high treason, carrying the death penalty, was laid against Riel on 6 July. (Despite the fact that Riel was an American citizen, the Canadian government held with the British government that he was also a British subject, since British citizenship

acquired through birth could never be renounced.) Even if Riel was a foreign national, however, he could still be tried for treason. The government chose to focus responsibility for the rebellion on Riel, which would allow leniency towards most of his followers. The trial began on 28 July in Regina, where feelings ran high. It was a political trial, infamously coloured in many ways by Macdonald's determination to have Riel found guilty and executed.

Riel passionately denied a plea of insanity introduced by his lawyers, realizing that to be declared insane (i.e., not responsible for his actions) would devastate his reputation and impugn his honour. The six-man jury (operating under the law of the North-West Territories) found him guilty but recommended mercy. It is not clear whether the jury brought in the mercy recommendation because it felt Riel's resistance was partially justified or because it did not really believe that he was responsible for his behaviour. In any case, because the charge was high treason, a guilty verdict brought a mandatory death sentence. The Canadian government could have

Big Bear (centre) trading at Fort Pitt, an HBC post on the North Saskatchewan River, 1884. In the same year the post was taken over by the North West Mounted Police. In April 1885, in the course of the uprising, Big Bear's band attacked the fort, which they evacuated and then burned. LAC, PA-118768.

Riel in the prisoner's box. He addressed the court twice during his trial, once after all the evidence had been presented (when he spoke for more than an hour) and once before sentence was pronounced. LAC, C-1879.

heeded the jury's recommendations, but refused to do so. Ottawa dismissed two appeals, and Riel was hanged at Regina on 16 November.

If Riel was treated without sympathy by the Canadian government, the punishments meted out to the First Nations, who were regarded as having joined Riel's resistance rather than acting on their own initiative, proved to be equally severe. The Macdonald government used the occasion of the rebellion and the violence committed by the leaders of the First Nations to crush the Aboriginal protests against the failure to observe the negotiated treaties. Eight warriors, including Wandering Spirit, were executed in late November of 1885, and before the courts were finished more than 50 others had been sentenced to imprisonment. Among the leaders, Poundmaker stood trial for treason and was sentenced to three years in prison. Released after a year, he died four months later. Big Bear received a similar sentence, but was released after a year and a half because of poor health and died soon after. The trials were most improper, conducted without full translation against people who understood little English and less of the law being employed. Few were properly represented in court. Most First Nations leaders and people tried to remain clear of the Métis uprising, but this did not save them from a subsequent campaign of repression by Assistant Indian Commissioner Hayter Reed, who argued that the rebellion had abrogated the treaties and who introduced a series of policies that made the First Nations totally dependent on the largesse of Canada.

The execution of Louis Riel had a lasting impact on Canada. In Quebec it strengthened French-Canadian nationalism and helped turn voters away from the Conservative Party, which they had supported since Confederation. On 22 November 1885, at a huge gathering in the public square in Montreal called the Champ de Mars, Honoré Mercier, the

'The Surrender of Poundmaker to Major General Middleton at Battleford, Saskatchewan, on May 26, 1885', oil on canvas, 1887, by R.W. Rutherford. LAC, C-002769.

Liberal leader in Quebec, joined Wilfrid Laurier in denouncing the government action. Mercier insisted: 'In killing Riel, Sir John has not only struck at the heart of our race but especially at the cause of justice and humanity which . . . demanded mercy for the prisoner of Regina, our poor friend of the North-West.' Laurier added: 'Had I been born on the banks of the Saskatchewan . . . I would myself have shouldered a musket to fight against the neglect of governments and the shameless greed of speculators.' The two leaders disagreed over Mercier's proposal that French Canadians leave the two major parties and form one of their own. Laurier insisted that Mercier's proposal would destroy Confederation. Symbolically, French Canada took the execution of Riel to represent the final exclusion of the franco-phone from the West. Few spoke of the symbolic

meaning for the Aboriginal peoples of the shearing of Big Bear's long hair when he was in captivity, or of the execution of Wandering Spirit.

The military defeat of the Métis, the humiliation of the First Nations, and the public execution of Louis Riel in November 1885 were only part of the reason why that year and that month were so significant, not only in the history of the West but in the history of Canada. In November 1885 workers drove the last spike at Craigellachie in eastern British Columbia, marking the completion of the Canadian Pacific Railway. The CPR had been resurrected in 1881 as a hybrid corporation controlled by private capitalists and financed largely by the state, which, along with public subsidies, gave it about 25 million acres (10,117,500 ha) of land along its right of way. Contemporaries actively debated the question

A CPR construction crew laying track at Malakwa, BC, early 1880s. LAC, C-001602.

The first transcontinental passenger train arrives at the foot of Howe Street in Vancouver, 23 May 1887. City of Vancouver Archives Photo Reference LGN 460.

of building in advance of settlement, particularly given the inducements needed to persuade hard-headed businessmen to proceed with construction. The Macdonald government defended the railway on the grounds of national interest. Since this concept is not measurable in dollar amounts, it is impossible to know whether the price was too high. Even before the line was completed, Macdonald used it to send troops west to help suppress the Métis uprising of 1885.

The construction of the CPR was a spectacular feat of engineering, partly thanks to the managerial skills of William Van Horne (1843–1915). The CPR was built chiefly on the backs of 6,500 Chinese coolie labourers especially imported for the job. Many died, and those who survived were summarily discharged when the work was completed. With the CPR finished, the Canadian government moved swiftly to limit Chinese immigration. With the Plains peoples and their Métis allies totally subjugated, Canada was open for settlement from coast to coast.

Conclusion

The West was to be an anglophone colony of Canada. Not only were First Nations, Métis, and Chinese cast aside as quickly as possible, but French Canadians

Historic Sites

1. *Charlottetown Province House:* The proclamation declaring Prince Edward Island a part of the Canadian union was read from the balcony of this house on 1 July 1873.
2. *Louis Riel House National Historic Site:* The home of Louis Riel's mother and family is located at 330 River Road in South St Vital.
3. *Regina:* At the end of every summer a group of local actors re-enacts the trial of Louis Riel.
4. *Batoche National Historic Site:* The village of Batoche on the South Saskatchewan River was the site of the last battle in the Northwest Rebellion of 1885.
5. *Fort Battleford National Historic Site:* A collection of buildings—now with reconstructed stockades and bastions—housed the North West Mounted Police.
6. *Craigellachie, British Columbia:* On the south side of Highway 1 south of Revelstoke, in the village of Craigellachie, are a plaque and display commemorating the driving of the 'Last Spike' by Lord Strathcona on 7 November 1885, thus joining the eastern and western constructions of the CPR.

were not expected to settle there in any substantial numbers. National consolidation was arguably complete in 1885, but much Canadian 'nationalism' still bore the distinctive mark of the Ontario WASP. Two cultures, French and English, were in firm opposition to each other, and other cultures were thoroughly marginalized. Trying to satisfy the nation's two main components would continue to be the most challenging task facing the Canadian government for many years.

How History Has Changed

Canada's Western Policy

Some of the most intense controversy in Canadian historiography has concerned the subject matter of this chapter, most particularly in regard to the western policy of the Canadian government and its treatment of the local inhabitants. To some extent Canada's western policy has been treated as a product of its attempts to create a strong national government. For the most part, though, the government's policy has been seen as separate from the larger debate over national versus provincial rights. The chief issues have revolved around the treatment of the Métis and Louis Riel and the way they were translated into the national political controversies of the day. The treatment of the Aboriginal peoples has also been emphasized in recent years, but is often kept separate from that of the Métis.

The principal debate has been over the treatment of the Métis by the federal government, especially in terms of their land claims. Much of the argument has centred on whether the problems over the distribution of Métis land were a result of deliberate obstructionist policies by the Canadian government or of difficulties beyond the control of the government. Douglas Sprague and others have insisted that the Métis were a stable and persistent population in the Red River period, and that behind their rapid disappearance from Manitoba after 1870—and their problems in their new homes—was a deliberate government policy to dispossess them of their land rights. Thomas Flanagan and Gerhard Ens, on the other hand, have maintained that the government treated the Métis more than fairly, and that most of the problems facing the Métis were essentially of their own making. Defenders of government Métis policy have, by and large, been able to separate it from Aboriginal policy, which is far less ambiguous.

The treatment of Louis Riel by historians has shifted substantially over the years since the nineteenth century. In his own lifetime, even people who defended Riel regarded him as cruel and insane. Recent studies have not only made him a more sympathetic character, but have turned him into a true Métis leader. Riel has now to some extent passed beyond biography into the realm of mythology.

Lurking behind the Métis debate itself is another issue, perhaps even more interesting and important. Sprague had raised the land claims issue when he was working as a researcher for the Manitoba Métis Federation. The Federation then used Sprague's research in its legal case against the federal government. Canada, in turn, hired its own historians—most notably Thomas Flanagan and Gerhard Ens—to research and prepare the documentation for a defence brief. For many historians, this use of subsidized scholarship for litigious purposes subverts the independent scholarly standing of those involved, turning them into what one critic has called 'hired guns'. When Sprague accuses the Canadian government of bad faith, even of provoking the 1885 Rebellion, or when Flanagan insists that Louis Riel received a fair trial in 1885, one may question whether their conclusions are not simply part of their briefs on behalf of their clients and that their research, far from being objective or independent, is driven by ideology. Much recent scholarship in Canada, not only on the Métis, has been conducted on behalf of litigants in complex court cases. Few Canadian historians believe any longer in 'objectivity' or complain about partisanship in historical writing—which has characterized Canadian historiography since its very beginning—but many still are committed to a philosophy of academic independence. It is fair enough to turn one's scholarship to one side or another of a highly charged political issue; but is it equally fair to do so as a subsidized or hired researcher? Flanagan, for example, has been in turn a mentor, colleague, campaign director, and chief policy adviser to Canada's Conservative Prime Minister, Stephen Harper, and was lambasted by Canada's major Native groups for his views on the Métis and other Aboriginal peoples.

Beyond the land claims stands the larger question of federal policy towards and treatment of the West. Most historians would concede that the Canadian government handled the West badly, but whether the treatment was malicious or simply incompetent is another matter, as is the question of whether the government's behaviour justified an armed uprising. One of the problems with viewing Canadian western policy as incompetent blundering, of course, is that the blunderer-in-chief comes to be seen as Prime Minister Macdonald himself, and not all Canadians are prepared to accept that Sir John A. may have had feet of clay.

Short Bibliography

Berger, Carl. *Honour and the Search for Influence: A History of the Royal Society in Canada.* Toronto, 1996. A study by Canada's premier historian of ideas.

Bolger, Francis. *Prince Edward Island and Confederation 1863–1873.* Charlottetown, 1964. The standard work on the subject.

Bumsted, J.M. *The Red River Rebellion.* Winnipeg, 1996. A revisionist account of the insurgency in 1869–70.

Carter, Sarah. *Lost Harvests: Prairie Indian Reserve Farmers and Government Policy.* Montreal and Kingston, 1990. Analysis of agriculture on prairie reserve farms from the time of the treaties to World War I, showing the extent to which the federal government failed to meet its obligations and how the Plains Indians tried to adapt to a sedentary lifestyle.

Cook, Ramsay. *Provincial Autonomy, Minority Rights and the Compact Theory 1867–1921.* Ottawa, 1969. A detailed investigation of the subject.

Creighton, Donald. *John A. Macdonald: The Old Chieftain.* Boston, 1965. Still the standard biography of the old man.

Ens, Gerhard. *Homeland to Hinterland: The Changing Worlds of the Red River Métis in the Nineteenth Century.* Toronto, 1996. A revisionist study that sees the Métis as responding seriously to the drastically changing economic circumstances of the nineteenth century.

Flanagan, Thomas. *Riel and the Rebellion: 1885 Reconsidered,* rev. edn. Saskatoon, 1998. A well-researched study that argues that Riel received a fair trial in 1885.

Pryke, Kenneth G. *Nova Scotia and Confederation 1864–1873.* Toronto, 1979. The standard work on the subject.

Reid, Dennis. *Our Own Country Canada: Being an Account of the National Aspirations of the Principal Landscape Artists in Montreal and Toronto 1869–1890.* Ottawa, 1979. A wonderful example of the integration of art history into the larger historical and social context.

Reid, Jennifer. *Louis Riel and the Creation of Modern Canada: Mythic Discourse and the Postcolonial State.* Albuquerque, 2008. An attempt to account for and analyze Louis Riel's transformation from historic to mythical figure.

St Germain, Jill. *Indian Treaty-Making Policy in the United States and Canada, 1867-1877.* Toronto, 2001. An illuminating comparative approach to treaty-making.

Shelton, W. George, ed. *British Columbia and Confederation.* Victoria, 1967. A useful collection of essays on the subject.

Sprague, D.N. *Canada and the Métis, 1869–1885.* Waterloo, Ont., 1988. The best statement of the case against the government with regard to the Métis and especially the Métis land question.

Stanley, George F.G. *Louis Riel.* Toronto, 1961. The standard biography.

Stonechild, Blair, and Bill Waiser. *Loyal till Death: Indians and the North-West Rebellions*. Calgary, 1997. A sympathetic account of the First Nations in the rebellions.

Swainger, Jonathan. *The Canadian Department of Justice and the Completion of Confederation 1867–78*. Vancouver, 2000. An important discussion of the creation of a federal justice system in the years after Confederation.

Thomas, L.H. *The Struggle for Responsible Government in the Northwest Territories, 1870–97*, 2nd edn. Toronto, 1978. Somewhat misleadingly titled, a judicious overview of the political history of the prairie West in the last third of the nineteenth century.

Thomson, Dale. *Alexander Mackenzie: Clear Grit*. Toronto, 1960. The only modern full-length study of a complex personality.

Ware, Tracy, ed. *A Northern Romanticism: Poets of the Confederation*. Ottawa, 2000. A representative collection of the works of the Confederation poets.

Wright, Barry, and Susan Binnie, eds. *Canadian State Trials, vol. III: Security Measures, 1840–1914*. Toronto, 2009. A collection of essays exploring the legal implications of government policy after the Rebellions of 1837 and before World War I, focusing particularly on the West and the rebellions of the 1880s.

Study Questions

1. Was the Métis action led by Louis Riel in 1869–70 a true rebellion? Explain why or why not.
2. Identify three ways in which railroads helped to 'complete' Confederation.
3. List the advantages and disadvantages that you would find if you settled on homestead land in the 1870s.
4. Why did Ontario spearhead the provincial rights movement?
5. What effect did the railroads have on the development of theatre arts during this period?
6. Give two reasons to explain why the Canadian nationality was so fragile in the post-Confederation period.
7. What were the main differences between the movements that Louis Riel led in 1869–70 and 1885?
8. Was there a single rebellion in 1885?
9. What sort of Canada does Charles G.D. Roberts envision in his 1886 poem?
10. How would you have felt about Canadian policy towards the West if you had lived in Saskatchewan in 1885?

 www.oupcanada.com/Bumsted4e

Visit the companion website for *A History of the Canadian Peoples*, fourth edition for further resources.

7 Becoming Modern, 1885–1914

Timeline

1886 W.S. Fielding introduces legislation in Nova Scotia calling for secession from the union. The first CPR transcontinental arrives in Manitoba.

1887 Honoré Mercier leads *nationaliste* Liberals to victory in Quebec. St Catharines opens first electric streetcar system in Canada.

1890 Manitoba government abolishes public funding for Catholic schools. CPR builds rail line through Maine to connect Moncton with Montreal.

1891 Sir John A. Macdonald dies.

1892 A great fire destroys St John's, Newfoundland.

1896 Wilfrid Laurier leads the Liberal Party to a national electoral victory. Gold is discovered in the Klondike. The Manitoba Schools Question becomes a national issue.

1898 A national referendum is held on prohibition of alcoholic beverages. Newfoundland completes a railway across the island.

1899 Canadian Northern Railway is incorporated. Alaska Boundary Dispute is referred to an international tribunal. Canada agrees to send volunteer troops to South Africa.

1900 Art Museum of Toronto is founded. Prohibition legislation is passed on Prince Edward Island.

1901 The first wireless message transmitted across the Atlantic is received on Signal Hill near St John's, Newfoundland.

1902 Ernest Thompson Seton founds Woodcraft Indians.

1903 Alaska Boundary Dispute between Canada and the United States is handed over to a joint commission of six 'impartial jurists of repute'.

1905 Saskatchewan and Alberta are created as provinces out of the North-West Territories. Ontario Conservatives finally win political control of the province.

1906 Ontario Hydro-Electric Commission is created.

1907 Development of Marquis wheat. Canadian Department of Interior begins paying bonuses to European immigrant agents for labourers. Canadian Art Club is founded in Toronto.

1908 Border crossings established at 38 points across the US–Canada border.

1909 Department of External Affairs is created.

1910 Steel Company of Canada is created by an amalgamation of smaller firms.

1911 Robert Borden's Conservatives take over federal government in the Reciprocity Election. Marius Barbeau is appointed as anthropologist in the Museum Branch of the Geological Survey of Canada. Noranda gold/copper mine opens in Quebec.

1912 Social Services Council of Canada is organized. Quebec's boundaries are extended to Hudson Bay.

Panning for gold. During the gold rushes in the Canadian Northwest of the last half of the nineteenth century, culminating with the Klondike discovery in 1896 in Yukon, prospectors and camp followers flocked to the region, hoping to strike it rich. Mining communities sprang up frequently and disappeared when the gold ran out. © PEMCO–Webster & Stevens Collection; Museum of History and Industry, Seattle/CORBIS.

In the years after Confederation, Canada became one of the richest nations in the world in terms of gross national product and per capita income. Given the advantage of hindsight, historians from comparably sized countries—such as Mexico, Brazil, or Argentina—can only envy Canada's privileged position of wealth, if not power, in this critical period. From the late 1870s to the end of World War I, Canada was among the top 10 of the world in industrial development. Though the country possessed rich agricultural and natural resources, much of the key to its success lay in the exploitation of these advantages by a burgeoning industrial sector. Canadians often saw only the weaknesses of the Canadian economy. From the vantage point of most of the world, however, Canada was rich, powerful, highly industrialized, and 'progressive', even if still a part of the British Empire. It possessed a vibrant labour movement. Before the Great War, Canada had created a self-sustaining internal economy and a dynamic foreign trade. While the nation was transforming its economy, it was also altering its society and culture. There was another round of immigration, and Canada became an increasingly urbanized country. This was also the great era of reform, both political and social. As well, there was a great national debate over Canada's place within the British Empire. The political system that made all these developments possible operated through the mediating influence of political parties.

As a result of both its geographical position and its colonial situation, Canada before 1914 was able to enjoy relative isolation from the turmoil of international politics, concentrating on its own domestic development. Like Americans, most Canadians were relatively inward-looking, even isolationist, in their attitudes towards the wider world. Most French Canadians saw themselves as an autonomous people without close European or international connections, while Canadians of British origin felt varying degrees of loyalty to Great Britain, which looked after most international affairs in the name of the Empire. Canada's corps of diplomats was tiny, confined to Washington, London, and Paris. After 1909 a small Department of External Affairs supervised and co-ordinated the nation's sporadic formal relations with the world. While most Canadians felt no need to be citizens of the world before 1914, they were not necessarily ignorant of it. The larger daily newspapers covered foreign affairs far more assiduously than their modern equivalents, for example.

The Developing Political and Constitutional System

The Fathers of Confederation had not written political parties into the Canadian Constitution. Nevertheless, by the mid-1880s a two-party system had evolved at both the federal and provincial levels that would remain unchanged until World War I. Indeed, this period was in many respects the golden age of Canadian party politics. Party affiliation was a serious matter. Being a Liberal or a Conservative was a commitment passed on from father to son; small towns had parallel Liberal and Conservative business establishments, including funeral parlours. The seeming vitality of the two-party system disguised, to some degree, the underlying tensions of Canadian federalism. Before 1914, however, the parties appeared flexible enough to contain various currents of conflict and disagreement. Both national parties developed consensual systems capable of holding differing ideologies, sections, and interest groups.

The key to the successful functioning of the national parties—and the allegiances of their adherents—was in large part the power of patronage. Both parties, in office, distributed honours and jobs to their leading supporters, carefully apportioning rewards to those whose qualifications were judged solely in terms of political service and loyalty. The patronage system rewarded chiefly those members of the Canadian professional and business elites (mainly from the so-called middle class) who ran the two parties. The system diminished ideological and regional differences, offering French Canadians their own opportunities for advancement. Patronage thus encouraged a stable party system in which matters of principle were less important than the division of the spoils of victory.

Despite their consensual utility, Canadian political parties had considerable difficulty in mediating the relationships between the federal and provincial levels of government. The rise of a strong movement for provincial rights, initiated by Ontario, joined by Quebec, and supported on occasion by all provinces, was almost inevitable. The chief, although not sole, bone of contention would be economic development. Provinces insisted that they, not the federal government, should control development within their boundaries. What was unexpected was the support for provincial rights provided by the Judicial Committee of the British Privy Council, the court of last resort for federal–provincial disagreements. In a series of landmark decisions stretching from the 1880s to the Great War, the Judicial Committee consistently reduced the power of the federal government and enhanced that of the provinces. Both anglophone and francophone voters tended to support this readjustment of Confederation. They saw the provinces as a check on the federal government's power, and they consistently supported provincial parties that wanted to confront Ottawa. Thus there was nothing unique about the 1887 victory in Quebec of the *nationaliste* Liberal government of Honoré Mercier (1840–94). W.S. Fielding (1848–1929) had won for the Liberals in Nova Scotia in 1884 on a platform of provincial rights. In 1886 Fielding introduced legislation calling for the secession of Nova Scotia from the union. Obviously, provincial parties could not afford too close an identification with their federal counterparts, particularly while the latter were in power. Only with the success of Laurier's Liberals in 1896 did the Ontario Tories escape the albatross of a federal Conservative Party, for example. By 1905 they won control of the province, which they would seldom relinquish over the remainder of the century.

A great irony of Confederation was that French Canada continued as the region upon which national political success had to be built. Until the death of Sir John A. Macdonald in 1891, the Conservatives had successfully appealed to Quebec with a judicious combination of local political patronage and national political policies. The execution of Louis Riel late in 1885 threatened that appeal, but the government's Quebec ministers held firm. The Grand Old Man's successors, including J.J. Abbott (1821–93), John S. Thompson (1844–94), and

Charles Tupper (1821–1915), simply did not have the magic. In 1896 Wilfrid Laurier (1841–1919) became the national *chef*. He had put together a coalition of provincial Liberal parties by softening the potential issues of division. Laurier's agonizing over the Manitoba Schools Question of the early 1890s, when his distaste for a unilingual policy for Manitoba schools was matched only by his refusal to prevent provinces from running affairs within their own general mandate, was a pure reflection of his approach. Laurier saw national unity and national harmony as identical and, not surprisingly, viewed a bicultural state as essential.

The Conservatives of Robert Borden (1854–1937) replaced Laurier's Liberals in 1911. The Tories split the Quebec vote while sweeping Ontario, thanks in large measure to the support of the Ontario provincial party. Key issues in the 1911 election were American reciprocity and imperial naval defence. Borden's victory was a triumph for Canadian imperial sentiment, anti-continentalism, and middle-class reform. Borden had set out his Halifax Platform in 1907, calling for civil service reform, public ownership of telephones and telegraphs, a reformed Senate, and free mail delivery in rural areas. Borden spoke for the 'progressive' forces of Anglo-Canadian society and reform, which had been marshalling strength since the mid-1880s. Laurier had enacted some of Borden's planks, including civil service reform in 1908, but the Conservatives still claimed the close imperial connection and had added the progressive mantle. Borden achieved some of his imperial vision only with the beginning of the Great War. The Conscription Crisis of 1917 completed the process, which began in 1911 with the defeat of Laurier, of the political isolation of French Canada. At the same time, neither the West nor the Maritimes were content, as events after the war's end soon demonstrated.

The Economic Infrastructure

Control of capital through chartered banks headquartered chiefly in central Canada was one of that region's great advantages. Unlike the United States,

Sir Wilfrid Laurier

Wilfrid Laurier, c. 1882. LAC, PA-013133.

The family heritage of Wilfrid Laurier (1841–1919), born in a small Quebec village outside Montreal, dated back to seventeenth-century Quebec. As part of his education, Laurier lived for two years with an English-speaking family and attended an English-speaking school. His facility in both languages was subsequently one of his great political strengths. After education at l'Assomption College and McGill University, he was called to the Quebec bar.

From his earliest days Laurier was a Liberal, and after election to Parliament in 1874 he soon joined the Mackenzie cabinet. Laurier was an outspoken critic of the ultramontane wing of the Catholic Church in Quebec and defender of both the Liberals as a party of moderation and of the laity as entitled to make their own choices free of clerical pressure. Like many French-Canadian Liberals of his generation, he not only wanted a non-denominational party but was also attracted to British history and to the British Constitution.

Somewhat chastened by political failure in the early 1880s, his career was rejuvenated by the execution of Louis Riel, whose constitutional

Canadian banking was always highly centralized. In 1914 in Canada there were only 26 banks operating 2,888 branches. Some of the larger banks (the Royal Bank, the Bank of Commerce) had more than 300 branches each. From the beginning, Canadian chartered banks focused less on serving local customers than on facilitating the transfer of commodities and funds. Their credit facilities, especially for outlying districts of the nation, were quite limited. The banking industry itself wrote Canadian banking legislation. The Canadian Bankers' Association was an organization of a few powerful men.

Although in 1913 Montreal-headquartered banks held half of the assets of all Canadian banks ($788 million of $1.55 billion), Quebec contained considerably fewer branch banks per capita than the remainder of the nation. The result was the founding by Alphonse Desjardins (1854–1920) of the caisses populaires, often run by curés in association with Catholic parishes. Financial institutions to compete locally with the chartered banks did develop, not only in the form of caisses populaires but as government savings banks, local savings banks, and credit unions. Their economic power was limited, however, and the chartered banks continued to grow. Banks with head offices in central Canada refused to make local loans and set local interest rates at high levels. Sir Edmund Walker (1848–1924), president of the Bank of Commerce, labelled regional complaints 'local grievances against what we regard as the interests of the country as a whole' (quoted in Naylor, 1975, I: 103).

grievances he championed. But Laurier resolutely refused to become a racial and religious nationalist, and he advocated conciliation between French and English. He exploited the clumsiness of both the Conservatives and French-Canadian clerics over the Manitoba Schools Question, insisting that he could effect a satisfactory compromise, which he did.

Once elected to office as Prime Minister in 1896, with the strong backing of Quebec voters, he appointed a strong cabinet composed mainly of provincial leaders with progressive ideas. Fortunately for the Liberal government, Canada was entering a period of great growth and economic boom, especially in the West, providing a tide upon which almost any government could have ridden successfully. The Liberals became involved with Canadian big business interests over the construction of two new transcontinental railroads, but eventually came to grief over military and imperial policy, issues that still divided English and French Canada. Laurier survived the Boer War by allowing English Canadians to participate as volunteers and by stifling all initiatives for closer imperial co-operation. He even managed to deal with the problem of increased German naval construction by introducing a Canadian navy instead of Canadian contributions to the British one.

One issue that helped defeat his government in 1911 came unexpectedly, when the United States offered Canada a reciprocal economic arrangement and Laurier accepted it enthusiastically. To its surprise, the Liberal government discovered that Canadians were not willing in boom times to pay the price of a potential loss of national sovereignty in return for American advantages, although the loss of Quebec support on imperial issues was probably more important, as was a perception that the Liberals had lost their reformist edge and were less progressive on social issues than were the Conservatives. Laurier supported Canadian entrance into World War I enthusiastically, but refused to co-operate in 1917 with the government over conscription or to join a coalition government committed to the question. He was deserted by many English-speaking Liberals, and in the election of November 1917 his support was reduced almost solely to Quebec seats.

Laurier was well known as a conciliator who sought compromise and opposed political extremism and sectional division in word and deed. In retrospect, one of his most important achievements may have been his refusal to allow his nation to become more closely integrated into the British Empire.

Transportation continued to be an essential ingredient of development. As in the age of the first railway boom of the 1850s, railways were both a means of development and a field of investment. Substantial railway construction involved significant public subsidies, often in the form of land grants along the right of way, as well as other boons. The CPR received from the government the completed line from Fort William to Selkirk, as well as the line from Kamloops to Port Moody. Moreover, it received a cash payment of $25 million, plus 25 million acres (10,117,500 ha) 'fairly fit for settlement', and various tax exemptions on its land. In addition, it had a monopoly position. Nor was the Canadian Pacific the only railway so favoured. Dozens of railways incorporated in Canada during these years. Local communities fought desperately for railways, seeing them as links to a prosperous future. Sir William Mackenzie (1849–1923) and Sir Donald Mann (1853–1934) constructed a second transcontinental line, the Canadian Northern Railway, which passed considerably to the north of the CPR. Everyone outside central Canada complained about the high costs of freight, but all Canadians relied on the railway. Passenger travel was swift and relatively inexpensive.

Energy was another essential. Canada always possessed rich potential energy resources. Coal never provided much advantage, but abundant water power did. Changing technology at the close of the nineteenth century enabled major natural waterfalls to be harnessed and others to be created through dams. Development for hydroelectric power was substantial in the early years of the twentieth century. No province had greater potential for hydroelectricity generation than Quebec. Unlike Ontario, which established the Ontario Hydro-Electric Commission in 1906 under the chairmanship of Sir Adam Beck (1857–1925), Quebec permitted its hydroelectric development to be carried out by private enterprise. The process of exploiting electricity, both for light and for power, was one of the great unsung technological developments of the age. Industry could use water power as an alternative to fossil fuel. Cheap hydroelectric power became an advantage for Canadian industry. The manufacturing community saw cheap power as essential to its growth and development. Hydroelectricity lit Canadian homes at relatively low cost. It fostered the growth of electric-powered public transportation, such as the tram and the trolley.

The period between 1880 and 1919 was a great age of science and technology throughout the Western world. Most fields of scientific endeavour transformed out of all recognition the basic theoretical assumptions that had dominated humankind for generations. The number of inventions that altered in practical ways how people lived and worked was astounding. Canada played little role at the frontiers of pure science. Its record in the technical application of science was somewhat better, as the activities of the Dominion Experimental Farms system (created by Ottawa in 1886) demonstrated. The great achievement of Canadian agricultural research in this period was the development of Marquis wheat in 1907 by Charles Edward Saunders (1867–1937). In both science and technology, however, Canada was fortunate to be able to borrow heavily from Great Britain and the United States. Most Canadian technical accomplishment came through adapting imported technology to Canadian conditions, although a number of useful Canadian inventions were introduced in this period.

Population growth was also necessary for economic development. Immigration provided much of that growth for Canada in this period, as in others. Between 1880 and 1920 nearly 4.5 million immigrants arrived in Canada, mainly although not exclusively from Europe and the United States. Beginning in the mid-1890s, the origins of the newcomers

shifted perceptibly. Most of the earlier immigrants came from the British Isles, while after 1896 large numbers came from Eastern and Southern Europe. In addition, Americans again began arriving in Canada in large numbers, their destinations the 'Last Best West' in Alberta and Saskatchewan. By 1901, 34 per cent of the newcomers to the prairie West came from other countries than Canada, with 33 per cent from the United States and 22 per cent from Britain. During the peak decade of immigration (1905–14), nearly 2.8 million people immigrated to Canada, with the numbers about equally divided among Central and Eastern Europe, the United States, and the British Isles. (A small number of Asians and people from the Near East were included in the total. Most of the Near East immigrants came

The Canadian Bank of Commerce building at 25 King Street West, designed by R.A. Waite and erected in 1889–90, was one of several new office buildings in Toronto that had some claim to architectural distinction and even grandeur. At seven-and-a-half storeys, it soared over neighbouring three- and four-storey buildings, and reflected the influence of the first skyscrapers in New York and Chicago. City of Toronto Archives, Micklethwaite Collection SC 1497 #21.

from Lebanon and were listed as 'Syrians' in the official records. Many of the victims on board the ill-fated passenger liner *Titanic* were 'Syrians' travelling in steerage on their way to Canada.) Between 1901 and 1911 alone, the Canadian population grew by 43 per cent. In the 1911 census, over 20 per cent of all Canadians enumerated had been born abroad. While many of the newcomers settled on farms, fully 70 per cent joined the labour force in industry and transportation. Canadian business and government specifically recruited many of the newcomers, often on a contract basis, to provide an industrial workforce. In 1907 the Canadian Department of the Interior began paying bonuses to European immigration agents for people who had labour experience, such as farmers, navvies, or miners. Much of this industrial workforce ended up in Canada's cities.

While the typical newcomer to Canada in these years continued to be the unassisted immigrant, arriving under his or her own power, either alone or as part of a family group, several other categories need to be singled out for special attention, particularly British 'orphans' and European contract labourers.

Canadians were generally more willing to accept immigrants from the British Isles than from any other place, although resentment was common against those Britons who looked down their noses at their 'colonial cousins'. On the other hand, many Canadians objected to the activities of British philanthropists and philanthropic institutions in employing Canada as a dumping ground for unwanted children of the urban poor. These children were recruited as cheap labour, mainly for Canadian farms and as domestic servants. The majority were young boys, but a substantial number were young girls as well. Nearly 100,000 of these 'home children' were sent to Canada before the Great War, most of them recruited in British slums. Many were encouraged to go by their parents; others were literally seized from parents and sent overseas 'for their own good'. The results were mixed, with the worst experiences probably suffered by children of both genders who were sent into rural homes, where many were badly exploited by their supposed benefactors. This immigration was constantly accompanied by opposition to its continuance. Much of the opposition to child

immigration came from the Canadian labour movement, especially between 1888 and 1895. It was concerned less with the treatment of the victims than with their presence as an unregulated low-wage component of the workforce.

Perhaps the most colourful of the philanthropists involved in child 'rescue' was the Dublin-born Thomas John Barnardo (1845–1900), who was personally responsible for sending more than 30,000 youngsters to Canada. Barnardo, always known as 'Doctor' Barnardo, actually scoured the streets of London for waifs, collecting thousands of pounds from the British public for his charity work. He used the money less to improve existing conditions than to expand the scope of his activities. Barnardo was a lightning rod for complaints of abuse and victimization. His activities were criticized on a number of occasions, and he came to take care that records were kept, using photographs and letters from children to demonstrate how well they were getting on. As for the children, one modern study of Barnardo children has concluded that some evidence exists that 9 per cent of the boys and 15 per cent of the girls were actually abused (Parker, 2009: 221). (In February 2010, British Prime Minister Gordon Brown met with a group of former immigrants and others to apologize for their treatment: *Globe and Mail*, 20 Feb. 2010, A3.)

Despite the emphasis on agricultural settlement and the concerns about the assimilability of non-British immigrants, a number of Canadian corporations insisted on their need for willing workers. For these companies, headed by the railroads, British immigrants were not desirable because they complained about wages and working conditions; farmers were unsuitable because they left their jobs at harvest time. The CPR turned increasingly after 1901 to contract workers, often from southern Italy. According to Donald Avery (1995: 30), these workers—supplied by labour agents working in Europe—could 'live for a year on the wages they earn in six months.' The railroads liked Bulgarians, Poles, and Italians because by working hard and living simply, they were 'peculiarly suited for the work'. A massive national railway construction program between 1900 and 1914 was sustained by 50,000 to 70,000 immigrant navvies (unskilled construction workers) per year. Mining corporations were equally attracted to Slavic and Italian workers, and by 1913 more than 300 labour agencies were recruiting more than 200,000 workers per year from abroad for labour in Canada. Several foreign governments protested the treatment of their nationals by labour agencies and Canadian employers, and both organized labour and nativist groups opposed the contract workers as being scabs. More than half of these workers were sojourners, who intended to use the savings from their earnings to return to their homelands, but a substantial minority would remain in Canada permanently. The Italians brought several new elements in their cultural baggage. Several secret societies modelled on the Sicilian Mafia and the Calabrian 'Ndrangheta provided a range of services to immigrants, sometimes also engaging in extortion activities that were attributed by the Canadian

media to the 'Black Hand'. A few Italians were also anarchists; one of their leaders, Luigi Galleani, was deported from Canada in 1903.

Another Round of Industrialization

Financial centralization and growing industrial capacity, particularly the shift from the processing of primary goods into the secondary manufacturing of finished goods, were major economic developments in Canada in the years 1880–1919. Continued industrialization always involved more than the construction of new and larger factories. Canadians needed to extend and rationalize transportation facilities. They had to mobilize investment, exploit resources, and recruit a labour force. Despite the National Policy, Ottawa did not maintain control over, or ownership in, the Canadian economy. The country's emergence on the international scene increased its vulnerability to world economic conditions and economic cycles. Moreover, its industrial development was distinctly uneven, with industrial growth well above the national average in Ontario, at the national average in Quebec, and well below the national average in the Maritime and western provinces. Larger urban centres, such as Montreal and Toronto, expanded constantly, while smaller communities fell steadily behind.

One of the keys to Canadian economic growth between 1885 and the Great War was an influx of foreign investment. Few nations depended so heavily on foreign capital to fuel economic growth as has Canada throughout its history. Investment in this era—particularly in the boom years 1900–13—was significant. Like other countries, Canada used most of its imported capital to finance large development projects, such as railways and hydroelectric generation. Canada's imports of capital came in the two forms of indirect (portfolio) investment and direct investment. These two types of investment reflected the respective activity of Canada's two largest financial partners. Much of the portfolio investment came from Great Britain. Much of the direct investment came from the United States. In terms of the foreign domination of the economy that resulted, the two types of investment were quite different. Direct

A 1907 poster exhorting immigrants to settle in western Canada. LAC, C-30621.

investment resulted in far greater control. At the time few Canadians agonized overly much about the extent or the origin of foreign ownership. Foreign control did not become a serious issue in Canadian economic theory or public life before the late 1950s. Until then, almost all Canadians might have agreed with the American entrepreneur Frank Clergue, who declared in 1901 that 'foreign money injected into the circulating medium of Canada' would 'remain forever to the everlasting blessing of thousands of its inhabitants' (quoted in Bliss, 1972: 38).

As students now learn routinely in introductory economics courses, portfolio investment represents money borrowed against securities, in this period mainly bonds. Bonds are a relatively safe investment. They do not carry management implications. The British preferred portfolio investment in Canada because their prosperous citizens wanted to clip coupons in their old age. Government (federal, provincial, municipal) and the railways did most of Canada's borrowing in Britain. The money went to finance transportation networks and public works. Little was available for private enterprise, almost none for venture capital. In the first years of the twentieth century, Canadian entrepreneurs exploited the British investment market in new ways. The chief innovation was the promotion of bond issues for giant industrial operations created from the merger of smaller companies. Nobody was more successful at merging than William Maxwell Aitken (1879–1964, later Lord Beaverbrook), son of a New Brunswick Presbyterian minister. His great triumph came in 1910 with the creation of the Steel Company of Canada, the bonds for which his Royal Securities firm sold in London. 'I believe in consolidations', Aitken told *Maclean's* magazine in 1911. 'They are more efficient. They give better service to the consumer. In a large country such as Canada, they reduce the distribution costs. They are good for the consumer' (quoted in Marchilson, 1996: 181). He was the most visible and sharpest operator in a movement that saw 58 giant corporations created in Canada between 1909 and 1912.

The United States was an importer of British capital before World War I and had little available for overseas portfolio investment. The Americans invested directly in Canada to gain access to Canadian raw materials and the Canadian market. They went heavily into the resource sector. They also invested in Canadian manufacturing to gain maximum access to the Canadian market. Less than half of American direct investment was in manufacturing, but the total amount involved was over $100 million by 1910. The protective tariff played an important role in encouraging American branch-plant investment. Early Canadian protectionism sought to foster employment. Canadians did not worry much about the outflow of profits or the influx of foreign managers. Canadians generally accepted that Canadian businessmen and investors were not very adventurous, preferring familiar fields and allowing the Yankees to take the chances. Far from endangering the Canadian identity, American investment fostered it. The alternative was immigration to the United States.

The Americans preferred to locate their branch plants in southern Ontario. This choice came for a variety of reasons. Americans were active in the heavy industries of Ontario, partly because Ontario was so close to the industrial heartland of the United States south of the Great Lakes. Moreover, Ontario deliberately encouraged Americans to invest in the processing of raw materials by allowing them virtually free access to the province's natural resources. Ontarians believed that they had all the requirements for self-sufficiency within their own borders. The province required that resources taken on Crown land be processed in Canada. 'Debarred from the opportunity of cutting logs for export, it is an absolute certainty that the American lumberman, in default of other sources of supply, will transfer his sawmill enterprises to Canadian soil' (quoted in Nelles, 1974: 217). American preference both contributed to and reflected the industrial development of Ontario.

After 1885 manufacturing replaced commerce as the chief propellant of urban growth in Ontario. Much of the new industrial plant involved sophisticated technological applications, often imported from the United States. Ontario became the centre of the Canadian iron and steel industry. The transformation of the older iron industry into the steel industry was symptomatic of the process that was occurring. Coal replaced charcoal as the source of heat. The refining process turned into two steps, first involving open-hearth furnaces and then a

Workers at looms, c. 1908. City of Toronto Archives, James Collection, Fonds 1244, 137.

steam-driven rolling mill. The result was a product with a slightly higher carbon content. Its name was steel. Mechanization occurred at every step in the manufacturing process. 'Gigantic automation' was the watchword at huge installations like Stelco's Hamilton plant and Algoma's Sault Ste Marie operation. Steel rails were the most common standard product. Ontario's manufacturing grew in a number of smaller urban centres.

Quebec manufacturing relied far less on heavy industry (and vast capitalization) than did manufacturing in Ontario. It depended far more on an industry based on labour and fussy mechanization, such as clothing, wood products, textiles, and food processing. Part of the explanation for the difference may reside in labour availability. Part may have been the availability of cheap hydroelectric power in

Quebec after 1900. Quebec had eliminated Ontario's early advantage in secondary over primary manufacturing by 1915. Montreal provided the greatest concentration of Quebec's manufacturing sector. By 1900 workers in that city represented about half the manufacturing labour in the province. It is easy to overemphasize the notorious lag between the two central Canadian provinces. They were more like one another than they were like the remainder of the nation. The industrial disparity between the central provinces and the others grew continually in the years before 1914.

While the absence of industrialization in the Canadian West was a consequence of the recentness of its settlement, this did not apply to the Maritime region. Here rural stagnation joined a crisis in the shipbuilding industry. The growth of new

Manufacturing Output, 1870–1890

One of the developments of the post-Confederation period was the tendency for the industrial output of the Maritime region to lose ground to Ontario and Quebec. The following table documents the change in output by province in various industrial sectors between 1870 and 1890.

Percentage Change in Manufacturing Output, 1870–1890

Industry	Nova Scotia	New Brunswick	Quebec	Ontario
All factories	128	42	104	116
Farm production (butter, cheese, and cloth)	60	67	50	34
All manufacturing	120	44	101	113
Consumer goods	160	95	100	119
Durable goods	30	−10	83	61
Intermediate goods	214	50	120	162
Chemical products	210	3	149	410
Clothing	224	49	125	277
Coal & petroleum products	164	321	365	−5
Food & beverages	361	292	122	82
Iron & steel products	142	21	92	90
Leather & fur products	−1	−12	50	41
Nonferric metal products	348	204	191	854
Nonmetallic mineral products	114	121	186	215
Printing	54	111	86	177
Paper products	48	−52	313	254
Rubber goods	na	Na	202	4311
Transport equipment	3	−38	154	26
Tobacco products	−78	64	162	263
Textiles	505	443	406	150
Wood products	213	2	64	153

Source: Kris Inwood, 'Maritime Industrialization from 1870 to 1910', *Acadiensis* 21, 1 (Autumn 1991): 147. Reprinted by permission.

technologies was partly to blame, but the problem was mainly a failure of the Maritime shippers' nerve. The shippers always viewed their ships as instruments of trade. Instead of reinvesting their capital in a modern shipbuilding industry, they and the business community of the region made a desperate effort to exploit the internal market. They accepted the National Policy and tried to work within it. The attempts at continentalism seemed initially successful in the 1880s, but rapidly turned to failure.

The reasons for the ultimate Maritime failure remain uncertain. Most Maritime entrepreneurs seemed to lack the financial resources to withstand the ups and downs of the economic cycles. They tended to blame many of their problems on high railway freight rates. At about the same time that the region's business community was moaning about railway rates, outside capital moved in and began buying up locally based companies. Montreal capitalists did most of the damage. They bought up and dismantled many burgeoning industries still servicing the local market.

Maritime entrepreneurs, convinced that they were at a substantial geographical disadvantage in competing with central Canada, ceased trying in most sectors after 1895. Instead, the region turned to the panacea of iron and steel. Surely the presence of local raw materials would make this industry a competitive one. Unfortunately, central Canadian interests soon took over the Maritime steel industry. By 1911 Montreal controlled much of the region's industrial enterprise. Toronto, on the other hand, moved into the region's wholesale and retail marketing sector. Between 1901 and 1921 the number of regional businesses that were branches of central Canadian firms more than doubled, from 416 to 950. The net result of both sorts of takeovers was a regional loss of economic autonomy. Outsiders siphoned capital away from the Maritimes, and when times got tough they closed stores and factories. The region was systematically deindustrialized and decommercialized. It would never recover its economic vitality.

Most of the businessmen who operated the industrializing economy were immigrants or sons of immigrants, with Scots farmers over-represented in both categories. Few had begun at the bottom of the social scale. French Canadians were seriously under-represented among large-scale entrepreneurs and industrialists, even within their own province. Most French-Canadian businesses remained small in scale, family-controlled, and confined chiefly to the province of Quebec. These businessmen did share an overall philosophy. They insisted on government involvement in large schemes of public development, such as railways. They accepted government power to grant monopolies of public service through charters or access to Crown lands through advantageous leases. They sought to minimize competition wherever possible, even if public regulation was the price paid for the reduction. Small businessmen who could not combine institutionally to control trade, such as the small retailers, fought hard for early closings and price-fixing. Business rhetoric about competition had less to do with extolling the virtues of free enterprise than with complaining about unfair competition. The business community insisted that what it wanted was a 'living profit', a reasonable return on investment of time and capital.

While few business leaders believed in policies of laissez-faire in the relationship between the state and business, the situation was quite different when it came to labour organizations. From the view of business, organized labour was an illegitimate combination designed to erode the right of the individual to run his business as he saw fit. Nevertheless, the growth of industrialization was conducive to expanding worker militancy. The Canadian state proved relatively receptive to the rights of labour to organize. Whereas in the United States public policy was almost universally hostile to labour organization, in Canada laws that legalized union activity were put on the books beginning in the 1880s. Many of the late nineteenth-century labour organizations in Canada were foreign imports, chiefly from the United States. If Canadian labour got much of its structure from the Americans, it drew much of its practical experience from Great Britain. For Canada as a whole, the Canadian Labour Congress formed in 1883 as an umbrella organization for local trade councils, and in 1892 it became the Trades and Labor Congress of Canada.

In this period most labour conflict revolved around the right to organize and the recognition of unions. Government acceptance of union activity in some ways increased the frequency of conflict. Moreover, the civil authorities frequently intervened in labour conflicts, usually in the name of public order and often on the side of management. Such intervention often produced violence. Strikes were certainly common everywhere in Canada, especially after 1900. In Ontario's 10 largest cities, between 1901 and 1914, there were 421

'Steel mills at Sydney, Cape Breton', oil on canvas, 1907, by the railway magnate Sir William Cornelius Van Horne. Built between 1900 and 1905, these two plants attracted hundreds of workers, creating an instant city. The Montreal Museum of Fine Arts, gift of the artist's grandson, William C. Van Horne. Photo: The Montreal Museum of Fine Arts, Brian Merrett.

strikes and lockouts involving 60,000 workers. In the Maritimes, 324 strikes occurred between 1901 and 1914. Except in the Far West, the majority of the workers involved in these confrontations were skilled rather than unskilled. By 1914 approximately 155,000 Canadians belonged to organized labour unions, many of them affiliated with American internationals.

Natural Resources

If Canada was to avoid eternal international balance-of-payment deficits (the plague of Third World countries in our own era) it obviously needed commodities to export. It found many of these in the natural resources sector. To a considerable extent Canada's resources were the old mainstays of the colonial staple economy, now produced under different guises. Resources not only earned money abroad, they encouraged manufacturing at home.

Agriculture

As if on some master schedule, the Canadian wheat economy continued to expand without pause. Fields of operation moved from central Canada to Manitoba and slightly later to the North-West Territories (which became the provinces

Arthur W. Puttee

Arthur W. Puttee (1868–1957) was born in Folkestone, England, and learned the printing trade in his father's shop. He was raised a Baptist, but turned to liberal Christianity and Unitarianism early in his adult life. He came to North America in 1888, initially establishing himself on a homestead in Portage la Prairie. Finding agricultural labour arduous, he headed to the United States to work as a journeyman printer, eventually returning to Manitoba and the composing staff of the *Manitoba Free Press*. Puttee was soon an active member of the Winnipeg Typographical Union (WTU), an important craft union in the city, and became its president in 1893. As a craft unionist, throughout his career Puttee preferred conciliation and arbitration to labour confrontation, although during his time in the WTU it faced technological threats from new linotyping machinery. The printers responded to the new technology by asserting the prerogatives of their craft, including union control over apprentices and operation of the new machinery. Puttee was serving as secretary of the WTU in 1896 when the union successfully struck the *Winnipeg Tribune*.

Printers were not only skilled artisans, but had to be literate. Many, including Puttee, went into politics. In Puttee's case, he used the Winnipeg Trades and Labor Council (WTLC) as a springboard, being an early advocate of the organization of a labour party in the city through a labour newspaper, *The People's Voice*, which he helped to purchase in 1897. Within a year he was editing and managing the paper. Puttee's ideological position of advocacy of independent political action by labour has been described as 'labourism'. In June 1899 he was nominated as an independent labour candidate for a Winnipeg seat in the House of Commons. His campaign appealed not only to organized labour but to 'the people', offering proposals both to expand political democracy and to protect labour against capitalism. Many of his campaign planks were common currency among progressive reformers in the United States and Canada. He advocated universal adult suffrage, proportional representation, initiative and referendum, and a popular veto on all legislation. He also favoured public ownership of all 'natural monopolies', and sought to raise most revenue by taxing 'land values'. He was elected in a close vote in January 1900, becoming both the youngest member of Parliament at the time and the first MP specifically elected as a labour candidate (although he joined several Ontario 'independents' in the House). He was re-elected in the November 1900 election, receiving much support from the Liberals.

In Parliament, Puttee saw himself as a citizens' representative as much as a representative of labour. His opposition to the protective tariff, railroad subsidies, and extensive immigration to Canada was particularly noteworthy. He was defeated in the 1904 general election and returned to Winnipeg to open a new printing company, Winnipeg Printing and Engraving, which took over the publication of *The People's Voice*. Puttee continued to advocate labour unionism, including the organization of the Canadian Labour Party based on the British model, but increasingly in Winnipeg he came to be seen as a conservative influence. In 1918 he opposed a general strike of civic employees and was pushed out of the WTLC by more radical and militant labour leaders. After 1918 he continued to run his printing company, but was no longer active in politics.

Source: Bryan Dewalt, 'Arthur W. Puttee: Labourism and Working-Class Politics in Winnipeg, 1894–1918', MA thesis, University of Manitoba, 1985.

of Saskatchewan and Alberta in 1905). Between 1870 and 1890 thousands of farmers, chiefly from Ontario, poured into the West. The number of acres of occupied land went from 2.5 million to over 6 million (1,011,750 to 2,428,200 ha) in the years 1881–91, while the acres of land under cultivation exploded from 279,000 to 1,429,000 (112,911 to 578,316 ha) in the same 10-year period. The opening of the CPR was critical for the production of western wheat. So, too, was the appearance of new wheat strains capable of maturation in the short prairie growing season.

Before the mid-1890s the typical prairie settler was an Ontario-born farmer who came west to make a new start. Despite the passage of the Dominion Lands Act of 1872, which made a fair amount of homestead land available, most farmers preferred to purchase land from companies set up by the great corporate benefactors of government land grants, especially the railways. Farmers believed (with some legitimacy) that homestead land was less likely to acquire rail transportation than was land owned by the railway itself. Although homestead land was free to the male settler (women could not apply for homesteads), successful farming still required substantial capital investment. Conservative estimates of the costs of 'farm-making' ranged from a minimum of $300 (the annual wage for an unskilled labourer) to $1,000. Most farmers brought money with them from the sale of land back East. The western farmer was a market farmer. Although the family grew as much food as possible for personal consumption, the farmer's instinct was to increase constantly his acreage under production. Before World War I, mechanization was limited mainly to harvesting. Animals (horses and oxen) did most of the ploughing and cultivation. Nevertheless, the individual farmer managed to cultivate considerable quantities of land, limited mainly by the size of his labour force. In 1898 Ontario-born A.J. Cotton (1857–1942) harvested a crop of over 17,000 bushels of top-grade wheat in Treherne, Manitoba.

Before the 1890s, western settlement was hampered by several factors. In the first place, the American West seemed a more attractive option to most potential new arrivals, with a longer growing season and better transportation networks. Between 1871 and 1891, more people from Canada had departed to the United States than had come

In western Canada, farmers' instincts were to increase acreage as much as possible, creating large, profitable farms. Here, farmers are seen breaking land in Pincher Creek, Alberta. Glenbow Archives, NA-2382-9.

to Canada from abroad. In the second place, Canadian immigration authorities had concentrated on recruiting British farmers, with only limited success. People with agricultural backgrounds in Britain were, on the whole, doing well and not anxious to move. Finally, the large private land companies that had received large land grants were not anxious to select their lands and release them onto the market, speculating that land would increase in value after the country was better settled. Beginning in the 1890s an open and aggressive Canadian immigration policy, conducted by both the federal and provincial governments, brought new settlers to the prairies. In 1896 a new Minister of the Interior (with responsibility for immigration) took office. Clifford Sifton (1861–1929) was an Ontario-born Manitoban who believed in massive agricultural immigration as the key to Canadian prosperity. The trick, he held, was to find suitable immigrants and to get them onto the land. Sifton decided to take his immigrant farmers from wherever in the world he could find them, rather than concentrating on people from the United Kingdom. He was prepared to recruit in Eastern Europe, especially on the steppes of Russia where grain cultivation was well established. Sifton saw a quality immigrant as a 'stalwart peasant in a sheep-skin coat born on the soil, whose fore-fathers have been farmers for ten generations, with a stout wife and a half-dozen children' (quoted in Petryshyn, 1985: 21). He was also prepared to recruit in the United States, which no longer had an unsettled frontier of its own, despite a previous Canadian reluctance to encourage American settlement. Changing conditions in both Eastern Europe and the United States worked to Canada's advantage.

THE UKRAINIANS

The Ukraine was a vast territory on the central and southern plains of Eastern Europe, and during the later nineteenth century 85 per cent of this territory was part of the Russian Empire, while 15 per cent belonged to the Austrian Empire. The first settlers from the Ukraine to Canada had come in the early 1890s, joining Mennonites and Hungarians as early arrivals from these European empires. In 1895, Dr Joseph Oleskiw, a Ukrainian academic who taught agriculture, visited Canada and proposed an extensive Ukrainian immigration to the Canadian West, which Clifford Sifton did his best to implement. Between 1896 and 1914, about 170,000 Ukrainians—chiefly from the overpopulated Austrian provinces of Galicia and Bukovyna—entered Canada, mainly settling on the prairies. In their homeland, these people had been experiencing increasing subdivision of their land and declining productivity because of lack of capital resulting from heavy taxation. By 1900, half of the landholdings in the provinces of Galicia and Bukovyna were less than two hectares in extent, and many small landholders were heavily in debt. The Ukrainians would probably have preferred to go to the United States, but they faced increasing immigration restrictions and an often hostile reception from the Americans, who no longer had any unsettled agricultural land to distribute to newcomers. Many of the immigrants came to Canada because of a secret agreement between the Canadian government and the North Atlantic Trading Company, which directed immigrants to Canada in return for under-the-table payments on a per capita basis. Indeed, steamship and railway companies were probably more successful recruiters of immigration outside the British Isles than was the Canadian government.

Canada may have been a second choice, but at least it encouraged Ukrainians to settle and it could make land available to them. Most Ukrainian immigrants were poor but not destitute. Like generations of immigrants before them, they had sold their land and possessions to purchase their passage. Like all immigrants of the time, they found the transatlantic passage in steerage to be a difficult experience. As their own historians have emphasized, the situation the Ukrainians entered in Canada was little different from that at home: bare survival on the land and an early death for those who failed. But they were stubborn—and hopeful. Many new arrivals found the quarter-section homestead concept—160 acres or one-fourth of a square mile township, the standard survey unit in the West—to be beyond their comprehension, partly because of its size and partly because of the difficulty of reproducing compact village communities like the ones they had left.

The first Ukrainians typically emigrated without many of their natural leaders, especially parish clergymen. They were particularly assisted by three members of the Ukrainian intelligentsia—Joseph Oleskiw, Kyrole Genik, and the Reverend Nestor Dmytriw—employed by the Canadian government as 'overseers' and advisers. These three men produced a substantial body of writing to assist the new arrivals. They emphasized the need for capital to establish a farm, the adoption of Canadian styles of dress, and the acquisition of free land. Canadian society received the Ukrainians with considerable suspicion, chiefly because they were obviously non-British 'foreigners' who spoke an alien language and practised different customs. Those who settled in the cities (especially Winnipeg's North End) in ethnic slum communities were most visible. But the willingness of the new arrivals to work hard was in their favour, at least before the onset of the Great War. After 1914, Austria-Hungary joined Germany as the enemy, and many Ukrainians in Canada became 'enemy aliens'.

Usually considered separately from the Ukrainians, although originating from the same region, the Doukhobors were a sectarian movement that broke away from the Russian Orthodox Church in the eighteenth century. The Doukhobors (the term literally means 'spirit wrestlers') became a Quaker-like pacifistic group that emphasized the brotherhood and sisterhood of all men and women and the validation of their beliefs not in books but in the 'book of life'. With the aid of Russian novelist Leo Tolstoy, the Doukhobors came to western Canada in search of refuge from Russian persecution. The first contingent was granted recognition as conscientious objectors by the Canadian government on 6 December 1898. Over the next few years, more than 7,500 Doukhobors arrived in Canada to settle on tracts reserved for them in what would become Saskatchewan and Alberta. They were joined by their leader, Peter Verigin (1859–1924), in 1903. In 1907 the Canadian government backed away from an earlier commitment to allow the Doukhobors to live and work communally, insisting instead on individual homesteading and an oath of allegiance. As a result, under the leadership of Verigin, communal-living Doukhobors bought land in the interior of British Columbia and moved into the Kootenay region, where they would subsequently struggle with the authorities over their beliefs.

THE AMERICANS

Although the Canadian press would occasionally complain about the 'Americanization' of the West and other places, most Americans had always been regarded as desirable settlers who 'understood the ways of the continent and its institutions' (Troper, 1972: 12). Many Americans, of course, had started their lives in British America before moving to the United States earlier in the century. Some exceptions to the favourable attitude towards Americans prevailed, however. Many Canadians objected to the pluralistic marriage practices of the Mormons, who were one of the earliest groups of immigrants into Alberta in the 1880s, and few Canadians showed any enthusiasm for the admission into their country of American blacks from Oklahoma and elsewhere. In addition to the Mormons, American cattle and sheep ranchers arrived before the 1890s, but after the well-publicized 'closing of the frontier' in the United States during that decade, the Canadian government made a real effort after 1896 to recruit American farmers of European origins for what would become known as 'The Last Best West'.

Canadian agents openly sought wealthy immigrants. One common form of recruitment was through personal correspondence from successful settlers to prospective ones, organized by the Department of Immigration. Much of the settlement in Saskatchewan and Alberta occurred in the so-called Palliser's Triangle, a dry-belt region with marginal rainfall. American farmers were alleged to be the best settlers of such land, as they were familiar with the techniques of dry farming. In a series of land rushes, thousands of American farmers settled the dry belt in the years between 1906 and 1914. They prospered because there was adequate rainfall during this period, but later abandoned the region when drought conditions returned.

By 1921 over 44 million acres (17,806,800 ha) of the prairies were under cultivation. According to one set of calculations, the wheat economy in 1901–11 contributed over 20 per cent of the growth in per capita income in Canada. While wheat was the big prairie crop, other crops were possible. Before the arrival of farmers, much of southern Alberta and southwestern Saskatchewan was the domain of ranchers, who grazed their cattle on open range leased from the federal government. At the height of the cattle boom in 1898, Canadian ranchers exported 213,000 live head. Most cattlemen were American, but a substantial minority were British, and polo-playing was common in early Alberta. Although ranchers insisted that much of the range land was unsuitable for farming because of water shortages, their obvious self-interest in an open range negated the force of much of their argument. Nevertheless, water remained a major potential problem in much of the West.

Mines and Timber

In 1890 Nova Scotia was the leading mining province in Canada, chiefly because of its rich coal resources. After that year, three factors hastened a great shift in Canadian mineral extraction. One was the development of new technologies to extract ore. Another was the increasing availability of railway transportation to remote areas. Most important of all, the international market created a new demand for metals that Canada had in abundance: copper, nickel, and silver. Almost overnight, Ontario and British Columbia became the leading mineral producers.

Although the most famous mining rush of the period was to the Yukon's Klondike district for gold, the Klondike was hardly typical of the mining industry. More representative were the mining towns that suddenly sprang up and equally rapidly closed down in the mountains of British Columbia and Alberta. Like most Canadian mines, these required considerable machinery and expertise to exploit, well beyond the resources of the individual miner. Well-capitalized corporations opened such mines, employing money and technology often imported from the United States. In Quebec, the most buoyant segment of the mineral industry between 1900 and 1920 was asbestos fibre, used chiefly in construction material consumed in the United States. The Canadian mining industry greatly benefited from the military requirements of the Great War.

A Ukrainian family harvesting wheat, 1918. LAC, PA-88504.

In the forest industry, the decline through permanent depletion of the white pine forests of eastern Canada pushed the centre of activity to the West. British Columbia had millions of acres of Douglas fir and cedar. The province started harvesting in the coastal regions close to water, but soon pushed inland. Most of its production went to American markets. The remaining forests of eastern Canada proved valuable for their softwood. The pulp and paper industry expanded rapidly, driven by an insatiable American demand for inexpensive newsprint. By 1915 wood pulp and paper represented one-third of the value of Canadian exports, virtually equal to wheat and grain in the overseas market. Quebec produced nearly one-half of Canada's wood pulp and paper.

The resource sector produced its own version of labour militancy. The sector was difficult to organize by traditional means. In mines and lumber camps, the distinction between skilled and unskilled labour had little meaning. Nevertheless, worker alienation was often extreme. In British Columbia, unrest was particularly strong among miners, who worked for large absentee corporations under difficult conditions. In this kind of environment, syndicalists and radicals (such as the Wobblies or the Impossibilists) did very well. They preached the need for the organization of all workers into general unions and the destruction of capitalism by revolution.

Urban and Rural Canada

In 1881 Canada had a population of 4,325,000, of whom 3,349,000 lived outside urban centres. Forty years later, of the nation's 8,788,000 inhabitants, only 4,811,000 resided in non-urban areas, and 1,659,000 lived in cities with populations over 100,000. While the non-urban population had grown over these years from 3,349,000 to 4,811,000, the number of city dwellers had burgeoned from 974,000 to 3,977,000. Urban growth was obviously a major trend of the period 1880–1918. Canada developed some very large metropolitan centres, but their residents did not constitute the entire urban population. If 1,659,000 Canadians lived in cities of over 100,000 in 1921, another 2.2 million lived in smaller centres, with 1,058,000 in towns of 5,000 to 29,999 people and 765,000 in towns of 1,000 to 4,999. Canadian urban growth in this era produced all sorts of new problems for the nation. At the same time, urban development was not the entire story for these years. As the statistics well demonstrate, before 1921 more Canadians continued to reside in rural than in urban areas. Rural Canada, although its earlier dominance was gradually eroding away, was still very important to the national ethos. Moreover, the very sense of the gradual loss of traditional rural values was critical for the Canadian psyche.

The City

As with most other aspects of Canadian development in this period, urban growth was uneven across the regions. Maritime cities grew fairly sluggishly. None could establish regional dominance. Indeed, Halifax lost ground as central Canada siphoned off its financial institutions. In Quebec, Montreal continued its path to the status of the Dominion's premier city, with Quebec City and other towns lagging far behind. In Ontario, Toronto was plainly the 'Queen City', although a number of smaller cities (Hamilton, London, and Kingston) were vibrant. Ottawa inhabited a world of its own as the nation's capital, as it always would. The most spectacular urban growth rates were in the West, which in this era spawned two major cities, Winnipeg and Vancouver, and two contenders for such a rank, Edmonton and Calgary. While western settlement usually suggests farms and agriculture, urban development in the West was strong from the outset. Land speculation drove local pretensions, and many communities aspired to be regional entrepôts. In the Prairie provinces the urban population grew from 103,000 to 606,000 between 1900 and 1916. City dwellers, who represented 25 per cent of the region's population in 1901, had increased to 35 per cent only 10 years later. By 1921 in British Columbia, Vancouver (117,217) and Victoria (38,727) contained 25 per cent of the population of that Pacific province.

The larger cities of Canada most clearly exposed the social problems of the later Victorian and subsequent Edwardian eras. The greatest problem was

Child Labour in Victorian Canada

The 1889 Royal Commission on the Relations of Labor and Capital documented through first-person testimony that a substantial number of children of both sexes between the ages of 10 and 14 were employed full-time (10 hours a day, six days a week) in the factories of Ontario and Quebec. They were paid between $1.00 and $2.00 per week, depending on their age and production during a time when the typical workingman earned $7.00 per week and females somewhat less. These children were subjected to heavy discipline, including corporal punishment. They were frequently fined when they fell behind quotas, and one factory even had a 'black hole' in which a child could be confined for hours or even days. Laws against the use of child labour, especially children under the age of 14, existed but were not enforced any more than were the laws calling for compulsory school attendance. Parents supported the employment of their children, even insisted upon it, as part of a 'family economy' that helped sustain many in the working classes of the nation. The absence of any clear concept of childhood beyond the early years helped contribute to the presence of children in factories and elsewhere in the Canadian industrial workforce, but such a pattern was only the tip of the iceberg when it came to the employment of children in Victorian Canada. Most of Canada remained agricultural, and in this sector of the economy the dominant economic institution was the family farm, which operated on the assumption that every family member beyond the earliest years worked to contribute to its survival and prosperity. Unlike the child factory workers, many of whom probably turned their earnings over to their families, the children working on the farm received no wages. Also unlike those employed in factories, of course, some of those children who worked on the family farm had a prospect of an inheritance at the end of the day, although usually only the older males and almost never the females benefited in this way. According to one recent study of prairie child labour in the Victorian period, the Canadian West could not have been successfully settled without the heavy use of child labour. 'Children contributed to production, took part in paid employment or other money-raising activities, worked at domestic and subsistence tasks, and thereby increased the supply of cash, food, and other necessary commodities to the family' (Rollings-Magnusson, 2009: 133–4). Indeed, settlement in Canada in any period was based on the exploitation of the unpaid labour of the family, including both women and children.

Although there were laws in place to protect child labourers, such as the children seen here separating the ore from the rock in a Quebec copper mine, these laws were not enforced. © McCord Museum, N-0000.94.58.

poverty. Existing evidence suggests that up to half of the Canadian urban working class lived below, or at best around, the poverty line. Most working-class families were glad to supplement the father's income with the earnings of wife and children in menial occupations. Given the grinding conditions of their lives, it is not surprising that many sought refuge in alcohol. Unbalanced diets and malnutrition were only the start of the problems of the poor. Their housing was typically overcrowded, with poor sanitation and a lack of open yards and spaces.

Home ownership was difficult, even for the middle classes, because mortgages were hard to obtain and were only of short duration, often no more than three or four years. Malnutrition and deplorable housing conditions combined to produce high overall death rates and high infant mortality rates in Canada's largest cities. The mortality differentials between the poor and the prosperous were substantial, ranging from 35.51 deaths per 1,000 in 1895 in one working-class ward in Montreal to less than 13 per 1,000 'above the hill'. Infant mortality rates in Canadian cities were little different from those in places like Calcutta and Bombay. The children of the urban poor often got little schooling. Moreover, the poor resisted pressures for compulsory education.

If the city had social problems, it also made possible a rich and varied cultural life. Before 1918 cultural life maintained an amateur tradition of considerable vitality. The major development in Canadian urban culture in this era was not so much the appearance of first-rate artists as the creation of an institutional infrastructure that might eventually enable them to emerge. The city made possible the development of cultural institutions in the form of both organizations and buildings to house them. The construction of museums, for example, was characteristic of the age. The Art Museum of Toronto appeared in 1900, the Royal Ontario Museum in 1912 (it opened in 1914). Equally characteristic of the era was the formation of artistic organizations. The Canadian Art Club (1907) was organized in Toronto, although its founders had no idea how to achieve their goal of introducing new Canadian painting to the entire nation. Formal art and music schools were organized in most of the larger urban centres, offering regularized instruction to neophyte painters and musicians. Theatrical buildings became a measure of a city's status. As early as 1891 Vancouver had a 1,200-seat opera house. Toronto's

The 'foreign' quarter of Winnipeg, c. 1909. Archives of Manitoba, Immigration 17 (N7936).

Royal Alexandra Theatre (1906–7) seated 1,525, and Winnipeg's Walker Theatre (1907, recently renovated as a theatrical venue) seated 2,000 in splendid comfort. These buildings operated continuously, housing mainly professional touring companies and local amateurs. Indigenous professional theatre emerged first in Montreal. There were 10 different professional companies at work in Montreal in the 1890s. In 1899 alone these companies gave 618 performances of 109 plays.

The extent of the growth of urban Canada between 1880 and 1919 was largely unanticipated. The large city cut against most of the dominant ideologies of the time, which were traditional and rural. The institutions of urban government were not well integrated into the overall Canadian political system. The British North America Act did not leave much room for the governance of cities that would have budgets and revenues as large as those of the provinces in which they were located. Urban government and urban politics operated outside the structures of Confederation, with their own agendas and distinct party labels. Most cities were slow to abandon property qualifications for voting. Local merchants and real estate promoters tended to dominate city councils, even in cities with a relatively democratic franchise. The ward system produced municipal politicians who curried favour with the electorate through corrupt practices ranging from the purchasing of votes to offers of 'jobs for the boys'.

No urban centre could expect to prosper in this era if it was not on a main-line railway. Contemporaries clearly recognized this reality. During the several outbursts of railway expansion—particularly between 1906 and 1915, when more than 14,000 new miles (22,530 km) of railway track

Interior of slum home, Winnipeg, c. 1915. Archives of Manitoba, Foote 1491 (N2438).

were laid in Canada—efforts by aspiring communities to become depots and junction points were prodigious. Conversely, rumours of new railway construction were sufficient to create a village where none had existed previously. The extremes to which communities would go to publicize themselves in order to attract railways were occasionally ludicrous and often expensive. Agricultural fairs, as well as the presence of town bands and sports teams, publicized communities. A marching brass band and a baseball team were two of the best advertisements an 'up-and-at-'em' town could enjoy. 'Bonusing'—financial inducements for railways and business entrepreneurs alike—was a way of life in this period.

If urban growth relied on railway networks, it operated in a context of fairly blatant and open land speculation. The attempted creation of every new city in western Canada began with a land boom. This stage of development usually ended with a collapse in land prices that required years of recovery. Many small businessmen in the West made a decent living selling out in one community just ahead of the bust and moving to a new townsite further down the rail line. The false fronts on western small-town stores were symbolic of the transitory nature of commitment. Speculation in land involved not merely businessmen—or the West. Almost all segments of local communities across Canada joined in real estate speculation whenever they could. Indeed, the attempt to turn a profit by investing in undeveloped land must surely be one of the most enduring features of Canadian life. Speculation was different from development. The former involved the holding of land for future profit, the latter the translation of land—often acquired at bargain prices—into immediate profit as sites for houses or factories.

Town and Suburb

In the larger urban centres land speculation and development were inseparable from the process of suburbanization. This trend combined with urban expansion away from the commercial core of most cities. There were three distinct motives for suburban expansion. Different types of suburbs were the result. The first motive dominated among the prospering business and professional classes, who moved to new residential suburbs to escape the noise, odours, and bustle of the central city. Horse droppings on busy city streets, for example, were a major problem before the Great War. Some of these suburbanites were attempting to separate themselves from the growing slums of the industrializing city. The architectural style most closely associated with the new suburban elites grew out of the English Arts and Crafts movement and became known as the English Domestic Revival. A second motive for suburban growth was the quest for lower land costs and lower taxes outside the central city. The result was the development of a number of industrial suburbs, such as Maisonneuve in Montreal, which flourished outside the city but were still within its orbit. The third motive was proximity to work. As industrial development moved into the cheaper outskirts, workers were forced to follow their jobs into often inadequate new housing. During this period, most large cities in Canada grew by a continuous process of absorbing outlying communities.

The genuine Canadian small town tended to fit one of two models. It was either a community serving a surrounding rural area, sometimes with a manufacturing plant or two, or a single-resource community, often remotely located, that had formed around a mine or mining/smelter operation. The resource town consisted almost exclusively of single males, with only a handful of women. There were precious few sources of entertainment other than booze and gambling. Many resource towns, though not all, were company towns. Such communities were both violent and restive, often centres of labour unrest.

The service community, on the other hand, was the centre of economic, social, and recreational life for its district. Before the advent of radio and television, the social life of small-town Canada bustled impressively. Organizations of all kinds proliferated and flourished. Most towns had a variety of lodges and an endless round of meetings, dances, and 'occasions'. These occasions included concerts, plays, sermons by visiting evangelical preachers, and lectures on temperance or exotic places. By the end of the Great War, most towns had a 'movie house' or a hall that exhibited motion pictures on a regular

Herbert Brown Ames on Poverty in Montreal

In 1897 the Montreal businessman Herbert Brown Ames published a series of articles in the *Montreal Star* that subsequently appeared as a book. The articles were based on his careful survey of social conditions in part of the west side of Montreal. The district he had selected probably offered a fair sample of working-class residences in Montreal at the end of the nineteenth century.

It will be remembered that, according to our industrious census, the total number of poor families was reckoned at 888 in 'the city below the hill'. Half of this number were by the writer selected as material for a second and more searching investigation, with a view of more fully examining the characteristics, conditions and causes of our west-end poverty. Four hundred and thirty-six families were sought for, and the first fact that was brought to the notice of the investigator was that 46 families, or 10 1/2 per cent of the above number, had left their former abodes, within the two months between the first and second canvass, drawing attention to one of the sad features of poverty's lot, viz., the constant necessity to move on because of inability to satisfy the claims of the landlord. If this ratio were maintained, and each month saw 5 per cent of the poor evicted, in a year not half these families could be found at the former addresses.

A second fact, made apparent by the special investigation, was that our west-end poverty was not the result of recent immigration. Quite the reverse from what would have been the case in New York or Chicago, hardly a dozen families were discovered that had not been residents of the city for at least three years. The vast majority were old residents who had lived in Montreal for the greater part of their lives. The presence of poverty, then, in the nether city is not chargeable to any considerable influx of foreign elements.

In the case of 323 families inquiries were made as to the causes, assigned by the people themselves, for their indigent condition. With 109 families, or 34 per cent the reply was 'irregularity of work'. The wage-earners were not without vocations but their employment was intermittent and often work ceased altogether for considerable periods. With 87 families or 28 per cent the answer was that the wage-earners had no work whatever, nor did there seem to be any immediate prospect of getting any. With 27 families, or 9 per cent, old age had unfitted and with a like number sickness had prevented the worker from earning the requisite support. Out of these 323 families, among the poorest of the poor, 62 per cent claimed to be able to better their condition were employment regular and abundant. That a certain percentage of the answers given did not state the real facts of the case is quite probable. Few are the families that will admit to a stranger that drink, crime or voluntary idleness is the cause of their misery, though in 7 per cent of the cases visited drunkenness was clearly at the bottom of the trouble. Still it is the belief of the investigator that the undeserving among the poor form a far smaller proportion than is generally imagined.

As to the composition of the family, out of 390 families, 86 were found wherein the head of the household was a widow, and 54 cases where the husband was too old or too ill to work, making in all 140 families, or 36 per cent of the whole, that might be called 'decapitated' family groups. In about two-thirds of the families, or in 64 per cent of the cases examined, there was an able-bodied man in the house, oftimes more than one, a man able to work and professing to be willing to do so. If these proportions may be taken as fairly indicating the average among the families of the poor, it is evident that at least one-third of them are in indigent circumstances through no fault of their own. . . .

Source: Ames, H.: *The City Below the Hill*, pp 74-76, © University of Toronto Press, 1972.

basis. Many small towns had exercised the local option permitted by liquor legislation and 'gone dry'. Small-town social relations were often strained, particularly between the middle classes and those who worked in the factories that many eastern small towns possessed. In the West, class conflict often pitted farmers against hired hands or the crews of threshing contractors. The possibility of outbreaks of violence was never far away.

Even more serious were the gender constraints inherent in the structure of small towns. Masculinity dominated the life of the town, in terms both of family relationships and especially of extracurricular activity. Local sports were controlled by notions of manliness, and most athletic organizations catered only to men. Local fraternal organizations were equally masculine and exclusionist, although occasionally they had women's auxiliaries. One of the most important underlying tensions in many (although not all) small towns was between church-related and other voluntary organizations. The church organizations were dominated by women and often sought reform, including prohibition of alcohol and elimination of gambling. The masculine-dominated voluntary structure was often, by implication, the chief target of these reformers. The attentive and careful reader can find all these tensions exhibited in the novels of small-town life that dominated Canadian literature in these years.

Rural Canada

A number of major changes occurred in Canadian agriculture during the period from 1880 to 1914. The most obvious was the enormous expansion of farming in the prairie West, concentrating single-mindedly on grain cultivation. Elsewhere, the era saw a major shift in eastern Canada towards specialized farming. In central Canada, farmers moved into specialized high-quality consumer production, becoming increasingly dependent on off-farm processing, particularly of cheese, butter, and meat. By 1900 Ontario had over 1,200 cheese factories, which captured over half of the British market. Ontario cheese makers were renowned around the world. Quebec farmers had greater difficulty in making the

change because of the marginality of much of their land. Specialty farming was very remunerative for those able to engage in it. The aristocrats of farming were the dairy farmers and the fruit farmers. Along with specialized farming came new technology, although the ubiquitous tractor did not replace the horse until after the Great War. More important were mechanical harvesters, centrifugal cream separators, and the introduction of refrigeration. Technology was essential to specialization. It was also capital-intensive. Not all farmers could make the shift. Those who could not often stagnated or failed absolutely. Between 1891 and 1921 the Maritime region lost 22,000 farms and 1,556,709 acres (630,000 ha) of farmland under cultivation. Unmodernized farms could not continue to support the entire family. By 1911 the *Farmer's Advocate* could refer to the 'perennial debates as to "Why the Boys Leave the Farm"'. While urban migration was one response, another was that farmers—and farm women—moved into the traditional resource industries of the nation. Males went to sea to fish or into the woods to cut timber. Females worked seasonally in factories, processing farm products or fish.

Although most athletic organizations catered only to men, by the turn of the twentieth century, hockey was being regularly played by women as well as men. Here is the Rossland Ladies' Hockey Team, c. 1900. Rossland Museum Archives, RHMA02-18-997.

The Town Directory of Treherne, Manitoba, 1895

In 1907 Alan Ross, a local poet in Treherne, Manitoba, published a small volume of his verse. It included the following poem, the subject of which is self-explanatory.

Town Directory 1895

E. Hamilton's our high school master;
D. Hamilton puts on the plaster;
Revds. McClung, Fraser and George Fill
On Sundays do our pulpits fill;
T.J. Lamont's our town M.D.;
One blacksmith's name is Thos. Lee;
Rogers sells dry goods and coffees;
Alexander keeps post office;
D. Williams and J.K. McLennan
Sell dry goods, cod, haddock finnan,
Ben Englewain repairs the clocks;
Our miller's name is Jas A. Cox;
James Telford Reid's our legal light
One retired farmer's called John White;
'Tis G.A. Anderson that carried
The business on for Massey-Harris;
And S.L. Taylor sells the pills,
That sometimes cure and sometimes kill;
C.W. Barkwell is town baker;
Ed Roberts is the undertaker;
Tom Roberts helps his brother Ed
Sell furniture and house the dead;

Joe Straube is town hardware man;
In athletics Paulin leads the van;
One livery's kept by the Parker Brothers;
And John Perrie keeps the other;
Jas. Stevenson keeps the 'Manitoba',
With parlor, dining-room, and lobby;
Fred Rocket keeps the 'Rocket House';
Our tailor's name is Harry House;
D. Harvie harness makes and collars
Watt Smith irons wagons, sleighs and rollers
And general blacksmith shop controls;
His carriage maker's William Bowles;
Andrew Ross supplies the butcher meat;
Malcolm McClarty shoes the feet;
H. Watson, Senior health inspector;
James McAdam's tax collector;
Claude Somerville's mill engineer;
John Coulter is mill charioteer;
James Emmond sues for delinquent debts,
And William Frame does serve the writs;
Robson deals in lumber, lime, and bricks . . . .

Source: Alan Ross, *Poems* (Treherne, Man.: The Treherne Times, 1907), 18.

Contemporaries often blamed the growing rural exodus on the social and cultural attractions of the city. While it might thus be tempting to visualize rural Canada as a vast wasteland of isolated and unlettered country bumpkins, such a view would be most inaccurate. Isolation did exist, as did educational limitations. On the other hand, a relatively efficient and inexpensive postal service provided contact with the wider world. People read books and discussed them at clubs that met in local churches. Clergymen often talked about controversial books and topics from their pulpits. Many farm families received at least one daily newspaper through the mail—seldom on the day of publication, but usually only a day or two later. Canadian dailies in this era provided more substantial fare than today. International coverage was much fuller, and many papers saw themselves as 'papers of record', often reproducing verbatim accounts of court trials and important meetings. In the spring of 1919, for example, the *Winnipeg Tribune* carried a full stenographer's report of the debates at the labour convention in Calgary, which agreed to 'an Industrial Organization of all workers'. Most rural folk also relied heavily for their edification on farm journals such as the *Grain Growers' Guide* (1908–28) and more general magazines like the *Christian Guardian*, the voice of the Methodist Church; it was begun in 1829 by Egerton Ryerson and continued under that name until 1925. The wide range of letters to the editor included in most of these periodicals suggests both their circulation and their vitality.

If rural Canadians had access to considerable information, they were also surprisingly able to get together socially with each other. The school and the church were two local institutions that served other functions besides providing formal education and worship services. School districts were usually the only sign of public organization in vast regions of rural Canada that were otherwise politically unorganized. The community jealously guarded its schoolhouse, which, from coast to coast, was typically of one room. The most common Quebec school in the 1913 census had one room, built at a cost of $1,200. Whether Protestant or Catholic, francophone or anglophone, rural Canadians took their religion seriously. Sermons provided topics for daily conversation. The activities of various auxiliary groups connected with any church, particularly the picnics and socials, were very popular. Winter did not shut down social life in rural areas, but permitted it to flower. The demands of the farm were much lighter in winter, while snow and ice provided a decent surface for horse-drawn sleighs and carrioles to travel about the countryside. 'A working day . . . was from about 4:30 a.m. to 11 o'clock at night,' reported one western farmer, 'but this was only in seeding and harvesting time. In the winter we used to really have fun' (quoted in Voisey, 1988: 158).

A number of diaries and journals kept by rural Canadians in this period have recently appeared in print. They provide two revelations for the modern reader. The first is the sheer volume of social interchange, especially among the young, that

actually occurred. The second is the extent to which Canadians of this era actively participated in their own entertainment rather than being amused as passive spectators by the activities of others. Canadians of both sexes and all ages routinely spent social evenings singing hymns and other songs. They created and performed their own skits and joined together in active games such as charades.

Rural life was not all bucolic pleasure, of course. The real reason for the rural exodus was not isolation but exploitation and lack of economic opportunity. The underside of life on the family farm was the exploitation and abuse of those who would not in the end inherit a substantial share in the property. The system was particularly hard on women, who usually did not share in the ownership of the farm and who seldom received remuneration for their labour. Western farmers especially were hostile to 'anachronistic' legal concepts such as dower rights. The homesteading system was generally unsympathetic to the rights of women to set up as independent farmers. For many women everywhere in Canada, the daily routine was even more continually demanding than it was for men. Women's responsibilities included not only the kitchen garden and the small livestock but care of the family itself. One consequence of the shift into specialized farming was that parts of the farm operation previously consigned to women that provided them with a small income ('egg money') were taken over by the males. Canadian rural society continued to be inherently patriarchal in its organization. Men owned the land and usually made the decisions, including when to uproot and resettle, often against the wishes of their wives. The figure of the rural patriarch as an intensely self-righteous, land-hungry, materialistic tyrant became a common motif in Canadian fiction of this and a slightly later period.

Despite the darker side, a vast majority of Canadians continued to hold rural values and to think of the nation largely in pastoral terms. Those who read Canadian poetry or looked at Canadian art found little but Canadian nature. Foreigners inevitably saw Canada as a completely undeveloped country and Canadians as an agricultural people. In the hands of the poets, Canadian nature was chiefly

Canada in 1898 and 1905.

'A Basket Social in P.E. Island'

'Preserve me from "pie socials"', wrote Lucy Maud Montgomery in her journal on 4 April 1899. 'They are the abomination of desolation.' The following more positive view was expressed by 'Welland Strong' (presumably a nom de plume) in a 1901 issue of the *Prince Edward Island Magazine*. Whoever the author may have been, he or she was quite right in thinking that the social was not distinctive to the Island, but appeared everywhere in rural Canada.

A Basket Social in P.E. Island
by Welland Strong

Basket socials may not be a form of amusement peculiar to Prince Edward Island, but in all events, I have never seen a place where they attained to such prominence, among the various schemes for getting money, as in this province. . . .

Often it happens that in country villages a debt is to be paid by a congregation, either a balance due on their church or perhaps for a new organ. Instead of raising the necessary amount by private subscription, the people decide upon a basket social, and word is sent to everyone. Upon hearing this the young ladies all begin to prepare baskets containing ample lunch for two people. These they carry, carefully wrapped in many sheets of paper, to the hall on the night of the social, and hand over to the committee in charge. The baskets are sold by auction, and the purchaser of each must share its contents with the young lady who brought it. Of course every young man is anxious to get the basket prepared by his 'best girl': but as the names are not announced until after the baskets are sold, many mistakes are made, and the remarks sometimes uttered, by fond lovers who have paid a high price for the wrong one, look much better in print when expressed by a dash.

Let us try to imagine ourselves in a hall in almost any country settlement on the evening devoted to one of these popular meetings. . . . The committee, composed of elders of the church, were kept busy finding seats for the ladies; taking care of the baskets handed to them, and doing the many little things necessary at all such entertainments. Now, however, we see them placing a row of chairs on the platform, and pushing the organ into a more convenient position. Hardly had this been done when there enter from a side door a number of ladies and gentlemen, who proceed to occupy the chairs. This is the village choir, and during the past week they have been practicing pieces to be sung to-night. . . .

Cheers, whistles and stamping of feet greeted the choir, who arose and, to the accompaniment of a hard-breathing organ, sang 'Jingle Bells'. The first verse was sung amid perfect silence, but in the second the crowd caught the rhythm of the piece and kept time to it with their feet, especially in the chorus, when a string of sleigh bells was used to make the effect more realistic. A recitation, 'Curfew shall not ring to-night,' given by a young lady, followed the chorus, but as most of the audience knew the piece by heart, very little attention was paid, and the greater portion of the piece remained almost unheard. But amid the din the speaker's voice could be heard every now and then, and bravely she struggled through until, with the saving of the lover, the piece ended and the 'Amen corner' burst into thunderous applause. Then came a fine-looking soloist— tenor in the choir and local auctioneer. He began 'Ten thousand leaves are falling,' but having pitched the song in too high a key, his voice broke and he stopped, his failure being greeted by frantic howls and advice from one of the small boys to 'start her at five thousand.' The programme went on; chorus following reading, and solo, chorus, the last few numbers being rendered 'midst an almost deafening noise and shouts of 'Bring on the baskets.'

When it ended the choir moved to one side of the platform, the schoolmaster who was to act as secretary and treasurer took his place at the table, and the auctioneer stepped forward holding in his hand the first basket, now unwrapped and decorated in a most fantastic manner with flags, flowers and coloured tissue paper. . . . After all the baskets have been sold, the names of the purchasers and ladies are read off by the secretary, and the baskets opened by them. Usually besides various kinds of cake and pie, the basket contains glasses and a bottle of home-made wine; but in case this has been left out, and also for the benefit of the older people, the committee furnish plenty of tea. When

the lunch has been disposed of, the men go to the nearest stables for their horses, which have been left there, while the young ladies gather their belongings, get muffled up ready for the drive home and, while waiting for their friends, sing a verse of 'God save the King.'

Sleigh after sleigh drives up to the door, the women and girls depart, and in a very few minutes no one remains in the hall save the members of the committee—counting over the money they have made and writing a report of the social to be published in the papers next day.

Source: *The Island Magazine* 46 (Fall/Winter 1999): 7–12. Reprinted with permission.

benign. Writers of prose sometimes depicted nature differently, often in terms of the victory of hardy settlers over the harsh landscape and climate. Many Canadian writers and painters of this period romanticized the farm and farming, none more so than Lucy Maud Montgomery. *Anne of Green Gables* summed up a major conflict of the era: the problem of reconciling the bucolic beauty and tranquility of the rural landscape with the need to leave it in order to fulfill one's ambitions. For large numbers of Canadians of this era, growing up meant leaving the farm.

Another form of romanticization of rural life was the collection of its folklore and folksongs. Marius Barbeau (1883–1969) was the first great Canadian collector of folk traditions, beginning in 1911 when he was appointed an anthropologist at the Museum Branch of the Geological Survey of Canada (now the National Museum of Canada). Barbeau recorded and preserved in archives thousands of songs and narratives that document not only the folk traditions of rural Quebec but also those of the Aboriginal peoples in British Columbia. The folkways and songs that Barbeau and others collected were part of the traditional rural experience of Canada. They preserved almost nothing of urban origin. The collectors desperately gathered up dialects, riddles, tall tales, and children's rhymes, all of which told more of the daily life of the people than most other historical evidence. Underlying the desperation was

the fear that these traditions would disappear in the rapidly changing society of the period.

The dominance in Canada of the myth of agriculture carried over into the various efforts of the period to turn Aboriginal peoples into 'peaceable agricultural labourers'. Agrarian ideology had the advantage of both justifying the dispossession of the Native peoples of their hunting grounds and providing them with an alternate way of life. Before the Great War most Canadians regarded agriculture as 'the mainspring of national greatness' and farming as a way of life that uplifted one 'morally and emotionally' (Carter, 1990: 20). Scientists saw agriculture as a crucial step in the ladder of progress. They perceived other ways of using the land, such as mining or lumbering, as tainted and inferior. The government displaced Aboriginals by treaties, then removed them to reserves and encouraged them to farm. Exhortation was not the same as useful practical assistance. Native Canadians needed a good deal of help to shift from a nomadic hunting/gathering existence to a settled agricultural one, and they did not consistently receive assistance. Government aid was sporadic, cheese-paring, and patronizing. After 1885 coercion replaced subsidization as the federal government's major weapon to impose agriculturalism on the reserves. Not surprisingly, the policy failed.

A final illustration of nature's appeal for Canadians came in the various back-to-nature

Sadie Allen's Diary, Summer 1892

Wed. June 29 [1892]. Well here it is just a beautiful day, fine and just warm enough to be pleasant. This is the third day of our holidays and I can't say I have enjoyed them very much so far. Yesterday it poured rain from dinner time until tea time, but still I was not very lonely because there is such a houseful of us. Besides, Aunt Rose (who came over a week ago tomorrow) came up and stayed all day, and she is just splendid company. In the morning I did my housework up and then trimmed May's sailor hat, and after dinner I got Winnie's ready for trimming and then made lemon filling for my Washington pie which I made yesterday and made frosting for it also. And I practised some and read some of a book called *Little Journey in the World* by the same author of *Baddeck and That Sort of Thing*. Mr. Bailey and Eddie White, Fred Henderson and Leonard Webster came up and spent the evening. We had lots of fun as usual over those Tiddlywinks. We had two tables, and when one side missed they had to go to the other table, and the best players kept their same places. There were Mr. B. and Nell, Win and Fred, Leonard and Bois, and Eddie and I. After playing we had a lot of music. Leonard sang 'They are After Me' and some other songs, and Mr. Bailey gave us a solo, then we had some Charades. We also made up an orchestra just for fun. Mr. B. played on the mouth organ (he plays just beautifully on it), and Leonard had the tambourine, Bois a tin whistle, Eddie another, and May the table bell, and Winnie played one piano and Nell accompanied her on the other, while I had the zither. Oh but we had fun over that.

Monday morning (day before yesterday) was fine but the afternoon was wet. I wrote a long letter to Ted before dinner. She wrote Nell and I while she was on her journey that they had stopped for a while at a little place a hundred miles from Port Arthur. Her mother told me yesterday that they both liked it in Winnipeg very much and Lottie was feeling very well only tired and sleepy. It is just three weeks I think from Monday since they left. For the past month back, part of the Lodge members were getting up a drama for the Lodge called *The Social Glass*. Nettie Evans, Mrs. Lodge, and Floss White and Eddie McDonald, Mr. Russell, Mr. Butler, Mr. Colwell, and Mr. Belyear and Es Hamilton are the ones that took part in it. So they gave it to the public last Monday evening. It was just fine. They had a full house and the band played between every act, some very pretty selections. They all took their parts splendidly. Hardly anybody knew Flo, when the curtain rose, and she was dressed as a bride in a light blue dress and her hair done up and flowers in it and she looked just sweet but so womanly. Es Hamilton was too comical for anything as Bob Brittle. Oh he was grand. Nettie Evans as Nettie Nettlebee could not have been better. It just suited her to a tee. 'She did love to make folks happy.' Will Butler was splendid as Fairly. He acted the delirium tremens fine and all the rest were good too. Though it was ridiculous and comical in lots of places, yet it was sad when you thought it was just real life. This social glass at first and then it gets to more and more until your own life is ruined by it and many many others.

Source: Mary Biggar Peck, ed., *A Full House and Fine Singing: Diaries and Letters of Sadie Harper Allen* (Fredericton: Goose Lane Press, 1992), 66–7.

movements. One form involved mounting crusades to preserve Canada's natural environment in the face of encroaching civilization. The fight for the conservation of Canadian wildlife involved the establishment of game reserves and legislation to curb indiscriminate hunting. The crusade's major victories came with the establishment of large numbers of national and provincial parks across Canada in the years before the Great War. Another expression of the back-to-nature movement was the summer cottage,

Canadians' fascination with the summer cottage had already taken hold before 1914. © McCord Museum, MP-1974.133.18.

which flourished among urbanites who could afford one by the early years of the twentieth century. Many refugees from the farm resolved their ambivalences through the summer cottage or summer travel, often into the wilderness. Thus, alongside the burgeoning Canadian cities came the growth of summer cottages and resort hotels, located at lakeside or seaside, and frequently directly served by rail. Weekend train services poured middle-class Canadians by the thousands into the Laurentians of Quebec, the Muskoka, Algonquin Park, and Haliburton districts of Ontario, and from Winnipeg into the Lake of the Woods district. The Canadian fascination with the summer cottage had taken firm hold before the Great War. During this same period, the establishment of a national park system had begun with the creation of Rocky Mountain Park (later Banff National Park) in 1886, and this and other parks in the Rocky

Mountains (Yoho, Glacier, Jasper, Waterton Lakes) of British Columbia and Alberta were conveniently reached by rail and, in some cases, the railways built expensive, sumptuous hotels to accommodate sojourners from the city.

While some Canadians settled temporarily into cottage or tourist hotel, others became fascinated with the recreational possibilities of wilderness travel. The waterways of Ontario and Quebec grew crowded with weekend canoeists enjoying a brief respite from the pressures of the city. Ernest Thompson Seton (1860–1946), who founded an organization called Woodcraft Indians in 1902, promoted a junior version of this outdoor activity from his apartment in New York City. Some of the best publicists for the canoe and the wilderness were painters, especially those who eventually formed the Group of Seven in 1920. Its members, mainly

English-born Torontonians making a living as commercial artists, had begun travelling north into the Georgian Bay and Algonquin wildernesses as early as 1911. This group captured the iconographic essence of wilderness Canada: a bleak and sombre but nonetheless curiously beautiful landscape of Jack pines, rock outcroppings, and storm-driven lakes, totally uninhabited by people.

Culture

In the years 1870–1914, most Canadians continued to amuse themselves at home, often performing imported theatrical works. Outside the home, the amateur tradition remained strong. In most fields of artistic endeavour, Britain and the United States remained the dominant influences. Perhaps the outstanding achievements in Canadian cultural production in this period occurred in fiction. Three developments stand out. One was the creation of the Canadian social novel. A second was the rise of a major figure in Canadian humour to carry on the earlier tradition of Haliburton and McCulloch. The third development, related to the previous two, was the emergence of several Canadian authors as international bestsellers. Some of these authors were women. All the successful authors were at their best in writing about the values of rural and small-town Canada at the end of the nineteenth century.

The best example of the social novel—also a novel of ideas—was *The Imperialist* by Sara Jeannette Duncan (1862–1912). Duncan had been born in Brantford and educated at the Toronto Normal School. She then became a pioneering female journalist, working for a long list of newspapers in the United States and Canada. In 1888 she and a female friend began a trip around the world, which she subsequently fictionalized. In 1904 she produced *The Imperialist*, a novel intended to describe the Imperial Question from the vantage point of the 'average Canadian of the average small town . . . whose views in the end [counted] for more than the opinions of the political leaders' (quoted in Klinck, 1965: 316). Duncan drew on her childhood experiences in Brantford to describe conditions in Elgin, a 'thriving manufacturing town, with a collegiate institute,

Lucy Maud Montgomery. Public Archives and Records Office of Prince Edward Island. Lucy Maud Montgomery 3110-1.

eleven churches, two newspapers, and an asylum for the deaf and dumb, to say nothing of a fire department unsurpassed for organization and achievement in the Province of Ontario' (Duncan, 1971 [1904]: 25). The opening chapter began with an account of the celebrations in Elgin on 24 May, the Queen's Birthday. Duncan interwove the issue of imperialism with the social values of late Victorian Canada. For her protagonist, young politician Lorne Murchison, Canada's continuation as a British nation was of moral rather than strategic importance.

Duncan was perhaps the first Canadian writer to recognize the literary potential of small-town Canada, especially for satirical purposes, but she was not the greatest. Stephen Leacock (1869–1944) had been born in England, but grew up on a farm near Lake Simcoe. Educated at Upper Canada College, the University of Toronto, and the University of

The Imperialist

It was the talk of the town, the pride of the market-place, Lorne Murchison's having been selected to accompany what was known as the Cruickshank deputation to England. . . .

'I expect you'll have the loveliest time you ever had in all your life. Do you think you'll be asked out much, Lorne?'

'I can't imagine who would ask me. We'll get off easy if the street boys don't shout, "What price Canucks?" at us! But I'll see England, Dora; I'll feel England, eat and drink and sleep and live in England, for a little while. Isn't the very name great? I'll be a better man for going, till I die. We're all right out here, but we're young and thin and weedy. They didn't grow so fast in England to begin with, and now they're rich with character and strong with conduct and hoary with ideals. I've been reading up the history of our political relations with England. It's astonishing what we've stuck to her through, but you can't help seeing why—it's for the moral advantage. Way down at the bottom, that's what it is. They've developed the finest human product there is, the cleanest, the most disinterested, and we want to keep up the relationship—It's important. Their talk about the value of their protection doesn't take in the situation as it is now. Who would touch us if we were running our own show?'

'I don't believe they are a bit better than we are,' replied Miss Millburn. 'I'm sure I haven't much opinion of the Englishmen that come out here. They don't think anything of getting into debt, and as often as not they drink, and they never know enough to—to come in out of the rain. . . .'

'Yes, but we are very apt to get the failures. The fellows their folks give five or six hundred pounds to and tell them they're not expected back till they're making a living. The best men find their level somewhere else, along recognized channels. Lord knows we don't want them—this country's for immigrants. We're manufacturing our own gentlemen quite fast enough for the demand.'

'I should think we were! Why, Lorne, Canadians—nice Canadians are just as gentlemanly as they can be! They'll compare with anybody. Perhaps Americans have got more style:' she weighed the matter; 'but Canadians are much better form, I think.'

Source: Sara Jeannette Duncan, *The Imperialist*, ed. Misao Dean (Peterborough, Ont.: Broadview Editions, 2005 [1904]), 123, 130–1. BROADVIEW PRESS.

Chicago, Leacock published a successful college textbook, *Elements of Political Science*, in 1906. He produced his first volume of humorous sketches, *Literary Lapses*, in 1910, and two years later published *Sunshine Sketches of a Little Town*. This was an affectionate satirical look at life in Mariposa, a fictionalized version of Orillia, the nearest town to his boyhood home. Leacock perfectly captured the hypocrisy, materialism, and inflated notions of importance possessed by Mariposa's residents. He followed this triumph with a much more savage satire of a North American city, obviously the Montreal in which he lived and taught (at McGill University). The work was entitled *Arcadian Adventures with the Idle Rich* (1914). In this book, which he pretended to set somewhere in the United States, Leacock began the transference of his satire from Canada to North America. He moved on from these early works to produce a volume of humorous sketches virtually every year, increasingly set in an international milieu. His books were very popular in Britain and the United States. Many critics feel that Leacock's best work was his early Canadian satire, in which he scourged Canadian pretensions.

Duncan and Leacock both achieved international reputations as writers of fiction, and they were joined by several other Canadians in the years between 1900 and 1914. One was the Presbyterian clergyman Charles W. Gordon (1860–1937), who under the pseudonym 'Ralph Connor' was probably the best-selling writer in English between 1899 and the Great War. Born in Glengarry County, Canada West, and educated at the University of Toronto and Edinburgh University, Gordon became minister of a Presbyterian church in Winnipeg, where he lived for the remainder of his life. Ralph Connor's first three books, published between 1899 and 1902, sold over five million copies. One of these, *Glengarry School Days: A Story of Early Days in Glengarry* (1902), was probably the best book he ever wrote. Like Duncan and Leacock, Connor excelled at the evocation of small-town life and mores, drawing from his personal experiences as a boy. He was not a great writer but knew how to sustain a narrative and to frame a moral crisis. Some of his work—including novels in which clerical examples of muscular Christianity faced a variety of frontier challenges—obviously struck a responsive chord in an international audience. Connor's heroes triumphed over sin, anarchy, and unregenerate people by sheer force of character, Christian conviction, goodness, and even physical strength; they represented what his generation saw as the forces of civilization and progress. Fellow Presbyterian Nellie McClung (1873–1951) also had great success with similar material, even less artfully rendered, in books such as *Sowing Seeds in Danny* (1908); her fame was more in the political arena.

A much superior artist was Lucy Maud Montgomery (1874–1942), whose *Anne of Green Gables* also first appeared in 1908. Montgomery's books lovingly described rural life and presented some of the standard dilemmas faced by her readers, ranging from growing up to having to leave the farm.

Imperialism, Reform, and Racism

Contemporaries often characterized Canadian political life in this era in terms of its lack of ideology and its predilection for what the French observer André Siegfried called the 'question of collective or individual interests for the candidates to exploit to their own advantage' (Siegfried, 1907: 142). Lurking only just beneath the surface, however, were some serious and profound issues. First was the so-called Canadian question, which bore in various ways upon the very future of the new nation. It often appeared to be a debate between those who sought to keep Canada within the British Empire and those who wanted it to assume full sovereignty. Into this discussion other matters merged subtly, including the 'race' question and the reform question. The former involved the future of French Canada within an evolving Anglo-American nation. The latter concerned the institution of political and social change through public policy. Debate and disagreement over the three loosely linked issues—imperialism, Anglo–French antagonisms, and reform—kept political Canada bubbling with scarcely suppressed excitement from the 1880s to the beginning of the Great War. Canada's involvement in the military conflict of Europe would bring those issues together, although it would not resolve them.

Imperialism

The period from 1880 to 1914 saw a resurgence of imperial development around the world. The French, the Germans, even the Americans, took up what Rudyard Kipling called the 'White man's burden' in underdeveloped regions of the world. About the same time, Great Britain began to shed its 'Little England' free trade sentiments. The world's shopkeeper discovered that substantial windfall profits came from exploiting the economies of Asia, Latin America, and Africa, especially the last. Canada first faced the implications of the resurgence of Britain's imperial pretensions in 1884 when the mother country asked it to contribute to an expedition to relieve General Charles Gordon, besieged by thousands of Muslim fundamentalists at Khartoum in the Egyptian Sudan. Sir John A. Macdonald's immediate response was negative, but he ultimately found it politic to allow Canadian civilian volunteers to assist the British army. By the end of the century Joseph Chamberlain at the Colonial Office was advocating that Britain's old settlement colonies be joined together in some political and economic union, the so-called Imperial Federation.

Encouraged by a new infusion of immigrants from Britain—nearly half a million between 1870 and 1896 and a million between 1896 and 1914—many anglophone Canadians began openly

Nellie Letitia McClung

Nellie McClung. The Canadian Press.

Born in Chatsworth, Ontario, Nellie McClung (née Mooney) (1873–1951) moved with her family to Manitoba in 1880. After attending normal school in Winnipeg, she taught in rural Manitoba for many years. She was active in temperance work and in suffrage agitation. In 1896 she married Robert Wesley McClung, a druggist, who promised, Nellie later reported, that 'I would not have to lay aside my ambitions if I married him.' Her emergence to prominence began when she entered an American short story competition in 1902 and was encouraged by an American publisher to expand the story into the novel that became *Sowing Seeds in Danny*, a light-hearted look at village life on the prairies published in 1908. The book sold over 100,000 copies, was in its seventeenth edition at the time her death, and brought her both fame and fortune.

She and her husband moved to Winnipeg with their four children in 1911, where she helped organize the Political Equality League in 1912. Frustrated with the difficulty of arousing male politicians to suffrage reform, after some humiliating experiences she turned herself into a first-rate platform speaker. In 1914 she organized the Mock Parliament of Women, in which women played all the political roles. McClung herself was Manitoba Premier Rodmond Roblin, one of the major opponents of women's right to vote. McClung and her associates, supporting the Liberal Party, were unable to defeat Roblin's government in the 1914 election, but it soon fell under the weight of a construction scandal. The Liberal government of Tobias Crawford soon made Manitoba the first province in Canada to grant women the right to vote.

Meanwhile, the McClungs had moved to Edmonton, where Nellie again led the fight for female suffrage. She was also a strong supporter of the war effort and the Red Cross. In 1921 she was elected to the Alberta legislature, where she championed a host of radical measures of the time, ranging from mothers' allowances to dower rights for women to sterilization of the mentally unfit. She was defeated in 1926 when her temperance stance became unpopular. Nellie subsequently helped in the successful fight for Canadian woman senators. The McClungs moved to Victoria in 1933. In her west coast years, she became a CBC governor (1936–42), a delegate to the League of Nations (1938), and an advocate of divorce reform.

She was throughout her life an active Methodist and subsequently a member of the United Church, and was prominent at the national and international levels in her church work. Apart from her first novel, none of her subsequent fiction has withstood the test of time very well. McClung did better with her autobiographical memoirs, all of which were highly regarded and reprinted. Like many early feminists, she was clearly a figure of her own time. She supported the Great War with almost bloodthirsty enthusiasm and was an active advocate of eugenics.

advocating Canada's active participation in the new British Empire. Their sense of imperial destiny was not necessarily anti-nationalistic. They saw no inconsistency between the promotion of a sense of Canadian unity and a larger British Empire. 'I am an Imperialist', argued Stephen Leacock in 1907, 'because I will not be a Colonial.' Leacock sought 'something other than mere colonial stagnation, something sounder than independence, nobler than annexation, greater in purpose than a Little Canada' (quoted in Bumsted, 1969, II: 78). Such pan-Britannic nationalism came to express itself concretely in demands for Imperial Federation. It was most prevalent in the province of Ontario.

Unfortunately for the imperialists, not all Canadians agreed with their arguments. Several strands of anti-imperial sentiment had emerged by the turn of the century. One strand, most closely identified with the political journalist Goldwin Smith (1823–1910), insisted that the geography of North America worked against Canadian nationalism. Smith advocated Canadian absorption into the United States. Fear of this development led many Canadians to oppose a new reciprocity agreement with the United States in 1911. Another strand, led by John S. Ewart (1849–1933), insisted on Canada's assumption of full sovereignty. Ewart argued that 'Colony implies inferiority—inferiority in culture, inferiority in wealth, inferiority in government, inferiority in foreign relations, inferiority and subordination' (Ewart, 1908: 6). Yet another perspective was enunciated by Henri Bourassa (1868–1912), who advocated a fully articulated bicultural Canadian nationalism. He wrote, 'My native land is all of Canada, a federation of separate races and autonomous provinces. The nation I wish to see grow up is the Canadian nation, made up of French Canadians and English Canadians' (quoted in Monière, 1981: 190). The Bourassa version of nationalism was considerably larger than the still prevalent traditional nationalism of French Canada.

Prof. Stephen B. Leacock, Montreal, 1914. II–202933 Notman Photographic Archives, McCord Museum of Canadian History, Montreal.

As the newspaper *La Vérité* put it in 1904, 'what we want to see flourish is French-Canadian patriotism; our people are the French-Canadian people; we will not say that our homeland is limited to the Province of Quebec, but it is French Canada. . . .'

The most common confrontations over the role of Canada within the Empire occurred in the context of imperial defence. At Queen Victoria's Jubilee celebration in June 1897, Laurier had fended off a regularization of colonial contributions to the British military. The question arose again in July 1899 when the mother country requested Canadian troops for the forthcoming war in South Africa against the Boers. When the shooting began on 11 October 1899, the popular press of English Canada responded with enthusiasm to the idea of an official Canadian contingent. But newspapers in French Canada opposed involvement. As *La Presse* editorialized, 'We French Canadians belong to one country, Canada: Canada is for us the whole world, but the English Canadians have two countries, one here and one across the sea.' The government compromised

On Imperialism and Nationalism

One of the opponents of Canadian imperialism was Henri Bourassa (1868–1952). In 1912 he explained his position in an address to the Canadian Club.

We speak of 'our Empire'. Have you ever considered how little we Canadians count in that Empire, the most wonderful fabric of human organization that has ever existed. Of course, as far as land is concerned, and water, and rocks, and mines, and forests, we occupy a large portion of the Empire. As to population we are only seven millions out of over four hundred millions. As to imperial powers, we have none. The people of the British Kingdom, forty millions in number, possess as their sole property the rest of that Empire. Suppose you except Canada with her seven millions, Australia with her four millions and a half, New Zealand with one million, and South Africa, with a little over one million of white people: apart from those semi-free states, the whole empire of India, the hundreds of Crown colonies, and those immense protectorates in Africa or Asia, no more belong to us than they belong to the Emperor of Germany, or to the President of the French Republic. We have no more to say as regards the government, the legislation, the administration, the revenue and the expenditure, and the defence of that territory, comprising four-fifths of the total population of the Empire, than have the coolies of India or the Zulus of Matabeleland! I am not saying this in disparagement of the system; I am simply putting our position as it is. At the present time, the seven millions of people in Canada have less voice, in law and in fact, in the ruling of that Empire, than one single sweeper in the streets of Liverpool, or one cabdriver on Fleet Street in London; he at least has one vote to give for or against the administration of that Empire, but we, the seven million Canadians, have no vote and no say whatever.

When I hear splendid phrases, magnificent orations, sounding sentences, about that 'Empire of ours', I am forcibly reminded of the pretension of a good fellow whom I had hired to look after the furnace of a building of which I had the management in Montreal. Every year, when the time came to

by sending volunteers, nearly 5,000 before the conflict was over. The defence issue emerged again in 1909, this time over naval policy. Under imperial pressure, Canada finally agreed to produce a naval unit of five cruisers and six destroyers. Both sides attacked Laurier's compromise Naval Service Bill of January 1910. The anglophone Tories insisted it did not provide enough assistance for the British, while in Quebec nationalists and Conservatives joined forces to fight for its repeal.

Reform

The reform movement of this period was rich and varied in its interests. It ranged from the women's suffrage movement to various efforts at social and humanitarian change. Mainstream Canadian reform movements had some features in common, however. Their leaders were members of the middle and professional classes who shared assumptions of the age about regeneration and social purity. Those of Protestant backgrounds tended to predominate, particularly in temperance/prohibition, public health, education, and women's suffrage. Women, because of their general nurturing role in society, played a major role in most reform movements. These women were often less concerned with restructuring gender roles in society than with the need for inculcating middle-class virtues or with helping the poor. French-Canadian women were significantly underrepresented in most national reform movements, partly because of the political isolation of Quebec and partly because the ideology of the traditional society greatly limited the place of women in that province.

purchase the coal for the winter, he used to exclaim, with a deep sense of his responsibilities: 'How dear it costs us to keep up our building!' Our right of ownership, of tutelage, of legislation, in the British Empire is exactly what the right of partnership of that stoker was in that building.

. . . [A]t the sixth Imperial Conference, the delegates from Australia, representing a courageous, intelligent, progressive British community, with a high sea trade amounting in imports and exports to $650,000,000 a year, asked the representatives of the British Government why the British authorities, without even thinking of asking the opinion of Canada, of Australia, of South Africa, and of New Zealand, had concluded with the great maritime powers the international treaty known as the Declaration of London, which may affect beneficially or otherwise the trade of the world in future naval wars. They enquired also if it would be possible to have at least one representative from the self-governing British colonies on the Board of Arbitration, eventually to be constituted, under the terms of that treaty, to adjudicate upon the seizures of trade and ships in times of war. Sir Edward Grey, undoubtedly one of the ablest men in British public life to-day, showed there, I think, his great tact and his extraordinary command of words and of diplomatic means. But, when all the courteous terms and all the frills were taken off, his answer amounted to this: On that board the negro President of Hayti could sit, the negro President of Liberia could sit, but the Prime Minister of Canada or of Australia could not sit, simply because Hayti and Liberia are nations, whilst Canada or Australia are not nations. He explained that the colonies were not consulted because they exist only through Great Britain, and that the moment Great Britain accepted that treaty it applied to us as to her. Undoubtedly true and another evidence, I think, to show that in the 'imperial partnership', in the enjoyment of that imperial citizenship of which we hear so much, there still remains a slight difference between the British citizen in England, Scotland and Ireland, and the British citizen of Canada: one is a member of a sovereign community, the other is the inhabitant of a subjected colony.

Source: H. Bourassa, *Canadian Club Addresses 1912* (Toronto: Warwick Bros & Rutter, 1912), 78–80.

The suffrage movement did emphasize the gender question. It addressed women's political powerlessness by attempting to win for them the right to vote. The movement was chiefly an urban one, dominated by well-educated women who saw political power as necessary to bring about other legislative change. The suffragist leaders were almost exclusively Canadian or British-born and belonged to the mainline Protestant churches. Well over half of these women were gainfully employed, mostly in journalism and writing. The suffragists gradually lost contact with working-class women, who were suspicious of the class biases in both the suffrage and reform movements. They also failed to gain the support of farm women because they did not understand rural issues, especially the concern over rural depopulation. Many rural women became involved in their own organizations designed to deal with their own problems, such as the Women's Institutes. Adelaide Hoodless (1857–1910) founded the first Institute at Stoney Creek, Ontario, in 1897. (In Henry James Morgan's biographical compilation *The Canadian Men and Women of the Time*, 2nd edn, 1912, she is listed under the entry for her husband John, who was an obscure furniture manufacturer in Hamilton.) Women's Institutes promoted appreciation of rural living, as well as encouraging better education for all women for motherhood and homemaking. In 1919 the Federated Women's Institutes of Canada organized with its motto 'For Home and Country'.

One female reform organization, the Woman's Christian Temperance Union, had both rural and urban memberships. Founded in 1874 in Picton, Ontario, the WCTU claimed 10,000 members by

The Americanization of Canada

In 1907 the American journalist Samuel E. Moffatt published a book entitled *The Americanization of Canada*, which extended Goldwin Smith's earlier arguments about the extent of Canadian integration into the United States.

In 1850, 147,711 persons of Canadian birth were living south of the border—about one-sixteenth of the number of people living in the British possessions at the same time. In 1860 the Canadian-born population of the United States had increased to 249,970, a gain of 76 per cent, while the general population of the Union was increasing at the rate of 35.6 per cent, and that of the British provinces at about 33.6. In 1870 there were 493,464 Canadians in the United States, an increase of 97.4 per cent for the decade against 22.6 per cent for that of the population of the Republic as a whole, and 16.2 per cent for that of the British colonies, now united in the Dominion of Canada. . . . While the population of the Republic was a little more than tripling in fifty years, and that of Canada was being multiplied by less than two and a half, the little Canada south of the boundary line saw the number of its inhabitants multiplied by eight. Of all the living persons of Canadian birth in 1900, more than one-fifth were settled in the United States. But if the statement stopped there it would be incomplete. In addition to the native Canadians in the United States in 1900, there were 527,301 persons of American birth but with both parents Canadian. There were also 425,617 with Canadian fathers and American mothers, and 344,470 with Canadian mothers and American fathers. Thus there were in all 2,480,613 persons in the United States of at least half Canadian blood, which is more than half the number of similar stock in Canada. . . .

In density of Canadian population, ignoring all other elements, Massachusetts stands first, exceeding any province of Canada, and Rhode Island second. The relative rank of the various Provinces and States previously named on this basis is:

1900 and had an influence far beyond that number. Despite its name, the WCTU wanted prohibition, soon seeing the elimination of alcoholic beverages as a panacea for many of the ills currently besetting Canadian society, such as crime, the abuse of women and children, political corruption, and general immorality. The WCTU was only one of several members of the Dominion Alliance for the Total Suppression of the Liquor Traffic. Like most Canadian reform movements, prohibition required state intervention to be effective, and this eventually led some of its supporters to women's suffrage. Laurier held a national referendum on prohibition in 1898. Although its supporters won a narrow victory, the Prime Minister refused to implement national legislation because only 20 per cent of the total electorate had supported the principle. The prohibitionists turned to the provinces, succeeding in getting legislation passed in Prince Edward Island in 1900 and in Nova Scotia in 1910. The local option was even more effective, since it involved local communities where prohibitionist sentiment could be strong. Prohibitionism exemplified both the best and the worst features of reform. It had little Catholic or urban working-class support. Moreover, it tended to clothe its single-minded arguments with intense moral fervour, often of the social purity variety.

Humanitarian reform, usually of urban abuses, often focused on the human victims of disastrous industrial social conditions. One of the main spearheads of such reform was the social gospel. Beginning in the Methodist Church and expanding to all Protestant denominations in Canada, the social

Canadian population per square mile

1	Massachusetts	64.2
2	Rhode Island	64.0
3	Prince Edward Island	45.36
4	Nova Scotia	20.6
5	New Brunswick	11.2
6	Connecticut	10.9
7	New Hampshire	10.8
8	Ontario	8.4
9	Michigan	7.1
10	Vermont	6.8 . . .

Classified in the same way, the principal Canadian cities in 1900–1 were:

1	Montreal	267,730
2	Toronto	208,040
3	Boston	84,336
4	Quebec	66,231
5	Chicago	64,615
6	Ottawa	49,718
7	Detroit	44,592
8	New York	40,400 . . .

Source: Samuel Erasmus Moffatt, *Americanization of Canada.* 1907.

gospel saw Christ as a social reformer and the institution of the Kingdom of God on earth as its (and his) mission. The growth of city missions and church settlement houses led to the establishment of the Social Services Council of Canada in 1912. The most prominent social gospeller was J.S. Woodsworth (1874–1942). Another branch of humanitarian reform involved various professionals who became concerned with social problems through their professional practices. Thus doctors, for example, were active in promoting a public health system and in recommending ways of improving public health care. Among the medical profession's public health recommendations was compulsory medical inspection of schoolchildren.

Schools and members of the teaching profession were also in the front lines of humanitarian reform. In this period educators pushed not only for improved schooling but for the schools to assume much of the burden of social services for the young by acting *in loco parentis* for the children of slum and ghetto dwellers. The pressure for compulsory school attendance legislation, extended on a province-by-province basis across the nation by 1914, was partly reformist in nature. Regular school attendance would provide a more suitable environment for children than roaming the streets or working in factories. The children might learn skills that would lift them out of their poverty and (in the case of immigrants) would become assimilated to the values of Canadian society. Educators clearly believed that using schools for reform purposes was in the best interests of Canadian society. It was also in their best interest. Compulsory education opened more

Clara Brett Martin

Clara Brett Martin, first female lawyer in the British Empire. Law Society of Upper Canada Archives, Archives Department collection, 'Photograph of Clara Brett Martin', P291.

The pioneering woman in the Canadian legal profession was Clara Brett Martin (1874–1923), who graduated with high honours in mathematics from Trinity College, Toronto, in 1890. In 1891 she petitioned the Law Society of Upper Canada to be registered as a student. The petition was denied, and she was advised to 'remove to the United States', where more than 20 states admitted women to the bar. Instead of leaving the country, Martin found an Ontario legislator willing to introduce a bill into the provincial legislature that would explicitly define the word 'person' in the Law Society's statutes as including females. This initiative was supported by Dr Emily Stowe, leader of the Dominion Woman's Enfranchisement Association, who gained the approval of Premier Oliver Mowat for the new legislation. By the time it was passed in 1892, the legislation was emasculated so that women could only become solicitors (not barristers), and then only at the discretion of the Law Society.

The Law Society subsequently again refused admission to Martin, and Oliver Mowat himself attended the next Law Society Convocation to move her admission. The Law Society agreed by the narrowest of margins, and Clara Martin became a student-at-law, accepted as an articling student by one of the most prestigious law firms in Toronto. Martin met much disapproval from within her law firm and was forced to change firms in 1893. She was also harassed in the lecture halls of Osgoode Hall and missed as many lectures as she possibly could. She eventually completed her degree and easily passed the bar examinations. Martin also pressed for revision of the legislation that allowed women to act only as solicitors, not barristers. She won this battle, too, and then had to face the Law Society again. A final controversy came over the dress code for female barristers, when women were required to wear their gowns over a black dress. Martin was finally admitted as a barrister and solicitor on 2 February 1897, the first woman in the British Empire entered into the legal profession. She practised for most of her legal career in her own firm in Toronto.

employment and introduced the educator as social expert, a professional who knew more about what was important for children than parents, particularly the parents of the disadvantaged. Compulsory education, medical examinations, school nurses, and lunch programs all were part of a new form of social engineering that would only increase in emphasis over the century.

In the course of time, many of the private agencies of reform became conscripted as quasi-public ones under provincial legislation. They served as arms of the state in the intermediate period before the establishment of permanent government bureaucracies. Thus private child welfare programs became officially responsible for abandoned, abused, and delinquent children. Despite this trend towards a

J.L. MacDonald's class in School District No. 3, Glenelg, Ontario, 1910. Fred W. Kelsey/LAC, C-15490.

public approach, the framework remained that of individual morality. The humanitarian reformers commonly linked vice, crime, and poverty. Even those who focused on poverty tended to attribute it to almost every other cause than the failure of the economic system to distribute wealth equitably. The concept of a basic minimum standard of living as the right of all members of society was slow to develop in Canada. Attacks on poverty in this period retained a certain class overtone, with a 'superior' class helping an 'inferior' one.

Another whole category of reformers sought structural alteration within the Canadian system. Their model was often sound business practice, for the leaders of this movement were usually successful businessmen. They sought the elimination of wasteful graft and corruption through political reform, the creation of publicly operated (and profitable) utilities to reduce unnecessary taxation, and the introduction of public planning. They tended to focus on the big city, although they spilled over in various directions. These reforms, which in the United States

were associated with the Progressive movement, all found allies within associated middle-class and professional groups. The City Beautiful Movement, for example, received much of its support from an expanding community of professional architects, who combined an urge to plan the city as a whole with aesthetic considerations of coherence, visual variety, and civic grandeur. Like Americans, many Canadians saw cities as the culmination of civilization, and many grand plans made their appearance on paper. Cities settled for a few monumental new buildings, such as the imposing legislative structures completed in many provinces before the war. Political reform of municipal government concentrated on 'throwing the rascals out', combined with structural changes to reduce the damage they could do when they were in. The changes often included the replacement of elective councils with more professional government by commission. Businessmen reformers also fought fierce battles over the question of the ownership of utilities. While the utilities barons complained of the attack on private enterprise, the corporate reformers countered by arguing that utilities were intrinsic monopolies that should be operated in the public interest. Much of the impulse behind reform of all sorts came from fear of class warfare and moral degeneration. The reformers did for the poor rather than with the poor. The results were a vast increase in the public concerns of the state and the beginning of the growth of a public bureaucracy to deal with social matters.

Racism: The Darker Side of Canada's Growth

Racialist thinking was at its height during this period. Part of the 'race question' in Canada was not about 'race' at all, of course, but about the conflict between French and English Canada. While there was no racial barrier between French and English, contemporaries accepted race-based arguments and analyses as 'scientific'. Many imperialists regarded the historical progress of the United States, Great Britain, and Canada as evidence of the special genius of the 'Anglo-Saxon race'. The French were acceptable partners because they, too, were a northern people. Out of the scientific theories of Charles Darwin came the conviction that inheritance was the key to evolution. Races were formed by natural selection, exhibiting quite unequal characteristics. In almost everyone's hierarchy, the dominant Canadian population was at the progressive top of the racial scale. Newcomers who could not or would not assimilate would inevitably lower the Canadian 'standard of civilization'. Sexual morality was an important component of the racism of the time.

Canadians saw the new immigration after 1896 as particularly troubling. Even that secular saint J.S. Woodsworth, the Methodist minister and social worker in Winnipeg who would become a leftist federal parliamentarian and the first leader of the Co-operative Commonwealth Federation (CCF), associated criminality with the newcomers. Many feared the potential degeneracy of the 'great northern race' through commingling with lesser stocks. Others concentrated on the campaigns for social purity, mixing restrictions on the consumption of alcoholic beverages with hostility to prostitution, venereal disease, and sexual exploitation. The first serious efforts at large-scale immigration restriction, designed mainly to keep out the 'degenerates', began in the early years of the century. Campaigns for social purity, immigration restriction, and exclusion of Asians all came out of the same stock of assumptions about heredity and environment that informed many other reform movements of the period. The reformers often emphasized social and moral aspects, directing their efforts chiefly against newcomers.

Immigration restrictions came in three senses. One was an insistence on the good health, good character, and resources of the individual immigrant. A second was an equally strong insistence on preventing group immigration by certain peoples deemed unassimilable, headed by Asians but also including American-born blacks. Efforts at a broader exclusionary practice involved bilateral negotiations with foreign nations to restrict the departure of their nationals, such as an exclusionary agreement with Japan in 1907 that followed anti-Asian riots in Vancouver. The third involved provincial legislation, mainly in British Columbia, to limit the rights of the unwanted. By 1907, the British Columbia legislature had disenfranchised nationals of China, Japan, and imperial India. Federal immigration policy was expressed mostly in informal ways before 1906, but thereafter, immigration authorities became much more concerned with formal regulation of the flow of newcomers, emulating the Americans in this regard.

In 1906 a new Immigration Act consolidated many earlier laws, barring large categories of people, including prostitutes and pimps, the insane, the mentally retarded, epileptics, and the 'deaf and dumb'. An expanded immigration service in 1908 for the first time began to monitor the border with the United States at 38 border crossings across the continent—before this time the border had been wide open with little checking of those crossing it in either direction—and was allowed to deport individuals who belonged to prohibited categories or become public charges. In 1908, another amendment to the Immigration Act provided that all immigration to Canada had to come via a continuous journey on a through ticket from the country of origin. This 'continuous journey' proviso was intended to make it more difficult for immigrants to Canada to evade immigration restrictions placed by the governments of their homelands, often established at Canadian insistence, and it effectively cut off immigration from India. Another restrictive Immigration Act in 1910 gave the cabinet the power to regulate immigration according to race and to keep out 'prohibited and undesirable classes'. Any group deemed unsuited to the climate or requirements of Canada could be deported on grounds of political or moral undesirability. Political grounds for rejection included the advocacy by a person not a Canadian citizen of the overthrow by force or violence of the government of Great Britain or Canada. The Act also introduced a head tax on all immigrants except the Japanese, who had been paying $500 since 1903 (9–10 Edward VII Chap 27, An Act respecting Immigration).

Perhaps the most extreme example of Canadian exclusionism occurred in May of 1914, when the Japanese vessel *Komagata Maru* arrived in Vancouver harbour with 376 passengers aboard. Of these, 165 had boarded at Hong Kong, 111 at Shanghai, 86 at Maji, and 14 at Yokohama. Of the passengers, 340 were Sikhs, a people who had been arriving in British Columbia for more than a decade. Most had been males from the Jat Sikh community in rural Punjab who came to Canada as sojourners, intending to return to their homes; according to official Canadian statistics, the number of East Indian adult females who entered Canada over the years 1904–7 was 14, and the number of children was 22. The East Indian community soon began to become organized and articulate. The Khalsa Diwan Society,

a fraternal organization with nationalist overtones, was organized in Vancouver in 1907. East Indian revolutionary agitators began their work in North America, including Canada. Separating the activities of Indian nationalists into those directed at abuses at home and in host countries is not easy. Much of our knowledge about the nationalists comes from information collected by police undercover agents, and must be understood in this context. The agents were convinced that the leading nationalists were advocates of violence and terrorism.

The *Komagata Maru*'s organizer expected that the Canadians would overlook the continuous voyage requirement when the ship docked in Vancouver and that the local community would raise the money for the head tax. He was right on the second count but wrong on the first. The Canadian government—backed by Vancouver municipal authorities and the British Columbia government, both of which became quite hysterical—refused to allow the passengers to land. Conditions on board ship deteriorated rapidly, and the incident quickly became an international one. Canadian immigration authorities attempted to storm the vessel by force but were driven off. Eventually the ship sailed out of Vancouver harbour under naval escort and headed back to India, a powerful symbol of Canada's exclusionism.

The sudden arrival of the Great War in September of 1914 would subsume these events in British Columbia, as it would virtually everything in Canadian life.

How History Has Changed

Canadian Immigration and Ethnicity

Before the 1960s, Canadian historians thought very little about the history of immigration and ethnicity. Immigration was viewed as a necessary step towards settlement, but was not a central feature of a Canada that was viewed chiefly in political, constitutional, and economic terms. No attention was paid to the overseas origins of the immigrants. While not all immigrants were successful, the focus was plainly on those who had managed to make a

new life and become Canadians, which was, after all, what immigration was all about. When the Canadian Parliament set up the Royal Commission on Bilingualism and Biculturalism in 1963, the Order-in-Council assumed that it would find that Canadian Confederation consisted of two founding races and some 'contribution made by the other ethnic groups'. To its surprise, the Commission found that the concept of two founding peoples took absolutely no account of the First Nations. As for the other ethnic groups, they proved to be much more substantial and articulate than the politicians could ever have imagined. Few of the ethnic groups had much concrete notion of their own history, however, which had been written chiefly by amateurs within their ranks who tended to gloss over or ignore the bad things that had happened along the way.

Within a few years, Canadian history was to be transformed by a number of concurrent trends. One was an emphasis on social history, on how the people (ordinary people) lived. Historians began to talk about writing history 'from the bottom up'. Thanks to the American civil rights movement of the 1960s, historians also began examining how ordinary people, especially minorities and the Aboriginal population, had been treated over the years. Instead of a celebratory history of successful settlement and development, the historical picture became far more mixed and nuanced. A final impetus for change was given by the policy of multiculturalism announced in 1971. That policy included substantial amounts of public money to be made available to both scholars and ethnic groups to study ethnicity, which inevitably led to further research on immigration.

And a concentration on research into immigration and ethnicity led almost inexorably to recognition of the racism expressed by the majority cultures and by the Canadian government towards many immigrants, ethnic minorities, and the Aboriginal communities of Canada.

By 1990 there was much outcry over historical mistreatment and much demand for redress by a variety of peoples: from the Japanese for their internment during World War II; from the Ukrainians for their internment during World War I; from the Chinese for the imposition of a discriminatory head tax; from the black residents of Africville in Nova Scotia for the destruction of their community. In that year the Mulroney government actually responded to a campaign from the Japanese community by agreeing to an apology and compensation for those people who had been interned, thus setting a precedent and opening the flood gates of redress. In 2009 the Harper government revised the manual given to all candidates for citizenship so that its potted history actually acknowledged many instances of public abuse of First Nations and various ethnic groups.

Short Bibliography

Avery, Donald. *Reluctant Host: Canada's Response to Immigrant Workers, 1896–1994*. Toronto, 1995. The best synthesis of the topic.

Bacchi, Carole. *Liberation Deferred? The Ideas of the English-Canadian Suffragists, 1877–1918*. Toronto, 1983. An analysis of English-Canadian suffragism, emphasizing the distinction between maternal and radical feminism.

Berger, Carl. *The Sense of Power: Studies in the Ideas of Canadian Imperialism, 1867–1914*. Toronto, 1970. The pioneer study of these ideas in Canada, and still easily the best.

Bliss, J.M. *A Living Profit: Studies in the Social History of Canadian Business, 1883–1911*. Toronto, 1974. A collection of stimulating essays on Canadian business in a critical period.

Bradbury, Bettina. *Working Families: Age, Gender, and Daily Survival in Industrializing Montreal*. Toronto, 1993. A valuable study on the effect of industrialization on the family and its strategies.

Carbert, Louise. *Agrarian Feminism: The Politics of Ontario Farm Women*. Toronto, 1995. The first full-length analysis of what farm women were up to before 1914.

Christie, Nancy. *Engendering the State: Family, Work, and Welfare in Canada*. Toronto, 2000. A recent and controversial work that locates the origins of the Canadian welfare state in the quest for stability for the family.

Copp, Terry. *The Anatomy of Poverty: The Condition of the Working Class in Montreal 1897–1929*. Toronto, 1974. An early study of the urban working class in Montreal, probably still the best analysis available.

Courville, Serge, and Normand Séguin. *Rural Life in Nineteenth-century Quebec*. Ottawa, 1989. A synthesis of a good deal of secondary literature, which emphasizes how similar rural French Canada was to English Canada.

English, John. *The Decline of Politics: The Conservatives and the Party System, 1901–20*. Toronto, 1977. The best study of politics before the Great War.

Heron, Craig. *Working in Steel: The Early Years in Canada, 1883–1935*. Toronto, 1988. A brilliant account of the origins of steelmaking in Canada, especially strong on labour issues.

Johnston, Hugh. *The Voyage of the Komagata Maru: The Sikh Challenge to Canada's Colour Bar*. Delhi, 1979. A dispassionate recounting of the story.

Linteau, Paul-André. *The Promoters' City: Building the Industrial Town of Maisonneuve, 1883–1918*. Toronto, 1985. A wonderful study of the creation of an industrial suburb in French Canada.

McCormack, A.R. *Reformers, Rebels, and Revolutionaries: The Western Canadian Radical Movement, 1899–1919*. Toronto, 1977. A work that resurrects and brings to life a collection of radicals previously neglected in the traditional literature.

McDonald, R.J. *Making Vancouver: Class, Status, and Social Boundaries, 1863–1913*. Vancouver, 1996. Urban social history that takes advantage of all the latest conceptualizations.

Magocsi, Paul Robert. *Encyclopedia of Canada's Peoples*. Toronto, 1999. A co-operative project by dozens of scholars providing a vast compendium of material on Canadian ethnicity.

Miller, Carman. *Painting the Map Red: Canada and the South African War, 1899–1902*. Montreal, 1993. The best study of Canada and the Boer War.

Parker, Roy. *Uprooted: The Shipment of Poor Children to Canada, 1867–1917*. Vancouver, 2008. A thorough scholarly synthesis of an emotive subject.

Petryshyn, Jaroslav, *Peasants in the Promised Land: Canaada and the Ukrainians, 1891-1914*. Toronto, 1985. A careful study of the early Ukrainian migration.

Rollings-Magnusson, Sandra. *Heavy Burdens on Small Shoulders: The Labour of Pioneer Children on the Canadian Prairies*. Edmonton, 2009. A recent study that suggests how much the settlement of the West depended on the work of children.

Sager, Eric, with Gerald Panting. *Maritime Capital: The Shipping Industry in Atlantic Canada, 1820–1914*. Montreal, 1990. A study, based on quantitative data, of an important industry.

Troper, Harold Martin. *Only Farmers Need Apply: Official Canadian Government Encouragement of Immigration from the United States, 1896–1911*. Toronto, 1972. The standard work on the topic.

Valverde, Mariana. *The Age of Light, Soap, and Water: Moral Reform in English Canada, 1885–1925*. Toronto, 1991. One of the few overall syntheses of the reform movement, focusing particularly on its moral dimensions.

Voisey, Paul. *Vulcan: The Making of a Prairie Community*. Toronto, 1988. Probably the best historical community study ever executed in Canada.

Walden, Keith. *Becoming Modern in Toronto: The Industrial Exhibition and the Shaping of a Late Victorian Culture*. Toronto, 1997. A recent work in cultural studies, deconstructing the Toronto Industrial Exhibition.

Study Questions

1. What role did the patronage system play in Canadian political parties in the years before the Great War?
2. How did the industrialization of the period 1885–1914 differ from that of the 1850s and 1860s?
3. Compare the major problems of urban and rural life in Canada in the early years of the twentieth century.
4. Are the differences between child labour in factories and on farms significant?
5. What does the poem 'Town Directory' tell us about Treherne, Manitoba, in 1895?
6. Discuss the relationship between the small town and the development of Canadian fiction, 1890–1914.
7. What were the linkages among imperialism, reform, and racism before the Great War?
8. Was Canada a country truly open to immigrants in this period? What were the limitations?

 www.oupcanada.com/Bumsted4e

Visit the companion website for *A History of the Canadian Peoples*, fourth edition for further resources.

8 Two Wars and a Depression, 1914–1945

Timeline

1914   Canada and Newfoundland enter the Great War.

1915   Canadian Expeditionary Force fights in the first Battle of Ypres. Ontario introduces Regulation 17.

1916   Canada introduces a business profits tax. The Newfoundland Regiment is decimated at the Battle of Beaumont Hamel.

1917   Canadian Expeditionary Force suffers heavy losses at Vimy in April. Canada introduces an income tax. Conscription crisis emerges over introduction of Military Service Act. Much of Halifax is destroyed in an explosion.

1918   The Great War ends. Spanish influenza epidemic begins.

1919   'Red Scare' begins. Government suppresses Winnipeg General Strike. First Congress of the League of Indians meets in Sault Ste Marie. *Canadian Bookman* is founded.

1920   Progressive Party is formed. First issues of *Canadian Forum*, *Canadian Historical Review*, and *The Dalhousie Review* appear. The Group of Seven holds its first exhibition of paintings.

1921   In a federal election, the Progressive Party wins 64 seats. William Lyon Mackenzie King's Liberals form the government. The Maritime Rights Movement is organized.

1923   Famous Players' Canadian Corporation takes over Allen Theatres.

1924   William Aberhart begins the Prophetic Bible Institute broadcasts over Calgary's CFCN.

1925   United Church of Canada is formed. Pacific Coast Hockey League folds.

1926   Governor General Byng refuses Prime Minister King a dissolution for a new election; a constitutional crisis ensues.

1929   Stock market collapses. Aird Commission report on public broadcasting favours nationalization of radio.

1930   Great Depression begins. R.B. Bennett's Conservatives are elected to power in Ottawa.

1931   Canadian government arrests and imprisons eight leaders of the Communist Party.

1932   Co-operative Commonwealth Federation is founded in Calgary. Bennett government forms the Canadian Radio Broadcasting Commission.

1933   Depression sees huge unemployment rolls. Regina Manifesto is adopted by the CCF. Maurice Duplessis becomes leader of the Conservative Party of Quebec. T. Dufferin Pattullo wins election in British Columbia.

1935   R.B. Bennett announces a 'New Deal' for Canada, but is defeated by W.L.M. King in the election. Social Credit under William Aberhart sweeps to power in Alberta. Duplessis forms the Union Nationale. The On-to-Ottawa Trek is suppressed at Regina.

1936   Canadian Broadcasting Corporation is formed.

1937   General Motors strike in Oshawa. Royal Commission on Dominion–Provincial Relations is appointed. Lord Tweedsmuir creates the Governor General's awards.

Canadian troops returning from action after defeating the Bavarians at Vimy Ridge in 1917. This was just one of many battles in which Canadians bravely fought during World War I. Canadian soldiers played an integral role in helping the Allied Forces claim victory in Europe. CWM 19920085-292, George Metcalf Archival Collection Canadian War Museum.

Continued

Timeline Continued

1939   Canada declares war on Germany. British Commonwealth Air Training Plan is founded.

1940   Royal Commission on Dominion–Provincial Relations recommends restructuring of public finances.

1941   Emily Carr wins Governor General's award for *Klee Wyck*. Hong Kong surrenders to Japan. Pearl Harbor attacked.

1942   Dieppe raid sees 2,700 Canadians killed or captured. National plebiscite held to release government from non-conscription pledge.

1943   Marsh report on social security is tabled in the House of Commons.

1944   Family Allowances Act and National Housing Act are passed.

The entrance of Canada into World War I marked a triumph of sorts for Canadian imperialism. Canada did not make its own declaration of war, but simply joined the British war effort. Before it ended, the war would inflict extremely heavy Canadian casualties: 60,661 killed in action and 172,000 wounded out of some 620,000 Canadians in uniform drawn from a population of only 8 million. The war gradually isolated French Canada and made possible sweeping national reforms on several fronts. Reform had always implied an interventionist state, and wartime conditions encouraged the Canadian government's intrusion into many new areas of life and work. The government's expenditures were enormous, but it managed to find the money to keep going, mainly through extensive borrowing. One of the new developments was a business profits tax, retroactive to the beginning of the war, introduced in 1916. Another was an income tax, first levied in 1917. Yet another was the nationalization of the railways. The war also accelerated and distorted virtually every economic development that Canada had experienced during the previous 40 years.

Canadians entered the war with no idea of its ultimate length, intensity, or futile savagery. The initial enthusiasm of English-speaking Canadians assumed a swift defeat of Germany and its allies. By 1917 support for the war effort emphasized the extent of the sacrifices already made. Families of the dead soldiers could emotionally rationalize their losses only by calling for more effort towards a final victory. Canada's military contribution was substantial. Nevertheless, Canadians who fought in Europe were almost exclusively volunteers. Serving as the shock troops of the British Empire, Canadians achieved an enviable reputation for bravery and fierceness. Their commanders continually placed them in the most difficult situations, and they performed well. The list of battles at which they fought heroically (and at heavy cost) was a long one, beginning at Ypres in 1915 and continuing through to the Belgian town of Mons, where fighting ended for the Canadians at 11 a.m. on 11 November 1918.

Life in the trenches—which was the main battle experience of most Canadian soldiers in World War I—was a nightmare, so hard to describe that most returning veterans did not really try. Loved ones at home seldom heard accounts of the trench experience, either in letters from the front or after the war. The social world of the trenches was a bizarre, surrealistic experience like no other to be found anywhere in the world. It is true that troops were rotated in and out of the front lines, but almost all experienced the danger and discomfort of life in the trenches at some point. Artillery shelling was constant, and reserves in the secondary and tertiary lines of fortifications were if anything shelled more heavily by large guns than those in the front lines; artillery crews always fired at longer-range targets for fear of hitting their own men. Periods of rotation were not standardized, and during times of crisis the stay in the front line could seem a lifetime. Actual attacks and offensives were relatively rare, but life in the trenches was extremely wearing; men faced not only the shelling and continual risk of sniper fire but difficulties in sleeping, bad food, and the ubiquitous mud, in which many men drowned. The worst thing about the mud was having to move through it. Most Canadian soldiers carried more than 60 pounds (27 kg) of equipment, and a mud-soaked greatcoat could weigh another 50 pounds (23 kg).

While in the front trenches, soldiers had to be constantly on the alert. They were regularly employed on 'fatigues', moving rations, stores, and wounded men, and repairing the trenches. Sleep deprivation was common. Soldiers suffered from the heat in summer and the cold in winter, and from rain virtually year-round. Corpses lay everywhere in the trenches and outside them, attracting rats and lice in great numbers. One Canadian remembered, 'Huge rats. So big they would eat a wounded man if he couldn't defend himself' (quoted in Ellis, 1975: 54). The trenches also stank of chloride of lime (a disinfectant), creosol (for the flies), human excrement and human sweat, and the putrefaction of decomposing bodies. Most soldiers were conscious not only of the stench but of the noise, especially the sounds of various sorts of artillery fire that were part of the continual bombardment in the trenches, particularly during offensives. Some could distinguish the various weapons by the noises they made. Dr Andrew Macphail, who served at the front with the 7th Canadian Field Ambulance, commented in his diary:

I amuse myself finding words to describe the sounds made by the various classes of guns. The 18 pounders thud, thud. The 4.7s bark like an infinite dachshund. The howitzers smash. The machine-guns rat-tat like the wood-pecker or the knocker of a door. A single rifle snaps like a dry twig when it is broken. Rapid rifle fire has a desolating sound; it is as if a load of small stones was being dumped from a Scotch cart. A large shell sounds exactly like a railway train; and shrapnel bursts as if boiler-plate were being torn into fragments, or as if the sky were made of sheet-iron, and had been riven by a thunderbolt. The whistle of the passing rifle bullet is unmistakable. (Macphail, 1915)

Many thought the worst things about the guns were the vibrations and the 'solid ceiling of sound'. By 1918 soldiers were also exposed to aerial attacks and bombardments. The Great War produced a new form of nervous illness, which came to be called 'shell shock', but which was really a combination of various assaults on the human nervous system.

Given the conditions under which the men operated, it becomes easier to understand how they could, from time to time, be led 'over the top' in open mass assaults or in raids in small parties—either way to risk death. Sleep-deprived and in a constant state of shock, most troops who actually engaged in battle were numb to virtually everything going on around them. They fought in a zombie-like state, and those who managed to return were totally exhausted. High command never really understood what the war was like in the trenches. The generals never appreciated that defensive firepower from a dug-in enemy meant that most attacks were nothing but human carnage. Field officers believed in the mystical value of intestinal fortitude. In April 1915, a Canadian regiment at Ypres withstood one of the first poison gas attacks, using for protection nothing but handkerchiefs soaked in urine. After beating back the enemy at great human cost and with other units retreating all around them, the regiment's colonel, supported by those remaining of his junior officers, volunteered to hold the line. He telephoned divisional headquarters and reported modestly, 'The 90th Rifles can hold their bit.' And they did. The

Lucy Maud Montgomery and the War

The following are excerpts from Lucy Maud Montgomery's journal for late 1914.

Monday, Dec. 7, 1914
Leaskdale, Ont.
A *Globe* headline today was 'The Germans Capture Lodz'.

This war is at least extending my knowledge of geography. Six months ago I did not know there was such a place in the world as Lodz. Had I heard it mentioned I would have known nothing about it and cared as little. To-day, the news that the Germans have captured it in their second drive for Warsaw made my heart sink into my boots. I know all about it now—its size, its standing, its military significance. And so of scores of other places whose names have been lettered on my memory in blood since that fateful 4th of August—Mlawa, Bzura, Jarolwav, Tomaskoff, Yser, Lys, Aisne, Marne, Prysmysl. At the last mentioned the newspaper wits have been poking fun since the siege of it began. Nobody seems to know how it is pronounced. I daresay the Austrians would think that Saskatchewan and Musquodoboit were about as bad.

The Manse, Leaskdale, Ont.
Thursday, Dec. 10, 1914

To-day at noon Ewan [her husband] came in jubilantly. 'Good news!' he said. I snatched the paper and read that a German squadron had been totally destroyed by a British one off the Falkland Isles. Coming after the long strain of the recent series of Russian reverses I rather went off my head. I waved the paper wildly in air as I danced around the dining room table and hurrahed. Yet hundreds of men were killed in the fight and hundreds of women's hearts will break because of it. Is that a cause for dancing and hurrahing? Oh, war makes us all very crude and selfish and primitive!

Saturday, Dec. 12, 1914

To-day's war news was better than it has been for some time—the second German invasion of Poland seems to have been definitely checked. Ever since it began—a fortnight or so ago—I have been wracked with dread. If Germany should smash Russia and then her victorious army back against the French and British lines! That thought was the Dweller on my Threshold. All through the forenoons I could manage to work and hold my dread at bay. But when at twelve I saw Ewan going out for the mail my nerve invariably collapsed. I could not do anything—it was of no use to try. I could not even read. I could only pace the floor like a caged tiger, nerving myself to meet the worst. Then when he came back I would snatch the *Globe* and desperately tear over the headlines. It has been agonizing.

Source: Mary Rubio and Elizabeth Waterston, eds, *The Selected Journals of L.M. Montgomery, vol. 2, 1910–1921* (Toronto: Oxford University Press, 1987), 157–8. Reprinted by permission of the publisher.

casualties in this one unit in this one battle ran at 20 officers and 550 men killed, wounded, missing, or gassed—out of a total complement of 900.

While dispatches spoke reassuringly of the value of the assaults and the heroism, the soldiers knew perfectly well that their sacrifices were achieving very little. Canadian casualties, like those of other settlement colonies, tended to run considerably higher than those of the armies of the European allies. Whether the colonials had less experience as soldiers, or were placed in the most dangerous places, or simply fought more savagely, is not entirely clear. On one

The Battle Diary of Deward Barnes

Deward Barnes was born in 1888 and enlisted at Toronto with the 180th Infantry Battalion on 26 February 1916 as an ordinary soldier. Throughout his wartime experience in France he kept a pocket diary, the entries in which he later transcribed in a larger diary. Deward was demobbed in 1919, returned to Canada, and lived in obscurity until his death in1967.

April 17, 1917 [near Mont-St. Eloi]: We were working on roads, reparing [sic] and filling in shell holes, in snow and rain. It was cold. We were at the Territorial Dump. 'Lousy,' we got back to Elk Trench and tried to sleep in dug-outs, but it was so lousy we had to get out and sleep in a trench full of mud. I had two rubber sheets, put one under me and one over. The rats were running over us all night. They didn't bother us, only you could hear and feel them running over your rubber sheet. This was an old trench, French, where they had battled nearly all through from the start of the war. Had been lost and retaken a few times and men had been blown to pieces, etc., then never found; the reason for so many rats.

8 May 1917 [in battle]. The shelling was terrible. It was realy [sic] heavy now as we got the whiz-bangs [German high-velocity artillery shells]. And he certain [sic] could send them fast. His field shells were a little lighter than ours, and he fired them faster. Always when he was going to make a drive in the monting [sic] he shelled all night long; where the British saved them up for zero hour and surprise. But Fritzie worried us. He never let up. He kept those whiz-gangs [sic] and heavies going fast from 2:00 a.m., until daybreak. . . . The whiz-bangs sounded just as thought [sic] they were just missing the tops of our trenches, and going over the hollow trench gave them a peculiar sharp sound, besides the whiz. It made you think of home. Our corporal told us not to be afraid, to look over, only don't move when a flare went up. The rain never stopped. The trenches were all caving in and puddles of mud and water. We were soaked through hours ago and thick with mud. We watched. We knew they were coming and fear had left me by that time. My eyes must have been half out of my head with excitement. . . . Finally, about 4 a.m. or just about daybreak, one of the boys says, 'There they are.' I couldn't see them just then and finally I saw one within a stone's throw away and then dozens of them. The front line of the Germans had been skirmishing and in the distance there were four lines of Germans. You could not see between them. . . . [An] officer came up to us (as he was helping the battalion get out) and said, 'Well, boys, we are done, do your duty and fight to the finish. We stuck, [f]ear had left us. I was never so cool before. I did not bayonet any, but some did. The Germans were behind us, some killed just as they were about to get into our trenches, some sitting on top of our trenches dead, but looked alive. . . . We hung on. . . . It was around 1:00 p.m. when the orders were sent to us from the rear to get back to the sunken road. It seemed miles back. We were the last to get out. It had been raining hard all the time, and the shells and the trenches caving in had buried men who had been wounded and killed. The trenches were full of dead Germans and our own men. In the front line your [sic] miss most of the shells but back farther it was terrible, hundreds of dead were lying on the part we saw alone. There were hands sticking out of the mud and just faces. Some looked peaceful and others out of shape. The sight was terrible. It was that stick clay. Every time you would go to lift your foot it would stick, and then stick to the other. You would sink to the tops of your boots in mud, trying not to step on faces, etc. And nothing to eat, no sleep, excited and dead tired and trying to get back as fast as you can. It was hell.

Source: Bruce Cane, ed., *It Made You Think of Home: The Haunting Journal of Deward Barnes, Canadian Expeditionary Force: 1916–1919* (Toronto: Dundurn Group, 2004), 67, 78–83. Reprinted by permission of The Dundurn Group.

horrible day in 1916 at Ypres, 684 Newfoundlanders were trapped by barbed wire and mowed down by German machine guns; 310 died. While it was possible to be invalided back to Britain ('Blight') or even Canada with a serious enough wound (often called 'a blighty'), most of the Canadian soldiers sent to Europe either died on the battlefield or remained on the lines until the Armistice.

Despite these sacrifices, the Canadian government had to fight hard for a voice in imperial war policy. It also worked hard to maintain separate Canadian unit and command structures. The arguments for autonomy—and the manpower necessary to sustain them—dragged the government ever deeper into the quagmire. By the time of Vimy in April 1917, Canada could no longer recruit new volunteers to replace the mounting casualties. The government saw conscription as the only solution. Conscription was a policy intensely opposed by

A recruitment poster. Archives of Ontario, MU 2052, #40, F 895 (1915). Recruiting Circulars.

many French Canadians. From the standpoint of Anglo-Canadians, French Canada had not borne its fair share of the burden of war. English Canada argued that less than 5 per cent of the Canadian volunteers had come from French Canada. On the other hand, French Canadians came to feel increasingly under attack by English Canada. As a symbol of their position they focused on the plight of francophones in Ontario, where in 1915 Regulation 17 had seemingly imposed unilingualism on the elementary school system. Virtually all French-Canadian members of Parliament opposed the Military Service Act, which became law in August 1917. In its wake, and with a federal election coming, a Union government was formed out of the Conservatives and those English-speaking members of the Liberal Party who had broken with Laurier over his opposition to conscription.

French Canada was not alone in becoming isolated by the war. Members of Canada's other ethnic minorities, many of them originating in parts of Germany and the Austro-Hungarian Empire, found themselves under attack. The government became increasingly repressive as the war continued. It interned 'aliens' by Order-in-Council and suppressed much of the foreign-language press. The Wartime Elections Act of September 1917 ruthlessly disenfranchised Canadians of enemy origin. Organized labour found itself shackled. The government introduced compulsory arbitration into all war industries in 1916. In the crisis year of 1917, the government announced its intention to outlaw all strikes and lockouts. The Union government was simultaneously bipartisan and sectional. It was able to implement several national reforms favoured by its Anglo-Canadian supporters. Many provinces had allowed women the vote earlier in the war. The Wartime Elections Act in 1917 granted the federal electoral franchise to women with close relatives in the war. In 1918 all women got the vote federally. Prohibition also triumphed nationally in 1918, not only to keep the soldiers pure and to ensure that the country to which they returned would be a better place to live but also to prevent waste and inefficiency. Daylight savings added an hour of light to the workday. Previous arguments about infringing personal liberty lost their cogency during wartime.

Canadian industry—at least in central Canada and industrial Nova Scotia—benefited directly from the war. By March 1915 over 200 firms had converted to munitions manufacture. Later in 1915 the government set up the Imperial Munitions Board, chaired by businessman Joseph Flavelle (1858–1939). Canadian munitions production increased dramatically, raising the export of iron and steel products from $68.5 million in 1915 to $441.1 million only two years later. The Canadian munitions industry employed 200,000 workers in 673 factories.

By 1917 the Imperial Munitions Board alone had an annual budget three times that of the federal government in 1914. In the latter years of the war nearly 40 per cent of Canadian manufacturing products found export markets. The high point came in 1918 when Canadian manufacturing exports reached $636 million and total exports peaked at $1.54 billion.

As for Canadian agriculture, it could not produce enough in the short run. From 1914 to 1919 in Canada as a whole, agricultural acreage under cultivation doubled. Wheat prices trebled, and western farmers expanded the size and number of their farms. The federal government created a national

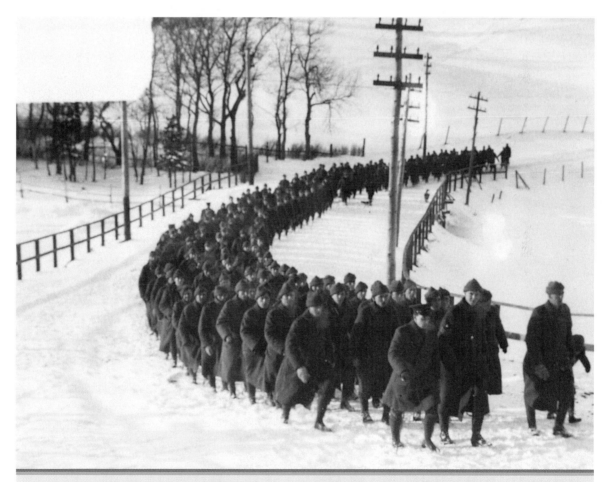

The Newfoundland Regiment, D Company, near St John's, 1915. On 1 July 1916 the Newfoundlanders would see their first action in France. Of the 801 who fought that day at Beaumont-Hamel, in the first engagement of the battle of the Somme, more than 700 were killed, wounded, or reported missing. The Rooms, Provincial Archives of Newfoundland and Labrador, E 22–45.

Wheat Board in 1917 to facilitate marketing. The number of prairie farms actually increased by 28 per cent between 1911 and 1921. Although the sons of Canadian farmers could gain exemption from conscription, by the time the draft was introduced in 1917 there were few young men left on the farms. Rural Canada, especially in the West, had outdone the remainder of the country in volunteer enlistment. The result was an increase in labour costs, which forced farmers to buy more agricultural equipment. Increased production also pushed up the price of land. Farmers therefore increased production by borrowing money at high rates of interest. Farm debt increased substantially. High prices also encouraged farmers to move cultivation onto marginal land while abandoning most of the tested techniques of soil and moisture conservation hitherto practised. The result of all this expansion would be an inevitable disaster when the price of grain and other crops ultimately fell on the international market.

One of many casualties of the war was civil liberty in Canada. The War Measures Act, passed at war's beginning, was a blank cheque allowing the government to censor writing and speech, as well as to arrest, detain, and even deport those regarded as obstructing the war effort. As a nation of immigrants, Canada inevitably contained citizens and residents whose homelands were part of the enemy, the so-called 'enemy aliens'. Although the bulk of such people were German, most of those persecuted and interned were citizens of the Austro-Hungarian Empire, chiefly people of Ukrainian origin. After

A Canadian battalion going 'over the top', October 1916. LAC, PA-648.

1917 and the Bolshevik Revolution, the activities of radical ethnic organizations came under heavy scrutiny, and the Dominion government was easily persuaded that the Ukrainian community was the centre of Bolshevism in Canada. Thus, on the eve of the Armistice, two Orders-in-Council suppressed the foreign-language press and most socialist/anarchist organizations.

The Great War had a profound impact on Canada in almost all aspects of life. Its rhetorical side was one of present sacrifice for future benefits. This war-to-end-all-wars would make the world safe for democracy. An era of full social justice would follow the great victory. That the Canadian government had ignored democratic civil liberties in fighting the war was an irony escaping most contemporaries.

The war's conclusion amounted to a triumph for Protestant Anglo-Canada, with little thought given to the tomorrows that would follow the coming of peace. A nation that had drawn heavily on its resources was really not ready to deal with the negative legacies of its efforts.

Only days after the Armistice was declared in November 1918, Prime Minister Sir Robert Borden went to Europe to head the Canadian delegation at the Peace Conference. Canada's participation at Paris beginning in January 1919 was less concerned with the disposition of European and international problems than it was with its own status in dealing with that disposition. This was a policy agreed upon in advance by the Union cabinet in Ottawa, although much Canadian public opinion would

During World War I, Ukrainians were one of several nationalities dubbed 'enemy aliens'. Many of these people were imprisoned in Canadian internment camps, such as the camp and internees shown here, at Castle Mountain, Alberta. Glenbow Archives, NA–1870–6.

Sir Robert Borden on Canadian Representation at Versailles

In his *Memoirs*, originally published in 1938 and based on his diaries kept at the time, Sir Robert Borden wrote the following.

The subject [of representation] was first debated informally at conferences between the British and Dominion Ministers, and afterwards in the formal meetings of the Imperial War Cabinet. It was assumed that only five places could be secured for the British Empire at the Peace Conference. The panel system, under which the representation of the British Empire at the sessions of the Peace Conference would be selected from day to day, as the nature of the subject demanded, was not regarded as satisfactory in itself.

Finally, I proposed that in the general representation of the British Dominions, the panel system might be utilized when necessary or appropriate but that there should be distinctive representation for each Dominion on the same basis as was to be accorded to the smaller nations of the Allied Powers. This proposal was eventually accepted at the preliminary conference in London between representatives of the British Empire, France, and Italy.

But all the difficulties had by no means been overcome. When the question of procedure, including that of representation, came before the Peace Conference on January 12, 1919, the proposal for distinctive representation for the British Dominions aroused strong opposition. The subject was further discussed in the British Empire Delegation, which was really the Imperial War Cabinet under another name; and the Dominions, standing firmly upon the principle recognized in London, declined to accept an inferior status. In the result, there insistence prevailed; and through a combination of the panel system together with their own distinctive representation, the Dominions secured a peculiarly effective position.

Elsewhere I have said, and here I emphatically repeat, that Canada and the other Dominions would have regarded the situation as intolerable if they, who numbered their dead by the hundred thousands in the fiercest struggle the world had ever known, should stand outside the council chamber of the Conference, while nations that had taken no direct or active part in the struggle stood within and determined the conditions of Peace. . . .

We were lodged at the Hotel Majestic where I had a very commodious bedroom and sitting-room. The British had brought over an entire staff for the hotel as they were afraid to utilize a French staff, lest important information leak out. As a result, we had typical English meals, altogether too heavy for persons habitually deprived of normal opportunities for exercise. I used to escape the dinners two or three times a week and content myself with an apple, a glass of water, and a long walk. This regimen enabled me to survive. On one occasion I avoided dinner for ten consecutive evenings.

[Feb. 4 1919] That evening, Foster [Sir George Foster] and I went with the Dowager Duchess of Sutherland to dine with Lord Brooke at the Café Escargot, where we had an excellent meal to which we did ample justice except the snails included in the menu. After dinner we attended the Theatre St. Martin to see *Cyrano de Bergerac*, beautifully acted but sad in its ending. We were invited to supper by the leading lady of the piece, 'Roxanne,' and at her apartment we met Percival Langdon of the *Morning Post*. We had an excellent supper and a most enjoyable time. This was one of the friskiest evenings of Foster's life, as we kept him up until 1:15. I told him I never would have embarked on such an adventure without his presence as chaperon.

Source: *Robert Laird Borden: His Memoirs, vol. 2, 1916–1920* (Toronto: Macmillan, 1938), 908.

have preferred to stay away from Versailles entirely. Canada and the other dominions banded together to insist on being treated as independent nations at the Peace Conference rather than as part of the British imperial delegation. The principal opponent to this change of policy was not the British government, but the United States, backed by other participants, who insisted that autonomous dominions would enhance the British voice in the deliberations, which did not answer the dominions' claim that their commitment of manpower (and casualties) during the war entitled them to a separate say in the outcome.

Sir Robert Borden proved to have an influence on the conference greater than Canada's actual power in world affairs. The first breakthrough came in early January 1919, when President Woodrow Wilson conceded a representative from each dominion at the peace table. Sir Robert Borden responded by calling a meeting of the dominions, refusing to accept one representative, and demanding two. Wilson agreed to two representatives from Canada, Australia, South Africa, and India, and one for New Zealand. Newfoundland would have to sit as part of the British delegation. The dominions subsequently got the right to separate membership on new international organizations coming out of the treaty, including the League of Nations, and a separate signature on the treaty and conventions. Membership in the League, of course, implied liability for any commitments undertaken by that organization. Canada had achieved a new status in world affairs. Whether that status justified the numbers of dead and wounded was another matter.

Once the Great War had ended, most Canadians did their best to put the conflict behind them. Many hoped for the emergence of a more just society. Stephen Leacock well expressed the ambivalence of the post-war period in *The Unsolved Riddle of Social Justice* (1919). Recognizing that industrial society did not normally employ its full potential, Leacock could only hope that the destructive energy of war could be harnessed for peacetime reform. The unsolved riddle was simply stated: 'With all our wealth, we are still poor.' Every child, Leacock insisted, should have 'adequate food, clothing, education and an opportunity in life'. Unemployment should become a 'social crime' (Bowker, 1973: 74–80). Leacock did not offer specific solutions. Such a collective transformation would not be easy to accomplish. There were too many unresolved economic, constitutional, and social problems. The development of Canada over the next quarter-century demonstrated that at least in peacetime, Canadians still had great trouble coming to terms with the paradox Leacock had identified in 1919. During the Great Depression especially, the state seemed impotent to improve conditions. The politicians blamed the Constitution. Beginning in 1939, however, Canada would again demonstrate its capacity for waging total war within the constraints of the British North America Act.

Returning to 'Normalcy'

During demobilization Canada experienced one of the most devastating epidemics of modern times, the Spanish flu outbreak of 1918–19. The situation was so desperate in November 1918 that the government actually attempted, without success, to postpone public celebration of the Armistice for fear of spreading infection. Canadian deaths from the flu ultimately ran to 50,000—only some 10,000 thousand fewer than the number of Canadians who had died in battle. Fatalities had shifted from the trenches to the home front.

Yet another form of infectious epidemic made its appearance in 1919 with the great 'Red Scare'. The Bolshevik Revolution of 1917–18 in Russia provided the Canadian government and businessmen with an example of what might happen if popular unrest got out of hand. Political paranoia was as catching as the flu. Both the government and the business community became almost hysterical over the possibility that the revolution was nigh. The immediate focus of their concern was the Winnipeg General Strike of June 1919, but it had been preceded by the organization of the One Big Union, formed in Calgary in February amid considerable anti-capitalistic rhetoric. As usual, the Canadian government responded to anything smacking of popular uprising with repression.

Most of the conditions and issues that initially produced labour unrest in Winnipeg in the spring of 1919 were traditional ones exacerbated by the war: workers sought recognition of union rights to organize, higher wages, and better working conditions. A walkout by workers in the city's metal trades and building industries was quickly joined by others (as many as 50,000) in a general sympathy strike. On 15 May the strikers voted to close down the city's services. Much of the rhetoric of the strike sounded extremely radical. Some labour leaders hoped to use the general strike as a weapon to bring capitalism to its knees. Many demobilized servicemen supported the strikers. Worried businessmen saw the general strike as a breakdown of public authority. Workers in other cities, such as Toronto and Vancouver, responded with declarations of support and threats of their own strikes. The Canadian government, represented locally by acting Minister of Justice

Arthur Meighen (1874–1960), responded decisively. He supplemented the army with local militia, the Royal North West Mounted Police, and 1,800 special constables. The Canadian Naturalization Act was hastily amended in early June 1919 to allow for the instant deportation of any foreign-born radicals who advocated revolution or who belonged to 'any organization entertaining or teaching disbelief in or opposition to organized government' (quoted in Avery, 1986: 222). Most strikers were British or Canadian-born, but both the general public and the returning veterans were easily persuaded that what was needed was to 'clean the aliens out of this community and ship them back to their happy homes in Europe which vomited them forth a decade ago' (quoted in Bumsted, 1994: 66).

Arthur Meighen effectively broke the strike on 17 June when he authorized the arrest of 10 strike leaders on charges of sedition. On the 21st—'Black

Despite efforts to protect themselves from the Spanish flu outbreak of 1918–19, approximately 50,000 people died in Canada from the diesease. The Canadian Press.

The Spanish Flu Pandemic

I had a little bird
And its name was Enza.
I opened the window
And in-flew-Enza.
(children's skipping song of 1918)

The wild card in Canada's post-war experience in late 1918 and early 1919 was the pandemic always known as the Spanish flu. There are no real questions about the incidence, the extent of sickness, or even the number of deaths caused by the disease, which ran rampant across Canada between September 1918 and March 1919. The problem is that it is impossible to document any real correlation between the flu and anything else going on in Canada at the time. Disease has always seemed to exist separately and independently from other historical factors. Contemporaries talked openly about the connection between the high cost of living and popular discontent, for example, but advanced few arguments about any relationship between fatal illness and the socio-political dissatisfaction of 1919.

Few historians dealing with the unsettled conditions in North America in 1919 mention the flu and popular attitudes in the same breath. The flu's almost unthinkable extent and impact across Canada at the end of the war seems to have eluded historical attention, perhaps partly because it was obviously not of human agency and was seldom seen by those who lived through it as anything other than a disease that struck at individuals and families. It was seen by its victims as a danger to their bodies but not as a social problem menacing the body politic. Even the rediscovery of the virulence of the pandemic by historians beginning in the 1980s—resulting in a major increase in information about it—has not produced many attempts to connect influenza in a careful way to other events occurring at the same time or only a few months later.

The likelihood is that more than one virus was responsible for the epidemic's course worldwide.

The likelihood also is that the several viruses either mutated, or became much more virulent, during their travels around the world, or that other strains succeeded in jumping from animals to humans by either adaptation or hybridization. Early evidence of the beginnings of the flu in its milder forms can be seen in various parts of the world. One outbreak occurred in San Sebastién on the northern coast of Spain in February of 1918. The Spanish experience gave the disease its name, unfairly since there was no real evidence that its actual origins were Spanish. In its early incarnations, this 'three-day fever'—as the American Expeditionary Force called it—was not terribly menacing. The symptoms were typically flu-like in a way familiar to all of us. The victim suddenly became ill, running a high fever. The face became red, every bone in the body ached, the body perspired considerably, and there was usually an accompanying headache. The period of feeling really sick usually lasted only 72 to 96 hours, during which time the victim was practically comatose, although after rising from his or her bed the victim remained weak for a further seven to 10 days. The disease was highly contagious.

At some point over the summer of 1918, this relatively mild influenza (with low mortality rates), which had affected Europe and the United States up to this point, mutated or morphed into a more virulent disease. The new variety (or varieties) was far more deadly. Some victims became extremely ill almost instantly with symptoms of extreme pneumonia, exhibiting high fevers and lungs full of fluid. Others gradually developed pneumonia after a few days of what appeared to be the ordinary flu. Associated with the new influenza was a cyanosis that discoloured the face and the feet with a dark bluish, almost black, cast and a cough bringing up blood-stained sputum and mucus. Unlike the earlier outbreaks, these new ones were highly fatal. There were reports at hospitals of corpses stacked up like cordwood.

Canadian troops returning home in the late spring and early summer brought the flu back to Canada from Europe. How many of the troops were carrying the earlier strains of the virus and how many the newly mutated ones will never be known, although clearly the virulent form was being introduced into the nation from somewhere. Troop ships, military camps, and soldier movement via the railroads were probably the major means of spreading the flu across Canada. The flu apparently did not usually hit on the whole very hard at the very old and the very young,

who were the typical victims of most epidemic diseases. It hit hardest at young adults, who were in most epidemics the most immune.

The flu devastated most large cities in Canada. In the rural districts, where houses were often far apart and isolated but relatively safe from infection unless it was introduced from outside, farm people often did exactly the wrong thing, fleeing to towns and villages to find companionship and medical assistance and thus increasing the likelihood of the spread of infection. Certainly the pandemic hit with especial fury against the First Nations. The death rate from influenza among Canadian Native peoples in these years overall was 37.7 per thousand, while the flu death rate per thousand was 14.3 in Toronto, 16.7 in Winnipeg, and 23.3 in Vancouver. Before it was over in the spring of 1919, approximately 50,000 Canadians had died.

Saturday'—a public demonstration of strikers and returned soldiers, marching towards the Winnipeg city hall, was met by a charge of Mounties on horseback. The result was a violent melee that injured many, killed two strikers, and led to the arrest of a number of 'foreign rioters'. This degree of violence, precipitated by the authorities, was unusual during the strike, perhaps because provincial prohibition in 1916 had closed bars and beverage rooms, making it difficult to get drunk and disorderly in public. Black Saturday happened despite the best efforts of the strike leaders to prevent the demonstration from going forward. The Strike Committee subsequently agreed to call off the strike if a Royal Commission investigated it and its underlying causes. The Royal Commission, called by the province of Manitoba, found that much of the labour unrest in Winnipeg was justified and that the strike's principal goal was to effect the introduction of collective bargaining. On the other hand, the Manitoba Court of Queen's Bench convicted most of the arrested leaders (who were either British- or Canadian-born) on charges of sedition. The Department of Immigration held deportation hearings for the 'foreigners' in camera. The use of the civil arm to suppress radicalism,

long a part of the Canadian tradition, was given a new meaning in post-war Winnipeg. Perhaps most significantly, the strike and its handling by the government demonstrated the fragility of the post-war readjustment. The next decade would further emphasize the problems.

Regional Protest in the 1920s

The decade of the 1920s is usually associated with prosperity, but in truth the period faced great economic difficulties. The boom did not begin until 1924 and it was quite limited in its influence. The depression of 1920–3 had seen world prices for resource products fall abruptly, while costs fell much more gradually. Prosperity finally came from substantial growth in new housing construction and a great wave of consumer spending, both understandable after the war and subsequent depression. There was a major expansion of consumer credit facilities to finance the new spending. An advertising industry quickly developed to promote consumerism. Speculative activities—in real estate, in the stock market, and in commodity futures—all flourished. So did gambling, both in the stock market and in games of chance; Canadians bet on almost anything. However, much of the boom was at best internal, at worst artificial. International markets, except in the United States, were very soft. The traditional resource sectors of the economy had suffered most from the worldwide fall in prices, although they recovered somewhat in the latter years of the decade. Only Ontario's economy really prospered, chiefly on the strength of the manufacture of the motor car both for domestic consumption and for export into a British Empire protecting itself against the Americans. The economy of the Maritime provinces continued to decline precipitously, since both the power revolution and the new industrialization bypassed them while foreign markets (especially for fish) continued to decline.

Despite the government's brutal suppression of the Winnipeg General Strike, industrial unrest remained high through 1925. The One Big Union, a radical and militant industrial union, flourished briefly in western Canada. In 1921 labour representatives sat in seven of nine provincial legislatures. In the federal election of that year, more than 30 labour candidates ran for office, although only four were actually elected. Labour unrest after Winnipeg was most prevalent in the geographical extremes of

The Winnipeg General Strike, 21 June 1919. Provincial Archives of Manitoba, N2771, Foote Collection 1705.

the country. There were a number of notable strikes in Cape Breton, Alberta, and British Columbia. In the coalfields, 22,000 miners were on strike in August 1922. Several unions were broken in some of the most bitter labour violence that Canada had ever seen. Tactics in the mining communities made Winnipeg seem like a Sunday school picnic. A number of movements, mainly regionally based, sprang up to protest inequalities in the national system. Their collective inability to effect much change—though they tried a variety of approaches—was, and is, instructive. One of the principal problems was the very difficulty of working together despite common complaints.

Certainly nobody felt harder done by after the Great War than the farmer. The movement of farm protest reached its height in the 1921 election, before the final wheat market collapse and the spread of drought conditions. Farmers in Anglo-Canada disliked inflation and had two specific economic grievances beyond the wheat price collapse of 1920. First, the wartime wheat marketing system had been abandoned by the government in 1919. Second, the government had failed to introduce serious tariff reform to lower the costs of farming. Behind these complaints was a long-standing farmer conviction that the political system operated to the advantage of profiteering central Canadian capitalists. Farmer discontent was national in scope, although western farmers were the most alienated. The new Progressive Party, formed in 1920, won 64 seats in the 1921 federal election in six provinces: 37 on the prairies, 24 in Ontario, one in New Brunswick, and two in British Columbia. Joining 50 Conservatives and 117 Liberals, the Progressives broke the established two-party tradition. But despite occasional farmer–labour alliances, the two major groups of malcontents were unable to unite politically for change.

Helen Jury Armstrong

Helen Armstrong (1875–1947) was born in Toronto and moved to Winnipeg from New York with her husband George, a labour leader, in 1905. She shared with her husband a firm belief in socialism and labour radicalism, and developed a considerable reputation as a feminist radical in Winnipeg during the Great War. She opposed the detention of 'aliens' and the introduction of conscription from numerous public platforms. In 1918 she was elected president of the Hotel and House Workers' Union in Winnipeg, and in February 1919 she resigned as president of the Women's Labour League when it supported the provincial Minimum Wage Board in recommendations that she felt were not in the best interests of female workers. Despite her break with the Women's Labour League, she ran the kitchen maintained by the League during the Winnipeg General Strike. It fed several hundred strikers every day. By this time she had acquired her nickname of 'Ma' Armstrong, and she would be subsequently dubbed by eastern newspapers 'the Wild Woman of the West'.

During the strike Armstrong was arrested on several occasions for 'disorderly conduct', usually the result of public demonstrations and agitations, often in support of female strikers. When her husband was arrested in June 1919 by the federal government for seditious libel, she became active in various campaigns to free him from arrest and, later, imprisonment. After George's incarceration in Stony Mountain Penitentiary, Helen organized concerts of children singing radical songs outside the prison. She ran unsuccessfully for the Winnipeg city council in 1923, and subsequently departed Canada for Chicago with her husband. She died in California. Virtually forgotten for many years, she more recently was the subject of a major documentary film, *The Notorious Mrs. Armstrong* (2001).

Coal Mining in Cape Breton

In 1990 Earle Peach wrote a memoir of what he called his 'childhood', which included an account of his first days at Number 22 Colliery, Birch Grove. He began working in the mines at the age of 17.

Mother had filled another lunch can. At five-thirty in the morning I slung it over my shoulder and tramped with a few others over the familiar path along the washer drain, past the old wash plant, through the woods to Morrison Lake, and along the lake to No. 22 Colliery. In the wash house Newfoundlanders, Frenchmen, Poles, Hungarians, MacDonalds, MacRaes, and Smiths, bleary-eyed and sleepy, flailed a writhing mass of limbs in all directions as they wrestled on their pit clothes. Bearlike torsos, dirty backs (many miners washed only their faces), clear backs, bristly backs incredibly muscular, small retracted penises, huge flopping penises—obscene, good natured kidding in a dozen dialects—these were the men who worked in the coal mine, and I was to become one of them. . . .

When a week or so had passed, it no longer seemed strange to walk down out of the brilliant sunlight, out of the fresh air, into total darkness that took five or ten minutes before one's eyes adjusted to the reduced light of one's headlamp and one's nose accepted the fetid, mouldy air of decay common to a mine. Air from a huge compressor on the surface was driven down a carefully constructed air course, circulated slowly through all the work areas, and returned up the main haulage way, ensuring that no significant accumulation of deadly gasses could occur. Yet in most places you were unaware of any body change. When you were working, sweat streamed from your body, but when you sat down for five minutes, you were shivering. Add to this the fact that you could seldom stand up without stooping except where the 'roof' had been 'brushed'; the coal seam was five feet thick, but in the air course, the chief haulage areas, an extra foot of shale was taken down chiefly to ensure that it would not fall down and block traffic or slow air circulation. This left a roof of solid stone generally considered safe. As coal seams went, the Gowrie seam was of generous thickness; the harbour seam on which Glace Bay collieries nos. 11 and 24 operated was only three and a half feet thick and required a good deal more stooping. . . .

At No. 22 Colliery the coal seam emerged to the surface, and . . . the main slope had been driven down the seam. At one-thousand-foot intervals, landings or levels were broken off east and west from the slope; the term 'level' is a relative one, for convenient operation preferred a slight slope in the level. At similar intervals along the level, 'headways' were driven up and 'deeps' driven down the slope of the seam, each conforming to the twenty degree angle. This might be more easily visualized by picturing a level as a road built horizontally across the mid-slope of a mountain; roads going up the mountain from it are headways, those leading down from it are deeps. At one-hundred-foot intervals up the headways and down the deeps, 'rooms' were broken off, assigned numbers, and turned over to a pair of miners known at that time as 'butties'; these did the actual mining. The average headway or deep could employ thirty pairs of miners paid by the ton for the coal they mined. A miner at the 'face' could earn fifteen to twenty-five dollars per day, which in 1926 was a lot of money, considerably more than the mine manager earned. Within their room a pair of miners were the lords of creation, and God help anyone or anything that prevented them from 'getting their coal out'. This was free enterprise, indeed.

Source: Earle Peach, *Memoirs of a Cape Breton Childhood* (Halifax: Nimbus, 1990), 112–13. Reprinted with permission.

Though they were entitled to become the official opposition, the Progressives were badly divided. Former Liberals wanted free trade, while the farm protestors sought more radical reform. The farm wing, led by Alberta's Henry Wise Wood (1860–1941), wanted to scrap the existing party system. It sought instead to focus on farmer grievances. The only actions the two wings could agree upon were negative. The Progressives would not become the official opposition, and they would not join in coalition with the Liberals, now led by William Lyon Mackenzie King (1874–1950). As a result, the inexperienced farmer MPs were unable to accomplish anything substantial in Ottawa when economic conditions in western Canada worsened. The King government provided token programs to gain the support of moderate Progressives. Meanwhile, drought and the worldwide collapse of wheat prices beginning in 1921 produced a widespread inability to meet mortgage payments. Much of the land in the dry-belt region reverted to the state for unpaid taxes. Its inhabitants went either to the cities or, in many cases, back to the United States. Surviving farmers became too disheartened to support a party that had accomplished little in Ottawa, and the Progressives quickly disappeared.

A similar fate befell the major eastern expression of protest, the Maritime Rights movement. Maritimers had difficulty joining western farmers in a common cause. The easterners sought not free trade but increased protectionism, as well as lower railway freight rates. The region was acutely conscious of its increasing impotency in Confederation, as its population base continued to decline proportionally to central Canada and the West. By the end of 1921, regional discontent found expression in the Maritime Rights movement, which combined an insistence on equitable freight rates with a series of particular provincial demands. The result was a widespread, if brief, public agitation. Eschewing the third-party route of the Progressives, the Maritime Rights

The 'dust bowl': the prairies in the 1930s. Agriculture and Agri-Food Canada. Reproduced with the permission of the Minister of Public Works and Government Services Canada, 2006.

leaders decided in 1923 to appeal to the remainder of the country over the head of Ottawa. Although a major national advertising and public relations campaign on behalf of Maritime concerns had some success, it was not enough. When Maritimers started voting Conservative in 1923 by-elections, this merely annoyed the King government. After a Royal Commission investigated Maritime grievances, the Liberals bought off the region with concessions on freight rates, subsidies, and port development. None of these concessions touched fundamental economic problems. In the end, working through the two-party system achieved no more than the creation of a third party. The inability of regional protest in the Maritimes and the West to find common ground was palpable—and significant. Neither side could see beyond its regional interests. Clever federal politicians, like Mackenzie King, could play the game of divide and rule with impunity.

While the West and the Maritimes produced their ineffectual protests, Quebec turned increasingly inward. It pursued a nationalism that was at

Ernest Lapointe

Ernest Lapointe. J. Russell & Sons/Library and Archives Canada/C-019104.

Ernest Lapointe (1876–1941) was born in St-Eloi, Quebec. He attended Rimouski College and then Laval University, being called to the bar in 1898. Six years later he became Kamouraska's Liberal MP. He was a staunch supporter of Wilfrid Laurier, but remained on the back benches for many years, although in Laurier's last days he was becoming more prominent, leading the Liberals in the debate over the Ontario Schools Question. In 1919 he was elected to Laurier's old riding in Quebec East. He came into his own under Mackenzie King, who appreciated his loyalty to the party and to the administration. King placed him in two patronage portfolios—Marine and Fisheries, 1921–4, and Justice, 1924–30 and 1935–41—and treated Lapointe as his lieutenant in Quebec. As Fisheries Minister, he signed the Halibut Treaty with the United States in 1923, the first treaty signed by Canada itself rather than Britain.

Lapointe went with King to the Imperial Conferences of 1926 and 1931, supporting Canadian autonomy in international matters all the way. Domestically, Lapointe was in favour of tariff reduction and provincial rights, although he was the Minister of Justice who disallowed Social Credit's reformist legislation in Alberta because it infringed on federal rights. He was very cautious about federal interference in Quebec. But he also used federal patronage to great effect in the province, leading many to call Quebec a Liberal fiefdom. At the beginning of World War II, Lapointe promised Quebec there would be no conscription, and thus brought the voters of the province on side for the Liberals and the war. His death in 1941 left Mackenzie King without a French-Canadian lieutenant of stature during most of the war.

least partly a reaction against its increasing sense of isolation from the remainder of Canada. The chief outlet for this nationalism was the journal *L'Action Française*, founded on the eve of the Conscription Crisis by the Ligue des droits de français. This movement began with a crusade to save the French language, but gradually shifted into broader issues. Inspiration for both movement and journal came from Abbé Lionel Groulx (1878–1967). Groulx worried about the survival of the traditional religion and culture in the face of an ever more materialistic environment. From the French-Canadian perspective, that environment was increasingly 'in the middle of an immense Anglo-Saxon ocean' (quoted in Cook, 1969b: 193). In the 1920s Groulx denied that he was a separatist, although his arguments pointed in that direction. He called for a commitment to build the Quebec economy, preparing for a future in which Confederation would come to an end. By the late 1920s, Groulx had proved more successful at refashioning the history of French Canada than at gaining widespread public support.

The Depression and Responses To It

The stock market failed in October 1929, with Wall Street leading the way in a record collapse of stock prices everywhere in North America. Contrary to popular opinion, this disaster was fairly independent of the Depression that followed it. That Depression was really the cumulative result of the worldwide fall in prices, which had never readjusted from the inflation of wartime and the deflation of the post-war period. An international inability to buy left Canada and other resource producers, such as Argentina and Australia, with decreased orders for their products. Trade deficits quickly mounted. Nations that owed Canada money were unable to pay. The dollar fell, and in 1931 so did a number of major Canadian financial institutions, brokerage agencies, and insurance companies. The country would not recover until after the eruption of another war in 1939. For most Canadians, the 1930s depression was always

the Great Depression. Canadians lived in its shadow for decades to come. Those generations who had experienced its effects were always sympathetic to calls for social justice.

What the Depression meant, first and foremost, was unemployment. Official statistics are totally meaningless as a measure of the extent of joblessness, much less its significance. According to the publication *Historical Statistics in Canada* (1983), reflecting contemporary government data, unemployment in Canada rose from 116,000 in 1929 to 741,000 in 1932 to 826,000 in 1933, ultimately declining to 411,000 in 1937 and increasing to 529,000 in 1939. These figures, while substantial enough in a nation of only 10 million, hardly reflected the reality. No farmers or fishers, or their families, counted among the ranks of the unemployed at this time. The government regarded them as self-employed businessmen. Women out of work did not count either. Thus unemployment in the depths of the Depression, around 1933, ran to more than 27 per cent in the non-agricultural sector, but probably more than 50 per cent overall. At the same time, a farmer whose expenses exceeded his income was probably better off than a jobless city dweller whose expenses similarly exceeded his income. Farmers at least had some land on which food could be grown. Moreover, provincial governments tended to respond to the plight of the farmers, who made up a substantial proportion of the electorate in many provinces. The rural population actually grew in this decade as members of farm families returned from the city to the family farm.

The fall in prices meant that times were good for those with jobs, although almost everyone held their breath each time payday rolled around. As for Canadian business corporations, outside the financial sector there was little permanent damage. Most large corporations ruthlessly retrenched and waited for better times. Canadian business corporations actually suffered losses only in 1932 because they had been too slow to limit operations. In 1933, the lowest point on the economic curve, they ended collectively in the black.

The real victims of the Depression were the urban unemployed, who found that their relief became the

By 1933, unemployment in Canada had risen to 50 per cent overall, forcing people to line up for jobs, food, and social assistance. Toronto Star/The Canadian Press.

great political football of the period. Traditionally, Canadian municipalities and private charities had cared for the poor and jobless. The challenge in the 1930s was more than any city could handle, at least without the full co-operation and assistance of senior levels of government. R.B. Bennett (1870–1947), Prime Minister from 1930 to 1935, personally assisted from his own pocket many people who wrote him begging letters while he was in office, but Bennett had long opposed the dole system and insisted that the provinces were responsible for social welfare. The provinces, in turn, maintained that they lacked the appropriate taxing power. They passed the problem to the municipalities, which had to support the unemployed on declining revenue from property taxes that provided about 80 per cent of municipal revenue. Municipal assistance was grudging, almost always taking the form of

credit vouchers to be redeemed at local stores rather than as cash, which might be spent on 'frivolities' or worse. The relief lines were not called 'the dole' for nothing. Cities often advised single unemployed men to go elsewhere and even paid their rail tickets out of town. The constitutional wrangling between the provinces and the federal government seemed quite irrelevant to Canadians looking for help.

Only in 1935, on the eve of a federal election, did R.B. Bennett become a convert to interventionist strategies. He announced his new policy, a 'New Deal' for Canada, in a live radio address to the nation early in January 1935, saying, 'I am for reform. I nail the flag of progress to the mast. I summon the power of the state to its support.' Bennett spoke of legislation regulating working conditions, insuring against unemployment, and extending credit to the farmer. Unfortunately for Bennett, his radio proclamations ran well ahead of the practical legislative program he and his cabinet had ready for Parliament. The Canadian electorate, moreover, was understandably suspicious of last-minute conversions. Instead, the voters brought back Mackenzie King's Liberals, who offered few promises but had the solid backing of Quebec.

R.B. Bennett's 'conversion' to New Dealism involved more than a desperate wish to return to office. It also represented a growing realization by large parts of the Canadian business and professional communities that stabilizing the nation's economy was necessary to prevent a more serious upheaval. Many leading businessmen and financiers were in favour of state intervention, not so much because they believed in social justice as because they wanted economic stability for capitalism. The prevailing political and economic system of Canada was under attack from many directions in the 1930s. Canadian politicians and businessmen did not

need to look to Germany or Italy to find examples of radical responses to economic problems. What European experience did point out, however, was that radicalism was not necessarily confined to the traditional left, to be associated with organized labour, socialism, or communism. The great fear was that a demagogue of any political persuasion would emerge, offering simple but final solutions to a frustrated electorate. Canada had its share of prospective demagogues. Most of their success came on the provincial rather than on the federal level, however. All were advocates of provincial rights. This blunted their national effectiveness. Agreeing to bash Ottawa together was never a very creative strategy unless agreement could be reached on what to do next. About all these leaders had in common were their own curious mixtures of radical rhetoric and fundamentally conservative attitudes.

Perhaps the most successful radical response came in Alberta, where the Social Credit Party

In this Depression-era photo, four men share a bed and three others sit on the floor. LAC, C-013236.

mobilized a population that had suffered heavily from drought and depression. The leader of Social Credit in Alberta was a Calgary radio preacher, William Aberhart (1878–1943), who since 1924 had used his Sunday broadcasts for the Prophetic Bible Institute over CFCN (Canada's most powerful radio station at the time) to build up a substantial personal following attracted to Protestant fundamentalism. In 1932 Aberhart added a secular dimension to his broadcasts, following his personal conversion to the economic ideas of a Scottish engineer named C.H. Douglas. An unconventional monetary theorist, Douglas claimed that capitalism's failure lay in its inability to translate its production into purchasing power for the mass of people. Douglas

advocated distributing money—'social credit'—to bridge the gap between production and consumption. Neither Aberhart nor his Alberta audience ever truly understood Douglas's monetary theories, but both understood that the state would issue a social dividend, eventually set by Aberhart at $25 per month, to all citizens as part of their cultural heritage. With the assistance of Ernest Manning (1908–96), Aberhart organized the Social Credit Party early in 1935. The new party swept to success at the polls, taking 56 of 63 seats and winning 54 per cent of the popular vote in the 1935 provincial election. The federal government (and courts) opposed much of its original legislative program, particularly mortgage, debt, and banking legislation, eventually

The Bennett Buggy

In his autobiographical account *O Little Town: Remembering Life in a Prairie Village*, Harlo L. Jones recalls the 'Bennett buggy'.

Among the buggies and wagons, there stood always a few examples of that symbol of the Depression, the Bennett buggy. The Bennett buggy was named, much to his chagrin, after R.B. Bennett, who had the misfortune to be Conservative Prime Minister of Canada from 1930 to 1935, during the worst years of the Depression. . . . There probably couldn't be a more fitting symbol of the Depression than the Bennett buggy. Originally it had been an automobile, most often a Model T Ford, and it is difficult to say whether the buggy evolved or the car devolved. At first it was nothing more than the automobile fitted with a tongue and whiffletrees so that a team of horses could be hitched to it for economical motive power. As time went on and it began to seem that the Depression would never end, various segments and parts were removed and those remaining re-arranged until little was left but the chassis with its rubber-tired wheels.

With engine, transmission and radiator removed, the front seat might migrate forward until it was between the strong wheels, or the cowling, windshield and front seat might move forward as a unit. Some form of box was built on the chassis to make a general utility vehicle. Whatever form each might take, all were called Bennett buggies. From the standpoint of the horses, their greatest advantage was that they pulled much more easily than wagons with steel-rimmed wheels—that is, until the tires wore out. Nor were the left-over parts all discarded. Automobile seats became sofas or seats on farm wagons. Generators became wind electrics, propeller-driven to generate power for primitive six-vo[lt] farm lighting systems. Worn out tires were sliced in two longitudinally to make circular watering troughs for poultry. Engine blocks and other steel parts that hadn't rusted away disappeared in the scrap drives of the Second World War.

Source: Harlo L. Jones, *O Little Town: Remembering Life in a Prairie Village* (Winnipeg: University of Manitoba Press, 1995), 170.

disallowing 13 Alberta Acts. Social Credit moved to more traditional fiscal practices, blaming Ottawa and eastern big business for its inability to enact its program. (Under Aberhart and, following his death in 1943, under Manning, Social Credit won nine successive elections in Alberta and governed the province until 1971.)

The emergent popular leader in Quebec was Maurice Duplessis (1890–1959). Duplessis came from a family of Conservatives. In 1933 he became leader of the highly fragmented Conservative Party of Quebec. He found allies in two burgeoning Quebec movements of the early 1930s: the Catholic social action of the École social populaire, and the Liberal radicalism of the Action libérale nationale (ALN). From Catholic social action Duplessis took a program of government intervention to redistribute wealth,

protect farmers and workers, and regulate large corporations, all within the context of the Christian law of justice and charity. From the ALN he took an emphasis upon economic nationalism that called for liberation from colonial oppression through agrarian reform, new labour legislation, the promotion of small industry and commerce, and the destruction of the great financial establishments of the province. Duplessis negotiated the merger of the ALN with the Conservatives in 1935 to form the Union Nationale. The new party campaigned on the ALN's reform platform, winning an easy victory in the 1936 provincial election with 76 out of 90 seats and 58 per cent of the popular vote. Now 'prime minister' of Quebec, Duplessis quickly abandoned the reform program that had brought him to power. Instead, he concentrated power in his own hands. His considerable

Premier William Aberhart (front row, third from left) and cabinet, Edmonton, Alberta, 1935. Glenbow Archives, ND–3–7103a.

success in office relied on a nationalistic concern for provincial autonomy in federal–provincial relations, anti-communism, and calculated paternalistic grants and patronage for the disadvantaged. He carefully cultivated the Catholic hierarchy in the province. The Union Nationale's economic program consisted chiefly in giving American entrepreneurs a free hand to develop the province's resources.

Other provinces besides Quebec and Alberta also produced populist political leaders, although within the context of traditional party labels. In British Columbia, T. Dufferin (Duff) Pattullo (1873–1956) had led his Liberal Party to power in 1933 without sounding very radical. In office, however, Pattullo gradually became a convert to state activism of the New Deal variety. His government was arguably the most interventionist in Canada, held back only by the province's shortage of revenue. In Ontario, Mitchell Hepburn (1896–1953) led a Liberal government with a series of flamboyant political gestures

Thomas Dufferin Pattullo

Thomas Dufferin Pattullo (1873–1956), usually known as 'Duff', was born in Woodstock, Ontario. He worked for Ontario newspapers before moving to the Yukon in 1897 as secretary to the commissioner of the Territory. He subsequently became acting assistant gold commissioner before leaving Dawson City in 1908 to open a brokerage firm. In Prince Rupert, he became a municipal political leader and then a member of the BC assembly (1916) and cabinet minister. He became provincial Liberal leader in 1928 and set about re-energizing the party and turning it from its previous conservative position to one of progressive liberalism far to the left of the federal Liberal Party. In 1933 Pattullo's Liberals won a large majority in an election fought chiefly against the newly founded CCF. The issue was socialism versus capitalism, and many voters failed to realize on how many points the Liberals and CCF were in agreement, with the CCF offering 'Humanity First' and the Liberals a 'New Deal' under the slogan 'Work and Wages'. Pattullo was something of a swashbuckler, and his insistence that the people were entitled to a decent standard of living guaranteed by government owed more to Franklin D. Roosevelt than to William Lyon Mackenzie King, the federal Liberal leader.

But the social reconstruction of British Columbia depended to a large extent on a new constitutional arrangement with the federal government, and Pattullo ended up fighting bitterly with Ottawa. He was unable to implement most of his ad hoc Keynesian views about pump-priming. In his early years in office, Pattullo was easily able to pass reform legislation that did not cost very much, but it was harder to find the money for social programs providing a decent standard of living. Pattullo settled for a program of public works. The defeat of the federal Tories in 1935 led Pattullo to hope for more assistance from Ottawa. Instead, Pattullo and King became involved in an unseemly struggle over provincial debts to Ottawa. British Columbia could not afford to implement Pattullo's cherished comprehensive health insurance scheme in 1937, the year the Liberals again faced the electorate. Although Pattullo's party was returned to office, he became more cautious and increasingly more hostile to the federal government. Standing foursquare for provincial rights, he was one of the chief critics of the Rowell-Sirois Commission when it recommended a transfer of functions to the federal government and a shift in taxation powers. Pattullo continued to advocate an enhanced role for government in the economy and in society, but by 'government' he meant government at the provincial level, not the federal level. The only exception was the responsibility for unemployment, which he always saw as a national and federal matter.

designed chiefly as self-advertisement. He achieved national prominence in April 1937, in the midst of a strike at the General Motors plant in Oshawa. More than 4,000 workers struck for an eight-hour day, better wages and working conditions, and recognition of the new union of United Automobile Workers. This union was an affiliate of the recently formed Congress of Industrial Organizations, which was organizing throughout the United States. Hepburn sided with General Motors and clashed publicly with the Prime Minister over Mackenzie King's refusal to send RCMP reinforcements for the local police. The Premier organized a volunteer force called Hepburn's Hussars. Both Pattullo and Hepburn got great political mileage out of their well-publicized clashes with Ottawa.

None of the prominent provincial political leaders of the 1930s had any serious socialist leanings. The most important alternative political response of the Depression years based in the socialist tradition came from the Co-operative Commonwealth Federation (CCF). A convention in Calgary in 1932 founded the CCF as a coalition of farmers' organizations, labour unions, and labour-socialist parties in the four western provinces. The League for Social Reconstruction (LSR) served as the CCF's midwife. The LSR, organized in 1931 by a number of prominent Canadian academics, believed in Fabian socialism. Like the Fabians, it was proudly non-Marxist and non-revolutionary, although vehemently committed to a welfare state and the state's takeover of key industries. At its first annual convention at Regina in 1933, the newly founded CCF adopted a political manifesto that promised a heady brew of political reform. The Regina Manifesto called for the nationalization (with compensation for the owners) of all industry 'essential to social planning'. It advocated a series of universal welfare measures for Canada—hospitalization, health care, unemployment insurance, and pensions—after amendments to the British North America Act to remove these areas from provincial jurisdiction.

The new party was an uneasy alliance of academics and public activists. It chose as leader the former Methodist minister James Shaver Woodsworth. Pacifist, idealist, and moralist, Woodsworth had since 1921 led a small cadre of labour-supported MPs

in Ottawa. The new party attracted over 300,000 votes in the 1933 British Columbia provincial elections, more than 30 per cent of the popular vote. In the 1935 federal election it obtained 8.9 per cent of the popular vote, which translated into seven CCF seats. During the 1930s the party would flourish only in BC and Saskatchewan, however. It did not attract broad-based popular support, particularly east of Ontario.

The nation's politicians and businessmen grimly viewed the CCF as a threat from the radical left, failing to appreciate that the new party provided a far more restrained left-wing approach than the Communist Party of Canada (CP). At the outset of the Great Depression, only the CP had sought to organize popular discontent, especially among the unemployed. The Communists operated under several disadvantages, however. One was the charge that they were members of an international conspiracy. The other was the Canadian government's willingness to repress the party in any way possible. Ottawa used section 98 of the Criminal Code, introduced in 1919 at the time of the first 'Red Scare', to outlaw the advocacy of revolution. It arrested eight Communist leaders in August of 1931. The courts quickly convicted and sentenced them, although the government gradually released them from prison after continual public demonstrations on their behalf. Nevertheless, the repression checked the momentum of the party. After 1933 the CCF took away some CP support. By mid-decade the CP found itself caught up in rapidly changing orders from the USSR and by events in Europe. In 1937 many Canadian Communists entered the European struggle by joining the Mackenzie-Papineau Battalion to fight in the Spanish Civil War.

The CP took the credit for organizing, through the Workers' Unity League, a mass march on Ottawa in 1935 known as the On-to-Ottawa Trek. The marchers came out of the unemployment relief camps in BC, where unemployed young men found their only refuge. Conditions in the camps were degrading. Not even the Communists claimed that the discontent was anything but spontaneous. The trek began in Vancouver and ended in Regina. The RCMP allowed a delegation of eight marchers to take their grievances

to Ottawa. The talks broke down and the delegation returned to Regina. At that point the Mounties moved in with baseball bat batons. The ensuing riot reduced downtown Regina to shambles and put 120 protestors in jail. Most of the remaining trekkers accepted offers of transportation back home. While the 1930s were punctuated from time to time by outbreaks of public discontent that turned to violence, as in Regina, two points must be emphasized about these incidents. The first is that with most of the spontaneous popular demonstrations, most of the damage to persons and property resulted from the authorities' efforts to break up what they regarded as ugly crowds. The second point is that much of the violence of the period resulted from confrontations between organized labour and the authorities. Clashes between police and strikers were common, as they always had been.

Canadian Society between the Wars

For more than half a century before 1919, Canada had been making a gradual transition from frontier nation to modern industrial state. This process

Strikers from the BC relief camps heading east as part of the 'On to Ottawa' trek; Kamloops, June 1935. LAC, C-029399.

basically continued unabated between the wars. Most of the emerging social patterns were not very different from those that affected all heavily industrialized countries. Urbanization advanced while rural (and especially agricultural) society declined in importance. The traditional family unit seemed under attack. Technology rapidly altered communication and transportation. It also profoundly affected the ways in which Canadians entertained themselves.

Immigration

Although the period 1914–45, which included two disruptive world wars and a major depression, is often viewed in Canada as the lull between two rounds of massive immigration, these years saw the admission of more than 1,700,000 newcomers, with more than 1,166,000 arriving between 1921 and 1931. The numbers were smaller during the Depression and World War II—140,000 from 1931 to 1941 and 50,000 1942 to 1945—but the most important feature of the period was the mounting negative attitude on the part of the Canadian authorities and citizens alike toward extensive immigration, with racism expressed against many ethnic groups. Exclusionary policies seemed increasingly in vogue. The main task of the Immigration Department, especially after 1930, seemed to be to figure out ways to keep immigrants out of the country, rather than of developing ways of allowing them to enter.

The Anglo-Canadian tradition had always been to reward soldiers with free land, and the Great War provided no exception. Providing returned veterans with land would support an agricultural community experiencing difficulties after the war, and soldier settlement began even before the war was over. In May 1919 soldier settlement was revamped to expand the amount of land available and to provide for a more generous supply of credit. Land in the West was taken from Indian reserves, and much of this land proved to be only marginally viable. By 1923 the failure rate among soldier-settlers ran at 21.5 per cent. An even larger problem was that soldier settlement absorbed a disproportionate amount of the money spent on veterans' benefits by the federal government. About 4 per cent of the total

number of able-bodied Canadian veterans got about 14 per cent of the money allocated for ex-soldiers. In a related vein was Empire Settlement, by which large numbers of Britons were recruited to come to Canada. The Canadian government was never very keen about Empire Settlement (which was an imperial scheme), persuaded as it was that most of those recruited were 'defectives' bring dumped by the United Kingdom. Despite the arrival of more than 100,000 British immigrants to Canada between 1922 and 1935—especially female domestics (20,000), intending farmers (10,000), and British farm families (3,500 families)—Empire Settlement did not work well, chiefly because the host country did not fully support it. British immigration became somewhat more popular after 1924, when the American government instituted a permanent quota system and exempted Canada from its provisions: between 1925 and 1932 nearly half a million Canadians would move to the United States.

The exodus of Canadians to the United States and boom conditions in Canada led in 1925 to the Canadian government signing an agreement with Canada's two major railroads. The Dominion now agreed that the railroads could recruit genuine European agriculturalists until 1928 from previously 'non-preferred' parts of Europe. Over the next half-decade, nearly 200,000 immigrants from Central and Eastern Europe were admitted to Canada, normally by co-operative arrangements among the railroads, their colonization companies, and various ethnic and religious organizations in Canada.

But exclusionary policies and practices were more common between the wars. One example of Canadian laggardness towards new immigrants can be found in the Canadian response to the persecution of the Armenian people by the Turkish government near the end of the Great War. Canadians responded to this genocide by raising hundreds of thousands of dollars to assist the refugee survivors. But the Canadian immigration authorities managed to combine two different standards for exclusion—refugee status and racial classification—to keep the number of Armenians allowed into Canada to a mere 1,200, during a period when 23,000 were admitted to the United States and 80,000 allowed into France. Most Armenians lacked proper passports, and Canada resolutely refused to recognize special identity certificates in lieu of passports. The Canadian Immigration Service also insisted on treating the Armenians as Asians, bringing into play all of the regulations designed to exclude people from Asia. They were required to have $250 in cash, to come to Canada via a continuous journey, and to meet Canada's occupational requirements as farmers experienced with North American conditions. The 1920s saw a further tightening of Dominion immigration policy directed at Asians, including a new agreement with the Japanese government to restrict the number of their nationals going to Canada to 150 per year and to put a stop to the so-called 'picture brides' (Japanese women coming to Canada to marry Canadian Japanese men whom they had never met).

Demographic Trends

Like all industrial countries, Canada experienced profound demographic changes. Some of these had been somewhat disguised by the federal government's failure, until 1921, to keep accurate national statistics beyond the census. Enormous infusions of new immigrants before 1914 also helped prevent the new demographic trends from becoming easily apparent, but they existed. By the 1941 census more Canadians lived in urban rather than rural places, a result of a substantial increase in urban residents, especially during the 1920s. Moreover, the 1941 census would be the last in which rural numbers and farm dwellers grew absolutely in number. Even before 1941, the impact of urbanization and industrialization was apparent.

First, mortality rates declined. In the critical area of infant mortality, the death rate had been steadily declining since the nineteenth century. Infant mortality took another major drop in the 1930s, while the overall death rate drifted perceptibly downward. By 1946 the median age at death was 63.1 for males and 65.3 for females. For the first time, Canadian society had begun to produce substantial numbers of people who would live beyond the age of productive labour; a rise in agitation for

old-age pensions in this period was hardly accidental. The main exception to the national trend was in the Aboriginal population. Their death rates ran to four times the national average; infant mortality was at least twice that of Canadian society as a whole. Large numbers of Native mothers died in childbirth. Moreover, Aboriginal people suffered up to three times more accidental deaths than Canada's population overall. They had a high suicide rate. Before 1940 most Aboriginal people died of communicable rather than chronic disease, with tuberculosis as the big killer. The decreasing death rate for Canadians in general resulted from an improved standard of living, including especially improvements in nutrition and hygiene as well as better medical treatment. In the years 1921–6, 270 out of every 1,000 Canadian deaths came from pulmonary and communicable disease. By 1946 such fatalities dropped to just over 60 out of every 1,000 Canadian deaths. Cardiovascular problems, renal disease, and cancer—all afflictions of an aging population—became more important killers.

Then fertility rates declined. The extent to which the fall in the birth rate resulted from conscious decisions on the part of women is not entirely clear, but the two were plainly related. Increased urbanization made large families less desirable. As industrialization took more women out of the home and into the workforce, child care became a serious problem. More women, especially those over 30 years old, began to limit the number of children they bore, practising some form of contraception. Birth rates had begun to fall in Canada before 1919 and continued to fall in the 1920s and 1930s. They recovered from an extremely low point in the middle of the Depression after 1941, increasing sharply after 1945. There were some significant internal differentials. One was between Quebec and the remainder of Canada. The birth rate in French Canada remained substantially higher than in the rest of the country, although it shared in the general decline. There was also a difference between urban and rural areas, with substantially higher birth rates in the latter. A third differential occurred between Catholics and Protestants, although certain Protestant subgroups, such as Mennonites

Canada and the Refugees from Nazi Germany, 1933–1939

From Adolf Hitler's assumption of office as German chancellor, it was clear that the Jews would be a target for persecution. Those Jews who could escape Germany did so, although they were unable to flee swiftly enough to escape the German annexations of the Rhineland, Austria, and Czechoslovakia. Most countries sheltering refugees made clear that they were providing only temporary shelter, and Canada felt it could not open its doors to a flood of people from Europe. Canadian policy was put in the hands of Frederick Charles Blair, a lifetime bureaucrat and well-known anti-Semite, who saw Jewish people as unassimilable. Blair kept the Jews out with the full approval of the Canadian cabinet. In 1938 he decided that the few Jews admitted to Canada as farmers were not really agriculturalists. That same year Canada reluctantly attended a conference at Evian, France, sponsored partly by the United States, to discuss the refugee problems of Europe. Canada was a nation with large amounts of vacant land, and many of its politicians and population feared—quite accurately—that the world community would be quite satisfied to resolve its problems with displaced persons by sending them to Canada. From Canada's perspective, there was no reason to become involved in a European mess not of its own making. Unfortunately, isolationism did not suit the times.

A handful of Jewish members of Parliament (there were only three after 1935), with the support of J.S. Woodsworth of the Co-operative Commonwealth Federation, proposed to the Canadian cabinet that Canada offer at this conference to admit 5,000 Jewish refugees over four years, with all costs to be assumed by the Jewish community in Canada, including guarantees that the newcomers would not become charity cases. The cabinet rejected this offer, chiefly on the grounds that such action could serve as the thin edge of the wedge. By 1938, of course, there were at least a million refugees to be dealt with. Canadian Undersecretary of State for External Affairs O.D. Skelton told the Americans that 'governments with unwanted minorities must . . . not be encouraged to think that harsh treatment at home is the key that will open the doors to immigration abroad' (quoted in Abella and Troper, 1991: 27). The Evian conference accomplished nothing except to demonstrate to the Nazis the lack of international support available to the Jews, thereby probably spurring further persecution, including the 'Kristallnacht' pogrom of late November 1938. On 23 November 1938 a delegation of Jews met with Prime Minister William Lyon Mackenzie King and T.A. Crerar, the minister of immigration, to plead for the admission of 10,000 refugees totally financed by the Jewish community. They were rebuffed, and the cabinet on 13 December 1938 agreed to maintain existing immigration regulations, which admitted only farmers with capital. Highly skilled professionals and intellectuals (including doctors, scientists, and musicians) were thus rejected as 'inadmissible'.

In May of 1939, nearly 1,000 German Jews left Hamburg on a luxury liner, the *St Louis*, some with entrance visas for Cuba. The Cubans rejected most of the passengers, and while Canada sat on the sidelines, the ship was forced to return to Europe. The most that could be said for the Canadian exclusion

and Mormons, had higher rates than the overall Catholic one. Finally, Aboriginal birth rates were at least twice the national average.

Another important new factor was divorce. The year 1918 saw 114 divorces in all of Canada, a rate of 1.4 per 100,000 people. By 1929 the divorce rate had reached 8.2 per 100,000, rising to 18.4 per 100,000 in 1939 and to 65.3 per 100,000 by 1947. Higher rates occurred partly because more Canadians gained access to divorce courts; Ontario

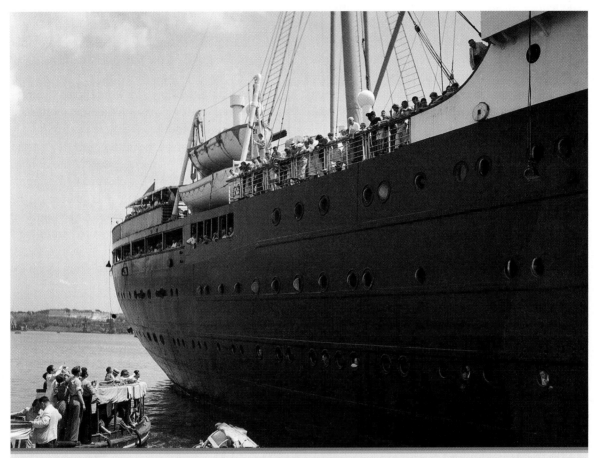

After being denied entry into Cuba, the SS *St Louis* was then sent away from the United States and Canada before returning to Europe, where many of its Jewish passengers were killed in the concentration camps. The Canadian Press.

of Jews was that it was consistent with past national policy, which had never been strongly influenced by humanitarian considerations. But for a nation as limited in world-renowned scientific, intellectual, and cultural talent as Canada, the result was a cruel—if totally deserved—shortfall. Even in the crassest of practical terms, Canadian policy was a disaster. But it was also inexcusable, in a moral sense, on the part of a nation that constantly lectured the rest of the world about its shortcomings.

courts obtained divorce jurisdiction in 1930. The increase also reflected changing attitudes, particularly among women, who instituted most divorce actions. Divorce statistics did not begin to measure the extent of marital dissolutions, however. Most dissolutions never reached a court. Especially during the Depression, husbands simply deserted their wives. Many contemporaries saw the increase in divorce as evidence of the disintegration of the Canadian family.

Technological Change

Despite the nation's uneven economic record between 1919 and 1945, Canadians in these years experienced an increase in the rate and nature of technological change. The new technologies had enormous impact on all aspects of Canadian life. On one level they forced governments to adopt a myriad of new policies. On another level they had tremendous psychological impact, particularly by militating against communalism in favour of the individual, family, or household.

One evident area of change was in the mass acceptance of the internal combustion engine in the form of the automobile and the tractor. Before 1920 automobile ownership had been almost entirely an urban phenomenon, but by 1920 it had become more general. In 1904 there were fewer than 5,000 motor vehicles in Canada. By 1920 there were 251,000, most of them built during the war. From 1918 to 1923 Canadian manufacturers, allied to US companies, were the second-largest car producers in the world. Canada was a major exporter, especially to the British Empire. By 1930 only the United States had more automobiles per capita than did Canada. In that year Canada had 1,061,000 automobiles registered. Also significant was the increase in the number of tractors employed on the nation's farms after 1918.

The automobile was individually owned and operated as an extension of a household. It represented private rather than public transportation. No other single product operated so insidiously against communalism as the automobile. It also had tremendous spinoff consequences. Automobiles required roads, which were a provincial and municipal responsibility. More than one-quarter of the $650 million increase in provincial and municipal debt between 1913 and 1921 resulted from capital expenditures on highways, streets, and bridges. Road mileage in Canada expanded from 385,000

A Toronto traffic jam, 1924: motorists out for a Sunday drive on the newly built Lakeshore Boulevard. City of Toronto Archives, James Collection, Fonds 1244, 2530.

miles (619,580 km) in 1922 to 565,000 miles (909,254 km) in 1942. Motorists wanted not only roads but properly paved ones. Although in 1945 nearly two-thirds of Canadian roads were still of earth construction, the other third had been paved or gravelled at considerable expense. Automobiles ran on petroleum products. Not only did they encourage petroleum production, chiefly in Alberta, but they also created the gasoline station, the repair garage, the roadside restaurant, and the motel— new service industries to provide for a newly mobile population. Door-to-door rather than station-to-station mobility was one of the principal effects of the automobile revolution. Both the automobile and the truck competed with the railways, which began their decline in the 1920s. Although the automobile provided an important source of tax revenue for both federal and provincial governments, neither Ottawa nor the provinces made any serious effort to control the use or construction of motor vehicles, aside from some fairly minimal rules of the road and the issuance of drivers' licences to almost all

comers. Despite its importance, the automobile and its 20,000 parts were produced entirely according to manufacturers' standards and consumers' desires, without government regulation. The car quickly became the symbol of North American independence and individuality. It also served as a combined status and sex symbol, and according to some critics, as a 'portable den of iniquity'.

Unlike the automobile, radio was treated by the federal government as a public matter deserving of regulation. The programs broadcast, rather than the radio receiver itself, became the target of government control. The transmission and reception of sound via radio waves had initially been developed before the Great War as an aid to ships at sea. The 1920s saw the mass marketing of the radio receiver in North America. In order to sell radios, it was necessary to provide something to listen to. By 1929, 85 broadcasting stations were operating in Canada under various ownerships. Private radio broadcasting in Canada was not all bad, but it was uneven. A Royal Commission on Broadcasting—the Aird

Household Equipment Ownership in Montreal, 1941

Heating			Radio	85.5
By stove	51.5%		Bathtub	83.9
Wood and coal	92.3		Telephone	44.9
Cooking Fuel			Vacuum cleaner	28.2
Wood and coal	17.7		Automobile	15.7
Gas & electric	80.6			
Refrigeration				
Mechanical	25.1			
Icebox	65.0			
None	5.1			

Source: Denyse Baillargeon, *Making Do: Women, Family, and Home in Montreal during the Great Depression* (Waterloo, Ont.: Wilfrid Laurier University Press, 2000), 187. Reprinted with permission.

Although this photo was staged, it conveys the avid interest that radio aroused in 1935. A receiver like this walnut-veneered Canadian General Electric model was a luxury that not many Depression-era Canadians could afford. LAC, C-80917.

Commission, appointed in 1928 and reporting in 1929—recommended the nationalization of radio. Its advice was not immediately taken. The Bennett government eventually introduced the Broadcasting Act of 1932, however, which led to the formation of the Canadian Radio Broadcasting Commission to establish a national network and to supervise private stations. In 1936 this Commission became the Canadian Broadcasting Corporation, with extensive English and French networks, and operated with federal financial support as an independent agency. No other Canadian cultural institution of its day was so closely associated with Canadian nationalism and Canadian culture than was the CBC. The CBC was not only pre-eminent but frequently unique in fostering Canadian culture. Often the battle seemed to be uphill, since Canadians usually preferred listening to the slick entertainment programming produced in the United States.

Prohibition and Church Union

The impetus for social reform died after 1918. To some extent, the movement was a victim of its own successes. For many Canadians, the achievement of prohibition and women's suffrage—the two principal reform goals of the pre-war period—meant that the struggle had been won. To some extent, reform was a victim of the Great War. Reformers had exhausted themselves in a war effort that had produced devastation but no final victory. The war had been a disillusioning experience for many.

The failure of the prohibition experiment symbolized the decline of reform. Despite considerable evidence that the elimination of alcoholic beverages had made a social difference—the jails were emptied in most places, since they were usually filled with prisoners who had committed alcohol-related offences—the supporters of prohibition were unable to stem the tide. The Ontario Alliance for the Total Suppression of the Liquor Trade claimed in 1922 that the number of convictions for offences associated with drink had declined from 17,143 in 1914 to 5,413 in 1921, and drunkenness cases decreased in the province's major cities from 16,590 in 1915 to 6,766 in 1921. Nevertheless, various provinces went 'wet' between 1920 and 1924, and the Liquor Control Act replaced the Ontario Temperance Act in 1927. Opposition to prohibition after the war found a new argument to add to the old one that private conduct was being publicly regulated: attempts to enforce prohibition encouraged people to flout the law and even created organized crime and vice. Too many people were prepared to ignore the law, said prohibition's opponents, who found more acceptable slogans of their own in 'Moderation' and 'Government Regulation'. In many provinces, the possibility of obtaining provincial revenue for tax-starved coffers led to the introduction of government control over the sale of alcohol. Taxing bad habits rather than forbidding them became part of the Canadian tradition.

While prohibition was dying, in 1925 the Methodist, Presbyterian, and Congregational churches (the first two were among Canada's largest denominations) merged as the United Church of Canada. As three of the most 'liberal' denominations in Canada, home of much of the social gospel commitment to Christian reform of secular society, they hoped to rejuvenate reform fervour through unification. Not all members of the three denominations were equally enthusiastic. Opposition to union was particularly strong among the Presbyterians. In the end, congregations could vote to stay out of the union. Thus 784 Presbyterian and eight Congregational congregations so declared, while 4,797 Methodist, 3,728 Presbyterian, and 166 Congregational congregations joined in the United Church of Canada. The new denomination became the most substantial Protestant communion of Canada, generally committed to liberal thinking and reform.

Racism

Canadian society between the wars continued to be profoundly racist. That point was demonstrable in a variety of ways, although it must be emphasized that very few Canadians saw their exclusionary attitudes as either socially undesirable or dysfunctional.

Imported from the United States, the Ku Klux Klan flourished in Canada during the 1920s. In the United States the revived Klan spread anti-black and anti-Catholic hate propaganda under the guise of a fraternal organization. In its secret rituals, fundamentalist Protestantism, and social operations, the Klan appeared to some Canadians to be little different from a host of other secret societies. The Klan assumed a Canadian face, posing as the defender of Britishness against the alien hordes and calling itself the 'Ku Klux Klan of the British Empire'. Although the Klan had some success everywhere in Canada, it made particular headway in the late 1920s in Saskatchewan, where by 1929 there were over 125 chapters. In that province it found support from a number of Protestant ministers, who objected to the increasingly liberal leanings of the main-line Protestant churches. It also gained acceptance as a way of opposing the patronage-style politics of the provincial Liberal government. Few of its members associated it with American-style cross burning or midnight lynch mobs.

Canada's treatment of its Aboriginal population continued to reflect both belief in the superiority of non-Native culture and antagonism towards the Native peoples. The Department of Indian Affairs assumed that assimilation was the only possible policy. Deputy Minister Duncan Campbell Scott stated in 1920 that 'Our object is to continue until there is not a single Indian in Canada that has not been absorbed into the body politic, and there is no Indian question, and no Indian Department.' Indian Affairs employed a variety of policies. It forced Aboriginal children into schools, usually residential ones far removed from their families. It forbade and actively suppressed the practice of traditional Native rituals like the potlatch. It carried out the Canadian government's legislative provisions to enfranchise the Aboriginal people, thus in theory making them full citizens and no longer wards of the state. Most of the resistance to these measures was passive, although there was the beginning of organization. The first congress of the League of Indians convened at Sault Ste Marie, Ontario, in September 1919. The League's objectives were 'to claim and protect the rights of all Indians in Canada by legitimate and just means' and to assert 'absolute control in retaining possession or disposition of our lands' (quoted in Cuthand, 1978: 31–2). The League and its successors met regularly thereafter.

In British Columbia, an anti-Oriental movement flourished during the interwar years. Much of the criticism of the 'menace' from Asia came from economic fears, although there was also a general concern for the racial integrity of the province as a white society. The general argument was that the newcomers would not assimilate, although there was considerable evidence that the Japanese, at least, were acculturating rapidly. Moving onto small holdings in the Fraser Valley and into salmon fishing along the coasts, the Japanese appeared to pose a potential military threat should their homeland—which was militarily aggressive in the Pacific from the beginning of the century—attempt to expand into Canada. If people from Asia were highly visible in some areas and in some industries, that fact was partly explained by their exclusion—in law and in practice—from so much of the life of the province.

Women

Canadian women emerged from the Great War with the vote in hand. A few feminist critics had argued that the vote was no panacea for women's second-class position in Canadian society. It did not even assure a high level of political involvement. Between the wars women did not very often run for public office or constitute a recognizable voting bloc. The flapper, with her bobbed hair, short skirts and spirit of independence, was the symbolic 'new woman' of the 1920s, but she was hardly typical. Most Canadian women did not smoke or sip cocktails or dance the

'black bottom'. About all they had in common with the flapper was that, like her, they worked outside the home. Quebec women began moving into the work-force after 1918. More women worked in Canada in 1931 than in 1921, mostly in dead-end jobs. The Depression was particularly difficult for women. Public opinion turned against married women holding jobs that could be done by men. Most relief programs were geared to men, partly because it was not thought that women would threaten the social order by rioting and demonstrating.

In the gradual elaboration of unemployment insurance, many radicals opposed gender discrimination

Charlotte Whitton

Charlotte Whitton (1896–1975) was born in Renfrew, Ontario, and was educated at Queen's University, where she had a spectacular academic record. In 1918 she was appointed assistant secretary to the Social Services Council of Canada. She was soon actively involved in social work and social work reform, and became first director of the Canadian Council on Child Welfare, which would become the Canadian Welfare Council, serving from 1926 to 1941. In this position she edited the journal *Social Welfare* and represented Canada on social issues at the League of Nations. She also campaigned courageously for improved standards in the care of children and juveniles, and insisted on the need for a more professional approach to social work. During her tenure as director of the Canadian Welfare Council she toured the nation, making frequent speeches and giving many lectures. Her major message during the 1930s was that while the Depression had made it impossible for private philanthropy to carry the social welfare load by itself, neither spending large sums of money on unemployment nor an active federal government was the answer to the problem. As an adviser to the Bennett government on federal unemployment relief, she offered the same opinions.

After her departure from the Welfare Council in 1941, Whitton became a private consultant on welfare matters. In 1943, in response to an invitation from new Progressive Conservative leader John Bracken, she published *The Dawn of an Ampler Life*, obviously intended to serve as a background document for the new party's social policy. (Bracken, a Progressive who had been Premier of Manitoba, had accepted the leadership of the Tories on the condition that 'Progressive' would be added to the name of the Conservative Party.) The reader would be hard-pressed to decide exactly what Whitton was recommending, but it clearly was considerably less state interventionist than most of the competing visions of the time, and it had little impact on the welfare debate. Whitton subsequently became notorious for her opposition to liberal divorce laws and to married women who held jobs. In 1950 she was elected controller of the city of Ottawa, succeeding to the mayor's post on the death of the incumbent, thus becoming the first female mayor of a major Canadian city. She was re-elected in 1952 and 1954, then again in 1960 and 1962. When not mayor, Whitton served the city as an alderman. She was famous for her outspoken opinions and keen wit.

but at the same time accepted the principle that married women should be supported by their husbands. Women's access to benefits was often limited without mention of gender. For example, traditionally female areas of employment—school teaching, nursing, domestic service performed in private homes—were excluded from UI coverage. Many husbands deserted their wives during the Depression, and even where the family remained together the wife did most of the work to keep it functioning. In the House of Commons in 1935, J.S. Woodsworth cited the case of a child murder and suicide in Winnipeg. The husband was unemployed and came home to find his children and wife dead. His wife had left a suicide note that read, 'I owe the drug store 44 cents farewell' (quoted in Pierson, 1990: 77–103).

Canadian Culture between the Wars

A resurgence of Canadian nationalism characterized the 1920s. The larger stories of the interwar period, however, were the blossoming of Canada's love affair with American popular culture and the simultaneous emergence of a number of significant homegrown writers and artists. By the 1930s Canadians no longer had to be apologetic about their cultural achievements, although the number of individuals who could actually make a living from their creative work remained fairly small.

The Great War may have been fought for the British Empire, but both its course and its outcome made Canadians more conscious of their nation's distinctiveness. In the 1920s Canadian nationalism wore a dual face. On the one hand, it had to reflect Canada's new international status. On the other, it felt it had to protect the country from being overwhelmed by foreign culture. The painter Arthur Lismer (1885–1969) wrote, 'After 1919, most creative people, whether in painting, writing or music, began to have a guilty feeling that Canada was as yet unwritten, unpainted, unsung. . . . In 1920 there was a job to be done' (quoted in Thompson and Seager, 1985: 158). That job was not simply to write books, paint pictures, and compose music that captured

Charlotte Whitton, the mayor of Ottawa (second from left), at the unveiling of commemorative bust of Agnes Macphail, the first woman elected to the House of Commons, outside the House, Ottawa, 1955. Also pictured (from left) are MP Margaret Aitken, Senator Cairine Wilson, and MP Ellen Fairclough. Duncan Cameron/LAC, PA-121765.

the true Canadian spirit. The task was also to organize national cultural organizations and institutions that would mobilize a new sense of national consciousness. A number of Canadian magazines and journals emerged to serve as vehicles for Canadian ideas. The *Canadian Bookman* appeared in 1919, and *Canadian Forum*, *Canadian Historical Review*, and *Dalhousie Review* in 1920. The Canadian Authors' Association, founded in 1921, backed campaigns promoting Canadian writers. In 1937 it succeeded in persuading the Governor General—the famous Scottish novelist John Buchan (1875–1940), Lord Tweedsmuir—to establish the prestigious Governor General's awards. In art, the Group of Seven consciously sought to create a Canadian mythology. According to their first exhibition catalogue, in 1920, their vision was simple: 'An Art must grow and flower in the land before the country will be a real home for its people' (quoted in Thompson and Seager, 1985: 162).

Between 1920 and 1940 over 750 Canadian novels were published. While most of these works

'As for Me and My House'

In 1941 (James) Sinclair Ross (1908–96) published a novel in New York entitled *As for Me and My House*. Set in Horizon, Saskatchewan, in the 1930s, the story is told from the vantage point of Mrs Bentley, the wife of a local clergyman.

Sunday Evening, April 30.

The wind keeps on. It's less than a week since the snowstorm, and the land is already dry again. The dust goes reeling up the street in stinging little scuds. Over the fields this morning on our way to Partridge Hill there were dark, foreboding clouds of it.

Service was difficult this morning. They were listening to the wind, not Philip, the whimpering and strumming through the eaves, and the dry hard crackle of sand against the windows. From the organ I could see their faces pinched and stiffened with anxiety. They sat in tense, bolt upright rows, most of the time their eyes on the ceiling, as if it were the sky and they were trying to read the weather. . . .

Philip and Paul and I stood on the school steps till the congregation were all gone. The horses pawed and stamped as if they, too, felt something ominous in the day. One after another the democrats and buggies rolled away with a whir of wheels like pebbly thunder. From the top of Partridge Hill where the schoolhouse stands we could see the prairie smoking with dust as if it had just been swept by fire. A frightening, wavering hum fled blind within the telephone wires. The wind struck in hard, clenched little blows; and even as we watched each other the dust formed in veins and wrinkles round our eyes. According to the signs, says Paul, it's going to be a dry and windy year all through. With the countryman's instincts for such things he was strangely depressed this morning. . . .

I found it hard myself to believe in the town outside, houses, streets, and solid earth. Mile after mile the wind poured by, and we were immersed and lost in it. I sat breathing from my throat, my muscles tense. To relax, I felt, would be to let the walls round me crumple in. . . .

It's the most nerve-wracking wind I've ever listened to. Sometimes it sinks a little, as if spent and out of breath, then comes high, shrill and importunate again. Sometimes it's blustering and rough, sometimes silent and sustained. Sometimes it's wind, sometimes frightened hands that shake the doors and windows. Sometimes it makes the little room and its smug, familiar furniture a dramatic inconsistency, sometimes a relief. I sit thinking about the dust, the farmers and the crops, wondering what another dried-out year will mean for us.

We're pinched already. They gave us fifteen dollars this week, but ten had to go for a payment on the car. I'm running bills already at the butcher shop and Dawson's store. Philip needs shoes and a hat. His Sunday suit is going at the cuffs again, and it's shiny at the seat and knees. I sent for a new spring hat for myself the other day, but it was just a dollar forty-five, and won't be much.

Source: Sinclair Ross, *As For Me and My House* (Toronto: McClelland & Stewart, 1970 [1941]), 37–9.

were escapist fiction, a number of Canadian novelists achieved national and even modest international reputations for their skill at their craft. Perhaps even more important, a small number of strong, confident, realistic novels appeared that formed the foundation of modern Canadian fiction. Not only was the move towards realism in line with international trends, but it responded to the nationalist demand for distinctively Canadian content. As for the visual arts, particularly during the Depression when most artists had to live at subsistence level, much work we now value highly was produced. Few visual artists in Canada could make a living from their work alone, but art schools were now sufficiently common in the larger Canadian cities to provide employment for painters and sculptors. British Columbia's Emily Carr (1871–1945) united art and literature in a highly original way. Combining French Post-Impressionism with Aboriginal form and colour, Carr gradually created a powerful and distinctive visual landscape. She also won a Governor General's award for *Klee Wyck* (1941), a collection of stories based on her visits to Native villages. By the time of her death, Carr's paintings were probably the visual icons the average Canadian could most easily associate with an individual artist. She had triumphed not only over the disadvantages of Canadian geography but over the limitations faced by any woman who aspired to more than a genteel 'dabbling' in art.

During the interwar period, radio, motion pictures, and the great expansion of professional sports all represented major American influences on the Canadian consciousness. In popular culture Canada made little effort at national distinctiveness. The loudest critics of insidious Americanization usually had no alternatives to offer other than a somewhat outworn Britishness. At the same time, Canada and Canadians were hardly innocent victims of American cultural imperialism. As a nation Canada had choices it failed or refused to exercise. As a people Canadians were willing—indeed, active—collaborators in cultural production, both at home and in the United States itself. A closer examination of motion pictures and hockey in this period is instructive.

In the world of film, Hollywood's success was also Canada's, since there was no shortage of Canadian talent involved in the formative years of Tinseltown. Mack Sennett, Sidney Olcott, Louis B. Mayer, Jack Warner, Walter Huston, Mary Pickford, Norma Shearer, and Marie Dressler—some of Hollywood's biggest and most influential names at the time—were Canadian-born. Pickford, Warner, and Mayer founded three of the major Hollywood studios between 1919 and 1924. Canada itself had only the beginnings of a film industry, consisting mainly of the seven films produced by Ernest Shipman, of which *Back to God's Country* (1919) is a Canadian silent film classic. Otherwise filmmaking in Canada was confined chiefly to newsreels and documentaries,

Emily Carr in the Cariboo region of British Columbia, 1904.

which were often appended to American features. By 1922 American studios were including Canadian receipts as part of domestic revenue, and in 1923 Famous Players' Canadian Corporation, a subsidiary of Pickford's studio, took over the leading Canadian cinema chain, Allen Theatres. At the height of the silent film era, Hollywood succeeded in monopolizing the distribution of film in Canada; Canadian exhibitors and cinema owners were not much concerned about where the product had originated so long as it was profitable.

Other nations around the world took some sort of defensive action against the Hollywood juggernaut, either placing quotas on imported films or providing tax incentives for local productions. Canada did neither, partly because a few of its citizens were so closely connected with the American film industry, partly because Canadians so clearly preferred Hollywood films to the alternatives. During the

Great Depression, when the Dream Factory provided blessed release from the cares and woes of everyday life for millions of Canadians, that dream was plainly American. Canadians continued to love American movies despite the inaccuracy with which Hollywood persistently treated Canadian geography, society, and history. Symbolically, the successive and successful film portrayals of that quintessential American, Abraham Lincoln, by two Canadian actors, Walter Huston (1884–1950) and Raymond Massey (1896–1983), only solidified the close identification of Canadians and Americans in the popular mind on both sides of the border.

The situation with professional hockey was equally interesting. The National Hockey Association (NHA) was organized in 1909 in eastern Canada. On the west coast, Frank and Lester Patrick, in 1911–12, formed the Pacific Coast Hockey League (PCHL), which defeated an NHA team for the Stanley Cup in 1915. In 1917 the National Hockey League (NHL) formed out of the NHA. The PCHL folded in 1925. That same year, the NHL granted a franchise lease to the Boston Bruins and became the top professional hockey league in North America. The New York Rangers and the Pittsburgh Pirates soon followed, and Chicago and Detroit received NHL franchises in 1927. Most of the American clubs were owned or managed by Canadians, and the players were almost entirely Canadian. Indeed, the Patrick brothers had brought players from their PCHL teams to the American-based NHL teams they acquired in the 1920s. The Toronto Maple Leafs acquired a physical presence when Maple Leaf Gardens was built as their home. At the opening on 12 November 1931, Foster Hewitt (1902–85) broadcast his first *Hockey Night in Canada*, describing the game from a gondola overlooking the rink. For three decades thereafter, his high-pitched voice—and his excited refrain, 'He shoots! He scores!'—*was* hockey for most Canadians. *Hockey Night in Canada* was the one and only Canadian-produced radio program on CBC that consistently outdrew American offerings with the Canadian listeners. Although the Depression benefited professional sports by creating a desperate need for escape, not all Canadians could afford to pay for admission. In Toronto, for example, ticket

prices of 50¢ and $1.25 resulted in many empty seats. By 1939 the NHL had suffered the loss of all but two of its Canadian teams, the Maple Leafs and the Montreal Canadiens. The centre of professional hockey power shifted to the United States, although Canadians still knew that virtually all the players came from Canada, where hockey was still a way of life on the frozen rivers and lakes of the nation in the winter months.

While Canada's film and hockey successes were mainly in Hollywood and in American arenas, a vital grassroots theatrical movement existed at home between the wars, almost entirely on the amateur level. It consisted of Little Theatre groups in most major cities and towns, hundreds of high school drama groups, dozens of university drama groups, and innumerable other drama and musical drama organizations sponsored by fraternal organizations, church groups, and labour unions. In most Canadian cities and towns, one group or another was rehearsing a play or a musical at any given time during the winter months. During the darkest days of the Depression, Canadian theatre blossomed, providing relief for many from the grim conditions of their lives. Protracted hard times, while discouraging some artists, also energized others, particularly those who sought cultural directions that would encourage a new spirit of social involvement and commitment.

During the Depression, a theatre of the left emerged in the major cities of Canada, particularly Vancouver, Toronto, Winnipeg, and Montreal, which spread to other places (like Timmins, Ontario) where 'progressive' people were to be found. In all of these places, there was a twin emphasis: first, on supplying theatre that spoke directly to its audiences about what was going on in Canada and the world; and second, on exemplifying the ideals of collective experience in theatrical production. The theatre of the left tended to exalt amateur values and participation. It also had far more Canadian content in its plays. The first tour of the Workers' Theatre, for example, included seven short plays, including *Eviction* (written by members of the Montreal Progressive Arts Club), *Farmers' Fight* (also written by the Montreal PAC), *Joe Derry* (written by Dorothy Livesay), and *War in the East* (written by Stanley Ryerson). Interestingly,

Radio Programming, 1939

Wednesday 2 August
Network Highlights

CBC

7:00   Songs of the World
7:30   Percy Faith's Music
8:00   Sunset Symphony
8:30   Nature Talk
9:15   Sunset Symphony
10:00   Everyman Theatre

NBC—BLUE

7:30   Idea Mart
8:00   Kay Kyser's Quiz
8:30   Fred Waring Orch.
10:30   Lights Out

CBS

9:00   Amos 'n' Andy
9:30   Paul Whiteman orch.

Station Programs

5:00   The Lone Ranger, sketch—CKY
5:00   Dinner Concert—CBC-CJRC, CBK
5:00   Fred Waring Orch—KFYR
5:30   Crackerjacks, songs—CBC-CJRC, CBK
5:30   Jimmy Allen, sketch—CKY
5:45   Howie Wing, sketch—CJRC
5:45   Waltz Time—CKY
5:45   Canadian Outdoor Days, Ozark Ripley—CBC-CBK . . .
7:00   Songs of the World, mixed choir, Montreal—CBC-CKY
7:00   Reports—CJRC

7:00   Horse and Buggy Days, songs of the 90s—KFYR
7:00   Percy Faith's Music; George Murray, Dorothy Alt, soloists, Toronto—CBC-CKY, CBK
7:30   Modern Music Maestros—CJRC
7:30   Idea Mart—KFYR
8:00   Interview from London, from BBC—CBC-CKY, CBK
8:00   Reports, Blaine Edwards, organ—CJRC
8:00   Kay Kyser's College, musical quiz—NBC—KFY until 9.
8:15   Teller of Curious Tales—CJRC
8:30   Dan McMurray's Nature Talk, Bank CBC-CKY, CBK
8:30   Five Esquires—CJRC
8:45   Lieder Recital—CBC-CKY, CBK
9:00   Canadian Press News—CBC-CKY, CBK
9:00   Reports; Piano Moods—CJRC
9:00   Amos 'n' Andy, sketch—CBS-WJR, WCCO, KMOX, KBL
9:00   Fred Waring Orch—NBC-KFTR, WHO, WLW
9:15   Summer Symphony, G. Waddington conducting from Walker Theatre, Winnipeg—CBC-CKY, CBK, CJRC, until 10.
9:30   Milt North Trio, WKNR
9:30   Tommy Dorsey Orch—NBC-KOR
9:30   Horace Heidt Orch—NBC-KFYR
9:30   Paul Whiteman Orch., guests—CBS-WCCO, KMOX, KSL
9:45   Reports—CJRC

Source: *Winnipeg Tribune*, 2 August 1939, 2.

progressive theatre groups did not shun the establishment-oriented Dominion Drama Festival (DDF) but instead competed frequently, seeking thereby to test their theatrical quality, apart from the political value of their work. The DDF adjudicators, in their turn, were sympathetic to the productions but often unenthusiastic about the doom and gloom of their themes, preferring lighter fare. In 1937, a four-person play entitled *Relief*, written by Minnie Evans Bicknell of Marshall, Saskatchewan, and performed

A Cabaret Song

One of the major songwriters for the cabarets of the left-wing Theatre of Action was Frank Gregory. These cabarets began in 1939 and continued through the early 1940s. The songs were heavily influenced by Tin Pan Alley and Broadway.

We Get Along

We never travel in Café society,
And Winchell never gives us notoriety—
   I guess we must be
   Socially insignificant
But we get along.

You'll never find us at the El Morocco,
We can't afford the latest Broadway socko—
   It seems we are just
   Socially insignificant.
But we get along.

Don't think we're satisfied
To sit and bide
Our time as we are:
   We're not the patient kind.
For in addition
We've got ambition,
But that can't get us far,
   With money and security so hard to find.

So that is why you'll never see our faces
In photographs of all the swellest places:
   You'd think we were born
   Socially insignificant,
But we get along.

Source: Quoted in Toby Gordon Ryan, *Stage Left Canadian Theatre in the Thirties: A Memoir* (Toronto: CTR Publications, 1981), 189. Courtesy CTR Publications.

by the Marshall Dramatic Club, was one of the finalists at the DDF. The play was a domestic tragedy performed in a naturalistic style in which the performers dealt with matters that were all too familiar in their daily lives, as the critics noted in their reviews. Toronto's Theatre of Action was particularly active in seeking out Canadian themes and Canadian playwrights. The thematic content of the drama preferred by the theatre of the left was undoubtedly one of the factors that limited its popular acceptance. Towards the end of the 1930s, however, influenced by the cabaret theatre of Kurt Weill and Bertolt Brecht as developed by left-wing American theatre groups, progressive theatre in Canada became more interested in musical theatre. Some of the cabaret productions actually featured songs that commented satirically on Canadian politics. This topical humour offered a lighter alternative to the fare presented by the more earnest theatre companies.

World War II

Canada went back to war on 10 September 1939. This time the government waited a week after the British declaration of war against Germany to join the conflict, thus emphasizing Canada's 'independent' status. The nation's entry into the war helped complete the process of economic recovery. Unprepared militarily, as in the Great War, Canada proved capable of mobilizing resources remarkably swiftly when required. Canada quickly accepted the British Commonwealth Air Training Plan as its major war commitment. The details of the scheme were agreed upon by Britain and Canada on 17 December 1939. Within months the program's first graduates emerged from Camp Borden, Ontario. It eventually graduated 131,533 Commonwealth airmen, 72,835 of whom were Canadian, at a cost of $1.6 billion. A nation of less than 12 million people would eventually put over 1 million of them into uniform. Using the War Measures Act, Canada succeeded in mobilizing economic resources in a way that had seemed impossible during the Depression. Tax arrangements between the Dominion and the provinces were restructured during the emergency, with the federal government collecting most of the revenue and making grants to the provinces to recover their operating expenses.

The economy was totally managed and regulated, a process associated with Ottawa's wartime economic czar, Clarence Decatur Howe (1886–1960). By 1943 unemployment was well under 2 per cent, a figure regarded in most quarters as full employment. Federal spending rose from 3.4 per cent of the gross national product (GNP) in 1939 to 37.6 per cent of GNP by 1944, totalling a full $4.4 billion in the latter year. Industrial growth was better distributed across the regions than in 1914–18, inflation was controlled, and consumption was regulated by shortages and rationing. Canada's total GNP rose from $5.6 billion in 1939 to $11.9 billion in 1945. The nation became one of the world's industrial giants, producing 850,000 motorized vehicles and over 16,000 military aircraft during the war. The government

Canadian soldiers, known for their bravery, were instrumental in liberating northwestern Europe from the Germans. Canadian Major David Currie (left, holding pistol) won the Victory Cross for his role in in helping to close the Falaise Gap in August 1944. CWM 20020045-2276 George Metcalf Archival Collection Canadian War Museum.

borrowed heavily from its own citizens, partly in the form of war bonds. While the achievement was impressive, it suggested that the riddle of social justice remained unsolved. Canada appeared far more capable of efficient use of its productive capacity to fight destructive wars abroad than to battle domestically with poverty and unemployment.

As in the Great War, Canadians fought well whenever called upon. As in the previous conflict, they were often employed as shock troops. In the disastrous landing of the 2nd Canadian Division at Dieppe in August 1942, nearly 2,700 of the 5,000 Canadians who embarked were either killed or captured. The First Canadian Army, formed in 1942 under the command of General A.G.L. McNaughton (1887–1966), was composed of five divisions that were eventually split between Italy and Northwest Europe. This army was independently commanded, although the Royal Canadian Air Force and the Royal Canadian Navy were mainly integrated with their British counterparts. Canadian flyers became noted for their work in bombers rather than in fighters, as in World War I. Many thousands of Canadians spent most or all of the war years in Britain, and a number brought back to Canada their British wives after the war.

The RCN grew to 365 ships, spending the war mainly protecting convoys on the North Atlantic route and achieving such expertise in this duty that in May 1943 a Canadian, Admiral L.W. Murray

The Story of War Bride Ruby McCreight

This narrative of a Canadian war bride begins in the third person but concludes in the first person.

Ruby was a lonely English girl from London, England. She was a widow with a three-year-old daughter. Ruby didn't make friends easily because she was hard of hearing and tended to keep to herself. At the time, she worked in a Legion waiting on tables and helping with the cleaning for the more than 400 soldiers of every nationality who called the Legion home. They could not go to their real homes on leave, so most of them stayed at the Legion.

Every New Year's Eve, the soldiers donned kitchen aprons and waited on the help. Everyone made jokes and enjoyed the antics and the soldier who waited on them.

The Canadian soldier who waited on Ruby spoke to her several times and even put a present on her plate, but she didn't answer him, she just tried to smile. Not many people knew she was hard of hearing.

After all the tables were cleared, the band began to play and couples started dancing. Ruby stood alone, just watching.

Suddenly Ruby's soldier approached her and gave her a note to read: 'I know you have trouble hearing. Are you as lonely as you look: I feel the same way; I miss my folks home in Canada. Would you keep me company and dance with me?' She surprised herself and danced with him several times. He saw her home, and after this he continued to see her at work and on the occasional date.

After seeing him for a little over six months, she took him home to meet her parents and her little girl. When the little girl saw him she ran to him and said: 'Daddy, you came home!'

She had seen her dad in uniform in a photo on her shelf, and seeing the soldier in uniform, she naturally assumed it was her father.

After the young girl was put to bed and Ruby and the soldier was [sic] alone, he asked, 'Well, how about it?'

'How about what?' Ruby asked.

'Being her daddy,' he replied.

This was in 1944. We were married in 1945 and came to Canada the next year. We have now been married for 46 years and we have five children—and are still as happy as the day we first met.

Source: David Helwig, ed., *Back Then: Voices of Memory 1915–1945* (n.p: Oberon Press, 1993), 102–3.

Life at Sea in a Canadian Corvette during the Second World War

One of Canada's major military functions during the war against Hitler was to provide escort service against Nazi submarines for convoys of ships plying the dangerous North Atlantic route. Much of this duty was carried out in small ships called corvettes. Built in Canadian shipyards and originally intended for coastal duty, the corvettes were manned by nearly 100,000 young Canadian sailors. Life aboard them was dangerous and uncomfortable, as the following account from Howard Cousins, leading signalman aboard HMCS *Algoma* in 1941–2, suggests.

The ship was your home and the weather had a direct effect on the degree of comfort that home provided. When the wind and seas built up, the comforts of your home were virtually non-existent. As the ship rolled and pitched, you were thrown around continuously, not daring to move without holding fast to something. The bridge was wet with spray, sometimes solid water.

The highly developed storm gear we have today was not available then. An oilskin coat worn over a duffel coat, a sou'wester on your head and sea-boots on your feet was the rig of the day. In theory, the oilskin coat overlapped the tops of the sea-boots. In practice, the wind whipping around the bridge caused the skirt of the coat to lift and flap. Before long water had seeped into your boots and soon your feet were wet and cold. Water also found its way down your neck. Some of us wore a towel around our neck, but before long the towel became soaked and water trickled down your chest and back.

A corvette on the crest of the wave could have one-third of the forward portion clear of the water. As the ship rolled and dropped down into the trough, it was almost a free fall. The poor blokes in the forecastle felt virtually weightless; anything on the lockers, shelves, and tables, including your meal, frequently floated off. When the ship smashed into the back of the next wave, it felt as if the ship had been dropped on concrete.

Drawing meals from the galley was awkward, to say the least. The galley was located aft of the wheelhouse and the duty messman had to collect the meals for his mess on a tray, then carry that tray along the open deck to the forecastle. With no hand available to hang on with, seas breaking over the side and down from the break of the forecastle, it was a perilous trip. Some meals did not make it.

I remember one occasion when the messman, having successfully made the trip, proudly stood at the head of the table as someone removed the oilskin protecting the food. The messman was starting to boast how good he was when the ship fell rapidly over the crest of a wave. When the ship was brought back up with the usual jolt, the messman and our food were thrown across the deck.

Bad weather also involved the laws of physics in the basic act of getting into your bed, which was a hammock suspended from steel rods on the deckhead. To get into your hammock, you grabbed the rod and swung yourself up and in. Timing was essential. If the ship was lifting to a sea, it was virtually impossible to push yourself off the deck, let along swing up into the hammock. On the other hand, if you waited until the ship was falling off the crest, a slight push of the toes was enough for you to float effortlessly up to the hammock.

Everyone's job became more difficult under bad weather conditions. . . . The cook often gave up and resorted to sandwiches. . . . No, home was not a place of comfort in bad weather, which did have one good thing going for it—there was very little chance that the convoy would be troubled with submarine attacks.

Source: M. Johnston, *Corvettes Canada: Convoy Veterans of WWII Tell Their True Stories* (Toronto: McGraw-Hill Ryerson, 1994), 113–15.

(1896–1971), was given command of the Canadian Northwest Atlantic theatre. Many other Canadians and Newfoundlanders served in the Canadian merchant marine, a thankless task that kept them out of the loop for veterans' benefits for many years. Canada ultimately had the third largest navy among the Allied powers, the fourth largest air force, and the fourth largest army. Such a contribution ought to have made it something of a power in the world, although the major powers—Britain, the United States, and the USSR—routinely treated Canada as little different from Allied nations such as Chile and Brazil, which had only token forces in the war. The superpowers admitted France to their council tables almost as soon as the nation was liberated, while ignoring Canada completely.

Canada fought chiefly in the European and North Atlantic theatres. Canadian assistance to American and British efforts in the Pacific and Southeast Asia was fairly minimal. In December 1941, however, two Canadian battalions were involved in the surrender of Hong Kong. The 1,421 men who returned home after years in Japanese prison camps had to fight for 23 years to win proper veterans' benefits from the Canadian government. As in the Great War, casualties in this conflict were heavy, with 42,642 Canadians giving up their lives. On the other hand, this was not a war of stalemate in the trenches. Instead, the establishment of beachheads was followed by a constant advance that involved liberating places held by the enemy. One innovation in this war was the active military service of women. As in 1914–18 large numbers of women were employed in the war industry, but by 1945 over 43,000 women were actually in uniform. A Gallup poll taken in 1944 indicated, however, that most Canadians, including 68 per cent of the women polled, believed that men should be given preference for employment in the

Japanese Canadians being relocated to camps in the interior of British Columbia, 1942. LAC, C-046355.

post-war reconstruction. As a result, the machinery for women's participation in the workforce, including daycare centres, was dismantled with unseemly haste at the war's end.

Dissent was met with persecution, as had been the case during the Great War. The Canadian government proved almost totally insensitive to pacifists' beliefs. It interned thousands of Canadians without trial, often for mere criticism of government policy. The most publicized abuse of the state's power was the treatment of the Japanese Canadians. Although the King government did not for a minute believe that Japanese Canadians represented any real military danger, it yielded to pressure from British Columbia and forcibly evacuated most Japanese Canadians from the west coast. Many were sent to internment camps in the interior of BC, and others were scattered across the country, their land seized and their property sold at auction. 'National emergency' was also used to justify the dissemination of propaganda, now called 'management of information'. Citizens needed to be educated in order to maintain faith and hope and to eliminate 'potential elements of disunity', a euphemism for criticism of the government. One major institution of information management was the National Film Board of Canada, under Scottish-born John Grierson (1898–1972), who believed in the integration of 'the loyalties and forces of the community in the name of positive and highly constructive ideas'. Grierson saw 'information services—propaganda if you like' as an inevitable consequence of the government's involvement in the crisis (quoted in Young, 1978: 217–40).

Internally, wartime policies revolved around two major questions: conscription and post-war reconstruction. In a national plebiscite held on the question of conscription in the spring of 1942, the nation voted 2,945,514 to 1,643,006 to release the government from an earlier pledge not to conscript for overseas service. Quebec voted strongly in the negative. The conscription issue emerged again in 1944, when the military insisted (as in 1917) that it was necessary to ship conscripts overseas, although they had been drafted with the promise that they would not be required to serve abroad. In the end, while conscripts were sent to Europe, few served as combatants before the war ended in May 1945. For the

King government, the increasing threat from the CCF became a problem as nagging as that of Quebec. As early as 1941 many Canadians had apparently come to realize that the failure to make a concerted assault on social injustice had been a result mainly of governments' refusal to act. Canada was now, in wartime, demonstrating how thoroughly the country could be mobilized if the will to do so was present. Public opinion in Anglo-Canada began turning to the social promises of the CCF. Indeed, in the September 1943 federal election, the CCF received the support of 29 per cent of the electorate at the polls, and in 1944 the Saskatchewan CCF wiped out a long-standing Liberal government in an election fought over social services.

King's Liberals had dragged their heels over social welfare reform. Federal unemployment insurance had been introduced in 1940, but other progressive legislation remained on hold. Now, in 1944, King declared in the House of Commons 'a wholly new conception of industry as being in the nature of social service for the benefit of all, not as something existing only for the benefit of a favoured few'. The introduction of social reform was necessary not only to deal with the threat from the CCF but also to prevent possible public disorder at the conclusion of the war and to assert the authority of the federal government. Once the political decision was made to implement social reform, there were plenty of schemes available, including a package in the *Report on Social Security for Canada* tabled in the House of Commons Special Committee on Social Security by economist Leonard Marsh (1906–82) in 1943. In the end, a full program of progressive legislation was never actually enacted before the end of the war. The Liberal government did introduce the Family Allowances Act of 1944, Canada's first social insurance program with universal coverage. It provided benefits to mothers of children under age 16. In 1944 the Liberals also passed the National Housing Act, described as 'An Act to Promote the Construction of New Houses, the Repair and Modernization of Existing Houses, the Improvement of Housing and Living Conditions and the Expansion of Employment in the Postwar Period'. The King government turned to the post-war period, however, with intentions of attacking the problem of social justice and the constitutional limitations of the British North America Act simultaneously.

Evacuation from Woodfibre, British Columbia, 1942

Takao Ujo Nakano published this account of his wartime experience in 1980.

Pearl Harbor, the opening strike of the Japan–U.S. conflict, shocked Woodfibre's inhabitants. The quiet town was completely transformed as rumours propagated rumours, fed by often conflicting reports. The Japanese community especially was in an uproar.

We Japanese, largely working-class immigrants, were, generally speaking, not given to sophisticated political thinking. Rather we had in common a blind faith in Japan's eventual victory. The extent of our reasoning, decidedly specious in retrospect, went something like this: The burst of energy at Pearl Harbor was exemplary. If the war were short, say of less than two years' duration, Japan stood to win. If it were prolonged, Japan, weakened by over a decade of aggression in Manchuria and China, admittedly might lose. Meanwhile, we kept receiving reports of Japanese victories in the Far East. We therefore resolved to bear the present uneasiness patiently.

In the weeks that followed, life in Woodfibre was indeed changed. I remember especially the compulsory nightly blackout, meant to thwart the activity of Japanese bombers that might fly over British Columbia. With Canadians thus anxious, some drastic move was inevitable. By mid-January of 1942, some of us faced the prospect of evacuation. At that time it was said that if the Issei [Japanese-born] men aged eighteen to forty-five went to the road camps, then the Issei men over forty-five, the Issei women and children, and all Nisei [Canadian-born of Japanese descent] would be allowed to remain where they were. We Issei men accordingly received an order to depart on March 16.

As the day of departure drew nearer, tension mounted in the Japanese community. The lot of us Issei men was held to be a sorry one indeed. The Rockies were terribly cold in March; some of us would likely freeze to death in the twenty-below temperature. Again, the steep mountains were subject to avalanches; road work in them would be very dangerous. And again, deep in the mountains, men could easily become isolated by the snow and starve when provisions failed to get through to them. With such conjectures, the families of Issei men spent anxious days and sleepless nights. But the order to depart was a government order. To accept it as fate was our sorry resolve. . . .

Source: Nakano, T.U.: 'Evacuation from Woodfibre, British Columbia, 1942', from *Within the Barbed Wire Fence: A Japanese Man's Account of His Internment in Canada*, pp 8–10, © University of Toronto Press, 1980.

Conclusion

Despite war fatalities, injustices, and some deprivation, World War II was, on balance, a unifying and positive experience for most Canadians. Full employment helped a good deal. Rationing provided a better-balanced diet. Limited leisure time and the absence of big-ticket consumer items, such as automobiles and household appliances, forced many Canadians to save, often by purchasing war bonds and savings stamps. By war's end, a 15-year deferral of expectations had built up a powerful urge among Canadians to enjoy material comforts, free from concern over life's vagaries and hazards. This population was fully conscious of the dangers of assuming that social protection could be left to the private individual. It was equally aware that the state could intervene in the process, if it so desired.

How History Has Changed

The Winnipeg General Strike

The historical interpretation of the Winnipeg General Strike of 1919 illustrates several different ways in which history changes. In the case of the Winnipeg General Strike, not only has one of the contemporary interpretations of its origins and meaning come to dominate, but its very importance in the nation's history has altered over time.

In 1919, there were two competing interpretations of the Winnipeg General Strike, both of them extreme. A conspiratorial one, propounded by its opponents, saw the strike as a daring attempt to overthrow the existing industrial and political system. The strikers themselves insisted that the strike was a legitimate, peaceful demonstration by labour to demand the right to organize and earn a living wage. Neither of these interpretations gained dominance at the time, and the strike—after a brief period in the national eye—was remembered solely as a local issue for many years. Only J.S. Woodsworth's prominence in Ottawa kept it before the larger Canadian public in the 1930s and 1940s. Textbooks written in the 1940s made little or no mention of the strike. This limited profile began to change in 1950 with the publication of Donald C. Masters's *The Winnipeg General Strike*. The strike gained in importance during the expansion of Canadian textbook publishing in the 1960s, as authors discovered that it was one of Canada's most highly polarized historical events,

ideal for 'conflicting interpretations' approaches. The strike's historical importance also benefited from an increased popularity of history 'from the bottom up' and from a new sympathy towards radical movements.

Since 1970 a number of serious, full-length academic studies have been published. Most have accepted the strikers' own interpretation, seeing the strikers as moderate gradualists, victimized by their opposition through the law and the courts. No one could be found to defend seriously the role or policy of the federal government in the strike, which was seen not as an incipient revolution but merely as a modest attempt to win collective bargaining. New studies have examined other aspects of the strike, such as the role of women, the role of the 'alien' and racism, and socialist ideology, but the strikers' own interpretation has now been clearly established as the dominant one.

In recent years, a number of historians have endeavoured to expand the scope of labour unrest before, during, and after the Winnipeg General Strike both chronologically and regionally. They have documented the presence of thousands of local strikes beginning in the years immediately before the war, and they have emphasized the number of sympathetic strikes in other urban centres in 1919. The result has been to render the situation in Winnipeg both more common and more general than was previously recognized.

Short Bibliography

Abella, Irving, and Harold Troper. *None Is Too Many: Canada and the Jews of Europe, 1933–1948*. Toronto, 1982. The standard work on the subject, judicious, fair, and scathing in its critique of Canadian policy.

Baillargeon, Denyse. *Making Do: Women, Family, and Home in Montreal during the Great Depression*. Waterloo, Ont.,

2000. A recent work exploring the role of women during the Depression.

Baum, Gregory. *Catholics and Canadian Socialism: Political Thought in the Thirties and Forties*. Toronto, 1980. A stimulating book emphasizing that not all Catholics were unsympathetic to social reform and socialism.

Berton, Pierre. *Hollywood's Canada: The Americanization of Our National Image*. Toronto, 1975. Perhaps Berton's best work, this explores the ways in which Hollywood has dealt with Canada and Canadian subjects.

Bumsted, J.M. *The Winnipeg General Strike of 1919: An Illustrated History*. Winnipeg, 1994. Makes the history of the strike accessible to the general audience.

Fedorowich, Kent. *Unfit for Heroes: Reconstitution and Soldier Settlement in the Empire between the Wars*. Manchester, 1995. Examination of the failed attempts to relocate British ex-soldiers as immigrants to rural areas in Canada and other Anglo countries.

Finkel, Alvin. *Business and Social Reform in the Thirties*. Toronto, 1979. A useful analysis of the relationship between business and social reform in the Depression, emphasizing that many businessmen saw reform as the only alternative to the destruction of capitalism.

Forbes, Ernest R. *The Maritime Rights Movement 1919–1927: A Study in Canadian Regionalism*. Montreal, 1979. A fascinating study of one movement of regional protest that failed.

Kaprelian-Churchill, Isabel. 'Armenian Refugees and Their Entry into Canada, 1919–1930', *Canadian Historical Review* 71, 1 (1990): 80–108.

Lévesque, Andrée. *Making and Breaking the Rules: Women in Quebec, 1919–1939*. Toronto, 1994. An important study of women in Quebec between the wars.

MacMillan, Margaret. *Paris 1919: Six Months That Changed the World*. New York, 2002. A Canadian-based historian's massive narrative of the Paris Peace Conference, including Canada's role put in context.

Morton, W.L. *The Progressive Party of Canada*. Toronto, 1950. The classic account, still generally valid.

Owram, Doug. *The Government Generation: Canadian Intellectuals and the State 1900–1945*. Toronto, 1986. A synthesis of secondary literature on the subject to the mid-1980s.

Peers, Frank. *The Politics of Canadian Broadcasting 1920–1951*. Toronto, 1969. A first-hand history of the development of Canadian broadcasting before television.

Safarian, A.E. *The Canadian Economy in the Great Depression*. Toronto, 1959. The standard account of the performance of the Canadian economy in the 1930s.

Stacey, C.P. *Arms, Men and Governments: The War Policies of Canada 1939–1945*. Ottawa, 1970. A useful survey of Canada's military policy during World War II.

Strong-Boag, Veronica. *The New Day Recalled: Lives of Girls and Women in English Canada 1919–1939*. Toronto, 1988. A survey of the changing (or unchanging) role of women in English Canada between the wars.

Sunahara, Ann. *The Politics of Racism: The Uprooting of Japanese Canadians during the Second World War*. Toronto, 1981. A sober and unsentimental account that does not hesitate to call this part of Canadian war policy racist.

Thompson, John Herd, and Allan Seager. *Canada 1922–1939: Decades of Discord*. Toronto, 1985. The best synthesis of the interwar years, rich in detail.

Tippett, Maria. *Making Culture: English-Canadian Institutions and the Arts before the Massey Commission*. Toronto, 1990. Perhaps the only overview of the cultural infrastructure of any part of Canada before 1951.

Trofimenkoff, Susan Mann. *Action Française: French-Canadian Nationalism in the Twenties*. Toronto, 1975. An analysis of nationalism, mainly in Quebec, in the 1920s, focusing on Abbé Groulx and his circle.

Study Questions

1. What was Stephen Leacock's 'unsolved riddle of social justice'? How did Canadians address this riddle in the interwar period?
2. Identify three causes of labour unrest in Canada after the Great War.
3. Explain why the Depression was a devastating experience for many Canadians.
4. What social and economic impacts did the automobile have on the Canadian public during this period?
5. Did gaining the vote substantially increase the political power of Canadian women? Explain.
6. In what ways could Canada's exclusionist immigration policy be defended?
7. Why was the 'theatre of the left' more active than the mainstream theatre in presenting Canadian themes during the 1930s?
8. For Canadians, in what ways was World War II a replay of World War I? In what ways was it different?

 www.oupcanada.com/Bumsted4e

Visit the companion website for *A History of the Canadian Peoples*, fourth edition for further resources.

9 Prospering Together, 1945–1960

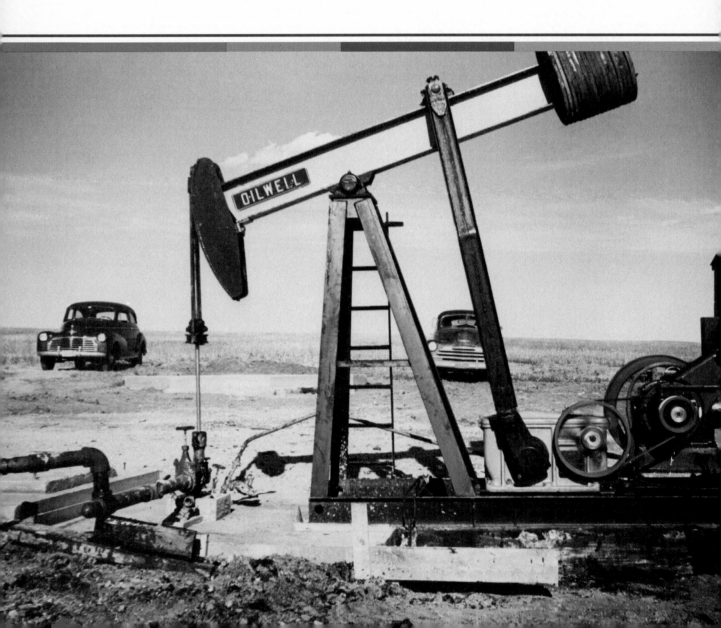

Timeline

1945   Liberal government is re-elected. Dominion–Provincial Conference on Reconstruction is convened. United Nations is founded in San Francisco. Gouzenko Affair. Cold War begins.

1947   Imperial Oil brings in Leduc, Alberta, oil field. Prime Minister King acknowledges Canada's 'moral obligation' to refugees and displaced persons in Europe.

1948   Mackenzie King resigns and is replaced by Louis St Laurent. Newfoundland holds two plebiscites on its future, choosing to join Canada. Canada becomes part of the Marshall Plan.

1949   Asbestos strike in Quebec. Newfoundland joins Confederation. Royal Commission on National Development in the Arts, Letters, and Sciences (Massey Commission) is appointed. North Atlantic Treaty Organization is formed.

1950   Canada joins Korean 'police action'. Interprovincial oil pipeline is built from Edmonton to Superior, Ontario.

1951   Old Age Security Act passed by Ottawa. Eaton's department stores' employees strike. Aluminum Company of Canada begins the Kitimat project in British Columbia.

1952   First CBC television stations are opened.

1953   Quebec's Tremblay Commission on Constitutional Problems makes its report. Mackenzie Highway is completed to Northwest Territories. Transmountain oil pipeline is built from Edmonton to Vancouver.

1954   British Empire Games in Vancouver sees mile run for the first time in less than four minutes by both Roger Bannister and John Landy. St Lawrence Seaway opens. First iron ore leaves Ungava, Quebec. Canada joins a joint commission on Vietnam.

1955   Canso Causeway is opened in Nova Scotia, linking Cape Breton to the mainland.

1956   Canadian Labour Congress is formed from a merger of the Canadian Congress of Labour and the Trades and Labor Congress of Canada. The Unemployment Assistance Act is passed by Parliament. Trans-Canada Pipeline debate weakens the Liberal government. First transatlantic telephone cable is completed between Newfoundland and Scotland. Distance Early Warning (DEW) line is established.

1957   Liberal government passes the Hospital Insurance Diagnostic Services Act. Diefenbaker's Tories win a minority government; St Laurent steps down. Lester B. Pearson wins the Nobel Peace Prize. Canada joins NORAD. The Canada Council is created.

1958   Inco strike. Lester B. Pearson is chosen Liberal leader. Diefenbaker Tories sweep the nation, including Quebec. Great Slave Railway is begun.

1959   Diefenbaker government decides to scrap the Avro Arrow. Maurice Duplessis dies.

1960   Royal Commission on Government Reorganization is appointed.

The 1940s and 1950s saw significant expansion in western Canada's oil and gas industries. The demand for Canadian natural resources prompted a period of economic growth for the country. Glenbow Archives NA-5103-20.

The post-World War II era, particularly before 1960, was a period of unparalleled economic growth and prosperity for Canada. Production and consumption moved steadily upward. Employment rose almost continuously. Canada substantially increased its workforce. Inflation was steady but almost never excessive. Interest rates were relatively low. The nation was in the midst of an uncharacteristic natural increase in its population growth rate that would become known as the baby boom. At the same time as many Canadians took advantage of the good times by conceiving children and moving to new homes in the suburbs, both the federal and provincial governments became active in providing new programs of social protection for their citizens. That network was not created without controversy, particularly of the constitutional variety, although the debate was still relatively muted until the 1960s. By that time, however, Canadian governments at all levels had become interventionist in a variety of areas, including culture.

Affluence

Economic prosperity and growth were at the root of all developments from 1946 to 1960 (and beyond). Almost all aspects of planning in both the public and private sectors were based on assumptions of constant growth, and such thinking seemed to work. Between 1946 and 1960, per capita income in Canada nearly doubled, thus increasing the Canadian standard of living. Canadians believed there were no limits to growth. Great Depressions were disasters of the past, and the standard of living could continue to rise. Politicians and their expert advisers argued that governments could now manage economies. They could correct for negative movements soon after they began. The operative economic wisdom was Keynesianism, named after the English economist John Maynard Keynes, whose writings provided much of the theoretical underpinning of the new affluence.

Quebec's Tremblay Commission on Constitutional Problems well described the prevailing wisdom in 1953:

> The objective envisaged was the maintenance of economic stability and full employment. . . . Both

expenditures and investments, by individuals as well as by companies, should, therefore, be encouraged. Moreover, the government should take a part in this, and co-operate in stabilizing the economy and in ensuring full employment by its own expenditures and investments. This would demand from it an appropriate fiscal and monetary policy, as well as a programme of carefully planned public works. . . . The new policy necessarily entailed a considerable number of social security measures regarded as indispensable for the correction of variations in the economic cycle.(Kwavnick, 1973: 183–4)

In truth, the overall pattern of affluence was neither solely attributable to government management nor distinctive to Canada. It was general across the Western industrial world. It started, in part, with the rebuilding of the war-torn economies of Europe and Asia. It continued with heavy expenditures on military defence during the Cold War. Filling consumer wants after a generation's deferral of expectations helped. Then prosperity continued under its own momentum for a time, aided by the baby boom.

Foreign trade was an important component of Canadian affluence. The volume of imports and exports increased substantially. Canada became integrated into the American trading market as Great Britain decreased in importance as a trading partner. The government set the value of the Canadian dollar in relation to the American dollar, and attempted to control Canadian foreign exchange and Canadian domestic banking through the Bank of Canada. After 1954, banks were allowed to extend consumer credit and mortgage loans, although before 1967 they were limited in the interest they could charge. Canada's monetary policy was to increase the supply of money in circulation, producing inflation that eventually would run out of control.

The relative importance of various sectors of the domestic economy shifted in these years. Agriculture declined from 25 per cent of the total workforce in 1946 to 11 per cent in 1961. The real growth areas were in the public sector, particularly public administration and the services necessary to manage the new state. In 1946 just over 15 per cent of Canadians were employed in the public sector, but by 1961 that

Most of the economic growth in Canada from 1946 to 1961 was in the public service sector. © McCord Museum, VIEW-26566.

figure had increased to just over 25 per cent. Many of the public service employees were highly educated white-collar workers, and by 1960 over half of Canadians held white-collar jobs. Women in 1960 made up about 30 per cent of the work force, with their pay about two-thirds that of males. Regional disparities in manufacturing continued and even grew. Central Canada, especially Ontario, experienced most of the gains in manufacturing. Ontario produced over 50 per cent of total manufacturing value added in the nation and dominated the manufacture of durable goods and big-ticket consumer items in many industries. In 1957, for example, Ontario turned out 98.8 per cent of Canada's motor vehicles, 90.7 per cent of its heavy industrial goods, 90 per cent of its agricultural implements, and 80.7

per cent of its major household appliances. Canadian manufacturing served two principal markets. One was the domestic consumer market, which exploded after 15 years of 'doing without'. The other was a huge market for military hardware to equip Canada's armed forces, which greatly increased in number after 1950. Canada was ambitious to produce home-grown equipment, but had to settle for subcontracting parts of Canadian orders through American branch plants. The Diefenbaker government's decision to scrap the Avro Arrow in 1959 ended the last serious Canadian venture in the independent development of military hardware.

The resource economy did reasonably well. Beginning in 1947, when Imperial Oil brought in the major oil field at Leduc, in southern Alberta, there was significant expansion in western Canadian oil and gas. Most of the risk was assumed by Americans, and the Alberta oil industry was quickly taken over by multinational firms. Oil and gas began to be transported by pipeline from the West into the major centres of population and industry. Potash provided a major new resource for Saskatchewan, and uranium was a short-lived bonanza for northern Ontario. The burning of fossil fuels and the development of nuclear power were the growth areas in the energy industry. Hydroelectric generation, which accounted for almost 95 per cent of Canada's electrical capacity in 1946, had dropped to just over 75 per cent by 1960 and would be down to only half that by the 1970s, despite massive hydroelectric projects in many provinces, especially Quebec and British Columbia.

In this period of growth, nobody paid much attention to environmental issues. Affluence rather than effluence was the watchword. Prior to 1960, Canadians were only dimly aware of the dangers of 'pollution', a word that had only just come into common use. Nuclear experts insisted that nuclear accidents were extremely unlikely and did not worry about the disposal of long half-life radioactive nuclear wastes. Petrochemical plants dumped waste into surrounding waters and paper-processing plants dumped poisonous mercury and other effluents into rivers and lakes. Solid industrial waste was usually buried, often used as landfill to create new housing estates near large urban centres, such as the Love Canal area in New York near Niagara Falls. Many inland rivers and lakes deteriorated into cesspools of industrial waste and human sewage. Acid rain spread, unrecognized as an international problem. Farmers dumped chemical fertilizers and weed-killers into the soil, where they eventually ended up in underground aquifers. Economic growth and development were the measures of all things, and the few Canadians preaching caution were often regarded as a lunatic fringe of troublemakers.

The boom of the post-war years encouraged the growth of American direct investment in Canada and the rise of the multinational corporation, which usually had headquarters in the United States and a branch-plant operation in Canada. By 1950 more than three-quarters of total foreign investment in the country was American, chiefly in mining,

manufacturing, and petroleum. In 1959 foreign-owned companies controlled nearly 60 per cent of assets in Canadian mining, over 60 per cent of the oil and gas industry, and over 50 per cent of Canadian manufacturing. The extent of foreign ownership of all major Canadian industries in 1959 was 34 per cent, of which 26 per cent was owned by United States residents. American ownership was especially prevalent in the highly profitable consumer area, where production flourished on the backs of American technology and American promotion of goods and brand names. American advertising and cultural values created consumer demand on a continental basis, and Canadian subsidiaries fulfilled this demand for the Canadian segment of their market. Not until 1957, however, did American investment and the growth of multinationals become important public issues. As late as 1956, one of the leading textbooks in Canadian economic history referred to foreign investment as 'one of the mainsprings of progress' without mentioning its less desirable aspects (Easterbrook and Aitken, 1956: 402). The foreign investment issue was brought to the public's attention by the Royal Commission on Canada's Economic Prospects, chaired by Walter Gordon. The report of the Commission, released after the Liberal government that had appointed it was defeated in 1957, observed that 'No other nation as highly industrialized as Canada has such a large proportion of industry controlled by non-resident concerns' (*Royal Commission on Canada's Economic Prospects*, 1958: 384). The Commission's concern was not immediately shared by the public, however.

Part of the critique of American multinationalism was related to Canada's scientific research and development policy. Critics noted that Canada spent a far smaller proportion of its science dollar on the development side of research and development. They added that industry in Canada contributed a far smaller share of scientific activity than in any other highly industrialized nation. The reasons for these lags, many insisted, were to be found in Canada's ability as a branch-plant economy to import technology developed elsewhere. In 1959, for example, industry was responsible for only 39 per cent of scientific research in Canada, as opposed to 58 per cent in Britain and 78 per cent in the United States. By

Waiting for the Queen

After a year of troubles, the people of the Northwest Territories got a lift from the news that the Queen would visit them on her tour of Canada. No reigning monarch had ever visited the Territories and the young, glamorous Queen Elizabeth II was utterly special. Her coronation, just a few years before, had had a fairy-tale quality about it. There was great excitement that she really was coming to the Territories. The visit was to be to Yellowknife on 20 July 1959. The date was perfect: school was out, days were long, flying was good. Groups of children were to be brought from all parts of the Territories and housed at government expense in the new hostel and hotels of the town. . . .

The twentieth of July was not a glorious, sunny day such as the north in summer can provide, but it was not raining and the temperature was mild. The crowd at the airfield to greet the Queen and the Duke of Edinburgh was enormous by NWT standards. They were mostly children, panting for the fair queen to arrive.

The Queen was coming from Whitehorse in the Yukon. Communications were poor: all we learned as we waited was that she would be a bit late. That added to the excitement when the great four-motored RCAF plane did finally come in. The impatience could scarcely be contained when, after careful taxiing into position, the stairs were put in place, the red carpet rolled to their foot, and the door of the plane at last opened. Would she be wearing her crown? What colour would her gown be?? What would she say? Finally someone did emerge—a man of medium height in a grey suit. No gown. No crown. No queen.

Nowhere else in Canada could the disappointment have been as great as at Yellowknife. No duke in a suit of any colour could do or say anything that would compensate. Queen Elizabeth, we were told, had become indisposed at Whitehorse and had to go directly to Edmonton. It later emerged that she was pregnant and some 'indisposition' led to medical advice against the strain of the trip to Yellowknife, the events there, and then the onward trip to Edmonton.

The Duke did his best. We all went to the gymnasium of the Sir John Franklin school for speeches, presentations, a walk about by him to talk to the children—but the magic had gone. The Duke, with a good show of interest, received gifts for the Queen from representatives of the different Indian tribes, the schoolchildren from far places, and most interestingly, an Inuit group. An artist among the latter had carved his own Queen out of the soapstone used for the sculptures that were beginning to get national and international recognition.

The sculptor had a magazine photograph of the Queen at her coronation to tell him what she looked like and what she wore—and there she was, about eighteen inches high, with a crown, a sceptre, and features that indeed were those of the Queen. It was beautifully done. The only thing the picture had not disclosed, because the Queen's gown was so long, was what she wore on her feet. When the carving was lifted out of its beautiful box so that it could be admired by the Duke from every angle, the sculptor's solution was revealed: the Queen was barefoot. Her feet and every one of her ten toes were beautifully carved.

Source: Robertson, G.: 'Waiting for the Queen' from *Memoirs of a Very Civil Servant: Mackenzie King to Pierre Trudeau*, pp 175–176, © University of Toronto Press, 2000.

this time, the federal government's outlays in scientific activity were in excess of $200 million per year, while in 1959 Canadian industry spent only $96.7 million on research and development at home.

Research money for the Avro Arrow was supplied not by A.V. Roe, but by the Canadian federal government. Moreover, 95 per cent of all Canadian patents between 1957 and 1961 involved foreign applicants, nearly

70 per cent of them American. Clearly Canada spent large sums of public money on scientific research, but the nation was not getting much industrial advantage from the expenditures. Canadian scientists had co-operated with American counterparts to produce the IBM 101 electronic statistical machine in time for it to analyze the 1951 Canadian census data. But before long, the new technology became American, and Canadians were never in the front lines of the micro-chip revolution of later years. In 1962, expenditure on research and development as a proportion of sales averaged 0.7 per cent by all Canadian manufacturers, as opposed to 2 per cent by American manufacturers and even larger proportions in Germany and Japan.

An increased role for organized labour accompanied other economic trends of the affluent society. Union membership increased and unions were organized in a number of new industries. World War II had marked a major turning point for Canadian labour, which had fought any number of bitter strikes during the Depression in search of an unfettered right to bargain collectively with employers. It received precious little support from government in this effort. The percentage of union members in the total civilian labour force had actually declined slightly between 1929 and 1939. During the war, however, the federal government had decided to co-opt labour into the war effort. Both Ottawa and the provinces began the slow process of altering labour legislation to recognize and protect the rights to organization and collective bargaining. The key breakthrough came in 1944 when the federal government, by war-time Order-in-Council, introduced PCO 1003. This order introduced recently adopted American principles of compulsory recognition and collective bargaining, creating the machinery necessary to protect

The 1949 Asbestos strike in Quebec. Metropolitan Toronto Reference Library.

both management and labour in contested cases. By 1946, 17.1 per cent of all workers and 27.9 per cent of non-agricultural workers belonged to unions.

With bargaining rights achieved, labour unions went on to hammer out working relationships with most of Canada's traditional industries. Improved working conditions and higher wages were the result. The process of coming to terms with employers was hardly a painless one. Throughout the 1950s there were never fewer than 159 strikes per year across Canada, involving between 49,000 and 112,000 workers annually. Important strikes that achieved national prominence included the Asbestos strike of 1949 in Quebec, the Eaton's strike of 1951, and the Inco strike of 1958 in Sudbury. A major breakthrough for public-sector unionism came at the very end of the 1950s when the postal employees organized and began demanding the right of collective bargaining. In 1956 the two largest Canadian umbrella organizations for labour—the Trades and Labor Congress of Canada and the Canadian Congress of Labour—merged as one consolidated body called the Canadian Labour Congress (CLC). This merger reduced jurisdictional disputes at the top of Canada's table of labour organization, although it did not deal with the question of the domination of so-called 'international' unions by their American members.

The Cold War

By 1945, Canada was probably already too deeply enmeshed in its linkages with the United States ever to cast them aside. Great Britain, financially strapped, was not likely to provide much of a counterweight. Canadian involvement in the Cold War was almost inescapable. There were numerous signs in the last years of World War II that the Russians and the Americans were the emergent world superpowers, eager to carve up the world into respective spheres of influence. Countries like Canada were virtually excluded from the process of peacemaking with the defeated enemies, as well as from most of the significant diplomatic manoeuvring of the post-war period. The nation found itself unable to translate its wartime manpower and resource commitments into any postwar place in the decision-making corridors of power that would remake the world. Canada protested privately about being left out of the surrender agreement with Germany, being left out of the drafting of a unilateral statement ending the war, and being left out of the Italian surrender. The final straw may have been the Allied decision to admit France (a nation that had allowed itself to be occupied by the Nazis and had fought Germany with only an army in exile) to the ranks of the 'Occupying Powers' of Berlin. As a result of the war, Canada did substantially increase its overseas diplomatic contacts, with 25 posts abroad in 1944 and 36 by 1947, but it hardly improved its international position. Towards the close of the war Canada tried to create some diplomatic distance from the Americans in their continual arm-wrestling with the Russians, but the notorious Gouzenko affair made it difficult for Ottawa to remain on sympathetic terms with the Russians.

Igor Gouzenko (1919–82) was an obscure cipher clerk in the Russian embassy in Ottawa. In September 1945 he brought material to the RCMP that demonstrated how the Russians had organized a spy ring in Canada during the war. Nowadays spying is taken for granted, but at the time Gouzenko's information and the subsequent arrests of Canadian citizens (including one member of Parliament) were absolutely shocking. Canada did not exchange ambassadors again with the Russians until after 1953. In public opinion polls in 1946, Canadians proved far more willing than people in other nations to believe that Russia sought to dominate the world. The Gouzenko incident would also send shock waves across the Western world, for loose ends from the files made it apparent that the Russians had suborned not only Canadians but their allies. Moreover, it became evident that the tight security connected with research on atomic energy carried on in Montreal had been breached. The Russians had received secret information that may have aided them in developing their own atomic bomb in 1949. With the two superpowers both possessing nuclear capability, the standoff that characterized the Cold War began in earnest. Unlike the British and French, the Canadian government declared its refusal to use nuclear power for military purposes.

Economic considerations impelled Canada in an inevitable direction as the international situation unfolded and the nation became America's docile junior partner. Prime Minister King was leery of a complete economic integration proposed by the Americans late in the war—and supported by many of his own civil servants—but Canada and the United States became closer trading partners than ever before. Moreover, when the American Congress approved the Marshall Plan early in 1948—by which the United States proposed to rebuild war-torn Europe with unrestricted gifts of money and goods—Canada was forced to do something. If European reconstruction was limited solely to American goods, Canadian trade would shrink to nothing. Canada needed market access into the American program, that is, permission for Europe to use American money to buy Canadian goods. The US readily agreed. King used North Atlantic security as a way out of continental free trade. A security treaty would not only deflect reciprocity but, as a multilateral arrangement, might provide a much-needed international counterbalance against American military domination. The Americans were not enthusiastic about a multilateral arrangement for North Atlantic security, but the Canadians pressed hard. Some Canadian diplomats even wanted non-Atlantic Commonwealth countries admitted, and Escott Reid, the deputy undersecretary of state for external affairs, sought a treaty that encompassed social and economic issues as well. The

Igor Gouzenko

Igor Gouzenko was born in Rogachov, USSR, on 13 January 1919, amid the turmoil of the aftermath of the Russian Revolution. In 1943 he was posted with his wife and son to Canada, officially serving as a secretary and interpreter at the Russian embassy in Ottawa. His superior was the Russian military attaché and head of Soviet military intelligence in Canada; Gouzenko was his cipher clerk, with access to much specialized information. In September 1945, Gouzenko was recalled to the Soviet Union, and he and his wife determined to defect rather than return home. Gouzenko was sensible enough to realize that his reception by the Canadian authorities would be greatly smoothed if he could provide secret documentation of some value to the West. On 5 September 1945, he returned in the evening to his office at the embassy and removed a collection of 109 documents that he had previously taken from the files. Arranging the documents around his body, he managed to leave the embassy building without being detected.

Gouzenko took the documents to the night editor at the *Ottawa Journal*, who recommended that he take them to the RCMP. He did so, and was told to come back in the morning. The entire Gouzenko family appeared at the Justice Building in Ottawa on 6 September but were turned away. They tried again at the *Ottawa Journal*, but were told politely, 'Nobody wants to say anything but nice things about Stalin these days.' Gouzenko went again to the Justice Building, then tried the Crown Attorney's office, where the family was met with sympathy but no assistance. They eventually returned to their apartment, where Gouzenko climbed a railing and spoke to an RCMP sergeant who was a neighbour. The Gouzenkos were sheltered in an adjacent apartment when a party from the Russian embassy broke into their apartment, where the RCMP discovered them searching for something. Gouzenko was then taken to RCMP headquarters.

Meanwhile, Gouzenko's visit to the Justice Building was brought to Prime Minister Mackenzie King's attention, but King refused to deal with the matter because it might jeopardize Canadian–Soviet relations. Gouzenko's interrogation by the RCMP indicated that his incredible stories were true. A Soviet spy ring was operating in Canada. Prime Minister King hesitated for five months before

Americans ultimately accepted the North Atlantic Treaty's military and security provisions, particularly the centralization of command under what would inevitably be an American general. They quietly scuttled other aspects of the alliance.

The Search for Middle-Power Status

By the time NATO was established in 1949, the Cold War had extended beyond Europe into Asia, where a Communist government headed by Chou En-lai had taken over China. Communism made gains in other places like Indochina and Korea, which had been partitioned after the war. The United States always saw these Communist governments as mere extensions of international communism rather than as movements of legitimate national liberation. In 1950 North Korea invaded American-supported South Korea. The Americans took advantage of a temporary Soviet boycott of the Security Council of the United Nations to invoke universal collective security. The Canadian government was in a quandary. It had no peacetime military of its own to send, nor was it enthusiastic about participating in collective security under the American aegis. Eventually a Canadian Army Special Force of 20,000 volunteers served in Korea, suffering 1,557 casualties and 312 fatalities. Most of the Canadians were involved after the Chinese had intervened on behalf of North Korea. Canada was more eager than the

appointing a Royal Commission on 13 February 1946 to take evidence from Gouzenko, whose testimony was detailed and totally credible. Canadian authorities accepted that Gouzenko would have to be given a new identity, and he only appeared in public with a hood covering his face. His revelations did not always lead to successful prosecutions, for the RCMP was clumsy in its investigations.

Gouzenko received little or no money from the Canadian government, but his disclosures in *Cosmopolitan Magazine* (February 1947) and his autobiography, *This Was My Choice* (1948), made him a rich man. Despite the establishment of a trust fund, Gouzenko was not able to hold on to his money and was subsequently reduced to soliciting interviews from the media. In 1954 he was interviewed by an American congressional subcommittee, an occasion that led to the publication of a novel under Gouzenko's name entitled *The Fall of a Titan*. This book won the Governor General's award for literature in 1954. A subsequent government investigation demonstrated Gouzenko was incapable of living within his means. The former spy spent his later years living on a tax-free pension of just over $1,000 a month. He died in 1982, apparently of natural causes.

Igor Gouzenko with a copy of his novel, *The Fall of a Titan*, 15 October 1954. LAC, PA-129625

United States for an armistice, but usually supported the Americans in public.

The Korean War increased the pressure for a military buildup. By 1953 the defence budget stood at nearly $2 billion, up tenfold since 1947. Public opinion in the 1950s consistently supported rearmament. The policy-makers at the Department of External Affairs did their best to give Canada an autonomous international presence, developing a Canadian reputation for sending small numbers of soldiers to trouble spots to supervise international agencies and monitor local conditions. Peacekeeping operations were carried out in Indochina and the Middle East, especially Cyprus. The nation's standing reached its high point in 1957 when Lester B. Pearson won the Nobel Peace Prize for his efforts to end the 1956 hostilities in Suez. Pearson, with American support, found a way for Britain and France to back out of an impossible situation created by their ill-conceived invasion of Egypt to protect the Suez Canal. Canada had earned its place among the 'middle powers', a characterization that became popular with Canada's international relations specialists at the same time as it flattered the nation's pretensions. But the world changed rapidly after Suez, and middle-power status altered with events.

The Retreat from Internationalism

Part of the gradual change in Canada's place in the world was a result of technology. When, in 1953, the USSR added a hydrogen bomb to its nuclear arsenal, Canadians became even more conscious that their nation sat uneasily between the two nuclear giants. Everyone's attention turned to air defence. Canada expanded the RCAF and began development of the famed CF-105 (the Avro Arrow). The United States pushed for increased electronic surveillance in the Arctic. In 1955 Canada agreed to allow the Americans to construct at their own expense a series of northern radar posts called the Distant Early Warning (or DEW) line. The Americans also pressed for an integrated bilateral air defence system, the North American Air Defense Command (NORAD), which was agreed to by the Diefenbaker government soon after it took office in 1957.

The Baby Boom and the Suburban Society

Canadians emerged from World War II with 15 years of disruption behind them. Normal expectations for family life had been interrupted in various ways. During the Depression, marriage and birth rates had decreased and the average age at marriage had risen. Between 1939 and 1952 the marriage rate jumped substantially, especially among the young. More family units were formed each year, while the birth rate and the annual immigration intake rose. Birth rates climbed because women who had married early tended to begin bearing children early as well—and to continue expanding their families while remaining at home. The result was a substantial increase in the total numbers of children in Canada between 1941 and 1961—the baby boom—a demographic phenomenon that occurred in the United States during the same period. As these children arrived at each stage of life in waves, their sheer numbers put heavy pressure on the facilities that had to accommodate them. The phenomenon hit primary education in the 1940s and then rolled progressively through the Canadian educational system and other aspects of society as the baby boomers got older. Secondary schools were affected in the 1950s, universities in the 1960s, employment in the later 1960s, and so on.

We do not entirely understand why this demographic blip occurred. Pent-up deferral of expectations during the Depression before the early 1940s is part of the answer, as is the absence of so many young men during the war. The fulfillment of deferred expectations, however, does not explain why an entire nation should suddenly decide to marry earlier and raise larger families. A better explanation is probably to be found in the fantasy package of a better life for post-war Canadians, fuelled by post-war affluence. The urge affected Quebecers as well as anglophone Canadians. Pierre Vallières described his father's post-war dream: 'We'll be at peace. The children will have all the room they need to play. We'll be masters in our own house. There will be no more stairs to go up and down. . . . Pierre won't hang around the alleys and sheds any more. . . . The owner

The North Atlantic Treaty, 1949

The North Atlantic Treaty was signed at Washington on 4 April 1949. The preamble and the first five articles are reprinted below.

The Parties to this Treaty reaffirm their faith in the purposes and principles of the Charter of the United Nations and their desire to live in peace with all peoples and all governments.

They are determined to safeguard the freedom, common heritage and civilization of their peoples, founded on the principles of democracy, individual liberty and the rule of law.

They work to promote stability and well-being in the North Atlantic area.

They are resolved to unite their efforts for collective defense and for the preservation of peace and security.

They therefore agree to this North Atlantic Treaty:

ARTICLE 1. The Parties undertake, as set forth in the Charter of the United Nations, to settle any international disputes in which they may be involved by peaceful means in such a manner that international peace and security, and justice, are not endangered, and to refrain in their international relations from the threat or use of force in any manner inconsistent with the purposes of the United Nations.

ARTICLE 2. The Parties will contribute toward the further development of peaceful and friendly international relations by strengthening their free institutions, by bringing about a better understanding of the principles upon which these institutions are founded, and by promoting conditions of stability and well-being. They will seek to eliminate conflict in their international economic policies and will encourage economic collaboration between any or all of them.

ARTICLE 3. In order more effectively to achieve the objectives of this Treaty, the Parties, separately and jointly, by means of continuous and effective self-help and mutual aid, will maintain and develop their individual and collective capacity to resist armed attack.

ARTICLE 4. The Parties will consult together whenever, in the opinion of any of them, the territorial integrity, political independence or security of any of the Parties is threatened.

ARTICLE 5. The Parties agree that an armed attack against one or more of them in Europe or North America shall be considered an attack against them all; and consequently they agree that, if such an armed attack occurs, each of them, in exercise of the right of individual or collective self-defense recognized by Article 51 of the Charter of the United Nations, will assist the Party or Parties so attacked by taking forthwith, individually and in concert with the other Parties, such action as it deems necessary, including the use of armed force, to restore and maintain the security of the North Atlantic area.

Any such armed attack and all measures taken as a result thereof shall immediately be reported to the Security Council. Such measures shall be terminated when the Security Council has taken the measures necessary to restore and maintain international peace and security.

Source: National Defence Headquarters, Department of National Defence, *The North Atlantic Treaty* (Ottawa: Queen's Printer, 1995) [includes a facsimile of the original treaty signed at Washington]. Reprinted by permission of the publisher.

was prepared to stretch the payments out over many years. . . . Life would become easier. . . . He would enlarge the house. A few years from now, Madeline and the "little ones" would have peace and comfort' (Vallières, 1971: 98). In 1945 the Vallières family moved to Longueuil-Annexe, one of the 'mushroom cities' that grew up around Montreal.

What Canadians thought they wanted—and what

Why Do Some Women Like Soap Opera?

The following analysis of Canadian women's attitudes towards radio programming, by Mary Jukes, appeared in the Canadian women's magazine *Chatelaine* in September 1948.

It was a warm spring day. The windows in the apartment were flung wide. Voices—male and female—mingled in what sounded like familiar domestic bickerings.

Words demanding, beseeching, agonizing, almost embarrassing in the tone confidential, sparked the morning air. They seemed to echo in the apartment well, coming from all the open windows. Almost in unison, the housewives in that particular apartment had tuned their dials and were treating themselves to a slice of throbbing domestic life, via soap opera.

How many Canadian women actually listen [to] and enjoy that kind of radio entertainment?

In the U.S.A., 58.3 per cent of the American women listen regularly to daytime serials of which there are 45. Of these, seven are released over the Canadian network. They are 'Road of Life', 'Big Sister', 'Lucy Linton', 'Life Can Be Beautiful', 'Ma Perkins', 'Pepper Young's Family' and 'Right to Happiness'. Another, 'Laura Ltd.', originates in Montreal, making eight. These daytime serials occupy two hours daily of Canadian broadcasting time.

Chatelaine went to its Consumer Council of 2,000 women, which gives an authentic cross-section of the thinking of Canadian women, from British Columbia to Prince Edward Island, drawn as it is from rural and urban groups of all ages and incomes.

The question was, 'As you know, the radio has quite a few daytime serial stories, frequently dealing with domestic problems. Do you enjoy them or not?'

Of all the replies, only 10 per cent confessed to enjoying them. But 35 per cent said they enjoyed some of them, which makes a total of 45 per cent enjoying one or more daytime serial[s].

More than a third of the women who enjoy soap opera give as their reason, 'It takes one's mind off one's own problems and troubles.' Murder mysteries probably do the same for the doctor who's glad to tear his thoughts away from Mrs. X's cardiogram. The president of the stock exchange who reads murder mysteries as an escape, might be able to agree with another third of *Chatelaine* Councilors who say, 'It makes married life seem easier.'

Over a fifth feel that soap opera adds the sentimental and romantic excitement lacking in the lives of so many women.

A tenth mention 'the sound of a human voice in a lonely house.'

Reasons favoring soap opera were stated in a straightforward unemotional kind of way. But when women don't approve of soap opera, their vehemence rises to a crusading height.

Over a quarter deplore the sob stuff, and the melodrama. Some even go so far as to call them immoral. More than a seventh complain that they don't resemble what goes on in everyday life. But the women who feel the strongest say, 'They are a waste of time and an insult to the intelligence.' A small group give as their reason for not listening a cryptic, 'Trouble of my own.'

But what would women do, if they were in a position to dictate radio-program policy?

To our astonishment 'Daily News' got the highest number of votes. Over three fifths of the women were in favor of this type of program. The next highest vote went to light opera or musical comedy tunes.

From there on preference was: Plays (good plays not crime or soap opera); quiz programs; news commentators; Sunday church services; symphonic music; discussion forums; weekday religious programs; women commentators; Canadian historical events; Canadian stars; book reviews; barn dance music. Those polling the least number of votes were crime plays and jazz music.

Source: *Chatelaine*, September 1948, as reprinted in Sylvia Fraser, ed., *Chatelaine: A Woman's Place: Seventy Years in the Lives of Canadian Women* (Toronto: Key Porter Books, 1997), 56–7.

the media told them was desirable—was a detached bungalow, preferably in a nice suburban neighbourhood, surrounded by green grass and inhabited by a traditional nuclear family. This fantasy included a wife who was a homemaker and a houseful of perfect children. 'Suburbia' was always less a geographical reality than a mental and emotional space. It is a convenient term that can be used to describe the idealized social world of the post-war period. After the war, a popular domestication of values extended into the ranks of the lower-middle and traditional working classes. Post-war suburbia was not only highly traditional in its gender roles but tended to be retrogressive in its emphasis on the role of the female as child-bearer and nurturer. In its consumer orientation, as well as in its child-centredness, it was a powerful force.

Houses became homes, easily the most expensive physical object possessed by their owners. So much time and emotional energy could be devoted to the edifice that it often seemed to possess its owners. The house focused the life of the nuclear family, while at the same time permitting individual members to have their own private space. Ideally, each child had a bedroom, for example, and a large recreation room in the basement provided a place for the children to play and gather. The kitchen was often too small for gathering, and the living room was, increasingly after 1950, the home of the television set. Advertising and articles in the media exalted the roles of housewife and mother as the epicentre of this world. Radio, television, and the record player all made it possible for popular culture to be consumed without ever leaving the house.

Central to any post-war middle-class household were its children, around whose upbringing the parents' lives increasingly revolved. The baby-boom generation grew up in a child-centred atmosphere in both home and school. Older standards of discipline and toughness in the parent–child relationship were replaced by permissiveness. New child-rearing attitudes found their popular expression in *The Pocket Book of Baby and Child Care* by the American pediatrician Benjamin Spock, which outsold the Bible in Canada after the war. Spock replaced more austere Canadian manuals. The book was one of the earliest mass-market paperbacks, sold over the counter at drugstores and supermarkets for less than 50 cents. In its pages the reader could find continual reassurance. Use your common sense, said Spock; almost anything reasonable is okay. 'Trust Yourself' was his first injunction. The good doctor came down hard against the use of coercion of any sort. In toilet training, for example, he insisted that 'Practically all those children who regularly go on soiling after 2 are those whose mothers have made a big issue of it and those who have become frightened by painful movements.' Spock explained that children passed through stages. Once parents recognized what stage of development their child had reached, they could understand otherwise incomprehensible behaviour, and recognize that seemingly exceptional problems were really quite common.

The baby boom combined with the attitudes of the permissively raised Spock generation and the new affluence to produce a category of adolescence segmented from and sandwiched between childhood and adult society. More and more young people were encouraged to remain in school longer. Progressive-minded educators treated them as a distinct social phenomenon. The authors of *Crestwood Heights*, a study of a wealthy Toronto suburb (1956), found a central theme in the 'difficulties experienced by the child in living up to the expectations of both parents and the school for "responsibility" and "independence".' They labelled the 16–19 age group as one of 'Dependent Independence'. The loss of community through urbanization and suburbanization provided a real challenge for social control. Kept out of the workforce, teenagers did not become full adults. Law and custom combined to prevent them from enjoying full adult privileges. These kids had considerable spending power. Encouraged to live at home, the youngsters were not often required to contribute their earnings (if any) to family maintenance. Instead, their parents gave them pocket money or allowances. Canadian teenagers rapidly became avid consumers, providing a market for fast food, clothing fads, acne medicine, cosmetics, and popular music. Melinda McCracken has explained that 'to be a real teenager you had to drink Cokes, eat hamburgers [known as nips in Winnipeg because

The baby-boom generation was child-centred, and Canadian youth rapidly became avid consumers. Chris Lund/National Film Board of Canada/Library and Archives Canada/PA-111396.

the local Salisbury House chain sold them as such], French fries [known in Winnipeg as chips, in the English fashion], go to the Dairy Queen, listen to the Top Forty and neck' (McCracken, 1975: 72).

Between 1946 and 1960 Canadian education, responding partly to the baby boom, partly to changing social expectations, transformed itself entirely. Canadians had long accepted the concept of universal education in the primary grades. In the 1940s and 1950s education for all was extended to secondary levels by raising the school-leaving age to 16. In 1945 there were 1,741,000 children in provincially controlled schools. By 1960–1 that figure had risen to 3,993,125. The expenditure per pupil in public schools nearly tripled between 1945 and 1958. Thousands of new schools had to be built to accommodate the increased student population. Teachers, who before 1946 had needed only a year or two of training in teachers' college, by the 1960s had to have a university degree. In 1956 the authors of *Crestwood Heights* observed that the flagship suburban community they had studied was, 'literally, built around its schools'. In 'Crestwood Heights' (Toronto's Forest Hill), education was 'aimed primarily at preparing pupils for a middle-class vocation in a highly-industrialized culture' (Seeley, Sim, and Loosley, 1972 [1956]: 224). Such was the goal of baby-boomer education all across Canada by the early 1960s.

Before the mid-1950s no one anticipated the arrival of a serious educational crisis, for in the decade after the war, classes in existing schools simply got larger while a few extra teachers were hired. But finally the problem of overcrowding became too obvious to ignore. Shortage of space was only partly a result of the baby boom. The new insistence on high school diplomas for everyone represented a profound social revolution and created a need for more room at the universities. Canadians saw more education as the key to dealing with modern industrial conditions. Curiously, however, Canada lagged badly behind other countries in terms of vocational and practical education, preferring instead to force the vast majority of its students into traditional academic endeavours. Much of the thinking that justified expanded education was imported from the United States, but these ideas increasingly were accepted by Canadian parents and taxpayers—particularly after 1957, when the Russians put Sputnik into orbit and inadvertently gave rise to a concerted campaign for educational reform throughout North America.

Immigration

Canada ended World War II with neither an immigration nor a refugee policy sufficient for the situations in which it would soon find itself, particularly internationally. The Canadian government and the Canadian people were, by and large, exclusionist, racist, and not very humane in their attitudes towards immigration. Over the next few years, this position would change, however. Circumstances, as well as slowly changing values, would literally force Canada to accept millions of immigrants, including both displaced persons and refugees (the distinction between the two was never entirely clear), and by 1962 the government would overhaul its immigration procedures to bring at least a formal end to racist immigration policy.

All of Canada's resources in late 1945 and early 1946 were devoted to transporting its troops home.

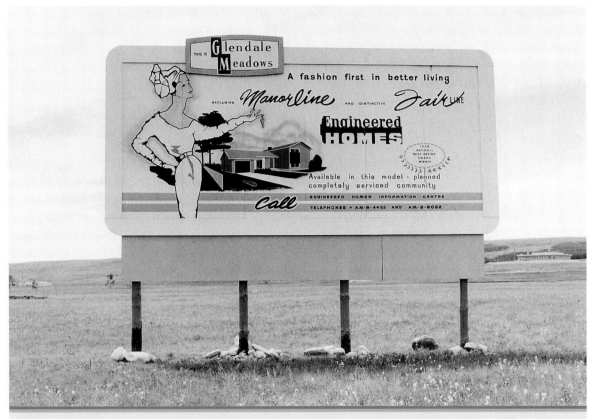

In the middle of the prairie outside Calgary, a billboard announces the new 'engineered' suburb of Glendale Meadows in August 1958. Photo Rosetti's Studio. Glenbow Archives, NA–5093–558.

Some of them had been in Britain since 1939. Partly as a result of the length of the stay abroad, almost 50,000 Canadian soldiers had found wives in Europe, mainly in the United Kingdom, although some soldiers had married women on the continent, especially in Holland. There were over 20,000 children from these marriages. Obviously these dependants would have to be allowed to accompany their soldier husbands and fathers back to Canada, and the Canadian Department of National Defence facilitated matters as expeditiously as possible, not only admitting these women and children without question, but also providing them with transport, documentation, and the transfer of money and possessions as well. The brides were informed there would be only a single one-way journey provided at government expense. Being uprooted was not an easy experience for many of these women, but they were for the most part welcomed enthusiastically in their new homes.

By the end of 1945, perhaps 2 million refugees and other displaced persons remained in allied territory, mostly in Germany but also in Austria and Italy. The majority had been housed in refugee camps. Few of these people had proper documentation, and more than a few had been Nazi soldiers and collaborators—even war criminals—who now posed as innocent victims. Establishing the legitimacy of each refugee was virtually impossible; therefore, Canadian officials did not want to accept immigrants from these camps. An investigation into immigration policy was conducted in May of 1946 by the Canadian Senate's Standing Committee on Immigration and Labour, which, to the surprise of immigration officials, supported such immigration. This report emphasized that 'Canada, as a humane and Christian nation, should do her share toward the relief of refugees and displaced persons' (Standing Committee of the Canadian Senate on Immigration and Labour, 1946: 628). The committee also criticized the government for its failure to produce a proper immigration policy.

The same month as the Senate hearings, the Canadian cabinet amended PC 695—the 1931 Order-in-Council still in effect—with PC 2071, permitting the admission of refugees with close relations in Canada. This was not intended to open Canada to a flood of immigrants. All existing immigration regulations were to be observed, and the definition of a first-degree relative was narrowly limited. Canadian immigration officials used the absence of inspection facilities as a reason for not processing first-degree relatives more rapidly. A Gallup poll in April of 1946 had indicated that two-thirds of Canadians opposed immigration from Europe. A subsequent poll in October of that year asked: if there were to be immigration, what nationalities would the respondent most like to keep out of Canada? The Japanese ranked first, the Jews second. Meanwhile, international pressure was building on Canada to help out with the refugee situation, and External Affairs became concerned that the United Nations might impose an arbitrary quota on Canada.

After months of debate in the Canadian press and in the cabinet, Prime Minister Mackenzie King read a formal statement on immigration policy to the House of Commons on 1 May 1947. King insisted that Canada wanted to encourage immigration, but also that Canada's 'absorptive capacity' must be taken into account. He did not further define 'absorptive capacity', which many Canadians chose to see as an economic measure. Others thought it a coded term for racism, an interpretation that gained force from King's spirited defence of the nation's right to pursue a discriminatory immigration policy that would not appreciably alter the makeup of the Canadian population, which, of course, was essentially of European descent. King further declared that although Canada's membership in international organizations did not oblige it to accept specific numbers of refugees and displaced persons (a barb directed towards External Affairs), 'We have, nevertheless, a moral obligation to assist in meeting the problem, and this obligation we are prepared to recognize' (quoted in Knowles, 1997: 132). In the wake of King's statement, five teams of immigration officials visited camps in Austria and Germany in the summer of 1947 to select potential immigrants. A new system of screening was put into effect, and an expansion of the term 'close relative' was introduced. Those selected were mainly under the labour selection category. They were granted visas and transported to a port of embarkation where they signed labour contracts. On arrival in Canada, each immigrant got money for railway tickets and meals. Most of the security concerns were over potential Communists rather than ex-Nazis.

Contributing to the new influx of displaced persons were fresh pressures on the Canadian government in 1947. First, the rampaging economic prosperity being supervised by C.D. Howe (Minister of Reconstruction and Supply) required more labour. 'The speeding up of the immigration movement', he insisted, had to be 'treated as a matter of high priority' (quoted in Margolian, 2000: 77). Second, the nature of the refugee lobby changed substantially. Symptomatic of this shift was the establishment in June 1947 of the Canadian Christian Council for Resettlement of Refugees (CCCRR). This organization was composed of various German immigrant-aid groups and concentrated on helping refugees from Germany and Austria, especially the *Volksdeutsche*, those Germans who had lived outside Germany's borders. With the assistance of the CCCRR, more than 120,000 refugees ultimately were admitted to Canada, placing the nation behind only the United States, Australia, and Israel as a receiver of refugees in the post-war period.

The influx of displaced persons to Canada from 1948 to 1952 was distinguished by several contradictory features. One was the inability of the Canadian authorities totally to prevent Jews from joining the flow, however hard they tried. Canada put Jews low on the list of desired immigrants, partly for cultural reasons but also because of what the authorities thought prospective employers expected of new immigrants, chiefly robust health and considerable strength. Most post-war Jews, it was argued, could not have coped with a regimen of hard physical labour. What clearly was needed was an alternate program. Jewish activists insisted that war criminals like Martin Bormann (Hitler's private secretary) could enter Canada more easily than Jews and, indeed, the immigrants of these years may well have included as many as 1,500 war criminals and Nazi collaborators. Another feature of these years was the arrival of the first 'boat people', as several thousand people from the Baltic area made their way independently to Canada aboard small and often unseaworthy vessels. They were usually greeted sympathetically and often allowed to remain by special Order-in-Council.

The hard-labour aspect of Canadian criteria for immigrants caused many problems for immigration officials. Early in 1948, for example, the Communists took over Czechoslovakia, forcing thousands to flee the country, including many of its civil servants. But such people were not eligible under existing immigration policy to enter Canada. One Canadian immigration official commented of the Czech diplomats clamouring for admission to Canada, 'As an ex-member of the profession, I may perhaps be forgiven if I suggest that the average diplomat is not likely to be very much use at anything else—particularly at the kind of initial jobs that are commonly available for immigrants' (quoted in Avery, 1995: 159). Highly trained professionals generally proved a major problem for nations receiving immigrants after the war; Canada was not exceptional in this regard. Local professional organizations and licensing authorities insisted on protecting the public from the unqualified, while the sorts of credentials offered by a displaced person from a European nation usually made little sense or seemed incomplete. Most receiving nations, including Canada, insisted that the professionals, especially the doctors, either take jobs where the receiving country's own nationals would not go—such as to the north, in Canada—or else requalify for their profession. Canada was not only unsympathetic to professionals but also to intellectuals and artists, such as those from Czechoslovakia.

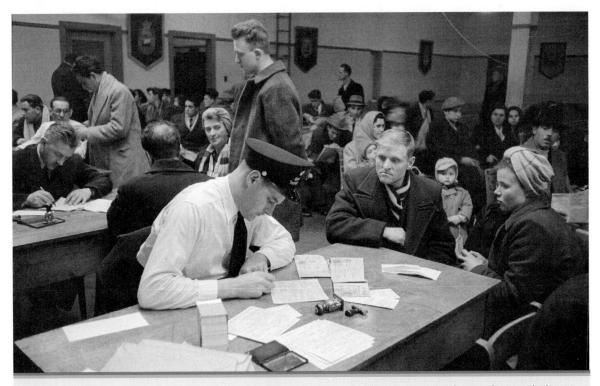

New arrivals are examined in Immigration Examination Hall at Pier 21 in Halifax, Nova Scotia. Chris Lund/National Film Board of Canada. Photothèque collection/Library and Archives Canada/PA-111579.

By 1949 Canada was finally brought to the realization that its concentration on human brawn was biting off its nose to spite its face. A new sponsorship program allowed up to 500 highly trained displaced persons into Canada, although it emphasized that most admitted could not immediately practise their skills. On the other hand, some countries, particularly the United States, had always been quite willing to accept skilled enemy aliens—even those openly Nazi—if they were scientists working in such areas as weapons research. Few scientists, no more than 50, were admitted to Canada before 1950. In a well-received book published in 1951, economist Mabel Timlin actually studied the question of 'absorptive capacity', concluding that Canada was capable of accepting larger numbers of immigrants from an economic standpoint and that such acceptance, by increasing the population, 'should mean a higher physical product per capita and hence higher real incomes for Canadian citizens' (Timlin, 1951: 122).

The displaced persons who came to Canada in the years immediately after the war shared much in common with one another. Most had suffered years of emotional turmoil, both in Europe and then in Canada. The sorts of jobs available to most immigrants, at the bottom of the occupational chain, tended to be in remote districts and subject to seasonal unemployment. The Canadian government provided little counselling or other assistance for the newcomers, leaving voluntary organizations to fill the gap as best they could. On the other hand, the post-war newcomers had the great psychological advantage of knowing that they could never return to a former life—thus providing a sense of finality and permanence to their new situation—and that almost any material conditions were better than those they had suffered in the refugee camps.

In June 1950, by Order-in-Council PC 2856, Canada expanded admissible categories of European immigrants to include any healthy individual of good character with needed skills and an ability to integrate. That same year saw the Department of Citizenship and Immigration established to replace a previous administrative structure in which immigration had been a branch of the Department of Mines and Resources. Canada now had an immigration policy of sorts, and a separate agency to administer it. In 1951 Canadian immigration policy reached out tentatively beyond Europe. The Canadian government agreed with the governments of India, Pakistan, and Ceylon to admit a few additional newcomers from each of these nations beyond the old quotas on Asians.

As many recognized by 1952, Canada desperately needed to overhaul and rethink its immigration policy. That goal was hardly achieved in the new immigration act of that year, produced after only four days of hearings by a House of Commons subcommittee that heard testimony mainly from the large transportation companies. Most of the other players involved in immigration, such as the trade unions and the ethnic organizations, were not heard at all. As a result the 1952 Act dealt mainly with administrative procedures rather than new initiatives. It expanded the discretionary powers of the cabinet and the Immigration Department to select immigrants, even on a case-by-case basis, but did not much alter the criteria used in the selection. Many found the Act concerned mainly with keeping people out. These included peculiar customs, unsuitability for Canadian conditions, and probable inability to become readily assimilated into full Canadian citizenship. The noisiest complaints about the 1952 Act came from the ethnic communities, who organized to lobby for their own particular agendas. The 1952 Act had little to say about refugees and nothing to say about the United Nations Refugee Convention of 1951, which provided a legal definition of a refugee as someone 'owing to well-founded fear of being persecuted for reasons of race, religion, nationality, membership of a particular social group or political opinion, is outside the country of his nationality and is unable or, owing to such fear, is unwilling to avail himself of the protection of that country; or who, not having a nationality and being outside the country of his former habitual residence as a result of such events, is unable or, owing to such fear, is unwilling to return to it.' Critics saw several reasons for the silence on refugees. One was the common belief that refugees were looking for temporary asylum rather than permanent resettlement. Another was the concern that not all refugees were necessarily responsible citizens driven out of their countries for the wrong reasons. Finally, there was the racial factor. Canada took some characteristic steps in 1956 when it decided as a humanitarian gesture to admit some of the 900,000 refugees living in camps in the Middle East. A Canadian immigration team visited camps in Jordan and Lebanon, selecting 98 potential citizens from the 575 candidates presented to them by international refugee organizations. Eventually, 39 heads of families were admitted to Canada in 1956. The tokenism manifest here is evident when the selection process is compared with that employed during and after the Hungarian uprising of November 1956.

Canadians had seen the events in Hungary unfold on their television screens, with young student 'freedom fighters' armed with nothing but stones facing Soviet tanks in the streets. Occurring as it did in the midst of the Cold War, the plight of the more than 200,000 refugees who fled to Austria quickly gained public sympathy. Immigration Minister Jack Pickersgill moved quickly, and before the end of November he announced the government's plan to provide free passage to Canada for every refugee who met Canadian admissions standards. By the spring of 1957, Canada had brought nearly 20,000 Hungarians to North America on board more than 200 chartered airplane flights, and by the end of the year another 10,000 Hungarians had arrived in Canada. These refugees were mainly young male students with urban backgrounds; many were Jewish. The new arrivals were, of course, fervently anti-Communist, which simultaneously made them popular with Cold Warriors—the House of Commons welcomed them enthusiastically almost to a person—and to some extent unpopular with some of the older generation of Hungarians in Canada, whose politics leaned further left. The enthusiasm of their welcome may have led some of the newcomers to assume that life in Canada

would be easier than it turned out to be, particularly as many suffered from severe trauma because of their experiences.

Not all the immigrants who came to Canada in the years after World War II remained in the country. One student of that immigration calculated that about 23 per cent of all post-war immigrants had left the country by 1961, and further estimated 'that Canada succeeded in retaining approximately 60 per cent of the immigrants who entered the country from the United States, about 70 per cent of those from Britain, and 80 per cent of those from other countries' (Richmond, 1967: 228). For most post-war European immigrants to Canada, their

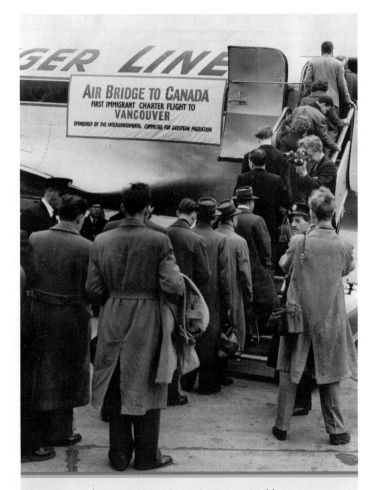

In 1957, nearly 20,000 Hungarian emigrants received free passage to Canada following the Hungarian uprising in 1956. Photo by Keystone/Getty Images.

commitment to their new nation was fairly strong. In many cases, immigrants had few family members and sometimes no country to which to return. In other cases, a return to a much less prosperous lifestyle at home was possible but hardly desirable. For the British, the years immediately after the war were ones of deprivation, but economic conditions gradually returned to normal in the United Kingdom, and social conditions under the 'welfare state' may even have improved, particularly for the working classes. In any case, upward of 100,000 British immigrants to Canada returned to their homeland during the 1950s. Most had been reasonably successful economically but had not substantially improved their social or occupational standing. Those who had married (and/or had children) in Canada were far more likely to remain, and single people, especially females, were far more likely to return home. The presence of close relatives in Canada was also important in the decision to remain.

In 1958 Prime Minister John Diefenbaker appointed a woman to the Immigration Department. Ellen Fairclough (1905–2004) was a Hamilton businesswoman and was the first female appointed to a federal cabinet post. Immigration was not expected by Diefenbaker to be a heavy responsibility, and Fairclough was given Indian Affairs as well. But a number of general problems related to immigration had surfaced by the later 1950s. Three were of critical importance. First and foremost were the ongoing difficulties with the sponsorship program, by which those already in the country could sponsor close relatives as immigrants. Second, there was the need for an expanded and liberalized selection policy, particularly in terms of attracting non-Europeans. Third, there was a need for administrative reform.

Fairclough first tackled the sponsorship program. With the virtual end of the European refugee influx in the early 1950s (except for the Hungarians), the basic way in which immigrants got to Canada was through being sponsored by close relatives already in the country. The sponsorship system, begun in 1946, had some advantages, as it authorized chain migration (by which one immigrant sponsored another) and provided a means of integrating the newcomers quickly into the Canadian community,

as well as of preventing them from becoming public charges. The national group that took greatest advantage of sponsorship was the Italians. More than 240,000 Italian immigrants arrived in Canada between 1946 and 1961, over 90 per cent of them sponsored by relatives, by far the heaviest proportion of sponsored arrivals among any immigrant group. Critics complained that many of these newcomers would not have qualified for admission had they not been sponsored.

Most family-sponsored Italians were either dependants (women, children, the elderly) not likely to enter the Canadian labour force, or unskilled males able to work only as labourers on heavy construction sites and thus likely to flood the unskilled job market. More than one-half (60 per cent) of these newcomers were from southern Italy, with the regions of Abruzzi, Molise, and Calabria providing the vast bulk of the immigrants. Most sponsors were male, and especially before 1956, males predominated in the immigration. But the chains gradually expanded, and by the later 1950s whole families and entire villages were coming to Canada. By the

The Honorable Ellen Fairclough. Photo by FPG/Archive Photos/Getty Images.

end of the decade, Immigration Department studies indicated that fewer than 10 per cent of these new arrivals would have been admitted to Canada under other circumstances. Because of the volume of Italian immigration, the Italian agents for immigrants to Canada committed fraudulent practices, chiefly the misrepresentation of facts on immigration applications. The Immigration Department began a deliberate bureaucratic slowdown of Italian immigration, as well as introducing an informal quota of 25,000 immigrants per year. The result was a huge backlog of cases, well in excess of 50,000.

Fairclough managed to get cabinet approval for an Order-in-Council of 1959 (PC 59/310), which limited the entry of non-dependent relatives into Canada. This limitation immediately affected the Italian flow but also the flow from other Mediterranean countries—such as Portugal and Greece—that featured large extended families and chain migration. The ethnic communities of these nations raised a wave of protest, claiming the new policy discriminated against them. 'Fairclough tried to defend her policy by pointing out that the sponsorship system was itself discriminatory since "well qualified Italians who wished to migrate to this country had little or no chance of having their applications considered unless they were in the sponsored categories"' (Avery, 1995: 176). She insisted that over the long term the limitation on sponsorship would produce a more diversified immigration. But she was forced to back down, stating that she was asking the cabinet to withdraw the Order-in-Council in favour of new regulations to be introduced later. This initiative failed partly because the issues were not clearly understood and partly because the government had not taken sufficient account of the vociferousness of the ethnic community; when push came to shove, the government did not want to alienate ethnic voters.

Post-war immigration greatly changed the face of Canada, especially in Ontario. Most of the new immigrants settled in the larger cities of the province, or in urban concentrations in other provinces. The Canadian city became honeycombed with ethnic neighbourhoods, featuring churches, markets, bakeries, restaurants, and clubs to cater to particular local tastes.

Aboriginals

As in earlier periods, one group that did not fully benefit from affluence and growth was the Aboriginal population. Improvements in First Nations medical care began in 1945 when responsibility for it was transferred from Indian Affairs to the Department of National Health and Welfare. This shift helped close gaps but did not eliminate them, chiefly because improved health care was not a panacea; it treated only the symptoms, not the causes of First Nations problems. At this time, infant mortality rates among Native peoples were greatly reduced for the first 28 days of life, but these rates continued to run four to five times the national average for the remainder of infants' first year. A change in major causes of death from infectious to chronic diseases occurred, but overall Indian and Inuit mortality rates still ran at more than twice the national average, and the incidence of death from accidental causes and suicide increased. Accidental and violent death was third on the list of killers for all Canadians, but first for First Nations—and this although automobile accidents were not common in most Native communities.

Alcohol was probably the major health hazard, less from long-term effects than from accidents and violence, neither of which could be dealt with effectively by improvements in medical service. Native people drank for the same reasons that other socio-culturally dislocated and economically disadvantaged people around the world did: out of frustration and a desire to escape. The First Nations were slow to organize to improve their conditions. A number of Saskatchewan groups merged into the Federation of Saskatchewan Indians at the end of the 1950s, however, and in 1961 the National Indian Council was formed 'to promote unity among Indian people, the betterment of people of Indian ancestry in Canada, and to create a better understanding of Indian and non-Indian relationships' (quoted in Patterson, 1972: 177).

The Growth of the State

Government at all levels—federal, provincial, and municipal—grew extremely rapidly after the war. For the Dominion government, the extension of its

Doctors and nurses of Indian and Northern Health Services check the health of Aboriginal people at a clinic at a Hudson's Bay Company post, 1945. Library and Archives Canada 1983-120 NPC.

power and authority represented a continuation of wartime momentum. For provincial governments, extensions of power were necessary to counter federal incursions in areas traditionally reserved for the provinces. All levels of government found the Canadian public responsive to the introduction of new social services, even if it was piecemeal. The emergence of a much more powerful and costly public sector was fuelled partly by increased social programs, partly by the growth of a Canadian public enterprise system after the war.

While the Canadian public enterprise system went back to the nineteenth century, the development of Crown corporations greatly accelerated during and especially after World War II. Both federal and provincial governments created Crown corporations, publicly owned and operated. They modelled management structures on private enterprise and usually administered these corporations on a hands-off basis. Many Crown corporations came into existence to provide important services that could not be profitably offered by private enterprise. There was a tendency for public enterprise, almost by definition, to risk unprofitability. The CCF government of Saskatchewan created many Crown corporations from the time of its election in 1944. One of the largest public enterprises of the 1950s, the St Lawrence Seaway, was a Crown corporation. For many rural Canadians the extension of electricity into all but the most remote corners of the country was a great development of the post-war period. Many provinces consolidated electric utilities in Crown corporations after the war to extend services. The federal government had hoped to expand Canada's social services after the war, at least partly to justify continuing control of the major tax fields it had acquired under wartime emergency conditions. At the Dominion–Provincial Conference on Reconstruction, which began on 6 August 1945 (the day the first atomic bomb was dropped on Japan), Ottawa discovered that not all the provinces were willing to withdraw permanently from the fields of personal and corporate income tax. Quebec and Ontario, particularly, were equally unenthusiastic about surrendering their constitutional rights to social services. The provincial rebuff to Ottawa in 1945 did not mean that the Dominion gave up on social security measures. Both funding and constitutional haggling, however, would be continuing problems.

While we often talk about the Canadian welfare state, there is little evidence that many people in Canada, much less in the federal government, had any notion of a truly comprehensive and integrated national social security system that would include full employment, housing, and education as social rights of all Canadians. Social protection in Canada would instead grow on a piecemeal basis through the activities of all levels of government. Sometimes new programs responded to overt public demand, sometimes they met obvious public need. Frequently job creation was the immediate rationale for a social program. Often a particular program of social protection was intended to provide a platform on which a government or political party could campaign. Political proponents of such programs hoped that the opposition would demur, thus providing a convenient election issue. Oppositions frequently failed to take the bait, accepting the programs and avoiding electoral battles. A patchwork of social programs thus emerged in fits and starts.

Canada ended the war with a limited federal pension program, a universal family allowance scheme, and housing legislation designed chiefly to provide employment. In 1945 Ottawa had also proposed to the provinces a national universal pension scheme for Canadians over 70 (with a means test provincially administered for those 65 to 69), a national

public assistance scheme for the unemployed, and a health insurance scheme to be shared by the provinces and the federal government. The almost inevitable demise of the Dominion–Provincial Conference on Reconstruction meant that federal progress on social protection moved ahead extremely slowly. Apart from the creation of the Central Mortgage and Housing Corporation to assist in providing low-cost mortgage loans to Canadian families and a limited home-building program (10,000 houses per year), little happened on the housing front in the 15 years after 1945. On the health-care front, the government in 1948 established a fund for health research and hospital construction, but did little else on health until 1957 when it passed the Hospital Insurance and Diagnostic Services Act. This legislation allowed the federal government to provide 50 per cent of the cost of provincial hospital insurance plans. A new Old Age Security Act of 1951 provided a $40-per-month pension to all Canadians over the age of 70, but still insisted on a means test for those between 65 and 69. In 1956 a limited federal Unemployment Assistance Act with a means test passed Parliament. Education remained almost entirely a provincial matter before 1960.

In 1945, the last year of the war, federal expenditure was just over $5 billion, with another $451 million spent by the provinces and $250 million by municipalities. In 1960 the Dominion still spent $5 billion, although far less on the military, but provincial governments now spent $2.5 billion and municipalities another $1.7 billion. Much of the increase went to social services. The result was a vast expansion in the numbers of government employees. In 1945, the last year of the war, the Dominion had 30,240 permanent civil servants and 85,668 temporary ones. At the beginning of 1961, it employed 337,416 Canadians, most of them 'permanent' and many of them female. Both provincial and municipal employment grew even faster. The provinces employed 50,000 in 1946 and 257,000 in 1966, while the municipalities increased from 56,000 in 1946 to 224,000 two decades later. By 1960 there was a sense (at least on the federal level) that matters could get out of hand. The Diefenbaker government in that year created the Royal Commission on Government Organization to

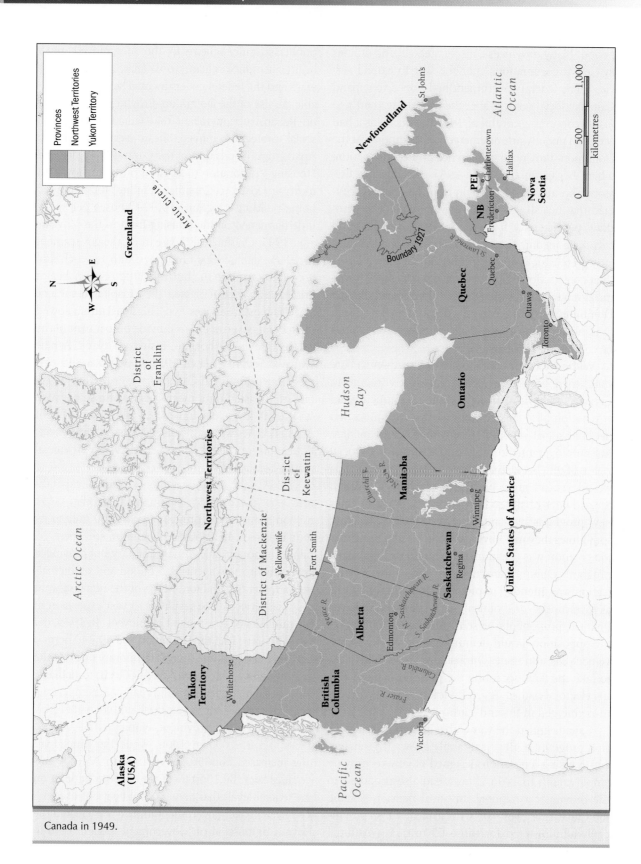

Canada in 1949.

improve efficiency and economy. It was chaired by J. Grant Glassco (1905–68).

The Shape of Politics

At the federal level there were two major parties, the Liberals and the Progressive Conservatives. In this period there were other federal parties as well, chiefly the CCF and Social Credit. The nature of the Canadian electoral system—particularly the 'first past the post' method of determining victorious candidates in single-member constituencies—combined with the continued presence of a multiplicity of parties to reduce to inconsequence the relationship between the popular vote and the number of seats in the House of Commons. True political mandates were difficult to find in such electoral results. The Liberals never won more than 50 per cent of the popular vote in any election in the period 1945–60, although they came close in 1949 and 1954. Only the Diefenbaker government of 1958 was elected by more than half of actual votes cast. The correlation between popular vote and number of seats could be quite low for both major and minor parties. The system tended to translate any edge in the popular vote for a major party into considerably larger numbers of seats and to dissipate votes for other parties. Third parties were much better off if their support was concentrated in a few ridings (as was true for Social Credit) and not spread widely across the country (as was the case for the CCF). In 1953, for example, the Liberals had 48.8 per cent of the popular vote to 31 per cent for the PCs, 11.3 per cent for the CCF, and 5.4 per cent for the Social Credit Party. These percentages translated into 171 Liberal seats, 51 PC, 23 CCF, and 15 Social Credit.

The Liberals had a number of advantages in the pursuit of continued federal power, of which two were absolutely critical. Above all they had the ongoing support of Quebec, which elected one of the largest blocks of seats in the House of Commons. Support from francophone Quebec had come to the Liberals in the 1890s, was solidified during the Conscription Crisis of the Great War, and was further confirmed by Mackenzie King's management of that same issue during World War II. The Liberals did not lose a federal election in Quebec between 1896 and 1958, usually winning more than three-quarters of the available seats. To triumph nationally without Quebec's support, an opposition party needed to win the vast majority of seats in the remainder of the country, including Ontario (in which the two major parties were always fairly evenly matched). The Tories did win anglophone Canada in 1957. Such a victory could produce only a minority government, however. The Diefenbaker sweep of 1958 was the exception that proved the rule. In other elections the Liberals were able to persuade Quebec's francophone voters that the competing parties were unsympathetic to French Canada.

The apparent Liberal stranglehold on Quebec had its impact on the other parties, particularly in terms of choice of leaders and electoral strategies. During this period, neither the Progressive Conservatives nor the CCF ever seriously considered selecting a leader from Quebec—not even a unilingual English-speaker, let alone a French Canadian. Nor did the other parties make much of an effort to campaign in French Canada, except in 1958. The Liberal Party, therefore, continued its historic collaboration with francophone Quebec. It alternated its leaders between anglophones and francophones, following Mackenzie King (1919–48) with Louis St Laurent (1948–57) and Lester B. Pearson (1958–68). This association tended to polarize Canadian federal politics. The Liberals also did well with other francophone voters, particularly the Acadians of New Brunswick.

But the Liberal political advantage was not confined to support from francophones. While national political parties needed to appeal to a broad spectrum of voters across the nation in order to gain power, only the Liberals consistently succeeded in this appeal, chiefly by staking out their political ground outside French Canada slightly to the left of centre. Mackenzie King had specialized in adopting the most popular goals of the welfare state, often lifting them shamelessly from the platform of the CCF, a practice his successors continued. The Liberals preferred to find urbane, well-educated leaders from the professional middle classes, oriented to federal service and politics. Each man had his own expertise. Mackenzie King was a professional labour

Louis Stephen St Laurent

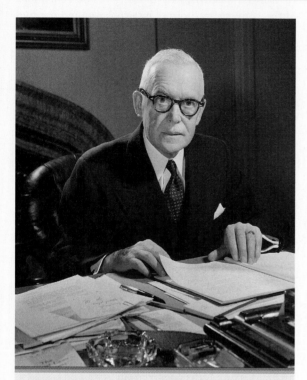

Prime Minister Louis St Laurent, December 1953. LAC, PA-144069.

Born in Compton, Quebec, Louis St Laurent (1882–1973) was the son of a French-Canadian father and an Irish mother, and was brought up in a bilingual environment. He graduated from Laval University in law in 1905 and became a law professor at Laval in 1915. For many years St Laurent was active and successful in the Quebec legal establishment, becoming president of the Canadian Bar Association in 1930 and serving as joint counsel for the Rowell-Sirois Commission in 1937.

Until 1941, St Laurent had managed to remain outside of politics. When Mackenzie King's Quebec lieutenant Ernest LaPointe died in 1941, however, King asked St Laurent to succeed Lapointe, and although he was nearly 60 years old at the time he agreed 'as a matter of patriotic duty'. He served throughout the war as Minister of Justice and in 1946 became Minister of External Affairs. He was elected King's successor as Liberal leader in August 1948 and became Prime Minister on 15 November of the same year, only the second French Canadian (and the first since Wilfrid Laurier) to hold the office. A gracious but relatively dispassionate man, he was successfully presented to the Canadian electorate by the Liberals in 1949 as 'Uncle Louis', everyone's favourite elder relation, folksy and lovable. This label stuck with him through his prime ministership. His party won easily on the strength of the performance of the economy.

In his first administration, St Laurent had a number of notable accomplishments to his credit. These included the admission of Newfoundland to Canada, the beginning of the Trans-Canada Highway, the Massey Commission, and the St Lawrence Seaway. In addition, his government improved health care and hospital insurance and introduced a better pension system. It easily won re-election in 1954. St Laurent's relationship with Quebec during the early 1950s was more problematic. During these years St Laurent made a number of concessions to Quebec, including giving Maurice Duplessis in 1954 the right to allow Quebecers to deduct the amount of new Quebec taxes from their federal taxes. 'When I get out of bed in the morning and bend over to get my socks,' remarked Quebec Liberal leader Georges Lapalme, 'I ask myself whether it will be Ottawa or Quebec City that will kick me in the behind.' In his second term St Laurent lacked energy and failed to restrain Minister of Trade and Commerce C.D. Howe, who exposed the government to much criticism by insisting on a premature parliamentary closure of debate on the Trans-Canada Pipeline Bill, leading to charges of Liberal arrogance in power.

consultant and negotiator who had studied economics at Chicago and Harvard and had written a well-known book entitled *Industry and Humanity* (1918). St Laurent was a former law professor at Laval, who became a highly successful corporation lawyer and president of the Canadian Bar Association. Pearson had begun as a history professor at the University of Toronto before joining the Department of External Affairs as a mandarin and professional diplomat. None of these men had earned a doctorate, but all held civilian appointments that in our own time would probably require one.

The Progressive Conservative Party also had three leaders in this period: John Bracken (1942–8), George Drew (1948–56), and John Diefenbaker (1956–67). Bracken and Drew had been successful provincial premiers with little federal experience, while Diefenbaker had been an opposition spokesman in the House of Commons from 1940. Bracken had been a university professor (of field husbandry) and administrator before entering politics. The other two had been small-town lawyers. All three were regarded as being to the left of their parties, and the PC party platforms of these years looked decidedly progressive. Diefenbaker was *sui generis*, a brilliant if old-fashioned public orator and genuine western populist. All the PC leaders had strong sympathies for the ordinary underprivileged Canadian, although only Diefenbaker managed to convince the public of his concerns. None of these men spoke French comfortably, and they left what campaigning was done in Quebec to others.

The Co-operative Commonwealth Federation had emerged from the war with high hopes, gaining 15.6 per cent of the popular vote and 28 members of Parliament in the 1945 federal election. Its popularity decreased regularly thereafter, however. By 1958 it was reduced to eight MPs and 9.5 per cent of the popular vote. This erosion of support came about partly because the CCF was mistakenly thought by some to be associated with international communism, and partly because much of the Canadian electorate regarded it as both too radical and too doctrinaire. The CCF showed no strength east of Ontario and was not a credible national alternative to the two major parties. After its 1958 defeat, the CCF remobilized through an alliance with organized labour (the Canadian Labour Congress), which in 1961 would produce the New Democratic Party under the leadership of former Saskatchewan Premier T.C. (Tommy) Douglas. The Social Credit Party won some scattered seats in Alberta and Saskatchewan after the war, but would achieve prominence only after Robert Thompson (b. 1914) became president of the Social Credit Association of Canada in 1960 and party leader in 1961.

Liberal dominance before 1957 was moderated less by the opposition parties than by other factors. One was the increased size and scope of the apparatus of bureaucracy, including a 'mandarinate' at the top of the civil service. Powerful senior civil servants stayed in their posts despite changes of minister or government. They provided most of the policy initiatives for the government. Another important limitation was the force of public opinion, which often restrained policy initiatives and provided a public sense of fair play. The Liberals under St Laurent lost the 1957 election for many reasons, but one of the most critical was a public sense that they had become too arrogant. Government closure of debate over the Trans-Canada Pipeline in 1956 served as a symbol for Liberal contempt of the democratic process. As the new leader in 1958, Lester Pearson blundered in, challenging the minority government of John Diefenbaker to resign in his favour without offering any compelling reasons for so doing.

At the provincial level, few provinces enjoyed genuine two-party politics. Long-governing parties with near monopolies were common, and even in Atlantic Canada, where there was a long tradition of trying to keep provincial and federal governments of the same party, the party in power was not necessarily Liberal. The Tories, under Robert Stanfield, took over Nova Scotia in 1956; Tories ran New Brunswick from 1951 to 1961. Quebec was controlled by Maurice Duplessis's Union Nationale. The Tory 'Big Blue Machine' ran Ontario, while Alberta (1935–72) and British Columbia (beginning in 1952) were governed by Social Credit. In British Columbia, W.A.C. Bennett (1900–79) took advantage of an electoral change (the preferential ballot), designed by a warring coalition to keep the socialists out of power, to

Thomas Clement Douglas

T.C. (Tommy) Douglas at the founding convention of the New Democratic Party in July 1961, when he was selected as its first leader. NAC, C-36219.

'Tommy' Douglas (1904–86) was born in Scotland, and his family immigrated to Winnipeg in 1919, just in time for the Winnipeg General Strike. After working in the printing trade, he began studying for the ministry at Brandon College in 1924, acquiring a commitment to the social gospel in the process. He moved to Saskatchewan upon ordination in 1930, where he founded a local branch of the Independent Labour Party and participated in the creation of the CCF. He ran successfully for the CCF in the federal election of 1935, and served two terms in Ottawa, where he became highly skilled at supporting unpopular issues, such as civil liberties during wartime. In 1944 he led the CCF provincial party to overwhelming victory in Saskatchewan by campaigning on the need for social reconstruction after the efforts of the war. Douglas formed the CCF's first provincial government and then served as Premier of the province for 17 years. His time in

office demonstrated that the party could not only run an effective government but successfully implement an innovative social services program.

Academics within and outside Canada were fascinated by the Saskatchewan experiment, since an agricultural province was the last place where political theory would have predicted success for a socialist party. Douglas began with expanding the province's health-care services and moved quickly to labour legislation, farm security, and school consolidation. The government also entered the insurance business in 1944, and in 1945 passed the Crown Corporations Act, which allowed it to establish a wide spectrum of government business enterprises. The recommendations of a Royal Commission on the management of northern resources were accepted; they emphasized conservation and sustainable development. Not all government initiatives, particularly in business enterprise, were successful, but the public takeover of Saskatchewan Government Telephones in 1947 and the Saskatchewan Power Commission in 1949 were generally popular. In 1948, the government established an extremely successful Arts Council. Many observers expected Douglas and the CCF to be a one-term wonder, but they managed to survive the first election in 1948 and several thereafter. The province became accustomed to the CCF approach, and it was not until the proposed introduction of medicare in 1960 that a well-organized opposition—led by the province's physicians, who entered into a bitter strike—appeared. Douglas stepped down in 1961 as provincial leader and re-entered federal politics, where he became the first leader of the NDP. Although he was unable to increase appreciably national support for the NDP, in the 1960s the party held the balance of power in several parliaments and pushed Liberal governments to the left. He left the leadership in 1971 and retired in 1979. In 2004, Canadians in a CBC poll elected Douglas the 'Greatest Canadian' of all time.

win enough seats to form a minority government in 1952. Continuing to exploit brilliantly the social polarities of a province divided into free enterprisers and socialists, Bennett never looked back. The CCF governed Saskatchewan. There was no provincial Liberal government west of Quebec between 1945 and 1960, although the coalition government of Manitoba was usually headed by a Liberal.

Liberal success in Newfoundland was a product chiefly of unusual local circumstances. Joseph R. Smallwood (1900–91) parlayed strong Liberal support for Confederation with Canada into an unbroken tenure as the province's first Premier from 1949 to 1971. After a somewhat complicated journey, Newfoundland joined Canada in 1949. Effectively bankrupt, the province had surrendered its elective government to Great Britain in 1933. It was governed until 1949 by an appointed commission, which balanced the budget but was not very popular. After 1945 the British government sought to get rid of its colonial obligations and ordered a national convention elected in 1946 to decide Newfoundland's future. In a preliminary referendum in 1948, 69,400 voters (44.5 per cent) voted for a return to the pre-1933 situation, 64,066 (41.1 per cent) voted for Confederation with Canada, and 22,311 (14.3 per cent) voted for the continuation of commission government. A second ballot held on 22 July 1948, which had an 84.9 per cent turnout, saw 78,323 Newfoundlanders (52.3 per cent) vote for Canada and 71,344 (47.66 per cent) for the resumption of Crown colony status. Confederation did best outside the Avalon Peninsula and St John's. The Canadian cabinet accepted the decision on 27 July 1948, allowing Smallwood, now leader of the Liberal Party, to head an interim government that easily won the province's first election in many years.

French Canada after World War II

The scope of social and economic change in French Canada, especially after 1939, went largely unheralded in the remainder of the nation until the 1960s. Pierre Elliott Trudeau began his editorial introduction to his book on the Asbestos strike of 1949—entitled 'The Province of Quebec at the Time of the Strike'—with the words, 'I surely do not have to belabour the point that in the half century preceding the asbestos strike, the material basis of Canadian society in general, and of Quebec society in particular, was radically altered' (Trudeau, 1974: 1). But in English Canada before 1960, the popular press was fascinated by Maurice Duplessis and his conservative Union Nationale; by ignoring the changes that were actually occurring, journalists presented a distorted picture of Quebec society. Duplessis mixed heavy-handed attacks on civil liberties and trade unions with traditional nationalism and laissez-faire economic policy, while ignoring the underlying social changes and debates occurring within Quebec. For many English-speaking Canadians, Quebec remained stereotyped as a priest-ridden rural society inhabited by a simple people. That Quebec had been lagging in the socio-economic aspects of modern industrialism made its rapid catch-up more internally unsettling and externally bewildering. As Trudeau had pointed out, by the 1950s Quebec was no longer behind the remainder of Canada in most social and economic indicators. Many Canadian commentators outside Quebec who were aware of the province's transformation assumed that the continued electoral success of Duplessis and the Union Nationale represented confusion on the part of many French Canadians. Since social and economic modernization should in the long run lead to French-Canadian assimilation into the majority society of North America, said external observers, in the short run it must be causing internal chaos.

The standard post-war assumptions about Quebec's modernization—that it meant short-term confusion and long-term loss of distinctiveness—were not particularly valid. The socio-economic transformation was accompanied by a series of profound ideological shifts within Quebec society that shook its very foundations. The patterns of that development ought to have been comprehensible to anyone familiar with what was happening elsewhere in developing societies. The power and authority of defenders of traditional Quebec nationalism, including the Roman Catholic Church, were being

Quebec Premier Maurice Duplessis giving a speech, 1950. Le Soleil/The Canadian Press.

for socio-economic change. While scorning international socialism because it would not pay sufficient attention to the particular cultural dimensions of French Canada, the new nationalists pre-empted much of the vocabulary and economic analysis of Marxism, including the essential concept of proletarian class solidarity. In their insistence on nationalism, they were hardly traditional Marxists. The post-war world, however, saw many examples of similar movements that combined Marxist analysis with national aspirations. The new nationalists—particularly the younger, more militant ones—were able to find intellectual allies and models everywhere. The external neo-Marxism most commonly cited came from the French ex-colonial world or from Latin America. The new nationalists had long insisted that the key to their program was an active and modern state. The homogeneous secular state represented the highest articulation of the nation and was the best means of liberating humanity. Traditionalist forces in Quebec had historically collaborated with forces in Canada to keep French Canadians in their place. The active state envisioned by the nationalists was Quebec, not Canada.

Opposition to the new nationalism came from a tiny but influential group of small-l liberal intellectuals centred on the journal *Cité libre*. This publication was founded by Pierre Elliott Trudeau (1919–2000) and Gérard Pelletier (1919–1997), among others, at the height of the Duplessis regime, to which it was a reaction. These liberals were as revisionist in spirit as the new nationalists, but simultaneously suspicious of what they regarded as simplistic doctrinaire thinking. They were committed to the new rationalism of the new social sciences. As Trudeau wrote in an oft-quoted manifesto:

swept away by a new secular nationalism that had become fully articulated under Duplessis. The main opposition to the new nationalism came less from the old nationalism than from a renewed current of nineteenth-century liberalism adapted to twentieth-century Quebec conditions. In the 1960s these two competing ideologies would find popular labels as 'separatism' and 'federalism'.

The new nationalism was profoundly different from the old in its intellectual assumptions, however similar the two versions could sound in rhetorical manifestos. In the first place, while often espousing Catholic values, the new nationalism was profoundly anticlerical. It opposed the entrenched role of the Church in Quebec society. In the second place, the new nationalism had no desire to return to a golden age of agricultural ruralism, but instead celebrated the new industrial and urban realities of modern Quebec. It insisted that Quebec nationalism had to be based on the aspirations of the newly emerging French-Canadian working class, which meant that nationalists had to lead in the battle

We must systematically question all political categories bequeathed to us by the intervening generation. . . . The time has arrived for us to borrow from architecture the discipline called 'functional', to cast aside the thousands of past prejudices which encumber the present, and to build for the new man. Overthrow all totems, transgress all taboos. Better still, consider them as dead ends. Without passion, let us be intelligent. (quoted in Behiels, 1985: 69)

Trudeau's small group was even more fiercely anti-clerical than the new nationalists, perhaps because its members still believed in the need for a revitalized Catholic humanism and criticized the Church from within. It was equally critical of traditional French-Canadian nationalism, which it regarded as outdated, inadequate, and oppressive. *Cité libre* preferred to locate French Canada within an open multicultural and multinational state and society.

Not only traditional nationalism but all nationalism was unprogressive and undemocratic.

At the end of the 1950s most Quebec intellectuals had arrived at some similar conclusions, however different the routes. The traditional nationalism in Quebec—of Catholicism, of the Union Nationale—led nowhere. The dead hand of the Church had to be removed. A modern state, secular and interventionist, was needed to complete Quebec's modernization.

Refus Global

In 1948, in Montreal, the painter Paul-Émile Borduas (1905–60) released a manifesto signed by himself and a number of other Quebec artists and intellectuals. An excerpt follows.

The magical harvest magically reaped from the field of the Unknown lies ready for use. All the true poets have worked at gathering it in. Its powers of transformation are as great as the violent reactions it originally provoked, and as remarkable as its later unavailability (after more than two centuries, there is not a single copy of Sade to be found in our bookshops; Isidore Ducasse, dead for over a century, a century of revolution and slaughter, is still, despite our having become inured to filth and corruption, too powerful for the queasy contemporary conscience).

All the elements of this treasure as yet remain inaccessible to our present-day society. Every precious part of it will be preserved intact for future use. It was built up with spontaneous enthusiasm, in spite of, and outside, the framework of civilization. And its social effects will only be felt once society's present needs are recognized.

Meanwhile our duty is plain.

The ways of society must be abandoned once and for all; we must free ourselves from its utilitarian spirit. We must not tolerate our mental or physical faculties' being wittingly left undeveloped. We must refuse to close our eyes to vice, to deceit perpetuated under the cloak of imparted knowledge, of services rendered, of payment due. We must refuse to be

trapped within the walls of the common mould—a strong citadel, but easy enough to escape. We must avoid silence (do with us what you will, but hear us you must), avoid fame, avoid privileges (except that of being heeded)—avoid them all as the stigma of evil, indifference, servility. We must refuse to serve, or to be used for, such despicable ends. We must avoid deliberate design as the harmful weapon of reason. Down with them both! Back they go!

MAKE WAY FOR MAGIC! MAKE WAY FOR OBJECTIVE MYSTERY!

MAKE WAY FOR LOVE!

MAKE WAY FOR WHAT IS NEEDED!

We accept full responsibility for the consequences of our refusal.

Self-interested plans are nothing but the stillborn product of their author.

While passionate action is animated with a life of its own.

We shall gladly take full responsibility for the future. Deliberate, rational effect can only fashion the present from the ashes of the past.

Our passions must necessarily, spontaneously, unpredictably forge the future. . . .

We need not worry about the future until we come to it.

Source: Ramsay Cook, ed., *French-Canadian Nationalism: An Anthology* (Toronto: Macmillan of Canada, 1969), 280–1. Reprinted with permission of the author.

There was some disagreement over the nature of this modern state. The new nationalists were inclined to see it as a liberating embodiment of French-Canadian collectivities, while the *Cité libre* people saw it more as a regulating mechanism. It only remained to persuade the general populace of the province of the need for change.

Signs of the profound changes that had occurred and were still occurring in Quebec could be seen in the province's intellectual and artistic communities. In 1948 Paul-Émile Borduas released his famous manifesto, written originally in 1947. *Refus global* was a rambling series of passionate, almost poetic utterances attacking virtually everything in Quebec society at the time. Some young painters were not satisfied with the combination of spontaneity and traditional spatial perspectives advocated by Borduas. Led by Fernand Leduc, they produced a manifesto in 1955—signed 'Les Plasticiens'—that was less inflammatory than *Refus global*, but that also insisted on artistic freedom. It said that its subscribers were drawn to 'plastic qualities: tone, texture, forms, lines, and the final unity between elements' (quoted in Davis, 1979: 18). Abstractionism quickly ceased to be regarded as particularly avant-garde in Quebec. In the theatre, some attempt was made to break out of the constraints imposed by realism. One particularly striking example was *Le Marcheur* (The Walker) by Yves Thériault, which was presented in 1950. It featured a dominant father (never seen on stage), who controlled the lives of everyone around him at the same time that he united them in their hatred for him. The father could be seen as the traditional French-Canadian paternal tyrant, or Premier Duplessis, or the Church.

Federal–Provincial Relations

The 1945–6 Dominion–Provincial Conference on Reconstruction had served as the arena for the renewal after the war of constitutional conflict between the Dominion and its provinces. In August 1945 the federal government tabled a comprehensive program for an extended welfare state based on the tax collection and economic policy of a strong central government. It sought the co-operation of the provinces to implement its plans. Ottawa wanted agreement that it could keep the emergency powers it had acquired to fight the war, especially the power to collect all major taxes. The Conference adjourned for study, finally meeting again in April 1946. At this point Quebec and Ontario in tandem simultaneously denounced centralization while insisting on a return to provincial autonomy. Ontario had some social programs of its own in the planning stages. Quebec, led by Duplessis, wanted to keep control of social powers in order not to have them implemented. In the wake of this meeting, the federal government offered a 'tax rental' scheme to the provinces, whereby it would collect certain taxes (on incomes, corporations, and inheritances) and distribute payment to the provinces. Ontario and Quebec went their own ways, but the remaining provinces (and Newfoundland after 1949) accepted tax rental, which (along with suitable constitutional amendment) had been recommended by the Rowell-Sirois Commission in 1940.

Constitutional revision was no easy matter to contemplate. As we have seen, conflict had been literally built into Confederation by the British North America Act. The Dominion of Canada was a federal state, with a central government in Ottawa and local governments in the provinces. While the intention of the Fathers of Confederation had been to produce a strong central government, they had been forced by the provinces (especially what would become Quebec) to guarantee them separate identities. These identities were protected through an explicit division of powers between federal and provincial governments in sections 91 and 92 of the British North America Act of 1867. The division thus created reflected the state of political thinking in the 1860s. It gave the federal arm the authority to create a viable national economy. It gave the provinces the power to protect what at the time were regarded as local and cultural matters. Some of the provincial powers, such as those over education, were acquired because the provinces demanded them. Others, such as the powers over the health and welfare of provincial inhabitants, were not regarded by the Fathers as critical for a national government. Lighthouses and post offices were more important than public medical care in the 1860s.

Over time the division of powers gave the provinces the responsibility, in whole or in part, for many of the expensive aspects of government, including health, education, and welfare. Provincial ability to raise the revenue needed to meet these obligations was limited, however. Many important aspects of welfare came to be shared among governments. The BNA Act's division of powers was clearly dated, ambiguous, and contentious. Despite the miracle of Canada's survival, the Constitution was constantly strained. Then, as now, critics of the existing system stressed its tensions, while its defenders lauded its capacity for survival.

One of the key problems was the settling of disputes over interpretation of the BNA Act itself. The Act provided for a judicature modelled on British arrangements, with a Supreme Court at the top. This Court, established in 1875, was not always the court of final recourse on constitutional matters. Until 1949 constitutional questions could be finally appealed to a British imperial court, the Judicial Committee of the Privy Council of the United Kingdom. In the years after Confederation, the JCPC had interpreted the Constitution in ways highly favourable to the provinces. Even with the successful elimination, after the war, of this example of continued colonialism, amendment of the Constitution was extremely difficult. Amending procedures were not spelled out in the Act itself. The convention had grown up that amendment required the consent of all provinces, which was not easy to obtain. Moreover, such amendment could ultimately be achieved only by an Act of the British Parliament.

By the mid-twentieth century, Canadian political leaders had worked out a variety of informal means for dealing with matters of constitutional disagreement. One of the most important was the federal-provincial conference, which was employed regularly after 1945 to deal with financial business and gradually came to address constitutional matters as well. So long as the Union Nationale government of Maurice Duplessis represented Quebec at these gatherings, Quebec stood by a traditional view of the 1867 arrangement. The province protected its existing powers fiercely, but did not particularly seek to expand them. Another dimension was added to the post-war constitutional situation through John Diefenbaker's insistence on the introduction of a Canadian Bill of Rights, however.

The Americans had produced their Bill of Rights (the first 10 amendments to their 1787 Constitution) as part of the process of ratifying the Constitution. In Canada, the British constitutional tradition insisted that Parliament was supreme, while the courts automatically protected against the abuse of power. The BNA Act had protected some minority rights, but had displayed little interest in the rights of the individual, which were crucial to the American approach. This notion of spelling out rights—for individuals or collective groups—was a potentially profound change in the Canadian Constitution. Diefenbaker's Bill for the Recognition and Protection of Human Rights and Fundamental Freedoms, fulfilling campaign promises of 1957 and 1958, passed the federal Parliament in 1960. As it was limited to the federal level, and the rights it protected could be overridden by national emergencies, it had little immediate impact. A full 10 years would go by before the Canadian Supreme Court would hear a case based on the Bill of Rights, but its implications for constitutional reform—particularly when combined with the growth of new and politically conscious minorities in the 1960s—were substantial.

At the end of the 1950s the Canadian Constitution stood on the cusp of great change. Canadians ought to have recognized that neither constitutional nor federal-provincial problems were solely the product of the presence of Quebec in Confederation. Nevertheless, the issue of Quebec became inextricably bound up with increasing federal-provincial tensions. Constitutional reform would become the panacea for the nation's divisions.

The Rise of Canadian Culture

Culture in Canada and Canadian Culture (the two were never quite synonymous) after World War II emerged as major public issues. This was a major

A Progressive Conservative Newspaper Editor Evaluates John Diefenbaker

Grattan O'Leary was editor of the *Ottawa Journal* for many years, wrote speeches for the Diefenbaker government, and was appointed to the Senate by Mr Diefenbaker in 1962.

I have never subscribed to the myth of Diefenbaker's greatness. At one time I felt Diefenbaker would be but a footnote to history. In recent years I have changed my mind about that. We had our fallings out, it is true. But there is no hatred or destructiveness in my feeling about John Diefenbaker, any more than in my feeling about any other person who held the arduous, demanding, and self-immolating responsibilities which he held. Men have faults equal to the sum of their abilities. Men's virtues spring from the same wellsprings wherefrom they derive their failings. . . .

If Diefenbaker could have achieved humility, compromise, a tendency to give a little—to show compassion for those around him—I am sure his greatness would have been written large. As it is, his legacy leaves doubt on the pages of history

Of course, the fires of controversy burned continuously around Diefenbaker and kept on doing so after he left the leadership, simply because of his refusal to compromise on any issue. Adherence to principle is a wonderful thing, but decisions on minor and even major problems are more easily found if there is a capacity to see another point of view. . . .

The Diefenbaker government was constantly running up against the harsh facts of life. The trade structure was what it was because of the necessities of our continental position; the United States was our best customer because the Americans needed what we had to sell and because it was more economical to obtain it from us than from someone else. By the end of six years the scope of achievements—both realized and merely contemplated—had been lost in a welter of confusion, contradictions, and confrontations.

What of John Diefenbaker's personality? A man who knew exactly what he wanted. A man imbued from early youth with the purpose of being Prime Minister; intemperate, messianic; a reformer, a crusader who could not stand or countenance divisions, as for those implied by special treatment of French Canada. Two nations, whether pronounced in English or in French, was anathema to him. There could be no compromise. . . . Almost fanatical in his determination to save us from ourselves, he refused to take into account the motivations of men and societies and was thus constantly in a position where he thought he was being betrayed by others. . . .

The Press Gallery wrote of him as an 'orator'—a distortion of language. For if oratory be what John Morley said it was—structure, beauty, and passion—no one could be more remote from it than John Diefenbaker. The choice and measured phrase of a Laurier or the poetry of a McGee were no more his than was the analytical power of a Meighen. But he could put on a performance.

Source: Grattan O'Leary, *Recollections of People, Press, and Politics* (Toronto: Macmillan of Canada, 1977), 134–6.

development of the post-war period. Culture had not been entirely ignored before 1945, but it had always taken a back seat to political and economic matters. Canada's cultural performance (or lack of it) was explained chiefly in terms of priorities. Culture was a luxury that would come only with political and economic maturity. Such maturity was now at hand. A number of parallel developments affecting culture occurred after 1945. One of the most obvious saw both federal and provincial governments attempt to articulate and implement public cultural policy. The policy initiatives were driven chiefly by concerns to protect homegrown culture from being overwhelmed by external influences. They helped create a variety of new cultural institutions in the post-war period. On the creative level, many contemporary artists began deliberately cultivating a naive or native style, with considerable public success, thus helping to breach the older boundaries of art and culture. Other artists enthusiastically joined international movements.

Canada was hardly alone in discovering that culture in its various forms was an important matter in the post-war world. Few nations, however, had a greater need for conscious cultural policy than Canada. It was a nation without a single unifying language and with at least two of what many after 1945 began to call 'founding cultures'. At the same time, francophones and anglophones often meant something quite different when they talked about culture. While nobody doubted that French Canada's culture was distinctive, defining the culture of the rest of the nation was more problematic. More than most nations, Canada was exposed to external cultural influences, particularly from its behemoth neighbour to the south, the United States. The Americans purveyed to Canada and then to the world a profoundly American cultural style, anchored in popular culture.

In 1945 (or at any point earlier), Canada had considerably more cultural activity than most Canadians would have recognized at the time. One of the problems was that cultural commentators relied on highly restrictive critical canons and categories. Much of Canada's cultural life went on outside

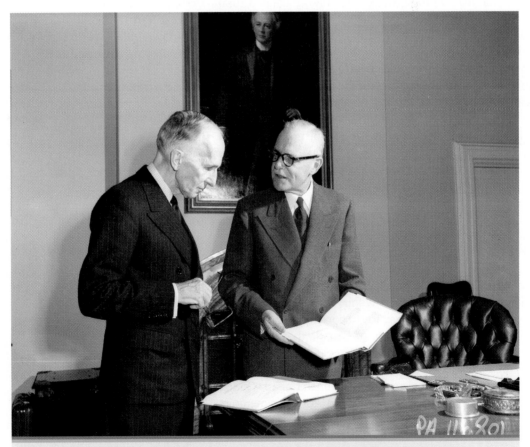

Vincent Massey (left), Chairman of the Royal Commission of Arts, Letters, and Sciences, presents Prime Minister Louis St Laurent with a copy of the Commission's official report. Chris Lund/National Film Board of Canada/Library and Archives Canada/PA-116801.

the boundaries of what critics and experts usually regarded as Culture with a capital C. Canadians became involved in culture on a non-professional basis for their own pleasure. The resultant culture came from folk traditions more than from high art. Moreover, it was not necessarily distinctly Canadian. By 1945, Canadian government—particularly at the federal level with the Public Archives, the National Gallery, the National Film Board, and the Canadian Broadcasting Corporation—already had a substantial if largely unrecognized role in culture. Prime Minister St Laurent was told during the 1949 elections that the Liberals might lose votes to the CCF from 'those Canadians who have a distinct national

Gabrielle Roy

Gabrielle Roy (1909–83) was born in Saint-Boniface, Manitoba, a francophone suburb of Winnipeg. She was educated at Winnipeg Normal School and taught for a number of years in the province, mainly in isolated rural communities. Thoroughly bilingual, in 1937 she travelled to Europe, where she spent two years before the approach of World War II forced her to return to Canada. Roy settled in Montreal, where she worked as a journalist while beginning to write fiction. Her observations of the working-class district of Saint-Henri served as the background for her first novel, *Bonheur d'occasion*, which was published in 1945. This work introduced an international readership to the complexities of working-class life in urban Quebec in the first years of World War II. Her characters are divided by their desire to make the most of military service and military prosperity after a decade of unemployment, while still susceptible to the general hostility felt by French Canada to involvement in an overseas war.

The novel won a French Prix Fémina, and after translation into English as *The Tin Flute*, it garnered a major American award as well from the Literary Guild of America. Typically for Canadian works, the novel was initially far more honoured outside the nation than within, although it did win the Governor General's award for fiction in 1947. Roy was invited to join the Royal Society of Canada that same year, which also saw her marriage to Dr Marcel Carbotte. Roy was far less regionally focused than most Quebec writers, and this was key to her popular success outside French Canada. Much of her later work was in the form of short stories or memoirs and was set in Manitoba or in the Arctic. She never returned to Manitoba to live, however, spending the remainder of her life in Europe and in Quebec. Roy wrote about the trials of ordinary people in a plain, accessible style. She was one of the first writers to depict Inuit characters in her fiction and to employ them as protagonists. Unusual among francophone writers in Canada, Roy saw virtually all of her work artfully translated into English.

Gabrielle Roy in the 1950s. LAC, C-18347.

consciousness and feel that more should be done to encourage national culture and strengthen national feeling'. As a result, St Laurent appointed the Royal Commission on National Development in the Arts, Letters, and Sciences, usually known as the Massey Commission after its chairman, Vincent Massey.

The Massey Commission existed because its time had come. It did not invent a cultural policy but merely publicized one. While its recommendations were crucial in increasing government involvement in the arts, they were precisely the ones envisioned in the Commission's terms of reference, which were in turn a product of considerable lobbying by well-established arts groups. The Commission held extensive public meetings, receiving 462 briefs and listening to 1,200 witnesses. The witnesses, reported its chairperson, represented '13 Federal Government institutions, 7 Provincial Governments, 87 national organizations, 262 local bodies and 35 private commercial radio stations' (*Report of the Royal Commission on National Development in the Arts, Letters and Sciences*, 1951: 8). In most respects the Massey

The Massey Commission Report, 1951

The Massey Commission was set up in 1949 to study and report on Canadian 'activities generally which are designed to enrich our national life, and to increase our own consciousness of our national heritage and knowledge of Canada abroad'. It made its report in 1951.

In writing this Report we have been forced to turn again and again to the dangerous neglect of the humanities and social sciences, studies essential to the maintenance of civilized life. It was suggested to us that the success of the National Research Council in the encouragement of scientific studies offered an example that should perhaps be followed in the establishment of a National Council for the Humanities and Social Sciences. We believe, however, that the implied parallel is misleading, that the essential nature and value of these studies makes it undesirable to isolate them in a separate body, that their present 'plight' may be partly explained, as we have previously suggested, by an effort to subject them too rigidly to scientific techniques and methods of organization. Moreover, we are convinced that, in our country particularly, encouragement of these studies must be carried on to a considerable extent through international exchanges, and through closer contacts with France, Great Britain and with other European countries where traditionally they are held in great respect. We think that the very important responsibility of encouraging these studies through a flexible scheme of scholarships and grants can best be carried out by an organization which will be obliged by its other responsibilities to keep in the closest touch with cultural affairs at home and abroad, and with universities, particularly with Canadian universities which, as we have seen, are the focal point for so many of our cultural activities.

We therefore recommend:

a. That a body be created to be known as the Canada Council for the Encouragement of the Arts, Letters, Humanities and Social Sciences to stimulate and to help voluntary organizations within these fields to foster Canada's cultural relations abroad, to perform the functions of a national commission for UNESCO, and to devise and administer a system of scholarships as recommended in Chapter XXII. . . .

Source: *Report of the Royal Commission on National Development in the Arts, Letters and Sciences 1949–1951* (Ottawa: King's Printer, 1951), 376–7.

Live Drama on Early Television

The following is a part of interviews conducted by Mary Jane Miller many years after the event with some of Canada's pioneer TV directors.

ROBERT ALLEN [1981]: In 1952, when television started, the CBC brought in a handful of people from various places, some more experienced than others. Some had been working in the theatre for one or two years. They all gathered here and began to learn how to do it. It is not easy for a director to learn to cope with the machinery of television. Moreover, he has to face a group of between thirty and fifty people in addition to the cast. We had at least three (sometimes four) cameras at the same time which you had to move from one place to another as the action shifted. The director had no chance to stop. When I think of the actual broadcast, the director was performing as much as the actors. Unlike film, with live television it was the director who determined everything. No retakes, no stopping to change reels. Just start and go.

MJM: The directors learned by doing it?

ALLEN: By doing it, yes. And there was the small group who continued to do it, until we all dropped dead, practically.

MJM: I can't get over the number of productions each of you did, one every two or three weeks. It must have been mad.

ALLEN: I was doing a ninety-minute show every three weeks. And the next morning I had to find another topic. Which meant reading, asking people, and in two or three days deciding what to do. I was also doing a half-hour of *Sunshine Sketches* every week. We were able to do stage plays on live television, because we cut the play. [There was no real adaptation.] We were on a treadmill, we were running fast enough not to worry about whether we were going to be shot down or not. [As far as censorship is concerned, always an issue in television, it was more difficult, because it went out live, for sponsors, politicians, or CBC brass to stop a show.]

PAUL ALMOND: It was really exciting. In those days of live television the most important thing was to catch the moment of drama—not at a dress rehearsal but on the air. You had to catch that elusive spark. Getting that live performance was quite different, you did it once. The art of trying to direct actors in those days was somehow to bring the performance to a peak at the right point—on the air. Just as the performances varied through the rough dress rehearsal (the first time, cast and crew did the drama 'at speed'), the dress rehearsal, and the show, so the camera would vary, it wouldn't just hit fixed marks. If a person was being tremendous on air we'd go in much closer, I'd say, 'closer, closer, she's terrific, closer!' and then suddenly, 'ok, pull back, wait a minute.' So everything happened spontaneously. The camera work was spontaneous with the acting because your shots reflected the intensity of the minute—which is impossible on film.

Source: Mary Jane Miller, *Rewind and Search: Conversations with the Makers and Decision-Makers of CBC Television Drama.* Montreal and Kingston, McGill-Queen's University Press, 1996, 4–5.

Commission looked backward instead of forward. It attempted to promote a Victorian vision of culture. It may have established most of the agenda of federal cultural policy for at least a generation to follow, but that agenda was narrowly conceived.

Despite its mandate to articulate a national cultural policy, especially in radio and television broadcasting, the Commission was chiefly interested in elite culture and elitist ways of dealing with it. What needed to be preserved was a culture of excellence that was 'resolutely Canadian'. In 1951 it recommended the creation of a national television service as quickly as possible. It also wanted both radio and television broadcasting to be 'vested in the

Family watching television, 1950s. Photo: Petrified Collection/Getty Images.

Canadian Broadcasting Corporation'. This monopoly would help 'to avoid excessive commercialism and to encourage Canadian content and the use of Canadian talent' (*Report of the Royal Commission on National Development in the Arts, Letters and Sciences*, 1951: 305). It supported the expansion of the National Film Board, the National Gallery, the National Museum, the Public Archives, the Library of Parliament, and the Historic Sites and Monuments Board of the National Parks Service. It also recommended the extension of the concept of the National Research Council (for scientific research) into the humanities and social sciences through the creation of a Council for the Arts, Letters, Humanities, and

Social Sciences. Much of its agenda would be implemented in piecemeal fashion by federal governments over the next decade. The Canada Council, for example, was established in 1957.

Not long after the Massey Commission had reported, the Royal Commission on Broadcasting was formed in 1955, chaired by Robert Fowler (1901–80) of Montreal. It made its final report in 1957. The Fowler Commission had to deal with the shift from radio to television and the prevalence of American-produced records, movies, and shows in both media. It insisted that the century-old Canadian answer to Americanization was for the government to provide 'conscious stimulation' through financial assistance, an approach it clearly favoured. In addition to subsidies and protective measures, the Fowler Commission recommended another cultural strategy: regulated competition with a 'mixed system of public and private ownership'. The Diefenbaker government translated Fowler's recommendations into its Broadcasting Act of 1958, creating the Board of Broadcast Governors to monitor broadcasting to ensure that the service would be 'basically Canadian in content and character' (*Report of the Royal Commission on Broadcasting*, 1957: 8–11).

In September 1952, the Canadian Broadcasting Corporation opened the nation's first two television stations in Toronto and Montreal, and over the next two years it extended its television coverage to seven other metropolitan areas. At the time, only 146,000 Canadians owned television receivers (or 'sets' as they were usually called).

They tuned their sets to American border stations and used increasingly elaborate antenna systems to draw in distant signals. Most Canadians thus missed entirely the first generation of American television programming, broadcast live from the studio, and tuned in only as US television moved from live to filmed programs and from New York to Hollywood. By 1952, *I Love Lucy* had been running in the States for over a year. But if Canada's love affair with the tube was slightly belated, the country rapidly caught

Robert Farnon

Robert Farnon was born in Toronto in 1917 and studied trumpet from his childhood. In the early 1930s he became active in the Toronto dance band scene and later joined orchestras at the CBC led by Percy Faith and Geoffrey Waddington. He was best known publicly in Canada for his participation in CBC's *Happy Gang* shows from 1937 to the early 1940s. At the same time, he developed a considerable reputation among musicians as a trumpet player, composer, and arranger. In 1943 he headed for Britain to become the conductor of the Canadian Band of the Allied Expeditionary Force. Many regarded this Canadian aggregation as superior to the UK band led by George Melachrino and the American band led by Glenn Miller because of Farnon's superior arrangements of tunes he copied off the short-wave radio. After the war Farnon became associated with the BBC, for which he wrote a succession of short program-signature tunes (including 'Jumping Bean' and 'Portrait of a Flirt') that made him one of the most listened to composers in the world, albeit with little public recognition. He also became known among his peers as the leading figure in what the British called 'light music'. He wrote over 30 movie soundtracks, did arrangements for most of the leading British bands, and settled in Guernsey in 1959. In the 1960s and 1970s he had a highly successful British recording career, leading his own orchestra, and was still winning awards, including a Grammy, in the 1990s. Farnon occasionally wrote music with Canadian associations, but he never returned to Canada on a permanent basis. He is a perfect example of a highly successful Canadian performer and artist who is virtually unknown in Canada because most of a distinguished career was spent outside the country.

up. By December 1954 there were nine stations and 1.2 million sets; by June 1955 there were 26 stations and 1.4 million sets, and by December 1957 there were 44 stations and nearly 3 million sets.

Television's popularity has been an international phenomenon transcending national circumstances and socio-economic conditions. Nevertheless, for Canadian society in the post-war years, television was the ideal technology. It fitted perfectly into the overall social and cultural dynamics of the time. Perhaps even more than the automobile or the detached bungalow on its carefully manicured plot of green grass, television symbolized the aspirations and emergent lifestyles of the new suburban generation of Canadians. Unlike other leisure-time activities that required 'going out', television was a completely domesticated entertainment package that drew Canadian families *into* their homes. Until the late 1960s, most families owned only one television set, located in the living room. Particularly on weekend evenings during the long Canadian winter, the only sign of life on entire blocks of residential neighbourhoods was the flickering glow of black-and-white television sets coming from otherwise darkened houses. The family could entertain friends who enjoyed the same popular programs, and everyone could enjoy snacks served on small metal 'TV tables' or even a meal taken from the freezer and heated (the 'TV dinner'). Some of what people watched was Canadian-produced, but most prime-time shows came from the Hollywood dream factory. Despite the popularity of Saturday evening's *Hockey Night in Canada*, first telecast in 1954, television served to draw Canadians ever deeper into the seductive world of American popular culture.

The post-war years were critical ones for popular culture in Canada. While governments wrestled with aspects of a cultural policy intended to protect Canadian culture and the Canadian identity from 'foreign' (read American) influence, their focus before 1960 was almost entirely on high culture. Few Canadians appreciated that the Americans were undergoing a cosmic shift of their own in cultural terms, particularly in the way they marshalled the media and their entire entertainment industry as delivery systems of American culture. One American scholar has described what happened as the shift from popular to mass culture. The secret of American success was an extraordinarily prosperous home economy, based partly on the extension of technological innovation into nearly every household. The result was a domestication of entertainment, moving it from the public arena to inside the home. Many of the new consumer goods, such as television sets and high-fidelity equipment, required the development of related cultural products—programs, recordings—to make the new gadgets essential to every family. The American entertainment industry was clearly up to the challenge. All aspects of American culture, including sports, were systematically brought into the web of the new entertainment industry. This would have a profound effect on Canadians.

After the war a handful of Canadian intellectuals became fascinated by the media's role in modern society. Given Canada's long history of wrestling with communications, this was perhaps not surprising. The Canadian scholar Marshall McLuhan (1911–80), following the lead of economic historian and communications theoretician Harold Adams Innis (1894–1952), would become the chief international guru of media culture, one of the first thinkers to arrive at and communicate some idea of the effect that electronic media were having on culture at every level. His first book, *The Mechanical Bride: Folklore of Industrial Man* (1951), examined comic strips, advertisements, and other promotional imagery of the American press to convey insights into 'that very common condition of industrial man in which he lives amid a great flowering of technical and mechanical imagery of whose rich human symbolism he is mainly unconscious' (McLuhan, 1951: 4). Like his mentor, Innis, McLuhan took the media seriously. Unlike Innis, however, McLuhan was not prepared to condemn the mechanization process and its introduction of a 'mass' dimension.

Categorizing culture has never been simple. One of the principal artistic developments of the post-war period—the commercialization of Inuit art—well demonstrates the problems. The Inuit of the Arctic had for centuries carved a complex image world in ivory and other materials, mainly for their own pleasure. In the late 1940s several Canadian artists working in the North, led by James Archibald Houston

The Impact of Science on Cultural Development

In 1948 the Canadian social scientist and economic historian Harold Innis (1894–1952) delivered a paper to the Conference of Commonwealth Universities in Oxford. A part of that paper follows.

The impact of science on cultural development has been evident in its contribution to technological advance, notably in communication and in the dissemination of knowledge. In turn it has been evident in the types of knowledge disseminated; that is to say, science lives its own life not only in the mechanism which is provided to distribute knowledge but also in the sort of knowledge which will be distributed. As information has been disseminated the demand for the miraculous, which has been one of the great contributions of science, has increased. To supply this demand for the miraculous has been a highly remunerative task, as evidenced by the publications of firms concerned with scientific works. Bury described the rapidly growing demand in England for books and lectures, making the results of science accessible and interesting to the lay public, as a remarkable feature of the second half of the nineteenth century. Popular literature explained the wonders of the physical world and at the same time flushed the imaginations of men with the consciousness that they were living in the era 'which, in itself vastly superior to any age of the past, need be burdened by no fear of decline or catastrophe but, trusting in the boundless resources of science, might surely defy fate.' 'Progress itself suggests that its value as a doctrine is only relative, corresponding to a certain not very advanced stage of civilization, just as Providence in its day was an idea of relative value, corresponding to a stage somewhat less advanced.' The average reader has been impressed by the miraculous, and the high priests of science, or perhaps it would be fair to say the pseudo-priests of science, have been extremely effective in developing all sorts of fantastic things, with great emphasis, of course, on the atomic bomb. I hoped to get through this paper without mentioning the atomic bomb, but found it impossible. . . .

The effects of obsession with science have become serious for the position of science itself. It has been held that the scientific mind can adapt itself more easily to tyranny than the literary mind, since 'art is individualism and science seeks the subjection of the individual to absolute laws', but Casaubon was probably right in saying that 'the encouragement of science and letters is almost always a personal influence.' The concept of the state in the Anglo-Saxon world has been favourable to the suppression or distortion of culture, particularly through its influence on science. Under the influence of the state, communication among themselves has become more difficult for scientists with the same political background and practically impossible for those with a different political background, because of the importance attached to war. Mathematics and music have been regarded as universal languages, particularly with the decline of Latin, but even mathematics is a tool and has become ineffective for purposes of communication in a highly technical civilization concerned with war.

Source: Harold Innis, 'A Critical Review', in Innis, *The Bias of Communication* (Toronto: University of Toronto Press, 1951), 192–3.

'Owl', stonecut, 1964, by Pauta Saila (1916–), printed by Echalook Pingwartok (b. 1942). Collection of the West Baffin Eskimo Co-operative Ltd, on loan to the McMichael Canadian Art Collection.

(1921–2005), encouraged the Inuit to offer their carvings for sale in the south through co-operative marketing. Later in the 1950s Houston would teach the Inuit how to translate their striking images into prints. The federal government encouraged commercialization, with the assistance of the Canadian Handicrafts Guild and the Hudson's Bay Company. Inuit artists quickly produced some of Canada's most distinctive images, known around the world. Their combination of folk tradition and deliberate commercialization, while not unique in this or any other period, resists facile generalizations.

Conclusion

Against a backdrop of economic prosperity and substantial population growth, Canada after the war finally appeared to be fulfilling its promise. Substantial strides were made on fronts as different as social welfare and cultural policy. 'Progress' was everywhere. Quebec's place within the Constitution had not yet emerged as a serious problem for the federal government, which by 1959 appeared to have established itself as a typical twentieth-century centralized state.

How History Has Changed

Understanding Suburbia

Although suburbs had existed in Canada before 1945, it was only after World War II that they became a contentious issue, particularly in the popular press. Two quite contrary interpretations of the meaning of the new suburbs predominated. One of these interpretations we can call the 'traditional' approach to suburbs, while the other can be labelled the 'metropolitan' approach.

The traditionalists saw the expansion of post-war suburbs in Canada as a return to earlier values of the nineteenth and earlier twentieth centuries. The suburbs were like small towns rather than part of the big city. They contained single-family dwellings with their own yards and lawns; these single-family dwellings housed traditional nuclear families in which the husband worked and the wife remained at home as a housewife and mother. The suburbs and the baby boom of the post-war period went well together, and the suburb was viewed as an ideal place to bring up kids, free from the evils of urban life. The suburban household marked a return to the values of domestication that had dominated the nineteenth century in Canada. The family lived in closer harmony. Fathers stayed at home in the evening rather than frequenting bars and other places of ill repute. The new suburbs quickly acquired churches (and synagogues), and they seemed to represent the promise of a return to earlier religious values.

The metropolitans, on the other hand, had a number of complaints about the new suburbs. One of these complaints was about their planning, which led to criticism on two seemingly opposite fronts. On one level, the suburbs were unplanned by speculators who moved into rural areas and put down large suburban estates in the middle of farmers' fields without much regard for infrastructure such as roads, schools, and shopping facilities. The developers kept the cost of their housing lower by avoiding the cost of improvement—beyond their own developments—as much as possible. The result was unplanned low-density suburban sprawl. On another level, however, the developers often overplanned within their own estates. They bulldozed the landscape and built identikit houses 'made of ticky-tacky', as American protest singer Malvina Reynolds described them in her song, 'Little Boxes'. Often, streets were segregated by income. The result was the encouragement of one of the greatest fears of post-war North American culture: a trend towards conformity, the loss of individuality, and the creation of a new mass culture based on home entertainment media such as the radio and later the television. The suburbs were regarded as being intellectually arid and later, in the 1960s, they were seen by feminist critics such as Betty Friedan as being prisons for housewives who were unable to fulfil their own destinies because they were stuck all day in the middle of nowhere.

Later historical writing on the suburb, both of the period 1945–65 and outside it, has emphasized that suburban development was nothing new in 1945 but had a long history in Canada. Moreover, the suburban picture of the post-war period was much too simplistic and mythological. Suburbs were far more complex in nature than the post-war debate over them had suggested.

Short Bibliography

Abella, Irving. *Nationalism, Communism, and Canadian Labour*. Toronto, 1973. A well-balanced analysis of the conceptual and practical problems besetting Canadian labour.

Bashevkin, Sylvia. *True Patriot Love: The Politics of Canadian Nationalism*. Toronto, 1991. A thoughtful study of the ways politicians and the state have attempted to harness Canadian nationalism to their own purposes.

Behiels, Michael. *Prelude to Quebec's Quiet Revolution: Liberalism versus Neo-Nationalism 1945–1960*. Montreal and Kingston, 1985. A fascinating treatment of the intellectual battle in Quebec in the years before the Quiet Revolution.

Bothwell, Robert, Ian Drummond, and John English. *Canada since 1945: Power, Politics, and Provincialism*, 2nd edn. Toronto, 1989. The best general account of the post-1945 period, though somewhat dated, fervently pro-federalist, and very Ontario-oriented.

Bryden, Kenneth. *Old Age Pensions and Policy-Making in Canada*. Montreal and London, 1984. A judicious study of a critical component of the welfare state.

Clark, S.D. *The Suburban Society*. Toronto, 1964. A study of the suburban phenomenon by the leading historical sociologist of his generation.

Doern, G. Bruce. *Science and Politics in Canada*. Montreal and London, 1972. A trenchant account of the history of Canadian science policy.

Guindon, Herbert. *Quebec Society: Tradition, Modernity, Nationhood*. Toronto, 1988. A useful overview of the recent history of Quebec.

Harris, Richard. *Creeping Conformity: How Canada Became Suburban, 1900–1960*. Toronto, 2004. A first-rate recent survey of the suburbanization process.

Iacovetta, Franca. *Such Hardworking People: Italian Immigrants in Postwar Toronto*. Montreal and Kingston, 1992. A comprehensive analysis of chain migration from southern Italy to Toronto in the 1950s and 1960s, and of Italian working-class life in Canada.

Korenik, Valerie. *Roughing It in the Suburbs: Reading Chatelaine Magazine in the Fifties and Sixties*. Toronto, 2000. A fascinating account of the relationship between suburbanization and popular culture in Canada's leading women's magazine.

Kostash, Myrna. *Long Way from Home: The Story of the Sixties Generation in Canada*. Toronto, 1980. A popular account of the 1960s, particularly useful for its take on the young.

Kwavnick, David, ed. *The Tremblay Report*. Toronto, 1972. An edited translation of the vital Quebec commission on constitutional problems of the early 1950s.

Litt, Paul. *The Muses, the Masseys and the Massey Commission*. Toronto, 1992. A revisionist study of the Massey Commission, which argues it was elitist and ineffective.

Owram, Doug. *Born at the Right Time: A History of the Baby Boom Generation*. Toronto, 1996. A scholarly attempt to understand the baby boomers.

Porter, John. *The Vertical Mosaic: An Analysis of Social Class and Power in Canada*. Toronto, 1965. The classic study that argued that a social hierarchy existed among Canadians based on ethnic origins.

Rea, K.J. *The Prosperous Years: The Economic History of Ontario, 1939–1975*. Toronto, 1985. A useful analysis of the period of affluence in Canada's largest province and of the centre of its industrial growth.

Richmond, Anthony. *Post-War Immigrants in Canada*. Toronto, 1967. A careful analysis of Canada's immediate post-war immigration policy and its outcomes.

Rutherford, Paul. *When Television Was Young: Primetime Canada 1952–1967*. Toronto, 1990. A scholarly treatment of the early history of the medium.

Safarian, A.E. *Foreign Ownership of Canadian Industry*. Toronto, 1966. A calm and dispassionate analysis of the hotly debated economic topic of the 1960s.

Seeley, John R., et al. *Crestwood Heights: A North American Suburb*. Toronto, 1956. A richly nuanced contemporary study of the Canadian suburban phenomenon, focusing on what was perhaps not a typical suburb.

Simeon, Richard, and Ian Robertson. *State, Society and the Development of Canadian Federalism*. Toronto, 1990. A useful overview of the recent historical development of federalism in Canada.

Stewart, Craig. *Arrow through the Heart: The Life and Times of Crawford Gordon & the Avro Arrow*. Toronto, 1998. Perhaps the best of the Arrow books, this one focuses on the man in charge of the project.

Trudeau, Pierre Elliott, ed. *The Asbestos Strike*. 1951, trans. Toronto, 1974. A fascinating study of one of the key events in Quebec in the early post-war years.

Study Questions

1. After World War I, a three-year economic depression struck Canada. World War II was followed by a prolonged economic boom. Identify and explain three changed conditions that might account for Canadian prosperity after World War II.
2. What was the main factor that made it possible for Canada to spend less than other developed nations on research and development while still benefiting from the latest technological advances?
3. What effects did the baby boom have on public education in Canada?
4. To what extent was suburbia an imagined world? How did this imagined world affect consumer spending patterns?
5. Give two reasons to account for rapid growth in the public sector of the economy between 1945 and 1960.
6. What were the chief factors that accounted for the Liberal Party's predominance at the federal level during this period?
7. How did immigration alter the face of Canada between 1945 and 1960?
8. Describe the main tenets of the 'new nationalism' that developed in Quebec after 1939.
9. What was the most important reason anglophone Canadians had so much trouble understanding the distinctiveness of their culture?
10. Who was Igor Gouzenko? What role did he play in the development of the Cold War between the West and the Soviet Union?

 www.oupcanada.com/Bumsted4e

Visit the companion website for *A History of the Canadian Peoples*, fourth edition for further resources.

10 Edging Towards the Abyss, 1958–1972

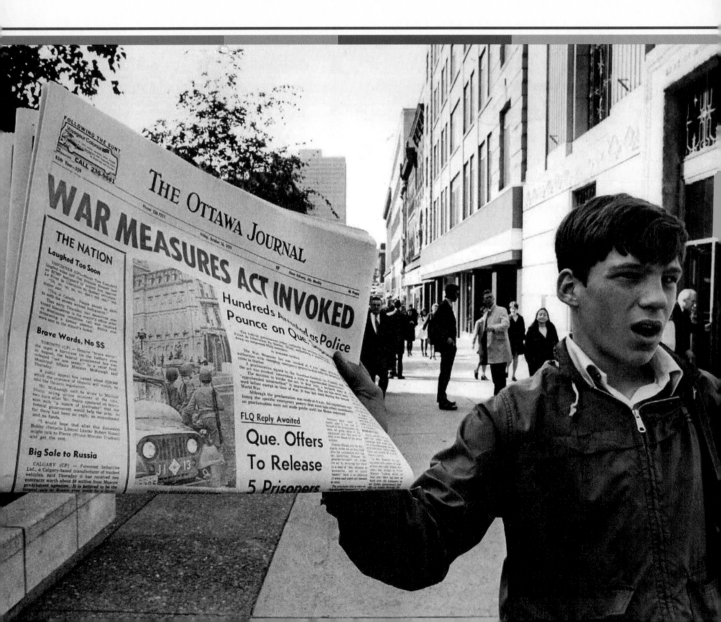

Timeline

1960   Introduction of Enovid. Royal Commission on Government Organization is created. Jean Lesage and the Liberals defeat the Union Nationale in Quebec. Bill of Rights passes federal Parliament.

1961   National Indian Council is founded. Canadian content regulations are introduced for television. CTV is formed. New Democratic Party is organized.

1962   Federal election returns a Diefenbaker minority government. Hydro-Québec is formed. Lesage government wins again with the slogan 'Maîtres chez nous'.

1963   Lester Pearson becomes Prime Minister at the head of a Liberal minority government. Parent Commission reports on education in Quebec. Royal Commission on Bilingualism and Biculturalism is formed.

1964   Family allowances are expanded. Brock University is founded. New Canadian flag is adopted.

1965   Student Union for Peace Action is founded. National Pension Plan is introduced, with a separate plan for Quebec. War on Poverty begins. Simon Fraser University and York University are opened.

1966   Federal Medical Act of 1966 is passed. Union Nationale defeats Liberals in Quebec.

1967   Canadian Centennial Year celebrations (including Expo 67). Official national anthem is adopted. Royal Commission on the Status of Women is appointed. National Hockey League is expanded, with no new Canadian teams. René Lévesque resigns from the Quebec Liberal Party.

1968   Michel Tremblay's play *Les Belles-Soeurs* is produced. Federal divorce reform is introduced. Canadian Métis Society and the National Indian Brotherhood are formed. Special Senate Committee on Poverty is established.

1969   Criminal Code amendments dealing with abortion and homosexuality are introduced. Sir George Williams University Computer Centre is occupied by protesting students. Montreal Expos begin play. White Paper on Indian policy is published. Pierre Trudeau's Liberals are elected with large majority. Official Languages Act is passed.

1970   Commission of Inquiry into the Non-Medical Use of Drugs (Le Dain Commission) delivers its interim report. Robert Bourassa's Liberals win over the Union Nationale in Quebec. October Crisis of 1970.

1971   New federal Unemployment Insurance Plan.

1972   'Waffle' purged from NDP. Bobby Hull signs with Winnipeg Jets of the World Hockey Association.

The October Crisis of 1970, precipitated by the FLQ kidnapping of a British diplomat and a Quebec cabinet minister, led to the invocation of the War Measures Act by Prime Minister Pierre Trudeau. This was the only time that this Act was implemented during peacetime. The Canadian Press/Peter Bregg.

Periods in history are seldom neat and tidy. Decades and centuries have a nasty tendency to spill over their technical dates. The era from 1958 to 1972 in Canada will always be labelled 'the sixties'. Life in those years was a bit like riding on a roller coaster. Revolution was in the air, but it never quite arrived. Everything seemed to be happening at roller-coaster speed. Although the ride was frequently quite exhilarating, the view from the front seemed to open into a bottomless abyss. Almost every positive development had its downside. The Canadian economy continued to grow, but the unpleasant side effects became more evident. Government sought to reform the legal system regarding divorce while the rates of marital breakdown reached epidemic proportions. The Roman Catholic Church internationally introduced a series of unprecedented reforms, but Canadians stopped attending all churches in record numbers. An increasing number of students at Canadian universities became concerned about American influence in Canada, only to be influenced themselves by American student reaction to the war in Vietnam. A variety of collective minorities began insisting on their rights, the acceptance of which would require the complete remaking of social justice—and, indeed, society—in Canada. The nation celebrated its Centennial in 1967, the most memorable event of which was probably an off-the-cuff public exclamation by French President Charles de Gaulle.

The usual picture of Canada after World War II shows a naive and complacent society that, with the aid of imported American ideas, suddenly questioned virtually all its values. There are a number of important qualifications to make to such a view. There was more ferment under the surface in post-war Canada than was recognized at the time. In many respects, ideas and behaviour that had previously been underground suddenly shifted into the public arena. Discontent was a product of the rising expectations caused by economic affluence. As is so often the case, much confrontation occurred because institutions did not change rapidly enough. Canadians were able to take over much of the American critical vocabulary because of their profound suspicions of the American system. Social critics in the United States struck a chord with Canadians who had similar feelings about the contradictions of American society and culture.

The 'Radical Sixties'

The era 1958–72 involved complex currents and countercurrents. Discussion of even the most major movements can only scratch the surface. Nonetheless, any account of the sixties must begin by considering three of the period's most striking developments: a broad societal shift towards liberalization; the appearance of a youth-centred counterculture; and the emergence of newly energized collective minorities in Canadian society. Sixties rhetoric was able to find a venue on radio and television. The reformers were the first radicals ever to have access to colour television. Only a few contemporaries ever managed to get beneath the rhetoric to understand the substance of the critique.

The Emancipation of Manners

The sixties have been credited with (or blamed for) a revolution in morality in which the traditional values of our Victorian ancestors were overturned virtually overnight. Firmly held moral beliefs do not collapse quite so rapidly or easily, of course. Rather, a belief system that was already in a state of decay and profoundly out of step with how people actually behaved in their daily lives was finally questioned and found wanting. A previous Canadian reluctance to examine morality ended. The brief upsurge of formal Christianity that had characterized the post-war era suddenly terminated. Canadians ceased attending church in droves. The phenomenon was especially evident in Catholic Quebec. The shifts involved were international ones that went much further elsewhere in the industrialized world than in Canada. By comparison with Sweden or California, for example, Canadian manners appear in retrospect to have remained quite old-fashioned.

The liberation of manners occurred simultaneously on several visible levels. The old media taboos against sexual explicitness, obscenity, and graphic depiction of violence virtually disappeared. Television attempted to maintain the traditional standards, but TV news itself constantly undermined that self-restraint with its coverage of what was happening in the world. The sixties were probably no more violent than any other period in human history. However, constant television coverage of the decade's more brutal events, increasingly in 'living' colour, brought them into everyone's living room. The memories of any Canadian who lived through the period include a veritable kaleidoscope of violent images: the assassinations of John F. Kennedy, his brother Robert, and Martin Luther King; the Paris and Chicago student riots of 1968; scenes in Vietnam (including the My Lai murders of innocent civilians and the defoliation of an entire ecosystem). Closer to home, there was the October Crisis of 1970. Canadians liked to believe that violence happened outside Canada, especially in the United States. Canadians somehow were nicer. On the eve of the October Crisis, the Guess Who, a Canadian rock group, had a monster hit, the lyrics of which pursued some of the most common metaphors of the time. 'American Woman' identified the United States with violence and Canada's relationship with its southern neighbour in sexual terms, a common conceit of the time.

As for sexuality, it became more explicit. Canadians began to talk and write openly about sexual intercourse, contraception, abortion, premarital sex, and homosexual behaviour. In place of the winks and nudges that had always accompanied certain 'unmentionable' topics, a refreshing frankness appeared. Many of the issues of sexuality revolved around women's ambition (hardly new) to gain control of their own bodies and reproductive functions. Part of the new development was the rapid spread of the use of Enovid, the oral contraceptive widely known as 'the pill' after its introduction in 1960. The pill seemed to offer an easier and more secure method of controlling conception. Its use became quite general before some of its unpleasant side effects came to light. One of the pill's advantages was that the woman herself was responsible for its proper administration. The birth rate had already begun declining in 1959, and probably would have continued to decline without the pill. Enovid symbolized a new sexual freedom—some said promiscuity—for

women that gradually made its way into the media. By the mid-1960s, popular magazines that had previously preached marriage, fidelity, and domesticity were now featuring lead articles on premarital sex, marital affairs, and cohabitation before marriage.

Language, at least as the media used it, was equally rapidly liberated. Canadian writers—whether in fiction, poetry, drama, film, or history—had usually employed a sanitized and almost unrecognizable version of spoken French or English. Earle Birney's comic war novel *Turvey* (1949) suggested the use of profanities by Canada's soldiers by means of dashes in the text. But *Turvey* only hinted at the larger reality. In everyday life many ordinary Canadians used not only profanities but a rich vocabulary of vulgar slang that could be found in few dictionaries of the day. In French Canada, that everyday language was called 'joual'. While earlier writers like Gabrielle Roy and Roger Lemelin had suggested its use, later writers such as Michel Tremblay (b. 1942) actually began to employ it. Tremblay's play *Les Belles-Soeurs*, written in 1965 but not produced until 1968 because of concerns about its language, cast its dialogue in joual. His later plays added sexually explicit themes, including transvestism and homosexuality. By 1970 both language and themes previously considered unsuitable became public across the country.

The state played its own part in the reformation of manners. Pierre Elliott Trudeau achieved a reputation that helped make him Prime Minister by presiding over a reformist Department of Justice from 1967 to 1968. He became associated with the federal reform of divorce in 1968, as well as with amendments (in 1969) to Canada's Criminal Code dealing with abortion and homosexuality. Trudeau's remark that the state had no place in the bedrooms of the nation struck a responsive chord. He was Prime Minister in 1969 when a commission was appointed to investigate the non-medical use of drugs. While its interim report, published in 1970, did not openly advocate the legalization of soft drugs, such as marijuana, its general arguments about the relationship of law and morality were symptomatic of the age. The commission maintained that the state had the right to limit the availability of potentially harmful substances through

Earle Birney, winner of the 1950 Leacock Medal. LAC, C-31956.

the Criminal Code. At the same time it added that it was not necessarily 'appropriate to use the criminal law to enforce morality, regardless of the potential for harm to the individual or society' (Addiction Research Foundation, 1970: 503–26).

The concept that it was not the state's function to enforce morality flew in the face of the Canadian tradition, which had always embodied morality in the Criminal Code. The new liberalism informed many of the legal reforms of the later 1960s. A number of Roman Catholic bishops, in a brief to a special joint committee of the legislature on divorce in 1967, stated that the legislator's goal should not be 'primarily the good of any religious group but the good of all society' (*Proceedings of the Special Joint Committee of the Senate and House of Commons on Divorce*, 1967: 1515–16). Such liberated thinking paved the way not only for a thorough reform of federal divorce legislation, making divorce easier

and quicker to obtain, but also for amendments to the Criminal Code in 1969 regarding abortion. Termination of pregnancy became legal if carried out by physicians in proper facilities, and following a certification by a special panel of doctors that 'the continuation of the pregnancy of such female person would or would be likely to endanger her life or health'. The Criminal Code was also amended in 1969 to exempt from prosecution 'indecent actions' by consenting couples over the age of 21 who performed such acts in private.

The reformation of manners, if not morals, based on the twin concepts that the state had no place in enforcing morality and that individuals were entitled to decide on the ways in which they harmed themselves, was largely in place by 1969. There were clear limits to liberalization, however. Since 1969 Canada has witnessed a resurgence of demands for state intervention in areas where liberalization was held to produce adverse consequences. Thus many women's groups have come to advocate stricter legislation on obscenity and indecency, particularly in the media, in order to protect women and children from sexual abuse.

The Counterculture

One of the most obvious manifestations of the ferment of the sixties was the rebellious reaction of young baby boomers against the values of their elders, a movement that came to be known as the counterculture. Many Canadian rebels of the period took much of the style and content of their protest from the Americans, although they had their own homegrown concerns, especially in Quebec. As in the United States, youthful rebellion in Canada had two wings, never mutually exclusive: a highly politicized movement of active revolution, often centred in the universities and occasionally tending to violence; and a less overtly political one of personal self-reformation and self-realization, centred in the 'hippies'. Student activists and hippies were often the same people. Even when different personnel were involved, the culture was usually much the same, anchored by sex, dope, and rock music. The participants in the two Canadian branches of youthful protest also had in common distinctly

The Use of Drugs

In 1969 the newly elected Trudeau government appointed a Commission of Inquiry into the Non-Medical Use of Drugs (the Le Dain Commission, after its chairman, Gerald Le Dain). That commission made its interim report in 1970, recommending that the government move towards decriminalization of 'soft' drugs such as cannabis. Its recommendations were largely unheeded. The interim report included a number of transcriptions from testimony before it, and those who gave testimony included the British rock musician John Lennon. The following testimony is from a university professor in eastern Canada.

I have enjoyed smoking marijuana and hashish several times, and I feel that if they are made legal, we have far more to gain than lose. I think they can be easily incorporated with our way of life in Canada without eroding any but purely materialistic or exploitative values. Marijuana does not provide an escape from reality any more than alcohol, sex or a drive in the country: we know we cannot be high all the time; we enjoy taking a trip (in both senses of the word) and we remember it with pleasure, but we know that we have to come back home again and go to work, and continue our everyday life. I have so often heard the argument that pot or hashish lead to hard drugs. For the vast majority of pot smokers, this is rubbish. It is the argument that temperance societies use against alcohol: social drinking leads to alcoholism. I have never had the slightest desire to shoot anything into my arm, nor do I want to try speed in any of its forms. There will always be a few disturbed people in our world, and I don't think that laws should be made for that tiny minority. . . .

I wrote to John Turner last winter deploring the persecution of young long-hairs by the police and the RCMP. As many people have observed, this leads not to a lessening of pot and hash smoking, but to a disrespect for the police. I would like to see the force more respected, because, as we all know, police need public support and sympathy in order to perform efficiently. What sympathy can they expect when they disguise themselves as hippies in order to infiltrate and arrest them? Hippies are not communists circa 1947, and this police tactic only degrades the officer who undertakes it, as well as the force in general. The hippies feel that the RCMP is acting out of ignorance and fear; they believe that pot-smoking is good, and there is no reason why they should change their minds: they are working from experience, and RCMP actions, no matter how 'legal', spring from institutionalized paranoia.

I am not underestimating the temporary upheaval which legalizing marijuana and hashish might cause in certain sectors—police, puritans, all those who wish to force their own limits of freedom and pleasure on the country as a whole. I think we should have the right to choose for ourselves whether we want to smoke or not. I think we have far more to gain than to lose by legalizing pot . . . .

Source: *Interim Report of the Commission of Inquiry into the Non-Medical Use of Drugs* (Ottawa: Queen's Printer, 1970), 292–3. Reproduced courtesy of The Privy Council Office, with the permission of the Minister of Public Works and Government Services, 2007.

middle-class backgrounds, for these were movements of affluence, not marginality.

The United States was the spiritual home of the sixties counterculture in English Canada. Americans had gone further than anyone else both in suburbanizing their culture and in universalizing education.

The rapidly expanding university campus provided an ideal spawning ground for youthful rebellion. The campus had helped generate, in the civil rights movement, a protest crusade that served as a model for subsequent agitation. Civil rights as a public concern focused attention on the rhetorical contradictions of mainstream American society, which preached equality for all while denying it to blacks. It also mobilized youthful idealism and demonstrated the techniques of the protest march and civil disobedience, as well as the symbolic values of popular song. When some American blacks left the civil rights movement, convinced that only violence could truly alter the status quo, they provided models for urban guerrilla activity, including the growing terrorist campaign in Quebec that was associated with separatism. (French-Canadian youths could identify with Pierre Vallières's *White Niggers of America*.)

In English Canada, what really ignited the revolt of youth was the war in Vietnam. In retrospect, the extent to which Vietnam dominated the period becomes even clearer to us than it was to people at the time. The war became the perfect symbol for the sixties generation of everything that was wrong with mainstream American society. It was equally exportable as an emblem of American Evil, representing everything that the rest of the world hated about the United States, including its arrogant assumption that it was always morally superior. For these reasons, Vietnam was central to the Canadian counterculture in a variety of ways. Hostility to American policy in Vietnam fuelled Canadian anti-Americanism, as a

Justice Minister Pierre Elliott Trudeau with Prime Minister Lester B. Pearson at the federal–provincial conference of February 1968. LAC, C-25001.

paperback book about the United States entitled *The New Romans: Candid Canadian Opinions of the U.S.* demonstrated in 1967. This hostility also connected young Canadians with the burgeoning American protest movements. Many Canadian university faculty members recruited during the decade were Americans, most of them recent graduate students critical of American policy. They were joined in their sympathies by an uncounted number of American war resisters (some said as many as 100,000 at the height of the war), the majority of whom sought refuge in communities of university students or hippies in large Canadian cities.

The youthful reaction advocated an eclectic kind of socialism—Marxist-influenced, democratically oriented, and idealistically verging on romanticism—that is usually referred to as the New Left. The movement was much better at explaining what was wrong with the present system than at proposing workable alternatives. It had no example of a large-scale society that operated on its principles. Nevertheless, Canadian student activists rose to positions of power in their universities, establishing several national organizations, such as the Student Union for Peace Action (1965). Student radicalism flourished at a few universities, such as Simon Fraser, York, and the Université de Montréal. Many of the less extreme student activists joined the Waffle wing of the NDP, which attempted to radicalize that party in the direction of economic nationalism and social reform. Perhaps the most publicized student protest in Canada occurred in February 1969 when the computer centre at Sir George Williams University (now Concordia) in Montreal was occupied for two weeks to protest racial intolerance and the 'military, imperialistic ambitions of Canada in the West Indies' (quoted in Forsythe, 1971: 9). The student protestors ended their occupation on 11 February by smashing the computers and damaging university equipment and records estimated to be worth millions of dollars. Ninety occupiers were arrested, including 41 blacks, many of whom came from the Caribbean region.

Despite the incident at Sir George Williams, youthful protest was not quite the same in Quebec as in Anglo-Canada. While Quebec's young were no less alienated than their anglophone compatriots,

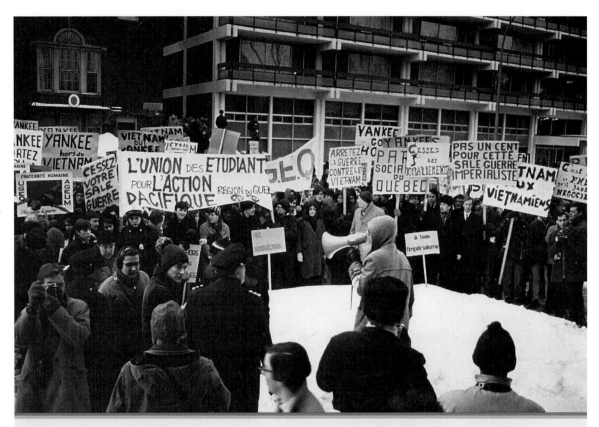

Anti-Vietnam War protestors make their way to the US Consulate in Montreal, 19 February 1966. LAC, PA-173623.

their anger found an outlet in opposition to Canadian federalism's colonial oppression of their own province. Young people of university age (although seldom at university) formed most of the active cells of the Front de libération du Québec (FLQ), including the one that provoked the October Crisis of 1970. The FLQ's rhetoric and tactics during the crisis were clearly modelled on extreme movements of protest in the United States and Europe. English-speaking Canadian students talked of the 'student as nigger', but French Canadians saw their entire society as comparable with that of the blacks in the US or an oppressed Third World nation (Kostash, 1980: 250). Radical young Quebecers were able to become part of a larger movement of protest and reform that cut across the age structure of Quebec society. Unlike their counterparts in English Canada, young protestors in Quebec were not cut off from the mainstream of adult society.

'The bureaucratic forms of organization shared by communism and capitalism', wrote one American activist, 'were embodiments of insult to the ideals of individualism, spontaneity, mutual trust and generosity that are the dominant themes of the new sensibility' (quoted in Kostash, 1980: 250). Such ideals motivated the hippies, who accordingly dropped out of mainstream society. Earlier generations of middle-class Canadians had dutifully struggled up the ladder of success. Many of the sixties generation lacked such ambition or direction. They were their parents' children, searching for personal self-fulfillment through any possible means. For some, the quest led to vulgarized versions of Eastern mystical religions. For others, it led to communes close to nature, often on remote islands. For the vast majority, it certainly meant experimenting with hallucinogenic drugs, particularly cannabis, and a sexual freedom bordering on promiscuity in an age when sexually

Canadian Writers View the United States

In 1968 the Canadian poet Al Purdy asked a number of his fellow writers in Canada to contribute their views of the United States to a collection he intended to publish. The following two poems came from George Jonas and Robin Mathews, respectively.

American Girl: A Canadian View

It is reassuring
To spend part of a night
With an American girl.

Chances are she will not resemble
The leaders of her nation
In speech, figure, or stance:

If she has imperialistic designs
She may draw you without a struggle
Into her sphere of influence.

Then you'll find her battledress
Fit for her private battles,
See not her battleships but hear her battlecries,
And melt (perhaps with a wistful smile)
Before the native napalm of her eyes.

But she'll seem to be prepared
To give as well as to accept
Some foreign aid

And by midnight or so
While the fires of her manifest destiny smoulder
You'll be all ready to slip across
The world's longest undefended border.

—*George Jonas*

Centennial Song

Canada, my beauty,
everybody's love,
white flower of diamond-studded North,
let me tell you that
a tired prostitute beyond her prime,
dejected, hungry,
full of malice and uncertain fear
would throw her charms away less openly,
would exercise more choice
than you have ever done,
would charge at least a reasonable rate,
would try to be
(within the perils of the trade)
a self-respecting whore;
And What Is More
even in her wildest state
of drunken self-delusion,
howling at a corner
where the newsies thrive,
she wouldn't let you see her
stopping people —
friends and neighbours,
even relatives,
shouting with paranoid insistence
upon decency and moral strength,
that she is living better now than ever,
friends with everyone, and that
despite all rumour, not a shred
of proof has ever been produced
to show that she
(as gossips say)
is being regularly screwed.

—*Robin Mathews*

Source: Al Purdy, ed., *The New Romans: Candid Canadian Opinions of the U.S.* (Edmonton: Hurtig, 1968), 53, 74. 'American Girl' reprinted by permission of the author.

transmitted diseases seemed easily treatable with antibiotics. Such experiments, together with a revolution in popular music, were the core of the sixties for participants and onlookers alike. Rock music was almost impossible to define, incorporating as it did so many musical styles ranging from black rhythm and blues to traditional folk music to Indian ragas to medieval Gregorian chant. Nevertheless, rock served as the symbol that both united the young and separated them from their parents.

It is impossible to define a precise moment at which the bubble of the sixties' youth energy burst. Many of the characteristics and tendencies of the period continued in fragmented fashion into the succeeding decades. But at the end of the sixties the naive beliefs of the young received a series of shocks when American student activists were ruthlessly suppressed at Chicago (1968) and Kent State (1970). At the same time, the central rallying point—American involvement in Vietnam—was gradually removed. In Canada, the founding of the Parti Québécois in 1968 provided a place within the system for many Quebec student activists. Two years later the October Crisis demonstrated how far some activists were prepared to go in the use of violence, and how far the Canadian state was prepared to go in suppressing it. The purging of the NDP's Waffle movement in 1972 perhaps completed the process of neutralizing

George Grant on 'Canadian Fate and Imperialism'

In 1969 the Canadian philosopher George Grant published a book of essays entitled *Technology and Empire*. An unrepentant Tory and classicist, Grant was a most unlikely guru for the radical generation of the time, but he was extremely popular in such circles.

To use the language of fate is to assert that all human beings come into a world they did not choose and live their lives within a universe they did not make. If one speaks in this way, one is often accused either of being pessimistic or of holding a tragic view of life. Neither of these accusations is correct. To say that one holds a tragic view of life would be to follow Nietzsche in thinking that Dionysian tragedy was a higher stance than that in Socrates; I do not think this. And the words optimistic and pessimistic are surely most accurately used, following Leibniz, to describe what one thinks about the nature of things, whether the world is good or not. It is quite possible to use the word 'fate', and to think that 'nature' is good, and not contradict oneself. It is in my opinion a sensible way to talk about events, though obviously it is far from the liberal dogmas within which most people are taught to think.

A central aspect of the fate of being a Canadian is that our very existing has at all times been bound up with the interplay of various world empires. One can better understand what it is to be Canadian if one understands that interplay. As no serious person is interested in history simply as antiquarianism but only as it illumines one's search for the good in the here and now, let me set the problem in its most contemporary form—Vietnam. What our fate is today becomes most evident in the light of Vietnam. It is clear that in that country the American empire has been demolishing a people, rather than allowing them to live outside the American orbit.

The Americans are forced to that ferocious demolition because they have chosen to draw the line against the Chinese empire in a country where nationalism and communism have been in large measure identified. How does this affect Canadians? On the one hand, many Canadians, whether their moral traditions come from Judaism, Christianity, the liberal enlightenment or a mixture, are not yet so empty that they can take lightly the destruction of a people—even in the case of Asians. On the other hand, the vast majority of Canadians are a product of western civilization and live entirely within the forms and assumptions of that enterprise. Today the enterprise of western civilization finds its spearhead in the American empire. In that sense our very lives are inevitably bound up in the meeting of that empire with the rest of the world, and the movements of war which draw the limits in that meeting. The depth of that common destiny with the Americans is shown in the fact that many Canadians who are forced to admit the sheer evil of what is being done in Vietnam say at the same time that we have no choice but to stand with the Americans as the pillar of western civilization. Beyond this kind of talk is of course the fact that this society is above all

a machine for greed, and our branch plant industry is making a packet out of the demolition of Vietnam.

Our involvement is much deeper than the immediate profits of particular wars. Our very form of life depends on our membership in the western industrial empire which is centred in the USA and which stretches out its hegemony into parts of western Europe and which controls South America and much of Africa and Asia. Somewhere in the minds of nearly all Canadians there is the recognition that our present form of life depends on our place as second-class members of that system. By 'second class' I do not imply a low status, because there are a large number of classes within it. It is much nicer to be a Canadian than a Brazilian or a Venezuelan, or for that matter an Englishman. . . .

Source: Excerpt from *Technology & Empire* copyright ©1969 by George Grant. Reproduced with permission of House of Anansi Press Inc., Toronto. <www.anansi.ca>.

---

activism, at least in English-speaking Canada. Some observers explained the collapse of the sixties youth movements in terms of demography. Young people got older and acquired jobs. Perhaps. In any event, by 1973 only memories of the 'good old days', often in the form of the lyrics of rock songs, were left for most of the sixties generation.

The Rise of Militant Collectivities

While much youthful protest disappeared at the end of the decade, the baby boomers had joined in some movements that outlasted the era. The sixties saw a number of previously disadvantaged groups in Canadian society emerge with articulated positions and demands. These included, among others, Aboriginal peoples, blacks, women, and homosexuals. To some extent, all these groups shared a common sense of liberation and heightened consciousness during the heady days of the sixties, as well as some common models and rhetoric. The several black movements in the United States, especially civil rights and black power, were generally influential. It was no accident that almost every group, including French Canadians, compared itself with

American blacks. While on one level other emerging collectivities could hardly avoid sympathizing with French Canada, on another level the arguments and aspirations of Quebec often seriously conflicted with those of other groups. Many collectivities sought to mobilize federal power to achieve their goals, often seeing the provinces and provincial rights as part of their problem.

As with so many other long-standing Canadian problems, that of the Aboriginal peoples moved into a new activist phase. Earlier, in the 1920s, the League of Indians, formed in 1919, had struggled for attention and against internal divisions. The state and the Canadian polity were not ready for a pan-Indian organization (Dickason, 2006: 222–3). In the 1960s Native leaders built partly on their own traditions of constructing organizations to speak for First Nations and Inuit concerns. In 1961 the National Indian Council (NIC) was founded. This organization was formed by Native people—many of whom had recently moved to the city—who hoped to combine the concerns of status and non-status Indians. Métis were also involved in the NIC. In 1968 political incompatibility led to the dissolution of the National Indian Council and the formation of two new groups:

In this photo, from left to right, are George Manuel, President of the National Indian Brotherhood, Aurilien Gill, 3rd Vice President of the Association of Indians, and Chief Max Louis, 2nd Vice President of the Association of Indians, at a news conference. The twentieth century saw a rise in Aboriginal activist groups that sought to bring Native issues to the political forefront. © Bettmann/Corbis.

the Canadian Métis Society (which in 1970 renamed itself the Native Council of Canada) representing Métis and non-status Indians, and the National Indian Brotherhood (which would become the Assembly of First Nations) representing status Indians. Activists were also able to take advantage of American models and Canadian federal policy, particularly the 1960 Bill of Rights. The search for new sources of raw materials for exploitation in the Canadian North threatened Aboriginal ways of life, forcing them into the political mainstream. By the end of the decade, an emerging Native militancy was able to marshal its forces to confront the federal government when it tried to rethink the Aboriginal problem.

In 1969 the Department of Indian Affairs, under Jean Chrétien (b. 1934), published a White Paper on federal Indian policy. All-encompassing in its reassessment, the document had three controversial recommendations: the abolition of the Indian Act (and the Department of Indian Affairs), which would eliminate status Indians; the transfer of First Nations lands from Crown trust into the hands of the First Nations; and the devolution of responsibility for Aboriginal people to the provinces. The White Paper touched off bitter criticism in all quarters, not least because it had been generated with little prior consultation with Native groups. It produced the first popular manifesto for Canadian Aboriginals in Harold Cardinal's *The Unjust Society: The Tragedy of Canada's Indians* (1969), which argued for the re-establishment of special rights within the strengthened contexts of treaties and the Indian Act.

The White Paper was consistent with federal policy towards all minorities, including French Canadians, at the end of the 1960s. It called for the advancement of the individual rather than the collective rights of Native peoples: 'The Government believes that its policies must lead to the full, free, and non-discriminatory participation of the Aboriginal people in Canadian society. Such a goal requires a break

Harold Cardinal

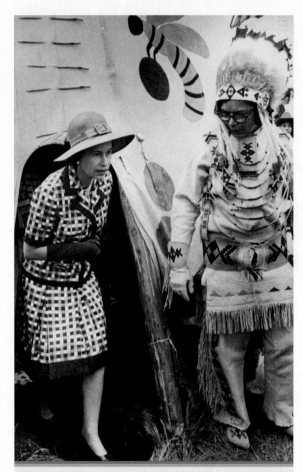

Alberta Indian Association President Harold Cardinal watches as Queen Elizabeth emerges from a teepee at an Indian Village in Calgary, 5 July 1973. CP Picture Archive/ Chuck Mitchell.

Harold Cardinal (1945–2005) was a member of the Sucker Creek Reserve band who became president of the Indian Association of Alberta at the young age of 23. He had read widely in the American rhetorical literature of the 1960s regarding Aboriginal peoples, and he responded to the federal government's 1969 White Paper on Indian policy—which called for the advancement of the individual rights of Aboriginals rather than their collective rights—with an angry, best-selling book entitled *The Unjust Society*, an obvious reference to Pierre Trudeau's 'Just Society'. Cardinal described the White Paper as a 'thinly disguised programme of extermination through assimilation', adding that the federal government, 'instead of acknowledging its legal and moral responsibilities to the Indians of Canada and honouring the treaties that the Indians signed in good faith, now proposes to wash its hands of Indians entirely, passing the buck to the provincial governments.'

Cardinal coined the term 'the Buckskin Curtain' to describe the separation between Europeans and First Nations in Canada, observing that while 'Canadian urbanites have walked blisters on their feet and fat off their rumps to raise money for under-developed countries outside Canada', Canadians generally did not 'give a damn' about the plight of their own Native people. He also attacked 'Uncle Tomahawks' among his own people who continually apologized for being Aboriginal. He noted with some irony that Native people who wore their normal clothing risked being confused with hippies. Cardinal was also a critic of Canada's 'two founding peoples' concept, pointing out that it did not recognize 'the role played by the Indian even before the founding of a nation state known as Canada'. He insisted that the First Nations were not separatists; they merely wanted their treaty and Aboriginal rights recognized so that they could take their place 'with the other cultural identities of Canada'. He subsequently helped write the 'Red Paper' in 1970, and in 1977 published *The Rebirth of Canada's Indians*, which attempted to outline a positive program for his people. He served briefly as director general of Indian affairs in Alberta, but spent much of his career in Native politics at both the provincial and national levels. In later life he took up an appointment at the University of Alberta.

with the past. It requires that the Aboriginal people's role of dependence be replaced by a role of equal status, opportunity, and responsibility, a role they can share with all other Canadians' (*Statement of the Government of Canada on Indian Policy*, 1969: 5). An assimilationist document, the White Paper insisted that treaties between the Crown and Aboriginals had involved only 'limited and minimal promises' that had been greatly exceeded in terms of the 'economic, educational, health, and welfare needs of the Indian people' by subsequent government performance (*Statement of the Government of Canada on Indian Policy*, 1969: 5). Allowing Aboriginal people full access to Canadian social services (many of which were administered provincially) would mark an advance over existing paternalism.

Ottawa seemed surprised that Native people responded so negatively to the White Paper, conveniently ignoring its implications for the concepts of treaty and Aboriginal rights. Prime Minister Trudeau defended the policy as an enlightened one, noting that 'the time is now to decide whether the Indians will be a race apart in Canada or whether they will be Canadians of full status.' He added, 'It's inconceivable, I think, that in a given society one section of the society have a treaty with the other section of the society. We must all be equal under the law' (Indian–Eskimo Association of Canada, 1970: Appendix 8).

Like other collectivities that discovered a new voice in the 1960s, Canadian women had been quietly preparing for their emergence (or re-emergence) for many years. Whether or not one took a patient view of the lengthy period of quiescence from the enfranchisement of women to the blossoming of the women's liberation movement— and most modern feminists understandably did not—some things had changed, and some political experience had been acquired. The Committee on Equality for Women, which organized in 1966 to lobby for a Royal Commission on the status of women, consisted of experienced leaders from 32 existing women's organizations united by their feminism. Their first delegation to Ottawa was ignored. Laura Sabia (1916–96), president of the Canadian Federation of University Women and leader of the call for a national evaluation of women's status,

responded with a classic sixties threat: she would lead a women's protest march on the capital. The Pearson government behaved characteristically. Although not convinced that women had many legitimate grievances, it dodged trouble by agreeing to an investigation 'to inquire and report upon the status of women in Canada, and to recommend what steps might be taken by the federal government to ensure for women equal opportunities with men in all aspects of Canadian society' (*Report of the Royal Commission on the Status of Women in Canada*, 1970: vii). The Royal Commission on the Status of Women, established in 1967, examined areas under provincial as well as federal jurisdiction and made its recommendations based on four operating assumptions: the right of women to choose to be employed outside the home; the obligation of parents and society to care for children; the special responsibilities of society to women because of maternity; and, perhaps most controversially, the need for positive action to overcome entrenched patterns of discrimination. The Commission's report provided a program that would occupy mainstream feminism for decades to come.

Virtually simultaneous with the Royal Commission was the emergence of the movement usually known as women's liberation. This articulate and militant branch of feminism had begun in the United States as an offshoot of the student movement, partly a product of the failure of male student leaders to take women seriously. Women's liberation shared much of its rhetoric with other leftist movements of decolonization. '[Woman] realizes in her subconscious what [Herbert] Marcuse says,' went one manifesto: 'Free election of masters does not abolish the masters or the slaves' (quoted in Kostash, 1980: 169). Not surprisingly, the liberationists found their organizing principles in issues of sexuality, particularly in the concept that 'woman's body is used as a commodity or medium of exchange' (quoted in Kostash, 1980: 196). True liberation would come only when women could control their own bodies, especially in sexual terms. Thus birth control and abortion became two central political questions, along with more mundane matters, such as daycare and equal pay for equal work. Such concerns brought feminists into conflict with what became known as male chauvinism at all levels of society. At the beginning of the 1970s, the women's movement stood poised at the edge of what appeared to be yet another New Day.

The minority perhaps most closely linked to the women's liberationists was composed of homosexuals and lesbians. Like the libbers, the gays (a term they much preferred to other more pejorative ones) focused their political attention on sexuality, particularly the offences enshrined in the Canadian Criminal Code. By the late 1950s more advanced legal and medical thinking had come to recognize the value of decriminalizing homosexual activity, at least between consenting adults. The sixties would see the expansion of this view, partly because of public lobbying by a number of gay organizations, such as the Association for Social Knowledge (1964), that emerged in the period. An increasing number of gay newspapers and journals also made their appearance. Like other minority groups, homosexuals and lesbians began to concentrate on constructing a positive rather than a destructive self-identity. The 1969 revisions to the Criminal Code did not legalize homosexuality and lesbianism, but they did have a considerable effect on the gay community. It was now possible, if still courageous, to acknowledge one's homosexuality (the usual term was 'coming out of the closet'). The ranks of openly practising gays greatly expanded. It was also possible to become more aggressive in support of more homosexual rights, and the first gay liberation organizations were formed in Vancouver, Montreal, Toronto, and Ottawa in 1970 and 1971. These groups led the way in advocating the protection of sexual orientation in any human rights legislation adopted by the government.

By the early 1970s a number of collectivities were making new demands for constitutional reform and political change. The political and constitutional agenda of Canada was no longer confined to such matters as extending the welfare state, satisfying Quebec, or redefining the federal–provincial relationship. It now had to take into account a variety of organized and articulate subgroups of Canadian society—of which Aboriginal peoples, blacks, women, and gays were only the most vocal—insisting that their needs also deserved attention.

A Still Buoyant Economy

Behind all the reform sentiment of the sixties was a persistently prosperous economy. Inflation (which ran at an annual average rate of 2.1 per cent between 1959 and 1968) and interest rates continued to be manageable. The nation continued to provide jobs for most of its expanding population, with unemployment rates under 6 per cent for most of the period. Critics might note that these rates were substantially higher than in other highly industrialized nations, where unemployment was under 2 per cent. But for the vast majority of Canadians, the performance of the economy seemed more than satisfactory, particularly after 1963, when a veritable explosion of construction projects began and foreign trade blossomed. Everywhere there were the visible signs of prosperity in the form of cranes and hard hats. Montreal and Toronto built subway systems. Large and small shopping malls sprouted up everywhere. Cultural facilities proliferated. Each province put up new university buildings. Less visible but equally important were a number of projects in the North, usually associated with hydroelectric expansion. The bellwether of the Canadian economy continued to be Ontario, still the only province with a mixed economy balanced between manufacturing and primary production. Ontario contained such a large proportion of the nation's people that its successes consistently raised national averages.

The averages disguised marked discrepancies and disparities. Some of them were regional. Overall, the most seriously disadvantaged area was the Atlantic region—the Maritime provinces plus Newfoundland. Per capita average income in this region was persistently more than 30 per cent below the figures for the other provinces, and a much larger proportion of the population than elsewhere worked in marginal primary resource extraction, which was often seasonal in nature. Even after taxes, Ontario's per capita income in 1970 was 70 per cent higher than Newfoundland's. Many commentators insisted, however, that the real regional disparity was between the industrial heartland of central Canada and the resource hinterland that constituted most of the remainder of the country. Canadians were naturally drawn to the more prosperous regions, while

Report of the Royal Commission on the Status of Women

In September 1970 the Royal Commission on the Status of Women tabled its report, which began with a statement of 'Criteria and Principles'.

. . . 4. We have been asked to inquire into and report upon the status of women in Canada and we have done so in the light of certain principles. A general principle is that everyone is entitled to the rights and freedoms proclaimed in the Universal Declaration of Human Rights. We have examined the status of women to learn whether or not they really have these positive rights and freedoms both in principle and in practice. Some of our recommendations should establish a measure of equality that is now lacking for men as well as for women.

5. Explicit in the Terms of Reference given us by the Government is our duty to ensure for women equal opportunities with men. We have interpreted this to mean that equality of opportunity for everyone should be the goal of Canadian society. The right to an adequate standard of living is without value to the person who has no means of achieving it. Freedom to choose a career means little if the opportunity to enter some occupations is restricted.

6. Our Terms of Reference also imply that the full use of human resources is in the national interest. We have explored the extent to which Canada develops and makes use of the skills and abilities of women.

7. Women and men, having the same rights and freedoms, share the same responsibilities. They should have an equal opportunity to fulfil this obligation. We have, therefore, examined the status of women and made recommendations in the belief that there should be equality of opportunity to share the responsibilities to society as well as its privileges and prerogatives.

8. In particular, the Commission adopted four principles: first, that women should be free to choose whether or not to take employment outside their homes. The circumstances which impede this free choice have been of specific interest to our inquiry. Where we have made recommendations to improve opportunities for women in the work world, our goal has not been to force married women to work for pay outside of the home but rather to eliminate the practical obstacles that prevent them from exercising this right. If a husband is willing to support his wife, or a wife her husband, the decision and responsibility belong to them.

9. The second is that the care of children is a responsibility to be shared by the mother, the father and society. Unless this shared responsibility is acknowledged and assumed, women cannot be accorded true equality.

10. The third principle specifically recognizes the child-bearing function of women. It is apparent that society has a responsibility for women because of pregnancy and child-birth, and special treatment related to maternity will always be necessary.

11. The fourth principle is that in certain areas women will for an interim period require special treatment to overcome the adverse effects of discriminatory practices. We consider such measures to be justified in a limited range of circumstances, and we anticipate that they should quickly lead to actual equality which would make their continuance unnecessary. The needs or capacities of women have not always been understood. Discrimination against women has in many instances been unintentional and special treatment will no longer be required if a positive effort to remove it is made for a short period. . . .

Source: *Report of the Royal Commission on the Status of Women* (Ottawa: Information Canada, 1970), xi–xii. Reproduced courtesy of The Privy Council Office, with the permission of the Minister of Public Works and Government Services, 2006.

Judy LaMarsh

Judy LaMarsh. The Canadian Press.

Julia Verlyn 'Judy' LaMarsh (1924–80) was born in Chatham, Ontario, and educated in Niagara Falls. After graduation from Hamilton Normal School, she served in the Canadian Woman's Army Corps from 1943 to 1946, translating Japanese documents. After the war she attended Victoria College and Osgoode Hall. In 1950 she joined her father's law firm. LaMarsh first ran for Parliament in 1960, winning a by-election in Niagara Falls. In 1962 she became part of the 'Truth Squad' that shadowed Prime Minister John Diefenbaker on his campaigns across the country, offering 'corrections' and 'constructive criticisms' to the Prime Minister's comments and speeches. This participation drew her to the attention of the media. A short, overweight woman, she took to wearing obvious wigs and knee-high leather boots. She was an extremely easy target for cartoonists to caricature, with increasing cruelty; and she was by her own account 'publicity prone', a situation hardly aided by her tendency to shoot from the lip. In 1963 she made a famous appearance at a benefit impersonating a gold-rush prostitute.

Upon re-election in 1963, LaMarsh was made a member of the Pearson cabinet and became Minister of Health and Welfare, a key portfolio that enabled her to capture many headlines. She personally helped draft the legislation for the Canada Pension Plan that was passed under her ministership. She was probably better known for having given up smoking while Minister of Health and Welfare, however. LaMarsh subsequently became Secretary of State, in charge of Canada's Centennial year, travelling thousands of miles to participate in celebrations and helping to entertain visiting dignitaries, including the royal couple. She also was partly responsible for the creation of the Royal Commission on the Status of Women. Not a fan of Pierre Elliott Trudeau, she made a negative comment about him that was caught on tape at the 1968 leadership convention. She subsequently retired from politics, leaving the incoming Parliament extremely short of women members. In retirement LaMarsh wrote a notorious memoir of her years in politics, *Bird in a Gilded Cage*, which received a huge advance and sold many thousands of copies.

the Atlantic region and Saskatchewan and Manitoba lost population in the 1960s through out-migration. A perception of disparity underlay much of the nation's political discontent. Some disparities were not regional at all, although they often had geographical overtones. Low wages, high unemployment, low labour force participation, and a limited tax base (constraining the financing of public services) together created higher incidences of inequality in some provinces. Young people under 25 were twice as likely to be unemployed as Canadians over that age, for example, and youth unemployment skyrocketed in marginal areas. Substantial evidence was advanced in this period showing that an individual's ethnic group, racial origin, and gender also affected economic success. And then there were the poor.

Table 10.1 Unemployment Rates by Region, 1961–1970

Year	Atlantic	Quebec	Ontario	Prairies	BC	Canada
1961	11.3	9.3	5.5	4.6	8.5	7.2
1962	10.8	7.5	4.3	3.9	6.6	5.9
1963	9.6	7.4	3.8	3.7	6.4	5.5
1964	8.2	6.3	3.3	3.1	5.3	4.7
1965	7.4	5.4	2.5	2.6	4.2	3.9
1966	6.4	4.7	2.5	2.1	4.6	3.6
1967	6.6	5.3	3.1	2.3	5.2	4.1
1968	7.3	6.5	3.6	2.9	6.0	4.8
1969	7.5	6.9	3.1	2.9	5.0	4.7
1970	7.6	6.9	4.3	4.4	7.7	5.9

Source: Department of Regional Economic Expansion/Industry Canada, *Major Economic Indicators, Provinces and Regions* (Ottawa: Queen's Printer, 1971), Table 2.4. Reproduced with the permission of the Ministry of Public Works and Government Services, 2006.

What constituted real poverty in Canada remained a matter of continual debate. What was indisputable, however, was the inequality of national personal income in Canada. The wealthiest 20 per cent of Canadians earned over 40 per cent of the income, and the poorest 20 per cent earned less than 6 per cent. Most of those in the poorest 20 per cent, it should be added, were employed.

Some of Canada's endemic economic problems were better publicized (if not better resolved) in the 1960s. There were a number of obvious weak points. One was in the food-producing sector. Canadian farmers continued to find that increased mechanization and use of fertilizers meant that fewer hands were needed to produce larger crops. Canadian farms became ever more capital-intensive, marginal lands less attractive, yet returns to the farmer remained sluggish. Most increases in food costs to the consumer were caused by non-agricultural factors, such as transportation and processing, rather than by increased returns to the farmer. The farm population in Canada had been declining absolutely for decades, and this era was no exception. Between the 1961 and 1971 censuses, the number of farm residents fell from 2,072,785 to 1,419,795. Drops were especially marked in Prince Edward Island and Manitoba. As for the fishery, the admission of Newfoundland to Confederation in 1949 only increased the numbers of fishers in serious difficulty. Experts' warnings about overfishing were ignored by governments eager to create programs to aid fishers and fishing communities.

By the end of the period, a handful of environmentalists had begun pointing out the damage being done by those reaping resources without concern for conservation practices and the consequences of pollution. American author Rachel Carson's *Silent Spring*, (1962) first called the attention of many Canadians to the evils of toxic chemicals in the environment, and the infamous story of Grassy Narrows in 1970 reinforced the message. At

Table 10.2 Percentage of Employment in Manufacturing by Region, 1961 and 1969, and Average Wage in Manufacturing, 1969

Region	Employment (000s)	1961 Share (%)	1969 Share (%)	Average Wage ($)
Atlantic	76.8	4.6	4.5	4,995
Quebec	527.0	33.6	31.2	5,542
Ontario	836.9	47.8	49.5	6,228
Prairies	119.8	6.9	7.1	5,888
BC	130.7	7.7	7.7	6,591

Source: Department of Regional Economic Expansion/Industry Canada, *Major Economic Indicators, Provinces and Regions* (Ottawa: Queen's Printer, 1971), Tables 3.3, 3.1. Reproduced with the permission of the Ministry of Public Works and Government Services, 2006.

Table 10.3	Average Income of Salaried Males in Fourteen Ethnic Groups, Quebec, 1961	
Ethnic Group	**In Dollars**	**Index**
General Average	3,469	100.0
British	4,940	142.4
Scandinavians	4,939	142.4
Dutch	4,891	140.9
Jewish	4,851	139.8
Russians	4,828	139.1
Germans	4,245	122.6
Poles	3,984	114.8
Asians	3,734	107.6
Ukrainians	3,733	107.6
Other Europeans	3,547	102.4
Hungarians	3,537	101.9
French Canadians	3,185	91.8
Italians	2,938	84.6
Native Indians	2,112	60.8

Source: *Canadian Dimension* 5, 8 (Feb. 1969): 17.

Grassy Narrows, in northwestern Ontario, a pulp mill upstream from the Grassy Narrows Reserve pumped lethal mercury into the waters from which the Aboriginals took their fish. Many inhabitants were systematically poisoned in the process.

Moreover, the issue of foreign ownership, first introduced by the Gordon Commission in 1958, took on a new life in the later 1960s when it became associated with American multinational corporations. Radical younger scholars such as Mel Watkins (b. 1932) called for the repatriation of the Canadian economy. Watkins headed the Task Force on the Structure of Canadian Industry, which in February 1968 released a report entitled *Foreign Ownership and the Structure of Canadian Industry* (the Watkins Report). Such critiques of American multinationalism merged with a widespread Canadian hostility to the policies of the United States, especially in Vietnam, as well as with the concerns of those worried about maintaining a distinctive Canadian identity. Public opinion shifted considerably between 1964 and 1972 over the question of further investment of

US capital in Canada. According to a 1964 Gallup poll, only 46 per cent of Canadians thought there was already enough American investment, and 33 per cent wanted more. By 1972, 67 per cent said that was enough, and only 22 per cent wanted further amounts.

Canadian nationalism emerged in the labour movement as well in the 1960s. This issue combined with others, particularly discontent among younger workers with the traditional nature of union leadership and organization. The older union leaders were not much interested in broad reform issues. They tried to dampen the reactions against local branches of international (i.e., American-dominated) unions that were seen as collaborators with American multinationals in both the 'sellout' of Canada and the maintenance of the 'military-industrial complex'. By the later 1960s many rank-and-file union members expressed discontent with American domination. The Americans took more money out of the country in dues than they returned in assistance; they failed to organize outside traditional industrial sectors; they often supported American military adventurism abroad; and, finally, they did not understand Canada and treated Canadian members with contempt. At least so went the complaints. Withdrawal from international unionism began seriously around 1970, and would increase over the next few years as wholly Canadian unions grew in numbers and membership. One of the major factors in the homegrown union movement was the success of public-sector unionism in the 1960s. In 1963 the Canadian Union of Public Employees organized, and in 1967 thousands of civil servants repudiated staff associations and formed the Public Service Alliance of Canada. Outside the civil service, but within the public sector, unionization was particularly marked in the teaching and health-care professions. Strikes by postal workers, teachers, and even policemen irritated large sectors of the Canadian public. Anger at the interruption of what many Canadians saw as essential services would eventually help make the unions easy targets in the 1970s as scapegoats for Canada's newly emergent economic problems.

Political Leadership

For much of the period, the Liberal hegemony of the King–St Laurent years appeared to be broken or at least bending. Not until the arrival of Pierre Trudeau did the Liberals get back on track, and that was at least partly because Trudeau represented a new style of political leadership, consonant with the age of television. John Diefenbaker, who became Prime Minister in 1957 and swept to a great victory in 1958, had a very old-fashioned political style. His bombastic speeches sounded as if they had been rhetorically crafted in the nineteenth century, and he revelled in being a House of Commons man, good in the specialized cut and thrust of debate in that legislative body. Diefenbaker inspired tremendous loyalty from some members of his party, but he seldom created confidence in his capacity to master public affairs. He was better at being the leader of the opposition than Prime Minister. Diefenbaker held a variety of contradictory positions; his latest biographer calls him a 'Rogue Tory'. He was a populist reformer at the head of a party that contained many genuine conservatives. He was simultaneously a Cold Warrior and a Canadian nationalist, holding both positions equally fervently. Despite his electoral successes in Quebec in 1957 and especially 1958, Diefenbaker was always associated (and associated himself) with English Canada. Diefenbaker's administration gave way to the Americans on the big principles while balking over the unpleasant consequences and details. Diefenbaker, moreover, was thoroughly detested by American President John F. Kennedy, who referred to 'the Chief' as one of the few men he

The revolutionary Avro Arrow, seen here in 1957, was scrapped by the Diefenbaker cabinet in 1959. This decision was the start of a heated debate regarding nuclear arms, which would eventually lead to the collapse of Diefenbaker government. Toronto Star/The Canadian Press.

had ever totally despised. Three related issues—the decision to scrap the Avro Arrow, the acceptance of American Bomarc-B missiles on Canadian soil, and the government's reaction to the Cuban Missile Crisis of 1962—illustrate the government's problems.

When Diefenbaker terminated the Avro Arrow project early in 1959, he did so for sound fiscal reasons. The plane had no prospective international market and would be inordinately expensive to build only for Canadian needs. The Prime Minister justified his decision in terms of changing military technology and strategy. An aircraft to intercept bombers would soon be obsolete, said Dief, and what Canada needed were missiles obtainable from the Friendly Giant. It turned out that Canada still needed fighters, however, and the country had to buy some very old F-101 Voodoos from the Americans. By cancelling Canada's principal technological breakthrough into the world of big military hardware in return for an agreement whereby parts of equipment purchased by Canada from the American defence industry would be assembled in Canada, Diefenbaker probably accepted reality. But the Bomarc-B missile was armed with a nuclear warhead, and Canada had a non-nuclear policy. Diefenbaker thus refused to allow the Bomarcs to be properly armed, erroneously insisting that they could be effective with non-nuclear warheads. The question took on new urgency in 1962 after President Kennedy confronted the USSR over the installation of Russian missile bases in Cuba. As Soviet ships carrying the missiles cruised westward towards Cuba and Kennedy threatened war if they did not turn back, NORAD automatically ordered DEFCON3, the state of readiness just short of war. Neither Diefenbaker nor his ministers were consulted—much less informed—about this decision. The Prime Minister was furious that a megalomaniac American President could, in effect, push the button that would destroy Canada.

In the end Nikita Khrushchev backed down in the fearsome game of nuclear chicken, but Cuba changed Canadian public opinion, which had tended to be against nuclear armament. The crisis provoked considerable media discussion of the government's prevarications and inconsistencies over nuclear and defence policy. NATO made it quite clear that Canada

was part of the nuclear system. Liberal leader Lester Pearson announced that the Liberals would stand by the nation's nuclear commitments even if the government that had made them would not. There was no point in housing nuclear weapons on Canadian soil if they could not be instantly deployed in the event of a crisis. Such defence blunders did Diefenbaker no good in the 1962 election. By January 1963 defence issues had reduced his cabinet to conflicting factions. The minority government fell shortly afterwards. Traditional Canadian nationalism as practised by John Diefenbaker was simply not compatible with the missile age.

During much of Diefenbaker's leadership of the Progressive Conservative Party from 1956 to 1967, his chief political opponent was Lester B. (Mike) Pearson. The contrast between the two men was instantly apparent, and the 'Dief and Mike' show (in the Commons and outside) was the joy of political cartoonists and satirists for that entire decade. Pearson was a soft-spoken former diplomat who had won a Nobel Peace Prize for conciliation in the Suez Crisis of 1956. Quietly ambitious, he had little House of Commons or domestic political experience. Apart from the 1958 election, the nation never gave either Pearson or Diefenbaker a mandate to govern, thus perhaps reflecting its suspicion of their qualifications. The voters preferred Diefenbaker in 1957, 1958, and 1962 (the first and the third elections producing minority governments), and Pearson in 1963 and 1965 (both times in a minority situation). Pearson was better able to govern with a minority, since his party could arrive at unofficial understandings with the CCF-NDP, something not possible for the Diefenbaker Tories. Pearson was no more able than Diefenbaker to rein in ambitious colleagues or provinces, however. The decade 1957–67 was one of constant federal political turmoil and federal–provincial hassles.

The returning Liberals, who regained power in 1963 under Pearson, spent most of the 1960s attempting to implement the integration of Canada's armed forces, mainly on the grounds that duplication of resources and command structures was an expensive luxury the nation could not afford. A unified Canadian military would be both leaner

White Paper on Defence, 1964

The White Paper on Defence was issued by the Pearson government in March 1964. This excerpt is from that document.

In the opinion of the government this solution [the gradual transfer of executive control of common requirements to the Chairman, Chiefs of Staff] does not adequately resolve the basic issues. If a single command structure is not established, co-ordination by the committee system will remain with all of its inevitable delays and frustrations.

The fundamental considerations are operational control and effectiveness, the streamlining of procedures and, in particular, the decision-making process, and the reduction of overhead. To the extent that operational control is exercised by Canada, it is the view of the government that it can be most effectively exercised by a single command. The question of duplication and unnecessary overhead, too, cannot be ignored. The present headquarters organization of the Department of National Defence is far too large. The fact that our field forces are modest creates a serious imbalance between the field and headquarters branches of the service. As it appears that we will have to maintain modest forces in being for many years to come, it is apparent that a re-organization is required.

Following the most careful and thoughtful consideration, the government has decided that there is only one adequate solution. It is the integration of the Armed Forces of Canada under a single Chief of Defence Staff and a single Defence Staff. This will be the first step toward a single unified defence force for Canada. The integrated control of all aspects of planning and operations should not only produce a more effective and co-ordinated defence posture for Canada, but should also result in considerable savings. Thus, integration will result in a substantial reduction of manpower strengths in headquarters, training and related establishments, along with other operating and maintenance costs. The total savings to be effected as a result of such reductions will make available funds for capital equipment purchases, and eventually make possible more equitable distribution of the defence dollar between equipment and housekeeping costs. Sufficient savings should accrue from unification to permit a goal of 25 per cent of the budget to be devoted to capital equipment being realized in the years ahead.

Two objections are given as reasons why integration should not be undertaken. First, that morale or 'esprit de corps' is weakened, and second, that competition is diminished. Neither of these objections will stand against careful scrutiny. 'Esprit de corps' by nature is associated with ship, or corps, or regiment, or squadron, as well as with the service. There is no thought of eliminating worthwhile traditions and there is no reason why morale should not be high—a direct result of effectiveness. Similarly, there will be no lack of competition. The sailors will press for more ships, the soldiers for more tanks and the airmen for more planes. This is as natural as breathing. Competition will not be lost but it will be contained at the service level.

Source: *White Paper on Defence*, March 1964 (Ottawa: Queen's Printer, 1964), 18–19. Reproduced courtesy of the Department of National Defence, with permission of the Ministry of Public Works and Government Services, 2007.

and meaner, capable of remaining within acceptable budget figures. A White Paper to this effect was released in March of 1964, and Bill C-90, which amended the National Defence Act by creating a single Chief of Defence Staff, was introduced into the House of Commons on 10 April 1964. The amendments producing a fully integrated military headquarters with a single chain of command received royal assent on 16 July 1964. The country and its politicians, however, continued to hold schizophrenic attitudes towards the Canadian military, its foreign obligations, and Canada's overseas role. Canada wanted to control its own destiny, which probably required a neutral stance internationally. Neutrality in international affairs would cost even more than the American and NATO alliances, however, so everyone pretended that Canada could hold the line on military spending and still honour its commitments through administrative reform. At the same time, Canada began a long, slow, gradual process of reducing its armed forces, a process that was still underway in the twenty-first century.

Despite Prime Minister Pearson's high profile as a successful world diplomat, his governments were not distinguished for their triumphs in the international arena. In fairness to Pearson, the world was changing in other ways not sympathetic to Canada's self-proclaimed role as a middle power. After 1960 the United Nations General Assembly opened its doors to dozens of Third World countries, most of them recently emerged from colonial status and quite hostile to the Western democracies. The new complexities of politics and expectations within the General Assembly, and in the various collateral UN organizations, worked against a highly developed and industrialized nation such as Canada—populated chiefly by the descendants of white Europeans—which also happened to be a junior partner of the United States. In UN bodies Canadian diplomats found themselves in the embarrassing position of defending the country's internal policy, particularly towards Aboriginal peoples, in the face of criticisms of racism and insensitivity to human rights. Canada was not in the same league as South Africa, perhaps, but its record on human rights was a hard one to explain internationally. At the same time, the success of the European Economic Community (first established in 1958) made Western European nations more important international players, while Japan had succeeded in restoring its industrial position. As a result, Canada became less important among the industrial nations at the same time that it became less credible in the Third World.

It was not only the configuration of world politics that had altered by the 1960s. So had the policy of

the United States. President Kennedy and his successor, Lyndon B. Johnson, were actually more hardbitten and confrontational Cold Warriors than their predecessors, Truman and Eisenhower. The latter had been extremely embarrassed in 1960 when the Russians shot down an American U-2 spy plane and captured its pilot, Francis Gary Powers. Kennedy, on the other hand, authorized dirty tricks by the CIA in foreign countries, and he made no apology when they were exposed. His only regret about the abortive 1961 Bay of Pigs invasion of Cuba by US-backed Cuban exiles, for example, was that it had failed. Most important, however, both Kennedy and Johnson permitted their governments to become ever more deeply involved in the quagmire of Southeast Asia. In 1945, Ho Chi Minh declared the Democratic Republic of Vietnam, with Hanoi as its capital, to be independent of French colonial control. When the French government proved incapable of defeating the armed 'insurgents', Canada in 1954 became involved in attempts at international control. It served as one of three members, with Poland and India, of a joint commission. Canada was actually eager to participate to bolster its middle-power pretensions in the world. The 1954 commission set the pattern for the next 20 years: one Iron Curtain nation, one Western ally of the United States, one neutral power, with votes often going against Canada as the American supporter. From the outset Canada had deceived itself into believing that it had a free hand to carry out its work without either upsetting the Americans or appearing to act merely as a lackey of the United States.

When the American administration gradually escalated both US involvement and the shooting war in Vietnam after 1963, Canada's position became increasingly anomalous, both on the commission and outside it. Lester Pearson was still hoping to mediate in April 1965 when he used the occasion of a speech in Philadelphia to suggest that the American government might pause in its bombing of North Vietnam to see if a negotiated settlement was possible. He was soon shown the error of his ways in no uncertain terms. In a private meeting with Lyndon Johnson shortly thereafter, the American President shook Pearson by his lapels and criticized Canadian presumptuousness with Texas profanity.

Vietnam certainly contributed to a new Canadian mood in the later 1960s, both in Ottawa and on the main streets of the nation. Canadians now sought to distance themselves from the policies of the 'Ugly Americans', although never by open withdrawal from the American defence umbrella.

The victory of Pierre Trudeau in 1968 marked a new era, which by the early 1970s saw a return to Liberal hegemony. The Tories had chosen Robert Stanfield (1914–2003) to succeed Diefenbaker. The soft-spoken Stanfield seemed a good match for Lester Pearson, but could not compete with the trendy and articulate Trudeau. Like the pop stars he seemed to emulate, Trudeau was capable of repackaging his image (and his policies) to suit conditions changing so fast they seemed to be 'blowin'' in the wind'. Not only was Trudeau a thoroughly bilingual French Canadian who was likely to appeal to Quebec, but he was continually able to convince the electorate that he was far more of a reformer than his subsequent policies would indicate. After years of apparently irresolute national leadership, Trudeau also seemed to be a strong figure. In some respects he was, as his behaviour in the October Crisis of 1970 demonstrated. The Prime Minister did not hesitate for a moment to invoke the War Measures Act and employ the military against the FLQ. Most of the nation appreciated his decisiveness.

The era was also characterized by a number of long-serving and highly visible provincial premiers, who provided considerable stability for the provincial cause in the regularly held federal–provincial conferences. While federal leadership had been ineffective for the 10 years before Trudeau, almost all the provinces had seemingly strong leaders. There continued to be little genuine two-party politics anywhere in Canada. Instead, dominant parties were usually in control. In Newfoundland Joey Smallwood still governed virtually unopposed. In New Brunswick Louis Robichaud was in control from 1960 to 1970. Ontario had John Robarts, Manitoba had Duff Roblin, Saskatchewan had Ross Thatcher, while Alberta still had Ernest Manning and British Columbia was led by W.A.C. Bennett. Few of these governments were Liberal. Ross Thatcher (1917–71) headed the only provincial Liberal government west of Quebec between 1945 and 1972,

John Diefenbaker and Lester Pearson, 30 January 1958. Duncan Cameron/LAC, PA-117093.

and he was a vociferous critic of the federal Liberals. By the early 1970s the only provincial governments controlled by the Liberals were in Prince Edward Island and Quebec. Pierre Trudeau's conception of liberalism and federalism certainly did not accord with that of Quebec's Liberal Premier, Robert Bourassa (1933–96).

No matter who was in charge and at what level, the size and scope of the apparatus of bureaucracy continually expanded. The scope of bureaucracy had political as well as economic implications. The larger it got, the harder it was to manage. A host of journalists and popular commentators attacked governments at all levels for mismanagement and waste, but as one commentator astutely pointed out, 'It is true that the initial motive for reforms may be the outsider's simple-minded belief that gigantic savings can be effected. But once set an investigation afoot and the economy motive gets quickly overlaid with the more subtle and difficult problems of improved service and efficiency' (Hodgetts, 1968: 7–8). The

Royal Commission on Government Organization, appointed by Diefenbaker in 1960, found itself unable to effect major changes in the bureaucracy, particularly in downsizing the scope of operations. All governments, including federal Liberal ones, increasingly found themselves entrapped by the actions of their predecessors and by the difficulties of dismantling systems once created. Government was becoming more difficult and the nation increasingly impossible to lead.

Immigration Reform

The conversion, within the space of a single generation, from a very insular and parochial nation to one that was relatively sophisticated and cosmopolitan, much more capable of toleration of ethnic differences, has been one of the most remarkable and underrated public changes in Canadian history. One factor in the change of attitude was World War II, a war in which over a million Canadians served in the military, more than half of them overseas. Unlike the Great War, which most Canadian soldiers spent in disgusting trenches on the continent of Europe, World War II actually gave Canadians some foreign experience. Over a quarter of a million troops spent up to four years in Great Britain, waiting for the Big Show of D-Day to begin and at least sometimes playing at being tourists. Canadian soldiers fought in Italy and through France, the Low Countries, and Germany. Such fighting was not nice but it was considerably more broadening than life in a muddy trench. That over 50,000 Canadians met foreign girls and got to know them well enough to propose marriage suggests some of the possibilities. The American popular song of World War I had queried, 'How you gonna keep 'em, down on the farm, after they've seen Paree?' That question was really much more relevant for Canada in 1945 than in 1918.

A second factor was the post-war immigration itself. Between 1946 and 1972 more than 3.5 million 'New

Canadians' entered the country, an average of about 135,000 per year. Even after emigration to other nations from Canada is subtracted (since people, especially recent arrivals, also *left* the country in substantial numbers), the net gain was well in excess of two million. By 1971, one in every four Canadians claimed an ethnic origin other than British, French, or Aboriginal. The changes are detailed in Table 10.4.

Proportionate to the total population, the post-World War II figures for immigration were not as significant as the earlier influxes of immigration to Canada before Confederation and before the Great War, but the post-war immigration was different. Unlike earlier arrivals, many of whom ended up on isolated farmsteads on the frontier, this population settled almost exclusively in the cities, especially those in Ontario and Quebec, transforming them enormously in the process. Before 1945, for example, Toronto had been a predominantly Anglo-Saxon city, in which only in certain areas could any language other than English be heard. By 1961 it was a city of ethnic neighbourhoods. Although Montreal had always been bilingual rather than unilingual, the sense of it as a polyglot city was present by the 1960s, as was the case in almost all of the

Table 10.4	Population by Ethnic Origin, 1951–1971		
Ethnic Group	1951	1961	1971
British Isles	6,709,685	7,996,669	9,624,115*
English	3,630,344	4,195,175	
Irish	1,439,635	1,753,351	
Scots	1,547,470	1,902,302	
Welsh, etc.	92,236	145,841	
French	4,319,167	5,540,346	6,180,120
Other European	2,553,722	4,116,849	4,959,680
Asiatic	72,827	121,753	285,540
Other**	354,028	462,630	518,850***

*By 1971 Statistics Canada had decided no longer to separate the British into national groups.
**Including Eskimo, Native Indian, Negro, West Indian, and not stated.
***Americans are included nowhere in this table because Statistics Canada did not regard the people of the United States as an ethnic group; Americans were listed under their 'national origins'.

larger cities of Canada west of the Atlantic region. The urban concentration of the post-war immigration made for the emergence of multi-ethnic cities.

A third factor in the new acceptance of cultural diversity was the rapid transformation into modern times of the rural communities of Canada between 1945 and 1960. In 1945 most rural Canadians lived in virtual isolation in a world of unpaved roads, horse-powered vehicles, cash shortages, and an absence of telephones and electricity. By 1960 the roads had been paved. The horse had been replaced by the tractor and the automobile. Farm families now had cash, from the monthly mothers' allowance cheque from the federal government, if from no other source. Virtually every family had a telephone, and the world of electricity meant milking machines, electric stoves, and refrigerators, as well as radios, television sets, and stereos. Rural and farm families had become plugged into the larger industrial economy rather than isolated from it, and there would be no going back.

Both the preference for urban life of post-war immigrants and the rural transformation helped contribute to a fourth factor in the change, which was the overall extent to which Canada became an urban nation in the years after 1945, especially in the provinces of Ontario and Quebec. This new wave of urbanization was based on a transportation shift to automobiles and trucks, the change from industrial to service production, and suburban development, as well as on the influx of immigrants and rural Canadians into the urban centres. In 1941 only 55 per cent of Canada's people lived in cities. That figure grew to 62.9 per cent in 1951 and 69.7 per cent in 1961. By 1971 over three-quarters of the Canadian population lived in an urban environment. Cities have usually been responsible for breaking down the old traditionalism of a society, and for long-resident Canadians in the post-war period, they did their job. It must be added that for many new arrivals, large cities and the resultant concentration of ethnic groups in complete communities meant that Canadian cities could actually slow acculturation rather than speed it up.

A fifth factor, related in part to rural transformation but involving the entire society, was the rapid modernization of Quebec. Between 1939 and 1960 Quebec caught up socially and economically with English-speaking Canada. The process involved substantial industrialization and urbanization. Quebec ceased to be a traditional society with its values based upon Catholicism. Symptomatically, the birth rate in Quebec in these years dropped from one of the highest in Canada to one of the lowest. The socio-economic transformation was accompanied by a series of profound ideological shifts within Quebec society that shook its foundations to the very core. The patterns of that development were relatively comprehensible to anyone familiar with what was happening elsewhere in developing societies. Traditional forms of defensive nationalism, including the power and authority of the Church, were eventually swept away by a new powerful and secular form of nationalism that had already become fully articulated in the years before 1960. The main opposition to the new nationalism came less from the old nationalism than from a renewed current of nineteenth-century liberalism adapted to twentieth-century Quebec conditions. In the 1960s, these two competing ideological currents would find popular labels in Quebec as 'separatism' and 'federalism'. Quebec's new internal nationalism meant that the province no longer served as a brake on federal policies of liberalization and that, instead, the province's demands helped contribute to change. The 'Quiet Revolution' of the 1960s would be a major impetus to a number of new Canadian policies. Most Quebecers were quite happy to accept ethnic minorities so long as they were prepared to speak French and associate themselves with the aspirations of Quebec. In the process of dealing with the new Quebec, a succession of Canadian governments would remake policy towards immigration and ethnic culture.

Finally, the new communications media, particularly the general expansion of television right across the Canadian population after 1950, increasingly plugged Canadians into the world. The very speed of the spread of television told its own story. The Canadian Broadcasting Corporation opened its first two television stations in Montreal and Toronto in September 1952. At the time of the introduction of Canadian television broadcasting, only 146,000

Canadians owned television receivers, tuning to American border stations and using increasingly elaborate antenna systems to draw in distant signals. By December 1954 there were nine stations and 1,200,000 sets; by June 1955 there were 26 stations and 1,400,000 sets; and by December 1957 there were 44 stations and nearly three million sets. The rate of set proliferation had been almost twice that of the United States, and the market for new receivers was virtually saturated within five years. By the early 1960s virtually the only sign of life in entire blocks of residential urban and suburban neighbourhoods—or on rural roads with their periodically scattered farmhouses—was the flickering dull glow of black-and-white television screens within otherwise darkened dwellings. Paradoxically, while television put Canadians back into their homes, it also helped force them out of their narrow insularity, not so much into their local communities as into the international world previously beyond their ken.

Just as immigration in the post-war period changed Canada's view of itself, so did immigration policy change the character of immigrants to Canada. As we saw in Chapter 9, Ellen Fairclough, the Minister of Immigration, sought unsuccessfully in 1959 to limit family immigration sponsorship to immediate family members, but she persisted with immigration reform. In 1962 she tabled in the House of Commons new immigration regulations that removed racial discrimination and introduced skill as the major criterion for unsponsored immigration. Such a policy was consistent with Prime Minister Diefenbaker's 1960 Bill of Rights, which rejected discrimination based on race, colour, national origin, religion, or gender. With this change to immigration policy, sponsored immigration—which was continued—almost immediately became by definition part of the old discriminatory system favouring European over non-European immigrants, since there were many more Canadians of European descent to sponsor new arrivals. According to the deputy minister of immigration:

Our prime objective in the proposed revision is to eliminate all discrimination based on colour, race or creed. This means that, if we continue to allow Greeks, Poles, Italians, Portuguese and

other Europeans to bring in the wide range of relatives presently admissible, we will have to do the same for Japanese, Chinese, Indians, Pakistanis, Africans, persons from the Arab world, the West Indies and so forth. The only possible result of this would be a substantially larger number of unskilled close relatives from these parts of the world to add to the influx of unskilled close relatives from Europe. (Quoted in Hawkins, 1972: 112)

To avoid this result, he added that it was going to be necessary to open the door to close relatives from all parts of the world and to reduce somehow the flow of European close relatives. However, Section 31(d) of the regulations did not open the sponsorship door to non-Europeans.

The new regulations also provided for an Immigration Board semi-independent of the Immigration Department to hear appeals, except in sponsorship cases. On the front of illegal Chinese immigration, the government decided to declare an 'amnesty' to all Chinese who had arrived illegally in Canada before 1 July 1960. This was the first of a long series of amnesties that would be declared to deal with illegal immigration to Canada. The Liberals complained in Parliament that this cosmic shift in Canadian policy had occurred without any public debate, which was of course true. Whether Canadian public opinion would have sustained such a non-racial policy in 1962 is, of course, quite doubtful. The new non-racial policy did not have an immediate impact on Canada because of the low level of immigration in the early 1960s. The low levels were a result of budget cutbacks to the Department of Immigration under the Diefenbaker government caused by financial rather than policy considerations. At the same time, it must be admitted that the Diefenbaker cabinet saw immigration as an unpleasant and necessary evil upon which as little money as possible should be spent.

Although there had been some shift in country of birth of immigrants after 1945, in 1965 Britain still provided nearly 30 per cent of the newcomers, continental Europe nearly half, and the United States 10 per cent, leaving only a little over 10 per cent of immigration originating in the remainder of the world. At this time, all of the top 10 'nations of origin' except the United States were still European. In 1966 the Liberal government of Lester B. Pearson epitomized much of the official Canadian philosophy of immigration when it put immigration under the same minister as manpower in the Department of Manpower and Immigration. The opposition in Parliament criticized the melding of immigration policy into the labour portfolio, preferring instead a department of citizenship and immigration. The deputy minister of the new Department of Manpower and Immigration found his task no easy one, reporting in his memoirs:

> Politicians were understandably chary of defining immigration policy at all precisely. On one hand, there was a broad public sentiment in favour of easy immigration; so many Canadians, if not immigrants themselves, had known parents or grandparents who were. There was also strong humanitarian sentiment on behalf of the oppressed and the deprived. And behind these general attitudes were powerful special interests: business wanting both skilled professionals and cheap labour; expanding universities wanting professors with doctorates not available in Canada; richer people wanting domestic servants. And, of course, recent immigrants wanted their relatives and friends to join them, and ethnic organizations had strong interests in the growth of their particular communities. (Kent, 1988: 407)

The new ministry sounded out public opinion in 1966 through the publication of a White Paper on Immigration Policy. This document argued for the recruitment of workers with high degrees of skills, regardless 'of race, colour or religion'. It also insisted that the government should not hesitate to keep out misfits and criminals. Public hearings on the White Paper by the Special Joint Committee of the Senate and House of Commons on Immigration began in November of 1966.

The Joint Committee heard a full spectrum of opinion from what Tom Kent has called the 'special interests'. The Confederation of National Trade Unions (CNTU) in Quebec opposed an emphasis on skills, insisting that such a policy would represent an international brain drain in which Canada would weaken Third World nations by taking their professionals. The Canadian Labour Congress agreed, adding that unskilled immigrant workers were needed to carry out 'tasks which native born or already established immigrants refuse to perform because of their better training'. The Mining Association of Canada definitely wanted at least 4,000 semi-skilled workers admitted per year, noting, 'The type of immigrant we have in mind has been the backbone of the labour force of the mining industry in the past. . . . a man has to be physically fit; but his education is not too important, so long as he can read or write.' Canadians would not work in mines, reported one witness from the mining interests, because 'there are no roads, no TVs, no cars, few girls, little or no liquor and most people recoil from the idea of working underground' (quoted in Avery, 1995: 181). No mention was made by this witness of the danger or relatively low pay experienced by miners. Most Canadian industrialists advocated the admission of the unskilled, although the Canadian Manufacturers' Association and the Canadian Medical Association both stressed the need for those who were technologically prepared. The Canadian Jewish Congress emphasized humanitarian concerns, 'the need for people to find asylum'. Many ethnic organizations applauded the new emphasis on skills, but most also insisted on the maintenance of the sponsorship category.

Having listened to the interest groups, the ministry moved quickly to major reform of immigration policy, instituting in 1968 a major new mechanism for immigration selection, the 'points system'. According to Tom Kent (1988: 410), 'If we could identify and define the various factors affecting a person's ability to settle in Canada, and attach relative weights to them, then immigration officers would have a consistent basis on which to assess potential immigrants.' Thus, education, employment opportunities, skills, age, and the immigration officer's assessment of potential were all to be awarded points adding up to a maximum total of 100. The points system—skills had only limited support from the hearing—was put in place apart from sponsorship, which was continued (although with reduced categories) because of its support from corporate Canada, trade unions, and ethnic groups.

A new procedure allowing for the application for immigration status from within the country was also introduced and would ultimately become one of the most controversial parts of the new immigration law. This last policy was prompted chiefly by the appearance as visitors in Canada of American draft evaders and was intended to regularize requests for landed immigrant status from this particular group of refugees. In the late 1960s as many as 100,000 Americans seeking to avoid service in the Vietnam War had come to Canada and were sheltered by Canadians and the Canadian government. The points system officially eliminated discrimination on the grounds of race or class but managed to perpetuate several traditional features of Canadian policy. By awarding large numbers of the points required for acceptance as an immigrant to Canada on the basis of occupation, education, language skills, and age, it continued both the economic rationale for immigration and the selectivity of the process.

The Beginning of International Drift

After Pierre Trudeau succeeded Pearson in April 1968, an undeclared and never co-ordinated policy of retreat from middle-power pretensions was accelerated. Trudeau had long been critical of Canada's foreign and defence policies. Soon after his accession to office, he initiated formal reviews, which the Departments of National Defence and External Affairs found most threatening. The Prime Minister was particularly eager to raise 'fundamental questions', such as whether there was really a Russian threat to world order, or whether the US '[would] sacrifice Europe and NATO before blowing up the world' (quoted in Granatstein and Bothwell, 1990: 17). The bureaucrats were not comfortable with such questions, nor were several of Trudeau's cabinet colleagues. Trudeau had a reputation as an internationalist, but he disliked the military, and ultimately

proved much more comfortable with domestic matters than external ones. For Trudeau, protecting the sovereignty of Canadian territory was far more important than international peacekeeping. Defence budgets continued to be cut and active Canadian involvement in NATO was pared to the lowest limits of allied acceptability. The best-known armed action by the Canadian military was its occupation of Quebec during the October Crisis of 1970. In 1973 Canada sent a large military mission to Vietnam to serve on a revised International Commission for Control and Supervision. Its purpose was to allow the Americans to withdraw from that troubled corner of the world, but the Commission was not able to act effectively. The Trudeau government called it home in mid-1973. Canada was no longer a self-defined middle power. It had no clear conception of its place or role in world affairs.

Canada's problem in the world was basically simple. Its economic indicators entitled it to major-league status, but its population was small and its close relationship with the United States inevitably consigned it to being a minor-league subsidiary player. The Canadian image abroad was as perplexing as its policies. On the one hand, the country continued its irritating habit of preaching from on high to nations that did not regard themselves as morally inferior. Catching Canada in hypocritical moral contradictions became a favourite international game. Canada's multilateral involvements limited its abilities to provide practical support for human rights issues, despite some internal pressures to adopt a more interventionist human rights position. On the other hand, Canada continued to be one of the most favoured destinations for immigrants from around the world. Ordinary people accepted that life was better in Canada. Indeed, surveys regularly listed Canada at the top of the international standard-of-living table.

Whatever the Department of External Affairs was or was not doing, Canadians themselves became citizens of the world in a way that would have been incomprehensible to earlier generations. By the early 1970s, relatively cheap airplane tickets to go anywhere in the world had become an accepted part of life. In the 1960s the kids had travelled the world, carrying backpacks festooned with the Canadian flag and sleeping in youth hostels. Now their parents followed them, staying in hotels that were just like those at home. Almost every Canadian family had at least one member with photographs of a major overseas expedition. Cheap airfares also brought relatives from abroad to visit Canada. All this travel combined with new immigration to make Canada an increasingly cosmopolitan place to live. Canadians drank less beer and more wine, much of it imported. They ate in restaurants with exotic cuisines, learned to cook similar food at home, and insisted that this type of food be available at their local supermarkets.

Pierre Trudeau's attempt to reorient Canadian foreign policy met with limited success. He managed to reduce Canada's military commitment to NATO and to reduce the size of Canada's armed forces. In 1972 the government produced a policy document that recommended a 'Third Option': less dependence upon the Americans. But if Canada moved away from the Americans, where would it go? The obvious answer was to Europe. Canada had waited too long and had become too closely identified with (not to mention integrated in) the American economy. The fizzle of the European initiative was followed by a similar effort in Asia, with perhaps slightly better success.

The Expansion of the Welfare State

Part of the reason for the continual expansion of government bureaucracy was regular (if unco-ordinated) expansion of the Canadian welfare state. Politicians viewed expanded social services as popular votegetters, and no political party strenuously opposed the principles of welfare democracy. Although the Diefenbaker government was not associated with any major program, it had initiated a number of reviews and Royal Commissions, the recommendations of which would pass into legislation under the Liberals. The minority Pearson government was pushed towards improved social insurance by the NDP, its own reforming wing, and competitive pressures from an ambitious Quebec and other provinces. Were Ottawa not to introduce new national programs, the federal government could well lose control of them to the wealthier and more aggressive provinces. The expansion in 1964 of family allowances to include children up to the age of 18 who were still in school merely imitated something introduced by the Lesage government in 1961. In 1965 the federal government attempted to introduce a national contributory pension scheme, but settled for one that allowed Quebec its own plan.

The changing demography of Canada guaranteed that there would be continual pressures on the government to improve the pension system. Those who wanted improved benefits were able to make common ground with those who sought to control costs. Both could agree on the superiority of a contributory scheme. The Medical Care Act of 1966 built on provincial initiatives with a cost-sharing arrangement. By 1968 all provinces and territories had agreed on cost-sharing arrangements with Ottawa that produced a social minimum in health care. For most Canadians, access to medical service (doctors and hospitalization) would thereafter be without charge. Occasionally cynicism triumphed. Early in 1965 Prime Minister Pearson wrote his cabinet ministers asking for suggestions of policy initiatives that would shift attention from political harassment by the opposition over mistakes and difficulties. The result was a Canadian variation of Lyndon Johnson's War on Poverty. Canada proposed a full utilization of human resources and an end to poverty. Actual reforms were not very significant.

The first Trudeau government, responding to the reform euphoria of the era, actually contemplated shifting the grounds of social protectionism in 'the Just Society'. To bureaucrats and political leaders in the late 1960s the emphasis of mainstream reform had been to carry out the agenda of the 1940s for the establishment of a 'social minimum' providing basic economic security for all Canadians. Now, at least briefly, they debated the possibility of expanding the welfare state to include some measure of income distribution. Poverty came to be seen as a serious problem worthy of public focus. The Economic Council of Canada in 1968 described the persistence of poverty in Canada as 'a disgrace'. Later that same year a Special Senate Committee on Poverty

Table 10.5	Expenditures on Personal Health Care as a Percentage of Gross Provincial Product and Personal Income, Ontario, 1960–1975	
Year	GPP	Personal Income
1960	3.76	4.62
1961	3.95	4.98
1962	4.04	5.04
1963	4.14	5.17
1964	4.15	5.40
1965	4.18	5.47
1966	4.08	5.35
1967	4.43	5.67
1968	4.69	5.99
1969	4.76	6.04
1970	5.06	6.32
1971	5.32	6.57
1972	5.17	6.18
1973	6.56	6.05
1974	6.38	8.23
1975	6.94	8.57

Source: K.J. Rea, *The Prosperous Years: The Economic History of Ontario 1939–75* (Toronto: University of Toronto Press, 1985), 119. Reprinted with permission.

was established under Senator David Croll's chairmanship. In 1971 this committee produced a report, *Poverty in Canada*, which insisted that nearly 2 million people in Canada lived below the poverty line. More radical critics, in *The Real Poverty Report* that same year, put the figure much higher.

Poverty not only characterized the lives of millions of Canadians, but it was structural, regional, and related to racial and sexual discrimination. A number of schemes were suggested, including a guaranteed income for low-income families as part of the family allowance package. The year 1970 had already seen the publication of a federal White Paper called 'Income Security for Canadians', which pointed out the escalating costs of social insurance and criticized the principle of universality that had previously governed Canadian policy. The ultimate

result was the new Unemployment Insurance Plan of 1971, which extended and increased coverage without actually addressing the concept of a guaranteed minimum income for all Canadians. At about the same time, Ottawa eliminated a separate fund for Canada pension contributions and began considering them as part of the general revenue of the government.

Reformers had long insisted that access to education was one of the social rights to which all Canadians were entitled. Increasing access meant creating new facilities. The presence of the baby-boom generation gave urgency to that implication. Parents were much attracted to the practical benefits of education in providing future employment and a better life for their children. The results in the 1960s were enormous pressures on education budgets and increasing demand for the production of more and better teachers. School authorities attempted to ease some of their problems by consolidating rural education through use of the ubiquitous yellow school bus, a process that continued into the early 1970s. Teachers acquired more formal credentials, became better paid, and organized themselves into a powerful professional lobby that was sometimes even unionized. By the late 1950s virtually everyone could agree on the need for universal high school education, and by 1970 over 90 per cent of Canadian children of high school age were in school. Increasing numbers of high school graduates were entitled to a university education, and the decade of the 1960s was the golden age of university expansion in Canada. Not only were new facilities constructed, but 20,000 new faculty members were recruited, most of them from the United States. By 1970 public spending on education had risen to 9 per cent of the gross national product, and represented nearly 20 per cent of all taxes levied by all three levels of government.

Before 1970 the disagreement between the universalists and the means testers had been relatively muted. Both sides could agree that there had been an absence of overall integrated planning in the growth of the welfare state. Little attention had been paid to the long-range implications of any policy. Bureaucracies and programs had been allowed to expand with no thought for tomorrow. The later

1960s had introduced a new ingredient into the mix, however. Governments began routinely spending more money than they were receiving.

Quebec

In the 1960s the average Anglo-Canadian discovered that Quebec was unhappy with Confederation. That discovery was part of the completion of Quebec's transformation into a secularized, urbanized, and industrialized region that differed little in many respects from its central Canadian neighbour, Ontario. The transformation was often associated with the Quiet Revolution in the first half of the decade, a term used by the media to describe the modernization of Quebec. The structural changes to French-Canadian society had already taken place before 1960, even though at the close of the 1950s traditional French-Canadian nationalism in Church and state, symbolized by the Union Nationale, still seemed to prevail. The critique of tradition had already been elaborated and the program of reform for Quebec was well articulated. All that remained was to fit the government of Quebec and popular aspirations together. That task was begun by the provincial Liberal Party, led by Jean Lesage (1912–80), which defeated the Union Nationale and came to power in 1960. The leading Liberal strategists did not realize at the time just how ready Quebec was for change, or how easily the traditional institutions and ways would crumble once they were confronted by an activist government composed of politicians drawn from Quebec's new middle and professional classes.

The first major step had to do with hydroelectricity. The tradition that had to be overcome was the long-standing Quebec fear, nurtured for decades by the Union Nationale, of anything resembling economic statism (or socialism or communism). *Anti-étatisme* in Quebec was not the same thing as a do-nothing government. Under Duplessis, the provincial government had spent a lot of money on public services, including many hydroelectric projects to assist rural electrification. What the Minister of Natural Resources, René Lévesque (1922–87), proposed on 12 February 1962, without consulting his colleagues, was the enforced government consolidation of all existing private hydroelectric companies into one massive Hydro-Québec. Hydroelectricity was an ideal place to fight the battle of nationalization, partly because electrical generation and supply was a public enterprise right across North America, partly because it directly touched the pocketbook of the rural Quebecer, who was most likely to oppose state action. Despite a famous 'Jamais!' from Premier Lesage, nationalization was quickly accepted by the Liberal cabinet as a winning campaign issue, and the Liberals took it to the province in 1962 with the slogan 'Maîtres chez nous'. Led by Lesage and a compelling Lévesque, the Liberals managed to turn Hydro-Québec into a symbol of the economic liberation of Quebec from its colonial status, thus co-opting the new nationalism with a vengeance. Liberal expenditures on welfare state reform and public enterprise tripled the provincial budget in the early 1960s, which saw provincial government involvement in almost every economic, industrial, and social activity in Quebec.

The other great symbolic reform of Lesage's Quiet Revolution was the secularization and modernization of Quebec's educational system. Since before Confederation, education had been in the hands of the Catholic Church, which staffed its schools chiefly with priests and nuns teaching a curriculum slow to change from the nineteenth-century classical one. By 1960 the Church itself was in trouble, not just in Quebec but around the world. Criticism of Quebec education was led by a Catholic clergyman, Brother Jean-Paul Desbiens (1927–2006), who published the best-selling *Les Insolences de Frère Untel* (translated in 1962 as *The Impertinences of Brother Anonymous*), based on a series of letters he had written to *Le Devoir* in 1959. The spate of responses to Frère Untel, many of them in the form of letters to editors of newspapers, demonstrated that he had struck a chord in the province. Lesage responded with a provincial commission of inquiry into education, chaired by the vice-rector of Laval University, Monseigneur Alphonse-Marie Parent. The commission's hearings produced a battery of complaints and indictments of the Quebec system, most of which the commission endorsed in its 1963 report. The

Parent Commission called not only for modernization along North American lines but for administration by a unitary secular authority. Armed with this endorsement, in 1964 the Lesage government passed Bill 60, which for the first time placed education in Quebec under provincial administration. Quebec education was thereafter rapidly brought up to national standards.

The Lesage government also sensed the importance of Frère Untel's call for the preservation and extension of French-Canadian culture and the French language. It had already created the Ministry of Cultural Affairs in 1961, which presided happily—with grants and other forms of support—over a veritable explosion of French-Canadian art and writing in the 1960s. The Ministry of Cultural Affairs in many ways typified the Quiet Revolution. The Lesage government was not so much the agent of change in Quebec as its *animateur*. As such it was the beneficiary of years of preparation by others. What the Liberals did was to identify some of the key problems, thus liberating the new-found aspirations of Quebec. Nevertheless, Lesage's government was defeated in 1966 by a rejuvenated Union Nationale under Daniel Johnson (1915–68), chiefly because it had failed to follow to its nationalist conclusion the logic of the revolution over which it had presided. The Union Nationale continued the Lesage program with louder nationalist rhetoric. In 1970 the party in turn was defeated by the

Lesage Endorses Hydro-Québec

In 1962 René Lévesque, as Quebec's Minister of Natural Resources, publicly committed himself to the nationalization of private hydroelectric companies in the province without gaining the support of his Premier and party leader, Jean Lesage. In his *Memoirs*, Lévesque recounted the resolution of the problem.

After having wished me in hell at one time because of my ideas on hydro, Lesage had curiously enough avoided opening the subject again. Since the others were thus prevented from expressing their opinions, I was left free to sell my wares. But certain ministers were growing more and more nervous, and others didn't hesitate to say I was taking up too much room and should be shut up or such talk would eventually put the government in danger. When the fall session came, then, suspense had built up even more. It was becoming urgent to put our cards on the table.

Thus, on September 3, cabinet was summoned to a special meeting in the chalet at Lac-à-l'épaule. Driving up there I reviewed all the elements to the dossier, including some last-minute figures that seemed to me to clinch the feasibility of our plan. But could one ever know? In politics so often there are reasons logic has nothing to do with.

The first night reinforced these doubts. The atmosphere was heavy. Most of my colleagues were in an ugly mood. Some really had it in for me, this nobody, this black sheep who was the cause of all their woes. Discussion seemed to start up, only to fizzle out again in back-room bickering. Some had taken a glass too many, and since Lesage was one of these, it soon became apparent that the evening was a write-off. It was so depressing I wondered if I hadn't better let the whole thing drop. But I had promised the team not to come back without a clear decision one way or another. So I stayed on and passed a very bad night.

Next morning things didn't look much better. Mornings after the nights before are always gloomy. At last, about eleven, Lesage decided to call the meeting to order and, to get the ball rolling, gave me the floor. After distributing copies of our memo, which certain members shoved disdainfully aside, I made a special effort to be as concise as possible, just hitting the highlights.

In rebuttal George Marler did his best to demolish me. . . . An old Liberal leader returning to Montreal

Liberals under the new party leader, Robert Bourassa, partly because it was squeezed between the Liberals and the newly formed Parti Québécois (PQ), partly because too many of its leaders had suffered fatal heart attacks (as had similarly happened to the Union Nationale a decade earlier when first Duplessis and then his successor, Paul Sauvé, died).

Quebec's attitude towards Confederation changed perceptibly during the 1960s. Under Duplessis, Quebec supported provincial rights to prevent Ottawa from taking control of them. Under Lesage and his successors, provincial powers were something to be exercised positively as Quebec built its own welfare state and accompanying bureaucracy. Quebec's newly empowered middle class became increasingly conscious of the powers beyond their reach. A substantial separatist movement developed in the province, its most visible example the FLQ. This organization, founded in March 1963, soon began a terrorist campaign to publicize its views. In November 1967, René Lévesque took a more traditional path towards political change when he resigned from the Quebec Liberal Party and began organizing the Parti Québécois, which was devoted to some form of independence. Along with increased constitutional militancy came increased fears for the future of the French language, with many French Canadians turning a suspicious eye on the immigrant groups in Quebec who were still educating their children in English. By 1970 no

after a tour of duty in Ottawa, he had been named to that little provincial senate called the Legislative Council, and it was from here Lesage had invited him to join the cabinet as his right-hand man in financial matters. He was reputed to have a very tight grasp on the purse strings. . . . That day Marler was not the eminent and phlegmatic notary who never raised his voice. . . . Insisting on the cost of the operation, on the danger of isolation Quebec might be exposed to, and on the opposition that was being manifested, particularly by the Chambers of Commerce, Marler had the bad idea to conclude by suggesting he might possibly resign. Lesage sat bolt upright and indignantly adjourned the meeting for lunch. . . .

Then suddenly everything was back on track again when early in the afternoon Lesage reopened the session and, after briefly summarizing the proposition, turned to Georges-Émile Lapalme, whom we hadn't heard from yet. 'Well, George, haven't you got anything to say? What do you think of this business?'

Lapalme took his time. As usual, behind those heavy glasses with their black frames that made him look like an evil owl, he stared long and without indulgence at the man who had taken his place.

He had been leader of the opposition during the last Duplessis years until he was replaced by Lesage in 1958, just on the eve of that string of events that at long last brought the Liberals back to power. Although he had consented to remain in the government, he was serving under a successor who would always be a usurper for him. This visibly gnawed at his vitals, and even though he adored the Ministry of Cultural Affairs that had been expressly created for him, he was too sensitive and deeply embittered to carry on much longer. In a few months he would be gone. But for the time being he was saving a surprise for us.

'Well, yeah . . .' he said, stretching his pauses, ' . . . is the project a good one? As for me, I'd say yes. . . . Is it feasible? . . . Yes, again. . . . But how should we go about it? That's the question . . .'

'Do you think,' Lesage continued, 'that we could make it an election issue?'

'Well, . . . it's a big deal. . . . Before we get involved in it, it wouldn't be a bad idea to go for a new mandate.'

'Good. Well, let's see now,' said Lesage, leafing through an agenda he had just pulled out of his pocket. 'How does November 14 strike you?'

Source: René Lévesque, *Memoirs*, trans. Philip Stratford (Toronto: McClelland & Stewart, 1986), 174–6.

Quebec politician wanted to be publicly associated with anything less than provincial autonomy. The first round of separatist agitation came to a climax in October 1970 when two cells of the FLQ kidnapped a British diplomat (Trade Commissioner James Cross) and a Quebec cabinet minister (Pierre Laporte), murdering the latter.

The Nation and Quebec

Although John Diefenbaker had come to power with the assistance of Quebec voters, neither 'the Chief' nor his English-Canadian supporters ever really attempted to understand Quebec's aspirations. It was left to the Liberal minority governments of Lester Pearson to respond to what was obviously a feistier Quebec. To some extent, most Canadians were prepared to be sympathetic with Quebec, since few could conceive of a nation without its francophone province. Pearson adopted three strategies. One was co-operative federalism, a concept exemplified in a series of agreements (1963–5) between Ottawa and the provinces, which accepted the need for consultation and flexibility, chiefly by having Ottawa give up many of the constitutional pretensions it had been insisting upon since the 1940s. This strategy ran aground because, as one political scientist put it, 'Quebec's demands for autonomy appeared to be insatiable' (Smiley, 1970: 48–66). Later critics would regard Ottawa's concessions as the beginning of the end for a strong federal state.

A second strategy dealt with the symbols of sovereignty, with the government looking towards reform before 1967 and the Centennial Year of Confederation. A new Canadian flag was adopted by Parliament in 1964 after the Liberals ended the

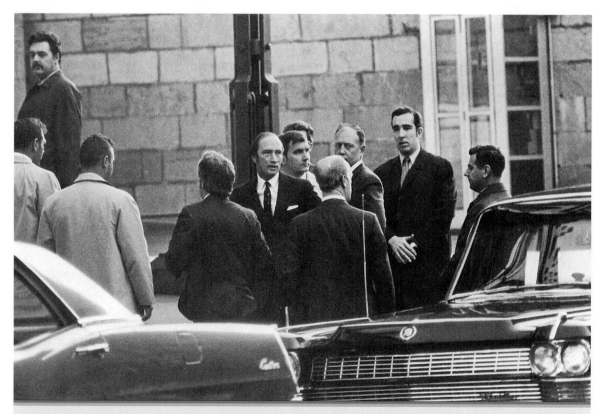

Prime Minister Pierre Trudeau arriving at the Notre-Dame basilica in Montreal for the funeral of Pierre Laporte, 20 October 1970. An FLQ cell had seized Laporte on 10 October, and his body was found a week later in the trunk of a car at the St-Hubert airport. His murder helped to justify the federal government in its imposition of the War Measures Act. LAC, PA-113490.

debate through closure; a new national anthem was approved in 1967. Centennial Year gave everyone a chance to display the new flag and sing the new anthem. Substantial amounts of money were spent on the celebration, with its centrepiece the Canadian Universal and International Exhibition at Montreal, familiarly known as Expo 67. The show was attended by millions of Canadians.

That summer an event occurred that shares an almost equal place in the history of the period. The occasion was the visit of French President Charles de Gaulle. From the outset, Ottawa and Quebec had jostled over protocol for the visit. On 24 July de Gaulle stood on the balcony of a Montreal hotel with open arms, receiving the tumultuous applause of half a million Quebecers. It was an emotional moment. He spoke of cherished memories such as the liberation of France in 1944. Then, before the huge crowd and a television audience of millions, he concluded: 'Vive Montréal! Vive le Québec! Vive le

The Ideology of the FLQ

On 5 October 1970 two armed men kidnapped British Trade Commissioner James Cross from his home in Montreal. A few hours later a communiqué from the abductors, a cell of the Front de liberation du Québec, was received. It was later broadcast as demanded by the abductors. Sandwiched in the middle of the document, between specific demands, the FLQ summarized its ideology.

. . . Through this move, the Front de libération du Québec wants to draw the attention of the world to the fate of French-speaking Québécois, a majority of which is jeered at and crushed on its own territory by a faulty political system (Canadian federalism) and by an economy dominated by the interests of American high finance, the racist and imperialist 'big bosses'. When you examine the origins of Confederation you are in a better position to understand what were the true interests ($$$) which inspired those who were called the Fathers of Confederation. Besides, in 1867, the Quebec people (Lower Canada) were not consulted as to the possibility of creating a Confederation of existing provinces. It was a question of big money and these questions are only sorted out by interested parties, the capitalists, those who possess and amass capital and the means of production and who, according to their sole needs and requirements decide on our whole lives as well as those of a race of people.

Thousand of Québécois have understood, as did our ancestors of 1837–38, that the only way to ensure our national as well as economic survival is total independence.

The Front de libération du Québec supports unconditionally the American blacks and those of Africa, the liberation movements of Latin America, of Palestine, and of Asia, the revolutionary Catholics of Northern Ireland and all those who fight for their freedom, their independence, and their dignity.

The Front de libération du Québec wants to salute the Cuban and Algerian people who are heroically fighting against imperialism and colonialism in all its forms, for a just society where man's exploitation by man is banished. However, we believe that the only true support we can give these people moving towards their liberations is to liberate ourselves first. During and after our struggle we shall offer much more than the usual sympathy of shocked intellectuals confronted with pictures showing aggression in a peaceful and blissful setting. . . .

WE SHALL OVERCOME. . . .

Source: Saywell, J.: 'The Ideology of the FLQ' from *Quebec '70: A Documentary Narrative*, pp 37–38, © University of Toronto Press, 1971.

Québec libre!' Whether de Gaulle had deliberately insulted the Canadian government and people (the official Pearson position) or had merely referred to Quebec's efforts to affirm its identity (the position of Quebec Premier Daniel Johnson) was irrelevant. The exclamation had been vociferously cheered, and the nation had been given yet another reminder of its deep division.

The final policy initiative of the Pearson Liberals was the concept of equal partnership, including the notions of cultural dualism and 'two founding cultures'. The Royal Commission on Bilingualism and Biculturalism was set up in 1963 to implement equal partnership. The Commission discovered, to its surprise, that not all Canadians believed in cultural dualism. It ended up recommending official bilingualism, which was implemented by the Official Languages Act of 1969. By the time bilingualism was formally adopted, Quebec had passed well beyond the stage of accepting its implications. Many political leaders were calling for a policy of unilingualism within the province. After the earlier entrance of Quebec's 'Three Wise Men' (Jean Marchand, Gérard Pelletier, and Pierre Trudeau) into Parliament and the cabinet in 1965, Pearson's resistance to Quebec had stiffened, however.

Quebec was not the home of all French Canadians, for there were hundreds of thousands of francophones living outside that province. The need to provide continuing protection for this outlying

The Canadian pavilion at Expo 67, dominated by a huge inverted pyramid. The dome beside it was clad with enlarged photos of Canadian scenes.

population was a principal argument of the federalists within Quebec. Francophones outside Quebec were understandably ardent federalists, and they were the chief beneficiaries of bilingualism and biculturalism. Only in New Brunswick were the francophones (the Acadians) sufficiently concentrated geographically and sufficiently numerous to regard themselves as a distinct people. The 1960s saw a renaissance of Acadian culture and a new political awareness that Acadian interests had to be served. Thus both major New Brunswick parties supported bilingualism, French-language education (including a university at Moncton), and the entrenchment of Acadian culture in the province. Bilingualism and biculturalism helped rejuvenate francophones elsewhere in Canada, most of whom were fluently bilingual. Not only did they gain advantages in obtaining federal employment in their regions, but their educational and cultural facilities received a good deal of financial assistance from the federal government as well, as did numerous other organized ethnic groups once multiculturalism became official policy.

'Non-charter' ethnic groups had vociferously informed the Royal Commission on Bilingualism and Biculturalism of their unhappiness with the concept of two languages and two cultures, insisting that such a policy offended those not part of the 'charter' community. The Commission had devoted a separate book of its final report to the 'other ethnic groups', and seemed to be suggesting that there was more to Canada than simply two cultures. Indeed, in 1971, as we have seen, more than one in every four Canadians was not a member of the charter communities. On 8 October 1971, Prime Minister Pierre Trudeau declared in the House of Commons a federal government policy of 'multiculturalism within a bilingual framework'. The policy would involve, he said, assistance to all Canadian cultural groups to continue to grow, to 'overcome cultural barriers to full participation in Canadian society', to interact with other cultural groups, and to become conversant in one of Canada's two official languages (quoted in Hansard, *Debates in the House of Commons*, 8 Oct. 1971). The reaction from Quebec was immediate and negative. French Canadians, probably quite accurately, saw the emphasis on multiculturalism as a way to deflect

the aspirations of Quebec by demonstrating that its linguistic and cultural aspirations were not unique and could not be considered apart from the needs of other communities in Canada. René Lévesque described multiculturalism as a 'red herring' designed 'to give the impression that we are all ethnics and do not have to worry about special status for Quebec.' Many French Canadians were incensed that Trudeau had chosen to link multiculturalism with language as well as culture. According to more than one commentator in Quebec, multiculturalism had reduced the Quebec fact to an ethnic phenomenon.

The government embodied multiculturalism in a Canadian Consultative Council on Multiculturalism, created in 1973, and in a separate section of the Department of the Secretary of State (the Multiculturalism Directorate), which was given funds to support multicultural activities of various sorts. Much of the funding was devoted to the support of ethnic research and scholarship, contributing to an explosion of ethnic studies, although money was also made available to ethnic organizations for various purposes and was subject to considerable criticism. The ethnic community was not united in its response to the funding for multiculturalism. Some members of the ethnic community itself complained that the funds were 'minuscule', while others pointed to the waste of money on meaningless projects. In the wake of the federal policy, various provincial governments also proclaimed policies of multiculturalism and began funding ethnic organizations and ethnic studies. The concept of multiculturalism was introduced into most provincial educational curricula to socialize schoolchildren to the new complexities of Canadian society, although not much was done about providing education in ethnic languages.

While multiculturalism was introduced as a highly politicized policy by a Prime Minister who did not really take minority ethnic causes very seriously, it struck a responsive chord with many Canadians. For Pierre Trudeau, multiculturalism was probably mainly part of a Quebec strategy that also may have been important as part of a conscious elimination of ethnic and racial discrimination. For many Canadians, however, it would become part of a new definition of national identity, a statement of the Canadian 'mosaic' in contradistinction to the American 'melting pot'. The mythology of the mosaic would become even more powerful after the introduction of the Canadian Charter of Rights (again by Trudeau) in 1982. Before long, many Canadians had quite forgotten the Prime Minister's contextualization of multiculturalism as being 'within a bilingual framework'. It would eventually become such a potent metaphor that many Canadians felt that their behaviour had to live up to its ideal.

Canadian Culture

In some senses, Canadian culture—quite apart from its multicultural aspects—came of age in the 1960s. Years of development of cultural infrastructure within the private sector, combined with a new government recognition of the need for conscious cultural policy and an enormous expansion of the Canadian university system, brought at least elite culture to a flowering. A national cultural policy, first articulated by the Massey Commission, was actually implemented under Diefenbaker and Pearson. Intended to foster a distinctive Canadian identity in the face of the ubiquitous Americans, it employed all possible cultural strategies, ranging from subsidies (the Canada Council) to protectionism (policy regarding Canadian magazines and Canadian content regulations for television introduced in 1961) to regulated competition (the Board of Broadcast Governors, established in 1958, licensed new television stations, which came together as a new television network in 1961 called CTV). Within the realm of 'serious' culture, Canadian governments at all levels were prepared to spend large amounts of money to produce works that would meet international standards. To considerable extent they succeeded. Whether the culture that resulted was Canadian Culture was, of course, another matter entirely.

Perhaps the greatest success story was in Canadian literature. Before the 1960s the market for, and interest in, works of literature by Canadian writers was not strong. There was no tradition of indigenous literary criticism, only a handful of literary periodicals, and almost no sense of a literary community anywhere outside Quebec. In 1976 critic Northrop Frye

noted 'the colossal verbal explosion that has taken place in Canada since 1960' (Frye, 1976: 849). That explosion saw a number of Canadian writers achieve international critical recognition. *The Apprenticeship of Duddy Kravitz* by Mordecai Richler (1931–2001), published in 1959, met with great popular success and established Richler as a major writer. Duddy Kravitz entered Canadian popular culture as an ethnic wheeler-dealer desperate for the security of land. Richler was not the first novelist to mine the rich vein of ethnicity in Canada, but he was the first to mythologize the urban ghetto, its inhabitants, and way of life. In 1966 he confessed: 'No matter how long I continue to live abroad, I do feel forever rooted in Montreal's St Urbain Street. This was my time, my place, and I have elected to get it exactly right' (quoted in Woodcock, 1979: 27).

Margaret Laurence (1926–89) was another Canadian novelist who created a mythologized Canadian space. Having lived with her husband in Somalia and Ghana from 1950 to 1957, she was residing in Jordan when her African novel *This Side of Jordan* (1960) appeared. Soon afterwards, she completed the first of her four 'Manawaka' novels, which brought her international acclaim. *The Stone Angel* (1961), *A Jest of God* (1966), *The Fire-Dwellers* (1969), and *The Diviners* (1974) could be read on many levels and were easily the most richly textured fiction ever produced by a Canadian writer. Laurence's setting may have been as far removed from urban Montreal as it was possible to get, but like Richler, she created a place out of what she knew. The mythical town of Manawaka, set somewhere on the Canadian prairies, was a strongly conceived and living entity, linking some powerful female protagonists struggling against hypocritical Scots-Canadian constrictions and their own pasts. Noting that she was not much aware that her 'so-called Canadian writing' was Canadian, Laurence once commented that 'this seems a good thing to me, for it suggests that one has been writing out of a background so closely known that no explanatory tags are necessary' (quoted in Woodcock, 1969: 9).

With a smaller readership than fiction commanded, poetry not only held its own but acquired a substantial audience. Irving Layton (1912–2006), Earle Birney (1904–95), and Al Purdy (1918–2001) were sent on reading tours by their publisher and became almost as adept in performance as in writing. Performance of a different kind marked the career of Leonard Cohen (b. 1934), who straddled the worlds of high and popular culture when he set some of his poems to music, wrote new songs, and sang them to his own guitar accompaniment. Cohen had played in a band in his teens and published his first book of poetry, *Let Us Compare Mythologies*, in 1956 at the age of 22. It was followed in the sixties by two novels, including his haunting classic *Beautiful Losers* (1966), and by several poetry collections that were exceptionally appealing to the younger generation in their imagery and themes. In 1968, he refused a Governor General's Award for his *Selected Poems*. In the same year his first record album, *Songs of Leonard Cohen*, appeared, soon to be followed by *Songs from a Room* (1969). A few of his songs had already been performed by Joan Baez and Judy Collins, but Cohen's own liturgical baritone was the perfect vehicle for popularizing them. By 1970 he was widely recognized as part of the pantheon of poet-singers that included Bob Dylan, Donovan Leitch, and Paul McCartney. Such songs as 'Suzanne', 'Bird on a Wire', 'It Seems so Long Ago, Nancy', and 'The Story of Isaac'—with its repeated image of an eagle becoming a vulture—entered the consciousness of the counter-culture. Cohen captured perfectly youth's scorn for hypocrisy. His songs counselled survival by withdrawal from the contests of life into a private world of the spirit, not in triumph or failure but in endurance through ceremony and self-understanding. These were powerful messages for the Woodstock generation. Ironically, while Cohen's songs contained almost no specific Canadian references, his sense of self-deprecation and self-abnegation was generally accepted as quintessentially Canadian.

The sixties also saw the creation of a number of small presses across the nation and the emergence of 'Can Lit' as an acceptable field of study. By 1970 virtually every Canadian university offered an undergraduate course in Canadian literature, and a critical canon had more or less been established, which naturally emphasized the distinctly Canadian qualities of Canadian writing. Without a new breed of scholarly critics who were prepared to take Canadian writing seriously—and without the subsidies that

Margaret Laurence, *c.* 1960. Dave Buchan/Vancouver Sun.

helped sustain author, critic, teacher, and journals—that writing would have developed more slowly. McClelland and Stewart's enduring New Canadian Library series began in 1958, offering during the sixties mainly reprints of classic and long out-of-print novels. *Canadian Literature*, 'the first review devoted only to the study of Canadian writers and writing', was founded in 1959 by George Woodcock (1912–95). The collectively written *Literary History of Canada* was published by the University of Toronto Press in 1965. At the beginning of his 'Conclusion' to the first edition of this work, Northrop Frye (1912–91) wrote:

This book is a tribute to the maturity of Canadian literary scholarship and criticism, whatever one thinks of the literature. Its authors have completely outgrown the view that evaluation is the end of criticism, instead of its incidental by-product. Had evaluation been their guiding principle, this book would, if written at all, have been only a huge debunking project, leaving Canadian literature a poor naked *alouette* plucked of every feather of decency and dignity. True, the book gives evidence on practically every one of its eight hundred odd pages, that what is really remarkable is not how little but how much good writing has been produced in Canada. (Klinck, 1965: 821)

For many critics, the challenge was to reveal quintessential Canadian qualities in the imaginative elements of the literature. Québécois fiction shared in the cultural flowering, with the anger and violence of language and subject matter, and with radical changes in syntax and formal structure, not only mirroring but fostering the spirit of liberation and the new goals of Quebec society.

The coming of age of Canadian writing was not matched by a similar maturation in Canadian book publishing, which found itself subject to several disturbing market trends, most notably an inability to make money in a retail climate dominated by foreign publishers. Ryerson Press, the oldest major publisher in Canada and supported by the United Church of Canada, was so much in debt that it was sold in 1970 to the American firm McGraw-Hill. In the same year, the Ontario government appointed a Royal Commission on Book Publishing (1970) and had to rescue McClelland and Stewart from an American takeover. Even though the federal government

Poems by Margaret Atwood

In 1971 Margaret Atwood published a small book of poems entitled *Power Politics*. The first selection below appeared on the opening page, as an epigraph.

you fit into me
like a hook into an eye

a fish hook
an open eye

* * * * *

After the agony in the guest
   bedroom, you lying by the
   overturned bed
   your face uplifted, neck propped
   against the windowsill, my arm
   under you, cool moon
   shining down through the window

wine mist rising
   around you, an almost-invisible halo

You say, Do you
   love me, do you love me

I answer you:
   I stretch your arms out
   one to either side
   your head slumps forward.

Later I take you home
   in a taxi, and you
   are sick in the bathtub.

Source: 'you fit into me' from *Power Politics* copyright © 1971, 1996 by Margaret Atwood. Reprinted by permission of House of Anansi Press. <www.anansi.ca>.

established a policy of giving support to Canadian-controlled publishing firms through such agencies as the Canadian Book Publishing Development Program and the Canada Council—as did provincial governments in various ways, including through the Ontario Arts Council—Canadian publishing had entered an era of chronic precariousness that the quality of the writing available to be published only served to emphasize. The relatively small market for English-language books in Canada, the enormous volume of foreign books available, the dominance of foreign-owned publishers, and the self-defeating policy of allowing full return of unsold books—all of these factors put Canadian-owned publishers at a competitive disadvantage. For authors even to be successfully published in the United States had its disadvantages, since the American publishers would sell their leftover books (known as 'remainders') in Canada at a fraction of the price the Canadian publisher was still asking for the same book. Publishers in Quebec experienced less difficulty than those in the rest of Canada, despite the small market. Apparently the people of Quebec were more willing to buy books about themselves and their culture from local publishers, and there was less American competition.

The effect of the socio-economic changes in Quebec on writing in that province was considerable. The influence was reciprocal: one fuelled the other. The literary transformation began in the late 1950s with *La Belle Bête* (1959) by the 20-year-old Marie-Claire Blais (b. 1939). This novel astonished the reading public (no less in its English translation, *Mad Shadows*) and scandalized the clergy with its portrayal of characters representing various kinds of moral and physical ugliness, and for its powerful impressionistic scenes of betrayal, disfigurement, pyromania, murder, and suicide. Blais was discovered outside Quebec by the American critic Edmund Wilson, who observed that she showed herself 'incapable of allowing life in French Canada to appear in a genial light or to seem to embody any sort of ideal' (Wilson, 1964: 147). The literary transformation that began in the late 1950s continued throughout the next decades. The anger and violence of language and subject matter, radical changes in syntax and formal structure, the freeing of style and content from the constraints

of tradition, not only mirrored but fostered the spirit of liberation and the new goals of Quebec society. This work was no longer called French-Canadian but 'Québécois' fiction. The journal *Parti pris* (1963–8), founded just after the first wave of FLQ bombings with an *indépendantiste* and Marxist perspective, published in January 1965 a special issue entitled *Pour une littérature québécoise*—giving a name, quickly adopted, to the current and future works of francophone writers in Quebec. That issue also promoted the use of joual in creative writing. The poet Paul Chamberland (b. 1939), one of the founding editors, wrote, '. . . any language must be shaken to its very foundations through the disfiguration inherent in our common speech, and in the lives of all of us.' Most of this literary explosion went unheeded in English-speaking Canada, partly because of the scarcity (and difficulty) of translations, but also, one suspects, because of the uncongenial spirit behind it.

Canadian scholarship, like other areas of elite culture, expanded and was strengthened in the 1960s. A

Northrop Frye, *c.* 1967. Brigdens Limited.

combination of grants from the Canada Council, the Social Sciences and Humanities Research Council of Canada (SSHRC), and the National Research Council, together with an increase in the number of Canadian universities, vastly added to the numbers of academics and research students. Canadian scholarship grew not only in volume but in reputation, achieving international recognition in many disciplines.

One field that had great difficulty coming to terms with the rapidly changing world of scholarship was Canadian history. Canadian historians almost by definition could not aspire to international repute, since in the broader scheme of things the history of Canada was of little interest to anyone outside the country. For most historians of Canada working within the English-speaking tradition, Canadian history was National History. The focus was unremittingly progressive. The country was settled, adopted representative government, turned responsible government into the union of the provinces, and with union moved gradually but inexorably towards full nationhood. Quebec, of course, had its own paradigm, equally nationalistic and political in nature. This comfortable mindset was overturned when younger historians began asking new questions about race, class, ethnicity, and gender that emerged out of the political turmoil of the late 1960s. These younger scholars also questioned the glaring neglect in the traditional approach towards Aboriginals, women, the working classes, and racial minorities. To these changes, Quebec historians added their own, often influenced by new European schools of analysis. Research and writing in Canadian economic and social history began to ask implicitly whether the old paradigm of nation-building was flexible and capacious enough to integrate the new methodologies and theories. By 1970 it was increasingly clear that the old fabric would not hold, although neither mainstream Canadian historians nor the revisionists had any idea of how to reweave it. Although the traditional synthesis had broken down, a new history had not yet appeared.

A new maturity and international acceptance of culture produced in Canada was to be found everywhere. We can see one major shift in the performing arts, where an amateur tradition of the 1950s was transformed quite swiftly into a full-fledged professional system operating from coast to coast. For example, Winnipeg—a middle-sized, geographically isolated urban centre with no particular tradition of cultural patronage—by 1970 was supporting a fully professional symphony orchestra; the Royal Winnipeg Ballet and other dance companies; an opera association mounting several works each year; the Manitoba Theatre Centre, an acclaimed model for regional theatre, whose impressive mainstage opened in 1970; an active art gallery; and a major concert hall. Thanks to various centennials, similar facilities and institutions soon existed in every major urban centre across Canada. By 1970 no important Canadian city or region was without its own professional theatre company, art gallery, and symphony orchestra.

Created with substantial public monies in the form of block grants from all levels of government, new arts institutions initially relied heavily on recent immigrants to Canada for professional expertise. Many of these professionals became teachers and sponsors of spinoff activities. It was not long before highly qualified younger Canadians were ready to step into these companies and organizations, and a substantial local audience had been developed. One of the secrets of public success in music and theatre was the introduction of annual subscription campaigns. Unlike audiences in New York, London, Paris, or Berlin, where tickets were sold for individual events, patrons of Canada's performing arts were asked to buy blocks of tickets in advance to guarantee an audience. If by 1970 the personnel in the performing and exhibitory arts were mainly Canadian, the repertoire on display tended to be largely an international one, both in origin and in style. Canadian artists, playwrights, composers, and choreographers still had trouble finding their own place and audience within the standard repertoire regardless of their style. How their art could be distinctly Canadian was an open question that ate away at the hearts of many Canadian creative people throughout the period.

The 1960s were also a critical decade for popular culture, particularly that valiant effort to keep the Canadian identity from being totally submerged by American influences. The record was mixed, as developments in Canadian sports well demonstrate. Nothing could be more quintessentially Canadian,

Marie-Claire Blais

Marie-Claire Blais.

M arie-Claire Blais was born in Quebec City in 1939. She received her early education from Catholic nuns, but soon became disillusioned with academic subjects, leaving school at age 15 to work in a factory. She subsequently attended Laval University and began writing. Her earliest novels, *La Belle Bête* and *Tête Blanche*, brought her to the attention of the distinguished literary critic Edmund Wilson, who described her in a *New Yorker* article on Canadian literature as the most promising young author in the country. As a result, she was able to study in Paris on a Guggenheim Fellowship. From the beginning, Blais's fiction had been experimental in language, form, and thematic content. She was one of the first Quebec novelists to break with realism, in favour of a surreal world of street dialogue and menacing sexuality.

In her work, Blais reflected major tensions in Quebec society. She was extremely conscious of the ways in which Quebec had oppressed its women. *Une saison dans la vie d'Emmanuel*, published in 1965, explores the life of a farm family during the months following the birth of the sixteenth child, Emmanuel, and emphasizes the brutality with which society responded to the older children's yearnings for something better. It won the Prix France-Canada and the Prix Médicis, and became a favourite topic for literary critics. Three semi-autobiographical novels with Pauline Archange as the central character, published between 1968 and 1970, echoed the critique of their parents by the younger generation in the 1960s.

In the 1970s Blais wrote about homosexuality. *Les nuits d'underground* (1978) was an evocative study of the everyday life of a lesbian frequenter of gay bars in Montreal. The later novels became increasingly characterized by stream-of-consciousness third-person narrative. Blais also published poetry and drama. For many readers, Blais became the epitome of the alienated artist and intellectual in modern Quebec society. Like the books of Gabrielle Roy, Blais's novels have all been translated into English, and she is one of a handful of Quebec novelists fully accessible to anglophones in Canada and beyond.

for example, than hockey. But that sport entered the post-war period in the hands of the American entertainment industry, and the situation never really altered. By the 1960s only at the NHL level did Canadian teams have any real representation (two of six teams, in Toronto and Montreal). At the minor-league level only Vancouver had a professional team. The NHL finally expanded in 1967, adding six new American franchises in what was hoped were hockey hotbeds like St Louis and Philadelphia. Not even

Vancouver, to its chagrin, could get a look-in. The chief argument against new Canadian teams was related to television. American TV viewers would not watch professional sports played by 'foreign' teams, said the experts, and the secret of expansion's success was a US national television contract. In 1969, on the other hand, the National Baseball League granted a franchise to a Montreal team to be called the Expos, demonstrating that if the local markets were big enough, the moguls could be won over, at least temporarily. As for the Canadian Football League, it entered its most successful decade to date. Teams became totally professional and drew considerable crowds. The fans appeared quite satisfied with the Canadian game and its differences from the American one—the size of the field, the number of downs, the 'rouge'—and with the large number of Canadians who, thanks to a quota system on imports, played it.

In September 1961 the federal government finally took some initiative on the problem of sports in Canada. Bill C-131, intended to 'encourage, promote

Bobby Hull

Bobby Hull, commissioner of the reincarnated World Hockey Association, displays the new team logo for the Halifax Icebreakers at a news conference in Halifax on 8 July 2004. The proposed new WHA never materialized. CP Photo/Andrew Vaughan).

Robert Marvin Hull Jr (a.k.a. 'the Golden Jet') was born in 1939 in Pointe Anne, Ontario. He began playing hockey at an early age and joined the Chicago Black Hawks of the National Hockey League in 1957. A left-winger, he was an intimidating presence on the ice, noted for his development of the 'slapshot', a technique for shooting the puck at the goalie at much increased speeds. He scored 50 or more goals five times, and led the Black Hawks to the Stanley Cup in 1961. He was first in the NHL in goals scored seven times and in total points scored three times.

In 1972 Hull signed a lucrative contract with the Winnipeg Jets of the upstart World Hockey Association, a league formed largely of Canadian teams that were unable to get NHL franchises. The NHL responded to this action by refusing to allow Hull to play for its team in the Canada–Russia hockey series of 1972. But Hull's signing gave the WHA considerable credibility. He won the WHA's most valuable player award in 1972–3 and led his team to several post-season championships in the 1970s. In 1980 he signed with the Hartford Whalers of the NHL and finished his career there. By his retirement, Hull had amassed in the NHL a total of 609 goals, 555 assists, and 1,164 points, and in the WHA 303 goals, 335 assists, and 639 total points. Whether those totals should be added together is the subject of continued controversy among hockey historians. After his retirement he maintained his public persona as television spokesman for several commercial products. He was elected to the Hockey Hall of Fame in 1983.

and develop fitness and amateur sport in Canada', passed both Houses of Parliament unanimously. Much of the bill's bipartisan political support was a result of public outcry over Canada's poor performance in international competitions, including hockey, and was part of the country's Cold War posturing. Speaking about amateur sports at that time, Opposition leader Lester Pearson (who had played lacrosse and hockey while at Oxford) said: 'all the publicity attached to international sport and the fact that certain societies use international sport, as they use everything else, for the advancement of prestige and political purposes, it is a matter of some consequence that we in Canada should do what we can to develop and regain the prestige we once had, to a greater extent than we now have in international competition' (quoted in Morrow, 1989: 328). Although the legislation was deliberately vague, it allowed the government to subsidize amateur coaches and teams, particularly in national and international competitions. In 1968 the National Advisory Council, set up under the Act to recommend policy and oversee its implementation, was shunted to one side in favour of professional bureaucrats within the Ministry of National Health and Welfare. Amateur sports in Canada had been taken under the wing of the welfare state. In that same year Pierre Trudeau promised in the election campaign a new study of sports in Canada. The 'Report of the Task Force on Sports for Canadians' was published in 1969. Despite the increased government involvement in and subsidization of amateur sports, in 1976 Canada acquired the dubious distinction of becoming the first (and so far only) nation to host the Olympic Games without winning a gold medal.

Conclusion

On the whole, the developments in sports were remarkably similar to those in other cultural sectors, and indeed the nation in general. By the early 1970s sport had been thoroughly drawn into the net of federal and provincial government policy, turned over to the bureaucrats and bean-counters. It had not yet answered the question of whether excellence and Canadian-ness were truly compatible, although the sense was that a sufficient expenditure of money would in the end resolve all problems. Unbeknownst to its participants, however, sport in Canada was about to share with other aspects of the Canadian experience a new sense of existing on the edge of some kind of precipice, about to free-fall into new and unknown territory. What consequences the fall would have were anybody's guess, although there were increasingly loud mutterings about the limits of growth. After 1972 Canadians would have to explore together the implications of a world in which not all things were possible. They would discover, as money and resources became more limited, that the infighting could be extremely fierce.

How History Has Changed

Perspectives on Sex

Like everything else in Canadian society and culture, historical writing has been subject to censorship and taboos, often self-imposed. The student will still look in vain in any textbook on Canadian history for any detailed examination of sexual activity or the excretory functions. It was acceptable to mention bathrooms, toilets, outhouses, and toilet paper (including the use of newspapers and department store catalogues in earlier eras), so long as there was no detailed discussion of what Canadians did in them or with them. Toilet behaviour is universal enough to be describable, but its very universality means that there is probably no need for explicitness; we can take such things pretty much for granted. As historians we could describe a sexual act only if one of our historical characters provided us with a documentable account of it, and most such personalities were amazingly reticent, even in their most revealing memoirs, about the existence of relationships, much less behaviour. Canadians were as astounded as Americans in the 1940s by the revelations of Dr Alfred Kinsey regarding sexuality in America. But even aside from explicit description of particular acts, the larger issues of sexuality have only very gradually become available as topics for public scrutiny. Modern historians have not themselves taken the lead in discussing sexuality, but have only responded to distinct shifts in public perceptions.

Although 'unnatural' sexual acts had been taboo in society for centuries and could be severely punished by the authorities when they were found, sexual deviancy emerged as an important social matter only in the later nineteenth century. In many cases, same-sex sexual activity was overlooked or regarded as tolerable in places where females were in short supply. Those concerned with social purity and 'race suicide' eventually attempted to preserve procreation from the evils of masturbation and other forms of 'perversion'. The newly emerging social sciences began to study deviancy, and various specific meanings of it became enshrined in the Canadian Criminal Code. A homosexual 'type' gradually began to emerge, and 'gross indecency' was first introduced to the Criminal Code in 1890. In general, Canada followed the United States and Great Britain in their understandings of what was permissible sexual practice. By the end of the 1890s, the concern of Canadians was with the immorality and degeneracy of what they regarded as deviant sexual activities. At the same time, the increasing social sophistication of Canadian society apparently led to an increase in organized underground behaviour of a deviant sort.

Unlike Britain and the United States, where historians began to study and write openly about both sexual activity and sexual deviancy by the 1950s, Canada had to wait until the 1980s for similar work to appear. Elsa Gidrow's autobiographical account of her lesbian experiences in Montreal during World War I appeared in print in 1986 (published in the United States), and Gary Kinsman's *The Regulation of Desire: Sexuality in Canada*—a thorough historical examination of the question—was first published only in 1987. Two factors led to a new openness of discussion. One was pressure from the gay community for a new Canadian attitude towards sexuality, including what Kinsman calls 'a more historically grounded perspective on gay and lesbian liberation: a view which understands the social forces that have both organized our oppression and made it possible for us to resist' (Kinsman, 1987: 15). Political pressure was evident in open protests by thousands of gays on the streets of Toronto in 1981 in response to police raids on bathhouses. The second factor was probably the emergence of AIDS, a disease that was from the outset associated with the homosexual community and that could not be discussed and analyzed apart from that community. In recent years 'Queer Studies' have become an acceptable approach for postmodern discourse. This is not surprising, since one major point of revisionist history depends on the postmodern insistence on the social construction of everything, including 'deviancy'.

Short Bibliography

Axelrod, Paul. *Scholars and Dollars: Politics, Economics and the Universities of Ontario 1945–80*. Toronto, 1982. An excellent study of the post-war universities in Ontario, emphasizing the expansion of existing universities and the creation of new ones, as well as distinct shifts in the justifications for higher education.

Behiels, Michael, ed. *Quebec since 1945*. Toronto, 1987. An admirable and comprehensive collection of articles on post-war Quebec.

Bergeron, Léandre. *The History of Quebec: A Patriote's Handbook*. Toronto, 1971. A translation of a radical 'people's' history of Quebec, strongly separatist in tone.

Cardinal, Harold. *The Unjust Society: The Tragedy of Canada's Indians*. Edmonton, 1969. The first attempt to tell the First Nations' story from the Native standpoint.

Clairmont, Donald, and Dennis Magill. *Africville: The Life and Death of a Canadian Black Community*, rev. edn. Toronto, 1987. A work that documents the destruction of Africville, a black community on the outskirts of Halifax, and insists it was improper and unnecessary.

Desbiens, Jean-Paul. *The Impertinences of Brother Anonymous*. Toronto, 1962. The famous critique of Quebec politics and culture that caused a furor when first published.

Forsyth, Dennis, ed. *Let the Niggers Burn: The Sir George Williams University Affair and Its Caribbean Aftermath*. Montreal, 1971. An account of the most famous Canadian incident of student protest.

Handler, Richard. *Nationalism and the Politics of Culture in Quebec*. Madison, Wis., 1981. A detailed analysis of the manifold ways in which Quebec nationalism has influenced Quebec culture and cultural policy.

Kinsman, Gary. *The Regulation of Desire: Sexuality in Canada*. Montreal, 1987. A pioneering study of sexuality and its treatment by the state.

Levitt, Kari. *Silent Surrender: The Multinational Corporation in Canada*. Toronto, 1970. The most notorious statement of the nationalist critique of foreign investment and the multicultural corporation in Canada.

Morton, W.L. *The Canadian Identity*. Toronto, 1961. An effort to discover the essence of Canada by one of its leading historians.

Royal Commission on Bilingualism and Biculturalism. 1969. *Report*, 6 vols. Ottawa: Queen's Printer. The key document in the struggle for bilingualism and biculturalism.

Saywell, John. *Quebec 70: A Documentary Narrative*. Toronto, 1971. A useful account of the FLQ crisis of 1970.

Simeon, Richard. *Federal–Provincial Diplomacy: The Making of Recent Policy in Canada*. Toronto, 1972. A fascinating study of the international implications of Canadian federalism.

Vallières, Pierre. *White Niggers of America*. Toronto, 1971. A brilliant polemical memoir about living as a French Canadian.

Weaver, Sally M. *Making Canada's Indian Policy: The Hidden Agenda 1968–1970*. Toronto, 1981. A sober account of Canadian Aboriginal policy in a crucial period of re-evaluation.

Study Questions

1. Identify at least one way in which Canadian manners were emancipated during the 1960s in each of the following areas: religion, the media, literature, sexuality, and the law.
2. Explain why the 'counterculture' was mainly a youthful phenomenon.
3. Canada was never directly involved in the Vietnam War. Why did this war have such a strong impact on Canadian society?
4. Identify four militant collectivities that arose in the 1960s. For each, summarize briefly their goals.
5. What do Tables 10.1 and 10.2 tell us about unemployment in the 1960s?
6. In what ways did the 'Quiet Revolution' change Quebec society?
7. Of the factors listed in the text as changing Canada's immigration policy, which in your view was most important?
9. What three policies did the Pearson government develop to deal with Quebec's aspirations? Comment on the effectiveness of these policies.

 www.oupcanada.com/Bumsted4e

Visit the companion website for *A History of the Canadian Peoples*, fourth edition for further resources.

11 Coming Apart, 1972–1992

Timeline

1972   Canada–Russia hockey series. Trudeau Liberals win in close election. NDP defeats W.A.C. Bennett in British Columbia.

1973   OPEC raises price of oil. Robert Bourassa's Liberals are elected in Quebec, but the Parti Québécois finishes strong.

1974   Trudeau Liberals win another close election. Trudeau imposes wage and price controls.

1976   Canadian Airline Pilots Association strikes. Montreal Olympics are held. Parti Québécois wins power in Quebec. Joe Clark is chosen leader of the Tories.

1977   Quebec government passes Bill 101.

1978   Task Force on National Unity tours Canada.

1979   Antonine Maillet publishes *Pélagie-la-Charette*. Joe Clark's Tories win minority government but the government falls in December.

1980   Trudeau's Liberals are swept back to power. Quebec referendum results in 60 per cent 'Non' and 40 per cent 'Oui' on question of sovereignty-association. Trudeau proposes constitutional reform.

1981   Supreme Court rules on federal constitutional initiative. The PQ is re-elected in Quebec. The 'Gang of Nine' cuts a deal on the Constitution. Revised constitutional package passes Parliament.

1982   A revised Constitution is approved by the British Parliament.

1983   Brian Mulroney replaces Joe Clark as Tory leader.

1984   Trudeau retires and is succeeded by John Turner. Brian Mulroney leads Progressive Conservatives to a federal sweep. The Cirque du Soleil is formed.

1985   PQ defeated by Robert Bourassa's Liberals. 22 June 1985: Air India bombing disaster.

1986   Mulroney government negotiates Free Trade Agreement with the US.

1987   Meech Lake agreement is reached between the federal and provincial governments.

1988   Mulroney's Tories win again. Mulroney signs redress agreement with National Association of Japanese Canadians. Ben Johnson wins a gold medal at Seoul Olympics, which is later revoked because of a positive steroid test.

1989   Fourteen female engineering students are gunned down in Montreal.

1990   Meech Lake Accord fails to be ratified by all provinces within required three years. Lucien Bouchard forms the Bloc Québécois. Mohawks confront Quebec government at Oka. Audrey McLaughlin is chosen as first female party leader in Canada. Jean Chrétien becomes Liberal leader.

1991   Goods and services tax officially introduced.

1992   Charlottetown Accord is reached. Toronto Blue Jays win World Series. National referendum rejects the Charlottetown Accord.

On 22 September 1988, Prime Minister Brian Mulroney and Art Miki, president of the Japanese-Canadian Association, signed a Redress Agreement, formally apologizing to the Japanese-Canadian community for their placement in internment camps and the confiscation of property during World War II. The Prime Minister acknowledged that this 'was unjust and violated principles of human rights as they are understood today.' The Canadian Press/Ron Poling.

After a quarter-century of optimism, the years after 1972 presented Canadians with a different picture. Everything, from the economy to the very nation itself, suddenly seemed to be in a state of confusion bordering on disintegration.

The Problems of Liberal Federalist Nationalism

Until the early 1970s the post-war era, for most Canadians, had been a time of affluence and optimism. It was characterized by a nationalism anchored by strong central federal government. This relatively positive climate had been achieved by policies dominated by twentieth-century small-l 'liberalism', a delicate balancing act that accepted an economic system based on private enterprise and corporate capitalism while also attempting to provide a social welfare safety net for the nation's citizens. Not all the resulting policies were influenced by Keynesian economics, but many of them were. Such policies were the operative ones for governments throughout the Western industrialized world. They were non-partisan. All major Canadian political parties, for example, at all levels of government—ranging provincially from the Socreds of the West to the separatists of Quebec—were essentially exponents of variants of liberalism with a small 'l'.

If the political consensus sought by all democratic governments in this period was formally dominated by liberal economics, the constitutional framework in which the liberalism was to operate increasingly produced conflict. For much of the period before 1970, the Liberal Party had combined liberal economics with a constitutionally centralized federalism. Although the Progressive Conservatives, in their six years of power between 1957 and 1963, had demonstrated different emphases, even they had not seriously contemplated overturning the broad framework. As we have seen, the Liberal consensus had come under attack in the 1960s, mainly from the left. It began seriously unravelling in the 1970s, and was in tatters by the beginning of the 1990s.

The Canadian political arena seemed incapable of dealing with both economic problems and constitutional problems simultaneously, at least at the same level of intensity. The period after 1972 saw an alternation of focus between the Constitution and the economy. The two questions were not entirely divorced, of course. One of the major arguments of the federalists was that only strong national policies could deal with the problems of the economy and with the demands of minorities not geographically embodied into provinces and regions. Moreover, while constitutional matters were largely under the control of Canadians, economic ones were chiefly international. After the election of a Tory government under Brian Mulroney in 1984, both nationalism and federalism were jettisoned for free trade and Meech Lake, while the principles of liberal economics were replaced by privatization, clawbacks, and deregulation.

No single factor or event can possibly be isolated as responsible for the collapse of the liberal federalist-nationalist consensus in Canada. Instead, a cumulation of what Marxist analysts would call 'contradictions'—matters that simply could not be resolved within the consensus—would eventually defy attempts at management, compromise, or hopeful neglect. The contradictions would come together at centre stage to produce a series of what the media liked to label 'crises'. Many of the pressures were not really of Canada's own making but were part of international trends over which no Canadian government had very much control. Increasingly both politicians and the public came to feel that all political responses were defensive reactions to unmanageable situations, and that all policies were merely band-aids placed over festering wounds. Public trust in the nation's political leaders declined as the consensus disintegrated and was not replaced by a new paradigm. Cynicism became entrenched at the core of the Canadian national psyche. To some imponderable extent, the increase in cynicism and the gradual emergence of ever more unalloyed self-interest as the mainspring of human action contributed to the further deterioration of the old consensus. World War II had been fought on the basic principles of the deferral of expectations and the need for national sacrifice for the greatest good of the greatest number—a classic liberal utilitarianism. Canadians, whether as private individuals or as voting citizens, became increasingly less willing to buy such arguments. They became ever more prepared to accept the calls of leaders who, by implication or open assertion, opposed either waiting or sharing.

In 1973 a ceasefire agreement allowed the United States to withdraw from Vietnam, and the American process of national disillusionment continued with the Watergate affair, in which an apparently successful President was eventually forced to resign on 9 August 1974 rather than risk removal from office by impeachment for years of lying to the public. In Canada, Vietnam seemed less important than the October Crisis, bringing to the fore the Parti Québécois, which succeeded in electing seven candidates in the 1970 Quebec election. Then on 6 October 1973—the Jewish holy day of Yom Kippur—the Arabs and Israelis went to war, as they had done periodically for many years. On this occasion, however, events in the Middle East had an immediate impact on the world and on Canada. The Arab oil exporters (who dominated the world market) embargoed shipments of oil to nations supporting Israel. Shortly thereafter, the Organization of Petroleum Exporting Countries (OPEC), which for 13 years had been a toothless cartel, managed to agree on another price increase, more substantial than the modest one announced before the Yom Kippur War. The price of oil more than tripled in 1973, and all Western industrialized nations suddenly realized how much their economies had depended on a constant supply of cheap oil.

Perhaps more than any other single commodity of the post-war era, oil symbolized the economics of the age of affluence as well as its North American problems. Cheap oil made possible the development of large, powerful, and comfortable automobiles— the 'Yank Tanks' as they were called in Canada before they briefly became the 'Detroit Dinosaurs'—that sat in every suburban driveway and clogged every freeway. Those freeways, of course, had been paved with materials conjured out of petroleum derivatives. The manufacture and sale of instantly obsolescent, gas-guzzling automobiles, as well as the construction of roads that connected thousands of new suburban developments and shopping malls, were major components of post-war economic prosperity in both the United States and Canada. Some saw the car as a symbol of post-war progress, while others saw it as a sex symbol. Either way, a 20-horsepower electric engine could hardly provide the same effect. The typical Detroit automobile not only consumed gas and oil as if there were no tomorrow, but discharged harmful hydrocarbons—serious contributors to the air pollution that increasingly affected everyone's health. Detroit engineering—never renowned for its flexibility—was slow to respond to the need for fuel efficiency brought about by significantly higher oil prices. By the time it had moved to smaller vehicles, the Japanese had taken command of the North American automobile market, a fact that strongly suggested a new world trading order.

If petroleum—literally as well as symbolically— fuelled the contradictions of the North American economy, it also exposed Canadians to a number of distinctly homegrown problems. Many of these matters had already been newsworthy before OPEC pulled the plug, but they seemed more urgent and apparent as the nation searched for a viable energy policy to respond to the 'crisis'. The Canadian petroleum industry, located chiefly in Alberta, was almost entirely owned and operated by multinational corporations, most (though not all) of them American-based. Oil, indeed, was one of those resources that most obviously epitomized the problems of foreign ownership that were addressed by a series of governments and task forces in the early 1970s. Moreover, although the petroleum still in the ground was a Crown resource, the Crown involved was the province and not the federal state. When the problems of jurisdiction over offshore oil were added to provincial control of oil as an internal natural resource, the result was a key item of potential dispute in federal–provincial relations. Most oil consumption in Canada occurred in the industrialized East, while most of the raw material was in the resource-rich West, a discrepancy that exacerbated regional tensions. Finally, increased petroleum prices had a ripple effect throughout both the Canadian and world economies. Prices rose overnight, and an already steady inflation soared to new highs at a time when Canadian labour unions had only recently succeeded in establishing themselves in many key industries, especially in the public sector. Having achieved full recognition of collective bargaining, union organizers next moved for improved working conditions and higher wages to match the cost of living. OPEC's price increases, with promises of more to come, thus affected Canada in several vulnerable areas: foreign ownership, federal–provincial relations, regional conflicts, and labour relations.

Virtually the only long-standing problem that oil did not seem to affect directly was Quebec. On 29 October 1973, only three weeks after the start of the Yom Kippur War, Quebecers went to the polls to elect a new provincial government. From the outset of the contest between the Liberals of Robert Bourassa and the Parti Québécois headed by René Lévesque, the chief issue had been the desirability of a separate Quebec. Both parties had worked to polarize the electorate on this simple issue. The result, on the surface, was a resounding victory for the Liberals: 1,600,000 votes (54.8 per cent of the total votes cast) to 897,000 for the PQ, and 102 seats in the legislature to six for the PQ. Nonetheless, the Péquistes had improved their performance over the 1970 election in almost every riding, and did exceptionally well among younger voters in Montreal. Post-election studies suggested that the majority of Liberal supporters had favoured federalism and a majority of PQ supporters wanted independence for Quebec. The anglophone voters were much more staunchly federalist than the francophones. In any event, separatism had suddenly become respectable. While no other province was prepared to join the PQ in the front lines of the quest for a new constitutional arrangement for Canada, resource-rich provinces like Alberta certainly favoured new guarantees of constitutional autonomy for the provinces.

The relationship between Quebec separatism and Canada's economic problems after 1973 was difficult to determine. In 1976 the PQ won a somewhat surprising victory, not necessarily to be interpreted as a mandate for separatism or sovereignty-association, although one of its pre-election platform planks was the promise of a referendum on sovereignty-association. When the referendum was held in May 1980, the 'Nons'—those opposed to sovereignty-association—won 60 per cent to 40 per cent. The PQ, however, were re-elected the next year. Especially after the referendum, the federal government under Pierre Trudeau turned its attention from the economy to the Constitution. Trudeau himself was not only a federalist Quebecer but a constitutional lawyer far more comfortable with the intricacies of the British North America Act than with oil-price equalization or economic planning. Oil and the Constitution were scarcely the only issues after 1973, but they were certainly front and centre for many years. The various attempts to resolve the problems they helped to create (as well as the ones they obscured) precipitated the deterioration of the post-war consensus.

Pressure for continual expansion of the welfare state came from many directions before 1980, because income security became essential to the federal government's power, representing as it did the main link between Ottawa and the people. After 1980, however, contrary tendencies became evident and eventually dominant. Canada's economic and social problems would continue to produce demands for expansion of social insurance, but with the erosion of revenue and intense international competition, the federal government increasingly focused on restraint and privatization. Before 1992, no major element of the existing welfare net had actually been eliminated, however. Pension benefits for the elderly even improved. But the government cumulatively reduced the universality of the system of family benefits through the income tax system. In unemployment compensation, revised regulations increased the waiting period, making it more difficult to use unemployment funds as income supplements. The notorious goods and services tax (GST) was a thoroughly regressive tax that hit hardest at the poor. Still, the greatest irony of government policy towards social welfare remained unchanged from the earlier part of the century. The government of Brian Mulroney was continually concerned about spending and the deficit, but had no trouble finding funds to support its military co-operation in the Gulf War of 1991. The unsolved riddle of social justice was still a challenge.

Robert Bourassa

Robert Bourassa was born 14 July 1933 on Parthenais Street in Montreal's East End. His father, Aubert Bourassa, was a documents clerk for the National Harbours Board, where he was made to work in English. His mother, Adrienne Courville, did not demand that Robert do household chores, permitting him to study instead. He attended the local St Pierre Claver parish school, then the Collège Brébeuf, then the Université de Montréal, where he was president of the French-Canada Association while studying law. He also wrote for the university newspaper, mostly advocating solidarity for the francophone minority. His first article for *Le Quartier latin* was an interview with Maurice Duplessis. Bourassa had excellent grades and received many scholarships and bursaries. He won the Mackenzie King scholarship of the Royal Society, the Governor General's medal, and a Ford Foundation bursary.

At the university Bourassa met Andrée Simard, who came from a family of rich industrialists in Sorel. They married in August 1958 and then went to London for further study. He got a job as financial adviser with the federal revenue department in 1960 and taught economics at the University of Ottawa. He first ran for elected office in 1966, winning his seat in the Mercier riding while the Liberals lost their majority. Bourassa joined the nationalist wing of the provincial Liberals, attempting to keep pace with Daniel Johnson, now Premier. He accompanied René Lévesque as part of the Montreal VIP delegation when de Gaulle made his famous speech. He was uncomfortable with de Gaulle's declaration, and told the St Laurent Kiwanis Club in November 1967, 'the economic aspect of a completely independent Quebec always leads to a stumbling block, no matter how you look at it, when it comes to the problem of suddenly instituting a Quebec currency.' Bourassa won on the first ballot at the Liberal leadership convention of

17 January 1970 and would begin his leadership career positioned ideologically halfway between Pierre Trudeau and Réne Lévesque. Bourassa as leadership candidate promised '100,000 jobs' and was elected Premier on 29 April 1970 on this same platform. Instead of creating jobs, he would spend the next five years passively resisting Trudeau's 'patriation' campaign and searching for 'social peace'. He tried to emphasize foreign investment, but got caught up in the October Crisis, in which he often appeared a weakling.

The FLQ manifesto that had to be read over Radio-Canada referred to 'Bourassa, the Simard canary, Trudeau the faggot'. After the Laporte kidnapping, it was Bourassa who wanted the War Measures Act invoked. 'If that's what you want', Trudeau told Bourassa, 'you'll have to ask me formally and say that you are faced with a state of potential insurrection.' The October Crisis, the subsequent constitutional negotiations that bypassed Quebec when Bourassa refused to accept the arrangements of the 1971 Victoria Charter, and the increased popularity of separatism all weakened Bourassa's power base. Although his government was easily re-elected in 1973, it collapsed in 1976 amid charges of scandal and corruption connected with the Olympic Games that same year. Bourassa retreated into private life, but re-emerged in 1983 as leader of the Liberals after the failure of Claude Ryan to provide a viable opposition to the Parti Québécois. In 1985 Bourassa led his party back to power, despite his personal defeat in the riding of Bertrand. Bourassa initially seemed to benefit from Prime Minister Mulroney's attempts to bring Quebec onside constitutionally at Meech Lake, but in the end the failure of Meech Lake and the subsequent defeat in a national referendum of the Charlottetown Accord damaged his reputation inside and outside Quebec. He resigned in 1994 after treatment for skin cancer and died in 1996.

The Shape of Federal Politics

The Ottawa scene from 1972 to 1992 divides into two periods, with the break coming in 1984. During most of the first period the Liberals under Trudeau clung tenaciously to power in a series of very close elections (1972, 1974, and 1980), although they were replaced in office briefly, in 1979, by a minority Tory administration headed by Joe Clark. This period was one of a gradual Liberal Party deterioration paralleling the unravelling of the small-l liberal consensus of the post-war era. In 1984 the Tories under Brian Mulroney swept to power in the most decisive election since 1945, exceeding even the Diefenbaker sweep of 1958 in percentage of popular votes and number of seats. As with most decisive electoral shifts in Canada, the one in 1984 involved a massive reorientation of votes in Quebec and Ontario. The change in Quebec was particularly critical, although it was not clear whether Quebec's party shift was a long-term one, or precisely what it meant. At the end of their tenures of office, both Trudeau and Mulroney engendered enormous currents of fierce voter hostility in a general atmosphere of public mistrust of politicians. This mistrust would continue for decades.

Whether Mulroney's Tories actually represented a different political vision that could serve as the basis for a new consensus was always an open question. Certainly they sought to move to the consensual centre, which public opinion polls and voting behaviour suggested had become dubious about many of the old assumptions, but there was no clear evidence that a new political paradigm was emerging from the shards of the old liberal one. Instead, the events of his second administration suggested that Mulroney, like Diefenbaker a generation earlier, was simply perplexed and confounded by the chaos of the disintegration of federalism. The problem of Quebec, which came to dominate public attention across Canada in the late 1980s and early 1990s, contributed to further confusion.

The Liberals

The fortunes of the federal Liberal Party between 1968 and 1984 became increasingly associated with Pierre Elliott Trudeau, its leader for most of that period. The identification was partly due to television's relentless search for visual images and Trudeau's brilliant mastery of the medium. But it was also a result of Trudeau's operating as a loner, not encouraging strong colleagues to emerge around him. Trudeau's 'arrogance', the term most often used to describe his behaviour, was personal, not political. As a French Canadian who had always firmly opposed Quebec separatism, he had little scope for manoeuvre when public opinion polarized in that province. As an equally strong federalist, he had no more time for western expressions of provincial or regional autonomy than he did for Quebec's. A central Canadian urban intellectual, he could not empathize with the problems of either the Atlantic region or western Canada. The East never deserted him, but by 1980 'western alienation' had reduced the number of Liberal MPs west of Ontario to two (both from Manitoba).

Never a fervent party man, Trudeau did not cultivate the grassroots. The powerful Liberal political organizations that had flourished before 1970 were allowed to wither away in most provinces, surfacing when federal patronage was to be dispensed but not at federal election time. Trudeau distressed many Canadians with forthrightness ('Just watch me' in regard to soldiers in the streets of Montreal during the October Crisis), vulgarity bordering on obscenity (one four-letter word in the House of Commons was transcribed as 'fuddle duddle', a raised-finger gesture to a western crowd appeared in newspapers across the nation), and personal unconventionality. Perhaps most damaging of all was an increasing tendency to treat almost everyone (members of his own caucus, the opposition, reporters, the voters) as ill-informed and irrational. Trudeau's public persona oscillated between that of a genial swinger (who could date Barbra Streisand) and that of a university professor facing a particularly stupid class.

Trudeau had announced his intention of retiring in 1979 following the Liberals' unexpected electoral defeat. But the Clark minority government fell before his replacement could be chosen. The Liberal caucus persuaded him to lead the party into the unanticipated election of 1980, and he remained in power for four more years. In 1984 Trudeau made

Prime Minister Trudeau and the newly elected Premier of Quebec, Robert Bourassa, at the federal–provincial conference of September 1970, in Ottawa. Duncan Cameron/LAC, PA-117468.

his retirement stick. He was succeeded by John Turner (b. 1929), who had waited in the wings for years. Chosen on 16 June 1984 as Liberal leader and becoming Prime Minister two weeks later, Turner dissolved Parliament on 9 July for the fateful 1984 election. Turner was born in England but was thoroughly bilingual. His decision regarding the election was a difficult one. He chose to run as a fresh face, on the momentum of his selection as leader, rather than remaining in office to attempt to improve the government's image. He had no new policies. Instead he was encumbered by the twin albatrosses of Trudeau's mounting unpopularity and the growing collapse of the liberal consensus. To everyone's surprise, he also proved utterly inept on television. The weak Liberal showing of 1984 (40 seats in the House of Commons) was hardly unexpected. Something better was hoped for by the party in 1988, however. In that election the Liberals did even worse in Quebec than in 1984, and Turner was a lame duck on election night. He was finally replaced in the summer of 1990 by Jean Chrétien (b. 1934), another veteran of earlier Liberal governments. Chrétien was a loyal party man and a proven campaigner. His leadership opponents had labelled him 'Yesterday's Man' with some justification, but lacked sufficient credibility or charisma to beat him.

The Progressive Conservatives

Robert Stanfield led the Tories to three successive defeats at the hands of the Trudeau Liberals. He was too low-key and uncompelling. Stanfield spoke French badly and his party did poorly in Quebec during his leadership (four seats in 1968, two in 1972, and three in 1974). He was followed as Tory leader by Alberta MP Joe (Charles Joseph) Clark (b. 1939), who emerged from nowhere as the compromise 'progressive' candidate at the 1976 leadership convention. 'Joe Who?' never did establish a distinct personality with the voters, except as a man who was accident-prone. In 1979 his Tories received 136 seats to 114 for the Liberals. Clark formed a minority government despite having won only two seats in Quebec (to 67 for the Liberals). He tried to govern as if he had a majority, mistakenly assuming either that other parties would support him in Parliament rather than face another election or that the nation would rally to his banner in a new election. Neither assumption was true. The NDP refused to support Clark, especially over the privatization of Petro-Canada. His government fell on a motion of non-confidence about the budget, involving gasoline pricing. Clark remained party leader after the disastrous election of 1980, but in June 1983 he was replaced by 'the Boy from Baie Comeau', Brian Mulroney (b. 1939).

Brian Mulroney entered Canadian politics at the highest level without ever having held public or elected office, although he had been active in the political backrooms for years. Unlike Clark, whose public utterances were unpolished and delivered in a boyish tenor (he reportedly took elocution lessons to lower his voice), Mulroney was a fluent speaker, perfectly bilingual, and possessed of one of the richest and most mellifluous voices ever heard in Canadian politics. He was an experienced labour lawyer and corporation executive, at his best at behind-the-scenes conciliation. Mulroney understood the need for Tory success in Quebec, and he brought a number of new faces into the campaign, some of whom were refugees from the old Union Nationale. In 1984 he successfully captured the centre of the new Canadian political spectrum. Although Mulroney's Tories promised they would not dismantle the existing welfare state, they put an ominous emphasis on 'fiscal responsibility'. They were equally committed to better relations between Canada and the United States, which meant less economic nationalism, as well as improved relations between Ottawa and the provinces (especially Quebec), which meant surrendering federalist pretensions.

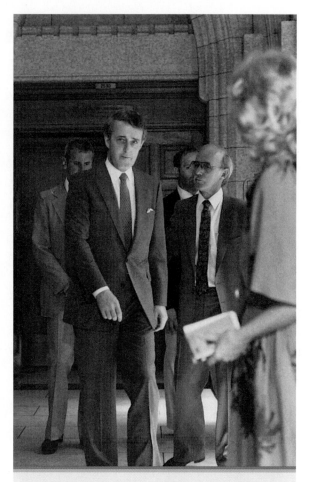

Brian Mulroney in 1983, the year before he became leader of the Progressive Conservative Party, mp for Central Nova, and leader of the Opposition. He was elected Prime Minister the following year. Ed McGibbon/LAC, PA-146485.

Once in office with an enormous majority, including 58 seats from Quebec, Mulroney succeeded in 1986 in negotiating a free trade agreement with the United States and the Meech Lake constitutional accord with the provinces. On the coattails of these successes the Tories won again in 1988, with 63 of their 169 seats coming from Quebec. Mulroney's second term was an unmitigated disaster. Given the amount of public support he had enjoyed in 1984 and 1988, the rapid growth of hostility to Mulroney in the early 1990s was quite remarkable. A variety of things went wrong. Government spending got quite out of hand. What was supposed to be a progressive tax reform, the GST, proved to be the most unpopular tax ever introduced in Canadian history, doubly resented for the way the Tories stacked the Senate to ensure its passage. The GST replaced previously hidden levies with an all-too-visible tax computed at the cash register. Unlike provincial sales taxes, it was applied to everything without exception. With the provincial taxes, the GST meant a surcharge of nearly 20 per cent in several provinces on most consumer spending. Meech Lake failed, and in a national referendum in October 1992 the nation rejected its successor, the Charlottetown Accord. Much of Canada came to believe that the Tory constitutional deals, especially with Quebec, not only made too many concessions but had actually stirred up unnecessary trouble.

Other National Parties

Throughout this period the New Democratic Party remained the constant third party. Its continuity was exemplified by the steadiness of its popular vote in federal elections, which ran between 15 and 20 per cent, and by the steadiness of its policies, which were indisputably federalist, nationalist, and liberal. Some complained that the party was not sufficiently socialist. It had certainly purged its socialist wing, the Waffle, in the early 1970s. But it was still unable to make inroads east of Ontario, and was consistently the big loser when the popular vote was translated into parliamentary seats. From 1971 to 1975 the NDP was led by David Lewis (1909–81), the son of Russian immigrants to Canada and a Rhodes scholar who had spent a lifetime associated with the CCF-NDP. His selection as leader followed a bitter fight with the radical caucus within the party. From 1972 to 1974 the Lewis-led NDP propped up the minority Liberal government, arguably turning it to the left, but paying for the collaboration at the polls in 1974.

In 1975 Ed Broadbent (b. 1936), a former political science professor at York University, succeeded Lewis. Broadbent's national position in Canada in the 1980s was a peculiar one. He consistently headed the polls as the most popular and trustworthy national leader, but his party was never able to increase its public support. In 1990 Broadbent was replaced by Audrey McLaughlin (b. 1936), a former social worker from the Yukon Territory who spoke halting French and had no appeal in Quebec. Her selection as the first female party leader in Canada, however, marked the NDP as yet again in advance of the other parties, for feminist issues were part of the unresolved agenda of Canadian politics in the 1990s.

The Provinces, the Constitution, and the Charter of Rights

The Shape of Provincial Politics

The provinces continued to have difficulty generating truly viable two-party or multi-party systems. Instead, most provinces operated through a single dominant party (often outside the two major federal ones) that remained in office in election after election, producing what C.B. Macpherson described for Alberta as a 'quasiparty' system. A single dominant party, Macpherson argued, satisfied voters and mediated local conflict by insisting that the important battle was against external forces symbolized by the Canadian federal government. Conflict with Ottawa had been an endemic feature of provincial politics and government since Confederation. Offers to outbash the opposition regarding Ottawa were standard fare in provincial elections, particularly highly contested ones. Party identification with government in Ottawa was always extremely dangerous when provincial rights issues were on the table.

In some ways the 1970s were hard on dominant parties in the provinces. Four long-dominant provincial parties went down to defeat: the Liberals in Newfoundland and Quebec, and the Socreds in Alberta and British Columbia. It was never clear whether the coincidence of these defeats was part of a much larger political shift, the product of changing economic circumstances, or mere accident. In any event, political veterans like Joey Smallwood, Ernest Manning, and W.A.C. Bennett were replaced by younger leaders such as Peter Lougheed (b. 1928) in Alberta, Brian Peckford (b. 1942) in Newfoundland, and Bill Bennett (b. 1932) in British Columbia. For the younger men, federal–provincial relations were not conditioned by depression, war, or post-war prosperity so much as by provincial self-interest ruthlessly pursued.

Federal–Provincial Relations

THE 1970S

Throughout the 1970s federal–provincial relations were dominated by oil, Quebec, and abortive constitutional reform. In June 1971, at the federal–provincial conference held in Victoria, the Trudeau administration made another effort to agree on a formula for constitutional repatriation that would satisfy Quebec's aspirations. Three points are worth noting about the 1971 discussions: first, entrenching rights in a charter was regarded as one way to reassure those who feared losing British constitutional protection; second, Quebec did not achieve a sufficiently distinctive place in Confederation to suit its demands; and finally, only Quebec and Ontario were given perpetual vetoes (other provinces could together mount a veto only using complicated co-operative formulas). The question of constitutional reform was not picked up again until 1980, by which time much had changed for both Canada and its provinces. Oil and the whole question of resource management had become subjects of continual tension between some of the provinces (led by Alberta) and the federal government after 1973. Before OPEC pulled the plug, Alberta had often single-handedly opposed Ottawa over resource management. With non-renewable resources now hot commodities, more provinces recognized the advantages of provincial autonomy. Only PEI, Manitoba, and New Brunswick were left to visualize their provincial self-interest as best served by a strong federal government. By 1980 the rich provinces, usually led by hard-headed businessmen who insisted that they put balance sheets ahead of sentiment, were ready to help dismantle Ottawa's centralized arrangements, especially in the area of social insurance programs.

THE PARTI QUÉBÉCOIS AND THE CONSTITUTION

The occasion for a new round of constitutional discussions was provided by the Parti Québécois, not through its electoral victory of 1976 but through its referendum on sovereignty-association of 1980. The PQ victory came as a shock to English-speaking Canada, although it was really quite predictable. The Bourassa government in Quebec had been badly shaken by charges of scandal and corruption on top of its seeming inability to deal expeditiously with either the separatists or Pierre Trudeau. It had lost considerable face when the Canadian Airline Pilots Association went on strike in June 1976, ostensibly over safety but really over bilingualism, an issue that only the federal government could resolve. Rumours of cost overruns and construction disasters in the preparations for the 1976 Summer Olympics in Montreal had been rife for years. Bourassa's government was not directly involved in the problems, which were primarily the responsibility of Mayor Jean Drapeau's Montreal government, but Drapeau was a Liberal ally and Bourassa had waffled over intervening. The province took over the Olympics construction only at the last minute. There were similar concerns over the control of the James Bay hydroelectric development, but in the summer of 1976 these were not so immediately visible in Montreal as the Olympics fiasco. A resurgent Parti Québécois won over many voters who did not normally support it, as the electorate simultaneously rejected Bourassa's Liberals and embraced Lévesque's party.

Issues are never tidy in any election. No evidence suggested that the PQ, despite its resounding victory, had received any mandate for its well-publicized sovereignty-association. The Parti Québécois had insisted that it would not act unilaterally on separation without a provincial referendum. Voters could thus support the reformist social democratic zeal of the PQ without signing on to its extremist constitutional position. English-speaking Canada, however, responded to the Quebec election by assuming that separatism had triumphed in Quebec. The nation had to be saved at any cost. Had Lévesque sought to renegotiate the constitutional issues in the immediate wake of the victory, he might have been offered some sort of two-nations formula, but the PQ was committed both to internal Quebec reform and to a democratic approach to separation.

René Lévesque on provincial election night, 29 October 1973. Duncan Cameron/LAC, PA-115039.

In office Lévesque's PQ successfully pursued policies of economic and linguistic nationalism. Its most controversial legislation was Bill 101, which went well beyond an earlier piece of Bourassa legislation (known as Bill 22) in its effort to turn Quebec into a unilingual francophone province. Bill 101 made it necessary for most Quebecers, regardless of their background or preference, to be educated in French-language schools. Only those temporarily resident in Quebec or whose parents had been educated in English-speaking schools in the province were exempted. The bill also insisted that French was the only legal medium in business and government, requiring the elimination of virtually all English-language signs in the province. In 1979 the Quebec government produced a White Paper detailing what it meant by sovereignty-association. It wanted 'a free, proud and adult national existence' within the context of a series of joint Quebec–Canada institutions, including a court of justice and a monetary authority

(Québec conseil exécutif, 1979). A totally independent Quebec, it insisted, would still have access to Canada and its economy. Outside the ranks of the converted, the scheme seemed far too lopsided in Quebec's favour. The proposal was a unilateral Quebec initiative.

As had been promised, there was a referendum, eventually scheduled for 20 May 1980. Referendums are notoriously tricky political instruments. They often encourage 'No' votes. Certainly the non-francophone population of Quebec (less than 20 per cent of the whole), although vehemently opposed to a '*Oui*' vote, were not by themselves numerous enough to reject sovereignty-association, but in the end almost 60 per cent of the province's voters and even a bare majority (52 per cent) of its francophones voted '*Non*'. This fairly decisive result left 40.5 per cent of the Quebec population, and just under half of its francophones, in favour of sovereignty-association. Nevertheless, Quebec had publicly rejected separation from Canada. The nation responded by breathing a collective sigh of relief and calling for a new federalism. Forgotten for the moment was the simple truth that pressure for change of the fundamental sort represented by separatism does not go away because of one setback at the ballot box.

THE FIRST ROUND OF CONSTITUTIONAL REVISIONS

Canadians had discussed and debated both national unity and constitutional change since the PQ victory in 1976. More than enough proposals for reform floated about the country. Many surfaced in the travelling

Chronology of Quebec Separatism

March 1963	Front de libération du Québec is founded.
November 1967	René Lévesque resigns from the Quebec Liberal Party and begins organizing the Parti Québécois.
25 June 1968	Pierre Trudeau is elected with a large Liberal majority.
7 July 1969	Canada becomes officially bilingual through the Official Languages Act.
October 1970	Kidnapping of James Cross and Pierre Laporte. War Measures Act is invoked.
29 Oct. 1973	PQ wins six seats in the Quebec election and becomes the official opposition.
15 Nov. 1976	PQ wins majority in Quebec election and takes over government.
26 Aug. 1977	Bill 101 makes French the official language of Quebec.
15 April 1980	Sovereignty referendum campaign begins.
14 May 1980	Trudeau promises constitutional reform.
20 May 1980	Sovereignty-association is defeated, 60 per cent to 40 per cent.
2 Oct. 1980	Trudeau announces that the Constitution will be repatriated.
13 April 1981	PQ wins a majority in the Quebec election.
2–5 Nov. 1981	Ottawa and nine anglophone provinces reach a deal on the Constitution. Lévesque claims he has been stabbed in the back.
1 July 1982	Queen gives royal consent to a new Constitution.
21 July 1985	René Lévesque retires.
3 October 1985	Pierre-Marc Johnson, new leader of the PQ, becomes Quebec Premier.
2 Dec. 1985	Liberals under Bourassa defeat Johnson's PQ and form a new government.
3 June 1987	Meech Lake Accord is negotiated.
1 Nov. 1987	Death of René Lévesque.
17 March 1988	Jacques Parizeau is elected new leader of the PQ.
2 June 1990	Meech Lake Accord fails when Manitoba and Newfoundland fail to ratify within deadline. Quebec says it will not take part in further constitutional deals.
25 June 1990	Seven independent Quebec MPs, led by Lucien Bouchard, form the Bloc Québécois.
28 Jan. 1991	Quebec Liberal Party calls for a decentralized Canada.
27 March 1991	Bélanger-Campeau Commission recommends a referendum on sovereignty by November 1992 if there is no deal with Canada.
24 Sept. 1991	Ottawa proposes recognition of Quebec as a distinct society, Senate reform, Aboriginal self-government, economic union, and adjustments to federal–provincial powers to give provinces more control.
12 March 1992	First formal federal–provincial meeting since the failure of Meech Lake.
7 July 1992	Federal government, nine provincial premiers (all but Quebec's), and Aboriginal leaders agree on a new formula for reform.

road show (known as the Task Force on National Unity) sent across Canada in 1978. Out of the flurry of activity and the myriad suggestions, several points were clear. One was that many Canadians—including a fair proportion of academics and lawyers, if not historians—were prepared to make relatively major alterations in the British North America Act, the document that served as the nation's Constitution. A second was that the vast majority of anglophone Canadians were prepared to make substantial concessions to keep Quebec within Confederation. A third point, perhaps less well understood by the public, was that the anglophone provinces of Canada—led by the western provinces of Alberta, British Columbia,

4 August 1992	Bourassa meets with other premiers and PM Mulroney.
19–23 Aug. 1992	Charlottetown Accord is negotiated, including Senate reform, Aboriginal self-government, an expanded House of Commons, some new power arrangements, and a provincial veto over future change to federal institutions.
18 Sept. 1992	National referendum campaign on Charlottetown begins.
26 Oct. 1992	Canadian voters reject Charlottetown, 54 per cent to 45 per cent.
25 Oct. 1993	Federal Liberals under Chrétien demolish the Tories and NDP; Bouchard's BQ forms the official opposition in Commons with 55 seats.
11 Jan. 1994	Bourassa resigns and is succeeded by Daniel Johnson.
12 Sept. 1994	PQ elected in Quebec and promises referendum on sovereignty.
12 June 1995	Parizeau, Bouchard, and Action Démocratique (ADQ) leader Mario Dumont form a coalition to fight for 'Oui' on referendum.
30 Oct. 1995	Sovereignty rejected, 50.7 per cent to 49.3 per cent; turnout for the referendum is an astonishing 93.5 per cent of eligible voters.
31 Oct. 1995	Parizeau resigns as PQ leader.
11 Jan. 1996	Lucien Bouchard is chosen PQ leader and Quebec Premier.
18 Jan. 1996	Bouchard resigns as BQ leader.
17 Feb. 1996	Michel Gauthier is chosen as head of BQ.
Sept. 1996	Quebec nationalist Guy Bertrand wins right in Quebec Superior Court to seek a court injunction against a new sovereignty referendum.
28 Feb. 1997	Federal Justice Minister Allan Rock insists Quebec has no right to declare independence from Canada unilaterally, even in the event of a pro-secession referendum.
March 1997	Gilles Duceppe elected Bloc leader.
2 June 1997	Bloc Québécois wins 44 Quebec seats in federal election to 26 for Liberals and 5 for Conservatives.
15 Sept. 1997	At a meeting of the anglophone premiers of Canada, seven principles are adopted to promote the distinctive character of Quebec, but the declaration is rejected by Premier Bouchard since it is not part of the Constitution.
20 Aug. 1998	Canadian Supreme Court rules that Quebec cannot unilaterally separate from Canada. After a clear majority vote in favour of sovereignty, Quebec would have to negotiate with Canada to 'address the interests' of various parties, including the linguistic and cultural minorities.
21 Sept. 1998	Parti Québécois National Council agrees not to hold another referendum until there is a good chance of winning it.
39 Nov 1998	Parti Québécois wins 77 seats of 125 in Quebec provincial election.
8 March 2001	Lucien Bouchard resigns from office and is replaced by Bernard Landry.
14 April 2003	Liberals under Jean Charest win Quebec election.
June 2005	Bernard Landry steps down as PQ leader.
Nov. 2005	André Boisclair, an acknowledged gay politician, is chosen as PQ leader.
23 Jan. 2006	Federal election sees Bloc win only 42 per cent of popular vote and 61 Quebec seats. This is regarded as a setback to the sovereignist movement.

and Saskatchewan and strongly supported by Nova Scotia and Newfoundland—had developed their own agenda for constitutional reform. These provinces saw Ottawa's federalism as operating almost exclusively in the interests of central Canada. They were quite prepared to take advantage of Quebec's moves towards greater autonomy, particularly if these pressures reduced Quebec's influence within Confederation and allowed for constitutional change in the best interests of other provinces. What the other provinces wanted most was unrestricted control over their own natural resources and reform of some of

Canadian Charter of Rights and Freedoms

The following clauses of the Charter of Rights and Freedoms are of most relevance to the present discussion. The Charter includes 34 clauses and can be accessed online at:
<www.efc.ca/pages/law/charter/charter.text.html>.

RIGHTS AND FREEDOMS IN CANADA.

1. The Canadian Charter of Rights and Freedoms guarantees the rights and freedoms set out in it subject only to such reasonable limits prescribed by law as can be demonstrably justified in a free and democratic society.

FUNDAMENTAL FREEDOMS.

2. Everyone has the following fundamental freedoms:
   (a) freedom of conscience and religion;
   (b) freedom of thought, belief, opinion and expression, including freedom of the press and other media of communication;
   (c) freedom of peaceful assembly; and
   (d) freedom of association.

DEMOCRATIC RIGHTS OF CITIENS.

3. Every citizen of Canada has the right to vote in an election of members of the House of Commons or of a legislative assembly and to be qualified for membership therein.

MAXIMUM DURATION OF LEGISLATIVE BODIES/
CONTINUATION IN SPECIAL CIRCUMSTANCES.

4. (1) No House of Commons and no legislative assembly shall continue for longer than five years from the date fixed for the return of the writs at a general election of its members.

(2) In time of real or apprehended war, invasion or insurrection, a House of Commons may be continued by Parliament and a legislative assembly may be continued by the legislature beyond five years if such continuation is not opposed by the votes of more than one-third of the members of the House of Commons or the legislative assembly, as the case may be.

ANNUAL SITTING OF LEGISLATIVE BODIES.

5. There shall be a sitting of Parliament and of each legislature at least once every twelve months.

MOBILITY RIGHTS OF CITIZENS/RIGHT TO MOVE AND GAIN LIVELIHOOD/AFFIRMATIVE ACTION PROGRAMS.

6. (1) Every citizen of Canada has the right to enter, remain in and leave Canada.

(2) Every citizen of Canada and every person who has the status of a permanent resident of Canada has the right
   (a) to move to and take up residence in any province; and
   (b) to pursue the gaining of a livelihood in any province.

(3) The rights specified in subsection (2) are subject to
   (a) any laws or practices of general application in force in a province other than those that discriminate among persons

Ottawa's governing institutions, notably the Senate and the Supreme Court, to reflect regional interests. The Trudeau government had seemed on the verge of conceding much of the provincial program when it was defeated in 1979. The Clark government had not dealt with the issue when it, too, failed at the polls.

The opportunity presented to Prime Minister Trudeau by the Quebec referendum, when he called a first ministers' conference for early June 1980, was real, if dangerous. Once the box of constitutional revision was opened, it might never be closed. From the federalist perspective, it was necessary to deal

primarily on the basis of province of present or previous residence; and

(b) any laws providing for reasonable residency requirements as a qualification for the receipt of publicly provided social services.

(4) Subsections (2) and (3) do not preclude any law, program or activity that has as its object the amelioration in a province of conditions of individuals in that province who were socially or economically disadvantaged if the rate of employment in that province is below the rate of employment in Canada. . . .

LIFE, LIBERTY AND SECURITY OF PERSON.

7. Everyone has the right to life, liberty and security of the person and the right not to be deprived thereof except in accordance with the principles of fundamental justice. . . .

TREATMENT OF PUNISHMENT.

12. Everyone has the right not to be subjected to any cruel and unusual treatment or punishment.

SELF-INCRIMINATION.

13. A witness who testifies in any proceedings has the right not to have any incriminating evidence so given used to incriminate that witness in any other proceedings, except in a prosecution for perjury or for the giving of contradictory evidence.

INTERPRETER.

14. A party or witness in any proceedings who does not understand or speak the language in which the proceedings are conducted or who is deaf has the right to the assistance of an interpreter.

EQUALITY BEFORE AND UNDER LAW AND EQUAL PROTECTION AND BENEFIT OF LAW/AFFIRMATIVE ACTION PROGRAMS.

15. (1) Every individual is equal before and under the law and has the right to the equal protection and equal benefit of the law without discrimination and, in particular, without discrimination based on race, national or ethnic origin, colour, religion, sex, age or mental or physical disability.

(2) Subsection (1) does not preclude any law, program or activity that has as its object the amelioration of conditions of disadvantaged individuals or groups including those that are disadvantaged because of race, national or ethnic origin, colour, religion, sex, age or mental or physical disability.

OFFICIAL LANGUAGES OF CANADA/OFFICIAL LANGUAGES OF NEW BRUNSWICK. ADVANCEMENT OF STATUS AND USE.

16. (1) English and French are the official languages of Canada and have equality of status and equal rights and privileges as to their use in all institutions of the Parliament and government of Canada.

(2) English and French are the official languages of New Brunswick and have equality of status and equal rights and privileges as to their use in all institutions of the legislature and government of New Brunswick.

(3) Nothing in this Charter limits the authority of Parliament or a legislature to advance the equality of status or use of English and French. . . .

with Quebec's aspirations without conceding too much to the other provinces, none of which was controlled by a Liberal government and all of which had their own visions of change. Ottawa's most consistent ally was Ontario, confirming regional charges that it had been the chief beneficiary of the old federalism. Quebec did not participate in the new discussions, but it could not be churlish about them. Its best strategy was to allow the anglophone provinces to initiate the dismantling of Confederation. Indeed, one of the principal characteristics of this round of constitutional discussion was that Quebec's concerns were not front and centre. General consensus was developed on economic issues, balancing provincial resource control against federal economic planning. But other questions remained difficult to resolve. Ottawa wanted to entrench a Charter of Rights in any new constitutional document, chiefly to guarantee francophone linguistic rights across the nation, but the majority of the provinces (including Quebec) objected to such a Charter as threatening their own rights. The provinces, for their part, wanted an amending formula that would allow all provinces the right of veto and the right to opt out of any amendments that they regarded as threatening their powers. This round of discussions broke down in September 1980. As Prime Minister Trudeau had been threatening for months, Ottawa prepared to take unilateral action.

Politically, the federal constitutional package developed in Ottawa was carefully calculated. As an ardent federalist, a trained constitutional lawyer, and an exponent of *realpolitik*, Pierre Trudeau was clearly in his element. The new proposal called for the elimination of recourse to the British Parliament for amendment of the British North America Act ('repatriation'). It also contained a Charter of Rights, which by establishing the rights of other collective minorities was intended to prevent the French Canadians from being treated as an exceptional case. The package also provided for a new method of amendment—through national referendum initiated in Ottawa—to be used in the event of provincial obstructionism. The Trudeau government was prepared to pass the package through the federal Parliament and send it to Britain for approval without

recourse to either the Supreme Court of Canada or the provinces, although it clearly infringed on the informal 'right' of the provinces to consent to constitutional change. Not surprisingly, the federal NDP supported this position, leaving the Progressive Conservative minority in Parliament to oppose it and voice the objections of nearly all the provinces except (again not surprisingly) Ontario.

Parliamentary amendments eliminated some of the least saleable features of the original proposal and introduced some new wrinkles, including the specific affirmation of 'aboriginal and treaty rights of the aboriginal peoples of Canada' (McWhinney, 1982: 176). The Liberal government had neatly set against each other two sets of rights, one the human rights protected in the entrenched Charter and the other the provincial rights ignored in both the amending process and the Charter itself. Eight of the provinces (excluding Ontario and New Brunswick), often unsympathetically referred to in the media as 'the Gang of Eight', organized as the leading opponents of unilateral repatriation, although Quebec and the English-speaking premiers had quite different views on positive reform.

The first major hurdle for the federal initiative was the Supreme Court of Canada, to which constitutional opinions from several provincial courts had gone on appeal. If the federal government won support from the Supreme Court, it would render untenable the provincial claim that the package was unconstitutional. While the Supreme Court deliberated, René Lévesque and the PQ won a resounding electoral victory in Quebec. The win did not, of course, resolve the deep contradiction that the PQ represented as a separatist party committed to non-separatist action, but it did reactivate Quebec on constitutional matters. Although the British government had refused to deal officially with the provincial premiers (much as it had in 1867 when Nova Scotia sent Joseph Howe to London), Canada's Native peoples set up their own lobbying office in London. They had some claim to direct treaty connections with the British Crown and a decent legal case. The Supreme Court of Canada handed down its ruling on 28 September 1981. Many Canadians had trouble comprehending both the process and the decision, since neither the constitutional nor the political role of the Canadian Court was as well understood as that of its American equivalent.

As one constitutional expert commented, the decision was, in legal terms, 'complex and baffling and technically unsatisfactory' (McWhinney, 1982: 80). In political terms, such complexity was doubtless exactly what the Supreme Court intended. Essentially, by a 7–2 decision, it declared the federal patriation process legal, since custom could not be enforced in courts. It then opined, by a 6–3 decision, that federal patriation was unconventional. Since most of the legal arguments against the process revolved around violations of constitutional 'convention' (or custom), these two opinions were mutually contradictory, although in law Ottawa had won. What the politicians could make of a result that said, in effect, that the federal package of repatriation was, strictly speaking, legal but at the same time improper was another matter.

In the end the nine English-speaking premiers, including seven of the original Gang of Eight, worked out a deal with Prime Minister Trudeau on 5 November 1981. Trudeau made substantial concessions—for example, abandoning the provision for a referendum. Ontario joined Quebec in agreeing to drop its right of veto in favour of a complex formula that ensured that either one or the other (but not both) would have to agree to any amendment. This represented less of a loss for Ottawa than for the central provinces, especially Quebec. At the same time, provinces that had refused to concur with constitutional change had the right to remain outside its provisions until they chose to opt in, a considerable move from Trudeau's earlier positions. Trudeau's greatest concessions were in the Charter of Rights, particularly the so-called 'notwithstanding' clause, which allowed any province to opt out of clauses in the Charter covering fundamental freedoms and legal and equality rights, although not other categories of rights, including language rights. There was disagreement over the intention of the negotiations regarding Native peoples, resulting in a temporary omission of the clause guaranteeing Aboriginal treaty rights, which subsequently had to be restored by Parliament. As for a definition of those rights

themselves, there was to be a constitutional conference to identify them.

The final compromise satisfied the nine anglophone premiers. It certainly strengthened in theory the rights of the provinces to opt out of the Charter on critical issues, including both Native rights and women's rights, through use of the 'notwithstanding' clause. Perhaps understandably, both Native groups and women's groups vowed to fight on in opposition to the package as revised. As for Quebec, all it had lost was some of its self-perceived distinctive status in Confederation. That loss would prove fairly crucial, however, for Quebec would consistently refuse to accept the constitutional reforms on the grounds that one of Canada's two 'national wills' had not been consulted. That position would lead to another attempt at provincial unanimity at Meech Lake in 1987.

The revised constitutional package passed the Canadian Parliament in December 1981 and the British Parliament early in 1982. The latter had resolutely refused to become involved in the various protests against the new agreement, thus surrendering its role as court of last resort against unconstitutional actions within Canada. Canadians at the time did not fully appreciate what had happened constitutionally or what the changes would mean. The principle of patriation had been purchased at considerable expense by the Trudeau government. The Charter of Rights did reflect the principle that collective and individual rights transcending the British North America Act (and its conception of relevant players) had to be carefully guarded. But in place of the earlier British constitutional position that the legislature (federal and provincial) was the source of protection, the Charter established the American constitutional notion that the court system would enforce fundamental rights over the legislature and the government responsible to it. In place of the earlier concept that Parliament was supreme, it introduced a whole new series of formal checks and balances limiting parliamentary supremacy.

A good example of the Charter principles in action would come in 1988, when Prime Minister Brian Mulroney signed a Redress Agreement between the National Association of Japanese Canadians and

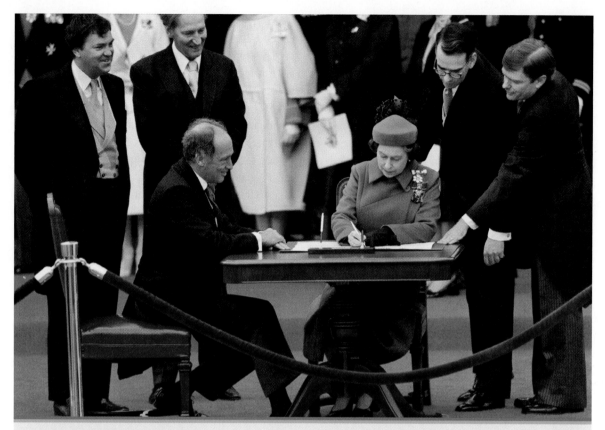

Prime Minister Trudeau looks on as Queen Elizabeth II signs Canada's constitutional proclamation in Ottawa, 17 April 1982. The Canadian Press/Ron Poling.

the Canadian government regarding the handling of Japanese Canadians during and after World War II. In letters to 20,000 Japanese Canadians in 1990, the Prime Minister acknowledged that the wartime treatment 'was unjust and violated principles of human rights as they are understood today'.

The new Constitution not only gave new powers to the provinces, it also recognized new and rather amorphous political collectivities in the Charter of Rights, which was somewhat less concerned than the American Bill of Rights with defining the rights of individuals and somewhat more concerned with delineating collective rights. Thus, in addition to providing equality before the law for individuals facing discrimination 'based on race, national or ethnic origin, colour, religion, sex, age or mental or physical disability' (section 15.1), the Charter also specifically permitted in section 15.2 'any law, program, or activity that has as its object the

amelioration of conditions of disadvantaged individuals or groups', including (but not limited to) those disadvantaged by discrimination as in section 15.1. Moreover, Aboriginal and treaty rights of the Aboriginal peoples, although deliberately not defined, were entrenched, as were sexual equality and multiculturalism. Although at first glance these Charter provisions seemed to represent the ultimate triumph of liberalism, in several respects they did not. In the first place, the liberal Charter provisions were balanced by the increased power given to the provinces to control their own resources and to call their own shots about the applicability of the Charter and any constitutional amendments. In the second place, the constitutional introduction of a whole series of new collectivities created further complications for an already overloaded political process. In the end this would help stifle the liberal impulse itself. Finally, the well-publicized antics of the politicians over the

Constitution contributed to a further reduction in the esteem with which those politicians were held by an increasingly cynical Canadian public.

CONSTITUTIONAL REVISION: ROUNDS TWO AND THREE

The 1982 Charter, with its explicit and implicit recognition of both collective and individual rights, was hardly the last word on the subject. A body of case law would have to be developed by the courts, especially the Supreme Court of Canada, which became the ultimate arbiter charged with interpreting the vague terminology of the document. Governments offered no clarification. The Charter simply became a wild card exercised by the Supreme Court of Canada on behalf of Canadians, arguably more amenable to change than the parliamentary system.

In 1987 the Mulroney government fastened on one of the loose ends of the 1982 constitutional process, Quebec's refusal to accept the 1982 Constitution. By this time René Lévesque had retired (in June 1985) and the PQ had been defeated in December 1985 by the Liberals under a rehabilitated Robert Bourassa. Once again in power, Bourassa offered to compromise. Mulroney summoned a new 'Gang of 10' to a closed-door session on 30 April 1987 at Meech Lake, where a revised constitutional arrangement acceptable to Quebec was worked out. While Quebec was to be constitutionally recognized as a 'distinct society' and given further concessions, including a veto over most amendments to the Constitution, there were also inducements to the other provinces, which would also enjoy some gains in autonomy. The federal government would compensate all provinces for programs they refused to join. Each province was given a veto over further amendments. There was to be regular discussion of Senate reform, although no particular formula was agreed upon. Nevertheless, there was a consensus among participants that the federal Parliament, and the legislatures of all 10 provinces, would have to approve the agreement by early June 1990—the lengthy time frame allowed for public hearings and feedback—or the arrangement was dead.

The three years permitted between the Meech Lake meeting and the deadline for approval created many difficulties. While the Mulroney government understandably insisted that no changes could be made in the agreement until it had been formally approved, not every provincial government felt bound by the particular terms accepted by whoever happened to be premier in April 1987. The subsequent public debate made clear that not all Canadians agreed with what was perceived as a further dismantling of central authority in favour not merely of Quebec but of all the provinces. The poorer have-not provinces—led by Manitoba, New Brunswick, and eventually Newfoundland—were concerned that few new federal programs would be mounted if the richer provinces had the option of receiving federal funds for their own programs. Other collectivities, such as Aboriginal peoples and women, worried that their rights were being bartered away to the provinces. Across the country, suggested revisions sprung up almost like grass, many of them offering structural panaceas, such as a reformed and more effective Senate.

As the deadline for acceptance loomed, only Manitoba and Newfoundland held out, the latter having rescinded an earlier legislative endorsement after Brian Peckford's Tories were defeated by the Liberals under Clyde Wells (b. 1937). Prime Minister Mulroney, drawing on his experience as a private-sector negotiator, called the premiers and other provincial political leaders into closed-door sessions designed to shame them into support on the eve of the deadline.

This tactic appeared to work, but in Manitoba, Cree leader and NDP MLA Elijah Harper (b. 1949) objected to the Accord on the grounds that it neglected Aboriginal people. Harper delayed debate on the Accord, preventing the legislature from voting to ratify it before the deadline. Since Manitoba was not going to approve, Newfoundland's Wells backed off from a previous commitment to gain his province's legislative endorsement. In the end, the two provinces refused endorsement and Meech Lake failed. Ominously, in the last days before the deadline, several Conservative MPs from Quebec, led by Minister of the Environment Lucien Bouchard (b. 1938), left the government to form a pro-separatist Bloc Québécois. In the post-mortems on Meech Lake, a

Not One of the Boys

Manitoba Liberal leader Sharon Carstairs had been one of the few consistent outspoken critics of the Meech Lake Accord. In June of 1990, with the deadline for ratification swift approaching, she was a member of an all-party delegation from Manitoba invited to Ottawa. There, she claimed, she was brow-beaten and lied to in order to get her support for Meech Lake, which she reluctantly gave. Her problems in Ottawa were nothing, however, in comparison with her problems when she returned to Manitoba, as she describes in this excerpt from her memoirs.

We arrived in Winnipeg in time for the sunrise. . . . After I had completed a scrum, Al Munroe, who had, of course, come to the airport to meet me, drove me home. . . . At the caucus meeting at 11:00 that morning, when I began to tell everyone about the worst week of my life, I broke down. I struggled to gain control but it was difficult. I realized that most of my colleagues were confused. . . . Several days later when I was somewhat restored, owing to a mild tranquillizer prescribed by Dr Gulzar Cheema, I was in the CBC studio having my make-up done prior to an interview when Mike McCourt dropped by to see me. McCourt was at this time the co-host of '24 Hours', the local 6:00 p.m. news show. Mike is a friend of both Otto Lang and Adrian Macdonald. He and his wife Lorraine had been at our home, and John [her husband] and I at theirs. When he asked me how I was doing I took it as a friendly question and not the question of a news reporter. I replied I was doing okay, nothing that a few tranquillizers and some sleep wouldn't cure.

A week later, long after I had stopped taking the pills, Mike McCourt conducted a series of interviews with the three leaders [Filmon, Doer, and Carstairs] about the impact of Meech week on us. One of my questions was, in paraphrase, 'I understand, Mrs Carstairs, you took some tranquillizers.' I suppose I could have lied, but that is not my style. Besides, I thought it important that the people of Manitoba understand in full the impact of that week on all of us. I suspect if I had said I had had a few stiff drinks no one would have looked askance. But somehow or other my use of tranquillizers, coupled with the fact that I was a woman, had a negative impact the likes of which I could not possibly have imagined. To be fair to Mike McCourt, I do not think he thought his remark would raise the question of my suitability for public life. It was clear, however, that there was a double standard at play here. When Pamela Wallin had asked John Turner, several years before, if he had a drinking problem, within days the story had turned from Turner's response to the acceptability of Wallin asking the question. No one in the media questioned the acceptability of Mike McCourt asking his question. During the same interview I also expressed the feeling that I was not sure I wanted to remain in public life. Again this was seen as a weakness on my part, and the phrase 'If you can't stand the heat get out of the kitchen' surfaced. I was dismayed by this reaction, and sick at heart.

It was not that I could not stand the heat; my diary for the week shows me at work every day and attending three or four events as well. I was simply not sure I wanted to remain in a profession where the ethics, in my opinion, had reached an all-time low. The NDP, in the election campaign to follow, actually broadcast a television ad with a woman answering, in response to a question, that she did not think she could vote for a woman who couldn't make up her mind whether to remain in public life or not.

Source: Sharon Carstairs, *Not One of the Boys* (Toronto: Macmillan Canada, 1993), 164–6.

number of points stood out. One was that after 1987 the popular support for Brian Mulroney (and the federal PCs) and Meech Lake had declined together. Quebec understandably interpreted the mounting hostility to Meech Lake in English-speaking Canada as directed specifically against the 'distinct society', but the fact was that most Canadians appeared to be prepared to allow Quebec its autonomy. What people objected to was the extension of that autonomy to the other provinces, a process that would balkanize the nation. Moreover, Elijah Harper's action called attention to Meech Lake's incompatibility with the collective rights recognized by the Canadian Charter. During the summer of 1990 the failure of Meech Lake was followed by an extremely nasty confrontation between Aboriginal peoples in Quebec, led by the Mohawks of Oka, and the Bourassa government. Bourassa called in the federal armed forces, as he had done in the October Crisis of 1970.

The crushing defeat in early September 1990 of one of the main supporters of Meech Lake, Premier David Peterson of Ontario, by the NDP led by Bob Rae (b. 1948) was perhaps another straw in the wind. Certainly the NDP's achievement of power (for the first time) in Ontario suggested that there might be a resurgence of the left. The NDP's victory proved illusory, as it was based chiefly on hostility to Peterson's government. Subsequent 1991 NDP victories in British Columbia and Saskatchewan only demonstrated the electorate's discontent and the NDP's inability to establish a new political paradigm.

The federal government spent most of 1991 attempting to figure out how to allow for 'democratic input' into the process of constitutional revision. The Mulroney administration was far too unpopular simply to force through legislation. Public hearings were followed by weekend conferences, none of which provided much direction. Canada had no tradition of consultative reform. In the end, another series of closed-door meetings between Ottawa and the anglophone provinces, subsequently joined by Quebec in August 1992 at Charlottetown, produced a revised package. This one offered Quebec a distinct society, the provinces a veto, the Aboriginal peoples self-government, and the country reform of both the

NDP MLA Elijah Harper sits in the Manitoba legislature holding an eagle feather for spiritual strength as he continues to delay debate on the Meech Lake Accord, 19 June 1990. The Canadian Press/Wayne Glowacki.

Supreme Court and the Senate. The nation voted on the package in a referendum on 26 October 1992, the day after the Toronto Blue Jays won the World Series. (The World Series was named after the New York newspaper the *World* and had no international implications.) To the simultaneous amusement and consternation of Canadians, in the opening ceremonies, the United States Marine Corps had inadvertently carried the Canadian flag upside down. The eventual victory sparked an outpouring of Canadian nationalism across the country. Some commentators openly feared for a country that could find togetherness only by celebrating the success of a collection of highly paid foreign athletes. How the win factored into the referendum is not known.

Six provinces (including Quebec) voted 'No'. The national totals were 44.8 per cent in favour of the agreement and 54.2 against (see Table 11.1). Polls indicated that Charlottetown failed because the majority of Canadians regarded the agreement as a

Table 11.1	Results by Province of the 26 October 1992 Referendum on the Charlottetown Accord	
Province/Territory	Percentage Yes	Percentage No
Newfoundland	62.9	36.5
Nova Scotia	48.5	51.1
Prince Edward Island	73.6	25.9
New Brunswick	61.3	38.0
Quebec	42.4	55.4
Ontario	49.8	49.6
Manitoba	37.9	61.7
Saskatchewan	45.5	55.1
Alberta	39.6	60.2
British Columbia	31.9	67.8
Northwest Territories	60.2	39.0
Yukon	43.4	56.1
National	44.8	54.2

increasingly widened the meaning of Aboriginal rights. These rights fall into several categories. The first are those rights that Aboriginal peoples have as a result of having been the first inhabitants of North America, and are usually called 'Aboriginal rights'. These include rights to land that the First Nations have occupied since before European intrusion, and a right to self-government. There are also 'treaty rights', which result from specific written arrangements between European governments, especially the British government and its Canadian successor, and First Nations peoples. Since the first arrival of the Europeans, treaties have been negotiated, chiefly to extinguish Native title to much of the land of North America. Aboriginal and treaty rights were entrenched without specifics in the Constitution Act of 1982 and in its Charter of Rights and Freedoms. This entrenchment has led the Canadian courts to become much more aggressive in defining and defending Aboriginal rights, especially in comparison with the American courts. The Canadian public

bad one. Poorer provinces favoured Charlottetown, while poorer, younger, and less well-educated Canadians opposed it. According to one poll, household income of $60,000 per year was the economic cutoff between 'Yes' and 'No', while a university degree was the educational one. Most of those who voted 'No' believed that their vote would have no negative consequences for the nation. Perhaps.

The Rise of Aboriginal Rights

The various debates over the Constitution and the Charter of Rights encouraged the emergence of new players and new issues in the constitutional mix. One of the most important new issues involved the Aboriginal peoples of the nation, who counted for over a million Canadians by 1991 and, with a very high birth rate, represented the most rapidly growing sector of the Canadian population.

Since Confederation, most First Nations have been paternally governed under the Indian Act. Beginning in the 1970s, the First Nations have

Table 11.2	Aboriginal and Métis People in Canada, by Province, 1991 Census	
Province	Aboriginals	Métis
Nfld	5,846	1,600
PEI	1,665	185
NS	19,950	1,590
NB	11,835	980
Quebec	112,590	19,475
Ontario	220,140	26,905
Manitoba	76,375	45,580
Sask.	69,390	32,840
Alberta	99,655	56,305
BC	140,570	22,290
Yukon	5,875	565
NWT	11,095	4,320
Total	783,980	212,650*

*This official figure probably under-represents the total by as much as 200,000.

Source: Statistics Canada.

has had great difficulty in understanding the concept of Aboriginal rights, although the ongoing saga is regularly reported in the media.

Aboriginal Title

In some parts of Canada, notably Labrador, northern Quebec, the Far North, and most of mainland British Columbia, historic land cession treaties were never negotiated, and consequently the Native peoples of these areas had no ascribed treaty rights and were in effect squatters on their own land. In 1969 Frank Calder of the Nisga'a people brought a court action before the British Columbia court, claiming Aboriginal title to 1,000 square miles in northwestern British Columbia. The case eventually reached the Supreme Court of Canada, which upheld a BC finding against Calder on a technicality. But despite the seeming defeat, the Supreme Court had agreed with Calder that there were such things as Aboriginal rights and title. As one of the judges wrote in his decision, 'The fact is that when the settlers came the Indians were there, organized in societies and occupying the land as their forefathers had done for centuries. This is what Indian title means' (quoted in Dickason with McNab, 2009: 325). Aboriginal title came up again in *Guerin v. the Queen* (1985), where the Supreme Court insisted that Aboriginal title predated European occupation and thus served as a check on the Crown's right to deal with lands. The recognition of Aboriginal title was temporarily set back by a decision of the BC Supreme Court in 1991 in the Gitksan–Wet'suwet'en case. Here Justice Allan McEachern rejected the claim to title, partly on the grounds of the absence of proper evidence. The judge did not regard Native oral history as sufficient, although he ruled that the plaintiffs had unextinguished non-exclusive Aboriginal rights, other than right of ownership. This ruling left major questions unresolved for several years.

The Economy

One of the many reasons for the failure of Keynesian economics was that after 1972 the system no longer worked according to its rules. Government management, even wage and price controls, could not prevent runaway inflation, high interest rates, high levels of unemployment, and substantial poverty. With the manufacturing economies of the industrialized world fully recovered and new competition from the industrializing world emerging daily, Canadian manufacturing was in serious structural trouble. So, too, were the farmers and the fishers. Symptomatically, the government's complex attempt, after 1973, to create a new national energy policy—based on a federally owned petroleum company to be called Petro-Canada—created only controversy.

As usual, Canadians had trouble understanding the intersection of international and domestic economic problems. They sought a reassuring way of comprehending their difficulties, for the notion that the country was internationally uncompetitive could not be seriously entertained. There were several potential scapegoats at hand. The bankers could have been blamed for the interest rates, or the businessmen for the unemployment. Instead, the country chose to fasten on the most visible and immediate of the trinity of troublesome indicators—inflation—and on a single factor to explain it. Polls taken in 1975 indicated that Canadians were willing to believe that the chief culprits on the inflation front were too-powerful labour unions demanding unreasonable wage settlements. Labour unions were understandably attempting to protect their members in the context of the new economic situation. They wanted wage increases to keep pace with inflation and opposed management efforts to rationalize or modernize their workforces through layoffs or by getting rid of redundancies. Strikes in many industries, including a much-publicized postal strike in the summer of 1975, made the demands of labour appear unreasonable. When police, firefighters, nurses, and teachers began taking similar steps, Canadians became alarmed. Not only were key public services threatened with interruption, but wage settlements in the public sector would have to be financed either with higher taxes or with deficit spending.

Although the extent of government deficits would not become a major public issue until later, by the early 1970s all levels of Canadian government were well into deficit financing. High interest rates made the government debt much more expensive to service. The economic problems of the period set into motion a series of automatic mechanisms, built into the social services safety net, that greatly increased public expenditures. Even without those economic problems, spending on social services constantly escalated according to some mysterious law of increased demand and expectation. The propensity to expand the civil service had its own logic. A variety of conservative economists now appeared to criticize the government's spending principles. Like the public, Pierre Trudeau's federal Liberals talked about the need for structural reform of the economy, but they were unable to confront the problems before the dangers posed by the PQ victory led to a renewed concern with the Constitution. Like all other governments around the world, Ottawa continued to spend more than it collected in taxes and revenue. In 1970 the per capita debt figure of the Canadian government was $795. By 1990 it was $14,317. Between 1981 and 1990, the total debt of the federal government soared from $100 billion to $380 billion. The last budget surplus had been in fiscal 1972–3.

Not surprisingly, the deficit was used as a weapon by conservatives opposed to the continued expansion of social assistance. These critics—headed by spokesmen for the business community—insisted that increases in social assistance programs were largely responsible for the problem, and they maintained that a balanced budget could be achieved only by making deep cuts in such programs. In reality, the deficit was caused mainly by the same people who worried most about it. Concern about deficits was accompanied by fear of runaway inflation, and the war against inflation was waged chiefly by the Bank of Canada through its control of interest rates. High interest rates created substantial unemployment, which in turn meant reductions in income tax revenues and increased expenditures on unemployment insurance and welfare. According to one economist, almost two-thirds of the 1992 deficit was caused by lost tax revenues from unemployment and increased costs of social assistance; the remainder was the result of high interest payments to creditors. A team of economists at the University of Toronto examined the reasons for the 1989–92 recession in Canada. They concluded that the chief factor was the Bank of Canada's consistent anti-inflationary/high interest policies. Many Canadians had been convinced by neo-liberal politicians and pundits, however, that dismantling the welfare state was the only way to deal with huge budgetary deficits. At the same time, most public opinion polls indicated that the vast majority of the electorate was not eager to surrender their social benefits.

Like the government, the Canadian consumer lived increasingly in Tomorrowland. Canadian consumer debt more than doubled in the 1980s, increasing in small but steady stages from 18.7 per cent of personal income to over 20 per cent. Much of that debt was incurred through the medium of

Table 11.3   Federal Government Debt (million dollars)

Dates	Net Federal Debt	Gross Federal Debt	Marketable Bonds	Treasury Bills	Savings Bonds	Other Securities	Pension Plans	Other Liabilities
					Components of the Gross Debt			
1866–7	76	93	69	—	—	—	—	24
1917–18	1,192	1,863	1,428	75	—	—	5	355
1949–50	11,645	16,723	12,882	450	891	850	175	1,475
1974–5	23,958	55,289	14,490	5,360	12,915	51	12,378	9,825
1983–4	162,250	210,841	58,994	41,700	38,204	3,228	37,988	30,727
1990–1	385,047	443,278	147,104	139,150	34,444	4,514	74,807	43,259

Source: *Canada Year Book 1994* (Ottawa: Statistics Canada, 1994), 304. Adapted from Statistics Canada, *Canada Year Book*, Catalogue 11-402, 1994, p. 304.

plastic credit cards. In the last year of the decade alone, the number of bank credit-card transactions increased from just over 100 billion to 150 billion. Residential mortgage debt nearly tripled. Over 10 years Canadian personal consumer debt (including mortgages) increased from 54.1 per cent of disposable personal income to 71.7 per cent, despite heavier taxes and truly debilitating interest rates.

Despite its talk of privatization, such as selling the assets of the Canada Development Investment Corporation, the Mulroney government backed away from an open confrontation with the welfare system. Instead, it took back benefits (such as the family allowance) from those with higher incomes and concentrated on increasing revenue through improving economic prosperity. The main vehicle for this increased prosperity was to be a new economic relationship with Canada's largest trading partner, the United States. The eventual Free Trade Agreement, characteristically negotiated in secret during 1986 and 1987, ran to 3,000 pages of legal technicalities. Tariffs would gradually be removed, leaving Canadians astonished to discover that tariffs were not much responsible for the disparity between what goods cost in American and Canadian stores. Canadians were equally surprised to find that 'free trade' did *not* apply to ordinary people shopping in the United States and returning to Canada with their purchases. The national debate over the deal generated little useful information. Not even the economic experts could safely predict the ultimate effects of the treaty, although most orthodox economists favoured it in principle. Some critics complained that the Canadian negotiators had gained less than useful access to the American market in return for continental economic integration. This was a futile argument, since most of that integration had already occurred. Only a fraction of total Canadian–American trade was actually affected by the treaty.

The most telling criticism was that the Free Trade Agreement did *not* revolutionize Canadian–American economic relations. Instead, the FTA was merely a cosmetic overhaul of the existing continental arrangement. Including the Mexicans in the North American Free Trade Agreement, which took effect in 1994, was potentially more significant, but

many observers could see few advantages to Canada in an economic partnership with a nation possessing a lower standard of living and cheaper labour.

After 1975 the Canadian economy more or less settled down to rates of unemployment, inflation, interest charges, housing costs, and taxation that would have previously been regarded as disastrous. Only food costs remained unaffected, which was not good news for the farmer. Indeed, agriculture re-emerged as a major economic problem for the nation. Despite quotas and marketing boards, the Canadian farmer continued to produce more than the market could consume, especially when that market was also being supplied by American farmers. No Canadian doubted that farmers were part of the backbone of Canadian society, but it was also obvious that farmers were leaving their farms in droves, both because they could not make a decent living and because of the continued attractions of the city's amenities. The government preferred financial assistance for farmers to higher food prices. The problem was that not all farmers would be supported. In 1986 Agriculture Canada admitted that its solution to the 'farm problem' was to encourage thousands of marginal farmers—perhaps up to 20 per cent of the total—to leave the business. To state openly that there were too many farmers was to play with political dynamite. That the government did so was a graphic illustration of how much the nation had changed since Confederation, which had been conceived in part to allow Canada to open a new agricultural frontier.

Although the opposition in Parliament wanted to know how the 'one-in-five' farmer would be chosen for elimination, there was no mystery about who was most at risk: younger entrant farmers, any farmer heavily in debt, and any 'inefficient' farmer. These categories were often mutually reinforcing. Young farmers often had to buy their land at inflated prices. To be efficient they needed to borrow money at high rates of interest in order to buy expensive equipment and machinery. When farm commodity prices turned downward, many farmers were in serious trouble, although it must be added that the costs of modern farming increasingly made it an uneconomic proposition for most farmers. The solution—significantly higher prices for farm crops—was simply not popular. Canadians were willing to pay increasing sums for more convenient packaging and marketing of the food they ate but were not prepared to put more money into the pocket of the farmer.

There were economic slowdowns in the early 1980s and early 1990s. From the standpoint of its conservative intentions, the welfare state worked. In both slowdowns the social protection apparatus clicked in, and while more families fell below the poverty line, there were few demonstrations in the streets. Canadians became conscious that jobs were harder to get and harder to keep. The young responded to the lack of jobs by seeking further education in courses that promised some immediate economic payoff, but they did not become radicalized. Perhaps they were too busy working to keep up the payments on their credit cards.

Canadian Society

A number of social trends characterized Canadian society in the 1970s and 1980s. One was a constant increase in the traditional indicators of 'instability'—divorce, suicide, rape, crime, and sexually transmitted diseases. Canada seemed to be coming apart socially as well as constitutionally and economically. Another trend was an increase in abuse (often violent) of others and extreme self-indulgence, both products of alienation. These trends were also linked to the power of the media, which on the one hand publicized what had long been occurring beneath the surface, and on the other hand produced new consumer fads, fashions, and even needs. A third trend involved the baby-boom generation, which was coming up to early retirement in the 1990s, at which point they would aggravate a fourth trend, the increasingly rapid growth in numbers of elderly Canadians. A final development of the era was the increased visibility of racial minorities, resulting in new social problems.

In 1974 a study found that suicide had become Canada's fifth-ranked cause of 'early death' (i.e., death between the ages of one and 70). Suicide rates continued to rise, and were especially serious among young males in general and young Aboriginal

males in particular, reaching epidemic proportions in some communities. A 1984 National Task Force on Suicide in Canada indicated that the causes were 'complex and multifactorial', adding that 'interprovincial studies appear to show that there has been a change in the contemporary fabric of society with lessened self-restraints and lowered morals (anomie). This coincides with a period of expanding economy, greater affluence as a whole, high-technology industrialization, and increased unemployment' (National Task Force on Suicide in Canada, 1984: 9). A similar explanation could have been advanced for many of Canada's 'morbidities'.

Another set of rising statistics related to crimes of violence against the person. From 1982 to 1987 crimes against property increased 0.1 per cent, while crimes of violence increased 30.1 per cent. On 23 June 1985, an Air India jet carrying mainly Canadian passengers exploded in mid-air over Ireland, victim of a bomb. Despite the suspicions, charges were not actually laid against Sikh extremists until 15 years later. From 1987 to 1991 violent offences increased another 29.8 per cent, while total criminal offences increased by only 11.5 per cent. On 6 December 1989 a lone gunman, apparently a misogynist, killed 14 female engineering students at the École Polytechnique in Montreal. This horrifying event occurred near the close of a year in which, according to one estimate, over 32,000 Canadian women had been raped. The number of divorces had been 32,389 in 1972, rising to 90,985 in 1987 before beginning to decline slightly in numbers. By the late 1980s it was estimated that well over half of all Canadian children born after 1980 would at some point experience life in a broken home. As divorce increased, marriage declined. Moreover, the number of common-law relationships more than doubled between 1981 and 1991.

The incidence of racial and sexual abuses of various kinds appeared to increase dramatically. The general professional consensus was that abuse had not become more common but that it was now more likely to be reported. Racial and sexual abuses that might have gone unrecorded in previous generations were now openly publicized. Wifebeating—for decades the most common domestic crime on the police blotter—became a matter of public concern. Not surprisingly, much of the abuse was directed against the less powerful—children, women, Aboriginal peoples, and visible minorities—by traditional authority figures ranging from fathers to pastors to teachers to policemen and judges. On one level it was possible to take solace in the fact that such improper behaviour was now being addressed. On another it was possible to argue that what had changed was not so much the behaviour of people in authority as society's willingness to tolerate the excesses of this type of behaviour. Both the extent of the abuse and the undermining of authority to which it contributed were distressing. Canadians could no longer believe that they were all good guys living in the Peaceable Kingdom, nor could they continue to believe in the inherent beneficence of authority figures or in the fairness of the Canadian judicial system.

The revelations of the post-1972 period, particularly in the 1980s, could only contribute to a growing national mood of sullen cynicism with regard to authority, which was hardly appeased by the unimaginative and self-seeking behaviour of the politicians. No institution proved itself above reproach, and all institutions demonstrated their willingness to cover up their inadequacies and failures. Some of the most shocking revelations came from Newfoundland, where a provincial inquiry in 1989 brought to light evidence of the sexual abuse of children by priests and brothers of the Roman Catholic Church at the Mount Cashel Orphanage. Such evidence was soon augmented by material indicating that the clergy of all the major denominations had been abusing Aboriginal children for years in residential schools and orphanages. The situation was not improved by the discovery that the Canadian system of justice was hardly very just, at least not when it came to Aboriginal people or accused murderers. The ways in which the system failed Donald Marshall, who

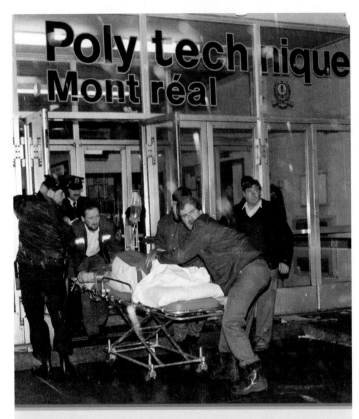

An injured person is wheeled out of the École Polytechnique in Montreal after a lone gunman, Marc Lapine, opened fire on 6 December 1989, killing 14 female students. The Canadian Press/Shaney Komulainen.

served 11 years in prison for a murder he did not commit, were particularly instructive in this regard.

Even the Red Cross, previously a model of institutional altruism, proved susceptible to incompetence and cover-up. The Canadian Red Cross had managed Canada's blood supply service since 1947, but the relationship between the government and the Red Cross had never been clearly defined. It remained unclear what government agency was responsible for assuring the safety of the blood supply, and for this reason it was difficult for the government to respond to problems when they emerged. In the late 1970s and early 1980s there were blood shortages in some parts of Canada, and this made the Red Cross reluctant to introduce screening measures that might further reduce the supply. As a consequence, the Canadian blood transfusion service in the early 1980s was sometimes (if infrequently) using blood

Air India Flight 182

This flight involved a Boeing 747–237B airplane registered to Air India named 'Emperor Kanishka', flying from Montreal/Mirabel International Airport to London Heathrow Airport and on to Palam International Airport in Delhi and Sahar International Airport in Bombay (Mumbai). It carried 307 passengers, including 82 children. Most of them were Canadians. It also carried a crew of 22. Flying over the Atlantic Ocean off the south coast of Ireland on 23 June 1985, the airplane was ripped open by the explosion of a bomb in the luggage compartment. It crashed into the sea. Not all of the bodies could be recovered, but autopsies on those that were indicated that some passengers had drowned. The bombing was the largest multiple murder in Canada's history, and the most serious terrorist incident employing aircraft anywhere in the world before 11 September 2001. Another bomb at the same time went off in Narita Airport in Japan, unloaded from a flight originating in Canada, but killed only two baggage handlers. The Canadian government had been warned by India of possible terrorist bombings on Air India flights, but there were no special security measures in place for the flight.

The chief suspects in the bombing were members of a Sikh separatist group named the Babbar Khalsa, several of whom were already under surveillance by the Canadian Security Intelligence Service (CSIS). Late in 1985 two members of Babbar Khalsa were arrested and charged by the RCMP with weapons offences, but no link to the Air India incident was established at the time. In 1991 one Sikh was convicted on charges relating to the Narita bombing, but no arrests were made in the Flight 182 bombing until 27 October 2000, when two men were charged with 329 counts of first-degree murder and other lesser offences. The chief witness against these men was the Sikh convicted in 1991, but at the subsequent trial he insisted he could not remember the events; he was later charged with perjury. The trial began in April 2003 and the verdict was delivered on 16 March 2005. Justice Ian Josephson declared at that time that the standard of proof beyond reasonable doubt was not met by the Crown, and the defendants were therefore not guilty.

The bombing demonstrated how lax security was at most airports and how easy it was for terrorists to be successful, but it was treated for many years as a one-time incident by most Canadians rather than as a harbinger of the future. For its part, the subsequent attempt to bring those responsible for the crime to justice demonstrated how difficult it was to gather and present incontrovertible and untainted evidence acceptable in court in such cases. A long overdue inquiry into the bombing, led by former Supreme Court Justice John Major, reported in mid-2010 on the woeful series of security failures leading up to and in the aftermath of the attack, and in June 2010, on the twenty-fifth anniversary of the tragedy, Prime Minister Stephen Harper issued a formal apology to the relatives of those killed.

---

infected both with the human immunodeficiency virus (HIV) and with infectious hepatitis C. Much of the infected blood was given to hemophiliacs, who because of their medical condition require a constant series of transfusions. Approximately 1,200 people were infected with HIV and 12,000 with hepatitis C through blood transfusions before the Red Cross introduced security measures to test for these viruses in 1985. Even after bringing the system back under control, it would take another dozen years to establish why the problem had occurred in the first place, as both government and Red Cross officials attempted to avoid the possible imputations of responsibility.

Other forms of abuse were self-inflicted, often related to short-term gratification without regard for

Table 11.4 Offences by Type, 1987–1991

Type	1987	1988	1989	1990	1991	Percentage change, rate/100,000 1987–91
Violent offences	219,381	232,606	248,579	269,381	296,680	+29.8%
Property offences	1,468,591	1,457,361	1,443,048	1,551,278	1,726,226	+12.8%
Other offences	1,276,036	1,265,861	1,300,005	1,343,397	1,470,454	+10%
Total	2,960,908	2,955,828	2,992,632	3,164,056	3,440,671	+11.5%

Source: Adapted from *Canada Year Book 1994* (Ottawa: Statistics Canada Catalogue no. 11–402, 1994), 222.

long-term consequences. The availability of drugs continued to increase steadily. Alcohol abuse continued unabated, along with substance abuse of many descriptions, including gasoline sniffing; and the use of steroids by athletes became common. Canada's most notorious substance abuser was the Olympic sprinter Ben Johnson (b. 1961), whose gold medal at Seoul in 1988 was ignominiously stripped from him for using steroids. Johnson initially denied the charge but eventually had to acknowledge his guilt at a well-publicized public inquiry. The most dangerous drug of all was tobacco. Canadian adults, reflecting the health consciousness of the baby boomers, led the way internationally in quitting smoking during the late 1980s. The young, however, remained undeterred by cigarette prices, which were often in excess of $6 per pack. One calculation revealed that tobacco would ultimately kill eight times as many 15-year-olds as automobile accidents, suicide, murder, AIDS, and drug abuse combined. Self-inflicted abuse was part of the new world of self-indulgence. Those who made their way to the top could reward themselves with luxuries and expensive toys. Sniffing cocaine became an indulgence of choice among the affluent. As for the poor, they had access to little pleasure that was not addictive and physically harmful.

Because AIDS is mainly a sexually transmitted disease, with a high incidence among homosexuals and the sexually adventurous, it became a favourite target for moralists in the 1980s. Many concerns were expressed that AIDS would encourage a judgemental response from Canadians with regard to both homosexuality and sexual freedom, but these concerns were not borne out in the available survey literature.

While surveys indicated that relatively few Canadians were morally judgemental, they also demonstrated much ignorance about AIDS and its prevention. Moreover, Canadians responded far less vigorously to the fear of infection than one might have expected, given the media attention AIDS received. In one Canadian study in 1989, for example, 63 per cent of those questioned knew that sexual intercourse was the most common way of becoming infected with AIDS, and about half identified homosexuals as the people most likely to become infected. Virtually everybody (90 per cent) believed that the best prevention was safe sex. Eighty-one per cent of those surveyed regarded having sex with one partner in a long-term relationship as a 'very effective' means of prevention, while 78 per cent considered complete sexual abstinence 'very effective'. Only 41 per cent rated condoms a 'very effective' method of protection against AIDS. At the same time, however, only 54 per cent of male and 41 per cent of female respondents said they had changed their sexual behaviour because of the risk of AIDS infection; truly safe sex was far from the Canadian norm. Not only did large numbers of respondents take no precautions, but the study suggested a tendency, particularly among males, for people with more knowledge of AIDS to take greater risks. Other studies suggested that only about half of Canadians between 15 and 19 years of age thought they were at risk from sexually transmitted disease, and thus about half of this age group presumably took no precautions. Chlamydia became far more common than AIDS among the young.

In many ways the post-1970 era was dominated by the baby-boom generation. Before 1970 the boomers had their chief impact on the educational system.

Donald Marshall Jr

Donald Marshall Jr (1953–2009) was born at Sydney, Nova Scotia. In late May 1971 he was arrested after a black companion named Sandy Seale was fatally stabbed while the two youths crossed a park late at night. A Mi'kmaq, Marshall had a reputation as a troublemaker. The Sydney police ignored contradictory evidence and testimony, and defence counsel did not bring them out at the trial. Marshall was convicted of murder and sentenced to life imprisonment. The police subsequently ignored evidence that a man named Roy Ebsary had committed the crime, and the Department of the Attorney General of Nova Scotia ignored evidence of judicial error because the defence had not raised the question. Marshall spent 11 years in prison, during which time his case was re-examined on three separate occasions before he was finally released on bail by the Nova Scotia Court of Appeal. Marshall was subsequently forced to prove his innocence (not simply the lack of real evidence of his guilt) in court. The Court of Appeal in its acquittal insisted that 'any miscarriage of justice' was 'more apparent than real' because Marshall had told a variety of stories under police interrogation.

Marshall understandably did not feel fully exonerated, and with his lawyer's assistance pressed for a public inquiry into the affair. Eventually Roy Ebsary was convicted of the death of Sandy Seale, and in 1986 the Nova Scotia government launched a Royal Commission to examine the Marshall case. The Commission heard from more than 100 witnesses during hearings in Sydney and Halifax in 1987. Witnesses testified to a pattern of incompetence and cover-up extending over many years. The Commission concluded that Marshall had been let down by the criminal justice system at virtually every turn. The miscarriage of justice—which would have been easily correctable by proper and professional behaviour on the part of those involved—was in part due to the fact that Marshall was Aboriginal. The Royal Commission's 1989 report was itself criticized for refusing to single out those most responsible for the cover-up.

Like most victims of judicial abuse, Marshall attempted to keep a low profile following his complete exoneration. But in 1993 he was arrested and prosecuted on three charges under the Fisheries Act for catching eels during the closed season in Pomquet Harbour, Nova Scotia. His lawyers argued that Marshall believed he was exempt from the fishery regulations because of treaties between the Crown and the Mi'kmaq in 1760 and 1761. Marshall was found guilty, a verdict subsequently affirmed by the Nova Scotia Supreme Court. But in 1999, the Supreme Court of Canada acquitted him on appeal, ruling that Marshall had a treaty right to a 'moderate livelihood' from the natural resources of his region. This landmark decision led to tension, violent standoffs, and acrimony in some Maritime communities as Mi'kmaq lobster fishers sought to claim their 'treaty right' and non-Native fishers and Fisheries and Oceans officials sought to stop them.

Now they put pressure on the employment system not only by their sheer numbers but by their educational qualifications. Not all were able to get the jobs for which they had prepared. The tightness of the job market, combined with the increased consumer requirements of the boom generation, produced more childless working couples and further lowered fertility rates. By the 1980s the baby boomers' demand for detached housing drove up housing prices in most of the nation's larger cities. Even after the inevitable bust, prices could never return to previous levels. In cities of premium-priced housing (such as Toronto and Vancouver), it was estimated that less than a quarter of those seeking to purchase their first house could qualify for a mortgage. Many boomers had money to spend on nice things: 'My Tastes Are

Simple', read one popular bumper sticker, 'I Like the Best.' Marketing strategies to reach these consumers included slick magazines distributed free to homes in neighbourhoods with the appropriate demographics. Articles featured various aspects of affluent lifestyles—home (re)decorating, gourmet foods eaten at home or in restaurants, and luxury travel. The boomers continued their fascination with the 1950s and 1960s pop and rock music of their youth. The music nostalgia industry thrived. Radio stations that for decades had tried to appeal to the kids suddenly shifted their programming to the 'Golden Oldies' in a

Roberta Bondar

The space shuttle *Discovery* was launched on 22 January 1992. The first Canadian female astronaut recalls the launch.

We're going to do it! I wonder briefly whether I'll have to use any of my bail-out training. Even in this modest amount of light, the bail-out cue is visible, stuck on a mid-deck locker. It is awe-inspiring to be sitting here, looking at a checklist in this green glow. Just beyond my black boots that will protect my feet if things get out of hand, the cue card details two bail-out sequences. The only thing left to think about now is keeping the differences in the two scenarios, or modes, clear in my mind. In the first one—that's before the liftoff—I need to take off the chute before rolling out of the chair. If I have to use the 'Mode 1 pad egress' to get out in any emergency situation on the launch pad, it will be unassisted and will take place in the next three minutes. One more time through the checklist:

> Visor down and locked.
> Pull the green apple.
> Pull the quick-disconnect/lap belts.
> Release chute.
> Evacuate.
> Slide wire.

In the second bail-out sequence, after the launch, I keep the parachute on. It's so automatic now. One glance at the cue card, and I'll plug into the right escape mode.

Dr Roberta Bondar. Canadian Space Agency photo.

As we leave the Earth, I sing to myself:

O Canada,
Our home and native land!
True patriot love . . .

Source: Roberta Bondar, *Touching the Earth* (Toronto: Key Porter Books, 1994), 20–1. Reprinted with permission by Key Porter Books Ltd. Copyright © Roberta Bondar, 1994.

blatant attempt to capture the largest single audience segment: middle-aged baby boomers.

The progressive aging of the Canadian population was neither a new development of the post-1970 period nor a distinctly Canadian one. By 1991 life expectancy for Canadian men had reached 74 years and over 80 years for women. The leading causes of death in Canada were all diseases of the old. The emerging conception of a 'crisis' was primarily connected with what seemed to be the increased costs associated with the elderly—pensions and health care—in the welfare states of the advanced world. Part of the problem was that the proportion of the population who were productive members of the workforce able to finance the care of the aging was constantly declining. In 1983 in Canada there were 18 people over 65 years old for every 100 aged 18–64. One prediction suggested that there would be 52 people over 65 for every 100 between 18 and 64 by 2031.

Pensions had always been based on the notion that the working generation would support the retired one. One study in the mid-1980s argued that by the year 2021 the funds required for public pensions would be three and one-half times greater than in 1976, given the continuation of the 1976 level of payments. Without a high level of pension support, the elderly would become an even greater proportion of Canadians below the poverty line. In 1986, 46.1 per cent of unattached females over the age of 65 were below that level. Longer life obviously meant more demands on the health-care system,

culminating in the potential need for expensive nursing home facilities. In 1986, only 9 per cent of Canada's elderly could be accommodated in nursing homes. Studies demonstrated that the cost of medical care for the last year of life was substantially greater than for the entire earlier lifespan. The problem was to decide when the last year had come and what medical strategy to adopt.

The increased visibility of racial minorities was especially evident in the nation's larger cities, where they tended to congregate. This concentration only encouraged racism. Despite higher levels of media attention, government expenditure, and Aboriginal self-consciousness, the demographic realities of Native life, while improving, continued to recall conditions in nations generally regarded as the most backward on the planet. Infant mortality and overall death rates ran high. Conditions on many remote reserves continued to be absolutely deplorable. It was not surprising that many Aboriginals migrated to cities like Winnipeg, where they met considerable social disapproval.

One of the most significant developments for Aboriginal peoples was the Mackenzie Valley Pipeline Inquiry, which played out in the years 1974–7. Inquiry chairman Justice Thomas Berger completely rewrote the rules for such inquiries by taking his hearings to the people in remote communities who would be most affected by the proposed pipeline and by paying close attention to what they said, but he stamped on the public (and

Table 11.5 Leading Causes of Death, 1990				
	Male		Female	
	No.	Rate	No.	Rate
Diseases of the circulatory system	38,823	296.3	36,266	269.0
Cancer	28,865	220.3	23,560	174.8
Respiratory diseases	9,351	71.4	6,921	51.3
Accidents and adverse effects	9,064	69.2	3,993	29.6
Diseases of the digestive system	3,961	28.2	3,303	24.5
Endocrine diseases, etc.	2,533	19.3	2,939	21.8
Diseases of the nervous system	2,275	17.4	2,580	19.1
All other causes	9,358	71.2	8,434	62.7
Total, causes	104,230	793.3	87,996	652.8

political) consciousness that development had to take into account the needs of Native peoples in a more thoroughgoing manner than had previously been the case. His report even became a best-seller (Berger, 1977). This was, arguably, the watershed event that brought Aboriginal issues into broad public awareness. It certainly made it impossible for the politicians to ignore Aboriginal peoples just a few years later when it came to crafting the Charter.

Immigration

While the Canadian population continued to drift off the farms, westward, and into the cities and surrounding suburbs, because of declining birth rates it also became increasingly dependent for its growth on immigration. That inflow increased its shift from the highly industrialized and earlier preferred nations of Western Europe and North America that had once represented Canada's sources of newcomers. Canada was no longer a special land of opportunity for citizens of the European Community, who lived in economies as prosperous. The new immigrants were largely from Third World countries in Africa, the Caribbean, Latin America, and Asia. The shift was facilitated by the changes in Canadian immigration policy and procedures. In 1973, Hong Kong, the Philippines, Jamaica, Trinidad, and India appeared among the top 10 countries of origin for Canadian immigrants.

In 1975 Immigration Minister Robert Andras tabled another government discussion document in the House of Commons, the so-called 'Green Paper'. A special joint committee of the House of Commons and Senate held almost 50 public hearings across Canada on the Green Paper. The hearings seemed to confirm that Canadians wanted to continue accepting relatively large numbers of new immigrants but not to open the nation's doors to unrestricted admissions. The result of the national discussion was another major Immigration Act, that of 1976, which stated Canadian goals regarding immigration and insisted on the need to plan for the future. The Act recognized three classes of immigrants: the family class (relatives of Canadian residents), the humanitarian class (refugees and displaced persons), and an independent class.

Immigration regulations were revised in 1978 to alter the points system by placing greater importance on practical experience and to change the refugee situation by creating a new program of refugee sponsorship. Most of the Vietnamese boat people, about 50,000, entered Canada under this plan between 1979 and 1984. Quebec was the only province to take full advantage of federal opportunities built into the legislation of 1976 and 1978 to assume new provincial powers in immigration matters. As a result, Quebec could now in practice select its own immigrants. Ontario and Nova Scotia also signed more limited immigration agreements with Ottawa. Whether or not Quebec could attract and hold its share of the immigration total was another matter entirely. Many immigrants were not enthusiastic about education in French for their children. Tough

By the mid-1980s, the majority of immigrants arriving in Canada came from countries in Asia. In this photo, a young Vietnamese boy waits with his family to be processed at an immigration centre in Montreal. © Owen Franken/Corbis.

language legislation led to considerable out-migration. Fewer francophones came to Quebec.

By the mid-1980s the traditional sources for Canadian immigrants were producing only about 30 per cent of the total and their share continued to drop. Moreover, the pattern was shifting simultaneously in other ways as well. Asia continued to be the principal supplier of immigrants. But the number of people from the Caribbean area increased and those from Central and South America continued to come, as did those coming from the Middle East and Africa. The 1980s also witnessed the rise again of the refugee question, both internationally and in Canada. Between the end of World War II and the new Immigration Act of 1978, more than 300,000 refugees—mainly European but including 7,000 Ugandan Asians in 1971 and 7,000 Chileans in 1973—had been admitted to Canada under the relaxation of formal regulations. Those fleeing strife and disasters came to Canada in increasing numbers, occasionally by unusual means, such as the lifeboat loads of Tamils who were picked up off the coast of Atlantic Canada in 1986. Debate over Canada's refugee admission policy after 1978 revolved around both overseas selection by visa and the issue of individuals already in Canada claiming refugee status without any previous processing or documentation (Dirks, 1995).

The visa question was an old one. The Canadian government has long tried to insist on proper visas for those entering the country. This policy forms a preliminary screen for identifying arrivals (immigrants or not) undesirable on medical or security grounds. When people applying for entry into Canada have visas issued by Canadian officials at foreign posts, the immigration officers know they have been pre-screened. Demand for visas for all visitors grew after the increased number of terrorist activities around the world beginning in the 1960s. The crash of an Air India airliner in 1985, in which Canadian authorities suspected that a bomb had been planted in Vancouver airport, reminded Canada of the problem. Despite its obvious advantages, however, insistence on visas has always been contentious in Canada for several reasons. First, political refugees may not have proper documentation and may be unable to get it. Humanitarian organizations in Canada vehemently opposed insisting on proper documentation for all visitors and immigrants. Second, visas may be hard to obtain in countries in which the Canadian presence is fairly limited. To get a visa may require lengthy travel to a national capital, for example, or even outside the country. As was well known, Canada used an absence of official presence as one way to reduce applications for immigration from some places. This was certainly the case for a country like Guyana. As a result, Canada in the 1980s did not insist on a strictly enforced visa policy. One of the most serious problems was caused by visitors who outstayed their permitted period for visits. Some suspected that these overstays were a way for people to get around the screening mechanisms. Nationals from some countries for which Canada did not require visas, chiefly India, Portugal, and Guyana, were particularly likely to overstay. It should be emphasized that potential immigrants who were able to afford to come to Canada as visitors and then remain in the country claiming refugee status were not usually impoverished peasants, but rather highly skilled professionals. Their entrance into their professions in Canada was hampered both by their use of the refugee route and by the typical reluctance of Canadian professional organizations to recognize foreign education and experience.

A related question was whether people would be allowed to apply for permanent residence (i.e., formally become 'landed immigrants') from inside the country. This issue again criss-crossed the problem of controlling immigration and the related problem of determining refugee status. By the early 1970s there was a substantial backlog of appeals from rejected applicants for landed status from those within and without the country, and in 1972 the regulation permitting application from within Canada was rescinded. But it continued to be possible to remain in the country by special minister's permit, a procedure employed mainly for family members of residents for compassionate reasons. Moreover, the practice of allowing a determination of refugee status from within, made possible by the 1976 and 1978 Immigration Acts, became increasingly common. The machinery of refugee status determination had not been intended as a way for avoiding routine admission procedures, but this was what it became in the later 1970s and early 1980s. The number of refugee claimants totally clogged the immigration system. Altered American regulations in 1986, which granted amnesty to illegal immigrants who arrived in the US before 1982, subjected those after 1982 to threat of deportation. Many of those threatened hoped to come to Canada, posing an additional burden on the system. An 'amnesty' was declared in 1986, allowing almost all refugees resident in Canada—some 63,000—to remain in the country as residents. In 1987 the Mulroney government introduced new legislation to deal with the refugee situation, but by the time the revised system went into operation there was already another major backlog, with over 122,000 residents claiming refugee status. Many of these claims were regarded by the authorities as patently improper. However, those whose cases had not been heard could not work and their families often went on provincial and municipal welfare. Ultimately, clearing the backlog took over three years.

While it was claimed that Canada's record with refugees was one of the best in the world—the nation allowed more refugees relative to its own population to immigrate than any other nation—many critics insisted that it needed to do far more. Canada's behaviour towards refugees was increasingly contrasted with its policy towards rich business people. Beginning in 1986 individuals with substantial amounts of capital (initially $250,000, later reduced to $150,000) could invest this money in projects approved by provincial governments and thereby gain admission to Canada. This scheme was heavily criticized in many quarters on a variety of grounds, including the charge that the imported capital helped drive up the real estate markets in a few Canadian cities, such as Vancouver and Toronto.

By the 1990s many Canadians had become concerned about the new patterns of immigration, which could be seen as finally confirming popular fears and paranoia expressed over many years. By 1991, the European share of Canadian immigration was down to 20.2 per cent. Even with the addition of those coming from the United States, newcomers of European origin represented less than one-quarter of the total of 230,781. In 1991, Africa sent 7.2 per cent of the total,

Asia 53 per cent, the Caribbean area 8.2 per cent, and South America 4.5 per cent. The top 10 sources for immigrants to Canada between 1981 and 1991 had been, in order, Hong Kong, Poland, the People's Republic of China, India, the United Kingdom, Vietnam, the Philippines, the United States, Portugal, and Lebanon. As these statistics indicate, the number of people in the underdeveloped nations of the world seeking admission to Canada had increased, and doubtless would continue to increase.

Most people from the underdeveloped nations were visibly different from the majority of the host population in Canada. Many of the newcomers represented racial, religious, and cultural backgrounds considerably unlike those of the traditional Canadian population, producing considerable potential strains on Canadian society. People of Third World origin, who had represented less than 1 per cent of the Canadian population in 1967, by 1986 represented 4.6 per cent, and those from the Third World totalled 30 per cent of all foreign-born in Canada. Between 1981 and 1991, the number of followers of Islam in Canada grew from 98,165 to 253,260, the number of Buddhists from 51,955 to 163.415, and the number of Sikhs from 67,715 to 147,440. In a Canada of high structural unemployment (close to 10 per cent even in times of 'prosperity') the newcomers might take jobs away from Canadians, a continued public fear however often researchers and immigration experts insisted that it was a myth. Moreover, for better or worse, in terms of locating themselves geographically, the new immigrants behaved in many ways little different from earlier ones. They flocked to a few large Canadian cities, mainly in English-speaking Canada, eschewing rural areas, Atlantic Canada, and Quebec. In the 1993 federal election, at least one political party, the Reform Party, began to talk openly of closing the door to immigration. Few Canadians were prepared to go that far, but many were worried about how a fair and just immigration policy could be developed.

In 1993 the Liberal government of Jean Chrétien announced that it would maintain a Canadian immigration intake at about 1 per cent of the total Canadian population. The resulting annual immigration figures since that date have been more than 200,000, up from the figures of the 1970s and 1980s. Such an intake did not begin to satisfy the demands of people from around the world who wanted to immigrate to Canada. It did mean that Canadian society would never be suddenly overwhelmed by people of different backgrounds. Nevertheless, over a protracted period, these sorts of numbers—especially if they continued to come from the Third World—would have a profound cumulative effect on the makeup of the Canadian population, including the languages spoken in this officially 'bilingual' country, as shown in Table 11.7.

Table 11.6   Immigrants Arriving by Place of Birth, 1981–1990

Place	Number	Percentage
Europe	351,511	26.4
Great Britain	81,460	6.1
Portugal	38,630	2.9
France	15,256	1.1
Greece	6,884	0.5
Italy	11,196	0.8
Poland	81,361	6.1
Other	116,724	8.8
Africa	72,941	5.5
Asia	619,089	46.5
Philippines	67,682	5.1
India	90,050	6.8
Hong Kong	96,982	7.3
China	74,235	5.6
Middle East	90,965	6.8
Other	199,175	15.0
North & Central America	114,073	8.6
US	63,106	4.7
Other	50,967	3.8
Caribbean & Bermuda	89,908	6.7
Australasia	5,877	0.4
South America	67,936	5.1
Oceania	10,040	0.8
Other	375	
Total	2,416,423	

Source: *Canada Year Book 1994* (Ottawa: Statistics Canada, 1994), 116. Adapted from Statistics Canada, *Canada Year Book*, Catalogue 11-402, 1994, p. 116.

Table 11.7   Canadian Population by Mother Tongue, 1996 Census

Total Population	28,528,125
Single Responses	28,125,560
English	16,890.615
French	6,636,660
Non-official languages	4,598,290
Chinese	715,640
Italian	484,500
German	450,140
Polish	213,410
Spanish	212,890
Portuguese	211,290
Punjabi	201,785
Ukrainian	162,695
Arabic	148,555
Dutch	133,805
Tagalog	133,215
Greek	121,180
Vietnamese	106,515
Cree	78,840
Inuktitut	26,960
Other non-official languages	1,198,870
Multiple Responses	402,560
Eng. & French	107,945
Eng. & non-off. lang.	249,545
French & non-off. lang.	35,845
Eng., Fr., & non-off. lang.	9,225

Source: Adapted from Statistics Canada, 1996 Census, nation tables.

Canadian Culture

After 1972 Canadians discovered that culture had not only moral, intellectual, and aesthetic dimensions but powerful economic implications as well. Canadian bureaucrats began to talk about 'cultural industries' instead of just culture, measuring jobs and spinoffs as well as enlightenment. At about the same time, governments began to discover how much money they had been putting into various aspects of culture since the halcyon days of the 1950s and 1960s. An additional debate over cultural policy focused on how both to limit and to supplement the vast public expenditures on activities ranging from university research to art events. To the extent that it was regarded as a non-essential, culture was extremely vulnerable to budget-cutting. Canadian cultural policy was hotly debated, particularly since the politicians sought to use cultural policy to other ends, notably in the area of multiculturalism. The always artificial distinction between commercial and non-commercial culture had now been partially overcome by the inclusion of cultural enterprise in the economy. Thus popular culture (including sports) came to be more frequently recognized as a legitimate part of culture.

Certainly one of the defining events of a lifetime for many Canadians was the Canada–Russia hockey series of 1972. The largest television audience ever

Summary of Game Eight, Canada-USSR Hockey Series, 1972

CANADA 6 USSR 5

FIRST PERIOD

1. 3:34 USSR, Yakushev (Liapkin, Maltsev)
2. 6:45 Canada, P. Esposito (Park)
3. 13:10 USSR, Lutchenko (Kharlamov)
4. 16:59 Canada, Park (Ratelle, D. Hull)

SECOND PERIOD

5. 0:21 USSR, Shadrin
6. 10:32 Canada, White (Gilbert, Ratelle)
7. 11:43 USSR, Yakushev
8. 16:44 USSR, Vasiliev (Shadrin)

THIRD PERIOD

9. 2:27 Canada, P. Esposito (P. Mahovlich)
10. 12:56 Canada, Cournoyer (P. Esposito, Park)
11. 19:26 Canada, Henderson (P. Esposito)

Penalties

2:25 White (holding)
3:44 Petrov (hooking)
3:44 Petrov (holding)
4:10 Parisé (interference, 10 min., misconduct and game misconduct)
9:27 Ellis (interference)
9:27 Tzigankov (interference)
9:46 Petrov (interference)
12:51 Cournoyer (interference)

Penalties

14:58 Stapleton (crosschecking)
18:06 Kuzkin (elbowing)

Penalties

3:41 Mishakov (major, fighting)
3:41 Gilbert (major, fighting)
4:27 Vasiliev (tripping)
15:24 D. Hull (highsticking)
15:24 Petrov (elbowing)

SHOTS ON GOAL

Canada	14	8	14	36
USSR	12	10	5	27

Source: Jack Ludwig, *Hockey Night in Moscow* (Toronto: McClelland & Stewart, 1972), 178.

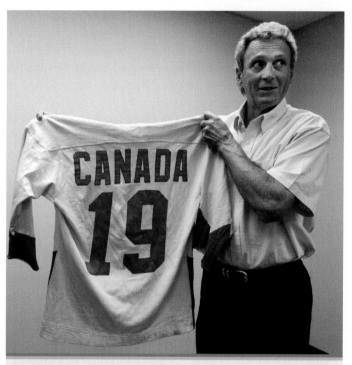

Paul Henderson holds up the hockey jersey he wore when he scored the game-winning goal in game eight of Canada–Russia Summit Series. The jersey was sold at auction for a record-breaking US$1,067,538 on 22 June 2010. Canadian Press/Nathan Denette.

entitled *Arts and Culture: A Statistical Profile* had estimated that in 1982 culture's share of the gross domestic product was $8 billion, calculated that there were 280,000 Canadian arts-related jobs in the 1981 census, and insisted that arts jobs were growing more quickly than the total labour force in all provinces. The 1986 Task Force on Funding in the Arts revised the economic dimensions of the cultural sector upward to $12 billion and the job numbers to 415,000. Despite the billions of dollars of public support, however, government spending on arts-related culture represented only about 2 per cent of the total of government expenditure at all levels. Moreover, little of the vast sum spent on culture trickled down to the primary producers—the writers, painters, actors, and composers. Government surveys of artists from 1978 to 1984 indicated that very few Canadians could make a living from the sale of their work or talents. Most held other employment, often in teaching. At the same time, the fact that even a few thousand Canadians could conceive of making a living as professional producers of culture certainly distinguished the post-1970 period from earlier times.

Little enough changed in terms of the distinctive Canadian content of culture in Canada, still seen by many observers as a major problem. The statistics were revealing. In book publishing, for example, titles published in Canada in 1984 (most written by Canadian authors) accounted for only 25 per cent of books sold. Nearly half the books sold to Canadians came directly from foreign sources. Twelve foreign-controlled firms in 1984 had 89 per cent of the sound-recording market in Canada, most for recordings made outside Canada. In one week in 1986 the top seven TV shows in English-speaking Canada were all American. The situation was quite different in French Canada, where all seven top shows were locally produced. In the 1980s there was great hope for satellite and cable technology, but while these improved access for many Canadian viewers, they did little for actual Canadian content.

assembled in Canada was glued to the TV, mesmerized by an unofficial sporting event, played for no historical trophy or recognized world title. Paul Henderson of the Toronto Maple Leafs scored the game- and series-winning goal with 34 seconds remaining in regulation time of the final game of the eight-game series. Despite this moment of national togetherness, the schism between francophone and anglophone cultures was constantly widening, and all levels of government continued to jostle for advantage. The result was a strong sense of diffusion and decentralization—some would say regionalization (although not merely geography was involved)—of what had once been perceived as a monolithic cultural establishment. Such developments paralleled and reinforced the retreat of centralism in the political and constitutional area, while contributing to the sense that Canadian society was unravelling.

By 1990 the *Canada Year Book* could call the cultural sector 'the fourth largest employer in Canada'. A few years earlier, a 1985 Statistics Canada compendium

Table 11.8 Percentage of Television Viewing Time Devoted to Canadian and Foreign Programming in Prime Time (7 p.m.–11 p.m.)

| | English | | | |
| | 1984–5 | | 1992–3 | |
	Canadian	Foreign	Canadian	Foreign
CBC	62.0	38.0	81.7	18.3
CTV	20.8	79.2	17.3	82.7
Global	7.9	92.1	17.4	82.6
Independent	16.4	83.6	17.9	82.1
	French			
SRC (Radio-Canada)	72.1	27.9	90.9	9.1
TVA	46.2	53.8	66.3	33.7
TOS	54.8	45.2	47.6	52.4

Source: *Globe and Mail*, 1 Feb. 1996, A21. Reprinted by permission of CBC.

Government support for High Culture further aided a respectable Canadian showing in areas of traditional activity, such as painting and literature. But at the very time Canadian High Culture was achieving international recognition, the idea of High Culture was breaking down. In addition, tensions were developing between what came to be labelled 'national' and 'regional' cultures, not to mention between French and English Canada. Before the late 1960s, a major problem for Canadian creators was receiving public exposure outside Toronto and Montreal.

The small presses and galleries that cropped up in the country, especially after 1970, became possible for several reasons. One was the allocation of new provincial funding for the arts, often from the revenues of publicly authorized gambling activities. In Quebec, cultural subsidies were a matter of high politics. Another was the emergence of local cultural entrepreneurs in what was now a large enough market for culture in second-tier cities such as Quebec, Halifax, and Winnipeg. Almost inevitably the new publishers and galleries tended to stress local themes and settings. Cultural regionalism grew to match political regionalism.

It began to appear that the very concept of a Canadian National Culture was an artificial one, impossible for most Canadian artists to realize in a fragmented nation. Precious few books published in Quebec were ever translated into English, for example. The success of multiculturalism and the changing face of immigration only complicated the situation further. One exception to all generalizations about culture in Canada began in 1984, when a group of young street performers in Montreal organized a festival that toured Quebec in celebration of the 450th anniversary of the landing of Jacques Cartier. The organizers built on a long tradition of the burlesque in Quebec and incorporated the more recent expression of avant-garde theatre in the province. The show toured in a large blue-and-yellow tent. It was a circus without animals or freaks, featuring acrobatic performances, brilliant costumes, and imaginative choreography with rock music accompaniment. This 'Cirque du Soleil', as it came to be called, was a huge success at Expo 86 in Vancouver. It took California by storm in 1987. The company toured the United States in 1988, went to Europe in 1990, and Japan in 1992. It established permanent circus shows in Las Vegas in 1992 and later at Walt Disney World in Florida. By the late 1980s it was recruiting performers around the world and began touring a number of different productions, with accompanying music composed by René Dupéré. Over the 1990s, the Cirque du Soleil became Canada's (or Quebec's) best-known cultural export, providing evidence that Canada could take the lead in the imaginative creation of culture that crossed all sorts of boundaries.

In early 1991, when the Quebec government of Robert Bourassa finally responded to the collapse of Meech Lake, it listed immigration, health, manpower, and cultural matters as the key areas in which it would demand increased constitutional powers. 'As far as culture is concerned, yes we should be in charge', announced Liberal Minister of Cultural Affairs Liza Frulla-Hébert in January 1991. 'We have to work toward being the one and only one giving the pulse of Quebec culture. Listen, culture belongs to Quebec' (*Winnipeg Free Press*, 25 Jan. 1991). No Canadian could doubt that in Quebec, culture was lively and distinctive, certainly better able to withstand American influence than elsewhere in Canada. Whether Quebec Culture was a National Culture became, in the end, a question more susceptible to political than intellectual answers.

International Affairs

After 1975, Canada returned to closer ties with the United States. Aside from perennial concern over

La Sagouine

She is seventy-two years old. She cleans. She is alone. The setting is simply made of her bucket, her mop and her rags. Her audience is in front of her, and all around her, but mostly at her feet, in her pail. She talks to that muddy water of hers. And it is from there that I heard her. A.M.

Sure 'nough, they came around fer the census. And don't you worry, they took a census of us all; . . . Well, some of the questions are tougher to answer than others. Like when they asked La Cruche what she does fer a livin . . . or when they asked Boy à Polyte to give the names of all his children . . . ain't easy.

That ain't all. Cause they got in their lists a question a lot tougher. Ah! There too, even Gapi didn' know what to answer. Yer nationality, they ask you. Citizenship 'n nationality. Hard to say.

. . . We live in America, but we ain't Americans. Nope, Americans, they work in 'em factories in the States, and in summer, they come around, visitin our beachers in their white trousers 'n speakin English. 'n they're rich, them Americans. 'n we ain't. Us, we live in Canada; so we figure we mus' be Canadians.

. . . Well, that ain't true either, cause the Dysarts, n'm the Carrolls, 'n the Jones, they just ain't like us, and they also live in Canada. If the're Canadians, we sure can't be the same. Case the're English, 'n us, we're French.

. . . Nope, we ain't completely French, can't say that: the French folks is the folks fr'm France, les Français de France, 'n fer that matter, we're even less Français de France than we're Americans. We're more like French Canadians, they told us.

Well, that ain't true either. French Canadians are those that live in Québec. They call 'em Canayens or Québécois. But how can we be Québécois if we ain't livin in Québec? Fer the love of Christ, where do we live?

. . . In Acadie, we was told, 'n we're supposed to be Acadjens. So, that's the way we decided to answer the question 'bout nationality: Acadjens we says to them. Now, then, we can be sure of one thing, we're the only ones to have that name. Well, them censors didn' wanna write down that word on their list. The way they sees it, seems l'Acadie ain't a country, 'n Acadjen ain't a nationality, cause of the fact it ain't written in Joe Graphy's books.

. . . Well, after that we didn' know what else to say, 'n we told them to give us the nationality they wanted. I think they put us down with the Injuns. . . .

Source: Antonine Maillet, *La Sagouine*, trans. Luis de Céspedes (Toronto: Simon & Pierre, 1979), 164–6. Reprinted by permission of The Dundurn Group.

trade figures and the occasional international conference attended by the Prime Minister, Canada's relations outside North America assumed a very low profile during the 1980s. Canadians expected precious little from foreign policy initiatives. The Free Trade Agreement with the Americans merely confirmed what everyone knew.

The key international developments of the 1980s were totally beyond Canada's control. The first was *glasnost*, the process of liberation from the repression of communism in the Soviet Union. The Soviet regime had been opening up for decades, but no one was prepared for the rapid changes of the later 1980s when the Russians made it clear that they were no longer prepared to prop up unpopular governments in Eastern Europe and wanted to shift their own internal priorities in what appeared to be capitalistic and democratic directions. The most obvious symbol of collapse was the razing of the Berlin Wall, which was demolished, along with the government of East Germany, in November 1989, clearing the way for

German reunification in late 1990. This event ultimately permitted Canada to close its last two military bases on German soil in 1993.

Conclusion

For many Canadians, especially those in English-speaking Canada, the years after 1972 were characterized by considerably less optimism and buoyancy than the previous quarter-century had been. In historical development, disparate events often come together in surprising ways to weave a complex web. This was the case with such seemingly unrelated trends as the rise of Quebec separatism; the growing power of the provinces; the international oil crisis; the shift away from trade protectionism and a managed economy; the weakening of Christian belief; and the passage through life of the baby boomers. The result was a Canadian society concerned mainly with hedonism and anxiety, displaying all the morbid symptoms that might have been expected.

How History Has Changed

Economic Theory

Differing historical interpretations often result from conflicting theories about how the world works. This has been particularly true of the Canadian economy. Between the end of World War II and the early 1970s, the dominant economic theory in Canada was associated with the English economist John Maynard Keynes. His theory had been developed in reaction to the economic conditions of the Great Depression. Keynes insisted that the best way to tackle the big economic problems—which he identified as stagnant economic growth and high unemployment rates—was by employing the taxing and spending powers of the state. When the economy slowed down, the pump needed to be primed, often through governmental spending on public works projects.

Like their predecessors, liberal democratic, Keynesians believed in market capitalism, properly

regulated. Canada's civil servants were more willing than the country's politicians to accept that full employment and an end to poverty required a thoroughly interventionist state. For the most part, the Keynesians were also proponents of the welfare state. Keynesianism went hand-in-hand with protectionist economies, and understandably dominated economic thinking in an age of economic growth and expansion. The most influential Keynesian in North America was the Canadian-born John Kenneth Galbraith. In a series of influential books, Galbraith insisted on pushing the new liberalism in a social democratic direction. Ironically, Galbraith's views were enthusiastically received by the Kennedy and Johnson administrations in the United States but more or less ignored in Canada.

Increasingly, after 1970, Keynes's interventionist views were challenged by another group of economic thinkers, often called Friedmanites after the American economist Milton Friedman. Friedman rejected state intervention in the economy, insisting that Keynesians exaggerated the utility of government taxing and spending in determining the level of national income and gross national product. The best policy (which came to be known as monetarism) was to control the stock of money in order to reduce inflation and otherwise to leave the economy to regulate itself. Warring on inflation benefited the creditor class more than the debtor class, and also worked to the advantage of foreign investors who were able to profit from an artificially favourable exchange rate. Many Friedmanites, including the master himself, opposed the welfare state. Friedman's most famous phrase was 'There is no such thing as a free lunch.' On the other hand, the monetarists, as part of their attitude towards the self-regulation of the market, also believed in free trade. In many ways

the worst feature of the debate over economic and social policy was the presumption on all sides that what was being purveyed was hard scientific truth rather than socio-political ideology.

Monetarism gained support from the business community as governments of the 1970s and 1980s went increasingly deeper into debt. Much of the debt was blamed on expensive social programs, although the federal and provincial budgets had been balanced during the years of the greatest expansion of social policy. In turn, the Keynesians insisted that government deficits were caused by anti-inflationary policies at the Bank of Canada. They charged these policies also caused unemployment, cut back on income tax revenues, and increased expenditures on unemployment compensation and welfare assistance.

Short Bibliography

Bashevkin, Sylvia. *True Patriot Love: The Politics of Canadian Nationalism*. Toronto, 1991. An important study of the way politicians have bent Canadian nationalism to their own purposes.

Berger, Thomas R. *Northern Frontier, Northern Homeland* (Report of the Mackenzie Valley Pipeline Inquiry), 2 vols. Ottawa, 1977. A key document in the history of social justice in Canada.

Bibby, Reginald. *Fragmented Gods: The Poverty and Potential of Religion in Canada*. Toronto, 1987. A perceptive account of the state of religion in Canada as of the mid-1980s, based on specially conducted national surveys and standard public opinion polls.

Cairns, Alan. *Disruptions: Constitutional Struggles, from the Charter to Meech Lake*. Toronto, 1991. An analysis of the constitutional problems of the 1980s by one of Canada's leading constitutional specialists.

Corse, Sarah. *Nationalism and Literature: The Politics of Culture in Canada and the United States*. Cambridge, 1997. A stimulating comparative study of recent cultural policy in the field of literature in the United States and Canada.

English, John. *Just Watch Me: The Life of Pierre Elliott Trudeau 1968–2000*. Toronto, 2009. A compelling account of Trudeau's years in power and beyond.

Frazer, William. *The Legacy of Keynes and Friedman: Economic Analysis, Money, and Ideology*. Westport, Conn., 1994. An intellectual history of one of the major ideological disagreements in North America in the late twentieth century.

Giangrande, Carole. *Down to Earth: The Crisis in Canadian Farming*. Toronto, 1985. A discussion of the reasons Canadian farmers were in serious financial trouble in the 1980s.

Gwyn, Richard. *The Northern Magus*. Toronto, 1980. A solid early biography of that complex Canadian, Pierre Elliott Trudeau.

Harris, Michael. *Unholy Orders: Tragedy at Mount Cashel*. Markham, Ont., 1990. An exposé of one of the first of Canada's sexual abuse scandals within a major religious denomination.

Jenish, D'Arcy. *Money to Burn: Trudeau, Mulroney, and the Bankruptcy of Canada*. Toronto, 1996. A partisan analysis of the 'crisis' of the deficit, presenting it as the major challenge to the present generation of Canadians.

McDonald, Neil, and Trevor McDonald. *Aboriginal Peoples: Past and Present: Summary of the History, Rights and Issues Relating to Aboriginal Peoples in Canada.* n.p., 2000. A good introduction to a complex question.

McQuaig, Linda. *Shooting the Hippo: Death by Deficit and Other Canadian Myths.* Toronto, 1995. A study by a leading radical economic and social analyst who insists that the deficit was an invented crisis, easily soluble.

McWhinney, Edward. *Canada and the Constitution, 1979–82.* Toronto, 1982. A well-balanced contemporary narrative.

Morgan, Nicole. *Implosion: An Analysis of the Growth of the Federal Public Service in Canada, 1945–1985.* Montreal, 1986. An explanation of the growth of Canada's federal bureaucracy.

Parsons, Vic. *Bad Blood: The Tragedy of the Canadian Tainted Blood Scandal.* Toronto, 1995. An angry look at one of the worst examples of the failure of public policy in the arena of public health.

Savoie, Donald. *The Politics of Public Spending in Canada.* Toronto, 1990. A dispassionate discussion of the financial crisis in Canada as of 1990.

Study Questions

1. What roles did the economy and the Constitution play in the disintegration of the liberal federalist-nationalist consensus during the 1970s?
2. In what ways did oil illustrate the excesses and weaknesses of the age of affluence?
3. After winning a second enormous majority for the Progressive Conservative Party in 1988, Brian Mulroney quickly became one of the most unpopular prime ministers in Canadian history. Identify and explain three reasons for his fall from grace.
4. If you think of the attempts at constitutional reform from 1980 to 1992 as a battle between the federal government and the provinces, who would you say won? Explain your answer.
5. What provisions did the Meech Lake Accord make regarding immigrants to Quebec? Why do you think Quebec wanted these provisions?
6. What did the Donald Marshall case reveal about the status of Aboriginal people in the Canadian justice system?
7. How did immigration remake Canadian society between 1980 and 1990?
8. In about 10 years, the Cirque du Soleil grew from a ragtag band of street performers to an international cultural institution. What factors led to the Cirque's success?

 www.oupcanada.com/Bumsted4e

Visit the companion website for *A History of the Canadian Peoples*, fourth edition for further resources.

12 Freefalling into the Twenty-First Century, 1992–2001

Timeline

1990   Japanese Canadians who lost property and were interned during World War II receive payment and written apology from Canadian government. Lucien Bouchard leaves PC Party, forms Bloc Québécois.

1991   Royal Commission on Aboriginal Peoples formed.

1992   Referendum on Charlottetown Accord.

1993   Kim Campbell is chosen leader of the Progressive Conservative Party and becomes Prime Minister of Canada in June. In October the Liberals win a great victory. Jean Charest becomes PC leader.

1994   NAFTA proclaimed. PQ victory in Quebec.

1995   Mike Harris's Tories demolish the NDP in Ontario. Separatism defeated in Quebec in close referendum vote. Quebec Nordiques leave for new home in Colorado.

1996   Sheldon Kennedy accuses his former hockey coach of sexual abuse.

1997   Liberals win another federal victory, PQ a victory in Quebec. Asia–Pacific Economic Co-operation (APEC) meeting held in Vancouver. Canada agrees to Kyoto Accord on greenhouse gases. Supreme Court hands down judgement in *Delgamuukw* case.

1998   Jean Charest steps down as federal PC leader to lead Quebec's provincial Liberal Party. Joe Clark becomes PC leader. United Church apologizes to Aboriginal people for residential school abuse.

1999   United Alternative convention held. Adrienne Clarkson becomes Governor General of Canada.

2000   Molson's 'I Am Canadian' advertising campaign begins. In July Stockwell Day is chosen over Preston Manning to lead the Canadian Alliance. In November the Liberals win their third term in office.

Rick Moranis and Dave Thomas are famous in Canada for portraying brothers Bob and Doug McKenzie, co-hosts of the fictional show 'The Great White North', a featured sketch on the comedy program *SCTV*. While much of the content on Canadian television was generally North American, these bumbling brothers brought toques, beer, and words like 'hosers' into North American households. Everett Collection–MGM/The Canadian Press.

If one listened to the journalists and the media pundits, Canada and Canadians lived in a constant state of crisis and turmoil in the 1990s, lurching from one emergency to the next without any road map to the future. While such may well have been the case, in this view there is little perspective. The 'news' almost by definition has no sense of history. Certainly Canada was not unique in its problems, which almost without exception were occurring in many other places around the world. Even the potential disintegration of the Canadian Confederation was hardly unique. Movements of national liberation were everywhere, and contrary to the situations in Bosnia, the USSR, and Sri Lanka—to name but a few troubled nations—at least in Canada the conflicting sides were not yet armed camps. Moreover, despite the nation's well-publicized problems, most of the population of the remainder of the world would have probably traded their situation for that of the average Canadian. Canada continued to rank at or near the top of everyone's world standard-of-living table. As for the claim that Canada lacked direction, this statement could have been equally true at any time in the past. With hindsight, historians can offer some notion of what the direction was and what the ultimate outcome would be. We can see an inexorable line from the Great Depression through World War II to the social service state, for example. Those who live in the midst of the maelstrom, however, can have little sense of how the issues and paradoxes of the moment will eventually be resolved. Nor can the participants in the chaos of the moment tell whether the resolution will be progressive or retrogressive, apocalyptic or gradual. About all we can say with assurance is that the future is—as it always has been—uncertain. That fact is not in itself a crisis. Moreover, all things are relative. By comparison with what happened in 2001 and after, the period of the 1990s seemed quite humdrum.

Politics

At the federal level, the most important political development of the mid-1990s was probably the triumph of the Liberal Party in the 1993 election, combined with the absolute collapse of the Progressive Conservative Party and its replacement by two openly antagonistic regional parties. National political parties had failed abysmally at the polls before (the Liberals in 1918, the Tories in 1940). Regional parties (such as the Progressive Party) had temporarily risen to prominence. What was new about the election of 1993, of course, was the emergence in the House of Commons of two regional parties of equal strength, the Reform Party and the Bloc Québécois, each committed to irreconcilable policies and their combined seats unequal to the large Liberal majority. These two regional parties both tended to draw their strength from voters who had previously supported the Tories. At the same time, the Liberals did win a major victory, but without any evidence of new policies.

By the close of 1992 it was clear that Prime Minister Brian Mulroney's popularity ratings, consistently lower than any other Canadian Prime Minister had ever previously experienced, were not likely to improve with time. At the leadership convention that ensued in June 1993, Kim Campbell (b. 1947) was chosen on the second ballot to lead the party. Campbell, a British Columbian who had originally been associated with the Social Credit party in that province, thus became Canada's first female Prime Minister. Although a relative newcomer to federal politics, she had more experience than Brian Mulroney at the time of selection. She had held two major cabinet portfolios beginning in 1989. The Tories apparently hoped that her gender and her refreshing 'candour' would lead the country to see Campbell as a fresh face, although her credentials in French Canada were hardly up to those of the man she had beaten out (Jean Charest of Quebec). Some observers, particularly among feminists, argued that Campbell had been chosen as a 'sacrificial lamb' to bear the brunt of the inevitable election defeat about to occur. In any case, like John Turner a decade earlier, Campbell inherited the enormous unpopularity of her predecessor. She had little time to establish a new government image before having to call an election.

Jean Chrétien's Liberals were in some ways well prepared for the contest, certainly financially, although the party platform was somewhat schizophrenic, committed to carrying on the welfare state while balancing the budget and reducing the deficit.

Jean Chrétien

Jean Chrétien, c. 1999. The Canadian Press/Tom Hanson.

Born in Shawinigan, Quebec, on 11 January 1934, he was the eighteenth of 19 children (not all of whom lived beyond infancy) born to a relatively poor family in the midst of the Depression. He attended Laval University, studying law, and practised in Trois-Rivières from his call to the bar in 1958 to his election to the House of Commons in 1963. A childhood illness left him deaf in one ear and partially paralyzed the left side of his face. After holding several parliamentary secretaryships, Chrétien served as Minister without Portfolio in 1967 and over the next 17 years held virtually every important portfolio in a series of Liberal governments, culminating as Secretary of State for External Affairs and Deputy Prime Minister in 1984 under John Turner.

Chrétien resigned his seat in 1986 and left public life for a few years, but was chosen head of the Liberal Party in 1990. He was the most prominent contender for the leadership, and many argued that he deserved it for long and loyal service to the party. He had many strengths. He was a proven campaigner, particularly in French Canada, and he cultivated the image of a guileless small-town French Canadian, more shrewd than clever. Never flashy, he had strong support within local Liberal organizations. His opponents tried to label him 'Yesterday's Man', and he offered no new visions, which may have been an advantage against his principal rivals, Sheila Copps and Paul Martin Jr.

Chrétien came to power in the Liberal sweep of 1993, and most of his 10 years as Prime Minister were spent without any serious opposition, either in the Commons or at the hustings. This lack of opposition made it possible for him to survive his own mistakes in judgement and the corruption of his Quebec associates. He was in constant hot water—over 'Peppergate' (the use by police of pepper spray on demonstrators during the 1997 APEC meeting in Vancouver), over his association with real estate promoters in his riding, over his physical response to a man who apparently sought to assassinate him.

Chrétien was hardly a brilliant campaigner, but he proved adequate to the task, much aided by a series of blunders by Campbell and her advisers. The worst occurred shortly before the end of the campaign, when Campbell was unable to distance herself quickly enough from a negative political ad campaign suggesting that Chrétien was handicapped. Negative campaigning in the media had become common in the United States, but this one backfired by generating popular sympathy for the Liberal leader. Submerged under the national media attention given to Campbell and Chrétien were a series of fascinating local races featuring a variety of third parties, of which the Reform Party and the Bloc Québécois proved on election day to be the most attractive to the voters. The Liberals did not so much receive a mandate as triumph over an otherwise badly divided field headed by the singularly inept Tories.

The Reform Party had been organized in October of 1987 by (Ernest) Preston Manning, son of the long-time Alberta Social Credit leader Ernest Manning. Its backbone was in traditional Alberta and British Columbia Socred constituencies, but it had some appeal as far east as Ontario among retired Canadians and young first-time voters. Preston Manning was a professional management consultant. He was a colourless speaker, but his lack of charisma was somewhat redeemed by a self-deprecating humour seldom seen among major political leaders. The Reform Party stood four-square for the traditional, often populist, values of the Anglo-Canadian West. It wanted to cut federal spending, to reform Parliament to make it more responsive to the popular will, and to provide for the equal treatment of provinces and citizens alike. The party had no time for the sovereignist pretensions of Quebec or for French-Canadian culture. Reform liked multiculturalism little better than biculturalism. Manning indicated his willingness to contemplate new limitations on immigration to Canada, although he was not pressed hard on the issue.

As for the Bloc Québécois, it was associated both within and without Quebec with its major campaign issue, the separation of that province from the Canadian Confederation, and with its leader, Lucien Bouchard. Born in St-Coeur-de-Marie in 1938, Bouchard had been a lawyer in Chicoutimi before his appointment as Canadian ambassador to France in 1985 by the Mulroney government. In the election of 1988 he had run as a successful PC candidate, but he had left the party before the 1992 referendum on the Charlottetown Accord to sit as an independent committed to a sovereign Quebec. The responses to Bouchard pointed to some interesting cultural differences between francophone Québécois and other Canadians. While many of the former found Bouchard compelling and charismatic in the traditional pattern of *le chef* (the best example of which had been Maurice Duplessis), anglophones inside and outside the province were not attracted to him in the slightest.

Not only were the PCs—soon led by Jean Charest (b. 1958)—reduced to a mere two seats on 25 October 1993, but both they and the NDP (with nine seats) lost official standing in the House of Commons. This loss of standing was particularly serious for the NDP, which had relied heavily on Commons financial support for its Ottawa infrastructure. With 54 seats to Reform's 53, the Bloc Québécois became the official opposition, offering the somewhat anomalous spectacle of 'Her Majesty's Loyal Opposition' committed to the destruction of the institution in which it was participating. The Liberals had a pretty easy time in most respects, since the opposition was unable to agree on very much and lacked numerical strength anyway. In power, the Chrétien government continued to exhibit the ambiguities of its campaign platform, trying to reduce federal expenditure and the deficit without doing serious damage to any of the major social programs—or its image. A major review of the entire welfare and unemployment system, headed by Lloyd Axworthy (b. 1939), ended up making essentially

Prime Minister designate Kim Campbell with Brian Mulroney outside the official residence at 24 Sussex Drive, Ottawa, 14 June 1993. The Canadian Press/Tom Hanson.

cosmetic changes to the system designed to make it more difficult to remain for long periods on social assistance or to use welfare to subsidize seasonal employment. The government predictably sought to save money by cutting deeply into cultural programs and the military, and by reducing the amount of transfer payments to the provinces for health and higher education. As the time for another election approached, the Liberals had precious little in positive accomplishment to take to the nation, however.

Despite the many weaknesses of Chrétien's government, the Liberals won easily in 1997. This victory was less the result of Liberal success than of opposition failure. The opposition forces were still divided regionally, with Bouchard's Bloc Québécois dominating in Quebec and Manning's Reform and Charest's Progressive Conservatives dividing the vote outside Quebec. While the PCs did best outside the West, Reform got all its 60 seats from the four western provinces, especially Alberta and British Columbia, where western alienation continued to be strong. The NDP still could not mount an eastern breakthrough and was hampered by its lack of a strong or imaginative platform; the party was badly divided between those who wanted to make it the radical alternative and those who thought such a stance would be the kiss of death. The Liberals collected 155 seats to 145 for the combined opposition, despite gathering only 38.4 per cent of the total vote.

The nation's most obvious political need was for a unified conservative opposition. This was far more difficult to obtain than might have been expected, given the potential prize of national political power were it accomplished. In April 1998, Jean Charest stepped down as leader of the national PCs to become leader of the Quebec Liberal Party. This

Opposition leader Preston Manning at a post-election news conference in Calgary, 3 June 1997. The Canadian Press/Frank Gunn.

shift of allegiance probably bothered the voters outside Quebec less than those within the province. Into the national gap stepped Joe Clark, the leader and ex-Prime Minister earlier dismissed from the leadership in favour of Brian Mulroney. Clark was popular with backroom Tories in eastern Canada, but hardly anybody else. In early 1999, 1,500 delegates assembled in Ottawa at a United Alternative convention, which hoped to lay the framework for a new political party of the right. Most of these delegates were members of the Reform Party, and there was little enthusiasm for this initiative from either the BQ (who were not invited) or the Tories (who were). The United Alternative turned into the Alliance party. Most Reform members shifted their allegiance, but Joe Clark resolutely remained outside the new umbrella. Preston Manning attempted unsuccessfully to become the Alliance's new leader, but was thwarted by a relative newcomer named Stockwell Day. Day was selected, in July 2000, probably because he seemed the only viable alternative to Manning, who graciously stepped aside as leader of the opposition in Day's favour. Manning had been rejected because he was perceived to be unacceptable outside western Canada. Unfortunately, Day proved to be less than compelling as a political leader. His first appearance in the role saw him don a wetsuit and ride a jet ski to meet the media. There was also the lingering problem of a lawsuit filed against him by a lawyer whom Day had criticized for defending a pedophile; the legal costs were assumed by the province of Alberta. Day was forced to lead the Alliance (officially the Canadian Reform Conservative Alliance) into an election within a few months of his selection and before he was able either to put his mark on the party platform or to develop any popular new initiatives.

In the 2000 federal election, the Liberals actually gained both in seats and in percentage of the popular vote. The number of Liberal seats increased to 172 and the party's percentage of the popular vote grew to 40.8 per cent. Some of the increase was at the expense of the Bloc Québécois, which dropped from 44 to 38 seats, although a number of seats were also taken from both the Progressive Conservatives and the NDP. The Alliance gained in seats over the Reform total in 1997, winning in 66 ridings, although still exclusively in western Canada. As leader of the opposition, Stockwell Day proved ineffective. Before long, leading members of his caucus, including Deborah Grey and house leader Chuck Strahl, were publicly criticizing Day's leadership. By April 2001, most of the caucus had turned against him and 13 walked out; six of the 13 subsequently returned.

Meanwhile, Prime Minister Chrétien came under attack in the House of Commons, in the media, and in his own caucus over his involvement with developers in his riding for whom he solicited government support. As well, there were a number of other ethically dubious interventions. The government's newly appointed ethics adviser ruled in all cases brought before him that Chrétien had broken no guidelines, but neither the opposition nor the public was entirely convinced. One of the chief issues in the Liberal caucus involved succession politics. Chrétien was widely expected to step down soon after his 2000 victory, and every potential leadership candidate tried to build up a financial war chest and support against the day the Prime Minister either announced his departure or authorized open campaigning for his successor.

Developments at the provincial level confirmed the split personality of the electorate. The public was concerned about the size of the deficits and was generally opposed to higher taxes, but at the same time was not at all enthusiastic about deep cuts in social programs. Whether these sentiments were held by the same people or by different groups of voters was not entirely clear. In Alberta, the Tory government of Ralph Klein (b. 1942) won a big election victory in 1993 on a platform of realistic government budgeting. Klein carried through with major budget cuts, although because of Alberta's relative wealth, these probably hurt less than they would have in a province like Nova Scotia. In Ontario, the NDP government of Bob Rae (b. 1948), which had not succeeded in controlling finances and had run afoul of the province's trade union movement in its attempts to cut the costs of its civil service, was demolished in 1995 by the Tories led by Mike Harris (b. 1945). The chief campaign issue was government spending. When Harris actually began to cut spending, however, the cries of wounded outrage were deafening.

Mario Dumont

Mario Dumont was born on 19 May 1970 in Cacouna, Quebec, a small town not far from Rivière-du-Loup. He first entered politics at the age of 16, when he became a member of the youth commission of the Quebec Liberal Party, subsequently serving on the executive of the Liberal youth commission. In 1991 he was elected chairman of the youth commission during the Liberal convention that adopted the Allaire report as party policy on the Constitution, and he was one of the leaders of the young people's wing of the Liberal Party in 1992. He campaigned against the Charlottetown Accord as co-chairman of the Network of Liberals, Voting No. In 1993 Dumont received his BA in economics from Concordia University in Quebec, and six months later (in January 1994) he was one of the founding members of the Action Démocratique du Québec. He was elected party president in March 1994 and became leader of the party at the age of 24 in April, when Jean Allaire resigned from the post. In September he led the ADQ in the general election and emerged as MNA for the riding of Rivière-du-Loup.

As leader of the ADQ, in June 1995 Dumont was a signatory (along with Jacques Parizeau and Lucien Bouchard) to the well-known tripartite pact on the campaign for Quebec sovereignty. His appearance in connection with this agreement was probably the first time most of Canada (or even Quebec) ever heard of him, and Dumont campaigned actively for sovereignty in the Quebec referendum of October 1995. Indeed, he was probably one of the few winners in the defeat of the referendum, since the campaign gave him an opportunity to become better known as one of the province's 'fresh faces' on the political front. He acquired his nickname of 'Super Mario' in emulation of the great hockey player Mario Lemieux (or perhaps via the video game of the same name). Re-elected from Rivière-du-Loup as MNA in 1998, Dumont helped lead his party to a stunning victory in the by-election in Saguenay in April 2002, taking advantage of the PQ's reputation as a reform party to stake out ground on the right and possibly make his party the logical successor to the mantle formerly worn by the Union Nationale. Dumont became leader of the opposition in the National Assembly in 2007, and resigned this post in 2009 to become a television talk-show host.

In Ontario, as elsewhere, there was some evidence from the polls that Canadians were actually prepared to pay higher taxes to preserve some of their social benefits, particularly in the health-care sector.

The reasons for the 1994 electoral victory of the Parti Québécois—or the mood of the electorate in that province—were, as usual, clouded by the sovereignty issue. The Bourassa government had not controlled spending, but the PQ did not present itself in the campaign as the party of fiscal restraint. In 1997 Bouchard's PQ easily won re-election over Jean Charest's Liberals by campaigning chiefly on a platform of preserving a 'zero deficit', which obviously meant deep cuts to education, social services, and health care. The party kept a low profile on separatism, and this probably only confused the electorate. The big winner in the 1997 election was the Action Démocratique du Quebec, led by an articulate young former Liberal named Mario Dumont (b. 1970) who advocated sovereignty-association. The ADQ presented a right-wing alternative to the two major parties and picked up much support from those who in earlier days would have supported the Union Nationale. Although the NDP was wiped out in 1995 in Ontario and in 2001 in British Columbia, in both cases standing accused of fiscal irresponsibility, it came to power in Manitoba in 1999 to replace a Tory government that had come to grief over mismanagement of health care. What was evident everywhere in Canada was that no politician or political party had any fresh ideas for resolving the fiscal dilemma.

The Constitution

Any hope that the referendum defeat of the Charlottetown Accord had put a lid on constitutional matters was ended by the 1994 PQ victory in Quebec. Led by Jacques Parizeau (b. 1930), the PQ moved inexorably towards another Quebec referendum on sovereignty. Parizeau had initially opposed sovereignty-association but gradually came to see it as a way to satisfy some soft nationalists. Realizing that one of the major problems with the 1980 referendum had been the uncertainty regarding both the question and any consequent action, Parizeau sought to tie down the new question. He had legislation passed defining the terms. In June 1995 he and the two other separatist leaders, the BQ's Bouchard and the ADQ's Dumont, agreed on a plan. Quebecers would be asked to authorize the Quebec government to open negotiations with Ottawa on sovereignty-association. If the province gave a mandate and if an agreement with Canada was not reached within a year, Quebec would unilaterally declare sovereignty. By joining forces, the three leaders hoped to allay fears that the Quebec government would, in Parizeau's words, 'jump the gun' on a declaration of sovereignty. The vote was soon set for 30 October 1995. The official question was 'Do you agree that Quebec should become sovereign, after having made a formal offer to Canada for a new Economic and Political Partnership, within the scope of the Bill respecting the future of Quebec and of the agreement signed on June 12, 1995?'

In the beginning the federalist ('*Non*') forces seemed to be well in control of the situation. Experts expected the usual ballot bonus for the federalists, who would turn out a higher proportion of their supporters. They also anticipated the usual conservative response to uncertainty. For the most part, Ottawa kept its distance from the campaign, allowing Liberal leader Daniel Johnson to carry the '*Non*' message to the electorate. The federal strategy was to do as little as possible to fuel the sovereignist position.

Then, with polls showing a marked advantage for the '*Non*' side, Lucien Bouchard actively entered the fray. Bouchard had only recently recovered from a rare bacterial infection that cost him a leg and nearly his life. He had not been originally expected to be an important campaigner, but the province was clearly not excited by Parizeau and Dumont. Bouchard introduced a new level of emotion into the campaign, simplifying the issues considerably. For many Quebecers, the need to move forward on the constitutional front became the key question in the referendum. When the need for constitutional change rather than the need for sovereignty became the real referendum question, the situation rapidly deteriorated for the federalist forces. What had earlier been a ho-hum campaign suddenly turned into a real barnburner. At the last minute, Prime Minister Chrétien revealed the panic in Ottawa by offering Quebec concessions, including yet another 'distinct society' constitutional proposal.

The vote turned into a cliff-hanger as virtually every eligible resident of Quebec cast his or her ballot. The final turnout—over 94 per cent of the total electorate—has seldom been matched except in police states with compulsory voting. Millions of Canadians remained tuned to their television sets until late in the evening, waiting for the decisive result. Finally, it became clear that the '*Non*' forces had won a narrow victory. In the end, 2,362,355 Quebecers (or 50.6 per cent) of the total voted '*Non*', while 2,308,054 (or 49.4 per cent) voted '*Oui*'. The young, the francophone, and the Quebecer outside Montreal led the way in voting '*Oui*'. There were many informal complaints about voting irregularities, but the vote was allowed to stand. Premier Parizeau had prepared a gracious speech of conciliation to accompany a sovereignist victory. In his bitter acknowledgement of failure on national radio and television, he was less gracious, blaming anglophones and ethnics for thwarting the aspirations of francophone Quebec. As Parizeau spoke, the cameras panned around the crowd of people gathered at '*Oui*' headquarters. Many were in tears. Parizeau's impulsive attack turned much public opinion against him, even within his own party. Within hours he announced his resignation. In February 1996 he would be officially replaced by Lucien Bouchard.

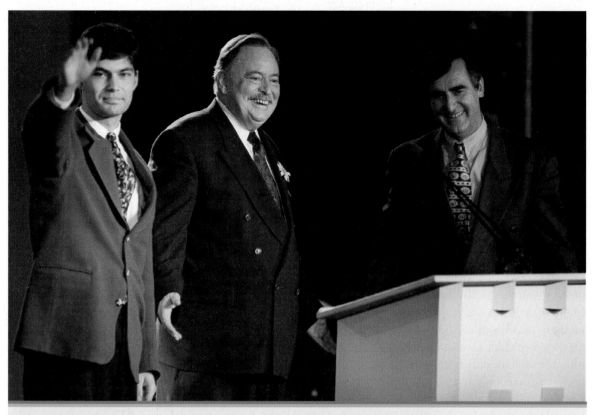

Mario Dumont, Jacques Parizeau, and Lucien Bouchard at a rally for 'Yes' supporters in Longueuil, Quebec, 29 October 1995. The referendum vote was held the following day. The Canadian Press/Paul Chiasson.

In the wake of the referendum, the Chrétien government passed a unilateral declaration in the Canadian Parliament that recognized Quebec as a distinct society, but as virtually everyone had come to appreciate, this gesture was too little too late. French Canadians in Quebec had made clear their desire for a new constitutional relationship with Canada. Virtually the only question remaining was whether or not a sovereign Quebec would remain within some sort of Canadian Confederation. Post-referendum polls continued to emphasize that Quebecers wanted to remain within Canada, but not under its present Constitution. Canadians turned to debate the next step in the ongoing constitutional process. One of the most difficult parts of this debate was trying to figure out a process for generating a new constitutional arrangement, since most of the previous approaches appeared discredited.

Any new constitutional arrangement would have to deal with more than merely the aspirations of Quebec. One of the most important additional items on the agenda for constitutional reform was the First Nations, who wanted the constitutional entrenchment of their conception of Aboriginal self-government. Although in many ways this position parallels Quebec's own position with respect to Canada, the province rejects Aboriginal claims to sovereignty within its jurisdiction. This refusal helps explain the insistence of the Quebec government in early 1996 that 'Quebec is indivisible.' The Constitution Act of 1982, while entrenching the existing Aboriginal and treaty rights of the First Nations, had not really come to terms with Aboriginal self-government, chiefly because the First Nations and Ottawa were so far apart on the subject, as was shown in the ensuing few years by three unproductive constitutional meetings of first ministers and Native leaders, which had been mandated in the new Constitution Act. The Aboriginal peoples have insisted that their government should be based on inherent jurisdiction as a historic right. For many Aboriginals this involves sovereign jurisdiction and the independent right to make laws and institutions for their people and their territory, since these rights were not surrendered with treaties. The militants object to the concept of Aboriginal self-government as an equivalent of municipal government, delegated to the First Nations by those jurisdictions (Ottawa and the provinces) that claim the sovereignty under the Crown and Constitution of Canada. As sovereign governments, First Nations would deal only as equals with Ottawa, which the Native people insist still owes them a heavy debt of financial responsibility. As municipal governments, they would become the agents of the senior governments, with only those powers allowed them by those governments. To recognize the First Nations (more than 500 bands) as sovereign would certainly be more possible in a Constitution that so accepted Quebec. For many Canadians, however, such recognition would not only further balkanize the country but would create independent jurisdictions within Canada that benefited from their Canadian affiliation but held no concurrent responsibilities under it. As the new millennium began, Quebec became more concerned with economic problems than with sovereignty issues, but all observers recognized that separatism could very easily slip back into the spotlight.

The Economy

The Canadian economy had now been running for a long time without correcting itself. In the 1990s some of the traditional indicators were positive for economic growth. Inflation was low, interest rates were low and constantly falling, and the Canadian dollar was lower against other world currencies. The resulting economic growth rate was slow, but constantly upward. Foreign trade continued to be buoyant, although mainly in the resource sector and associated industries. On the other hand, construction starts were stagnant and sales of new cars were lower than had been the case since the early 1980s. The Americans chipped ominously away at the Free Trade Agreement whenever doing so worked to their advantage. The buoyant real estate market of

the 1980s was no more, even in the still overheated British Columbia economy. Household debt was up to 89 per cent of disposable income. Most important, official unemployment rates were over 10 per cent nationally, while some of the regional figures were alarming, with rates above the national average east of Ontario and below it from Ontario westward. Official unemployment in Newfoundland in 1994 was 20.4 per cent, and in Quebec 12.2 per cent. These figures, of course, included only the people still looking for work. Many of those previously employed in dead industries like the Atlantic fishery had simply given up, as had quite a few of the young.

Finding a job was not easy. Keeping one was equally difficult. Downsizing continued to be the order of the day. Governments at all levels were attempting to reduce their workforces, and almost every private enterprise was trying (with some success) to make do with less. Even those who still had their jobs lived in constant fear of the next round of rationalization. As for the rationalizers, there was growing evidence that downsizing was no more self-correcting than other economic strategies. According to hopeful economic theory, once business profits went up substantially, excess profits would be reinvested in expansion. This was at least partly the thinking behind the practice of keeping business taxes low in what came to be known as 'Reaganomics', after the American President who had campaigned on this view. What often seemed to be happening in the 1990s, however, was that the increasing profits were simply distributed to the shareholders. Nonetheless, governments hesitated to increase the tax rates.

Perhaps as disturbing as the nagging fear of the chop for those who still had jobs was the absence of recognizable new career growth areas for those seeking to prepare themselves for employment. The education counsellors had virtually run out of suggestions for viable careers. There were still plenty of jobs in the part-time, semi-skilled (and low-paid) end of the workforce. 'Working at McDonald's' became the catchphrase. 'McJobs' became the term encompassing all such employment, which had no attractive future whatsoever and provided few or no fringe benefits. The younger generation faced with such employment prospects came to label itself Generation X. The post-baby boomers who, through no fault of their own, had arrived at adulthood after all the decent jobs were taken had little to look forward to. Generation X was both hedonistic and bitter, a volatile combination. The creation of new jobs was high on the wish list for most Canadians, but particularly for the young.

One economic growth area continued in household appliances and equipment. What had once been luxury items now became necessities, and new gadgets were being introduced every day. As had been the case for over a century with household equipment, constant reductions in price through technological innovation made mass marketing possible. In 1980 few homes had microwave ovens. By the mid-1990s over 80 per cent of households owned them. By 1994 more than half of Canadian households possessed a gas barbecue, and over 25 per cent of Canadian homes had some kind of air conditioning. Compact-disc players and home computers had exploded from a standing start in the late 1980s, and by 1995 were in over 50 per cent of households. Much of the electronic household gadgetry was assembled abroad, providing jobs only on the retail sales and highly technical service ends. At the same time, there was obviously room for employment in computers. Canadians established some reputation for software development.

Connected to the enormous expansion of the home computer were the growth of e-mail and the use of computer networks for both business and personal communication. By 1996 the Internet—another communications medium in which Canadians had taken the lead, especially in terms of usage— had become so popular and overloaded that it no longer worked very well. Never designed for mass participation, the Internet had grown without any regulation whatsoever, which was part of its attraction and would increasingly become part of its problem. While there was a future in the computer and

the microchip, this was a highly technical business that required special skills and special aptitudes. Business publications were full of stories of successful Canadian initiatives involving the glitzy new technologies, but they never explained how this would translate into large-scale employment for average Canadians.

The high-tech industries collapsed into chaos on 11 September 2001, the day a group of terrorists succeeded in orchestrating an air attack on the United States involving four hijacked airliners. This 'meltdown' might have occurred differently under other circumstances, but there was plenty of evidence that the technological sector had expanded far too rapidly and with far too little attention being paid to proper management and accounting practices. What was collapsing was a typical overheated boom. Osama bin Laden and his conspirators were allowed to take entirely too much credit for the economic chaos that followed '9/11'.

The private enterprise philosophy associated with the growth of schools of management at the universities had, by the 1990s, been operative for nearly 20 years. There was precious little evidence, however, that the economic thinking of the free

By 1995, over 50 per cent of households had a home computer. In this photo, a young girl finishes her report for school on her family's computer, c. 1994. Photo © Steve Skjold/Alamy.

enterprisers had produced a more satisfactory economy for most Canadians than had Keynesianism. Unemployment remained high nationally and was even higher in certain regions and among certain age groups. Like earlier economic pundits, the private enterprisers insisted that their theories had not yet been given a fair chance, but few Canadians wanted to take the gamble. As for the free trade agreements made with the Americans, the jury remained undecided, although there was increasing evidence that they were not unqualified successes. The North American Free Trade Agreement (NAFTA), which extended the earlier Free Trade Agreement (FTA) to include Mexico, took effect on 1 January 1994 with very little controversy and even less publicity. Subsequently, a number of well-publicized incidents suggested that there was little in NAFTA to protect Canadian business from American vested interests, if those interests sought to exercise their power. Thus the American softwood lumber industry, in the most highly publicized case, successfully argued that their Canadian counterparts were competing unfairly by pursuing policies that were perfectly acceptable under NAFTA. The result was the introduction of heavy surcharges on imports of Canadian lumber into the United States. As for Mexico, it became a haven for automobile manufacturers seeking to escape the high wages paid in Ontario. By the beginning of the new century, moreover, even the financial press in Canada—always sympathetic to free trade—began to run stories about the hollowing out of Canadian business. This process, by which management and executive power is taken out of the country and placed at head office, usually in the United States, had long been one of the major concerns of the opponents of free trade.

Globalization

Scholarly studies in the 1970s and 1980s had often called into question the market view of industrial development, but regional economic integration gave a new boost to convergence theories. These theories predicted the gradual spread across the globe of similar patterns of economic life once constraints were removed. While the academic economists were careful to confine their theories to the economic realm, the business press and other popularizers quickly applied such thinking to a variety of forces, such as new communications technologies and the mobility of capital, and identified something that came to be labelled 'globalization'. The term first appeared sometime in the late 1980s. Kenichi Omae's *The Borderless World: Power and Strategy in the Interlinked Economy* (1990) was probably the key text. The globalizers argued that international flows of capital, services, goods, and people, in a world of instant communications and liberal trade policies, were not being controlled—indeed, could not be controlled—by traditional national agencies.

The proposed Multilateral Agreement on Investment (MAI) became the epitome of the new order in which a rampant international capitalism would sweep everything before it. This global treaty on investment aligned the capital-exporting nations of the industrial West against the less developed nations. The Organization for Economic Co-operation and Development (OECD), which consisted of the 29 most highly developed nations of the world (including Canada), set a target date of 1997 for the introduction of the new world order. The MAI generated an enormous amount of opposition, not just from the developing countries, but from the developed nations as well. Much of the consciousness-raising and organization behind this opposition was made possible by the Internet, which thus demonstrated that it could be a force of resistance as well as of liberalization. In this case, the Internet served as the principal medium for anti-globalization activists to organize and to publicize an international arrangement that the bankers and politicians had deliberately kept out of the public eye as much as possible. The critics argued that the MAI gave to multinational corporations a series of political powers that had for several centuries been regulated by the nation-state. Under the MAI, international corporations could be treated no differently from domestic ones, and the nation-state could impose no unusual performance requirements upon them. While the introduction of the MAI was quietly abandoned in the face of considerable opposition and criticism, the threat of some form of multilateral agreement by the rich nations of the West remained very much in place. The morphing of the General Agreement on Tariffs and Trade (GATT) in 1995 into the more highly institutionalized and powerful World Trade Organization (WTO) suggested the direction of the threat. Such a spectre fuelled many of the fierce public demonstrations at various economic summit meetings held by the leading industrial nations in the late twentieth and early twenty-first centuries.

Perhaps the most publicized Canadian reaction occurred at the Asia–Pacific Economic Co-operation (APEC) meeting in Vancouver in November 1997. APEC was a meeting of 18 nations proposing a free trade zone in the vast Pacific region of the globe. Demonstrators were alarmed by this example of globalization (one group of University of British Columbia opponents argued, 'if you thought NAFTA was scary, wait until you hear about APEC.'). But the APEC meetings provoked other concerns as well. Many demonstrators were upset that Canada was hosting several heads of state whose record on human rights was undistinguished, including Jiang Zemin of China and General Suharto of Indonesia. UBC students were unhappy that the meeting was being held on their campus (at the Museum of Anthropology) without their consent. Student demonstrators were doused by the RCMP with pepper spray when they did not move aside quickly enough, resulting in what came to be called 'Peppergate'. The RCMP insisted that it was only responding to orders from the Canadian government, while Prime Minister Chrétien's response was: 'Pepper? I put that on my plate.' A formal investigation was held to get to the bottom of the matter. It did not really resolve the question of who was responsible for the pepper spray, although in the process the reputation of the Prime Minister's Office was probably damaged by its failure to fully co-operate in releasing top-secret government files. The Canadian public became increasingly sensitized to the dangers of secrecy and stonewalling.

The MAI and its various offshoots posed a somewhat different problem for Canada than did North American free trade. Both were held by their critics to threaten the Canadian nation-state, but free trade encouraged mainly a North American economic integration, while globalization went much further. A number of pundits saw continental economic integration as leading inevitably to political and social integration (or 'convergence', as it came to be called), although most theories dealt with the economic arena. In the late 1990s, Conrad Black's new newspaper, the *National Post*, became a vocal advocate of total North American integration, although the paper softened its stance after being purchased by the Asper family early in the new millennium. Convergence theory is not monolithic. Instead, a number of alternative scenarios have been advanced by various convergence theorists. One scenario emphasizes strong market forces and weakened governments. Another talks about imitation of the best way to operate—the mimicking of

Prime Minister Jean Chrétien and Environment Minister David Anderson shake hands following the House of Commons vote on ratification of the Kyoto Accord, 10 December 2002. The Canadian Press/Tom Hanson.

Kyoto Protocol to the United Nations Framework Convention on Climate Change

The Kyoto Accord of 1997 has been one of the most controversial international agreements that Canada has ever signed. The opening pages of this document, reprinted below, illustrate the complexity of the issues with which the Canadian public must now deal on a routine basis.

The Parties to this Protocol, Being Parties to the United Nations Framework Convention on Climate Change, hereinafter referred to as 'the Convention', In pursuit of the ultimate objective of the Convention as stated in its Article 2, Recalling the provisions of the Convention, Being guided by Article 3 of the Convention, Pursuant to the Berlin Mandate adopted by decision 1/CP.1 of the Conference of the Parties to the Convention at its first session, Have agreed as follows:

Article 1

For the purposes of this Protocol, the definitions contained in Article 1 of the Convention shall apply. In addition:

1. 'Conference of the Parties' means the Conference of the Parties to the Convention.
2. 'Convention' means the United Nations Framework Convention on Climate Change, adopted in New York on 9 May 1992.
3. 'Intergovernmental Panel on Climate Change' means the Intergovernmental Panel on Climate Change established in 1988 jointly by the World Meteorological Organization and the United Nations Environment Programme.
4. 'Montreal Protocol' means the Montreal Protocol on Substances that Deplete the Ozone Layer, adopted in Montreal on 16 September 1987 and as subsequently adjusted and amended.
5. 'Parties present and voting' means Parties present and casting an affirmative or negative vote.
6. 'Party' means, unless the context otherwise indicates, a Party to this Protocol.
7. 'Party included in Annex I' means a Party included in Annex I to the Convention, as may be amended, or a Party which has made a notification under Article 4, paragraph 2(g), of the Convention.

Article 2

1. Each Party included in Annex I in achieving its quantified emission limitation and reduction commitments under Article 3, in order to promote sustainable development, shall:
   (a) Implement and/or further elaborate policies and measures in accordance with its national circumstances, such as: (i) Enhancement of energy efficiency in relevant sectors of the national economy; (ii) Protection and enhancement of sinks and reservoirs of greenhouse gases not controlled by the Montreal Protocol, taking into account its commitments under relevant international environmental agreements; promotion of sustainable forest management practices, afforestation and reforestation; (iii) Promotion of sustainable forms of agriculture in light of climate change considerations; (iv) Promotion, research, development and increased use of new and renewable forms of energy, of carbon dioxide sequestration technologies and of advanced and innovative environmentally sound technologies; FCCC/CP/1997/L.7/Add.1 (v) Progressive reduction or phasing out of market imperfections, fiscal incentives, tax and duty exemptions and subsidies in all greenhouse gas emitting sectors that run counter to the objective of the Convention and apply market instruments; (vi) Encouragement of appropriate reforms in relevant sectors aimed at promoting policies and measures which limit or reduce emissions of greenhouse gases

not controlled by the Montreal Protocol;
(vii) Measures to limit and/or reduce emissions of greenhouse gases not controlled by the Montreal Protocol in the transport sector;
(viii) Limitation and/or reduction of methane through recovery and use in waste management, as well as in the production, transport and distribution of energy;

(b) Cooperate with other such Parties to enhance the individual and combined effectiveness of their policies and measures adopted under this Article, pursuant to Article 4, paragraph 2(e)(i), of the Convention. To this end, these Parties shall take steps to share their experience and exchange information on such policies and measures, including developing ways of improving their comparability, transparency and effectiveness. The Conference of the Parties serving as the meeting of the Parties to this Protocol shall, at its first session or as soon as practicable thereafter, consider ways to facilitate such cooperation, taking into account all relevant information.

2. The Parties included in Annex I shall pursue limitation or reduction of emissions of greenhouse gases not controlled by the Montreal Protocol from aviation and marine bunker fuels, working through the International Civil Aviation Organization and the International Maritime Organization, respectively.

3. The Parties included in Annex I shall strive to implement policies and measures under this Article in such a way as to minimize adverse effects, including the adverse effects of climate change, effects on international trade, and social, environmental and economic impacts on other Parties, especially developing country Parties and in particular those identified in Article 4, paragraphs 8 and 9 of the Convention, taking into account Article 3 of the Convention. The Conference of the Parties serving as the meeting of the Parties to this Protocol may take further action, as appropriate, to promote the implementation of the provisions of this paragraph.

4. The Conference of the Parties serving as the meeting of the Parties to this Protocol, if it decides that it would be beneficial to coordinate any of the policies and measures in paragraph 1(a) above, taking into account different national circumstances and potential effects, shall consider ways and means to elaborate the coordination of such policies and measures.

Article 3

1. The Parties included in Annex I shall, individually or jointly, ensure that their aggregate anthropogenic carbon dioxide equivalent emissions of the greenhouse gases listed in Annex A do not exceed their assigned amounts, calculated pursuant to their quantified emission limitation and reduction commitments inscribed in Annex B and in accordance with the provisions of this Article, with a view to reducing their overall emissions of such gases by at least 5 per cent below 1990 levels in the commitment period 2008 to 2012.

2. Each Party included in Annex I shall, by 2005, have made demonstrable progress in achieving its commitments under this Protocol.

3. The net changes in greenhouse gas emissions from sources and removals by sinks resulting from direct human-induced land use change and forestry activities, limited to afforestation, reforestation, and deforestation since 1990, measured as verifiable changes in stocks in each commitment period shall be used to meet the commitments in this Article of each Party included in Annex I. The greenhouse gas emissions from sources and removals by sinks associated with those activities shall be reported in a transparent and verifiable manner and reviewed in accordance with Articles 7 and 8.

4. Prior to the first session of the Conference of the Parties serving as the meeting of the Parties to this Protocol, each Party included in Annex I shall provide for consideration by the Subsidiary Body for Scientific and Technological Advice data to establish its level of carbon stocks in 1990 and to enable an estimate to be made of its changes in carbon stocks in subsequent years. The Conference of the Parties serving as the meeting of the Parties to this Protocol shall, at its first session or as soon as practicable thereafter, decide upon modalities, rules and guidelines as to how and which additional human-induced activities related to changes in greenhouse gas emissions and removals in the agricultural soil and land use change and forestry categories, shall be added to, or subtracted from, the assigned amount for Parties included in Annex I, taking into account uncertainties, transparency in reporting, verifiability, the methodological work of the Intergovernmental Panel on Climate Change, the advice provided by the Subsidiary Body for Scientific and Technological Advice in accordance with Article 5 and the decisions of the Conference of the Parties. Such a decision shall apply in the second and subsequent commitment periods. A Party may choose to apply such a decision on these additional human-induced activities for its first commitment period, provided that these activities have taken place since 1990. . . .

Source: *Kyoto Protocol to the United Nations Framework Convention on Climate Change* (New York: United Nations, 1998), 1–3, at: <unfccc.int/resource/docs/convkp/kpeng.pdf>.

'best practices'—as a consequence of institutional competition. A third scenario speaks of convergence through enforced international agreement, as in the European Economic Community or in NAFTA. A minority of theorists would insist that not just external forces but concomitant internal ones are necessary to bring about convergence. And not all economists agree that convergence is necessarily the way of the future. Most of those who disagree emphasize the continued ability of the nation-state to resist and adjust to new pressures. In the jargon of the economist, the 'border effect' continues to be a silent but powerful retardant to convergence. Moreover, there is now an explicit backlash within many nations to integration and globalization, and this is producing new political alliances and new ways of preserving the power of the nation-state.

A related economic problem for Canada involved the extent to which the nation could afford to be pressured by the international community on environmental concerns. In 1997 an international summit meeting at Kyoto, Japan, had agreed on a world protocol for environmental improvement, most notably through reducing the emission of hydrocarbon gases that many scientists blamed for the so-called 'greenhouse effect' and other pollution. The extent of the greenhouse effect was still being debated, in the public press if not by the scientific community. But the larger question involved the economic costs of complying with Kyoto. The lead in the creation of the Kyoto Accord had been taken by the nations of industrialized Europe, which for a variety of reasons had managed to go much further in reducing industrial pollution than had North America. Europe was supported by a developing world community that either had little polluting industry or did not intend to observe the protocol. The Americans bowed out of the Kyoto Accord, calling it too expensive to implement. As one of the few nations in the world seriously affected, Canada continued to debate the question, although in typically Canadian fashion Kyoto got tied up in constitutional hassles between the federal and provincial governments over jurisdiction.

External Affairs

The demise of communism did not occur without difficulty. In many of the Iron Curtain nations, it turned out that the Communist regime had been the only force supporting unity and stability, whatever the price. Movements of national liberation tore apart the USSR itself, as well as other ethnically complex constructions, such as Yugoslavia. Civil war among Serbs, Croats, and Muslims in Bosnia became an international concern. The transition to a capitalistic economy was so painful that many citizens of the old Soviet bloc began voting in free elections for their former Communist masters. By the mid-1990s it was clear that the Cold War was indeed dead. What would replace it as a principal of international dynamics was not so clear.

The elimination of Communist repression did not necessarily save the world for democracy. As if to demonstrate the fragility of international peace, in the summer of 1990 the Iraqi army invaded Kuwait, one of the small independent oil-rich principalities on the Persian Gulf. The world witnessed the unusual spectacle of American–Russian co-operation at the United Nations, and elsewhere, in opposition to Saddam Hussein's move. With Russian approval, President George H.W. Bush sent American forces to the Persian Gulf. Canada contributed three ancient destroyers to the international force. For the first time, Canada's military involvement abroad did not feature the army but regular naval and air force units. Paradoxically, despite earlier military unification, the Canadian services did not act jointly as a national force in this conflict, at least partly because the forces of other nations (especially the United States) were still organized more conventionally. The Canadians did co-operate very successfully with their allies. The Canadian navy considered its work in the Gulf War highly successful, particularly given the equipment with which it had to operate. The Canadian government got just what it wanted: an active, limited, and relatively inexpensive (about $1 billion) operation within a coalition in which Canadians served apart from direct American control.

In some ways the collapse of the Cold War temporarily opened up new ways for Canadians to offer their services to the world. Canadian peacekeepers were in constant demand around the world, ultimately serving in such trouble spots as Somalia and Bosnia with a singular lack of effectiveness. Canada also flirted with the dangers of diplomatic isolation in 1995, as its attempts to enforce limits on offshore fishing led to an open confrontation with the Spaniards. Fortunately, there was enough support for the Canadian position behind the scenes to discourage Spanish militancy. The crisis was resolved peacefully.

Canadian involvement in the United Nations' Balkan peacekeeping was suggested by the Mulroney government as early as 1990 and reiterated in 1991, but the Mulroney initiative was not popular with Canada's allies. The British foreign secretary told Mulroney, 'Trouble with you Canadians is you think there is a solution to every problem' (quoted in Gammer, 2001: 81). Nevertheless, Canada persisted in driving the United Nations and NATO forward on the Balkan peacekeeping front, and it could hardly avoid contributing to a peacekeeping force for

Peacekeeping in Cambodia: Corporal Corena Letandre of the Canadian Forces' 2 Service Battalion comforts a hospitalized child. Reproduced courtesy of the Department of National Defence, with the permission of the Ministry of Public Works and Government Services, 2006.

Bosnia in 1993 despite recognition of the difficulties of the situation. To a considerable extent, Canadian commanders on the scene were, if anything, more aggressive than the government had intended, and the military did its best to adapt to Canada's doctrines of interventionism in the early 1990s.

Lack of success, lack of funding, and some nasty scandals reduced the credibility of Canada's military to the point that by 1997 the nation could fully anticipate that Canada's armed forces would no longer be serving anywhere in the world but at home. The Somalia Commission of Inquiry concluded:

> Many of the leaders called before us to discuss their roles in the various phases of the deployment refused to acknowledge error. When pressed, they blamed their subordinates who, in turn, cast responsibility upon those below

The Somalia Affair

In 1997 a Commission of Inquiry made its final report on the behaviour of Canadian troops in Somalia in 1993. The following extract explains the background to the inquiry.

In the spring, summer, and fall of 1992, the United Nations, concerned about the breakdown of national government in Somalia and the spectre of famine there, sought international help to restore some semblance of law and order in Somalia and feed its starving citizens. Canada, among other nations, was asked to help. After months of planning and training, and after a change in the nature of the United Nations mission from a peacekeeping mission to a peace enforcement mission, Canadian Forces personnel, as part of a coalition of forces led by the United States, were deployed for service to Somalia, mainly in December 1992. Many of the Canadian personnel involved in the deployment belonged to the Canadian Airborne Regiment Battle Group (CARBG), itself made up largely of soldiers from the Canadian Airborne Regiment (a paratroop battalion), with other army personnel added to it, including A Squadron, an armoured car squadron from the Royal Canadian Dragoons, a mortar platoon from 1st Battalion, the Royal Canadian Regiment, and an engineer squadron from 2 Combat Engineer Regiment.

On the night of March 16–17, 1993, near the city of Belet Huen, Somalia, soldiers of the Canadian Airborne Regiment beat to death a bound 16-year-old Somali youth, Shidane Arone. Canadians were shocked, and they began to ask hard questions. How could Canadian soldiers beat to death a young man held in their custody? Was the Canadian Airborne Regiment suitable or operationally ready to go to Somalia? Was racism a factor in improper conduct within the Regiment? Before long, Canadian media began to publicize accounts of other incidents involving questionable conduct by Canadian soldiers in Somalia. Major Barry Armstrong, surgeon to the Canadian Airborne Regiment, acting in fulfilment of his military duties, alleged that an earlier incident on March 4, 1993, where an intruder was shot dead and another was wounded by Canadian Airborne soldiers, appeared to have been an execution-style killing. And so, other questions arose: Were incidents in Somalia covered up, and, if so, how far up the chain of command did the cover-up extend? Did the Canadian Forces and the Department of National Defence respond appropriately to the allegations of cover-up? And perhaps most problematic of all, were the mistreatment of Shidane Arone and other incidents of misconduct caused by a few 'bad apples', or were they symptomatic of deeper institutional problems in the Canadian military at the time—problems relating to command and control, accountability, leadership, or training? If so, did these problems still exist?

The Canadian Forces responded in many ways to the death of Shidane Arone and other incidents that occurred in Somalia. Several courts martial, arising mostly though not exclusively from misconduct them. They assumed this posture reluctantly—but there is no honour to be found here—only after their initial claims, that the root of many of the most serious problems resided with 'a few bad apples', proved hollow.

We can only hope that Somalia represents the nadir of the fortunes of the Canadian Forces. There seems to be little room to slide lower. One thing is certain, however: left uncorrected, the problems that surfaced in the desert in Somalia and in the boardrooms at National Defence Headquarters will continue to spawn military ignominy. The victim will be Canada and its international reputation.

A total withdrawal from Europe had been delayed by peacekeeping in Yugoslavia, but in early 1996 Canada announced it was acting unilaterally to bring its forces home. Somalia and Bosnia were both

relating to the death of Shidane Arone, were launched and concluded. A court martial trial began against Master Corporal Clayton Matchee, the person who allegedly beat Shidane Arone to death. The trial did not proceed, however, because injuries resulting from an apparent suicide attempt rendered MCpl Matchee unfit to stand trial. The most prominent court martial was arguably that of Private Kyle Brown, who was convicted of manslaughter and torture in the death of Mr Arone. In some cases, appeals of the courts martial arising from the Somalia operation were launched. Other individuals involved suffered sanctions less severe than imprisonment upon conviction.

But perhaps more important, the Canadian Forces recognized the need for additional measures to respond to public concern about what happened in Somalia. Accordingly, the Chief of the Defence Staff of the Canadian Forces appointed an internal board of inquiry under section 45 of the National Defence Act to look into issues arising from the Somalia operation. The board conducted the first phase of its work from April to July 1993. The board's final report made several recommendations for change. However, its terms of reference were restricted in two ways. First, to avoid challenges to its jurisdiction under the Canadian Charter of Rights and Freedoms, it was essentially precluded from looking into incidents that could give rise to court martial proceedings. . . . Second, its focus was on

issues such as leadership and discipline relating to the CARBG, which included the antecedents of the CARBG in Canada and higher headquarters in Somalia before and during its deployment there. Thus, it had no authority to look into the actions or omissions of persons at the highest levels of the chain of command within the Canadian Forces. As well, the hearings were not open to the public. It was intended that there would be a second phase of the inquiry to address issues not addressed in its first phase.

Critics argued that an open inquiry was needed to get to the truth of what happened and why. Representatives of the Liberal Party of Canada, the official opposition at the time the board of inquiry was established, argued for an open public inquiry under the National Defence Act. When the Liberals gained power after the 1993 federal election, they continued to express this view. However, as more revelations suggesting possible cover-up and other disclosures were made, the Government eventually decided to establish a public inquiry independent of the military that would have the power to subpoena witnesses not belonging to the military. As a result, on March 20, 1995, this Commission of Inquiry, governed by the federal Inquiries Act, was created. This act sets out the statutory powers and responsibilities of inquiries, generally giving us broad powers to summon and enforce the attendance of witnesses and to require the production of documents.

Source: *Dishonoured Legacy: The Lessons of the Somalia Affair: Report of the Commission of Inquiry into the Deployment of Canadian Forces to Somalia: Executive Summary* (Ottawa: Minister of Public Works and Government Services, 1997), I, 1–3; notes omitted. Reproduced courtesy of the Privy Council Office, with the permission of the Minister of Public Works and Government Services, 2006.

public relations disasters that marked an end to a new Canadian willingness to intervene in local disputes. In the former, supposedly highly disciplined Canadian soldiers brutalized the locals. In the latter, Canadian peacekeepers seemed unable to accomplish anything positive and were often held as impotent hostages by the warring factions.

In the end, the Chrétien government chose to return to a more traditional interpretation of peacekeeping, in which Canada served as a neutral arbitrator rather than an interventionist peacekeeper. To a considerable extent the withdrawal to neutral peacekeeping was a product of the failure of the military to be successful, complicated by the military insistence that success required better hardware and increased expenditures. Chrétien cancelled several large orders for new hardware the military commanders deemed necessary to keep the forces competitive. Public exposure of Canadian soldiers' racism and brutality towards one another did little for either image or morale. One battalion of paratroopers, the Canadian Airborne, was totally disbanded. Canadian troops did yeoman duty in two domestic emergencies, a major flood in Manitoba in May 1997 and a devastating ice storm in Quebec in January 1998. Both actions served to refurbish the military's public image and self-confidence.

The disarray of the military and the withdrawal from an active peacekeeping role in Africa seemed symptomatic of Canada's international posture. The idealism of earlier days was now replaced by incompetence and impotence. Public opinion polls by the end of the century routinely reported that Canadians no longer expected to be defended from foreign aggression by their own military.

Canadian Society

The Immigrants

Straddling the gap between international concerns and domestic policy was immigration, one of the 'hot button' issues of the decade. The fundamental questions were the same as always. How many immigrants should Canada admit, particularly given the shortage of employment opportunities for members of Generation X and the fragility of the nation's urban infrastructure? By the 1990s, many of the immigrants to Canada came from the Third World.

The new Canadian immigrants came from six vastly different regions: Africa, the Caribbean, the Middle East, and three regions of Asia—South Asia, Southeast Asia, and Asia proper. Most were members of visible minorities. A substantial number were Muslims. The 1991 census indicated 253,265 Muslims. Ten years later the census counted 579,740 adherents of Islam. Many of the new arrivals were political refugees from highly repressive regimes, and their situation in Canada was dominated by that previous experience. There were bad memories, and guilt about loved ones left behind. Many newcomers to Canada suffered from depression and required extensive psychological assistance to manage from day to day. Those who became caught in the refugee backlog of the 1980s—which meant they were unable legally to work until their status had been formally determined—were obviously often seriously disadvantaged. The Canadian government in July 1994 finally made it possible for failed refugees to become legitimate permanent residents. The visible minorities from the Third World settled almost exclusively in the large cities of Ontario and Quebec, as well as in Vancouver. They were also most likely

Table 12.1	Top 10 Source Countries of Immigrants to Canada, 1991–2001	
China, People's Republic	197,355	
India	158,170	
Philippines	122,075	
Yugoslavia	67,750	
Sri Lanka	67,585	
Pakistan	57,940	
Taiwan	53,750	
US	51,440	
Iran	47,075	
Poland	43,370	
Total top 10 countries	859,450	(46.9%)
All other countries	922,300	(53.1%)

to be the targets of racial hostility, both from the general population and from law enforcement agencies. Most immigrants were not refugees, but those who were often experienced poor service from public assistance programs. As usual, the newcomers clustered in poorer urban sections, where they often became associated in the public mind with the problem of ethnic gangs.

Multiculturalism contributed to the positive reception of the immigrants, although many commentators complained that Canada failed to state adequate limits on what the larger society would accept, encouraging the newcomers to believe that they could continue traditions that were not generally approved in their new home while carrying on battles inherited from the old country. Further complicating immigrant reception in Canada was what became known as 'deskilling'. According to one study, 'the landed immigrant cohort of 2000 was dominated by one single occupational group: professional occupations in natural and applied sciences' (Couton, 2002). Canadian employers and professional bodies (usually governed under provincial jurisdiction) have long insisted that their employees and members have Canadian work experience and have looked with suspicion on foreign credentials, which are held to be non-transferable because of the problem of guaranteeing quality. This problem would be recognized after 2000 and addressed by several governments.

The Aged

While all symptoms of social morbidity continued their alarming progress, perhaps the most disturbing trends occurred at the opposite ends of the life cycle, particularly among the aging. The first of the baby boomers were coming up to (early) retirement, soon to be followed by the deluge. That the system was really not ready for this event became increasingly clear. In 1995 the Canadian Institute of Actuaries (CIA) reported that in 1992 retired Canadians (numbering 19 per cent of the working-age population) had paid $9 billion in taxes and received $54.4 billion in public funds in a variety of forms, including medical treatment. By 2030 the

percentage of retired Canadians would be up to 39 per cent of those eligible to work. The payout at 1992 rates would be well beyond the capacity of the system to absorb. The present system worked only because the demand upon it had not yet grown sufficiently. The CIA concluded that the present system of social insurance payments was not 'sustainable in [its] current form. Contributions will rise. Benefits will be cut; retirement ages deferred; universality curtailed.' Surveys suggested that many Canadians had begun to appreciate the difficulties, although most were still confused and few had any solutions. According to one survey, most Canadians feared that the Canada Pension Plan would be unable to look after their retirement, but fewer than 15 per cent had more than $10,000 put away somewhere apart from their CPP pensions. The age at which most Canadians still expected to retire was 59, although the experts and the politicians were now suggesting that such an age was simply a pipe dream for most people.

Retirement pensions were only part of the problem. The other major concern was health care, the cost of which continued to spiral upward despite desperate efforts by provincial governments to bring it under control through cost-cutting and privatization. Per capita health-care expenditure (in constant 1986 dollars) had progressively and annually increased from $1,257.25 in 1975 to $1,896.27 in 1993. The proportion of gross domestic product devoted to health care had gone up from 7.1 per cent in 1975 to 10.1 per cent in 1993. Although these Canadian figures were not as alarming as the corresponding American ones—the proportion of GDP given to health care in the US had increased from 8.4 per cent in 1975 to 14.4 per cent in 1993—they pointed to a financial crisis if they were not capped somehow. Much of the increasing cost involved care for the elderly, and life expectancy continued to advance. The baby boom and increased life expectancy together produced the demographic prospect of ever larger numbers of elderly people making increasing demands on the health-care system.

While provincial governments closed hospitals and reduced the numbers of beds available within those remaining, Canadians began to debate hard questions, such as the extent to which the terminally ill should be offered the expensive treatment that medical science now had at its disposal. Even if the elderly were not given expensive treatment, their increasing numbers produced a housing problem. Only one out of every four Canadians expected to have to look after his or her parents in old age, which was far too low an estimate of future realities. But even if all Canadians took in their still functioning elderly, the numbers of those requiring extensive care beyond the home were bound to increase enormously. Dealing with seniors was clearly the most important problem facing the social insurance system, particularly given the national sense that deficit financing was already too high. One could only sympathize with the younger generation, unable to establish themselves in careers but still being asked to finance the post-retirement years of their elders. According to one study by the Research for Public Policy group, younger Canadians would have to pay increasingly more in taxes than they would ever receive in social benefits to maintain the present structure, which was not only 'unsustainable' but 'immoral'. But this was not the only morality question surrounding health care. Much of the cost of the health-care system continued to be absorbed in looking after seniors in their last months of life. Few Canadians wished to do less, whatever the cost. Despite all the rhetoric, health care was still more of an ideological issue than a practical one for most Canadians. While some might want the opportunity to jump queues to get their needs looked after more quickly, not many Canadians really sought to cut into the basic principle of universal health care available to all. For many, access to free health care had become one of the major factors of the Canadian identity. According to one oft-quoted comedian, a Canadian was an unarmed American with free and universal health-care coverage.

Redress for Historic Abuse

Early in 1990, thousands of Canadians received from the Minister of State for Multiculturalism and Citizenship a letter enclosing a substantial cheque and an 'acknowledgement signed by the Prime Minister'. The recipients were Japanese Canadians who had been uprooted from their homes in 1942 by the Canadian government. The cheque was for 'redress' (or compensation, as it was usually called), and the document from the Prime Minister acknowledged that 'the treatment of Japanese Canadians during and after World War II was unjust and violated principles of human rights as they are understood today.' Japanese Canadians had first organized to seek redress in 1977, at the time of the centennial of the first arrival of Japanese in Canada. The government of Pierre Trudeau had refused to consider action on this issue, but the Progressive Conservative opposition was more sympathetic. After Brian Mulroney's Tories swept to power in 1984, the Japanese renewed their efforts, which led finally on 22 September 1988 to the signature of the Prime Minister on a Redress Agreement between the National Association of Japanese Canadians and the Canadian government (Miki and Kobayashi, 1991). This agreement symbolized the changed attitudes towards both ethnicity and redress at the end of the twentieth century. The government's action with respect to the Japanese encouraged a variety of other groups to apply for redress, including the Ukrainian aliens interned by Canada during the Great War and the Acadians deported from Nova Scotia in the 1750s.

When the unsinkable ship the *Titanic* went down in the Atlantic Ocean in 1912, it took with it over 100 Canadian victims. The literature on the *Titanic* demonstrates quite clearly that the tragedy could have been prevented, and that responsibility for the disaster was systemic and widely distributed. But what is perhaps often forgotten is that most of the survivors and the families of the victims never seriously considered demanding a public inquiry or government compensation. Nor did they engage in class-action litigation in the courts to the same end. Disasters in Canada were traditionally regarded as acts of God. The federal government did supply compensation for victims of the Halifax Explosion of 1917, but that was because the disaster was regarded as a war matter. When the notion of public assistance for disaster losses began to take hold in Canada after World War II, compensation was not initially regarded as a matter of right or of reparation. Rather, it was one of relief and generosity, which meant that it was not really compensation at all. Victims of the Manitoba Flood of 1950 received assistance from the

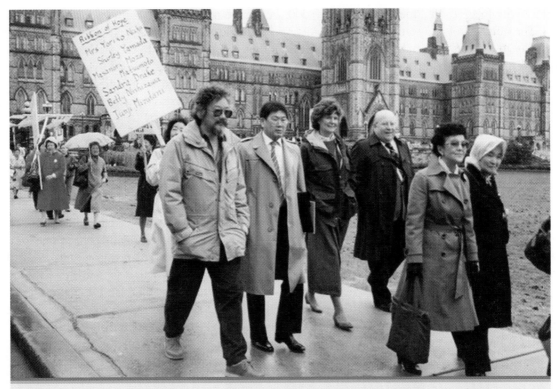

David Suzuki marches at the Redress Rally on Parliament Hill on 14 April 1988. A few months later the government signed the Redress Agreement, officially offering an apology to Japanese Canadians. Reprinted with permission from Gordon King Photography.

federal and provincial governments, as well as from a privately raised relief fund. We do not understand just how disaster relief gradually became translated into a right of compensation, but by the 1990s that concept was clearly in place.

Part of the shift was doubtless associated with the rise of insurance to cover various sorts of damage, including malpractice and accidental injury to property and person, and the increasing insistence on dealing with such matters in the courts. Seeking damages for injury through the courts is, of course, something that has been with us as long as there have been civil courts. The practice was greatly escalated in the United States after World War II, with juries awarding ever larger damage amounts, often exceeding the defendant's ability to pay them. In the process, the concept of liability was transformed by the courts. In recent years, simple damage suits have grown into class actions, in which a large, amorphous body of victims engages in litigation. Prime

examples of such actions, of course, are the cases that have been introduced against various tobacco companies for illnesses resulting from smoking. We may not understand the way this trend developed, but it is perfectly clear that one of the major social issues in Canada in the last third of the twentieth century was the appearance of the idea that someone must be held responsible for every negative consequence. (A related concept is that every victim is entitled to compensation for his or her injury.) In the context of Canada's Aboriginal peoples this clearly was the outstanding social issue in Canada at the end of the century.

Aboriginal Peoples

In 1996 there were some 554,000 status Indians in Canada. Two-thirds of them lived on about 2,600 reserves in over 600 registered bands, and the remainder resided chiefly in larger southern cities such as Winnipeg. In addition, there were 41,000 Inuit. The numbers of non-status Indians and Métis are harder to estimate. The number accepted by the government is 210,000, but the total across Canada is probably at least 500,000. Despite increased levels of media attention, government expenditures, and Aboriginal self-awareness, the realities of Native life—while improving—continue to recall conditions in the poorest underdeveloped countries of the world. In the 1990s, the First Nations for the first time were popularly perceived as an important Canadian political 'problem', perhaps the most important and controversial one of the decade. The immediate crisis was not over the demographics of Native life, although particular cases of violence and abuse continued to make newspaper headlines. The problem was really three related issues that came to prominence in the nineties. The first was how to deal with the land rights of the indigenous peoples. The second was how to deal with Native administration and the Aboriginal insistence on the right to self-government. The third was how to make reparations for earlier mistreatment of Aboriginals, particularly in the residential school system of Canada.

LAND RIGHTS

The Aboriginal peoples had long attempted to claim their land rights. Those claims came under three headings. First were the claims resulting from agreements or treaties made with the Crown, whether before Confederation, between 1871 and 1921 (the so-called numbered treaties, 1–11), or in modern times. Second were claims based on continuing Aboriginal title (established historically). Finally, there were specific claims, usually involving either improper seizure of land or government failure to pay proper compensation for lands seized legally. In 1969, the Trudeau government established the Indian Claims Commission to deal with land claims, but the slow pace of negotiations soon led the Aboriginal peoples to turn to the courts for redress. A series of landmark court decisions, many of them in the Supreme Court of Canada, gradually produced new policies from the federal and provincial governments. Over the ensuing years, a number of historic agreements would be reached with Aboriginal peoples, although the settlement

of claims was a slow, labyrinthian process. Literally hundreds of land claims have been raised, and not all have been dealt with, either through negotiations or through the courts. By and large, the courts have not so much settled land claims as maintained the Aboriginal right to hold them and to negotiate them with the government.

In 1973, the Supreme Court of Canada ruled in the *Calder* case that the Nisga'a of British Columbia had Aboriginal title to their land that had never been extinguished. Mr Justice Wilfred Judson concluded: 'The fact is that when the settlers came the Indians were there, organized in societies and occupying the land as their forefathers had done for centuries. This is what Indian title means. What they are asserting in this action is that they had a right to continue to live on their lands as their forefathers had lived and that this right has never been lawfully extinguished.' Mr Justice Emmett Hall added, 'What emerges from the . . . evidence is that the Nishgas in fact are and were from time immemorial a distinctive cultural entity with concepts of ownership indigenous to their culture and capable of articulation under the common law. . . .' In August 1973, Minister of Indian Affairs Jean Chrétien stated publicly that the federal government was committed to settling Aboriginal land claims.

A Supreme Court ruling in 1973 that the Quebec government could not continue with its James Bay hydroelectric project until it had resolved Aboriginal claims led to the historic James Bay and Northern Quebec Agreement in 1975 between the province and the James Bay Cree and Inuit, which is generally considered to be the first modern land claim agreement. It provided for $225 million in financial compensation, as well as establishing landownership and usage in the region of northern Quebec. Aboriginal rights and treaty rights were recognized in the 1982 Constitution Act, although individual cases would have to be decided by the courts. In 1984, in a final ruling in *Guerin v. The Queen* (a case brought in 1975 by the Musqueam Indian band in Vancouver), the Supreme Court of Canada recognized that Aboriginal rights in Canada predated Confederation.

In 1984 a suit filed in the Supreme Court of British Columbia by 35 Gitksan and 13 Wet'suwet'en chiefs contested 58,000 square kilometres of land in the province. The case (known as the *Delgamuukw* case) was heard from 1987 to 1990, and a decision was brought down on 8 March 1991. Before this decision, the Supreme Court of Canada had ruled in 1990 in *Sparrow v. The Queen* that section 35 of the Constitution Act protected Aboriginal rights, which it insisted must be dealt with by the courts in a generous manner. In his decision in the *Delgamuukw* case, Chief Justice Allan McEachern of the BC court denied the plaintiffs the right to exclusive landownership and self-government, in large measure because he rejected the oral history on which the claims had been based. As a result of this case, the government of British Columbia and the First Nations agreed to a treaty-making process. In the meantime, however, the plaintiffs in *Delgamuukw* appealed, and were rejected again on their major points in 1993. Another appeal was heard by the Supreme Court of Canada, with a decision handed down on 11 December 1997. The Supreme Court did not rule on title, indicating that the case would be better resolved through negotiations. But it did indicate that oral histories are 'a repository of historical knowledge for a culture' (quoted in Dickason with McNab, 2009: 330–1), and that the courts must 'come to terms with the oral histories of Aboriginal societies, which for many Aboriginal Nations, are the only record of their past' (Chief Justice Lamer, in *Delgamuukw v. British Columbia*, 3 S.C.R., 1997). On 16 July 1998, the federal and British Columbia governments signed a final agreement with the Nisga'a people, which granted them 1,930 square kilometres of land, self-government, and a large amount of cash; as part of the agreement, the Nisga'a gave up their tax-free status under the Indian Act.

ABORIGINAL SELF-GOVERNMENT

Aboriginal self-government was another long-standing question in Canada (Engelstad and Bird, 1992). The First Nations insisted that the assertion of ultimate sovereignty over the land by the Crown interfered with neither Aboriginal land rights nor the rights of Aboriginals to govern themselves according to their own laws in their traditional territories. Considerable historical evidence exists to indicate that historically the Crown did not usually attempt to assert its direct political authority over Aboriginal land. Exactly how

the government or the courts viewed the legal relationship between the Crown and the First Nations was and is another matter entirely. In most instances, Aboriginal self-government follows the municipal model, with local councils ultimately responsible to the Crown, although several First Nations organizations insist that it must become something more (Royal Commission on Aboriginal Peoples, 1993).

In May 1993, the federal government agreed not only to settle the Inuit land claims to the eastern Arctic, but to establish a new territory (to be called Nunavut) with a new form of Aboriginal self-government, that is, an inclusive public government not run exclusively by or for the Aboriginal people. In fact, however, because the Inuit comprise close to 85 per cent of the Nunavut population, it will remain a self-governing Aboriginal territory for the foreseeable future. This arrangement came after agreement in principle had been reached in 1990. The demand for self-government originated with the Inuit, who had refused to surrender it in the years of discussion over land rights. The new territory, which was hived off from the Northwest Territories, came into existence on 1 April 1999. In Nunavut's legislative assembly, Inuktitut and English are the two official languages. Some observers have argued that Nunavut is not really run by the Inuit, since the federal government continues to have a strong presence through its agencies, co-management boards, and financial dealings with the territory. Instead, they say, Nunavut has something more like a highly traditional colonial government (Wall, 2000: 143–67).

RESIDENTIAL SCHOOLS

The beginnings of the residential school system long predated Confederation. In the seventeenth century, schools were usually part of the missionary work of the churches, designed both to educate Aboriginal people and to assimilate them into European society. Residential schools came in a variety of forms, although in the twentieth century the most common were the so-called industrial schools. They were located in almost every province and territory. The government of Canada shared in the administration of these schools from at least 1874. By the end of the nineteenth century, the schools had shifted from being church institutions partly funded by the

Delgamuukw v. British Columbia

Late in 1997 the Supreme Court of Canada handed down a judgement on appeal from the Court of Appeal of British Columbia. The case had been brought to the Supreme Court by Delgamuukw (a.k.a. Earl Muldoe) on behalf of a number of Gitksan and Wet'suwet'en 'houses' upon the earlier rejection of their Aboriginal claims by the British Columbia court. A portion of the judgement follows, specifically some of the dissenting opinion of Justices La Forest and L'Heureux-Dubé. This indicates the complexity of the reasoning involved.

The reasons of La Forest and L'Heureux-Dubé JJ. were delivered by

187   LA FOREST J.—I have read the reasons of the Chief Justice, and while I agree with his conclusion, I disagree with various aspects of his reasons and in particular, with the methodology he uses to prove that aboriginal peoples have a general right of occupation of certain lands (often referred to as 'aboriginal title').

188   I begin by considering why a new trial is necessary in this case. It is true, as the Chief Justice points out, that the amalgamation of the appellants' individual claims represents a defect in the pleadings and, technically speaking, this prevents us from considering the merits of the case. However, in my view, there is a more substantive problem with the pleadings in this case. Before this Court, the appellants sought a declaration of 'aboriginal title' but attempted, in essence, to prove that they had complete control over the territory in question. The appellants effectively argued on appeal, as they did at trial, that by virtue of their social and land tenure systems—consisting of Chief authority, Houses, feasts, crests, and totem poles—they acquired an absolute interest in the claimed territory, including ownership of and jurisdiction over the land. The problem with this approach is that it requires proof of governance and control as opposed to proof of general occupation of the affected land. Only the latter is the sine qua non of 'aboriginal title'. It follows that what the appellants sought by way of declaration from this Court and what

they set out to prove by way of the evidence were two different matters. In light of this substantive defect in the pleadings, a new trial should be ordered to permit a reassessment of the matter on the basis of these reasons.

189   In my view, the foundation of 'aboriginal title' was succinctly described by Judson J. in *Calder v. Attorney-General of British Columbia*, [1973] S.C.R. 313, where, at p. 328, he stated: 'the fact is that when the settlers came, the Indians were there, organized in societies and occupying the land as their forefathers had done for centuries. This is what Indian title means . . . .' Relying in part on Judson J.'s remarks, Dickson J. (as he then was) wrote in *Guerin v. The Queen*, [1984] 2 S.C.R. 335, at p. 382, that aboriginal peoples have a 'legal right to occupy and possess certain lands, the ultimate title to which is in the Crown'. As well, in *Canadian Pacific Ltd. v. Paul*, [1988] 2 S.C.R. 654, this Court stated, at p. 678: 'The inescapable conclusion from the Court's analysis of Indian title up to this point is that the Indian interest in land is truly *sui generic*. It is more than the right to enjoyment and occupancy although . . . it is difficult to describe what more in traditional property law terminology'. More recently, Judson J.'s views were reiterated in *R. v. Van der Peet*, [1996] 2 S.C.R. 507. There Lamer C.J. wrote for the majority, at para. 30, that the doctrine of aboriginal rights (one aspect of which is 'aboriginal title') arises from 'one simple fact: when Europeans arrived in North America, aboriginal peoples *were already here*, living in communities on the land, and participating in

distinctive cultures, as they had done for centuries' (emphasis in original).

190   It follows from these cases that the aboriginal right of possession is derived from the historic occupation and use of ancestral lands by aboriginal peoples. Put another way, 'aboriginal title' is based on the continued occupation and use of the land as part of the aboriginal peoples' traditional way of life. This *sui generis* interest is not equated with fee simple ownership; nor can it be described with reference to traditional property law concepts. The best description of 'aboriginal title', as set out above, is a broad and general one derived from Judson J.'s pronouncements in *Calder, supra*. Adopting the same approach, Dickson J. wrote in *Guerin, supra*, that the aboriginal right of occupancy is further characterized by two principal features. First, this *sui generic* interest in the land is personal in that it is generally inalienable except to the Crown. Second, in dealing with this interest, the Crown is subject to a fiduciary obligation to treat aboriginal peoples fairly. Dickson J. went on to conclude, at p. 382, that '[a]ny description of Indian title which goes beyond these two features is both unnecessary and potentially misleading'. I share his views and am therefore reluctant to define more precisely the 'right [of aboriginal peoples] to continue to live on their lands as their forefathers had lived'; see *Calder*, at p. 328.

191   The approach I adopt, in defining the aboriginal right of occupancy, is also a highly contextual one. More specifically, I find it necessary to make a distinction between: (1) the recognition of a general right to occupy and possess ancestral lands; and (2) the recognition of a discrete right to engage in an aboriginal activity in a particular area. I defined the latter in *R. v. Côté*, [1996] 3 S.C.R. 139, at para. 97, as 'the traditional use, by a tribe of Indians, that has continued from pre-contact times of a particular area for a particular purpose'. The

issue in *Côté*, as in *Van der Peet*, was whether the use of a particular fishing spot was really an aspect of the aboriginal peoples' way of life in pre-contact times; see also in the *Van der Peet* trilogy *R. v. Gladstone*, [1996] 2 S.C.R. 723, and *R. v. N.T.C. Smokehouse Ltd.*, [1996] 2 S.C.R. 672. In all those cases, the fishing rights asserted by the aboriginal claimants were not associated with a more general occupancy of the affected land. By contrast, the present case deals with a general claim to occupy and possess vast tracts of territory (58,000 square kilometres). This type of generalized land claim is not merely a bundle of discrete aboriginal rights to engage in specific activities. Rather, it is, as the Chief Justice states, at para. 111, the 'right to use land for a variety of activities, not all of which need be aspects of practices, customs and traditions which are integral to the distinctive cultures of aboriginal societies'. These land-based activities are, of course, related to the aboriginal society's habits and mode of life.

192   I note, as well, that in defining the nature of 'aboriginal title', one should generally not be concerned with statutory provisions and regulations dealing with reserve lands. In *Guerin, supra*, this Court held that the interest of an Indian band in a reserve is derived from, and is of the same nature as, the interest of an aboriginal society in its traditional tribal lands. Accordingly, the Court treated the aboriginal interest in reserve lands as one of occupation and possession while recognizing that the underlying title to those lands was in the Crown. It was not decided in *Guerin, supra*, and it by no means follows, that specific statutory provisions governing reserve lands should automatically apply to traditional tribal lands. For this reason, I am unable to assume that specific 'reserve' provisions of the Indian Act, R.S.C., 1985, c. I-5, and the Indian Oil and Gas Act, R.S.C., 1985, c. I-7, apply to huge tracts of land which are subject to an aboriginal right of occupancy.

Source: *Delgamuukw v. British Columbia*, [1997] 3 S.C.R. 1010.

Canada in 1999.

government to being government institutions operated by the churches. Their purpose also shifted, from assimilating students into European society to preparing them for life on controlled reserves. From an early date, there was an undercurrent of abuse and intimidation connected with the schools, for their rationale was based on the (often forcible) removal of children from their families in order to 'civilize' them and convert them to Christianity. Most of the schools had rules against speaking Native languages and practising Native religious beliefs; these rules were typically enforced through corporal punishment and their effect was to denigrate Aboriginal cultures.

In 1969, the government of Canada took over the administration of the schools and they gradually disappeared, the last closing in 1996. Both churches and government were slow to respond formally to the tide of complaints from the Aboriginal community about the treatment of their children in the residential schools, although stories of abuse were recounted before every commission that investigated the treatment of Aboriginal people in Canada, including the Royal Commission on Aboriginal Peoples (1991–6). The Anglican Church formally apologized to the Aboriginal community for its part in the schools only in 1993, and the federal government and the United Church in 1998.

In the 1990s, Aboriginal victims of the residential schools began to take the federal government to court over their treatment. The government in its turn insisted on involving the various churches as co-defendants, in the process virtually bankrupting at least the Anglican Church of Canada and a number of its dioceses. By the end of the decade there were more than 8,000 such cases pending. Early in January 1998, the government of Canada announced a program ('Gathering Strength—Canada's Aboriginal Action Plan') to deal with past injustices, based on reconciliation and concrete action for the future. The government issued a statement of reconciliation acknowledging its part in the residential schools and apologizing for its actions. It offered $350 million to help heal the injuries, but was not able to come to terms with the litigants. In 2007, a $1.9 billion agreement of reparations to survivors was agreed upon. Finally, on 11 June 2008, Prime Minister Harper, on behalf of the Canadian government, made a formal apology in the House of Commons, attended by the leaders of five national Aboriginal organizations and by many residential school survivors, for the damage caused by the schools to individuals, families, and communities. A month earlier, in May 2008, an Indian Residential Schools Truth and Reconciliation Commission was established, but this symbolically significant body got off to a rocky start, with its head, an Ontario judge of Aboriginal descent, resigning within months and the other two commissioners stepping down a few months later. A reconstituted Commission began its work in June 2009 under the leadership of Justice Murray Sinclair, the first Aboriginal judge in the Manitoba court system.

Contemporary Abuse

Charges of sexual abuse were not confined to incidents far in Canada's past. In September 1996, the National Hockey League's Sheldon Kennedy (b. 1969) told the Calgary police that between the ages of 14 and 19 he had been sexually abused more than 350 times by his nationally known hockey coach. The coach admitted the offences and was sentenced to prison early in 1997. After the sentencing, Kennedy's interviews with the press created a considerable controversy. One question that was asked repeatedly was whether the whistle should have been blown much earlier on the abusive coach. The main question, however, centred on the extent to which Kennedy's experience was an aberration. Kennedy did his best to help others, particularly in a campaign to raise funds for a home for sexual abuse victims. Despite his well-publicized in-line skate across Canada in 1998, this venture foundered under the burden of bad management.

Other cases of abuse continued to surface in the media, usually involving authority figures who took advantage of their positions. Understandably, such cases always involved a concern that the good reputation of the vast majority of authority figures would be sullied by the behaviour of a few bad actors. Much evidence suggested that abusive behaviour was not common, but attempts on the part of higher authorities to deny it or sweep it under the carpet were all too frequent. The problem was not confined to Canada. In 2002, the international furor over abusive behaviour by priests of the Roman Catholic Church forced the Vatican for the first time to deal publicly with the issue.

Canadian Culture

Economic restraint hit hard at Canada's cultural industries, almost all of which had relied heavily on public subsidies. Cutbacks were inevitably accompanied by exhortations to financial responsibility and efforts to seek assistance from the private rather than the public sector. To the mid-1990s, much of the slack was taken up by cost-cutting and private fundraising. Ways of raising money became increasingly imaginative and required far more attention from cultural administrators. Too much of the increased revenue, said some critics, came from state-run gambling and privately run lotteries. Public involvement in fundraising was not necessarily a bad thing, for those in the community who helped

The United Church Apology to First Nations Peoples regarding Residential Schools, 26 October 1998

At the conclusion of a four-day meeting of the United Church's General Council Executive, the moderator of the United Church, the Right Reverend Bill Phipps, read the following announcement.

I am here today as Moderator of the United Church of Canada to speak the words that many people have wanted to hear for a very long time. On behalf of the United Church of Canada I apologize for the pain and suffering that our church's involvement in the Indian Residential School system has caused. We are aware of some of the damage that this cruel and ill-conceived system of assimilation has perpetrated on Canada's First Nations people. For this we are truly and most humbly sorry.

To those individuals who were physically, sexually and mentally abused as students of the Indian Residential Schools in which the United Church of Canada was involved, I offer you our most sincere apology. You did nothing wrong. You were and are the victims of evil acts that cannot under any circumstances be justified or excused. We pray that you will hear the sincerity of our words today and that you will witness the living out of this apology in our actions in the future.

We know that many within our church will still not understand why each of us must bear the scar, the blame for this horrendous period in Canadian history. But the truth is we are the bearers of many blessings from our ancestors, and therefore we must also bear their burdens. We must now seek ways of healing ourselves, as well as our relationships with First Nations peoples. This apology is not an end in itself. We are in the midst of a long and painful journey. A journey that began with the United Church's Apology of 1986, to our Statement of Repentance in 1997 and now moving with this apology with regard to Indian Residential Schools. As Moderator of the United Church of Canada I urge each and every member of the church, to reflect on these issues and to join us as we travel this difficult road of repentance, reconciliation and healing.

Source: Excerpt, 'Apology to Former Students of United Church Indian Residential Schools, and to Their Families and Communities' (1998) by The Right Reverend Bill Phipps, Moderator of The United Church of Canada. <www.united-church.ca/beliefs/policies/1998/a623>. Used with permission.

raise money developed close ties with the enterprise. Few of the mainline establishment organizations in dance, classical music, and the theatre were actually forced out of existence, although everyone complained that there was no room for experimentation and risk-taking in the new financial climate. A few specialized operations bit the dust, and several symphony orchestras were threatened with extinction by militant musicians' unions. Nevertheless, despite the constant cries of crisis, the private sector did seem able to fill most of the gaps in the establishment world of haute culture.

Curiously enough, popular culture seemed more genuinely affected by fiscal restraint than did elite culture. The long decline of the Canadian Broadcasting Corporation continued unabated, and Parliament carried on with annual cuts to the corporation's operating budget. Across the corporation as a whole, regional production was the first to suffer. The CBC's problems were many. Not all services ought to have been in equal trouble, however. The radio services were generally acknowledged to be the best in the world. Radio-Canada's television operation in French consistently outdrew the opposition, producing almost all of the most-watched television programs in Quebec.

The sinkhole was English-language television, which had never been able to carve out a satisfactory niche for itself in an increasingly complex viewing world. The introduction of a variety of new Canadian-based cable networks in 1994 further eroded the CBC's position as a showcase for Canadian programming. Few seemed willing to scrap the television service, however. Another government commission, this one chaired by Pierre Juneau, recommended an increase in Canadian content, an end to commercial

Royal Canadian Air Farce cast members Luba Goy, Don Ferguson, John Morgan, and Roger Abbott with politician Preston Manning (seated left). Air Farce Productions Inc.

advertising, and additional revenue from taxes on the competing services. CBC-TV would no longer have to compete in the world of commercial television but would instead become a Canadian version of America's Public Broadcasting System, appealing to the higher instincts of the viewing public. There was no certainty that these recommendations would be accepted. What was definite was that the corporation would have to make do with less. Huge staff cuts were announced, with more to follow. Like employees of almost every other enterprise in Canada, those at the CBC could only look forward to further downsizing.

The prospects for Canadian content were improved to some extent by the expansion of specialty cable channels on television, although much of the new production came in the form of cooking shows and competitive sports channels. No shortage of Canadian talent existed in the field of comedy. *Saturday Night Live* and *SCTV* were both successful comedy programs of the late 1980s featuring a number of Canadian comedians who subsequently had major careers in the United States. *The Kids in the Hall*—with an all-Canadian cast—flourished in the early 1990s. Most of the humour on these shows was generically North American in content, but the McKenzie brothers from *SCTV*, portrayed by Rick Moranis and Dave Thomas, were an exception: two small-town Canadians—'hosers'—who swilled beer, sported toques, talked incessantly about hockey, and struck a chord in their considerable audience. *The Red Green Show* satirized the same kind of rural Canada. It was particularly subtle in its approach, superficially accepting the masculine values of the hunting-and-fishing set while constantly poking fun at them as well. Several of the show's catchphrases, including 'Keep your stick on the ice', passed into the larger national vocabulary. More directly political was the *Royal Canadian Air Farce*. Its 'chicken cannon' regularly blasted a Canadian prominent in the current news.

One of the most powerful examples of Canadian content came in television commercials produced by the Molson Brewing Company, the makers of the beer labelled 'Canadian'. Molson released a number of ads with subtly anti-American themes, and in March 2000 produced a nationalist 'rant' entitled 'I

Am Canadian', which was the talk of the nation for many months. The rant was very simple. An ordinary Joe stands before a slide display of Canadian backgrounds while he recites his litany, which included such lines as: 'I believe in peace keeping, not policing, diversity, not assimilation, and that the beaver is a truly proud and noble animal.' According to one account, high school students chanted the rant spontaneously in the corridors of their schools (*Calgary Herald*, 30 Apr. 2000). Many commentators wondered why it was a beer company and not the government that was involved in promoting Canadian pride. Characteristically, the Americans did not seem to notice the commercial at all.

It was not clear whether the problems of professional sports in Canada were caused by budgetary restraint in the public sector, although it *was* clear that sports teams in Canada could no longer be sustained by massive infusions of indirect aid from the public purse, often in the form of arena facilities. This changing attitude combined with other factors to cause a number of disasters. One was an international market in player salaries with which Canadian teams could not successfully compete. The Canadian Football League, faced with escalating costs and declining attendance in the later 1980s and early 1990s, responded aggressively to its problems by expanding directly into the United States. This strategy proved absolutely disastrous. The new American franchises all folded after a season or two, leaving behind nothing but confusion and a trail of debt. The CFL regrouped and actually achieved some success as an acknowledged minor league protected by the National Football League. As for hockey, American integration finally caught up with it. The Quebec Nordiques left Canada for Colorado in 1995 and the Winnipeg Jets announced their departure for Phoenix, Arizona, early in 1996. Many experts calculated that the Edmonton Oilers, Calgary Flames, and Ottawa Senators could not be far behind, although all three teams continued to hang on into 2010 despite claims of financial losses. The National Hockey League, now run by high-powered American business executives, decided that Canadian franchises in smaller cities were not sufficiently profitable. The NHL refused to share television revenue equally and

Practising Islam in Toronto and Edmonton

We are Muslims, we believe in the Islamic religion, and we practised it in our country. People from all over the world, every continent, every country maybe, come to Canada, so all the religions are here. We go to mosque on Fridays instead of Sunday like the Christians. On Saturday and Sunday, there are certain religious classes, but sometimes it is difficult to get transportation. The nearest mosque is on Dundas [Street, in Toronto]. It's too far away, so sometimes it is difficult to get there. I'm Muslim, but I'm not a very religious person. We have our own clothes and our own culture. We like and are very proud to wear our traditional dresses in the summertime. Whether you are very religious or not, winter is your master because you have to wear what the other people wear. But in the summertime, we are very comfortable wearing our dresses, our style. If you are married, you have to cover your hair. That's for religious purposes. We have different sheekh (religious leaders). Those are in the top ranks of the religion. In some circles, if you are a woman, whether you are married or not, you have to cover your body except for maybe your eyes, your face. Our tradition is the Somali tradition. We cover our hair and our body. We are all Muslim, but some wear short dresses the way that they like. They pray five times a day, but they wear whatever they like, and others have some restrictions, but it depends, just like Catholicism.

We pray five times a day. Sometimes we pray as a family, but it is not compulsory to do it together. Amina prays on her own and the others do so as well, but on the weekend, if we are all together, we pray together in the morning (Subah), at noon (Duhur), evening (Asar), (Macrib) and the final prayers (Isha). That's five prayers. We pray before sunrise, after two o'clock, at six, at nine, and at ten we pray the last one before we go to bed. If it is not possible for them to pray during the day, when they come home, they have a late prayer.

Source: Elizabeth McLuhan, ed., *Safe Haven: The Refugee Experience of Five Families* (Toronto: Multicultural History Society of Ontario, 1995), 192–4.

One of the Five Pillars of Islam that we used to always follow before we came to Canada was to pray five times daily and to attend the mosque on Fridays. Generally speaking, the places from which we came and their style of life was organized in such a way that neither of these posed any real difficulties. What are we to do here, when the work day is so closely regulated by the clock? Some people bring prayer rugs to work and then use their breaks and part of their lunch time for their prayers. Others have had to give up some of their daily prayers. Almost no one has been able to get time off from work on Fridays, so working people generally attend mosque very early in the morning or after work. Ramadan also poses some difficulties, but of a different kind. During the month of Ramadan [the ninth month of the Islamic year] we are supposed to refrain from all food and drink from dawn to dusk. Again, where we come from the days and nights are about equal, so that with practice this fast goes smoothly. But try it in Edmonton, where the late summer days are almost eighteen hours long!

Source: Norman Buchignani and Doreen M. Indra, with Ram Srivastava, *Continuous Journey: A Social History of South Asians in Canada* (Toronto: McClelland & Stewart, 1985), 188–9. Reprinted by permission of the author.

made impossible demands in terms of the facilities and financing of arenas, thus literally forcing the franchises to move to greener pastures.

A similar situation prevailed in baseball. The Montreal Expos had responded to years of money-losing seasons in 1994 by dismantling a team that might have won the World Series had not a players' strike led to cancellation of the post-season. Eventually, the American executives decided to eliminate the team altogether, and Major League Baseball took over control of the team for a few years, with some home games being played in Puerto Rico, until it finally found a new home in Washington, DC, in 2005. In professional basketball, the Vancouver Grizzlies moved to Memphis in 2001, the team's unsuccessful financial record since the establishment of the franchise in 1994 aggravated by a series of bad management decisions.

For many years Canadians have insisted that hockey must be maintained as Canada's national sport. In recent years the federal government has indicated its willingness to add NHL hockey to the list of cultural items that it is committed to protecting. Exactly where hockey fits into the overall cultural picture is as difficult to assess as the nature

of its problems. The very extent of the integration of hockey into the American entertainment industry is one of the difficulties—as the agonized discussion over the transfer of hockey icon Wayne Gretzky from Edmonton to Los Angeles demonstrated in August 1988. But globalization is just as serious a problem. Since the 1980s the number of Canadian-born hockey players in the NHL has steadily declined, and the number of Canadian-born superstars has declined even more precipitously.

Since the professionals now stock the teams in international hockey, Canadian teams have not been able to dominate the annual world championships or the Winter Olympics (with the exception of the 2002 and 2010 Games). Indeed, they had not been dominant in international competition for the previous half-century because Canadian amateurs were competing against essentially professional teams from the Soviet bloc countries. Many critics

Members of the Canadian women's hockey team pose with their coach, Danielle Sauvageau, and their gold medals after defeating the US team 3–2 at the Salt Lake City Winter Olympics, 21 February 2002. The Canadian Press/Mike Ridewood.

have suggested that the Canadian system has failed to produce large numbers of highly skilled players because it is not sufficiently committed to elite development, although Canada's success in the men's junior (under-20) world ice hockey championships would seem to challenge this analysis: during the 1990s the Canadian junior team won seven world championships, including five in a row, and then won five more consecutive world titles from 2005 to 2009. It is also worth noting that the Canadian national women's hockey team won seven consecutive world titles without consoling many Canadians about the situation in men's hockey. Canadian women's hockey at the international level was one of the great sports success stories of the 1990s—not to mention the 2002 and 2006 Olympics—but the women's team was still unable to make many inroads into a sport dominated by the ethos of the male professionals.

Conclusion

While in the larger scheme of things one pattern of historical development has always been cyclical, few analysts believed that Canada could ever return to the optimistic prosperity of the 1950s. Instead, the road ahead seemed at best to consist of a series of hard choices. How Canadians and their political leaders would come to terms with such decisions was an open question, even before the attack on the World Trade Center on 11 September 2001 changed the world.

How History Has Changed

Theoretical Developments

The period since 1990 has been characterized by two seemingly contradictory developments in the writing of Canadian history. One has been a remarkable resurgence of what is usually called 'popular history', written or produced to be accessible to a larger audience. Popular history has not been confined to books, but has increasingly found a place in the media, particularly on television, where separate specialty channels devoted exclusively to history serve up a 24-hour-a-day menu of documentaries, historical films, and historical 'reality' television programming. The concentration on biography in many of the documentaries has become a major trend. This trend has not been confined to Canada. An American magazine recently argued that 'Pop culture has become the salvation of interest in history' (*Vanity Fair*, May 2002). Evidence of the new financial stakes involved in popular history has included the reports of large-scale plagiarism by some of the most successful practitioners. Pop history is part of a general international movement caused in large part by the other new development, also an international one: the emergence of cultural studies and new social theory as influences on the discourse of younger academic historians in Canada. Much of the new academic writing draws heavily on linguistic and epistemological theory, and its arcane style can make it almost entirely incomprehensible to the average reader.

A large part of the new body of theory was developed in post-war Europe. Structuralism (derived from the linguistic theories of Ferdinand de Saussure) uses the rules of language to provide the basis for a collection of laws to govern analysis. It tends to operate without much reference to time or chronology, and is hostile to inductive analysis and human agency. Semiotics (associated with the work of Roland Barthes and Louis Althusser) is a subset of structuralism that looks for meaning in human communication by analyzing its variations as signs. Post-structuralism (associated with Jacques Derrida and Michel Foucault) exists most commonly in the form of deconstructionism, in which a text is broken down and stripped of all its mystifications. These theorists believe that texts do not necessarily say what their authors intended, but have subtexts that are never constant and are always changing in meaning. For them, language has no permanence of meaning and hence all knowledge is arbitrary and relative. There is no truth, only the interpretation of the moment. Postmodernism builds on the philosophical ideas of Friedrich Nietzsche and Martin Heidegger, both critics of modern rationalist thought. Like the linguistic theorists, these philosophers (both of whom were extremely popular in Nazi Germany) argued there were no facts, only interpretations, and no objective truth or truths, but only perceptions that depend entirely on the point of view of individuals and groups. Obviously the new history seeks in large measure to undermine the old history, developed in the Renaissance and refined by the Enlightenment, which tended to see historical study as analogous to science in its accumulation of objective and 'provable' knowledge. Popular history flourishes in the face of the new history partly because it avoids any confrontation with theory. It presents narratives that are not treated as problematic but as factual.

The underlying problems of epistemology and methodology currently debated in some historical circles do not often intrude on survey courses in Canadian history, but students need to be aware of their existence.

Short Bibliography

Bibby, Reginald. *The Bibby Report: Social Trends Canadian Style*. Toronto, 1995. A useful survey of material about Canadian society in the 1990s.

Clarke, Tony. *MAI: The Multilateral Agreement on Investment and the Threat to Canadian Sovereignty*. Toronto, 1997. An impassioned defence of Canadian sovereignty in the age of globalization.

Driedger, Leo. *Multi-Ethnic Canada: Identities & Inequalities*. Toronto, 1996. A careful scholarly study of ethnicity in modern Canada.

Engelstad, Diane, and John Bird, eds. *Nation to Nation: Aboriginal Sovereignty and the Future of Canada*. Toronto, 1992. A collection of essays on Aboriginal governance.

Long, David, and Olive Patricia Dickason, eds. *Visions of the Heart: Canadian Aboriginal Issues*, 2nd edn. Toronto, 2000. An important collection of essays that serves as an introduction to the First Nations and their problems at century's end.

Mackey, Eva, *The House of Difference: Cultural Politics and National Identity in Canada*. Toronto, 2002. A provocative analysis of the new cultural agendas of the political parties in the 1990s.

Magder, Ted. *Canada's Hollywood: The Canadian State and Feature Films*. Toronto, 1993. An important analysis of the failures of Canadian cultural policy, particularly in the area of film.

Magosci, Paul Robert, ed. *Encyclopedia of Canada's Peoples*. Toronto, 1999. A monument to the scholarship of the 1990s in Canada.

Miki, Roy, and Cassandra Kobayashi. *Justice in Our Time: The Japanese Canadian Redress Settlement*. Vancouver, 1991. An account of the redress process involving the Japanese, written by one of the participants.

Randall, Stephen, and Herman W. Konrad, eds. *NAFTA in Transition*. Calgary, 1995. A collection of essays on NAFTA that includes an important study by John Thompson of Canadian cultural policy.

Report of the Sub-Committee on the Study of Sport in Canada. Ottawa, 1998. The first attempt by Parliament to study sport in Canada, chaired by David Mills. The report begins with the premise that professional sport is an important part of the fabric of sport in the nation.

Silver, Jim. *Thin Ice: Money, Politics, and the Demise of an NHL Franchise*. Halifax, 1995. A case study of the problems of professional sport in contemporary Canada.

Watson, William. *Globalization and the Meaning of Canadian Life*. Toronto, 1998. A relatively sanguine account of globalization and its Canadian impact.

Windshuttle, Keith. *The Killing of History: How Literary Critics and Social Theorists Are Murdering Our Past*. New York, 1997. Despite its sensationalist title, this book is a responsible and intelligent critique of the relationship between historical study and new postmodern theories, written by an Australian historian.

Study Questions

1. List and explain three factors that contributed to the collapse of the Progressive Conservative Party in the federal election of 1993.
2. What was the main reason for the opposition's failure to mount a successful challenge to the Liberal domination of Parliament after 1993?
3. Define in your own words the term 'globalization'.
4. Explain why Canada's aging population created a crisis in health care.
5. Why did sexual abuse become an important social issue in the 1990s?
6. What significant gains did Canada's Aboriginal peoples make in regard to land rights in the 1990s?
7. In one sense the 'I Am Canadian' rant was just another beer commercial. Why did it become such a popular phenomenon?

 www.oupcanada.com/Bumsted4e

Visit the companion website for *A History of the Canadian Peoples*, fourth edition for further resources.

13 From 9/11 to the G20

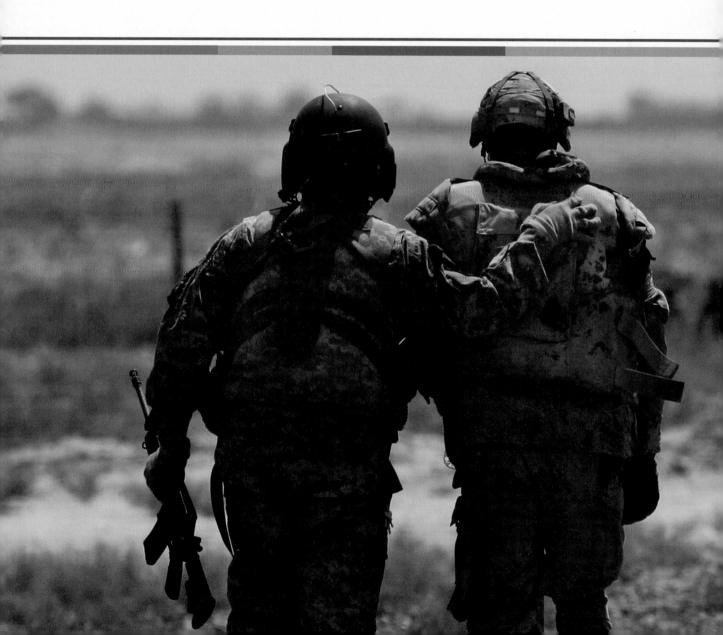

The twenty-first century opened with an apprehended crisis: fears that millions of computers worldwide would not click over into the new century (as 1999 had to shift to 2000) proved largely illusory. Its first decade for most people in Canada was probably bookended by 9/11 and the nation's hosting of two major international events in 2010—the Winter Olympics in Vancouver and the G8 and G20 summits in Huntsville, Ontario, and Toronto. Neither of these latter two events was an unqualified public relations triumph. In between, Canadians were subjected to a daily menu of unbelievable events, which usually turned out to be true, and to a series of crises proclaimed by the media, many of which turned out to be false.

After 9/11

On 11 September 2001, a series of events occurred that shook Americans—and the world—to their very core. A number of small cadres of terrorists prepared to die in the course of their actions hijacked four American commercial airliners. Two of the planes were flown directly into the World Trade Center towers in New York City, which subsequently collapsed in a literal inferno with the loss of close to 3,000 people, many of them firefighters. One of the planes was flown into the Pentagon, causing considerable damage, while the fourth crashed in a field in Pennsylvania after what was apparently an open confrontation between the hijackers and the passengers. The incidents demonstrated graphically how vulnerable the United States was to committed terrorists—many of those involved in 9/11 had even learned to pilot the airliners while living in the US—and the Americans became suddenly very security-conscious.

Horrific as the events of that day were for Americans and Canadians alike, their true significance became apparent only as the shock waves continued to spread across the continent and the world. The United States government and its citizens understandably treated the successful terrorist attack as a national disaster and responded with a variety of extreme measures, in which Canada became inescapably entwined, even as the nation tried to stand apart from many of them. As a consequence, Canadian–American relations jumped to the front of the newspaper headlines and remained there.

The War on Terrorism and the War in Iraq

Despite increasing evidence of internal economic and social integration between the United States and Canada at the beginning of the twenty-first century, which some disputed, the somewhat paradoxical truth was that, internationally, the political and philosophical gulf between the two nations was widening, especially in terms of their respective views of the world (Adams, 2003). In the new era after the collapse of the Soviet Union and the end of the Cold War, the United States was left standing as the only superpower in the world, while Canada continued its long-standing policy of multilateralism and support of international co-operation combined with a skeptical view of the American unilateral use of power, partly an automatic reaction to distance itself from the American juggernaut. The events of 9/11 widened the gulf. While Canada's immediate response to the mass terrorism was enormous sympathy for the United States, combined with a spontaneous welcoming of thousands of American air travellers inadvertently forced out of the sky into Canadian airports, Canada would have much difficulty with the Bush administration's 'with us or against us' position with respect to the 'war on terrorism' declared by President Bush, especially as the Americans widened the war to focus on Iraq. Canada recognized the need for increased border security and supported the United States in its naval operations in the Persian Gulf. It also contributed 850 troops to a military task force in Afghanistan in early 2002, the first deployment of Canadian ground troops in combat since Korea. After August 2003 it

A medic with the US Army comforts an injured Canadian soldier outside of Salavat, in the Panjwayi district, southwest of Kandahar, Afghanistan, June 2010. In early 2002, Canada sent a military task force to Afghanistan, the first deployment of Canadian ground troops in combat since Korea. The Canadian Press/Anja Niedringhaus.

would become the largest single contributor to the United Nations' International Security Assistance Force (ISAF) in Afghanistan.

A willingness to join a military invasion of Iraq became the litmus test of any nation's friendship with the United States. Every nation allied to the Americans except Great Britain failed the test. President Bush and his administration began insisting that Iraq had 'weapons of mass destruction' (WMD) and was behind most international terrorism, while Canada insisted (according to External Affairs Minister Bill Graham) that 'Iraq under Saddam Hussein is clearly always a threat, but we have no evidence he is in possession of weapons of mass destruction or that he would intend to use them at this time.' Moreover, Canada would join in military action against Iraq only in concert with the United Nations. Prime Minister Chrétien repeated these views before a meeting with President Bush on 9 September 2002. Three days later, Bush addressed the United Nations and continued his accusations that the Hussein regime possessed WMD and supported terrorists. Meanwhile, the Chrétien government backed action against Iraq in the UN but refused to get behind unilateral action, not long before the American Congress voted to allow Bush to use force in Iraq 'as he determines to be necessary and appropriate'.

Relations between the two nations were aggravated when a close associate of the Prime Minister, Françoise Ducros, accused President Bush of being 'a moron'. Chrétien was eventually forced to accept her resignation amid increasing international debate over the evidence for the existence of WMD and public opinion polls indicating that nearly two-thirds of the Canadian public opposed Canada's connection in a war with Iraq without UN support; the opposition was even stronger in Quebec. Early in 2003, Chrétien told a journalist, 'If I have to say no, I will. If I have to say yes, I will. We are an independent country.' Canada proved unconvinced by the 'case' for Iraqi complicity in terrorism and possession of WMD that was delivered by Secretary of State Colin Powell to the UN Security Council on 5 February 2003. A spokesman for the Prime Minister's Office said the Canadian government wanted hard evidence, not accusations. Many Canadians became concerned that Ottawa was not being supportive of the United States, and Canada offered to send a battalion headquarters and soldiers to Afghanistan in order to free American troops for Iraq.

At the United Nations in February 2003, Canada sought to fill its traditional role as compromiser to break the log-jam between the American (and British) insistence on force in Iraq and other nations that were willing to go no further than a resolution

On 9 September 2002, Prime Minister Jean Chrétien met with US President George W. Bush to discuss Canada's involvement in any military action against Iraq. The Canadian Press/Jason Kryk.

calling for further arms inspection. Since Canada at this time did not have a seat on the Security Council, however, its influence was muted. In addition, the perception of the Canadian government's benevolence towards the United States was greatly weakened when Carolyn Parrish, a Liberal backbencher, said of the Americans, 'I hate those bastards.' She would apologize, but the damage was done; a State Department official called the comment part of a 'disturbing pattern' (*Calgary Herald*, 1 Mar. 2003). Canada continued to try to find a formula at the UN, calling at an open Security Council meeting for an authorization of war against Iraq if that nation failed to meet the UN's disarmament ultimatum by 1 April 2003. Leading protagonists on both sides rejected this plan, the Americans for allowing Saddam too much time, others for proposing a deadline at all.

In the end, the American President acted unilaterally and began the war. For its part, the Canadian House of Commons voted to remain out of the military action, although the Chrétien government said it would reconsider the decision if the Iraqis used weapons of mass destruction against the invaders. The American ambassador to Canada expressed his disappointment at the Canadian action, and President Bush pointedly cancelled an upcoming visit to Ottawa. Shortly after the initial 'shock and awe' bombardment of Baghdad by the Americans, the ambassador told the Economic Club of Toronto on 25 March that 'We [the United States] are at war to liberate Iraq, to protect the people of the United States and other countries from the devastating impact of Iraqi weapons of mass destruction being used by terrorists or the Iraqi government to kill thousands of innocent civilians' (*Globe and Mail*, 26 Mar. 2003). The trouble with this justification for the invasion, of course, was that it was not documentable. On 1 May 2003, the American President declared the war over. No weapons of mass destruction had been found, and none ever were, because they existed only in the minds of the American military. The Americans eventually admitted they were mistaken.

The problem was that 'victory' did not bring peace to Iraq. The United States continued to have to commit large numbers of troops to occupation and attempted pacification of the country; the war increasingly came to look like another Vietnam. Prime Minister Chrétien was forced from power in 2003 for reasons that had little to do with Iraq, and President Bush got a surprising (to many observers) endorsement for his war in the 2004 presidential election. But the Iraq invasion clearly damaged Canadian–American relations. Washington was understandably disappointed that a nation prospering under the American defence umbrella should adopt such an independent policy, while Canada became increasingly convinced that the Americans had made a terrible mistake in the invasion of Iraq. The Iraq War and attitudes towards the Bush administration demonstrated how far apart the American public was from the Canadian public, despite so-called convergence. Whether 9/11 and the Iraq War were solely responsible for the bad turn in Canadian–American relations in the early years of the new millennium was another question entirely. The answer was almost certainly not, for many of the ongoing problems were a product of the complexities of two thoroughly integrated economies in which the power relationships in a variety of ways were not equal.

Homeland Security

The immediate response of the American government to 9/11 was to insist on improved security and safety, especially within the borders of the United States. Part of President Bush's proclaimed 'war on terrorism' involved much tighter security. The initial focus was on airports, where security had indeed gotten very lax, but it soon spread to border crossings from Canada into the United States. The result was long lines in airports and at border crossings. From the beginning, the American ambition—shared by most Western European nations—was for the total elimination of terrorist activity. This, of course, was quite impossible to achieve, given the democratization of technology and the willingness of the new breed of terrorists to sacrifice their own lives in the course of carrying out their attacks. As an earlier generation of terrorists had fully appreciated by the 1960s and even earlier, terrorist activity brought those involved enormous political power, much more than legitimate democratic protest. Few acts of terror were more successful than political kid-nappings, although random bombings probably ran a close second. The public in Western democracies proved to have a very low pain threshold. Perhaps the worst feature of the search for unattainable total security was that each terrorist incident led to increased efforts to prevent the next one, often by singularly dubious methods and the sacrifice of basic human rights. The American security services before 9/11 underestimated the possibility of campaigns of terrorism within the American homeland using essentially homemade weapons of mass destruction produced in kitchens, and, after 9/11, overestimated the possibility that the Iraqis had huge stockpiles of such weapons produced in laboratories and factor-ies. No sensible person could possibly advise the American or Canadian publics to learn to live with a low level of terrorist fatalities on the grounds that the alternative would be far worse, but rationally such was probably the case.

Canadians have never faced the same level of terrorist threats as have the Americans (and per-haps their allies in the Iraq War, especially Great Britain), chiefly because Canada was not perceived as an important enough enemy to the terrorists. At the same time, the Americans became convinced that Canada was harbouring terrorists and serving as a staging area for terrorist attacks. Thus, despite the arrest of a number of alleged terrorists in the Toronto area in early June of 2006, the chief threat to Canada from terrorism was in the American secur-ity response, which greatly complicated the previ-ously open border in terms of the movement of both people and goods, and would do the same after every major incident. The American media covered the terrorism arrests much more closely than did their Canadian counterparts. The Americans did not sac-rifice economic prosperity through tightened secur-ity; it simply became another cost of doing business, added onto the final price. But the cost to Canadians is likely to be enormous, not least in terms of the end of the open border.

For nearly 200 years, Canadians and Americans had enjoyed a special relationship along their com-mon border. That relationship has occasionally been difficult, but before 9/11 few observers would have

conceived of a continent in which passports would be required to cross the border, as the United States by 2006 was uncategorically demanding. As origin-ally envisioned, at the end of 2006, every Canadian entering the United States by air or sea would need a passport or other identity document establish-ing the bearer's identity and citizenship, and at the end of 2007 the requirement would be extended to land travel. In late May 2006 the United States Senate extended the deadlines for the introduction of this policy another year. With the implementa-tion of this policy shift, Canadians ceased to have a special travel status in terms of the United States but were treated like all other visitors. Passport demand by Canadians rose significantly after 9/11. Less than 30 per cent of Canadians held a passport in 2000, and the figure was expected to rise to 50 per

After 9/11, the American government tightened security, establishing a colour-coded system to notify citizens of any change in security levels. Photo © moodboard/Alamy.

Omar Khadr

Courtroom sketch of Omar Khadr during his hearing in April 2010. Photo © POOL/Reuters/Corbis.

Omar Khadr (b. 1986) is a Canadian citizen born in Toronto whose treatment by the United States and his own government has not only been very controversial but, for many, symptomatic of the abuse of human rights involved in the battle against terrorism. Khadr's father was a member of Al Qaeda and a personal friend of Osama bin Laden. He took his son to Pakistan, and then to Afghanistan, where the boy became involved in the fighting, accused of throwing a grenade at and killing an American soldier, although doubts remain that he would have been able to have thrown the grenade, given his condition and his location in the building where he was found. Badly wounded himself, the 15-year-old—by definition, a child soldier—was captured by the Americans on 27 July 2002 and taken to their detention centre at Guantanamo Bay, Cuba, in October of that year, where he was treated as an adult, constantly interrogated, and subjected to long periods of solitary confinement. He made several confessions, which he subsequently repudiated.

The Canadian government was never very supportive of Khadr during his confinement, and has resolutely refused to ask for his repatriation despite the pleas of many Canadian and international organizations. A series of Canadian courts have ruled that Khadr was being treated improperly by the Canadian government. The Supreme Court of Canada in January 2010 ruled 9–0 that Canada had violated Khadr's rights under the Charter of Rights, but stopped short of ordering his return to Canada. By this time a large majority of the Canadian people believed that Khadr had been victimized. In July of 2010, the Federal Court of Canada issued an ultimatum to the Conservative government: act on the Khadr file within a week by providing 'a list of remedies for its breach of Omar Khadr's constitutional rights', as the earlier ruling had instructed, or the Court could be compelled to act for the government (*Toronto Star*, 6 July 2010, 6). After several military tribunals failed to get off the ground, with military-appointed lawyers for Khadr resigning, being let go by Khadr, or being summarily replaced by the American military, a new trial was scheduled to begin in July 2010, then delayed until mid-August, just over eight years after Khadr's capture. It appeared to be a case that both the Canadian Harper government and the US administration of Barack Obama, who had promised to close down the Guantanamo detention centre, wished would just go away.

In the end a deal was made. Khadr pleaded guilty to murder in violation of the rules of war, and apologized to the widow of his 'victim.' The Americans were prepared to repatriate him to Canada after one more year in prison.

cent by 2008. Passport Canada had changed from producing travel documents to providing identity documents, including new passports with embedded digital chips. As of 2010, it was still possible for Canadians to enter the United States without passports, providing they had other approved documentation including a photograph. Any Canadian failure to pay serious attention to American security demands designed to produce that elusive goal of total security clouded the Canadian–American relationship. At the same time, many recent immigrants to Canada come from countries that feel threatened by aggressive American security and are inherently anti-American (Keeble, 2005). Further complicating the border situation is the fact that the United States has been trying to decide how to deal with millions of illegal immigrants from Mexico. As Canadian politicians keep trying to tell the Americans, the two borders are quite different and cannot be treated with common policies, such as the construction of a wall along the border.

The Tale of Two Mad Cows

Bovine spongiform encephalopathy (BSE), more commonly known as 'Mad Cow Disease', is a neurological disorder found in cattle. How it is transmitted is not yet clear, although the suspicion is that the feeding of diseased animal meat-and-bone meal to live animals somehow plays a major part. Much evidence exists of a relationship between a serious if rare human disorder called Creutzfeldt-Jakob disease (CJD) and BSE in animals. CJD is a degenerative brain disease that is invariably fatal. It affects one in every million persons worldwide and is characterized by rapid progressive mental deterioration. The worst outbreak of BSE occurred in Europe in 1992 and 1993. In Great Britain thousands of herds were infected and many cattle were destroyed.

North America seemed to be amazingly free of BSE until early in the new millennium (O'Neill, 2005). In May of 2003, Canada announced its first case of BSE, discovered in Alberta. A few months later the first case of BSE turned up in the state of Washington, and the infected cow was traced back to Canada. The Americans immediately responded by closing

their border to Canadian cattle and kept it closed on health grounds until well into 2005. Therein was the problem. Farmers in western Canada, as a result of the removal of quotas and tariffs from the continental trade in beef and cattle by the FTA and NAFTA and flat prices for grain, had shifted much of their production activity into cattle in the 1990s, increasing exports of cattle from 500,000 head in 1988 to 1.5 million head in 2002, and raising beef exports from 200,000 metric tons to over 1 million metric tons. The three Prairie provinces (especially Alberta) contained most of the cattle producers and operators of feedlots. Beef cattle became western Canada's most important agricultural crop, and the nation's farmers after 2003 lost billions of dollars. The impact on Canada of the embargo was far more serious than in the United States, and both federal and provincial governments were forced to provide emergency aid for farmers. The increased beef exports from Canada after 1990 had not been greeted with enthusiasm in the cattle-producing states south of the border, where constant complaints were made of unfair practices and dumping. On the other hand, American cattle producers embraced the embargo and American state courts have supported its continuance, despite the further appearance of only a handful of cases of mad cow disease on either side of the border. At issue has been the establishment of an international agreement on a standard of minimal risk. Both nations agree on the need for scientific management of BSE, but they have disagreed over acceptable standards of infection. How many cases constitute an epidemic? Canada introduced more stringent regulations on meatpacking and animal feed than have the Americans, but this does not seem to have affected the raising of the ban.

The situation over the international trade in cattle was exacerbated by several factors. One was the extent of inequality in a highly interdependent trade relationship. The Canadian farm industry was much more dependent on the cattle trade than were the Americans, especially since Canadians had restructured the beef industry to suit the new trade conditions by leaving more slaughterhouse and meatpacking functions to the Americans and concentrating more on the export of live cattle. Another was the difficulty of finding mechanisms of dispute resolution between the two nations under conditions as complex as these. The Canadians argued that the Americans had over-reacted, and were supported in this insistence by several international agencies, which had little effect on the policies of the United States Department of Agriculture. The best solution clearly was high-level bilateral negotiation between the two governments on an agreed standard of risk, and here the prevalent sense on both sides of the border of a deteriorating Canadian–American relationship undoubtedly complicated the diplomatic process. As the Americans continued to keep the border closed to Canadian cattle, the Canadians became increasingly convinced that they were somehow being punished for their failure to support the United States in Iraq. Canadian frustration with American policies was the result. The border was still not fully opened as of this writing.

Softwood Lumber

Unlike the mad cow business, which emerged suddenly in 2003, the dispute over softwood lumber—the easy-to-saw lumber used in most building construction—is a long-standing one (see McKinney, 2004). What has been chiefly at issue is whether Canadian timber practices constitute unfair subsidies for the Canadian lumber industry, as charged by the American lumber industry's Coalition for Fair Lumber Imports, a lobbying group heavily subsidized by the major American lumber producers. Interestingly enough, many consumer groups and advocates in the United States have been highly critical of the CFLI. Most Canadian timber is owned by the Crown and the fee for harvesting on public lands ('stumpage rights') is set by administrative practice rather than by open auction as in the United States.

In 1982 the CFLI petitioned the American Department of Commerce to apply countervailing duties on Canadian lumber imported to the United States, on the grounds that it was unfairly subsidized. Because the Canadian system was not confined to a single industry, countervailing duties were regarded as not applicable, and the CFLI did not appeal this ruling. But the American industry returned to its

crusade in 1986 and won a decision for a tariff of 15 per cent. This action led Canada to agree to a Memorandum of Understanding and a phasing in of the tariff. In 1991 Canada withdrew from this agreement on the grounds that it had changed its practices, and the question of the tariff was referred to procedures instituted under the FTA. A binational panel of three Canadians and two Americans heard the case. The panellists voted strictly along national lines and found for Canada in a very controversial decision objected to by the United States on all sorts of procedural and substantive grounds. In 1996 the two nations came to an agreement limiting Canadian lumber exports to the United States from certain provinces (British Columbia, Alberta, Ontario, and Quebec) to 14.7 billion board feet annually. This understanding ended in 2001 and a replacement could not be negotiated. During the course of this agreement provinces that harvested lumber from private land (mainly in the Maritimes) greatly increased their market share in the United States because their lumber was not subject to tariff.

Another petition from the American lumber industry in 2001 asked for the imposition of countervailing duties and penalties against Canadian lumber exporters for dumping. Both requests were supported by the Bush administration. The United States Department of Commerce levied both charges on 25 April 2002, announcing a tariff of 18 per cent and combined levy of 27.22 per cent against Canadian lumber. Canada appealed to a NAFTA panel, which ruled in August 2003 that while the Canadian lumber industry was subsidized, the American tariff was much too high. Only weeks later a World Trade Organization panel also found the tariffs much too high. It also ruled that Canadian stumpage rights were clearly a 'financial benefit' to Canadian companies, but not enough to be a labelled a subsidy. The Americans insisted they had won because the panels had supported the American charge of subsidization and the concept of tariffs, while the Canadians maintained that they had won because the panels had found the subsidies much too high, almost punitive. The Americans appealed the NAFTA ruling to an 'extraordinary challenge panel' on the grounds that earlier decisions in favour of Canada ignored trade rules. On

10 August 2005 this panel sustained the earlier decision. The Canadian government called for the United States to stop collecting duties and to refund those collected over the years since 2002. The Americans rejected the NAFTA ruling and refused to scrap the duties. They subsequently agreed to comply with the cessation of collection, although whether they would refund anything remained unclear. Yet another NAFTA panel ruled in March 2006 that Canadian softwood exports were not subsidized.

By this time the Canadian election had resulted in a Conservative minority government, a situation that continued to prevail through 2010. The Conservatives would be more supportive of the American government and more compliant towards American demands. Prime Minister Stephen Harper sent friendly signals to the Bush administration and met with President Bush at Cancun, Mexico, at the end of March 2006. Not long after this meeting,

the United States and Canada announced they had reached an understanding for ending the softwood dispute. Under it, the Americans would return most (80 per cent) of the duties collected over the past four years, while Canadian lumber would be restricted to its present 34 per cent of the American market. Canada would levy an export tax on lumber exported to the United States if the price dropped under $355 per thousand board feet. This agreement was announced in Parliament on 27 April 2006. It was immediately criticized by the British Columbia lumber industry as a sellout to the Americans that compromised Canadian sovereignty.

The softwood lumber dispute is a perfect example of a legitimate disagreement between the United States and Canada that had little to do with 9/11, but a lot to do with internal politics and international law and most of all to do with power relationships. As in many disputes between the two nations under

Prime Minister Stephen Harper's first Conservative minority government was elected in 2006. In this photo, the new cabinet is sworn in at Rideau Hall on 6 February 2006. The Canadian Press/Jake Wright.

the FTA and NAFTA agreements, the American government found difficulty in accepting rulings that went against it under the conflict resolution provisions of the treaties, and there were no ways Canada had of enforcing the favourable decisions it had received. As in most such cases, bilateral negotiation to resolve a dispute that should have been settled within the framework of the treaties was the ultimate outcome. In this case, the result of the bilateral discussions was almost certainly less satisfactory to Canada than the NAFTA rulings suggested.

Energy

On 14 August 2003, one of the hottest days of the summer, the lights went out for 50 million North Americans—10 million in Ontario and 40 million in eight American states. The cause of the blackout was not the heat, but rather a cascading failure in the transmission grid that supplied these regions, mainly involving automatic disconnects. Fingers were initially pointed at various culprits, the Americans blaming the Canadians, the Canadians denying responsibility, and much of the public fearful of a terrorist attack. As cooler heads prevailed, discussion centred on deregulation of the electricity market, which had reduced profits and hence incentives for new power lines and security backups. A joint working group commissioned by the American and Canadian governments concluded after a lengthy investigation that many electric companies had not complied with voluntary reliability standards and recommended government regulation. For 50 million people, however, the immediate issue was loss of power and considerable personal inconvenience. Television cameras caught hundreds of thousands of commuters in New York City walking to their homes in New Jersey and Long Island, and they were only a small part of the commuters affected. Just as the loss cascaded across the grid, so, too, did its implications. Public transit ground to a halt, many gas stations were unable to pump fuel, and highways were crowded with automobiles that had run out of gas; oil refineries closed and were slow to open. Telephones mainly worked, but systems quickly overloaded. Cable television and Internet were

virtually shut down. Industrial closures were widespread, and 140 miners were stranded underground in the Falconbridge mine in Sudbury, Ontario. The eventual cost was estimated to be in the range of $6 billion on both sides of the border. Many political pundits claimed that the Ontario Tories lost a provincial election in October 2003 because of the blackout. It was clear that the Tories had not appropriately expanded the province's power facilities, and unlike other political leaders, Premier Ernie Eves was not visible on television for many hours after the disaster began (he was away from Toronto on holiday). The failure certainly highlighted the interdependence of the grid and emphasized, as well, its vulnerability to terrorist attacks. For the first time since blackouts in the 1960s, North Americans were made aware of their reliance on interdependent energy sources. Energy issues leaped to the fore and would remain there.

The interdependence of the Canadian–American energy relationship—in oil, natural gas, electricity generation and transmission, and even in water management (for water supplies much of Canada's electricity)—continued to grow throughout the first decade of the twenty-first century (Gattinger, 2005). Rises in energy prices, fears over security in the energy sector after 9/11, deregulation and market restructuring, concern over the continuation of oil from the Middle East, the catastrophic oil leak in the Gulf of Mexico that began in April 2010, all played their part in increasing the complexity of the energy relationship and its problems. The economic pressures for oil from the Alberta tar sands caused unanticipated environmental damage as producers hastened to pump the oil south (*Washington Post*, 31 May 2006). Continental co-ordination was increasingly required to manage energy matters (Doern and Gattinger, 2003).

The Canadian–American energy relationship has been shaped in the early years of the twenty-first century by a number of factors. First, Canada within its own boundaries has had a surplus of energy in all three major energy sectors, while the United States saw demand exceed supply in both petroleum and natural gas. Canada's energy resources lie in less densely populated parts of the country, creating disagreement between energy-consuming provinces (Ontario and Quebec) and energy-producing provinces, as well as between developers and residents (often Aboriginal peoples) in the resource-rich regions. This means that internal Canadian energy policy is a hot domestic political issue on several fronts. Second, American energy demands and energy policy are continual and extensive, thus shaping the continental market far into the future. The pressure is and will continue to be upon Canada to open up and develop its energy resources for the American market, perhaps more rapidly than is in Canada's best interests. This pressure will prove particularly intense if oil prices continue to rise and gas at the pumps remains at unprecedented high levels. Third, various trade agreements and other integrations have to some considerable extent limited the options of Canadian policy; Canada can no longer establish two-tier pricing policies as it did in the National Energy Program, for example, or attempt through federal action to control the amount of energy sold to the United States. Dealing with continental energy resources has become less a political issue and more a management issue, involving players from various levels of government and from the private sector. The Americans, moreover, would dearly love to add water (whether defined as energy or resource) to the existing package of complexity.

Global Issues

The Environment

Many of the global questions that faced Canadians and their governments in the first years of the new millennium had continental implications that were in one way or another connected with international ones. Global warming, for example, was part of an environmental envelope that the United States government tended to downplay as much as possible. By 2006 many experts began to fear that increasingly unstable and extreme weather events, including hurricanes and floods, were all part of the warming problem that the United States refused to address. The global spread of epidemic disease, quite apart from its potential relationship to 'weapons of mass

destruction', also suggested, as with terrorism, the impossibility of eradication in a modern world of international mobility. As for Canadian 'peacekeeping', which by 2006 involved Canadian forces in a shooting war in Afghanistan, especially in Kandahar province, it was clearly a part of Canada's response to Iraq.

By 2006 two absolutely contradictory and irreconcilable conclusions had been reached about global warming (see, e.g., Kolbert, 2006; Michaels, 2005; Reay, 2005). On the one hand, almost all scientists and experts were agreed that global warming was for real and had to be addressed. The evidence was overwhelming, they said. A few skeptics still insisted that this was a natural process of the weather cycle, but most agreed that the greenhouse gases emitted by the industrialized nations—notably the United States and Canada—were indeed increasing the amounts of heat-trapping gases in the atmosphere. Since the eighteenth century, the average global temperature has risen by 0.7 degrees Celsius, and projections are that it will rise 2 degrees above pre-industrial levels by the middle of the twenty-first century. Unfortunately, global warming does not simply mean higher temperatures but a variety of other results: melting ice caps, higher sea levels, more frequent floods and hurricanes, and loss of biodiversity, as well as food shortages. The world, say most scientists, has already been subjected to the early harbingers of extreme global change. On the other hand, while scientists were convinced that something had to be done immediately, several governments—including those of the United States and Canada—had reached the conclusion that little could be done practically to reduce significantly carbon dioxide pollution, at least by using the mechanism of the Kyoto Protocol. The chief problems were that too many nations did not buy into Kyoto and refused, as well, to cut emissions, insisting that the cost—a shift away from the capitalist paradigm of an ever-increasing economy—was too high for the gains. Distressingly, substantial publicity about the greenhouse effect and Kyoto had failed to penetrate very far into the Canadian public's consciousness. A poll conducted in the spring of 2006 indicated that two-thirds of Canadians knew nothing about the details of Kyoto (*Winnipeg Free Press*, 29 May 2006, 7). Public awareness only decreased thereafter.

What may prove to be the final blow to Kyoto was struck by the Canadian government in May of 2006 when it called for the gradual elimination of Kyoto with no alternative suggested to replace it (*Globe and Mail*, 20 May 2006, 1, 5). At the same time, the government also cancelled 'Project Green', the Liberal government's controversial $12 billion seven-year plan to implement Kyoto. An independent study released after the project was terminated argued that it would 'fail dramatically to meet national objectives and yet will entail a substantial cost', with much of the money to be spent abroad (*Winnipeg Free Press*, 29 May 2006, 7). While the Liberal government had been a strong supporter of Kyoto, at least in theory, the Conservatives had long been suspicious of it, concerned in part that it put Canada at odds with the United States, which was highly critical of the protocol, in part that adherence would be very expensive and damage Canada's global economic competitiveness. Over the ensuing years, the Harper minority government continued to be unwilling to sign on to unilateral action to reduce greenhouse gases or in other ways to act to affect global warming in a positive manner, insisting that only concerted international decisions and close co-operation with the United States would be effective. Although it has pledged the reduction of carbon emissions, it has not offered many specific measures to do so. At the United Nations Climate Change Conference held in Copenhagen in December 2009, most observers regarded the Canadian government as especially obstructive of any real progress on the key issues.

Pandemic Disease

While international co-operation on greenhouse gases seemed impossible to achieve, a much higher degree of agreement appeared to be possible on other fronts, including pandemic disease. Quick action by the authorities in 2003 kept under control a potentially serious outbreak of severe acute respiratory syndrome (SARS), apparently brought from Hong Kong to Greater Toronto, although the

advisory of the World Health Organization against unnecessary travel to Toronto had serious implications in the short run for the city's tourist industry (Koh et al., 2005). Health authorities internationally seemed better equipped than usual to prevent local epidemics of highly contagious diseases (mainly of the influenza variety) from turning into pandemics. Canadian medical researchers have established themselves in the front lines of virus research. At the same time, experts warned that various communicable diseases, including H5Nl (avian flu), could easily cripple the international economy, which requires the smooth transit of goods. In some ways the problems are related to the same ones that affect the environment and security. Most people (in Canada as elsewhere) would prefer to believe that a disaster won't happen and refuse to pay attention to the doomsayers, and most governments are as concerned with trade and tourism as they are with saving lives. Furthermore, most defence mechanisms are predicated on reducing the danger rate to its absolute minimum and contain few backup plans if any disease breaches the first line of protection. In 2009, an apprehended international epidemic of swine flu of the H1N1 variety again proved that the Canadian public was skeptical of the efficacy of a massive inoculation program well advertised by its government as essential to prevent disaster. In the end, less than 50 per cent of the population was inoculated amid considerable confusion over the production and distribution of vaccine. Fortunately, the outbreak proved far less serious than experts had earlier feared.

The War in Iraq and Peacekeeping in Afghanistan

As we have seen in earlier chapters, a series of Canadian governments dating back to the 1960s have engaged in 'smoke and mirror' operations to convince the Canadian public that a continually decreasing percentage of the federal budget being devoted to the military was compatible with both national security and Canadian international obligations. After 2003, and as a consequence of 9/11, this military illusion was finally breached. In 2002, Canada committed military forces to Afghanistan as

Toronto residents wait in line to receive the H1N1 vaccine at the East York Civic Centre in October 2009. REUTERS/Mike Cassese.

a necessary gesture to its overall alliance with the United States. Those military forces were stepped up in number and their role increased by the new Conservative government in 2006 (Khan, 2006). Afghanistan was divided into military sectors and Canada given responsibility for the southeastern section of the country—Kandahar—in which the guerrilla fighting against the Taliban was the most intense. Few Canadians listened carefully as the Department of National Defence DND announced on 16 May 2005 that the Canadians would move from Kabul to Kandahar, a move that clearly implied a change in military policy. Newly elected Prime Minister Harper subsequently visited the Canadian troops on 12–13 March 2006, telling them that the government—and soldiers—would be there for a long time. At the same time, he refused to hold a parliamentary debate on Afghanistan, saying, 'In such a debate, such a lack of strength by any Canadian party would weaken our troops, and possibly place our troops in more danger' (Kahn, 2006). What the Liberal and then the Tory governments had done without actually saying so, of course, was to shift the role of its troops from peacekeepers to combatants. Canada was now committed to a new style of war, in which peacekeeping and humanitarian activities were combined with combat missions; the Canadian military command now had to think in terms of 'the enemy' rather than in terms of the minimum use of force. Moreover, that command was headed on the ground by a one-star general, with many senior military and civilian figures above him. Interestingly enough, all four parties in Parliament supported both the original mission and its refocusing. The result of the shift, of course, was a raised level of casualties, including in mid-May 2006 the death of the first female Canadian soldier ever killed in combat. Canadians began to complain that soldiers were being killed without a clear rationale. On 17 May 2006, in a tight vote of 149 to 145, the House of Commons extended for two years the mandate for a continued Canadian presence in Afghanistan. In 2008 Prime Minister Harper pledged that Canada would leave Afghanistan in 2011. As of mid-July 2010, a year before the date of withdrawal, Canada had roughly 2,500 Canadian Forces personnel in Afghanistan, and had experienced 151 deaths of soldiers and four of civilians.

When Stanley McChrystal, the American general in charge of American and NATO involvement in Afghanistan, was fired by President Obama in June 2010 for what amounted to insubordination—after he and some subordinates were quoted in a *Rolling Stone* magazine article as making comments critical of the Obama administration—General David Petraeus was appointed to take command, on 4 July 2010. Petraeus earlier had been the commander of forces in Iraq during the troop surge in that country that appeared to change the direction of that conflict, and now he moved into the command position in yet another war where expanded US involvement in the form of a 'surge' was underway. As in Iraq, he cautioned that real change on the ground would take time, and emphasized the need for absolute co-ordination and co-operation among the forces in Afghanistan. What Canada's role would become in the months and years to come remained an open

The coffin of Capt. Nichola Goddard arrives at the military cemetery for a full military burial ceremony in Ottawa, 7 June 2006. Goddard is Canada's first woman soldier to be killed in combat; she died 17 May 2006 fighting Taliban insurgents in Afghanistan. The Canadian Press/Tom Hanson.

question, but clearly there would be heavy pressure not to pull out of Afghanistan in accordance with the commitment in Parliament. In November 2010, the government indeed reversed the commitment and announced it would remain in Afghanistan, providing training personnel rather than armed combatants.

One of the many casualties of the Afghan involvement was the virtual end of Canadian peacekeeping operations around the world. Canada could no longer continue this international role with over 2,000 troops in Afghanistan. At the end of March 2006, the Canadian Forces made a final withdrawal of 190 soldiers from the Golan Heights, where a Canadian presence had been maintained since shortly after the Yom Kippur (October) War of 1973. After this withdrawal, Canada would have fewer than 60 peacekeepers serving under the United Nations flag, and most of those were policemen rather than soldiers. Few Canadians seemed aware—or cared very much—about what was happening.

Lebanon

For many years Lebanon was an overall part of the Middle Eastern crisis on which the spotlight occasionally focused. A sporadic civil war was fought in the country between 1975 and 1990. During this war, thousands of Lebanese left the country and immigrated to Canada, where they took up Canadian citizenship. This movement was encouraged by the Canadian government, which made special concessions to allow Lebanese with Canadian relatives—Lebanese had immigrated to Canada in small numbers since the 1880s—to enter the country. By the 2001 census there were officially 142,635 people of Lebanese origin in Canada, but unofficial estimates put the total at closer to 250,000. Most were francophones who settled in Quebec, although there were also communities in Ottawa, Edmonton, and Toronto. In 1982 Israel invaded Lebanon to uproot a Palestinian government that had grown up there. The invasion was successful in reducing Palestinian raiding on Israel, but led to the growth of the Shiite Hezbollah movement unalterably opposed to Israel and the Israeli presence in Lebanon. Hezbollah came to control most of southern Lebanon and especially the city of Beirut, and claimed that the withdrawal

of Israeli troops from the country in 2000 represented its victory. Beginning in 1990 and especially after the Israeli withdrawal of 2000, Lebanon had been rebuilt and returned to something resembling normalcy. As many as 40,000 Canadians, part of the Lebanese diaspora, returned to Lebanon after 1990 and especially after 2000, either for extended visits with family or as permanent residents. By 2006, although few people in Canada realized the fact, there were as many as 40,000 Canadian citizens now resident in Lebanon. Not surprisingly, these people, along with other former Lebanese now citizens of Western countries, became trapped in the escalating violence between Hezbollah and Israel in 2006.

Canada, along with other Western countries, offered to evacuate its citizens who could travel successfully to the Mediterranean coast. The journey was a difficult one, and undoubtedly kept down the numbers who managed to take advantage of the offer. In the end, about 10,000 Canadian citizens resident in Lebanon were returned to Canada by air and sea. The remainder—except for the eight members of a Lebanese-Canadian family who were killed by an Israeli attack—waited for a ceasefire, which finally was brokered by the United Nations in mid-August. Part of the complex agreement called for a UN force of up to 15,000 peacekeepers to be stationed in southern Lebanon.

Canadian Politics

The Meltdown of the Liberal Party

While Canadian–American relations, and probably Canada's international relations, were perceptibly shifting, so, too, was domestic politics. The two shifts did not seem much connected, and probably were not. Few of the international dimensions of events after 9/11 seemed to have much impact on domestic politics, except for the public approval Prime Minister Chrétien enjoyed in refusing to support the United States in Iraq. Chrétien's substantial majority in the House of Commons in the 2000 election, of course, had been largely illusory, caused by a plethora of parties with popular support combined with structural factors such as the Canadian electoral system. A true Liberal victory would have seen the popular support for the extra parties decline rather than increase. In any case, from the very beginning of the new Parliament, the Liberal caucus was full of squabbling as a number of contenders tried to position themselves to replace Chrétien, who was perceived as on his way out. The Prime Minister was probably preparing to retire, but he wanted this to be on his terms and not those of the party. Having introduced a series of budgets that took advantage of a virtually unprecedented period of economic prosperity for Canada, which made both budget surpluses and many new policy initiatives possible, Finance Minister Paul Martin quickly emerged as the front-runner. He retired from the cabinet and ran a double campaign in 2002, both to force Chrétien out and to position himself to replace him.

A smooth—some said 'slick'—bilingual businessman whose father had served in Liberal cabinets under four prime ministers, Martin's personal portfolio and its management would become problems for the Liberals. But his most serious problem was in distancing himself from Liberal corruption, particularly in Quebec, while still maintaining French-Canadian support. By 2002 it was clear that there were two Liberal parties in Canada, one led by Chrétien and the other by Martin. Liberal Party discipline was nearly non-existent, and various hopefuls floated policy balloons that often contradicted each other. The government was embarrassed by the gun control fiasco. In December of 2002, the Auditor General of Canada revealed that a gun control program originally expected to cost $119 million—with registration fees providing a return of $117 million, for a net cost of just $2 million—would end up costing more than $1 billion, and even then would be incomplete. This example of political mismanagement was soon joined by further evidence of political incompetence and illegal behaviour at all levels. The gun fiasco continued to haunt the Liberals throughout the decade.

By the time in November 2003 when Martin was chosen leader of the Liberal Party, a year of mudslinging had left virtually everyone in the party soiled, dirtied, and exhausted. The Canadian public had been exposed to more rumours and charges of wrongdoing than could possibly be swept under the rug. Many of the rumours involved a federal program in Quebec designed to counter separatism in the province by a judicious expenditure of money for federalist advertising. The corruption issue heated up in November 2003 when Auditor General Sheila Fraser introduced sponsorship and advertising affairs in Quebec in her annual report to Parliament. Martin attempted to deal with the problem by appointing a commission of inquiry, headed by Mr Justice John Gomery of Quebec and firing the former head of the program, Alphonso Gagliano, who subsequently became Canadian ambassador to Denmark; other bureaucrats would later be fired. The Gomery Inquiry brought to the fore a number of associates of former Prime Minister Chrétien, each of whom denied any wrongdoing in not very convincing testimony. Several of these individuals were subsequently arrested by the RCMP for fraud. Chrétien called for Gomery to resign on grounds that he was biased. Gomery refused. The Inquiry in the spring of 2004 did not manage to implicate Prime Minister Martin (Gomery would later exonerate him completely), and Martin called an election on 23 May 2004.

The Resurgence of Canadian Conservatism

By this time, closed-door meetings between the Canadian Alliance and the Progressive Conservative Party in late 2003 had resulted in the creation of the new Conservative Party of Canada (CPC), ratified by postal ballot among the Alliance and by regional conventions among the PCs. The 2000 election had made clear that the Liberals would govern forever if they continually faced a divided conservative opposition complicated by a sovereigntist party in Quebec. The two conservative parties had some difficulty in merging, since they represented different conservative traditions in Canada. The Progressive Conservatives, based mainly in eastern Canada at the provincial level, tended to be strong Canadian nationalists and supporters of state-run social programs, while the Alliance, as the heir to the western-dominated Reform Party, was more socially conservative, with strong roots in fundamentalist religion, and populist in its opposition to centralized federalism. The Alliance had moved increasingly to the centre, however, as it became clear that a truly right-wing party could not flourish electorally in Canada. The new party was a neo-conservative one much like the American Republican Party under George Bush. It was socially conservative, favourably disposed to the international use of military force, populist, and free enterprising. On 20 March 2004, Stephen Harper was elected leader of the CPC. Harper had succeeded Stockwell Day as leader of the Alliance in early 2003 and had helped engineer the merger of the two conservative parties. He was relatively young (b. 1959), articulate, and extremely self-assured; his French was passable and getting better.

The Canadian federal election of 28 June 2004 was a relatively quiet affair. Instead of five parties with hopes of electoral success there were only four. Most observers watched carefully the campaign performance of the recently united Conservative Party of Canada under its new leader. The Tories behaved responsibly and with considerable discipline. They suggested that they were pro-American and pro-business but did not actually say so. Their campaign platform called for high government expenditures and differed from the Liberals mainly on high-profile social issues—abortion, same-sex marriage, the death penalty—where it called for free parliamentary votes. Naturally, the Tories emphasized accountability and transparency in government. Unable to find a handle of attack in the Tory platform or campaign, Prime Minister Martin was reduced to charging that the Conservatives had a 'hidden agenda' (presumably to cut health care and social services as soon as possible). Canadians in a series of polls had made it quite clear that they would cling tenaciously to universal health-care coverage despite its cost. The leader of the NDP, a thoroughly bilingual and personally attractive Jack Layton, joined Martin in criticizing the phantom Tory campaign platform. This phantom platform may in the end have defeated the Conservatives. At the last minute, many voters had a sudden change of mind away from the Tories, leading to results considerably different from the last opinion polls taken, which had suggested a Conservative victory. The Liberals were returned instead with a minority government. The NDP won 38 seats, while the Bloc Québécois won 54 (all in Quebec) but had no place to go given the lack of support in Quebec for extreme measures.

Minority Governments, 2004–2010

The Liberal minority government of 2004 was an inherently unstable one, and political jockeying continued throughout most of 2005. When the NDP tried to gain more social concessions as the price of its continued support, Martin refused, and the Liberal government fell 171–133 on a confidence motion in the House of Commons on 28 November 2005.

The election campaign of 2006, like the previous campaign, was relatively dull, not least because it was spread out over the Christmas/New Year holiday season. Many of the candidates, especially among the Liberals, appeared to be merely going through the motions. The buzz in the hundreds of Tim Horton's restaurants across the country (now owned by American interests but still regarded as where ordinary Canadians drank their morning coffee and 'rolled up the rim to win') was simple: 'it's time for a change.' The Liberals had been in power for too long and had lost both their integrity and their links with the electorate. The Liberals, the BQ, and the NDP all lost seats to the CPC, as the threat of the 'hidden agenda' was less effective than in 2004. Harper managed to keep a lid on right-wing pronouncements from his more conservative candidates, and in the end he had sufficient parliamentary votes to become Prime Minister. As he had promised, Paul Martin resigned as party leader as soon as the votes were counted.

As a minority Prime Minister, Harper had a difficult task ahead of him. He apparently understood that he still did not have the complete trust of the electorate and would have to govern the nation in such a way as to avoid major outcries until he could eventually obtain a majority through another election. One action Harper took was to abandon the Kelowna Accord for Aboriginal peoples. He did so without raising much initial outcry, except from Aboriginal leaders, although western provincial premiers soon joined the chorus of those protesting the death of Kelowna (*Winnipeg Free Press*, 30 May 2006). One senior federal cabinet minister said, 'I'm convinced that actually delivering the goods is more important than 10-year plans that don't deliver anything' (*Vancouver Province*, 3 May 2006).

Another action of the Prime Minister was to continue to insist on tight control over communication

Stephen Harper

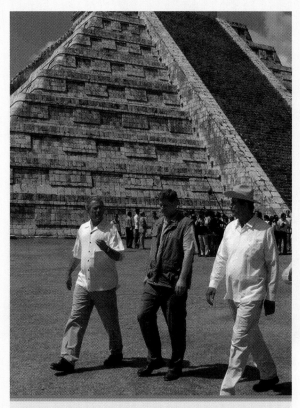

US President George Bush, Canadian Prime Minister Stephen Harper, and Mexican President Vicente Fox tour the ancient Maya ruins of Chichen-Itza in the Yucatan, 30 March 2006, during their first encounter of the two-day three-nation summit in Mexico. Photo by Gustavo Benitez/ Residencia de la Republica/KRT/ABACAPRESS.COM. © Abaca Press/2004. All rights reserved.

Born in Toronto in 1959, Stephen Harper was educated at Richview Collegiate Institute in Etobicoke before moving to Alberta, where he worked as a computer programmer before attending the University of Calgary. He received a BA in 1985 and an MA (Economics) in 1991 from Calgary. A supporter of the Liberal Party in high school, he opposed the Trudeau government's energy policy and became chief aide to Tory MP Jim Hawkes in 1985 before leaving the PC Party in 1986.

Harper was quickly recruited by Preston Manning for the incipient Reform Party, made a speech at its founding convention in 1987, and served as Chief Policy Officer in 1988 at the time of the drafting of the 1988 election platform. He ran for Parliament in the 1988 federal election but was defeated by Jim Hawkes. Harper subsequently became executive assistant to Deborah Grey in 1989 and wrote speeches for her until 1993. As Reform's policy officer to 1992, Harper argued that Reform needed to expand its regional base and criticized radical extremism. He broke with Manning in 1992 over the Charlottetown Accord, which Harper wholeheartedly opposed, and defeated Hawkes in the 1993 election. In the Reform Party caucus, Harper quickly developed a reputation as a bright newcomer, opposed to centralizing federalism and socially conservative; he opposed same-sex marriage and gun control legislation, for example.

But Harper was never comfortable in the Reform Party or with Preston Manning's leadership, seeing both as too populist, and he resigned his parliamentary seat in early 1997 to become an officer of the National Citizens' Coalition. He opposed appeasement of Quebec separatism, arguing that 'Quebec separatists are the problem and they need to be fixed.' After the Canadian Alliance was formed in 2000 and chose Stockwell Day as leader, Harper co-authored with a number of prominent Alberta politicians, including 2006 Alberta Conservative leadership candidate Ted Morton, the 'Alberta Agenda', which called for the provincial government to 'build firewalls around Alberta' to prevent continued redistribution of Alberta's wealth to less affluent provinces. He also insisted that Canada 'appears content to become a second-tier socialist country.' Harper ran for the Alliance leadership against Stockwell Day in March 2002 and won on the first ballot. He became leader of the opposition two months later, resigning the post early in 2004 to run for the leadership of the newly united Conservative Party of Canada. He won easily.

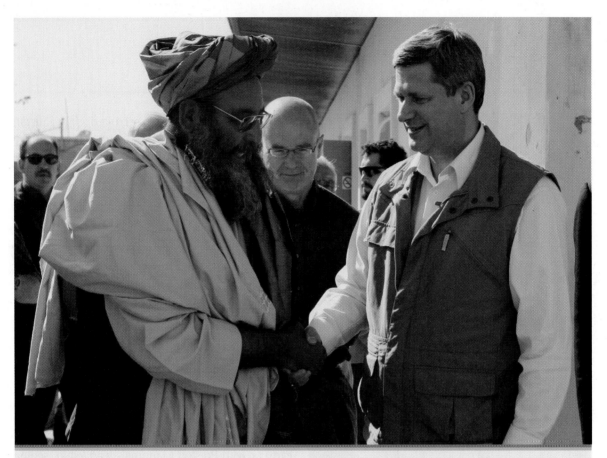

Prime Minister Stephen Harper shakes hands with Kandahar elder Mulah Akibullah following their meeting in Kandahar, Afghanistan, 13 March 2006. The Canadian Press/Tom Hanson.

between cabinet and caucus members and the parliamentary press corps. This was a natural consequence of minority status, since the government could not count on controlling the agenda in Parliament. Within a few weeks Harper was complaining that the Ottawa journalists did not like him, while the national press chafed about 'managed news'. The Tories had to avoid becoming too dependent for their tenure on the BQ and had to pick the appropriate moment to go to the nation for a new mandate; a huge lead in the polls could quickly disappear under the reality of an election or as a consequence of news that could not be managed. A surprise photo op for the newly elected PM in Kandahar might work, but when flag-draped coffins began to return regularly from Afghanistan, or when Harper called the heavy Israeli bombing of Lebanon in the summer of 2006 a 'measured' response and a family

of eight Lebanese Canadians from Montreal visiting in the country were killed, the news quickly became less manageable.

The government would clearly be aided for some time by the disarray within the Liberal Party. No prominent Liberal—and precious few were around—came immediately forward to replace Martin. The result was a scramble among a number of lesser lights—as many as 11 or 12—and some fairly ludicrous infighting, such as over the question of how bilingual some of the candidates truly were. For months, as a joke, ordinary Canadians went about their business announcing that they were not candidates for the Liberal leadership. On 2 December 2006, the Liberals at an exciting convention chose Stéphane Dion as their new leader. Dion was victorious as a third candidate, because too many supporters of the two leading contenders, Michael Ignatieff and Bob Rae, refused to accept the victory of the other man. Dion had little experience at government, spoke English hesitantly, and offered no program except enthusiasm for environmental issues. Clearly out of his depth, he resigned after a disastrous defeat of his party in the 2008 election. He was replaced by Ignatieff, whose family background was impeccable but who had spent most of his adult years outside the country as a university academic, in Great Britain and the United States. His career path opened him to charges that he had come back home only because of the chance to become prime minister. Such insinuations were even made publicly in a series of prominently displayed television commercials sponsored by the Tory party in 2009.

Two political realities dominated Canadian federal politics as the second decade of the century began. First, none of the parties or leaders had particularly impressed the Canadian electorate, which seemed content with minority government. Second, Canadians continued to share in the current international cynicism about politics and politicians, especially after the economic meltdowns caused, in large part, by the failure of governments around the world to control greedy behaviour. The voters cheered visibly as the Canadian Auditor General, for example, sought early in 2010 to audit the expenses accounts of members of Parliament, who initially resisted tooth and nail.

The Canadian Economy

One of the factors mitigating and cushioning developments that would otherwise in mid-decade have been terrible blows was an extremely buoyant economy. Canada converted a protracted period of high commodity prices and high domestic construction demand into general employment growth that seemed to have no end. By 2006 the nation had seen 13 years of employment increases, with unemployment rates at a 30-year low. Over this period employment growth had averaged 2 per cent per year. That Canada was merely sharing in an international boom that seemed bottomless did not dampen Canadian enthusiasm for the situation. Construction was fuelled by a policy of low interest rates maintained by the Bank of Canada and by a

rapidly rising demand for housing that inexorably drove up prices. Inflation remained manageable. The Canadian government ran high surpluses and the Canadian international balance sheet saw substantial balances in the nation's favour as well. By 2006 the biggest threat to Canadian prosperity was the weakening American dollar, which was worth only a few cents more than the Canadian one. Analysts warned that the international value of the Canadian dollar was reducing the country's international competitiveness. The solution was higher interest rates, but if raised too high, these would take the steam out of housing. Greatly increased oil prices—gasoline at the pump reached over a dollar a litre in the spring of 2006—were also a danger to the continued smooth running of the Canadian economy.

Some weak spots had persisted in Canadian prosperity from the twentieth century. Farmers continued to suffer, both from mad cow disease and from unusual weather conditions (drought and floods). Canada's share of international tourism was down, chiefly because American traffic across the international border decreased substantially. Americans stayed home because of security threats, because of perceived Canadian hostility to the United States, because of the lessening value of the American dollar, and because of increased Yankee boredom with what Canada had on offer for tourists: clean air, clean beaches, and attractive scenery. The decreased tourist trade had a significant effect everywhere in the country, but especially in the Maritime region, which had become almost totally dependent on visitors in the summer. Despite the problems of farmers, the three western provinces of British Columbia, Alberta, and Saskatchewan posted the most substantial rates of job creation and economic development. For many younger entrants into the job market, only part-time work without proper job security or fringe benefits was available, however.

Then came the financial crisis of 2008–9, which had its origins in the United States and spread worldwide. It was triggered in the first instance by the collapse of an overinflated real estate market. American mortgages had been easy to obtain and encouraged buyers to think that they could always trade up. Many homebuyers were encouraged to buy houses beyond their means, and when the bubble burst, defaults and foreclosures spiralled. Many financial institutions had tied securities to mortgages in new ways, and as the housing market went down, these securities and the credit based upon them proved worthless. Government regulation had not kept pace with the innovative nature of the credit expansion, and there was much chicanery in the system as well. Both financial institutions and individuals were over-leveraged, i.e., in debt beyond their capacity to pay. Financial experts did not appreciate the danger sufficiently early. Internationally, more than $1 trillion was lost on bad loans, and most of the largest investment bankers on Wall Street and around the world were forced into insolvency, from which governments had to bail them out. Canadian banking was better regulated and more conservative, so it was not much involved in either the bubble or the ensuing banking crisis, although the Canadian economy was badly hit by the international consequences. Like other governments, Canada's was forced to intervene to save institutions from collapse, particularly in the automotive industry, and to create employment through public spending.

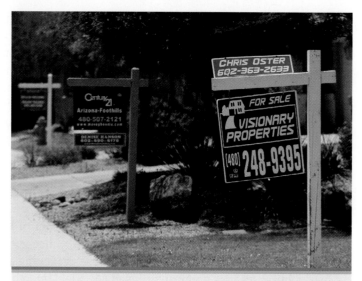

As a result of the economic recession in 2008–9, thousands of people in the US who could no longer afford to pay their mortgages were forced to sell their homes or face foreclosure. REUTERS/Joshua Lott.

Canadian Society and Culture in an Age of Meltdown

Given the volatility of the first years of the new millennium, it was hardly surprising that social and cultural signals in Canada often tended to be mixed and difficult to interpret. Only a few examples can be given here.

Boomers, Sandwiches, and Boomerangs

The constraints of economic life in the twenty-first century have led to an increased visibility in certain social phenomena relating to households and families: sandwiched parents and boomerang kids. Sandwiched parents, all members of the baby-boom generation, are those caring simultaneously for aging parents on one hand and adult children on the other hand. In 2002, according to Statistics Canada, 2.6 million Canadians aged 45–64 had children under 25 living at home (Turcotte, 2006). One-third of parents whose youngest child was between 20 and 34 had at least one child living at home, and one-quarter had an adult child who had returned to the parental home after leaving it at least once—the so-called 'boomerang generation'. At the same time, 27 per cent of the Canadians with children at home also provided elder care, and 21 per cent cared for two seniors. The reason for having to look after the elders is simple enough, but the 'boomerang' kids are a more complex business. Their numbers have increased significantly enough since earlier eras to represent a recognizable trend. Most adult children living at home do so because of high housing costs, high university tuition fees and/or high debts accumulated to attend university, and low wages after graduation. The probability of having adult children at home was substantially increased if parents lived in a single family dwelling in one of the larger cities of Ontario. Only 17 per cent of parents in rural areas or in small towns were likely to have adult children living at home.

Religion and Church Attendance

Some of the mixed messages regarding religious faith in Canada were especially confusing. Polls and studies persistently revealed that most Canadians believed in God and that many had enjoyed spiritual experiences, but regular church attendance in Canada, especially in the mainline churches, continued to fall off. The Roman Catholic Church was particularly hard-hit by revelations that for years it had covered up systematic sexual abuse by many of its priests. In 1946, 67 per cent of adult Canadians attended church regularly, but by 2001 that rate was down to 20 per cent. One poll taken in April 2006 indicated that regular attendance had decreased 4 per cent since 1996 and that less than half of the Canadians polled went to church more often than once a year. Attendance was lowest in Quebec, but every province had pockets of high attendance rates and low attendance rates. Curiously enough, this attitude towards church attendance in Canada was quite different from that in the United States, where almost 40 per cent of Americans went to church at least once a week, a figure that has remained unchanged since 1900. The difference, many observers suggested, was that the Americans had many more evangelical congregations. In any event, these church-going statistics suggest a substantial difference in values between the United States and Canada in an important aspect of daily life, and provided a challenge to those who claimed that American and Canadian basic values were converging.

That both Americans and Canadian Christians were questing for something spiritual they were not currently getting in church was well demonstrated by the bookstore success of Dan Brown's controversial novel, *The Da Vinci Code*, which sparked a subgenre of religious literature dealing with alternate interpretations of early Christianity labelled as heresy and suppressed by the early Church in the fourth century. Most of this literature dealt with the Gnostic writings of early Christianity. Many of these writings offered a far more human Jesus and a far less dogmatic

approach to belief. They marked the fruits of several generations of scholarship on early texts. How the mainline churches would respond to this evidence of interest in spiritual matters was another matter.

Health and Health Care

The efficacy of the Canadian health-care system—and its cost—were the subjects of continual controversy throughout the first years of the new century. Canadians heard a fair bit about their system, much of it ill-informed, in the course of the American debate over health care in 2009 and 2010. Continual questions were raised over affordability, particularly in light of the aging of the Canadian population (see Chapters 11 and 12). A report, for example, by the Parliamentary Budget Officer, issued on 18 February 2010, asked again whether the federal government's fiscal structure was sustainable, given the increasing number of Canadians out of the workforce but making greater demands on health care and other elderly benefits. It concluded that sustainability was impossible without significant reform to the structure. Other 'think-tank' reports, such as one by TD Bank economists for the Ontario Health Minister, shared the concern, claiming that if current trends continued, 'health-care expenditures would make up 80 per cent of total program spending by 2030, up from 46 per cent today. All other programs, such as education, would be funded out of the remaining 20 per cent' (*Globe and Mail*, 27 May 2010, A4). Not all experts agreed. A substantial minority insisted that health-care costs would not greatly increase as the population aged, since the next generations of older citizens would be healthier and require less medical attention for much of their extended life expectancy. Less debatable were the statistics on infant mortality. Figures for 2008 released by Statistics Canada were widely publicized in the press. These showed that while the number of deaths of infants under one per 1,000 live births was still declining in Canada, it was declining less than in many other developed nations. Indeed, Canada had fallen internationally from number 6 to number 24 on this sensitive indicator of the general health of the population.

Canada's Alternate Religion: Hockey

By the new millennium, Canadians clearly understood that the spread of hockey, especially in Europe, made it impossible for Canada to dominate international tournaments on a regular basis, although the national junior team regularly outperformed expectations. Thus it was particularly satisfying at the 2002 Winter Olympics when Canada's men's and the women's hockey teams both won gold medals. Nothing on the international level, however, prepared Canadians for 15 September 2004, the day the National Hockey League's commissioner, Gary Bettman, locked out the league's players after a protracted bout of unsatisfactory labour negotiations. The lockout lasted until mid-July of 2005. The 2004–5 season was finally cancelled on 14 February 2005. The NHL insisted that players' salaries had gotten out of hand; the NHL Players Association replied that salaries had escalated because of greedy owners who couldn't resist signing high-priced free agents. The majority of Canadian fans found both sides at fault, trapped into positions from which they could not extricate themselves without losing face. The eventual deal included a salary cap and a mechanism connecting salaries and revenue.

Canadians had watched in horror over the years as American big business messed around with a perfectly good game. Many observers agreed that the lockout was the ultimate by-product of the failure of the league to expand successfully into the southern United States and to convince Americans that they wanted to watch hockey on television on a regular basis. Empty seats in the south and a lack of a national American television contract spelled fiscal disaster for many owners. The league took advantage of the stoppage in play to study how the game could be made 'better', i.e., more exciting for fans, particularly those who did not understand the fine points of play. A series of new rules were introduced to encourage more end-to-end rushes and to make defence more difficult, particularly against the league's skilled superstars. At the 2010 Vancouver Olympics, both Canada's men's and women's teams again won gold medals, which pleased Canadians even if the victories did not necessarily vindicate the National Hockey League.

The Internet

Canadians continued to demonstrate an extraordinary willingness to try and use new technologies. The nation was particularly advanced in terms of the Internet, where Canadian broadband users were proportionally more numerous than in the United States and were continuing to increase. By 2004, almost 70 per cent of the adult Canadian population had access to and used the Internet, and by 2007, 81 per cent of online households would have broadband connections. This meant that Internet usage had penetrated more deeply in Canada than in the United States among the middle-aged, between the ages of 35 and 54, and among the older population. Only a few nations in Asia had higher rates of usage among the young than did Canada. The Internet was changing communications virtually overnight. Online telephonic connections were growing rapidly, and radio listening via the Internet was cutting into normal patterns of radio usage. The technology was so new that nobody fully understood either its possibilities or its liabilities. The medium's capacity for being monitored was considerable. Canadian intelligence got on the trail of the alleged Toronto terrorists of June 2006 through the Internet. The susceptibility to monitoring also meant that invasions of privacy could easily occur. The best example of this tendency was an increasing criticism of Facebook, a social networking application that became increasingly ubiquitous in the later years of the decade.

Canadian Popular Culture

Despite continued dire predictions of the convergence of Canadian and American culture, as we have seen in this chapter all evidence suggests that Canadian identity and Canadian values were stubbornly holding their own against the onslaught of the American media. Canadian popular music, at least in English Canada, has become increasingly full of Canadian places and Canadian references, and the sitcom *Corner Gas*—with its setting in rural Saskatchewan— became very popular at home (Jackson, 2005). The continued success of Tim Horton's restaurants proves that Canadian consumers can be very comfortable

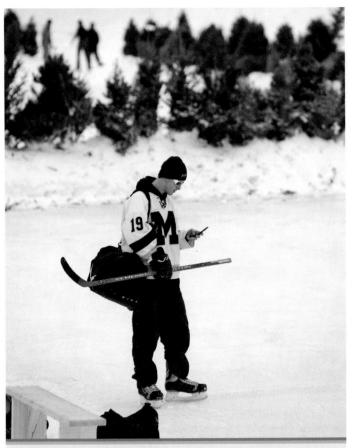

In Winnipeg, Manitoba, a young man juggles two of Canada's favourite pastimes: hockey and texting. Text messaging has become a popular method of communication for young Canadians. Photo © Ken Gillespie/Alamy.

before the official opening of the Games called into question the 'win at any cost' nature of Canada's 'Own the Podium' program, amid charges that Canada was not allowing visiting athletes equal access to practise at competitive venues. Criticism of 'Own the Podium' continued throughout the Games, although it very nearly achieved its objective of bringing Canada more medals than were won by any other nation. As for the hosting of the international summits, much criticism was levelled at the security costs of over $1 billion, particularly for the G20 gathering held in Toronto. Canadians were in the process treated to the sight of thousands of Toronto policemen equipped with helmets, clubs, and riot shields battling protestors on the streets of the city. In the aftermath of this summit, several different inquiries, none federal, were established to explore police actions and what went wrong. It seemed unlikely that any of these would seek or find answers to the most pertinent questions: Why did security cost over $1 billion? Why was the G20 summit held in the heart of a locked-down downtown Toronto?

The summits reminded Canadians that their nation was but a small part of a world that was, according to the alarmists, teetering on the brink of catastrophe in the early years of the new millennium. The only question for many seemed to be which disaster would trigger Armageddon. Would it be world terrorism, or global warming, or pandemic disease, or some currently unsuspected difficulty? Amid all the predictions of doom and gloom, however, Canadians managed to carry on. The number of gardening centres and the sales of garden plants increased enormously in the new millennium, as did the sales of gourmet foods. Home renovation and cooking programs became extremely popular on TV and were reflected in the explosion of domestic reconstruction and redecorating projects across the country.

with American ownership of Canadian icons, and Tim Horton's management accepted its responsibility by agreeing to open a branch in Afghanistan for Canadian troops.

Conclusion

In 2010 Canada exposed itself to international scrutiny on several occasions, first at the Vancouver Winter Olympics and then at the G8 and G20 international summits, held at Deerhurst Resort near Huntsville, Ontario, and in Toronto over a single week in June. On neither of these occasions did Canada enjoy an unqualified triumph. At the Winter Olympics, the death of a Georgian luger in a training run just hours

Protestors confront riot police in downtown Toronto during G20 protests in June 2010. Some protestors vandalized storefronts and destroyed city property, resulting in widespread criticism of the Toronto Police Service. The Canadian Press/Christian Lapid.

Although Canadians are having some trouble living with the new uncertainties, we should not conclude on a negative note. Today most Canadians live longer, earn more, are better educated, travel more, and possess more consumer goods than they did in the 1950s. Few would wish to return to the period in which there were no life-saving drugs, little family planning, and a minimal welfare and healthcare system. Fewer still would want to go further back, to the time when only men could vote, ballots were open, and unabashed sexism and racism were taken for granted. On every international indicator of quality of life—health standards, cultural achievement, environmental protection, infrastructure, gross national product per capita, political rights and civil liberties, and per capita purchasing power—Canada has continued to rank at or near the top. The statistics only confirm what Canadians themselves instinctively know: Canada is a great country and a good place to live.

Interpreting the Present

One of the most difficult challenges the historian of the present faces is to try to isolate the trends and developments that will still seem important to future generations. The headlines offer one criterion in this respect, but it is a limited one because of the difficulty of anticipating the future. There are several problems. One is whether the headline events and personalities of the present will be interpreted the same way in the future. An important consideration here will be whether the headline-maker continues to fit into an important trend or trends or whether he, she, or it comes to represent some sort of historical dead end. The issue usually will not involve the appearance of vast quantities of fresh information upon which to make a judgement. It is unlikely that much new personal material on Jean Chrétien or Brian Mulroney, for example, is going to surface over the next quarter-century, although the 2010 report of the Schreiber Inquiry into the private business dealings of a German businessman and former Prime Minister Brian Mulroney did provide some unexpected revelations into Mulroney's personality and character. More important is what will happen to Chrétien's or Mulroney's political vision and party, and whether it is kept rhetorically alive by their successors. If neither flourishes, the two prime ministers, despite their relative longevity in office, will certainly seem less influential over the long haul. If free trade is eventually repudiated by Canada, Mulroney will seem less important. Unlike Pierre Trudeau, neither man succeeded in creating a positive larger-than-life mythology for himself during his time in office. Trudeau's mythology can already be seen as flourishing quite apart from his historical record.

As for the interpretation of Canadian involvement in Afghanistan, much depends on how that business plays out militarily. If Afghanistan turns out to be a disaster, Prime Minister Harper could well be remembered, like President Kennedy with Vietnam, as the man who got us involved—even though neither leader, in fact, initiated his nation's involvement. If intervention in Afghanistan works, Harper and the Harper government might well be seen as having made the courageous decision.

On the whole, most political leaders today leave office somewhere near the bottom as far as their reputations are concerned. One of the chief characteristics of twenty-first century politics, as we have seen, is an abiding public suspicion of politicians, not just in Canada but around the world. In the short run, what we are likely to remember are the Gomery Commission and the Schreiber Inquiry. In this sense, reputations can only get better.

As for the people these politicians seek to appeal to and lead, as we saw in Chapter 11 the human face of Canada is changing, especially in Canada's largest cities. In March 2010 Statistics Canada reported that the so-called 'visible minorities' would form the majority of Toronto residents by the year 2017, thus making 'whites' or Euro-Canadians the new 'visible minority' in that city. By 2031, according to Statistics Canada's 'reference scenario', which assumes that current demographic trends are maintained, 63 per cent of Toronto residents would be people of colour and, in Vancouver, the visible minorities (a term that does not include Aboriginal peoples) would make up 59 per cent of the population (Statistics Canada, 2010). Indeed, by 2031, over 71 per cent of the visible minorities in Canada would live in the three census metropolitan areas of Toronto, Vancouver, and Montreal. What these demographic changes will mean to Canadian society and politics, and to the changing history of Canada as has been discussed in this book, only the future can determine.

Short Bibliography

Adams, Michael. *Fire and Ice: The United States, Canada, and the Myth of Converging Values*. Toronto, 2003. A study arguing that the United States and Canada were not becoming socially more alike.

Doern, Bruce, and Monica Gattinger. *Power Switch: Energy Regulatory Governance in the 21st Century*. Toronto, 2003. A careful analysis of how energy was regulated.

Drache, Daniel. *Borders Matter: Homeland Security and the Search for North America*. Halifax, 2004. A Canadian nationalist looks at the homeland security issue.

Koh, Tommy, et al., eds. *The New Global Threat: Severe Acute Respiratory Syndrome and Its Impacts*. River Edge, NJ, 2003. A multi-authored and international account of SARS.

Kolbert, Elizabeth. *Field Notes for a Catastrophe: Man, Nature, and Climate Change*. New York, 2006. A powerful vision of world disaster.

McDougall, John N. *Drifting Together: The Political Economy of Canada–US Integration*. Toronto, 2006. Argues the case for convergence.

McKinney, Joseph. *Political Economy of the U.S.–Canada Softwood Lumber Trade*. Orono, Maine, 2004. An analysis of the softwood lumber business, sympathetic to the United States.

Study Questions

1. Would Canadian–American Relations in the early twenty-first century have been very much different without 9/11? Why or why not?
2. Why did the Liberal Party lose the 2005 election?
3. What was the 'mad cow' kerfuffle really about?

 www.oupcanada.com/Bumsted4e

Visit the companion website for *A History of the Canadian Peoples*, fourth edition for further resources.

Epilogue

At Canada Day in 2010, the Canadian media almost unanimously agreed in proclaiming with much self-congratulation that the country had finally come of age and was ready to take its place as a leader on the world stage. The evidence, of course, was Canada's successful hosting of the 2010 Winter Olympics, followed by its hosting of the G8 and G20 summits. At the latter, Prime Minister Harper managed to lead an international consensus in favour of an international campaign for improved pre-natal and maternal care, as well as an agreement on balancing budgets and controlling deficits. In regard to fiscal responsibility, Canada was generally admired around the world for its policy before and during the Great Meltdown. The nation had virtually eliminated its federal deficit a dozen years earlier (thanks chiefly to a super-buoyant economy that had produced unexpectedly rich government revenues, and no thanks to the present government in power) and now stood as a model to its allies. Canada certainly was much more admired for its fiscal policy than it had been a few months earlier for its environmental obstructionism at the Copenhagen summit on climate change, although editorial memories are often short, especially on Canada Day. Whether the Canada that would face the world after 1 July 2010 would be the fiscally successful one or the environmentally dubious one was another matter.

As we have seen, several of the seemingly serious problems that had faced Canada at the beginning of the millennium had more or less sorted themselves out during its first decade. Canadian–American relations were far less hostile, partly because the Canadian government had symbolically given way on several major economic bones of contention and was now a more or less compliant junior partner. An electoral alternative to the Liberals had been found in the newly minted Conservative Party and the Canadian electorate had voted it into power as a minority government. Whether the Conservatives could form a stable majority government was still unclear, however. On the other hand, other problems, such as global warming and Canada's involvement in the war in Afghanistan, only got more complicated. While old questions in the Middle East reappeared with new implications for Canada, the threat of international terrorism escalated.

Global Warming, Energy, and Oil Spills

By the end of the first decade of the new millennium, several developments had virtually cancelled each other out on the global warming front. On the one hand, most respectable scientific opinion was agreed that global warming caused by carbon dioxide emissions was a reality, and most scientific skepticism had moved to an insistence that the recent extreme weather patterns observed in the world—such as an increased incidence of hurricanes in the Caribbean and eastern Atlantic region—were not connected with the emissions. On the other hand, it was also clear that the economies of the developed nations of the world were far too dependent on fossil fuels to be able to effectively reduce their use. The Kyoto Accord was, for all intents and purposes, toast. Some other mechanism would have to be found to reduce the 'carbon footprints' that increasingly were causing potential chaos.

Adding further complexity to the global warming/energy picture was an enormous spike in the price of a barrel of standard crude oil after September 2003, when the price had stood under $25 a barrel. By July 2006, that price had reached $78.40 per barrel and manifested itself in escalating prices for gasoline at the pump in both the United States and Canada. While experts acknowledged the influence of such factors as the Iraq War and the Middle East crisis on prices, many believed that the fundamental cause for the higher prices was the recognition that the supply of easily exploited oil was rapidly running out. The climbing pump prices had some limited effect on consumer choices—the Detroit automakers, which for some years had kept up their market share through the production of gas-guzzling sport utility vehicles (SUVs), suddenly discovered that the SUV was substantially less popular; some reduction in summer tourist travel by automobile could be observed; and 'hybrid' vehicles that relied partially on other energy sources became marketable. The most interesting point of consumer reaction to stratospheric gas prices in both the US and Canada was how little change at first occurred, apparently confirming the general perception that North Americans might complain about energy prices, but would pay them rather than greatly alter their behaviour. Subsequently, it must be added, a temporary consumer shift from gas guzzlers almost destroyed the Detroit Big Three during the Great Meltdown. Not surprisingly, Canada's raw resources became much coveted around the world. In November of 2010, for example, the federal government refused to allow an Australian company to purchase the nation's largest producer of potash, claiming the deal was not of sufficient 'strategic benefit' to Canada.

The environmental disaster in the Gulf of Mexico created by the explosion and sinking of the Deepwater Horizon oil-drilling rig and the subsequent wellhead blowout on the ocean floor, which took months to contain, simply added to the public confusion. As almost everyone acknowledged, underwater oil wells were absolutely essential—as was the oil from the environmentally 'dirty' Athabasca tar sands in Alberta—and public attention focused on how technology and corporate culture had failed in the Gulf of Mexico crisis rather than on whether such deep-sea drilling should be allowed in the first place. Canadians could take some solace in the fact that none of their offshore wells had caused a disaster—yet—but only if they closed their eyes to what was happening to the environment in Alberta. A business-as-usual mindset, rather than any serious rethinking about standards of living and North American society's voracious appetite for oil, was reflected when the Alberta government, in the midst of the Gulf of Mexico crisis, paid for a half-page ad in the *Washington Post* that appeared the day after Canada Day. The implicit message, in light of the Gulf crisis, was that the tar sands aren't so dirty after all; the explicit message was that Alberta, with its 'reliable' and 'secure' resource, was eager to help the Americans by providing oil, as well as a new Keystone Pipeline to siphon unrefined bitumen—along with many new refinery jobs and environmental damage—to the American neighbours to the south (Wingrove, 2010). Environmental groups on both sides of the border increased their opposition to the proposed pipeline, and these protests were ratcheted up a notch when, in late July 2010, a pipeline owned by Calgary-based Enbridge broke in southern Michigan, spilling over 3 million litres of Alberta crude oil into the Kalamazoo River. The enormity of the Gulf of Mexico oil spill as an environmental disaster should by all rights lead to a massive paradigm shift in Canadian attitudes on the environment, but there is not much evidence that any such thing will happen.

The War in Afghanistan

While few Canadians appeared to recognize that the nature of the Canadian involvement in the war in Afghanistan had changed in 2005, they were gradually forced to accept that Canadian casualties had greatly increased and might increase still more. By October of 2006, nearly 40 Canadian soldiers had been killed in that conflict; by mid-2010 the figure passed 150. Each dead soldier was brought back to Canada and buried with great ceremony and publicity. By comparison with American losses in Iraq, the Canadian numbers were minuscule, but to some extent that was exactly the point. The dead were small enough in number so that each one could be mourned individually. A continuation of this pattern was bound to keep public opinion uneasy with the war, and the nation always seemed on the verge of a great national debate over Canadian military policy. That debate had not yet occurred, and was still being deferred. In November of 2010 all parties in Parliament backed away from challenging the government's about-face—without consulting Parliament—on Canadian withdrawal from Afghanistan, apparently preferring to avoid the issue rather than threaten the precarious balance of power in Parliament and perhaps provoke an election.

Renewed International Terrorism and Other Threats to Air Travel

On 10 August 2006, Scotland Yard announced that it had foiled a terrorist plot designed to blow up, in a co-ordinated fashion, as many as 10 aircraft flying from the United Kingdom to the United States. The plot involved liquid explosives hidden in carry-on luggage, then mixed and detonated on the aircraft. The conspirators were, for the most part, Muslims born in Britain. None of the flights involved Canadian airliners or Canadian destinations, but Canada fully participated in the unprecedented security response to the threat. Airport searches became more intense, and virtually all carry-on baggage, including all liquids, was temporarily forbidden; passengers were even denied any reading material beyond that obtained at the boarding gate. Lengthy delays were inevitable, and the result, of course, was utter chaos, beginning in London's Heathrow Airport and radiating around the world. Many observers feared that the eventual result of the new threats and restrictions would be the end of air travel as it had developed since the introduction of the jet airplane. The question about the future of air travel was raised again in 2010 in another context, as a volcanic eruption in Iceland spewed dangerous black clouds across the major flight paths from North America to Europe and forced the closure of air travel across the Atlantic for days on end, a reminder of how dependent the world had become on smoothly functioning international transportation.

And indeed, even a casual perusal of the daily newspapers (or increasingly, newspaper websites) made abundantly evident that the world had become extraordinarily interdependent in ways that ought to have altered the policies and behaviour of nations far more than it had.

But hope springs eternal.

References

Abella, Irving, and Harold Troper. 1991. *None Is Too Many: Canada and the Jews of Europe, 1933–1948*, rev. edn. Toronto: Lester and Orpen Dennys.

Abraham, Thomas. 2005. *Twenty-First Century Plague: The Story of SARS*. Baltimore: Johns Hopkins University Press.

Adams, Michael. 2003. *Fire and Ice: The United States, Canada and the Myth of Converging Values*. Toronto: Penguin.

Addiction Research Foundation. 1970. *Summary with Comments on the Interim Report of the Commission of Inquiry into the Non-Medical Use of Drugs*. Toronto: Addiction Research Foundation.

Akins, T.B., ed. 1869. *Selections from the Public Documents of the Province of Nova Scotia*. Halifax: n.p.

Allen, Robert S. 1992. *His Majesty's Indian Allies: British Indian Policy in the Defence of Canada, 1774–1815*. Toronto: Dundurn Press.

Arthur, E. 1986. *Toronto: No Mean City*. Toronto: University of Toronto Press.

Avery, Donald. 1986. 'The Radical Alien and the Winnipeg General Strike of 1919', in J.M. Bumsted, ed., *Interpreting Canada's Past*, vol. 2. Toronto: Oxford University Press, 222–39.

———. 1995. *Reluctant Host: Canada's Response to Immigrant Workers, 1896–1994*. Toronto: McClelland & Stewart.

Axtell, James. 2001. *Natives and Newcomers: The Cultural Origins of North America*. New York: Oxford University Press.

Bakker, Peter. 1989. 'Two Basque Loanwords in Micmac', *International Journal of American Linguistics* 55, 2: 258–60.

Ballantyne, R. 1879. *Hudson's Bay: or, Everyday Life in the Wilds of North America*. London: T. Nelson and Sons.

Barnholden, Michael. 2009. *Circumstances Alter Photographs: Captain James Peters' Reports from the War of 1885*. Vancouver: Talonbooks.

Behiels, Michael D. 1985. *Prelude to Quebec's Quiet Revolution: Liberalism versus Neo-Nationalism, 1945–1960*. Montreal and Kingston: McGill-Queen's University Press.

Bell, W.P. 1990. *The 'Foreign Protestants' and the Settlement of Nova Scotia: The History of a Piece of Arrested British Colonial Policy in the 18th Century*. Fredericton, NB: Acadiensis Press.

Benson, A.B., ed. 1937. *The America of 1750: Peter Kalm's Travel in North America*, 2 vols. New York: Dover.

Berger, Carl. 1986. 'The True North Strong and Free', in J.M. Bumsted, ed., *Interpreting Canada's Past*, vol. 2. Toronto: Oxford University Press, 154–60.

Berger, Thomas R. 1977. *Northern Frontier, Northern Homeland*, 2 vols. Report of the Mackenzie Valley Pipeline Inquiry. Ottawa: Supply and Services Canada.

Binnie-Clark, G. 1914. *Wheat and Woman*. Toronto: Bell & Cockburn.

Bliss, Michael. 1972. 'Canadianizing American Business: The Roots of the Branch Plant', in I. Lumsden, ed., *Close the 49th Parallel: The Americanization of Canada*. Toronto: University of Toronto Press.

Bourassa, Henri. 1912. *Canadian Club Addresses 1912*. Toronto: Warwick Bros & Rutter.

Bowker, A., ed. 1973. *The Social Criticism of Stephen Leacock: The Unsolved Riddle of Social Justice and Other Essays*. Toronto: University of Toronto Press.

Brebner, J.B. 1927. *New England's Outpost: Acadia before the Conquest of Canada*. New York: Columbia University Press.

Brode, P. 1984. *Sir John Beverley Robinson*. Toronto: University of Toronto Press.

Bumsted, J.M., ed. 1969. *Documentary Problems in Canadian History*. Georgetown, Ont.: Irwin-Dorsey.

———. 1971. *Henry Alline, 1748–1784*. Toronto: University of Toronto Press.

———, ed. 1986. *Understanding the Loyalists*. Sackville, NB: Mount Allison University Press.

———. 1994. *The Winnipeg General Strike of 1919: An Illustrated History*. Winnipeg: Watson and Dwyer.

Calgary Herald, 1 March 2003.

Campbell, Patrick. 1937. *Travels in the Interior Inhabited Parts of North America in the Years 1791 and 1792*, ed. H.H. Langton. Toronto: Champlain Society.

Canada Year Book. 1959. Ottawa: Queen's Printer.

———. 1990. Ottawa: Queen's Printer.

———. 1994. Ottawa: Statistics Canada.

Carr, E.H. 1964. *What Is History?* Harmondsworth, UK: Penguin.

Carson, Rachel. 1962. *Silent Spring*. Boston: Houghton Mifflin.

Carter, Sarah. 1990. *Lost Harvests: Prairie Indian Reserve Farmers and Government Policy*. Montreal and Kingston: McGill-Queen's University Press.

Cell, Gillian, ed. 1982. *Newfoundland Discovered: English Attempts at Colonisation, 1610–1630*. London: Hakluyt Society.

Christensen, Deanna. 2000. *Ahtahkakoop: The Epic Account of a Plains Cree Head Chief, His People, and Their Struggle for Survival, 1816–1896*. Shell Lake, Sask.: Ahtahkakoop Publishing.

Clark, Arthur H. 1968. *Acadia: The Geography of Early Nova Scotia to 1760*. Madison: University of Wisconsin Press.

Clark, C.S. 1898. *Of Toronto the Good: A Social Study*. Montreal: Toronto Publishing Co.

Clark, E.A. 1988. 'Cumberland Planters and the Aftermath of the Attack on Fort Cumberland', in M. Conrad, ed., *They Planted Well: New England Planters in Maritime Canada*. Fredericton, NB: Acadiensis Press.

Commission of Inquiry into the Non-Medical Use of Drugs. 1970. *Interim Report*. Ottawa: Queen's Printer.

Conrad, Margaret, et al., eds. 1988. *No Place Like Home: Diaries and Letters of Nova Scotia Women 1771–1938*. Halifax: Formac.

Cook, Ramsay. 1969a. *Provincial Autonomy: Minority Rights and the Compact Theory, 1867–1921*. Ottawa: Queen's Printer.

———, ed. 1969b. *French-Canadian Nationalism: An Anthology*. Toronto: Macmillan.

Couton, Philippe. 2002. 'Highly Skilled Immigrants: Recent Trends and Issues', *Isuma: Canadian Journal of Policy Research* 3, 2 (Fall).

Craig, G.M., ed. 1963. *Lord Durham's Report*. Toronto: McClelland & Stewart.

Cuff, R.D., and J.L. Granatstein. 1977. *The Ties That Bind: Canadian–American Relations in Wartime from the Great War to the Cold War*. Toronto: Samuel Stevens Hakkert & Co.

Cuthand, S. 1978. 'The Native Peoples of the Prairie Provinces in the 1920s and 1930s', in I.A.L. Getty and D.B. Smith, eds, *One Century Later: Western Canadian Reserve Indians since Treaty 7*. Vancouver: University of British Columbia Press, 31–2.

Davis, Ann. 1979. *Frontiers of Our Dreams: Quebec Painting in the 1940's and 1950's*. Winnipeg: Winnipeg Art Gallery.

Department of Regional Economic Expansion. 1971. *Major Economic Indicators, Provinces and Regions*. Ottawa: Queen's Printer.

Dickason, Olive Patricia. 2002. *Canada's First Nations: A History of Founding Peoples from Earliest Times*, 3rd edn. Toronto: Oxford University Press.

———. 2006. *A Concise History of Canada's First Nations*, adapted by Moira Jean Calder. Toronto: Oxford University Press.

——— with David T. McNab. 2009. *Canada's First Nations: A History of Founding Peoples from Earliest Times*, 4th edn. Toronto: Oxford University Press.

Dirks, Gerald E. 1995. *Controversy and Complexity: Canadian Immigration Policy during the 1980s*. Montreal and Kingston: McGill-Queen's University Press.

Doern, Bruce, and Monica Gattinger. 2003. *Power Switch: Energy Regulatory Governance in the 21st Century*. Toronto: University of Toronto Press.

Dollier de Casson, F. 1928 [1868]. *A History of Montreal 1640–1672*, ed. and trans. R. Flenley. London: J.M. Dent & Sons.

Drache, Daniel, 2004. *Borders Matter: Homeland Security and the Search for North America*. Halifax: Fernwood.

Duncan, Sara Jeannette. 1971 [1904]. *The Imperialist*. Toronto: McClelland & Stewart.

Durand, E. 1981. *Vignettes of Early Winnipeg*. Winnipeg: Frances McColl.

Dyer, G., and T. Viljoen. 1990. *The Defense of Canada: In the Arms of the Empire 1760–1939*. Toronto: McClelland & Stewart.

Easterbrook, W.T., and M.H. Watkins. 1962. *Approaches to Canadian Economic History*. Toronto: McClelland & Stewart.

——— and G.J. Aitken. 1956. *Canadian Economic History*. Toronto: Macmillan.

Eccles, W.J. 1983. *The Canadian Frontier 1534–1760*, rev. edn. Albuquerque: University of New Mexico Press.

Ellis, John. 1975. *Eye Deep in Hell: Trench Warfare in World War I*. Baltimore: Johns Hopkins University Press, reprint 1989.

Engelstad, Diane, and John Bird, eds. 1992. *Nation to Nation: Aboriginal Sovereignty and the Future of Canada*. Toronto: Anansi.

Ewart, J.S. 1908. *The Kingdom of Canada: Imperial Federation, the Colonial Conferences, the Alaska Boundary and Other Essays*. Toronto: Morang.

Fairley, M., ed. 1960. *The Selected Writings of William Lyon Mackenzie*. Toronto: Oxford University Press.

Fingard, Judith. 1988. 'The Relief of the Unemployed Poor in Saint John, Halifax, and St John's, 1815–1860', in P.A. Buckner and D. Frank, eds, *The Acadiensis Reader*, vol. 1. Fredericton, NB: Acadiensis Press.

Fisher, R. 1977. *Contact and Conflict: Indian–European Relations in British Columbia 1774–1890*. Vancouver: University of British Columbia Press.

Forsythe, D., ed. 1971. *Let the Niggers Burn: The Sir George Williams University Affair and Its Caribbean Aftermath*. Montreal: Black Rose.

Frye, Northrop. 1976. 'Conclusion', in C.F. Klinck, ed., *Literary History of Canada*, rev. edn. Toronto: University of Toronto Press, 849.

Gage, Thomas. Papers. William Clements Library, University of Michigan.

Gammer, Nicholas. 2001. *From Peacekeeping to Peacemaking: Canada's Response to the Yugoslav Crisis*. Montreal and Kingston: McGill-Queen's University Press.

Gattinger, Monica. 2005. 'From Government to Governance in the Energy Sector: The State of the Canada–U.S. Energy Relationship', *American Review of Canadian Studies* 35, 2: 321–52.

Gérin-Lajoie, A. 1977 [1874]. *Jean Rivard*, trans. V. Bruce. Toronto: McClelland & Stewart.

Gerry, Thomas M.F. 1990–1. '"I Am Translated": Anna Jameson's Sketches and *Winter and Summer Rambles in Canada*', *Journal of Canadian Studies* 25, 4 (Winter).

Globe and Mail, 26 March 2003, 20 May 2006.

Granatstein, J.L., and R. Bothwell. 1990. *Pirouette: Pierre Trudeau and Canadian Foreign Policy*. Toronto: University of Toronto Press.

Grant, George. 1965. *Lament for a Nation: The Defeat of Canadian Nationalism*. Toronto: Macmillan.

Grant, G.M., ed. 1876. Picturesque Canada. Toronto: Hunter, Rose & Co.

Gray, Charlotte. 1999. *Sisters in the Wilderness: The Lives of Susanna Moodie and Catharine Parr Traill*. Toronto: Viking.

Gray, J. 1966. *The Winter Years: The Depression on the Prairies*. Toronto: Macmillan.

Gunn, G.E. 1966. *The Political History of Newfoundland, 1832–1864*. Toronto: University of Toronto Press.

Haliburton, Thomas Chandler. 1838. *The Clockmaker: or The Sayings and Doings of Samuel Slick of Slickville*. London: Richard Bentley.

Halpenny, F.G., ed. 1976. *The Dictionary of Canadian Biography*, vol. 9. Toronto: University of Toronto Press.

Harper, J. Russell. 1966. *Painting in Canada: A History*, 2nd edn. Toronto.

Hatch, R. 1970. *Thrust for Canada*. Boston: Houghton Mifflin.

Hawkins, Freda. 1972. *Canada and Immigration: Public Policy and Public Concern*. Montreal and Kingston: McGill Queen's University Press.

Hind, H.Y. 1869. *The Dominion of Canada: Containing a Historical Sketch of the Preliminaries and Organization of Confederation*. Toronto: L. Stebbins.

Hodgetts, J.E. 1968. 'The Changing Nature of the Public Service', in L.D. Musoff, ed., *The Changing Public Service*. Berkeley: University of California Press, 7–18.

Indian–Eskimo Association of Canada. 1970. *Native Rights in Canada*. Toronto: Indian–Eskimo Association of Canada.

Innis, H. 1948. *The Diary of Simeon Perkins, 1766–1780*, vol. 1. Toronto: Champlain Society.

Jackson, David J. 2005. 'Peace, Order, and Good Songs: Popular Music and English-Canadian Culture', *American Review of Canadian Studies* 35, 2 (Spring): 25–44.

Johnston, M. 1994. *Corvettes Canada: Convoy Veterans of WWII Tell Their True Stories*. Toronto: McGraw-Hill Ryerson.

Kahn, Agnan R. 2006. 'Canada's Kandahar Balancing Act', *Maclean's*, 26 May.

Kealey, Greg, ed. 1973. *Canada Investigates Industrialism: The Royal Commission on the Relations of Labour and Capital, 1889*, abridged. Toronto: University of Toronto Press.

Keeble, Edna. 2005. 'Defining Canadian Security Continuities and Discontinuities', *American Review of Canadian Studies* 35, 1 (Spring): 1–23.

Keefer, T.C. 1853. *Philosophy of Railroads, Published by Order of the Directors of the St Lawrence and Ottawa Grand Junction Railway Company*, 4th edn. Montreal: J. Lovell.

Kent, Tom. 1988. *A Public Purpose: An Experience of Liberal Opposition and Canadian Government*. Montreal and Kingston: McGill-Queen's University Press.

Kert, Faye Margaret. 1997. *Prize and Prejudice: Privateering and Naval Prize in Atlantic Canada in the War of 1812*. St John's: International Maritime History Association.

Kinsman, Gary. 1987. *The Regulation of Desire: Sexuality in Canada*. Montreal: Black Rose Books.

Klinck. Carl, ed. 1976. *Literary History of Canada: Canadian Literature in English*, 2nd edn, 3 vols. Toronto: University of Toronto Press.

Knowles, Valerie. 1997. *Strangers at Our Gates: Canadian Immigration and Immigration Policy, 1540–1997*. Toronto: Dundurn Press.

Koh, Tommy, et al., eds. 2003. *The New Global Threat: Severe Acute Respiratory Syndrome and Its Impacts*. Singapore: World Scientific Publishing.

Kolbert, Elizabeth. 2006. *Field Notes for a Catastrophe: Man, Nature, and Climate Change*. New York: Bloomsbury.

Kostash, M. 1980. *Long Way from Home: The Story of the Sixties Generation in Canada*. Toronto: James Lorimer.

Kwavnick, David, ed. 1973. *The Tremblay Report*. Toronto: McClelland & Stewart.

Lévesque, René. 1986. *Memoirs*, trans. Philip Stratford. Toronto: McClelland & Stewart.

Library and Archives Canada. 1745. 'Representation of the State of His Majesty's Province of Nova Scotia', 8 Nov.

Lower, A.R.M. 1973. *Great Britain's Woodyard: British North America and the Timber Trade, 1762–1870*. Montreal and Kingston: McGill-Queen's University Press.

Lucas, C.P., ed. 1912. *Lord Durham's Report*, 3 vols. Oxford: Clarendon Press.

McArthur, D.A. 1924. 'The Teaching of Canadian History', *Ontario Historical Society Papers* 21.

MacBeath, G. 1966. 'Charles de Saint-Étienne de La Tour', in G. Brown, ed., *Dictionary of Canadian Biography*. Toronto: University of Toronto Press, 592–6.

McCracken, M. 1975. *Memories Are Made of This: What It Was Like to Grow Up in the Fifties*. Toronto: James Lorimer.

MacDonell, Sister M. 1982. *The Emigrant Experience: Songs of Highland Emigrants in North America*. Toronto: University of Toronto Press.

McKinney, Joseph S. 2004. *Political Economy of the U.S.–Canada Softwood Lumber Trade*. Orono: University of Maine Press.

McLuhan, Marshall. 1951. *The Mechanical Bride: Folklore of Industrial Man*. New York: Vanguard Press.

Macphail, Andrew. 1915. Diary, vol. 1, 28 Dec. Macphail Papers, Library and Archives Canada.

McWhinney, E. 1982. *Canada and the Constitution 1979–1982*. Toronto: University of Toronto Press.

Magocsi, Paul Robert, ed. 1999. *Encyclopedia of Canada's Peoples*. Toronto: University of Toronto Press.

Marchilson, Gregory. 1996. *Profits and Politics: Beaverbrook and the Gilded Age of Canadian Finance*. Toronto: University of Toronto Press.

Margolian, John. 2000. *Unauthorized Entry: The Truth about Nazi War Criminals in Canada, 1946–1956*. Toronto: University of Toronto Press.

Marshall, J., ed. 1967. *Word from New France: The Selected Letters of Marie de l'Incarnation*. Toronto: Oxford University Press.

Marwick, Arthur. 1970. *The Nature of History*. London and Basingstoke: Macmillan.

Masters, D.C. 1936. *The Reciprocity Treaty of 1854*. London: Longmans Green & Company.

Michaels, Patrick J., ed. 2005. *Shattered Consensus: The True State of Global Warming*. Lanham, Md: Rowman & Littlefield.

Miki, Roy, and Cassandra Kobayashi. 1991. *Justice in Our Time: The Japanese Canadian Redress Settlement*. Vancouver: Talonbooks.

Mills, David. 1988. *The Idea of Loyalty in Upper Canada, 1784–1850*. Montreal and Kingston: McGill-Queen's University Press.

Monière, D. 1981. *Ideologies on Quebec: The Historical Development*. Toronto: University of Toronto Press.

Moodie, Susanna. 1852. *Roughing It in the Bush, or, Life in Canada*, vol. 1. London: Richard Bentley.

Moogk, Peter. 2000. *La Nouvelle France: The Making of French Canada, A Cultural History*. East Lansing: Michigan State University Press.

Morrow, Don. 1989. *A Concise History of Sport in Canada*. Toronto: Oxford University Press.

Morton, W.L., ed. 1970. *Monck Letters and Journals 1863–1868: Canada from Government House at Confederation*. Toronto: McClelland & Stewart.

National Task Force on Suicide in Canada. 1984. *Suicide in Canada*. Ottawa: Queen's Printer.

Naylor, R.T. 1975. *The History of Canadian Business, 1867–1914*, vol. 1. Toronto: James Lorimer.

Neatby, Hilda. 1972. *The Quebec Act: Protest and Policy*. Toronto: Prentice-Hall of Canada.

Nelles, H.V. 1974. *The Politics of Development: Forests, Mines & Hydro-Electric Power in Ontario, 1849–1941*. Toronto: Macmillan.

Nevitte, Neil. 1996. *The Decline of Deference: Canadian Value Change in Cross-National Perspective*. Peterborough, Ont.: Broadview Press.

Niagara Spectator, 11 December 1817.

O'Neill, Kate. 2005. 'How Two Cows Make a Crisis: U.S.–Canada Trade Relations and Mad Cow Disease', *American Review of Canadian Studies* 35, 2: 295–319.

Ormsby, Margaret. 1958. *British Columbia: A History*. Toronto: Macmillan of Canada.

Parker, Roy. 2009. *Uprooted: The Shipment of Poor Children to Canada, 1867–1917*. Vancouver: University of British Columbia Press.

Patterson, E.P. 1972. *The Canadian Indian: A History since 1500*. Toronto: Collier-Macmillan.

Perlin, George. 1997. 'The Constraints of Public Opinion: Diverging or Converging Paths?', in Keith Banting, George Hoberg, and Richard Simeon, eds, *Degrees of Freedom: Canada and the United States in a Changing World*. Montreal and Kingston: McGill-Queen's University Press.

Petryshyn, Jaroslav. 1985. *Peasants in the Promised Land: Canada and the Ukrainians, 1891–1914*. Toronto: James Lorimer.

Pope, Sir J. 1930. *Memoirs of the Rt Hon. Sir John A. MacDonald*, vol. 1. Toronto: Oxford University Press.

Preston, R.A., ed. 1974. *For Friends at Home: A Scottish Emigrant's Letters from Canada, California and the Cariboo 1844–1864*. Montreal and Kingston: McGill-Queen's University Press.

Prince, Bryan. 2009. *A Shadow on the Household: One Enslaved Family's Incredible Struggle for Freedom*. Toronto: McClelland & Stewart.

Proceedings of the Special Joint Committee of the Senate and House of Commons on Divorce. 1967. Ottawa: Queen's Printer.

Province, The (Vancouver), 3 May 2006.

Pryke, K.G. 1979. *Nova Scotia and Confederation, 1864–1874*. Toronto: University of Toronto Press.

Quaife, M.M., ed. 1962. *The Western Country in the 17th Century: The Memoirs of Antoine Lamothe Cadillac and Pierre Liette*. New York: Citadel Press.

Québec conseil exécutif. 1979. *Québec–Canada, a New Deal: The Québec Government Proposal for a New Partnership between Equals, Sovereignty-Association.* Québec: Québec conseil executif.

Radforth, Ian, 2004. *Royal Spectacle: The 1860 Visit of the Prince of Wales to Canada and the United States.* Toronto: University of Toronto Press.

Rasporich, A.W. 1969. 'National Awakening: Canada at Mid-Century', in J.M. Bumsted, ed., *Documentary Problems in Canadian History*, vol. 1. Georgetown, Ont.: Irwin-Dorsey, 225.

Rea, K.J. 1985. *The Prosperous Years: The Economic History of Ontario 1939–75.* Toronto: University of Toronto Press.

Reay, Dave. 2005. *Climate Change Begins at Home: Life on the Two-Way Street of Global Warming.* New York and London: Palgrave.

Recollections of the War of 1812. 1964. Toronto: Baxter Publishing Company.

Report of the Royal Commission on Broadcasting. 1957. Ottawa: King's Printer.

Report of the Royal Commission on National Development in the Arts, Letters and Sciences. 1951. Toronto: King's Printer.

Report of the Royal Commission on the Status of Women in Canada. 1970. Ottawa: Queen's Printer.

Richmond, Anthony. 1967. *Post-War Immigrants in Canada.* Toronto: University of Toronto Press.

Robertson, J.R. 1911. *The Diary of Mrs John Graves Simcoe, Wife of the First Lieutenant-Governor of the Province of Upper Canada, 1792–1796.* Toronto: W. Briggs.

Rollings-Magnusson, Sandra. 2009. *Heavy Burdens on Small Shoulders: The Labour of Pioneer Children on the Canadian Prairies.* Edmonton: University of Alberta Press.

Royal Commission on Aboriginal Peoples. 1993. *Partners in Confederation: Aboriginal Peoples, Self-government, and the Constitution.* Ottawa: Queen's Printer.

Royal Commission on Canada's Economic Prospects. 1958. Ottawa: Queen's Printer.

Royal Commission on the Donald Marshall, Jr, Prosecution, vol. 1: Findings and Recommendations. 1989. Halifax: The Commission.

Royal Society of Canada. 1932. *Fifty Years' Retrospective 1882–1932.* Toronto: University of Toronto Press.

Rubio, M., and E. Waterston, eds. 1987. *The Selected Journals of L.M. Montgomery, vol. 2: 1910–1921.* Toronto: Oxford University Press.

Rutherford, Paul. 1982. *A Victorian Authority: The Daily Press in Late Nineteenth-Century Canada.* Toronto: University of Toronto Press.

Saywell, J. 1971. *Quebec 70: A Documentary Narrative.* Toronto: University of Toronto Press.

Seed, Patricia, 1995. *Ceremonies of Possession in Europe's Conquest of the New World, 1492–1640.* Cambridge: Cambridge University Press.

Seeley, J.R., R.A. Sim, and E. Loosley. 1972. *Crestwood Heights: A North American Suburb.* Toronto: University of Toronto Press.

Shkilnyk, Anastasia. 1985. *A Poison Stronger Than Love: The Destruction of an Ojibwa Community.* New Haven: Yale University Press.

Siegfried, André. 1907. *The Race Question in Canada.* London: E. Nash.

Smiley, Donald V. 1970. 'Canadian Federalism and the Resolution of Federal–Provincial Conflicts', in F. Vaughan et al., eds, *Contemporary Issues in Canadian Politics.* Toronto: Prentice-Hall, 48–66.

Special Committee on Social Security. 1943. *Report on Social Security for Canada, Prepared by Dr L.C. Marsh for the Advisory Committee on Reconstruction.* Ottawa: King's Printer.

Stacey, C.P. 1970. *Arms, Man and Governments: The War Policies of Canada 1939–1945.* Ottawa: Queen's Printer.

———. 1981. *Canada and the Age of Conflict: A History of Canadian External Policies, vol. 2: 1921–1948.* Toronto: Macmillan.

Standing Committee of the Canadian Senate on Immigration and Labour. 1946. *Senate Report no. 6.* Ottawa: King's Printer.

Stanley, G.F.G. 1977. *Canada Invaded, 1775–1776.* Toronto: Canadian War Museum.

Statement of the Government of Canada on Indian Policy. 1969. Ottawa: Queen's Printer.

Statistics Canada. 1957. *Manufacturing Industries of Canada 1957.* Ottawa: Queen's Printer.

———. 2010. 'Study: Projections of the Diversity of the Canadian Population', *The Daily*, 9 Mar. At: <www.statcan.gc.ca/daily-quotiden/100309/dq100309a-eng.htm>.

Steele, S. 1915. *Forty Years in Canada: Reminiscences of the Great North-West . . . .* Toronto: McClelland, Goodchild & Stewart.

Stephens, H.F. 1890. *Jacques Cartier and His Four Voyages to Canada: An Essay with Historical, Explanatory and Philological Notes.* Montreal: W. Drysdale & Co.

Swainger, Jonathan. 2000. *The Canadian Department of Justice and the Completion of Confederation 1867–1878.* Vancouver: University of British Columbia Press.

Sykes, E.C. 1912. *A Home-Help in Canada.* London: G. Bell & Sons.

Thompson, John Herd, and Allan Seager. 1985. *Canada, 1922–1939: Decades of Discord.* Toronto: McClelland & Stewart.

Timlin, Mabel. 1951. *Does Canada Need More People?* Toronto: Oxford University Press.

Titley, Brian. 2009. *The Indian Commissioners: Agents of the State and Indian Policy in Canada's Prairie West, 1873–1932.* Edmonton: University of Alberta Press.

Toronto Star, 6 July 2010, 6.

Traill, Catharine Parr. 1846. *The Backwoods of Canada*. London: M.A. Nattali.

Troper, Harold Martin. 1972. *Only Farmers Need Apply: Official Canadian Government Encouragement of Immigration from the United States, 1896–1911*. Toronto: Griffin House.

Trudeau, Pierre Elliott, ed. 1974. *The Asbestos Strike*. Toronto (translation of 1951 edition).

Trudel, Marcel. 1973. *The Beginnings of New France 1524–1663*. Toronto: McClelland & Stewart.

Turcotte, Martin. 2006. 'Parents with Adult Children Living at Home', *Canadian Social Trends* (Spring): 2–9.

Vallières, Pierre. 1971. *White Niggers of America*. Toronto: McClelland & Stewart.

Voisey, P. 1988. *Vulcan: The Making of a Prairie Community*. Toronto: University of Toronto Press.

Waite, Peter B. 1962. *The Life and Times of Confederation, 1864–1867: Politics, Newspapers, and the Union of British North America*. Toronto: University of Toronto Press.

———, ed. 1963. *Confederation Debates in the Province of Canada*. Toronto: McClelland & Stewart.

Wall, Denis. 2000. 'Aboriginal Self-Government in Canada: The Cases of Nunavut and the Alberta Métis Settlements', in David Long and Olive Patricia Dickason, eds, *Visions of the Heart: Canadian Aboriginal Issues*, 2nd edn. Toronto: Harcourt Brace, 143–67.

Washington Post, 31 May 2006.

White, Richard. 1991. *The Middle Ground: Indians, Empires and Republics in the Great Lakes Region, 1650–1815*. New York: Cambridge University Press.

Williamson, J.A., ed. 1962. *The Cabot Voyages and British Discoveries under Henry VII*. Cambridge: Hakluyt Society of the University Press.

Williamson, M. 1970. *Robert Harris, 1849–1919: An Unconventional Biography*. Toronto: McClelland & Stewart.

Wilson, Edmund. 1964. *O Canada: An American's Notes on Canadian Culture*. New York: Farrar, Straus and Giroux.

Wingrove, Josh. 2010. 'Stelmach buys U.S. ad touting oil sands', *Globe and Mail*, 2 July. At: <www.theglobeandmail.com/news/politics/stelmach-buys-us-ad-touting-oil-sands/article1627312>.

Winnipeg Free Press, 13 Mar. 2006, 29 May 2006, 30 May 2006.

Woodcock, George, ed. 1969. *The Sixties: Writers and Writing of the Decade*. Vancouver: University of British Columbia Press.

———. 1979. *The Canadians*. Don Mills, Ont.: Fitzhenry & Whiteside.

Wright, E.C. 1955. *The Loyalists of New Brunswick*. Fredericton, NB: University of New Brunswick Press.

Wynn, G. 1980. *Timber Colony: A Historical Geography of Early 19th Century New Brunswick*. Toronto: University of Toronto Press.

Young, W. 1978. 'Academics and Social Scientists versus the Press: The Policies of the Bureau of Public Information and the Wartime Information Board, 1939 to 1945', in *CHA Historical Papers, a Selection from the Papers Presented at the Annual Meeting of the Canadian Historical Association* (1978).

Index